THE BOOK ®

Ford Escort
Service and Repair Manual

Steve Rendle and John S Mead

(0686 - 296 - 5Y12)

Models covered

Ford Escort front-wheel-drive Hatchback, Cabriolet, Estate, Van and Combi, including XR3, XR3i, RS Turbo and special/limited editions

1117 cc, 1118 cc, 1296 cc, 1297 cc, 1392 cc & 1597 cc petrol engines

Does not cover Diesel engine, CTX (automatic) transmission, RS 1600i models, or revised Escort range introduced in September 1990

ABCDE
FGHIJ
KL

4

© Haynes Publishing 1996

A book in the **Haynes Service and Repair Manual Series**

ISBN 1 85960 083 2

British Library Cataloguing in Publication Data
A catalogue record for this book is available from the British Library.

Printed by **J H Haynes & Co. Ltd, Sparkford, Nr Yeovil, Somerset BA22 7JJ**

Haynes Publishing
Sparkford, Nr Yeovil, Somerset BA22 7JJ, England

Haynes North America, Inc
861 Lawrence Drive, Newbury Park, California 91320, USA

Editions Haynes S.A.
147/149, rue Saint Honoré, 75001 PARIS, France

Contents

LIVING WITH YOUR FORD ESCORT

Roadside Repairs

Weekly checks

Lubricants, fluids and tyre pressures

MAINTENANCE

Routine Maintenance and Servicing

Contents

Introduced in September 1980, the Ford Escort soon established itself as Britain and Europe's best-selling car.

The cars feature front-wheel-drive from a transverse engine/transmission arrangement with independent front and rear suspension on Saloon and Estate models, dual circuit brakes and four or five-speed manual or three-speed automatic transmission.

The model range is extensive including three or five-door Hatchback Saloon, Estate, soft-top Cabriolet and Van versions, available with overhead valve or overhead camshaft engines. High performance models in the range are the Escort XR3, XR3i with fuel-injection, and RS Turbo with fuel-injection and turbocharger.

Extensive modifications to all models were introduced in 1986, with changes to engine sizes and specification, revised body styling and interior, and a number of steering, suspension, and transmission improvements. 1986 also saw the introduction of Ford's unique Anti-lock Braking System as standard equipment on RS Turbo models and a low cost option on certain other models.

Ford Escort XR3i (1986 model)

The Ford Escort Team

Haynes manuals are produced by dedicated and enthusiastic people working in close co-operation. The team responsible for the creation of this book included:

Authors	Steve Rendle John Mead
Sub-editor	Sophie Yar
Editor & Page Make-up	Steve Churchill
Workshop manager	Paul Buckland
Photo Scans	John Martin Paul Tanswell
Cover illustration & Line Art	Roger Healing

We hope the book will help you to get the maximum enjoyment from your car. By carrying out routine maintenance as described you will ensure your car's reliability and preserve its resale value.

Ford Escort 5-door Estate

Acknowledgements

Thanks are due to Champion Spark Plug who supplied the illustrations showing spark plug conditions. Certain other illustrations are the copyright of Ford Motor Company Limited, and are used with their permission. Thanks are also due to Sykes-Pickavant Limited, who supplied some of the workshop tools, and to all those people at Sparkford who helped in the production of this manual.

We take great pride in the accuracy of information given in this manual, but vehicle manufacturers make alterations and design changes during the production run of a particular vehicle of which they do not inform us. No liability can be accepted by the authors or publishers for loss, damage or injury caused by errors in, or omissions from, the information given.

Working on your car can be dangerous. This page shows just some of the potential risks and hazards, with the aim of creating a safety-conscious attitude.

General hazards

Scalding

• Don't remove the radiator or expansion tank cap while the engine is hot.
• Engine oil, automatic transmission fluid or power steering fluid may also be dangerously hot if the engine has recently been running.

Burning

• Beware of burns from the exhaust system and from any part of the engine. Brake discs and drums can also be extremely hot immediately after use.

Crushing

• When working under or near a raised vehicle, always supplement the jack with axle stands, or use drive-on ramps. *Never venture under a car which is only supported by a jack.*
• Take care if loosening or tightening high-torque nuts when the vehicle is on stands. Initial loosening and final tightening should be done with the wheels on the ground.

Fire

• Fuel is highly flammable; fuel vapour is explosive.
• Don't let fuel spill onto a hot engine.
• Do not smoke or allow naked lights (including pilot lights) anywhere near a vehicle being worked on. Also beware of creating sparks (electrically or by use of tools).
• Fuel vapour is heavier than air, so don't work on the fuel system with the vehicle over an inspection pit.
• Another cause of fire is an electrical overload or short-circuit. Take care when repairing or modifying the vehicle wiring.
• Keep a fire extinguisher handy, of a type suitable for use on fuel and electrical fires.

Electric shock

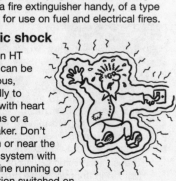

• Ignition HT voltage can be dangerous, especially to people with heart problems or a pacemaker. Don't work on or near the ignition system with the engine running or the ignition switched on.

• Mains voltage is also dangerous. Make sure that any mains-operated equipment is correctly earthed. Mains power points should be protected by a residual current device (RCD) circuit breaker.

Fume or gas intoxication

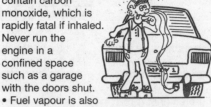

• Exhaust fumes are poisonous; they often contain carbon monoxide, which is rapidly fatal if inhaled. Never run the engine in a confined space such as a garage with the doors shut.
• Fuel vapour is also poisonous, as are the vapours from some cleaning solvents and paint thinners.

Poisonous or irritant substances

• Avoid skin contact with battery acid and with any fuel, fluid or lubricant, especially antifreeze, brake hydraulic fluid and Diesel fuel. Don't syphon them by mouth. If such a substance is swallowed or gets into the eyes, seek medical advice.
• Prolonged contact with used engine oil can cause skin cancer. Wear gloves or use a barrier cream if necessary. Change out of oil-soaked clothes and do not keep oily rags in your pocket.
• Air conditioning refrigerant forms a poisonous gas if exposed to a naked flame (including a cigarette). It can also cause skin burns on contact.

Asbestos

• Asbestos dust can cause cancer if inhaled or swallowed. Asbestos may be found in gaskets and in brake and clutch linings. When dealing with such components it is safest to assume that they contain asbestos.

Special hazards

Hydrofluoric acid

• This extremely corrosive acid is formed when certain types of synthetic rubber, found in some O-rings, oil seals, fuel hoses etc, are exposed to temperatures above 400ºC. The rubber changes into a charred or sticky substance containing the acid. *Once formed, the acid remains dangerous for years. If it gets onto the skin, it may be necessary to amputate the limb concerned.*
• When dealing with a vehicle which has suffered a fire, or with components salvaged from such a vehicle, wear protective gloves and discard them after use.

The battery

• Batteries contain sulphuric acid, which attacks clothing, eyes and skin. Take care when topping-up or carrying the battery.
• The hydrogen gas given off by the battery is highly explosive. Never cause a spark or allow a naked light nearby. Be careful when connecting and disconnecting battery chargers or jump leads.

Air bags

• Air bags can cause injury if they go off accidentally. Take care when removing the steering wheel and/or facia. Special storage instructions may apply.

Diesel injection equipment

• Diesel injection pumps supply fuel at very high pressure. Take care when working on the fuel injectors and fuel pipes.

⚠ *Warning: Never expose the hands, face or any other part of the body to injector spray; the fuel can penetrate the skin with potentially fatal results.*

Remember...

DO

• Do use eye protection when using power tools, and when working under the vehicle.

• Do wear gloves or use barrier cream to protect your hands when necessary.

• Do get someone to check periodically that all is well when working alone on the vehicle.

• Do keep loose clothing and long hair well out of the way of moving mechanical parts.

• Do remove rings, wristwatch etc, before working on the vehicle – especially the electrical system.

• Do ensure that any lifting or jacking equipment has a safe working load rating adequate for the job.

DON'T

• Don't attempt to lift a heavy component which may be beyond your capability – get assistance.

• Don't rush to finish a job, or take unverified short cuts.

• Don't use ill-fitting tools which may slip and cause injury.

• Don't leave tools or parts lying around where someone can trip over them. Mop up oil and fuel spills at once.

• Don't allow children or pets to play in or near a vehicle being worked on.

The following pages are intended to help in dealing with common roadside emergencies and breakdowns. You will find more detailed fault finding information at the back of the manual, and repair information in the main chapters.

If your car won't start and the starter motor doesn't turn

☐ If it's a model with automatic transmission, make sure the selector is in 'P' or 'N'.
☐ Open the bonnet and make sure that the battery terminals are clean and tight.
☐ Switch on the headlights and try to start the engine. If the headlights go very dim when you're trying to start, the battery is probably flat. Get out of trouble by jump starting (see next page) using a friend's car.

If your car won't start even though the starter motor turns as normal

☐ Is there fuel in the tank?
☐ Is there moisture on electrical components under the bonnet? Switch off the ignition, then wipe off any obvious dampness with a dry cloth. Spray a water-repellent aerosol product (WD-40 or equivalent) on ignition and fuel system electrical connectors like those shown in the photos. Pay special attention to the ignition coil wiring connector and HT leads. (Note that Diesel engines don't normally suffer from damp.)

A Check that the spark plug HT leads are securely connected by pushing them onto the plugs.

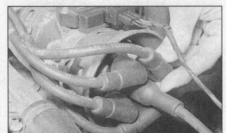

B Check that the HT leads are securely connected to the distributor (where fitted) and the wiring connector is securely connected.

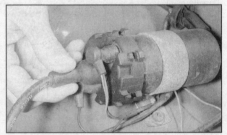

C Check that the HT lead and wiring connector are securely connected to the ignition HT coil.

Check that electrical connections are secure (with the ignition switched off) and spray them with a water dispersant spray like WD40 if you suspect a problem due to damp

D Check the security and condition of the battery terminals.

The ignition system wiring plug on top of the distributor may cause problems if not connected securely.

Booster battery (jump) starting

When jump-starting a car using a booster battery, observe the following precautions:

✔ Before connecting the booster battery, make sure that the ignition is switched off.

✔ Ensure that all electrical equipment (lights, heater, wipers, etc) is switched off.

✔ Make sure that the booster battery is the same voltage as the discharged one in the vehicle.

✔ If the battery is being jump-started from the battery in another vehicle, the two vehcles MUST NOT TOUCH each other.

✔ Make sure that the transmission is in neutral (or PARK, in the case of automatic transmission).

1 Connect one end of the red jump lead to the positive (+) terminal of the flat battery

2 Connect the other end of the red lead to the positive (+) terminal of the booster battery.

3 Connect one end of the black jump lead to the negative (-) terminal of the booster battery

4 Connect the other end of the black jump lead to a bolt or bracket on the engine block, well away from the battery, on the vehicle to be started.

5 Make sure that the jump leads will not come into contact with the fan, drive-belts or other moving parts of the engine.

6 Start the engine using the booster battery, then with the engine running at idle speed, disconnect the jump leads in the reverse order of connection.

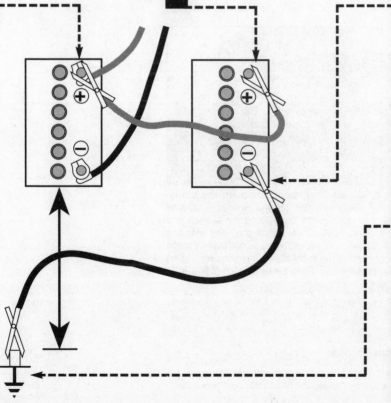

Wheel changing

Some of the details shown here will vary according to model. For instance, the location of the spare wheel and jack is not the same on all cars. However, the basic principles apply to all vehicles.

Warning: Do not change a wheel in a situation where you risk being hit by other traffic. On busy roads, try to stop in a lay-by or a gateway. Be wary of passing traffic while changing the wheel – it is easy to become distracted by the job in hand.

Preparation

☐ When a puncture occurs, stop as soon as it is safe to do so.

☐ Park on firm level ground, if possible, and well out of the way of other traffic.

☐ Use hazard warning lights if necessary.

☐ If you have one, use a warning triangle to alert other drivers of your presence.

☐ Apply the handbrake and engage first or reverse gear (or Park on models with automatic transmission).

☐ Chock the wheel diagonally opposite the one being removed – a couple of large stones will do for this.

☐ If the ground is soft, use a flat piece of wood to spread the load under the jack.

Changing the wheel

1 Remove the spare wheel, jack and wheel brace from their location in the luggage compartment, underneath the carpeting. Prise off the wheel trim (if fitted) using the wheel brace supplied.

2 Using the wheel nut wrench, initially slacken the nuts on the wheel to be removed.

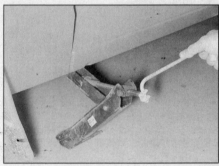

3 Engage the jack with the sill jacking point nearest the wheel to be raised. Turn the jack handle to raise the wheel clear of the ground.

4 Once the wheel is clear of the ground, remove the wheel nuts, and lift off the wheel.

5 Locate the spare wheel on the studs, then refit the original wheel nuts, and hand tighten them using the wrench in a diagonal sequence. Lower the vehicle to the ground, and withdraw the jack. Finally tighten the wheel nuts using the wrench, with hand pressure only. Refit the wheel trim (if fitted).

Finally...

☐ Remove the wheel chocks.

☐ Stow the jack and tools in the correct locations in the car.

☐ Check the tyre pressure on the wheel just fitted. If it is low, or if you don't have a pressure gauge with you, drive slowly to the nearest garage and inflate the tyre to the right pressure.

☐ Have the damaged tyre or wheel repaired as soon as possible.

Identifying leaks

Puddles on the garage floor or drive, or obvious wetness under the bonnet or underneath the car, suggest a leak that needs investigating. It can sometimes be difficult to decide where the leak is coming from, especially if the engine bay is very dirty already. Leaking oil or fluid can also be blown rearwards by the passage of air under the car, giving a false impression of where the problem lies.

 Warning: Most automotive oils and fluids are poisonous. Wash them off skin, and change out of contaminated clothing, without delay.

HAYNES HiNT *The smell of a fluid leaking from the car may provide a clue to what's leaking. Some fluids are distinctively coloured. It may help to clean the car carefully and to park it over some clean paper overnight as an aid to locating the source of the leak.*
Remember that some leaks may only occur while the engine is running.

Sump oil

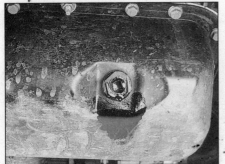

Engine oil may leak from the drain plug...

Oil from filter

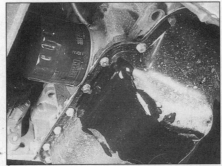

...or from the base of the oil filter.

Gearbox oil

Gearbox oil can leak from the seals at the inboard ends of the driveshafts.

Antifreeze

Leaking antifreeze often leaves a crystalline deposit like this.

Brake fluid

A leak occurring at a wheel is almost certainly brake fluid.

Power steering fluid

Power steering fluid may leak from the pipe connectors on the steering rack.

Towing

When all else fails, you may find yourself having to get a tow home – or of course you may be helping somebody else. Long-distance recovery should only be done by a garage or breakdown service. For shorter distances, DIY towing using another car is easy enough, but observe the following points:

☐ Use a proper tow-rope – they are not expensive. The vehicle being towed must display an 'ON TOW' sign in its rear window.
☐ Always turn the ignition key to the 'on' position when the vehicle is being towed, so that the steering lock is released, and that the direction indicator and brake lights will work.
☐ Only attach the tow-rope to the towing eyes provided.
☐ Before being towed, release the handbrake and select neutral on the transmission.
☐ Note that greater-than-usual pedal pressure will be required to operate the brakes, since the vacuum servo unit is only operational with the engine running.
☐ On models with power steering, greater-than-usual steering effort will also be required.

☐ The driver of the car being towed must keep the tow-rope taut at all times to avoid snatching.
☐ Make sure that both drivers know the route before setting off.
☐ Only drive at moderate speeds and keep the distance towed to a minimum. Drive smoothly and allow plenty of time for slowing down at junctions.
☐ On models with automatic transmission, special precautions apply. If in doubt, do not tow, or transmission damage may result.

Introduction

There are some very simple checks which need only take a few minutes to carry out, but which could save you a lot of inconvenience and expense.

These "Weekly checks" require no great skill or special tools, and the small amount of time they take to perform could prove to be very well spent, for example;

☐ Keeping an eye on tyre condition and pressures, will not only help to stop them wearing out prematurely, but could also save your life.

☐ Many breakdowns are caused by electrical problems. Battery-related faults are particularly common, and a quick check on a regular basis will often prevent the majority of these.

☐ If your car develops a brake fluid leak, the first time you might know about it is when your brakes don't work properly. Checking the level regularly will give advance warning of this kind of problem.

☐ If the oil or coolant levels run low, the cost of repairing any engine damage will be far greater than fixing the leak, for example.

Underbonnet check points

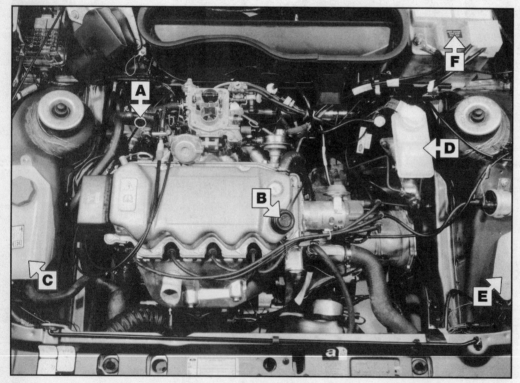

◀ **1.4 litre CVH**

A Engine oil level dipstick
B Engine oil filler cap
C Coolant expansion tank
D Brake fluid reservoir
E Windscreen washer reservoir
F Battery

◀ 1.6 litre RS Turbo

A Engine oil level dipstick

B Engine oil filler cap

C Coolant expansion tank

D Brake fluid reservoir

E Windscreen washer reservoir

F Battery

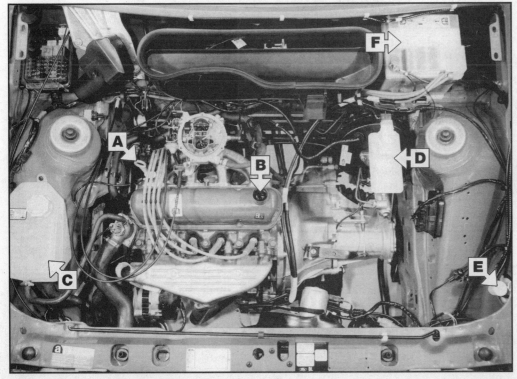

◀ 1.3 litre HCS

A Engine oil level dipstick

B Engine oil filler cap

C Coolant expansion tank

D Brake fluid reservoir

E Windscreen washer reservoir

F Battery

Air cleaner removed for clarity

Engine oil level

Before you start

✔ Make sure that your car is on level ground.
✔ Check the oil level before the car is driven, or at least 5 minutes after the engine has been switched off.

 HAYNES HiNT *If the oil is checked immediately after driving the vehicle, some of the oil will remain in the upper engine components, resulting in an inaccurate reading on the dipstick!*

The correct oil

Modern engines place great demands on their oil. It is very important that the correct oil for your car is used (See "Lubricants, fluids and tyre pressures").

Car Care

● If you have to add oil frequently, you should check whether you have any oil leaks. Place some clean paper under the car overnight, and check for stains in the morning. If there are no leaks, the engine may be burning oil *(see "Fault Finding").*

● Always maintain the level between the upper and lower dipstick marks (see photo 3). If the level is too low severe engine damage may occur. Oil seal failure may result if the engine is overfilled by adding too much oil.

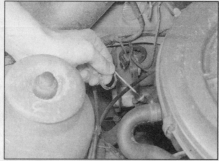

1 The dipstick location is at the rear right-hand corner of the engine. (see *"Underbonnet check points"* on pages 0•10 and 0•11). Withdraw the dipstick.

2 Using a clean rag or paper towel remove all oil from the dipstick. Insert the clean dipstick into the tube as far as it will go, then withdraw it again.

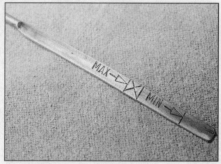

3 Note the oil level on the end of the dipstick, which should be between the hatched area on the dipstick. Approximately 1.0 litre of oil will raise the level from the lower mark to the upper mark.

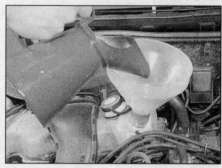

4 Oil is added through the filler cap. Pull off the cap and top-up the level; a funnel may help to reduce spillage. Add the oil slowly, checking the level on the dipstick often. Don't overfill (see *"Car Care" left*).

Coolant level

⚠ *Warning: DO NOT attempt to remove the expansion tank pressure cap when the engine is hot, as there is a very great risk of scalding. Do not leave open containers of coolant about, as it is poisonous.*

Car Care

● With a sealed-type cooling system, adding coolant should not be necessary on a regular basis. If frequent topping-up is required, it is likely there is a leak. Check the radiator, all hoses and joint faces for signs of staining or wetness, and rectify as necessary.

● It is important that antifreeze is used in the cooling system all year round, not just during the winter months. Don't top-up with water alone, as the antifreeze will become too diluted.

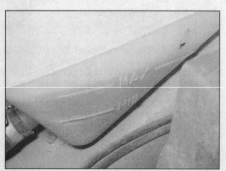

1 The coolant level varies with engine temperature. When cold, the coolant level should be between the "MAX" and "MIN" marks. When the engine is hot, the level may rise slightly above the "MAX" mark.

2 If topping up is necessary, **wait until the engine is cold**. Slowly unscrew the pressure cap on the expansion tank (or thermostat housing on early 1.1 litre models), to release any pressure present in the cooling system, and remove it.

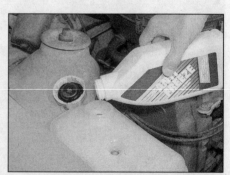

3 Add a mixture of water and antifreeze to the expansion tank **only** until the coolant level is up to the "MAX" mark. Refit the cap and tighten it securely.

Brake fluid level

Warning:
● **Brake fluid can harm your eyes and damage painted surfaces, so use extreme caution when handling and pouring it.**
● **Do not use fluid that has been standing open for some time, as it absorbs moisture from the air, which can cause a dangerous loss of braking effectiveness.**

HAYNES HINT
• *Make sure that your car is on level ground.*
• *The fluid level in the reservoir will drop slightly as the brake pads wear down, but the fluid level must never be allowed to drop below the "MIN" mark.*

Safety First!

● If the reservoir requires repeated topping-up this is an indication of a fluid leak somewhere in the system, which should be investigated immediately.

● If a leak is suspected, the car should not be driven until the braking system has been checked. Never take any risks where brakes are concerned.

1 The "MAX" and "MIN" marks are indicated on the side of the reservoir. The fluid level must be kept between the marks at all times.

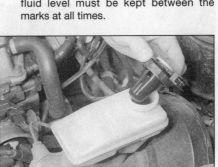

3 When adding fluid, it's a good idea to inspect the reservoir. The system should be drained and refilled if dirt is seen in the fluid (see Chapter 9 for details).

2 If topping-up is necessary, first wipe clean the area around the filler cap. Unplug the wiring connector and unscrew the reservoir cap.

4 Carefully add fluid, taking care not to spill it onto the surrounding components. Use only the specified fluid; mixing different types can cause damage to the system. After topping-up to the correct level, securely refit the cap and wipe off any spilt fluid.

Screen washer fluid level

Screenwash additives not only keep the winscreen clean during foul weather, they also prevent the washer system freezing in cold weather - which is when you are likely to need it most. Don't top up using plain water as the screenwash will become too diluted, and will freeze during cold weather. *On no account use coolant antifreeze in the washer system - this could discolour or damage paintwork.*

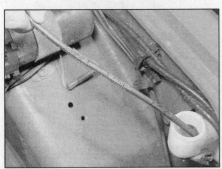

1 Fluid for the windscreen washer system is stored in a plastic reservoir, the filler neck of which is located at the left-hand front corner of the engine compartment. Some models are fitted with a dipstick to show the level of fluid. The reservoir for the rear screen wash is located in the luggage compartment.

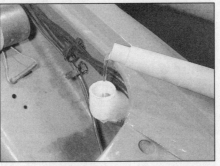

2 Top-up the reservoir using plain water at first followed by . . .

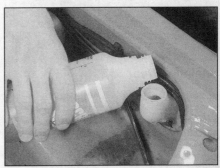

3 . . . screenwash additive in the quantities recommended on the bottle.

Tyre condition and pressure

It is very important that tyres are in good condition, and at the correct pressure - having a tyre failure at any speed is highly dangerous. Tyre wear is influenced by driving style - harsh braking and acceleration, or fast cornering, will all produce more rapid tyre wear. As a general rule, the front tyres wear out faster than the rears. Interchanging the tyres from front to rear ("rotating" the tyres) may result in more even wear. However, if this is completely effective, you may have the expense of replacing all four tyres at once! Remove any nails or stones embedded in the tread before they penetrate the tyre to cause deflation. If removal of a nail does reveal that

the tyre has been punctured, refit the nail so that its point of penetration is marked. Then immediately change the wheel, and have the tyre repaired by a tyre dealer.

Regularly check the tyres for damage in the form of cuts or bulges, especially in the sidewalls. Periodically remove the wheels, and clean any dirt or mud from the inside and outside surfaces. Examine the wheel rims for signs of rusting, corrosion or other damage. Light alloy wheels are easily damaged by "kerbing" whilst parking; steel wheels may also become dented or buckled. A new wheel is very often the only way to overcome severe damage.

New tyres should be balanced when they are fitted, but it may become necessary to re-balance them as they wear, or if the balance weights fitted to the wheel rim should fall off. Unbalanced tyres will wear more quickly, as will the steering and suspension components. Wheel imbalance is normally signified by vibration, particularly at a certain speed (typically around 50 mph). If this vibration is felt only through the steering, then it is likely that just the front wheels need balancing. If, however, the vibration is felt through the whole car, the rear wheels could be out of balance. Wheel balancing should be carried out by a tyre dealer or garage.

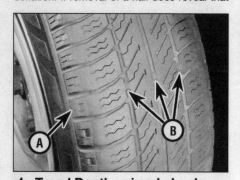

1 Tread Depth - visual check

The original tyres have tread wear safety bands (B), which will appear when the tread depth reaches approximately 1.6 mm. The band positions are indicated by a triangular mark on the tyre sidewall (A).

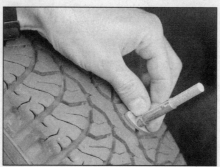

2 Tread Depth - manual check

Alternatively, tread wear can be monitored with a simple, inexpensive device known as a tread depth indicator gauge.

3 Tyre Pressure Check

Check the tyre pressures regularly with the tyres cold. Do not adjust the tyre pressures immediately after the vehicle has been used, or an inaccurate setting will result. Tyre pressures are shown on Page 0•16.

Tyre tread wear patterns

Shoulder Wear

Underinflation (wear on both sides)
Under-inflation will cause overheating of the tyre, because the tyre will flex too much, and the tread will not sit correctly on the road surface. This will cause a loss of grip and excessive wear, not to mention the danger of sudden tyre failure due to heat build-up.
Check and adjust pressures
Incorrect wheel camber (wear on one side)
Repair or renew suspension parts
Hard cornering
Reduce speed!

Centre Wear

Overinflation
Over-inflation will cause rapid wear of the centre part of the tyre tread, coupled with reduced grip, harsher ride, and the danger of shock damage occurring in the tyre casing.
Check and adjust pressures

If you sometimes have to inflate your car's tyres to the higher pressures specified for maximum load or sustained high speed, don't forget to reduce the pressures to normal afterwards.

Uneven Wear

Front tyres may wear unevenly as a result of wheel misalignment. Most tyre dealers and garages can check and adjust the wheel alignment (or "tracking") for a modest charge.
Incorrect camber or castor
Repair or renew suspension parts
Malfunctioning suspension
Repair or renew suspension parts
Unbalanced wheel
Balance tyres
Incorrect toe setting
Adjust front wheel alignment
Note: *The feathered edge of the tread which typifies toe wear is best checked by feel.*

Battery

Caution: Before carrying out any work on the vehicle battery, read the precautions given in "Safety first" at the start of this manual.

✔ Make sure that the battery tray is in good condition, and that the clamp is tight. Corrosion on the tray, retaining clamp and the battery itself can be removed with a solution of water and baking soda. Thoroughly rinse all cleaned areas with water. Any metal parts damaged by corrosion should be covered with a zinc-based primer, then painted.

✔ Periodically (approximately every three months), check the charge condition of the battery as described in Chapter 5A.

✔ If the battery is flat, and you need to jump start your vehicle, see *Roadside Repairs*.

HAYNES HiNT

Battery corrosion can be kept to a minimum by applying a layer of petroleum jelly to the clamps and terminals after they are reconnected.

1 The battery is located on the left-hand side of the engine compartment. The exterior of the battery should be inspected periodically for damage such as a cracked case or cover.

3 If corrosion (white, fluffy deposits) is evident, remove the cables from the battery terminals, clean them with a small wire brush, then refit them. Automotive stores sell a tool for cleaning the battery post . . .

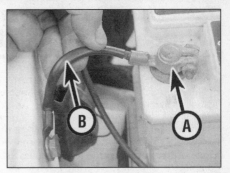

2 Check the tightness of battery clamps (A) to ensure good electrical connections. You should not be able to move them. Also check each cable (B) for cracks and frayed conductors.

4 . . . as well as the battery cable clamps

Wiper blades

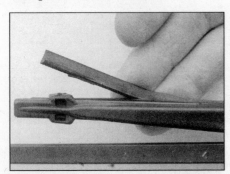

1 Check the condition of the wiper blades; if they are cracked or show any signs of deterioration, or if the glass swept area is smeared, renew them. Wiper blades should be renewed annually.

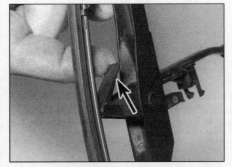

2 To remove a windscreen wiper blade, pull the arm fully away from the screen until it locks. Swivel the blade through 90°, press the locking tab with your fingers and slide the blade out of the arm's hooked end.

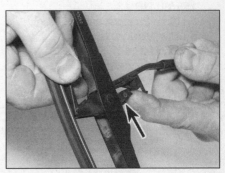

3 Don't forget to check the tailgate wiper blade as well. To remove the blade, depress the retaining tab and slide the blade out of the hooked end of the arm.

Lubricants and fluids

Component or system	Lubricant type/specification
Engine	Multigrade engine oil, viscosity range SAE 10W/30 to 20W/50 to API SG/CD or better
Cooling system	Antifreeze to Ford specification SSM-97B-9103-A
Braking system	Brake fluid to Ford specification SAM-6C 9103-A
Manual transmission	Hypoid gear oil, viscosity SAE 80EP to Ford specification SQM-2C 9008-A
Automatic transmission:	
prefix number E3RP	ATF to Ford specification SQM-2C 9010-A or ESP-M2C 138-CJ
prefix number E6RP	ATF to Ford specification ESP-M2C 166-H

Tyre pressures

Tyre pressures - cold in bar (lbf/in^2):	Front	Rear
Saloon and Estate models:		
145 SR 13 (pre-1986 models):		
Up to 3 occupants	1.8 (26)	1.8 (26)
Fully laden	2.0 (29)	2.3 (33)
145 SR 13: (1986-on models):		
Up to 3 occupants	1.6 (23)	2.0 (29)
Fully laden	2.0 (29)	2.3 (33)
155 SR/TR 13 (manual transmission models):		
Up to 3 occupants	1.6 (23)	2.0 (29)
Fully laden	2.0 (29)	2.3 (33)
155 SR/TR 13 (automatic transmission models):		
Up to 3 occupants	1.8 (26)	2.0 (29)
Fully laden	2.0 (29)	2.3 (33)
175/70 SR/HR 13:		
Up to 3 occupants	1.8 (26)	1.8 (26)
Fully laden	2.0 (29)	2.3 (33)
175/65 HR 14:		
Up to 3 occupants	1.6 (23)	2.0 (29)
Fully laden	2.0 (29)	2.3 (33)
185/60 HR 13:		
Up to 3 occupants	1.8 (26)	1.8 (26)
Fully laden	2.0 (29)	2.3 (33)
185/60 HR 14:		
Up to 3 occupants	1.6 (23)	2.0 (29)
Fully laden	2.0 (29)	2.3 (33)
195/50 VR 15:		
Up to 3 occupants	1.8 (26)	1.8 (26)
Fully laden	1.8 (26)	2.0 (29)
Van models:		
155 SR 13:		
Up to 3 occupants	1.8 (26)	1.8 (26)
Fully laden	1.8 (26)	2.6 (38)
165 RR 13:		
Up to 3 occupants	1.8 (26)	1.8 (26)
Fully laden	1.8 (26)	3.0 (44)

Increase the above pressures by 0.1 bar (1.5 lbf/in^2) for every 6 mph (10 kph) above 100 mph (160 kph) for sustained high speed use

Chapter 1
Routine maintenance and servicing

Contents

Degrees of difficulty

Easy, suitable for novice with little experience	**Fairly easy,** suitable for beginner with some experience	**Fairly difficult,** suitable for competent DIY mechanic	**Difficult,** suitable for experienced DIY mechanic	**Very difficult,** suitable for expert DIY or professional

Engine

Oil filter type .... Champion C104
Valve clearances (cold):
  OHV engines:
    Inlet .... 0.22 mm (0.008 in)
    Exhaust .... 0.59 mm (0.023 in)
  HCS engines:
    Inlet .... 0.22 mm (0.008 in)
    Exhaust .... 0.32 mm (0.012 in)

Cooling system

Recommended antifreeze concentration .... 45% by volume

Fuel system

Idle speed:
  Carburettor models:
    All except Weber 2V TLDM carburettor .... 750 to 850 rpm
    Weber 2V TLDM carburettor .... 700 to 800 rpm
  Bosch K-Jetronic fuel injection models .... 750 to 850 rpm
  Bosch KE-Jetronic fuel injection models:
    1985 models .... 800 to 900 rpm
    1986 models onwards .... 920 to 960 rpm
  Electronic Fuel Injection (EFI) models .... 900 ± 50 rpm
Idle mixture CO content:
  Bosch K-Jetronic fuel injection models .... 1.0 to 1.5 %
  Bosch KE-Jetronic fuel injection models:
    1985 models .... 0.25 to 0.75%
    1986 models onwards .... 0.5 to 1.1%
  Electronic Fuel Injection (EFI) models .... 0.8 ± 0.25% (cooling fan running)
Air filter element type:
  1.1 litre and 1.3 litre OHV engines .... Champion W153
  1.1 litre and 1.3 litre HCS engines .... Champion W225
  1.1 litre and 1.3 litre CVH engines .... Champion W127
  1.4 litre CVH engine:
    Carburettor engines .... Champion W179
    Central Fuel Injection (CFI) engines .... Champion W201
  1.6 litre CVH engine (except XR3 models):
    Up to 1986 .... Champion W169
    1986 to October 1988 .... Champion W201
    October 1988 on .... Champion W226
  1.6 litre CVH engine (XR3 models) .... Champion W201

Ignition system

Contact breaker points gap:
  Bosch distributor .... 0.40 to 0.50 mm (0.016 to 0.02 in)
  Lucas distributor .... 0.40 to 0.59 mm (0.016 to 0.023 in)
Dwell angle (contact breaker ignition system) .... 48° to 52°
Ignition timing *:
OHV engines:
  Up to 1984 (contact breaker) .... 12° BTDC at idle speed
  1984-on (contact breaker) and all electronic ignition .... 6° BTDC at idle speed
CVH engines (all models) .... 12° BTDC at idle speed
* Note: *Ignition timing on models with either a Distributorless Ignition Sytem (DIS) or a programmed ignition system (ESC) cannot be adjusted. Refer to Chapter 5, Part B for further information.*
Spark plugs:
Type:
  OHV and HCS engines .... Champion RS9YCC or RS9YC
  CVH engines:
    Carburettor models .... Champion RC7YCC or RC7YC
    Bosch K-Jetronic fuel injection and
    Electronic Fuel Injection (EFI) models .... Champion C6YCC or RC6YC
    Bosch KE-Jetronic fuel injection models .... Champion C61YC
    Central Fuel Injection (CFI) models .... Champion RC7YCC or RC7YC4
Electrode gap:
  All except HCS and CFI models:
    RS9YCC, RC7YCC, C6YCC spark plugs .... 0.8 mm (0.032 in)
    RS9YC, RC7YC, RC6YC, ... 0.7 mm (0.028 in)
  HCS and CFI models .... 1.0 mm (0.039 in)

Brakes

Minimum front brake disc pad thickness	1.5 mm (0.06 in)
Minimum rear brake shoe lining thickness	1.0 mm (0.04 in)

Tyres

Tyre pressures	See "*Weekly checks*" on page 0•16

Torque wrench settings

	Nm	lbf ft
Exhaust manifold nuts - RS Turbo models	14 to 17	10 to 13
Turbocharger-to-manifold nuts	21 to 26	15 to 19
Spark plugs:		
OHV and HCS engines	13 to 20	10 to 15
CVH engines	25 to 38	18 to 28
Seat belt anchor bolts	29 to 41	21 to 30
Roadwheel bolts	70 to 100	52 to 74

Capacities

Engine oil (drain and refill)

OHV engine:	
With filter change	3.25 litres (5.7 pints)
Without filter change	2.75 litres (4.8 pints)
CVH engine:	
Carburettor engines with filter change:	
Pre-July 1982	3.75 litres (6.6 pints)
July 1982 onwards	3.50 litres (6.2 pints)
Carburettor engines without filter change:	
Pre-July 1982	3.50 litres (6.2 pints)
July 1982 onwards	3.25 litres (5.7 pints)
Fuel-injected engines with filter change	3.85 litres (6.8 pints)
Fuel-injected engines without filter change	3.60 litres (6.3 pints)

Fuel tank

All models (except XR3i and Van) pre-May 1983	40 litres (8.8 gallons)
All other models (except Van)	48 litres (10.6 gallons)
Van	50 litres (11.0 gallons)

Cooling system

1.1 litre OHV engine	6.7 litres (11.8 pints)
1.1 litre CVH engine:	
With small radiator	6.2 litres (11.0 pints)
With large radiator	7.2 litres (12.6 pints)
1.3 litre OHV engine	7.1 litres (12.5 pints)
1.3 litre CVH engine:	
Pre-1986	7.1 litres (12.5 pints)
1986 onwards	7.6 litres (13.3 pints)
1.4 litre CVH engine	7.6 litres (13.3 pints)
1.6 litre CVH engine:	
Pre-1986	6.9 litres (12.1 pints)
1986 onwards	7.8 litres (13.7 pints)

Transmission

4-speed manual	2.8 litres (4.9 pints)
5-speed manual	3.1 litres (5.5 pints)
Automatic transmission	7.9 litres (13.9 pints)

Ford Escort maintenance schedule

The maintenance intervals in this manual are provided with the assumption that you, not the dealer, will be carrying out the work. These are the minimum maintenance intervals recommended by the manufacturer for vehicles driven daily. If you wish to keep your vehicle in peak condition at all times, you may wish to perform some of these procedures more often. We encourage frequent maintenance, because it enhances the efficiency, performance and resale value of your vehicle.

If the vehicle is driven in dusty areas, used to tow a trailer, or driven frequently at slow speeds (idling in traffic) or on short journeys, more frequent maintenance intervals are recommended.

When the vehicle is new, it should be serviced by a factory-authorised dealer service department, in order to preserve the factory warranty.

Every 250 miles (400 km) or weekly

☐ See *"Weekly checks"*

Every 6000 miles (10 000 km) or 6 months – whichever comes first

In addition to all the items in the 250 mile (400 km) service, carry out the following:

☐ Renew the engine oil and filter (Section 6)
☐ On OHV and HCS engines, remove and clean the oil filler cap (Section 7)
☐ Check the hoses, hose clips and visible joint gaskets for leaks and any signs of corrosion or deterioration (Section 8)
☐ Visually check the fuel pipes and hoses for security, chafing, leaks and corrosion (Section 8)
☐ Check the fuel tank for leaks and any sign of damage or corrosion (Section 8)
☐ On RS Turbo models check the tightness of the exhaust manifold retaining nuts (Section 9)
☐ Check and if necessary adjust the idle speed and mixture settings (Section 10)
☐ Clean the distributor cap, coil tower and HT leads and check for tracking (Section 11)
☐ On contact breaker point distributors lubricate the distributor shaft and cam (Section 12)
☐ On contact breaker point distributors check and if necessary adjust the points gap (dwell angle), then check the ignition timing (Sections 13 and 14)
☐ On RS Turbo models renew the spark plugs (Section 15)
☐ Check the front disc pad thickness (Section 16)
☐ Check the rear brake shoe lining thickness (Section 17)
☐ Check the steering and suspension components for any signs of damage and wear (Section 18)
☐ Check the security of the front suspension lower arm balljoint (Section 18)
☐ Check the seat belt webbing for cuts or damage and check the seat belt operation (Section 19)
☐ Carefully inspect the paintwork for damage and the bodywork for corrosion (Chapter 11)
☐ Check the condition and adjustment of the alternator drivebelt (Section 20)

Every 12 000 miles (20 000 km) or 12 months - whichever comes first

In addition to all the items in the 6000 mile (10 000 km) service, carry out the following:

☐ On OHV and HCS engines check and if necessary adjust the valve clearances (Section 21)
☐ Check the exhaust system condition and security (Section 22)
☐ On RS Turbo models check the tightness of the turbocharger-to-manifold nuts (Section 23)
☐ Renew the spark plugs (Sections 24 and 15)
☐ On contact breaker point distributors renew the contact breaker points (Section 25)
☐ Check and if necessary top-up the manual transmission oil (Section 26)
☐ Check the automatic transmission fluid level - where applicable (Section 27)
☐ Check the operation of the automatic transmission selector mechanism (Section 28)
☐ Check the driveshafts for damage or distortion and check the condition of the constant velocity joint bellows (Section 29)
☐ Inspect the roadwheels for damage (Section 30)
☐ Check the tightness of the roadwheel bolts (Section 30)
☐ Lubricate all hinges, door locks, check straps and the bonnet release mechanism (Section 31)
☐ Check the operation of all door, tailgate, bonnet release and window regulator components (Section 31)
☐ Carry out a road test (Section 32)

Every 24 000 miles (40 000 km) or 2 years - whichever comes first

In addition to all the items in the 12 000 mile (20 000 km) and 6000 mile (10 000 km) services, carry out the following:

☐ Renew the coolant (Section 33)
☐ Renew the air cleaner element (Section 34)
☐ On CVH engines renew the crankcase emission control filter (Section 35)
☐ On fuel-injected engines renew the fuel filter (Section 36)

Every 36 000 miles (60 000 km) or 3 years - whichever comes first

In addition to all the items listed in the previous services, carry out the following:

☐ On CVH engines renew the timing belt (Section 37)
☐ Make a thorough inspection of all brake components and rubber seals for signs of leaks, general deterioration and wear (Section 38)
☐ Renew the brake fluid (Section 39)

Engine and under bonnet component location on 1986 1.4 litre models (air cleaner removed for clarity)

1 Fuse and relay box
2 Windscreen wiper motor
3 Engine oil dipstick
4 Carburettor
5 Fuel pump
6 Battery negative terminal
7 Brake master cylinder reservoir
8 Distributor
9 Ignition coil
10 Washer reservoir
11 Thermostat housing
12 Oil filler cap
13 Vehicle identification plate
14 Engine tuning decal
15 Cooling system expansion tank
16 Suspension strut top mounting

Engine and under bonnet component locations on 1986 RS Turbo models

1 Fuse and relay box
2 Windscreen wiper motor
3 Crankcase emission control filter
4 Engine oil dipstick
5 Throttle housing
6 Inlet manifold
7 Throttle position sensor
8 Charge air temperature sensor
9 Distributor
10 Brake master cylinder reservoir
11 Battery negative terminal
12 Ignition coil
13 Fuel filter
14 Washer reservoir
15 Air cleaner
16 Fuel distributor
17 Inlet air hose
18 Turbocharger
19 Vehicle identification plate
20 Engine tuning decal
21 Cooling system expansion tank
22 Suspension strut top mounting

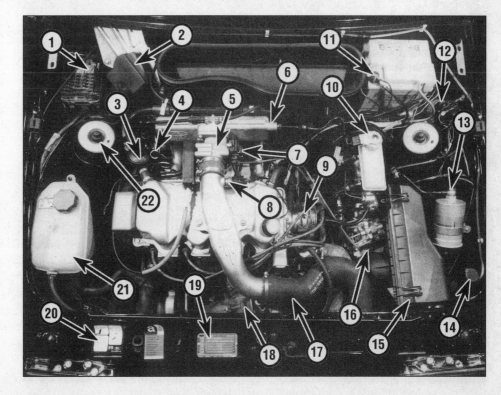

Engine and underbonnet components location on 1989 1.3 litre HCS model (air cleaner removed for clarity)

1 Ventilation air inlet duct
2 Battery
3 Bonnet hinge
4 Suspension strut upper mounting
5 Brake system fluid reservoir
6 Ignition system ESC module
7 Windscreen washer reservoir filler cap
8 Transmission housing
9 Clutch release lever
10 Cooling fan motor
11 Starter motor
12 Engine oil filler neck (cap removed)
13 Exhaust manifold shield
14 Alternator
15 Coolant thermostat and fan thermal switch
16 Coolant expansion tank
17 Spark plug HT leads
18 Engine oil dipstick
19 Throttle cable
20 Choke cable
21 Carburettor
22 Fusebox
23 Windscreen wiper motor

Front underbody view of a 1986 1.4 litre Saloon model

1 Anti-roll bar clamp
2 Anti-roll bar
3 Front suspension lower arm
4 Steering tie-rod
5 Transmission support crossmember
6 Gearchange rod
7 Gearchange stabiliser
8 Driveshaft
9 Engine oil drain plug
10 Brake caliper
11 Alternator
12 Exhaust front pipe
13 Starter motor

Rear underbody view of a 1986 1.4 litre Saloon model

1 Fuel filler pipe
2 Suspension lower arm
3 Tie-bar
4 Tie-bar front mounting
5 Fuel tank
6 Handbrake cable adjuster
7 Exhaust mounting
8 Exhaust intermediate silencer
9 Exhaust rear silencer
10 Rear towing eye

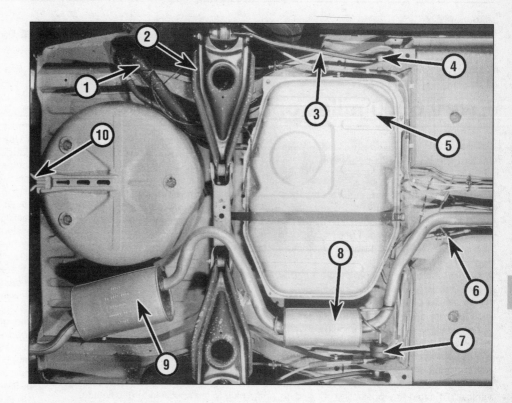

1 Introduction

General information

This Chapter is designed to help the home mechanic maintain his/her vehicle for safety, economy, long life and peak performance.

The Chapter contains a master maintenance schedule, followed by Sections dealing specifically with each task on the schedule. Visual checks, adjustments, component renewal and other helpful items are included. Refer to the accompanying illustrations of the engine compartment and the underside of the vehicle for the locations of the various components.

Servicing of your vehicle in accordance with the mileage/time maintenance schedule and the following Sections will provide a planned maintenance program, which should result in a long and reliable service life. This is a comprehensive plan, so maintaining some items but not others at the specified service intervals will not produce the same results.

As you service your vehicle, you will discover that many of the procedures can - and should - be grouped together because of the particular procedure being performed, or because of the close proximity of two otherwise unrelated components to one another. For example, if the vehicle is raised for any reason, the exhaust can be inspected at the same time as the suspension and steering components.

The first step in this maintenance program is to prepare yourself before the actual work begins. Read through all the Sections relevant to the work to be carried out, then make a list and gather together all the parts and tools required. If a problem is encountered, seek advice from a parts specialist, or a dealer service department.

2 Intensive maintenance

If, from the time the vehicle is new, the routine maintenance schedule is followed closely and frequent checks are made of fluid levels and high wear items, as suggested throughout this manual, the engine will be kept in relatively good running condition and the need for additional work will be minimised.

It is possible that there will be times when the engine is running poorly due to the lack of regular maintenance. This is even more likely if a used vehicle, which has not received regular and frequent maintenance checks, is purchased. In such cases, additional work may need to be carried out, outside of the regular maintenance intervals.

If engine wear is suspected, a compression test will provide valuable information regarding the overall performance of the main internal components. Such a test can be used as a basis to decide on the extent of the work to be carried out. If for example a compression test indicates serious internal engine wear, conventional maintenance as described in this Chapter will not greatly improve the performance of the engine, and may prove a waste of time and money, unless extensive overhaul work is carried out first.

The following series of operations are those most often required to improve the performance of a generally poor-running engine.

a) Clean, inspect and test the battery (Section 5).
b) Check the levels of all the engine related fluids (Section 3).
c) Check the condition and tension of the alternator drivebelt (Section 20).
d) Check the condition of the spark plugs and renew if necessary (Section 15).
e) Check the condition of the air cleaner element, and renew if necessary (Section 34).
f) Check the condition of all hoses and check for fluid leaks.
g) Check and if necessary adjust the idle speed (where possible) (Section 10).

1

Weekly checks

3 Fluid level checks

See "Weekly checks" starting on Page 0•10.

4 Tyre checks

See "Weekly checks" starting on Page 0•10.

5 Battery check

See "Weekly checks" starting on Page 0•10.

Every 6000 miles or 6 months

6 Engine oil and filter renewal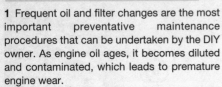

1 Frequent oil and filter changes are the most important preventative maintenance procedures that can be undertaken by the DIY owner. As engine oil ages, it becomes diluted and contaminated, which leads to premature engine wear.

2 Before starting this procedure, gather together all the necessary tools and materials. Also make sure that you have plenty of clean rags and newspapers handy to mop up any spills. Ideally, the engine oil should be warm, as it will drain better and more built-up sludge will be removed with it. Take care, however, not to touch the exhaust or any other hot parts of the engine when working under the vehicle. To avoid any possibility of scalding, and to protect yourself from possible skin irritants and other harmful contaminants in used engine oils, it is advisable to wear rubber gloves when carrying out this work. Access to the underside of the vehicle will be greatly improved if it can be raised on a lift, driven onto ramps or jacked up and supported on axle stands (see "Jacking and Vehicle Support"). Whichever method is chosen, make sure that the vehicle remains as level as possible, to enable the oil to drain fully.

3 Remove the oil filler cap from the rocker cover, then position a container beneath the sump.

4 Clean the drain plug and the area around it, then slacken it using a suitable socket or spanner (see illustration). If possible, try to keep the plug pressed into the sump while unscrewing it by hand the last couple of turns. As the plug releases from the threads, move it away sharply so the stream of oil issuing from the sump runs into the container, not up your sleeve!

5 Allow some time for the old oil to drain, noting that it may be necessary to reposition the container as the oil flow slows to a trickle.

6 After all the oil has drained, wipe off the drain plug with a clean rag and check the condition of the sealing washer. Renew the washer if necessary. Clean the area around the drain plug opening, then refit and tighten the plug to the specified torque setting.

7 Move the container into position under the oil filter. The oil filter is located at the rear of the cylinder block, and is accessible from under the vehicle (see illustration)

8 Using an oil filter removal tool, slacken the filter initially. Loosely wrap some rags around the oil filter, then unscrew it and immediately position it with its open end uppermost to prevent further spillage of oil. Remove the oil filter from the engine compartment and empty the oil into the container.

9 Use a clean rag to remove all oil, dirt and sludge from the filter sealing area on the engine. Check the old filter to make sure that the rubber sealing ring hasn't stuck to the engine. If it has, carefully remove it.

10 Apply a light coating of clean oil to the sealing ring on the new filter, then screw it into position on the engine. Tighten the filter firmly by hand only - do not use any tools. Wipe clean the exterior of the oil filter.

11 Remove the old oil and all tools from under the vehicle, then (if applicable) lower the vehicle to the ground.

12 Fill the engine with the specified quantity and grade of oil, as described in "Weekly checks". Pour the oil in slowly, otherwise it may overflow from the top of the rocker cover. Check that the oil level is up to the correct level on the dipstick, then refit and tighten the oil filler cap.

13 Run the engine for a few minutes, and check that there are no leaks around the oil filter seal and the sump drain plug.

14 Switch off the engine and wait a few minutes for the oil to settle in the sump once more. With the new oil circulated and the filter now completely full, recheck the level on the dipstick and add more oil if necessary.

15 Dispose of the used engine oil safely with reference to "General repair procedures" in the Reference Sections at the end of this manual.

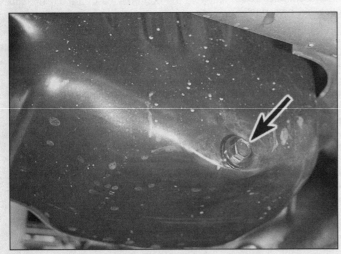

6.4 Engine oil drain plug (arrowed) - CVH engine

6.7 Oil filter location - CVH engine

7 Oil filler cap cleaning - OHV and HCS engines

1 Simply pull the oil filler cap from the rocker cover and, where applicable, disconnect the hose(s) from the cap.
2 Inspect the filler cap, and if necessary clean the cap using clean petrol to remove any deposits.
3 Ensure that the cap is completely dry before refitting.

8 Fluid leak check

1 Visually inspect the engine joint faces, gaskets and seals for any signs of water or oil leaks. Pay particular attention to the areas around the rocker cover, cylinder head, oil filter and sump joint faces. Bear in mind that over a period of time some very slight seepage from these areas is to be expected but what you are really looking for is any indication of a serious leak. Should a leak be found, renew the offending gasket or oil seal by referring to the appropriate Chapter(s) in this manual.
2 Similarly, check the transmission for oil leaks, and investigate and rectify and problems found.
3 Check the security and condition of all the engine related pipes and hoses. Ensure that all cable-ties or securing clips are in place and in good condition. Clips which are broken or missing can lead to chafing of the hoses, pipes or wiring which could cause more serious problems in the future.
4 Carefully check the condition of all coolant, fuel and brake hoses. Renew any hose which is cracked, swollen or deteriorated. Cracks will show up better if the hose is squeezed. Pay close attention to the hose clips that secure the hoses to the system components. Hose clips can pinch and puncture hoses, resulting in leaks. If wire type hose clips are used, it may be a good idea to replace them with screw-type clips.
5 With the vehicle raised, inspect the fuel tank and filler neck for punctures, cracks and other damage. The connection between the filler neck and tank is especially critical. Sometimes a rubber filler neck or connecting hose will leak due to loose retaining clamps or deteriorated rubber.
6 Similarly, inspect all brake hoses and metal pipes. If any damage or deterioration is discovered, do not drive the vehicle until the necessary repair work has been carried out. Renew any damaged sections of hose or pipe.
7 Carefully check all rubber hoses and metal fuel lines leading away from the petrol tank. Check for loose connections, deteriorated hoses, crimped lines and other damage. Pay particular attention to the vent pipes and hoses which often loop up around the filler neck and can become blocked or crimped.

Follow the lines to the front of the vehicle carefully inspecting them all the way. Renew damaged sections as necessary.
8 From within the engine compartment, check the security of all fuel hose attachments and pipe unions, and inspect the fuel hoses and vacuum hoses for kinks, chafing and deterioration.
9 Where applicable, check the condition of the oil cooler hoses and pipes.
10 Check the condition of all exposed wiring harnesses.
11 Also check the engine and transmission components for signs of fluid leaks.

9 Exhaust manifold nut check - RS Turbo models

Check the tightness of the exhaust manifold securing nuts using a torque wrench.

10 Idle speed and mixture adjustment

Caution: Certain adjustment points in the fuel system are protected by "tamperproof" caps, plugs or seals. In some EEC countries (though not yet in the UK) it is an offence to drive a vehicle with broken or missing tamperproof seals. Before disturbing a tamperproof seal, satisfy yourself that you will not be breaking any local or national laws by doing so, and fit a new seal after adjustment is complete where required by law. Do not break tamperproof seals on a vehicle which is still under warranty.

Note: *Before carrying out any carburettor adjustment, ensure that the contact breaker points, ignition timing and spark plug gaps (as applicable) are set as specified and that the distributor is operating correctly (where applicable). To carry out the adjustments an accurate tachometer will be required and the use of an exhaust gas analyser (CO meter) is also preferable.*

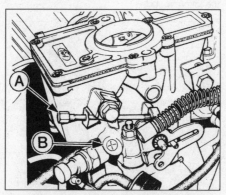

10.6 Idle speed adjustment screw (A) and mixture adjustment screw (B) - Ford VV carburettor

Models with Ford VV carburettor

Idle speed

1 With the engine at normal operating temperature, connect a tachometer in accordance with the manufacturer's instructions.
2 Disconnect the wiring multi-plug from the radiator cooling fan thermostatic switch in the thermostat housing and bridge the two contacts in the plug using a suitable length of wire. This is necessary so that the cooling fan runs continuously during adjustment.
3 On automatic transmission models slacken the adjuster screw on the throttle valve shaft lever to give clearance of 2 to 3 mm (0.079 to 0.118 in) - see Chapter 7, Part B.
4 Ensure that the air cleaner is fitted and that its vacuum hoses are not in any way trapped or pinched, particularly between the air cleaner body and the top face of the carburettor.
5 Run the engine at 3000 rpm for 30 seconds, then allow it to idle and note the idle speed. If using an exhaust gas analyser it should be noted that initially the CO% reading will rise, but then fall and stabilise after a period of 5 to 25 seconds. The CO reading should then be as specified.

Idle mixture

6 If necessary, adjust the idle speed adjustment screw to give the specified idle speed **(see illustration)**.
7 Adjustment of the CO content (mixture) is not normally required during routine maintenance, but if the reading noted in paragraph 5 is not as given in the Specifications first remove the tamperproof plug, prising it free using a small screwdriver.
8 Run the engine at 3000 rpm for 30 seconds, then allow it to idle. Adjust the mixture screw **(see illustration 10.6)** within 30 seconds. If more time is required run the engine at 3000 rpm again for 30 seconds.
9 Adjust the idle speed if necessary and recheck the CO content.
10 Fit a new tamperproof plug to the mixture adjuster screw on completion. It should be noted that mixture adjustment without a CO analyser is not accurate and therefore not recommended.
11 On completion disconnect the instruments, remove the cooling fan bridging wire and reconnect the multi-plug.
12 On automatic transmission models adjust the downshift linkage (Chapter 7, Part B).

Models with Weber 2V carburettor

13 The procedure is the same as for the Ford VV carburettor as described previously in this Section, but the adjusting screw locations are as shown **(see illustrations)**.

Models with Bosch K-Jetronic fuel injection system

14 The idle speed and fuel mixture adjustments will normally only be required after the installation of new components.

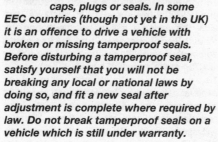

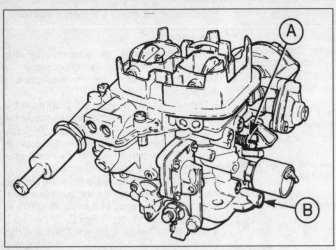

10.13a Weber 2V carburettor idle speed adjustment screw (A) and mixture screw (B) - XR3 and 1.4 litre models

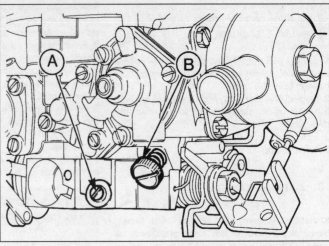

10.13b Weber 2V carburettor mixture adjustment screw (A) and idle speed adjustment screw (B) - 1.6 litre models

Refer to the caution at the beginning of this Section before proceeding.

15 On early models the idle speed adjustment screw is located on the rear of the throttle housing, but access is severely limited unless the heater plenum chamber top cover is removed as described in Chapter 4, Part B **(see illustration)**.

16 On later models the idle speed adjustment screw is located on top of the throttle housing beneath a tamperproof plug **(see illustration)**.

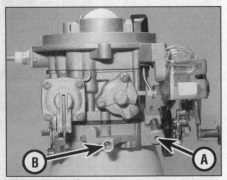

10.13c Idle speed screw (A) and mixture adjustment screw (B) on Weber 2V TLDM carburettor (1.1 and 1.3 HCS engines)

Hook out the plug with a sharp pointed tool to gain access.

17 Before making any adjustments, warm the engine up to normal operating temperature and connect a tachometer in accordance with the manufacturer's instructions.

18 Increase the engine speed to 3000 rpm and hold it at this speed for 30 seconds, then allow the engine to idle, check the tachometer reading and if necessary turn the idle speed adjustment screw as required until the engine is idling at the specified speed.

19 To check the mixture adjustment an exhaust gas analyser is needed and should be connected in accordance with the manufacturer's instructions. A 3 mm Allen key will also be required to make any adjustments.

20 Before making any adjustments to the mixture, ensure that the idle speed is correct.

21 Remove the tamperproof plug from the top of the mixture adjustment screw tube on top of the fuel distributor **(see illustration)**.

22 Stabilise the exhaust gases (paragraph 18).

23 Insert the Allen key into the mixture screw tube and engage the adjusting screw. Turn the screw as necessary until the correct CO reading is obtained, then if required readjust the idling speed.

24 If the mixture adjustment cannot be finalised within 30 seconds from the moment of stabilising the exhaust gases, repeat the operations in paragraph 18 before continuing the adjustment procedure.

25 On completion fit a new tamperproof plug and disconnect the tachometer and exhaust gas analyser.

Models with Bosch KE-Jetronic fuel injection system

26 The idle speed and fuel mixture adjustments will normally only be required after the installation of new components.

27 The idle speed adjustment screw is located on the side of the throttle housing **(see illustration)**.

28 Before making any adjustments, warm the engine up to normal operating temperature and connect a tachometer in accordance with the manufacturer's instructions.

29 Disconnect the wiring multi-plug at the pressure actuator on the side of the fuel distributor **(see illustration)**.

30 Increase the engine speed to 3000 rpm and hold it at this speed for 30 seconds, then allow the engine to idle. Check the tachometer reading and if necessary turn the

10.15 Idle speed adjustment screw (arrowed) on early K-Jetronic systems

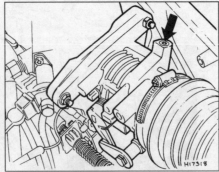

10.16 K-Jetronic system idle speed adjustment screw (arrowed) on later models

10.21 K-Jetronic system mixture adjustment screw location (arrowed)

10.27 Idle speed adjustment screw (arrowed) on KE-Jetronic system

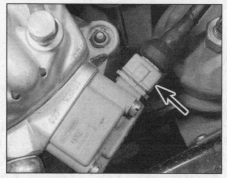

10.29 Pressure actuator wiring multi-plug (arrowed) - KE-Jetronic system

10.33 KE-Jetronic system mixture adjustment tamperproof plug (arrowed)

idle speed adjustment screw as required until the engine is idling at the specified speed.

31 To check the mixture adjustment an exhaust gas analyser is needed and should be connected in accordance with the manufacturer's instructions. A 3 mm Allen key will also be required to make any adjustments.

32 Before proceeding ensure that the idle speed is correct.

33 Unscrew the tamperproof plug from the mixture adjustment orifice on top of the fuel distributor **(see illustration)**.

34 Stabilise the exhaust gases (paragraph 30).

35 Insert the Allen key into the mixture adjustment orifice and push down to engage the adjustment screw. Turn the adjustment screw clockwise to increase the CO reading and anti-clockwise to decrease it. Remove the Allen key, plug the orifice and check the CO reading.

36 If the mixture adjustment cannot be finalised within 30 seconds from the moment of stabilising the exhaust gases, repeat the operations in paragraph 30 before continuing the adjustment procedure. Make sure that the Allen key is removed before increasing the engine speed otherwise the fuel distributor will be damaged.

37 Continue adjustment until the correct CO reading is obtained, then if necessary readjust the idle speed.

38 Refit the tamperproof screw and reconnect the pressure actuator multi-plug. Disconnect the tachometer and exhaust gas analyser.

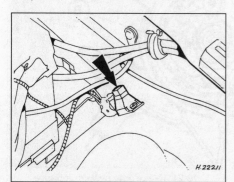

10.45 CO adjustment potentiometer location (arrowed) - 1.6 EFI engine

Models with Central (single-point) Fuel Injection (CFI) system

39 Both the idle speed and mixture are controlled by the engine management system. Adjustment requires the use of specialist equipment. If the idle speed is suspected of being incorrect, the vehicle must be taken to a Ford dealer for diagnostic checks and, if necessary, adjustment.

Models with Electronic Fuel Injection (EFI) system

40 Idle speed is controlled by the EEC IV module, and cannot be adjusted.

41 To adjust the mixture (CO content), first run the engine until it reaches normal operating temperature.

42 Connect a CO meter and a tachometer in accordance with the manufacturer's instructions.

43 Clear any excess fuel in the inlet manifold by running the engine at 3000 rpm for approximately 15 seconds, then allow the engine to idle.

44 Wait for the test instrument readings to stabilise, then record the CO content and the idle speed.

45 If adjustment of the CO content is required, remove the tamperproof cap from the CO adjustment potentiometer (located on the wing panel behind the left-hand suspension turret) and adjust the screw to obtain the correct CO setting at the specified idle speed **(see illustration)**. Note that any adjustment must be made within 30 seconds of the instrument readings stabilising, otherwise the procedure described in paragraph 43 must be repeated.

46 On completion of adjustment, stop the engine and disconnect all test equipment. Fit a new tamperproof cap to the CO adjustment potentiometer.

11 Ignition system component check

1 Where applicable, remove the distributor cap and thoroughly clean it inside and out with a dry lint-free cloth. Examine the four HT lead segments inside the cap. If the segments appear badly burnt or pitted, renew the cap.

Make sure that the carbon brush in the centre of the cap is free to move and that it protrudes significantly from its holder.

2 Check the distributor cap for signs of tracking (indicated by thin black lines on the surface of the cap). Renew the cap if tracking is evident.

3 Wipe clean the HT leads and the coil tower.

4 Check the condition and security of all leads and wiring associated with the ignition system. Make sure that no chafing is occurring on any of the wires and that all connections are secure, clean and free from corrosion.

12 Distributor lubrication - models with contact breaker distributor

1 Remove the distributor cap and the rotor arm.

2 Apply a couple of drops of light oil to the felt pad in the top of the shaft.

3 Wipe clean the distributor cam, then apply a trace of high melting-point grease to the four cam lobes.

4 Refit the rotor arm and the distributor cap.

13 Contact breaker points adjustment - models with contact breaker distributor

1 Spring back the retaining clips or undo the screws as appropriate and lift off the distributor cap.

2 Withdraw the rotor arm from the distributor shaft.

3 Using a screwdriver, gently prise the contact breaker points open to examine the condition of their faces. If they are rough, pitted or dirty they should be renewed as described in the next Section.

4 Assuming that the points are in a satisfactory condition or that they have just been renewed, the gap between the two faces should be checked and if necessary adjusted. This can be done using feeler blades as described in the following paragraphs, or preferably by using the more accurate dwell angle method as described from paragraph 8 onwards.

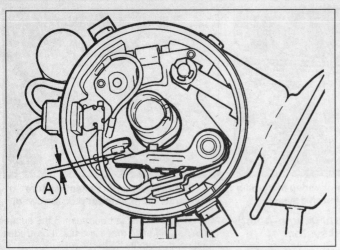

13.5a Contact breaker points gap (A) - Bosch distributor

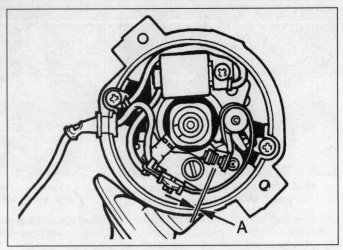

13.5b Contact breaker points gap (A) - Lucas distributor

5 To adjust the points using feeler blades, turn the crankshaft using a spanner on the crankshaft pulley bolt until the heel of the contact breaker arm is on the peak of one of the four cam lobes and the points are fully open. A feeler blade of thickness equal to the contact breaker points gap as given in the Specifications should now just slide between the point faces **(see illustrations)**.

6 If adjustment is required, slacken the retaining screw slightly and move the fixed point as necessary to achieve the desired gap **(see illustrations)**. After adjustment tighten the retaining screw and recheck the gap.

> **HAYNES HiNT** *The points can be easily moved by engaging a screwdriver in the slot on the end of the fixed point and levering against the corresponding slot or raised pips on the baseplate.*

7 Refit the rotor arm and the distributor cap.

8 If a dwell meter is available adjust the contact breaker points by measuring and setting the dwell angle as follows.

9 The dwell angle is the number of degrees of distributor cam rotation during which the contact breaker points are closed; ie the period from when the points close after being opened by one cam lobe, until they are opened again by the next cam lobe. The advantages of setting the points by this method are that any wear of the distributor shaft or cam lobes is taken into account and the inaccuracies associated with using feeler blades are eliminated. Also, on 1.1 litre CVH engines the static ignition timing is accurately set in production and adjustment of the ignition timing in service has been deleted from the maintenance schedule. Therefore dwell angle adjustment is far more critical on these engines.

10 In general a dwell meter should be used in accordance with the manufacturer's instructions. However, the use of one type of meter is outlined as follows.

11 Remove the distributor cap and rotor arm and connect one lead of the dwell meter to the "+" terminal on the coil and the other lead to the coil "-" terminal.

12 Whilst an assistant turns on the ignition and cranks the engine on the starter, observe the reading on the dwell meter scale. With the engine cranking the reading should be equal to the dwell angle given in the Specifications.

13 If the dwell angle is too small, the contact breaker points gap should be reduced and if the dwell angle is excessive the gap should be increased.

14 Adjust the points gap while the engine is cranking using the method described in paragraph 6. When the dwell angle is satisfactory, disconnect the meter, then refit the rotor arm and distributor cap.

15 Check the ignition timing (Section 14).

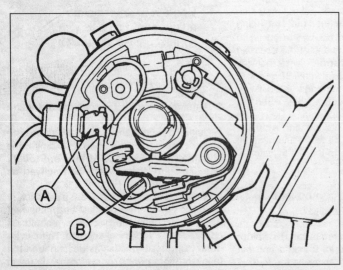

13.6a Contact breaker point components - Bosch distributor
A LT lead connector   B Contact breaker retaining screw

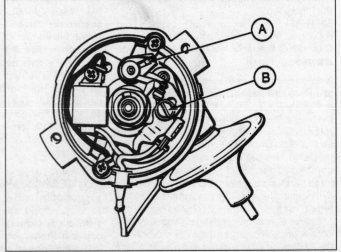

13.6b Contact breaker point components - Lucas distributor
A Secondary movement cam and peg   B Contact breaker retaining screw

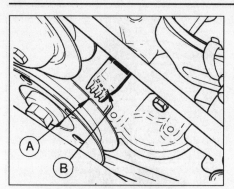

**14.5a Timing mark identification -
OHV engines**
A Notch on crankshaft pulley
B Timing scale cast into timing cover

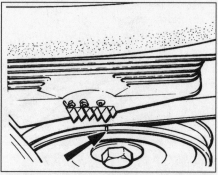

**14.5b Crankshaft pulley notch (arrowed)
and timing scale - CVH engine**

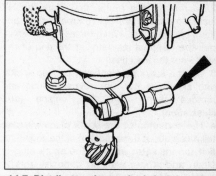

**14.7 Distributor clamp pinch-bolt location
(arrowed) - OHV engines**

14 Ignition timing check - models with contact breaker distributor

Note: *With modern ignition systems the only suitable way to time the ignition accurately is with a stroboscopic timing light. However, for initial setting up purposes (ie after major overhaul, or if the timing has been otherwise completely lost) a basic initial static setting may be used to get the engine started Once the engine is running, the timing should be accurately set using the timing light. Before carrying out any of the following, ensure that the contact breaker points are correctly adjusted as described in Section 13.*

1 In order that the engine can run efficiently, it is necessary for a spark to occur at the spark plug and ignite the fuel/air mixture at the instant just before the piston on the compression stroke reaches the top of its travel. The precise instant at which the spark occurs is determined by the ignition timing and this is quoted in degrees before top dead centre (BTDC).

2 If the timing is being checked as a maintenance or service procedure, refer to paragraph 11 onwards. If the distributor has been dismantled or renewed, or if its position on the engine has been altered, obtain an initial static setting as follows.

Static setting

3 Pull off the plug lead and remove No 1 spark plug (nearest the crankshaft pulley).
4 Place a finger over the plug hole and turn the crankshaft in the normal direction of rotation (clockwise from the crankshaft pulley end) until pressure is felt in No 1 cylinder. This indicates that the piston is commencing its compression stroke. The crankshaft can be turned with a spanner on the pulley bolt.
5 Continue turning the crankshaft until the notch on the pulley is aligned with the appropriate mark on the timing scale for the engine being worked on (see Specifications). On OHV engines the timing scale is cast into the timing cover and situated just above and to the right of the pulley. On CVH engines the

scale is moulded into the timing belt cover and is situated directly above the pulley. On all engines the "O" mark on the scale represents Top Dead Centre (TDC) and the raised projections to the left of TDC are in increments of 4° BTDC **(see illustrations)**.
6 Remove the distributor cap and check that the rotor arm is pointing towards the No 1 spark plug lead segment in the cap.
7 Slacken the distributor clamp pinch bolt (OHV engines) or the three distributor flange securing bolts (CVH engines) **(see illustration)**.
8 Turn the distributor body anti-clockwise slightly until the contact breaker points are closed, then slowly turn the distributor body clockwise until the points just open. Hold the distributor body in this position and tighten the clamp pinch bolt or flange securing bolts as applicable.
9 Refit the distributor cap, No 1 spark plug and the plug lead.
10 It should now be possible to start and run the engine enabling the timing to be accurately checked with a timing light as follows.

Stroboscopic setting

11 Refer to the Specifications for the timing setting applicable to the engine being worked on and then highlight the appropriate mark on the timing scale and the notch in the pulley with a dab of white paint (see paragraph 5).
12 Connect a timing light to the engine in accordance with the manufacturer's instructions (usually between No 1 spark plug and plug lead).
13 Disconnect the vacuum hose at the distributor vacuum unit and plug the hose.
14 Start the engine and allow it to idle.
15 Point the timing light at the timing marks. They should appear to be stationary with the crankshaft pulley notch in alignment with the appropriate notch on the scale.
16 If adjustment is necessary (ie the marks are not aligned) slacken the distributor clamp pinch bolt or flange securing bolts as applicable, and turn the distributor body as necessary to align the marks. Tighten the pinch bolt or flange bolts when the setting is correct.

17 A secondary use of the timing light is to check that the centrifugal and vacuum advance functions of the distributor are working.
18 The tests are not of course precise as would be the case if sophisticated equipment were used, but will at least indicate the serviceability of the unit.
19 With the engine idling, timing light connected and vacuum pipe disconnected and plugged as described in the preceding paragraphs, increase the engine speed to 2000 rpm and note the approximate distance which the pulley mark moves out of alignment with the mark on the scale.
20 Reconnect the vacuum pipe to the distributor and repeat the test when for the same increase in engine speed, the alignment differential of the timing marks should be greater than previously observed.
21 If the timing marks did not appear to move during the first test, a fault in the distributor centrifugal advance mechanism is indicated. No increased movement of the marks during the second test indicates a punctured diaphragm in the vacuum unit, or a leak in the vacuum line.
22 On completion of the adjustments and checks, switch off the engine and disconnect the timing light.

15 Spark plug renewal - RS Turbo models

1 The correct functioning of the spark plugs is vital for the correct running and efficiency of the engine. It is essential that the plugs fitted are appropriate for the engine, and the suitable type is specified at the end of this chapter. If this type is used and the engine is in good condition, the spark plugs should not need attention between scheduled replacement intervals. Spark plug cleaning is rarely necessary and should not be attempted unless specialised equipment is available as damage can easily be caused to the firing ends.

2 To remove the plugs, first mark the HT leads to ensure correct refitment, then pull them off the plugs. When removing the leads, pull the terminal insulator at the end of the lead - not the lead itself.

3 Using a spark plug spanner or deep socket and extension bar, unscrew the plugs and remove them from the engine **(see illustration)**.

4 The condition of the spark plugs will also tell much about the condition of the engine.

5 If the insulator nose of the spark plug is clean and white, with no deposits, this is indicative of a weak mixture, or too hot a plug. (A hot plug transfers heat away from the electrode slowly - a cold plug transfers it away quickly.)

6 If the tip and insulator nose are covered with hard black-looking deposits, then this is indicative that the mixture is too rich. Should the plug be black and oily, then it is likely that the engine is fairly worn, as well as the mixture being too rich.

7 If the insulator nose is covered with light tan to greyish brown deposits, then the mixture is correct and it is likely that the engine is in good condition.

8 The spark plug gap is of considerable importance, as if it is too large or too small, the size of the spark and its efficiency will be seriously impaired. The spark plug gap should be set to the figure given in the Specifications at the beginning of this Chapter.

15.10a Measuring the spark plug gap with a wire gauge . . .

15.10b . . . and adjusting the gap using a special adjusting tool

15.3 Tools required for spark plug removal, gap adjustment and refitting

9 To set it, measure the gap with a feeler blade, and then bend open, or close, the outer plug electrode until the correct gap is achieved **(see illustration)**. The centre electrode should never be bent as this may crack the insulation and cause plug failure, if nothing worse.

10 Special spark plug electrode cap adjusting tools are available from most motor accessory shops **(see illustrations)**.

11 Before fitting the plugs first ensure that the plug threads and the seating area in the cylinder head are clean, dry and free of carbon.

12 Screw the plugs in by hand initially and then fully tighten to the specified torque. If a torque wrench is not available, tighten the plugs until initial resistance is felt, then tighten by a further 1/16 of a turn for the taper seat plugs fitted to OHV engines, or 1/4 of a turn for the gasket seat type fitted to CVH engines. Do not over-tighten the spark plugs, otherwise damage to the threads may occur and they will also be extremely difficult to remove in the future.

HAYNES HiNT

It is very often difficult to insert spark plugs into their holes without cross-threading them. To avoid this possibility, fit a short length of 5/16-inch internal diameter rubber hose over the end of the spark plug. The flexible hose acts as a universal joint to help align the plug with the plug hole. Should the plug begin to cross-thread, the hose will slip on the spark plug, preventing thread damage to the aluminium cylinder head.

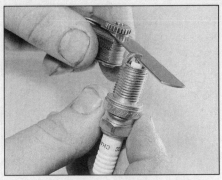

15.9 Measuring the spark plug gap with a feeler blade

13 Refit the plug leads in the correct order ensuring that they are a secure fit over the plug ends. Periodically wipe the leads clean to reduce the risk of HT leakage by arcing and remove any traces of corrosion that may occur on the end fittings.

16 Front brake disc pad check

1 Place a mirror between the roadwheel and the caliper and check the thickness of the friction material of the disc pads **(see illustration)**. If the material has worn down to the specified minimum or less, the pads must be renewed as an axle set (four pads).

2 For a comprehensive check, the brake pads should be removed and cleaned. This will permit the operation of the caliper to be checked, and the condition of the brake disc itself to be examined on both sides. Refer to Chapter 9 for further information.

17 Rear brake shoe lining check

1 Due to the fact that the rear brake drums are combined with the hubs, which makes removal of the drums more complicated than is the case with detachable drums, inspection of the shoe linings can be carried out at the

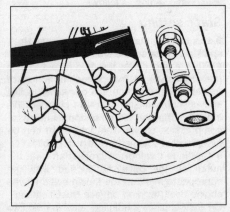

16.1 Checking the front disc pad wear using a mirror

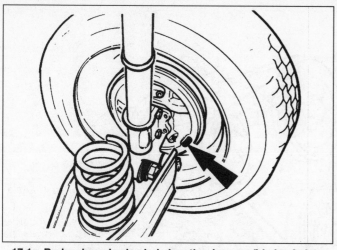

17.1a Brake shoe viewing hole location (arrowed) in backplate

17.1b Checking rear brake lining wear with a mirror

specified intervals by prising out the small inspection plug from the brake backplate and observing the linings through the hole using a mirror **(see illustrations)**.

2 A minimum thickness of friction material must always be observed on the shoes. If it is worn down to this level, renew the shoes.

3 Do not attempt to re-line shoes yourself but always obtain factory re-lined shoes.

4 Renew the shoes in an axle set (four shoes), even if only one is worn to the minimum.

18 Suspension and steering check

Front suspension and steering check

1 Raise the front of the vehicle, and securely support it on axle stands (see "*Jacking and Vehicle Support*").

2 Visually inspect the balljoint dust covers and the steering rack-and-pinion gaiters for splits, chafing or deterioration **(see illustration)**. Any wear of these components will cause loss of lubricant, together with dirt and water entry, resulting in rapid deterioration of the balljoints or steering gear.

3 Grasp the roadwheel at the 12 o'clock and 6 o'clock positions, and try to rock it **(see illustration)**. Very slight free play may be felt, but if the movement is appreciable, further investigation is necessary to determine the source. Continue rocking the wheel while an assistant depresses the footbrake. If the movement is now eliminated or significantly reduced, it is likely that the hub bearings are at fault. If the free play is still evident with the footbrake depressed, then there is wear in the suspension joints or mountings.

4 Now grasp the wheel at the 9 o'clock and 3 o'clock positions, and try to rock it as before. Any movement felt now may again be caused by wear in the hub bearings or the steering track-rod balljoints. If the inner or outer balljoint is worn, the visual movement will be obvious.

5 Using a large screwdriver or flat bar, check for wear in the suspension mounting bushes by levering between the relevant suspension component and its attachment point. Some movement is to be expected as the mountings are made of rubber, but excessive wear should be obvious. Also check the condition of any visible rubber bushes, looking for splits, cracks or contamination of the rubber.

6 With the car standing on its wheels, have an assistant turn the steering wheel back and forth about an eighth of a turn each way. There should be very little, if any, lost movement between the steering wheel and roadwheels. If this is not the case, closely observe the joints and mountings previously described, but in addition, check the steering column universal joints for wear, and the rack-and-pinion steering gear itself.

7 Visually check that each lower arm balljoint is correctly located in the hub carrier, ensuring that the Torx type pinch-bolt is fully engaged in the groove in the balljoint stud.

Suspension strut/shock absorber check

8 Check for any signs of fluid leakage around the suspension strut/shock absorber body, or from the rubber gaiter around the piston rod.

Should any fluid be noticed, the suspension strut/shock absorber is defective internally, and should be renewed. **Note:** *Suspension struts/shock absorbers should always be renewed in pairs on the same axle.*

9 The efficiency of the suspension strut/shock absorber may be checked by bouncing the vehicle at each corner. Generally speaking, the body will return to its normal position and stop after being depressed. If it rises and returns on a rebound, the suspension strut/shock absorber is probably suspect. Examine also the suspension strut/shock absorber upper and lower mountings for any signs of wear.

19 Seat belt check

1 Periodically check the belts for fraying or other damage. If evident, renew the belt.

2 If the belts become dirty, wipe them with a damp cloth using a little detergent only.

3 Check the tightness of the anchor bolts and if they are ever disconnected, make quite sure that the original sequence of fitting of washers, bushes and anchor plates is retained.

1

18.2 Checking a steering gear gaiter

18.3 Rocking the roadwheel to check steering/suspension components

20 Alternator drivebelt check

1 A conventional vee drivebelt is used to drive both the alternators and water pump pulleys on OHV and HCS engines, and the alternator pulley only on CVH engines, power being transmitted via a pulley on the engine crankshaft.

2 To remove the drivebelt, slacken the alternator mounting bolts and the bolts on the adjuster link and push the alternator in towards the engine as far as possible **(see illustration)**.

3 Withdraw the belt from the pulleys. In some instances it may also be necessary to remove the adjuster link-to-alternator bolt to avoid straining the drivebelt.

4 Fit the belt by slipping it over the pulley rims. If necessary remove the adjuster link-to-alternator bolt, if not already done, to avoid straining the belt. Never be tempted to remove or refit the drivebelt by prising it over a pulley rim otherwise the pulley or the drivebelt internal webbing will be damaged.

5 To tension the belt pull the alternator away from the engine until the belt is fairly taut, and tighten the adjuster link-to-alternator bolt. Check that the total deflection of the belt, using finger pressure at a point midway between the alternator and crankshaft or water pump pulleys, is 10 mm (0.4 in) **(see illustrations)**. A little trial and error may be necessary to obtain the correct tension. If the belt is too slack, it will slip in the pulleys and soon become glazed or burnt. This is often indicated by a screeching noise as the engine is accelerated, particularly when the headlights or other electrical accessories are

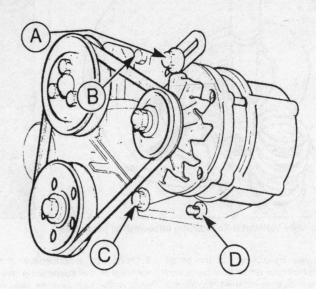

20.2 Alternator mounting and adjuster link bolts

A Adjuster link-to-alternator bolt
B Adjuster link-to-engine bolt

C and D Alternator mounting bolts

switched on. If the belt is too tight the bearings in the water pump and/or alternator will soon be damaged.

6 Once the tension is correct, tighten the remaining adjuster link bolt, front mounting bolt and rear mounting bolt in that order.

7 If a new belt has been fitted the tension should be rechecked and adjusted again if necessary after the engine has run for approximately ten minutes.

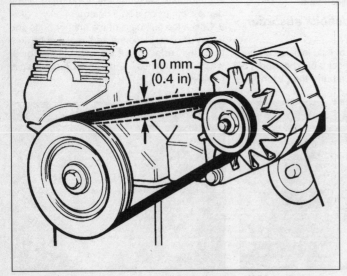

20.5a Drivebelt tension checking point - CVH engines

10 mm (0.4 in)

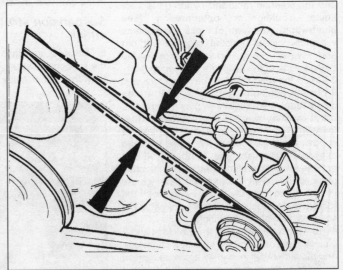

20.5b Drivebelt tension checking point - OHV engines

Every 12 000 miles or 12 months

21 Valve clearance adjustment - OHV and HCS engines

OHV engines

1 This operation should be carried out with the engine cold and the air cleaner and rocker cover removed.

2 Using a ring spanner or socket on the crankshaft pulley bolt, turn the crankshaft in a clockwise direction until No 1 piston is at TDC on its compression stroke. This can be verified by checking that the pulley and timing cover marks are in alignment and that the valves of No 4 cylinder are rocking. When the valves are rocking, this means that the slightest rotation of the crankshaft pulley in either direction will cause one rocker arm to move up and the other to move down.

3 Numbering from the thermostat housing end of the cylinder head, the valves are identified as follows:

Valve No		Cylinder No
1	Exhaust	1
2	Inlet	1
3	Exhaust	2
4	Inlet	2
5	Exhaust	3
6	Inlet	3
7	Exhaust	4
8	Inlet	4

4 Adjust the valve clearances by following the sequence given in the following table. Turn the crankshaft pulley 180° (half a turn) after adjusting each pair:

Valves rocking	Valves to adjust
7 and 8	1 (Exhaust), 2 (Inlet)
5 and 6	3 (Exhaust), 4 (Inlet)
1 and 2	7 (Exhaust), 8 (Inlet)
3 and 4	5 (Exhaust), 6 (Inlet)

5 The clearances for the inlet and exhaust valves are different (see Specifications). Use a feeler blade of the appropriate thickness to check each clearance between the end of the valve stem and the rocker arm. The gauge should be a stiff sliding fit. If it is not, turn the adjuster bolt with a ring spanner. These bolts are of stiff thread type and require no locking nut. Turn the bolt clockwise to reduce the clearance and anti-clockwise to increase it (see illustration).

6 Refit the air cleaner and rocker cover on completion of adjustment.

HCS engines

7 The procedure is as described previously for OHV engines, but note that the valve arrangement has been altered and is now as shown below. Take care not to overtighten the rocker cover bolts on refitting, as this can result in leaks.

Valve No		Cylinder No
1	Exhaust	1
2	Inlet	1
3	Exhaust	2
4	Inlet	2
5	Inlet	3
6	Exhaust	3
7	Inlet	4
8	Exhaust	4

22 Exhaust system check

With the vehicle raised on a hoist or supported on axle stands (see "Jacking and Vehicle Support"), check the exhaust system for signs of leaks, corrosion or damage and check the rubber mountings for condition and security (see illustration). Where damage or corrosion are evident, renew the system complete or in sections, as applicable, using the information given in Chapter 4, Part E.

23 Turbocharger-to-manifold nut check - RS Turbo models

Check the tightness of the turbocharger-to-exhaust manifold securing nuts using a torque wrench.

24 Spark plug renewal

The procedure is as described for RS Turbo models in Section 15.

25 Contact breaker points renewal

1 Spring back the retaining clips or undo the screws as appropriate and lift off the distributor cap.

2 Withdraw the rotor arm from the distributor shaft.

3 On the Bosch distributor disconnect the contact breaker points LT lead at the spade connector. On the Lucas distributor ease the contact breaker spring arm out of the plastic insulator and slide the combined LT and condenser lead out of the hooked end of the spring arm.

4 Undo the retaining screw and withdraw the contact breaker points from the distributor baseplate. Take care not to drop the screw and washer inside the distributor during removal and refitting. If possible use a magnetic screwdriver, or alternatively, retain the screw on the end of the screwdriver using a dab of grease.

5 Wipe clean the distributor cam, then apply a trace of high-melting-point grease to the four cam lobes. Also, on OHV engines apply two drops of light oil to the felt pad at the top of the distributor shaft.

21.5 Valve clearance adjustment

22.1 Exhaust silencer mounting

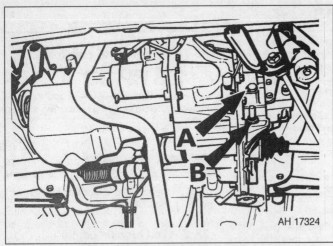

26.1a Transmission oil filler plug (A) and selector shaft locking mechanism cap (B)

26.1b Allen type transmission filler plug (arrowed) as fitted to later models

6 Locate the new contact breaker points on the baseplate and secure with the retaining screw, lightly tightened only at this stage. On the Lucas distributor ensure that the secondary movement cam is engaged with the peg, and that both washers are refitted with the retaining screw **(see illustration 13.6b)**.

7 Reconnect the LT lead, then refer to Section 13 and adjust the contact breaker points gap.

26 Manual transmission oil level check

1 With the car on level ground wipe the area around the filler plug, then unscrew the plug using a socket spanner, or on later versions a suitable Torx or Allen key or socket bit, as applicable. Access can be gained from above or below the car **(see illustrations)**.

2 Locate the aluminium build code tag, which is secured to one of the transmission housing upper bolts, and note the transmission part number stamped on the tag. If the last letter of the part number suffix is a D then the transmission was manufactured prior to August 1985. Transmissions manufactured

from August 1985 have an E as the last letter of the part number suffix.

3 On the early type transmission (suffix letter D) the oil level must be maintained between 5 and 10 mm (0.2 and 0.4 in) below the lower edge of the filler plug hole.

4 If the transmission is of the later type (suffix letter E) the oil level must be maintained between 0 and 5 mm (0.2 in) below the lower edge of the filler plug hole.

5 To simplify the checking procedure a dipstick can be made from thin rod bent at right angles and having marks on one "leg" made with a file at 5 mm (0.2 in) intervals. Rest the unmarked leg on the lower edge of the filler plug hole with the marked leg immersed in the oil. Remove the dipstick, read off the level and top-up if necessary using the specified grade of oil. Refit the filler plug on completion.

6 Renewal of the transmission oil is not a service requirement, but if draining is necessary prior to a repair or overhaul task place a suitable container beneath the selector shaft locking mechanism cap nut located just below the filler plug **(see illustration)**. Unscrew the cap nut, remove the spring and interlock pin and allow the oil to drain.

⚠️ *Caution: Take care when unscrewing the cap nut as the tension of the spring may cause the pin to fly out as the cap nut is released. Refit the pin, spring and cap nut when draining is complete, but apply sealer to the cap nut threads (see Specifications). Note that from 1986 onwards the cap nut is shrouded by the transmission support crossmember and cannot be removed in situ. On these models draining can only be carried out after removal of the transmission from the car.*

27 Automatic transmission fluid level check

1 The automatic transmission fluid level must be checked when the engine and transmission are at normal operating temperature; preferably after a short journey.

2 Park the car on level ground, then fully apply the handbrake.

3 With the engine running at its normal idle speed, apply the footbrake and simultaneously move the selector lever through the full range of positions three times then move it back to the P position. Allow the engine to run at idle for a further period of one minute.

4 With the engine still idling, extract the transmission fluid level dipstick and wipe it dry, with a clean non-fluffy cloth. Fully reinsert the dipstick and then extract it again and check the fluid level mark, which must be between the "MAX" and "MIN" markings **(see illustration)**

5 If topping-up is necessary, use only the specified fluid type and pour it through the dipstick tube, but take care not to overfill. The level must not exceed the "MAX" mark.

26.6 Selector shaft locking mechanism cap nut (arrowed)

27.4 Transmission fluid level dipstick location and level markings

6 An improved type of transmission fluid is used in later models and before topping-up or refilling it is necessary to identify the transmission being worked on so that the correct fluid may be obtained.

7 Locate the transmission identification number which is stamped on a metal tag attached to the top of the valve body cover **(see illustration)**. If, at the end of the second line on the metal tag, the prefix E3RP- appears, then the transmission is of the early type. If the prefix is E6RP- then the unit is of the later type. Later transmissions can also be identified by having a black dipstick stating the fluid specification and type. Having determined whether the transmission is of the early or later type, refer to *"Lubricants and fluids"* for the fluid requirement. *Under no circumstances may the later type fluid be used in the early type transmission, and vice versa.*

8 If the fluid level was below the minimum mark when checked or is in constant need of topping-up, check around the transmission for any signs of excessive fluid leaks, and if present then they must be rectified without delay.

9 If the colour of the fluid is dark brown or black this denotes the sign of a worn brake band or transmission clutches in which case have your Ford dealer check the transmission at the earliest opportunity.

28 Automatic transmission selector mechanism check

Carry out a thorough road test, ensuring that all gearchanges occur smoothly without snatching, and without an increase in engine speed between changes. Check that all gear positions can be engaged with the appropriate movement of the selector lever, and with the vehicle at rest. Check the operation of the parking pawl when "P" is selected.

29 Driveshaft check

1 Carry out a thorough inspection of the driveshafts and joints as follows.

2 Jack up the front of the car and support it securely on axle stands (see *"Jacking and Vehicle Support"*).

3 Slowly rotate the roadwheel and inspect the condition of the outer joint rubber bellows. Check for signs of cracking, splits or deterioration of the rubber which may allow the grease to escape and lead to water and grit entry into the joint **(see illustration)**. Also check the security and condition of the retaining clips. Repeat these checks on the inner constant velocity joints. If any damage or deterioration is found, the bellows should be renewed as described in Chapter 8.

4 Continue rotating the roadwheel and check for any distortion or damage to the driveshaft.

27.7 Transmission identification number on valve body tag

Check for any free play in the joints by first holding the driveshaft and attempting to rotate the wheel. Repeat this check by holding the inner joint and attempting to rotate the driveshaft. Any appreciable movement indicates wear in the joints, wear in the driveshaft splines or loose retaining nut.

5 Road test the car and listen for a metallic clicking from the front as the car is driven slowly in a circle with the steering on full lock. If a clicking noise is heard this indicates wear in the outer constant velocity joint caused by excessive clearance between the balls in the joint and the recesses in which they operate. Remove and inspect the joint (Chapter 8).

6 If vibration, consistent with road speed, is felt through the car when accelerating, there is a possibility of wear in the inner constant velocity joint. If so, renewal of the driveshaft inner joint will be necessary.

30 Roadwheel check

Check the wheel rims for distortion, damage and excessive run-out. Also make sure that the balance weights are secure with no obvious signs that any are missing.

Check the torque of the wheel bolts.

31 Hinge and lock check and lubrication

1 Work around the vehicle, and lubricate the bonnet, door and tailgate hinges with a light machine oil such as Duckhams Home Oil.

29.3 Checking driveshaft outer joint rubber bellows

2 Lightly lubricate the bonnet release mechanism and exposed sections of inner cable with a smear of grease.

3 Check the security and operation of all hinges, latches and locks, adjusting them where required. Where applicable, check the operation of the central locking system.

4 Check the condition and operation of the tailgate struts, renewing them if either is leaking or is no longer able to support the tailgate securely when raised.

32 Road test

Instruments and electrical equipment

1 Check the operation of all instruments and electrical equipment.

2 Make sure that all instruments read correctly, and switch on all electrical equipment in turn to check that it functions properly.

Steering and suspension

3 Check for any abnormalities in the steering, suspension, handling or road "feel".

4 Drive the vehicle, and check that there are no unusual vibrations or noises.

5 Check that the steering feels positive, with no excessive "sloppiness", or roughness, and check for any suspension noises when cornering, or when driving over bumps.

Drivetrain

6 Check the performance of the engine, clutch, transmission and driveshafts.

7 Listen for any unusual noises from the engine, clutch and transmission.

8 Make sure that the engine runs smoothly when idling, and that there is no hesitation when accelerating.

9 Where applicable, check that the clutch action is smooth and progressive, that the drive is taken up smoothly, and that the pedal travel is not excessive. Also listen for any noises when the clutch pedal is depressed.

10 Check that all gears can be engaged smoothly, without noise, and that the gear lever action is not abnormally vague or "notchy".

11 Listen for a metallic clicking sound from the front of the vehicle, as the vehicle is driven slowly in a circle with the steering on full lock.

1

Carry out this check in both directions. If a clicking noise is heard, this indicates wear in a driveshaft joint, in which case, the complete driveshaft must be renewed (see Chapter 8).

Check the operation and performance of the braking system

12 Make sure that the vehicle does not pull to one side when braking, and that the wheels do not lock prematurely when braking hard.

13 Check that there is no vibration through the steering when braking.

14 Check that the handbrake operates correctly, without excessive movement of the lever, and that it holds the vehicle stationary on a slope.

15 Test the operation of the brake servo unit as follows. With the engine off, depress the footbrake four or five times to exhaust the vacuum. Start the engine, holding the brake pedal depressed. As the engine starts, there should be a noticeable "give" in the brake pedal as vacuum builds up. Allow the engine to run for at least two minutes, and then switch it off. If the brake pedal is depressed now, it should be possible to detect a hiss from the servo as the pedal is depressed. After about four or five applications, no further hissing should be heard, and the pedal should feel considerably firmer.

Every 24 000 miles or 2 years

33 Coolant renewal

Cooling system draining

1 It is preferable to drain the system when the coolant is cold. If it must be drained when hot, release the pressure cap on the thermostat housing (or expansion tank on later models) very slowly, having first covered it with a cloth to avoid any possibility of scalding. Having relieved the pressure, remove the cap.

2 Set the heater control to the maximum heat position.

3 Check to see if a drain plug is fitted to the lower left-hand side of the radiator. If so, place a suitable container beneath the radiator, unscrew the plug and allow the coolant to drain **(see illustration)**.

4 If a drain plug is not fitted, place the container beneath the radiator bottom hose. Slacken the clip, release the hose and allow the coolant to drain.

5 A cylinder block drain plug is also fitted to certain models on the forward facing side of the cylinder block, towards the flywheel end. Where this is the case, unscrew the plug and allow the cylinder block to drain into the container **(see illustrations)**.

Cooling system flushing

6 Providing that the correct mixture of antifreeze and water has previously been maintained in the system, then no flushing should be necessary and the system can be refilled immediately as described in the following paragraphs.

7 Where the system has been neglected however, and rust or sludge is evident at draining, then the system should be flushed through using a cold water hose inserted into the thermostat housing (thermostat removed - see Chapter 3). Continue flushing until the water flows clean from the disconnected bottom hose, radiator drain plug and cylinder block drain plug, as applicable. If, after a reasonable period the water still does not run clear, the radiator can be flushed with a good proprietary cleaning system.

8 If the radiator is suspected of being clogged, remove and reverse flush it as described in Chapter 3.

9 When the coolant is being changed, it is recommended that the overflow pipe is disconnected from the expansion tank and the coolant drained from the tank. If the interior of the tank is dirty, remove it and thoroughly clean it out.

10 After draining or flushing, reconnect all disconnected hoses and refit the drain plugs where applicable.

Cooling system filling

11 Using the correct antifreeze mixture (See following sub-Section) fill the system through the thermostat housing filler neck slowly until the coolant is nearly overflowing. Wait a few moments for trapped air to escape and add more coolant. Repeat until the level does not drop and refit the cap. Pour similar strength coolant into the expansion tank up to the "MAX" mark and fit the cap.

12 On later models with a screw type pressure cap on the expansion tank, fill the system in the same way, but through the expansion tank rather than the thermostat housing.

13 On all models start the engine and run it to normal operating temperature then switch off. Once it has cooled, check and carry out any final topping-up to the expansion tank only.

Antifreeze mixture

14 Never operate the vehicle with plain water in the cooling system. Apart from the danger of freezing during winter conditions, an important secondary purpose of antifreeze is to inhibit the formation of rust and to reduce corrosion.

15 The coolant must be renewed at the intervals specified. Although the antifreeze properties of the coolant will remain indefinitely, the effectiveness of the rust and corrosion inhibitors will gradually weaken.

33.3 Radiator drain plug location (arrowed)

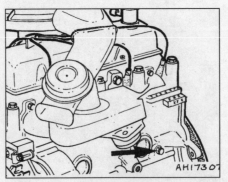

33.5a Cylinder block drain plug location (arrowed) - OHV engines

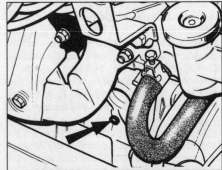

33.5b Cylinder block drain plug location (arrowed) - CVH engines

34.1a Removing the air cleaner retaining screws on a 1.3 litre CVH engine . . .

34.1b . . . and air cleaner retaining screw locations on 1.4 litre CVH engine

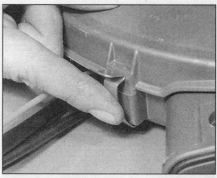

34.2 Release the air cleaner lid retaining clips, where fitted

16 It is recommended that Ford Super Plus antifreeze is used for filling and topping-up, as it has been specially formulated for use in Ford mixed metal engines (see "Lubricants and fluids").

17 A solution of 45% antifreeze must be maintained in the system all year round which will provide adequate protection against frost, rust and corrosion.

18 After filling with antifreeze, a label should be attached to the radiator stating the type of antifreeze and the date installed. Any subsequent topping-up should be made with the same type and concentration of antifreeze.

19 Do not use engine antifreeze in the screen washer system, as it will cause damage to the vehicle paintwork. Screen wash antifreeze is available from most motor accessory shops.

34 Air cleaner element renewal

Carburettor and Central Fuel Injection (CFI) models

1 To remove the air cleaner lid undo and remove the retaining screws or bolts on the top face of the lid (see illustrations).

2 Where applicable release the lid retaining clips around the side of the air cleaner body (see illustration).

3 Lift off the lid, remove and discard the paper element and wipe out the inside of the air cleaner body and lid (see illustration).

4 Place a new element in position and refit the lid.

Bosch K-Jetronic fuel injection models

5 Disconnect the battery earth lead.

6 Unscrew and loosen off the air ducting-to-sensor plate unit securing band, then separate the two (see illustrations).

7 Carefully pull free the shut-off valve hose from the air ducting connector. The hose is a press fit (see illustration).

8 Unscrew and remove the six air sensor plate-to-cleaner top cover retaining screws, but leave the plate unit in position.

9 Prise free and release the air cleaner cover retaining clips and detach the hose from the cover at the front (see illustration).

10 Carefully lift the sensor plate clear, together with its gasket, and pivot it back out of the way. Withdraw the shut-off valve from the rear end of the cleaner case cover, then lift out the cover and remove the element from the casing (see illustrations).

11 If the air cleaner casing is to be removed you will need to detach the fuel filter from the side of the cleaner casing (leave the fuel lines attached to the filter) and the air inlet hose from the front end of the case. Unscrew and remove the casing retaining nuts from the inner wing panel and lift out the casing.

12 Refitting is the reversal of the removal procedure. Wipe the casing clean before inserting the new element. When fitting the

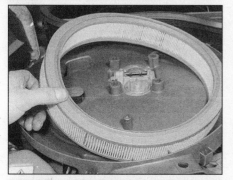

34. 3 Removing the air cleaner element

34.6a Slacken the securing band screw . . .

1

34.6b . . . and lift the air duct away from the sensor plate unit - K-Jetronic system

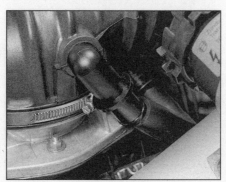

34.7 Detach the shut-off valve hose - K-Jetronic system

34.9 Detach the hose from the front of the air cleaner cover - K-Jetronic system

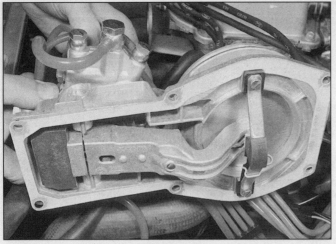

34.10a Lift the sensor plate clear . . .

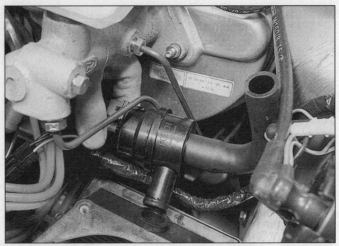

34.10b . . . withdraw the shut-off valve . . .

34.10c . . . lift out the cover . . .

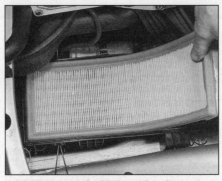

34.10d . . . and withdraw the element – K-Jetronic system

34.12 Locating the sensor unit gasket

sensor plate unit into position on the top cover check that the gasket is in good condition and aligned correctly **(see illustration)**.

13 Check that all connections are secure on completion.

Bosch KE-Jetronic fuel injection models

14 Undo the two bolts securing the air cleaner assembly to the air sensor plate unit and remove the air cleaner assembly **(see illustration)**.

15 Unclip the retaining clips and lift off the air cleaner top cover. Remove the filter element **(see illustration)**.

16 Clean the inside of the air cleaner body and fit a new filter element. Place the top cover in position and secure with the clips.

17 Refit the unit to the air sensor plate and secure with the two bolts.

Electronic Fuel Injection (EFI) models

18 Proceed as described in paragraphs 15 and 16.

35 Crankcase emission control filter renewal - CVH engines

Carburettor and Central Fuel Injection (CFI) engines

1 Where fitted, the crankcase ventilation filter is located in the base of the air cleaner.

2 The filter can be renewed by pulling it out of the air cleaner after disconnecting the hoses **(see illustration)**.

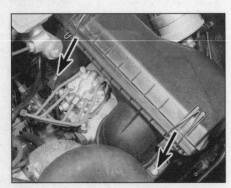

34.14 KE-Jetronic air cleaner retaining bolts (arrowed)

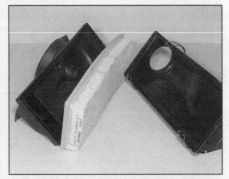

34.15 Lift off the air cleaner and remove the element - KE-Jetronic system

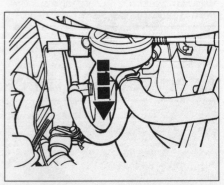

35.2 Crankcase ventilation filter renewal on CVH engines with carburettor

35.4 Crankcase ventilation filter location on KE-Jetronic fuel injection engines

36.3 Fuel filter inlet pipe (A), outlet pipe (B) and clamp screw (C)

3 Ensure that the sealing grommet is in position in the air cleaner before pushing a new filter into place.

Bosch K-Jetronic and KE-Jetronic fuel injection engines

4 The filter is located on the right-hand side of the engine and can be removed after disconnecting the hoses (see illustration). On early versions, detach the filter from its support bracket.
5 Refitting is a reversal of removal, ensuring that the hoses are correctly reconnected.

Electronic Fuel Injection (EFI) engines

6 The filter is located in the hose run to the air cleaner. Note the locations of the hoses to ensure correct reconnection.

36 Fuel filter renewal - fuel injection engines

Warning: This procedure may result in some fuel spillage. Before carrying out any operation on the fuel system refer to the precautions given in Safety First! at the beginning of this manual and follow them implicitly. Petrol is a highly dangerous and volatile liquid and the precautions necessary when handling it cannot be overstressed.

Bosch K-Jetronic and KE-Jetronic fuel injection models

1 Disconnect the battery negative lead.
2 Relieve the system pressure (Chapter 4, Part B).
3 Place absorbent rags beneath the filter and disconnect the fuel inlet and outlet connections (see illustration).
4 Slacken the clamp bracket screw and withdraw the filter from the bracket.
5 Refitting is the reversal of removal, but ensure that the arrows on the filter body point in the direction of fuel flow; ie towards the outlet pipe union. On completion check for fuel leaks with the engine running.

Central Fuel Injection (CFI) models

6 Disconnect the battery negative lead.
7 Position a suitable container beneath the fuel filter to catch any escaping fuel, then slowly slacken the fuel inlet pipe union, allowing the pressure in the fuel line to dissipate. When fully dissipated, disconnect the fuel inlet and outlet pipe unions. Take adequate fire precautions.
8 Note the orientation of the flow direction markings on the filter casing, then remove the clamp bolt and withdraw the filter from the vehicle. Note that the filter will still contain fuel, and care should be taken to avoid spillage.

9 Refitting is a reversal of the removal procedure, but ensure that the flow direction markings on the filter casing are correctly orientated, and tighten the unions to the specified torque.
10 On completion, switch the ignition on and off at least five times, and check for fuel leakage.

Electronic Fuel Injection (EFI) models

11 The filter is located in the engine compartment.
12 Depressurise the fuel system as described in Chapter 4, Part D, then disconnect the inlet and outlet unions from the filter.
13 Note the orientation of the flow direction markings on the filter casing, then remove the clamp bolt and withdraw the filter from the vehicle. Note that the filter will still contain fuel, and care should be taken to avoid spillage.
14 Refitting is a reversal of the removal procedure, but ensure that the flow direction markings on the filter casing are correctly orientated, and tighten the unions to the specified torque.
15 On completion, switch the ignition on and off at least five times, and check for fuel leakage.

Every 36 000 miles or 3 years

37 Timing belt renewal - CVH engines

Refer to Chapter 2, Part B.

38 Brake components check

1 Inspect the thickness of the friction linings on the disc pads and brake shoes (as described earlier in this Chapter) at the intervals specified.

2 The rigid and flexible hydraulic pipes and hoses should be inspected for leaks or damage regularly. Although the rigid lines are plastic-coated in order to preserve them against corrosion, check for damage which may have occurred through flying stones, careless jacking or the traversing of rough ground.

3 Bend the hydraulic flexible hoses sharply with the fingers and examine the surface of the hose for signs of cracking or perishing of the rubber. Renew if evident.

4 Renew the brake fluid at the specified intervals and examine all rubber components (including master cylinder and piston seals) with a critical eye, renewing where necessary.

39 Brake fluid renewal

⚠️ *Warning: Brake hydraulic fluid can harm your eyes and damage painted surfaces, so use extreme caution when handling and pouring it. Do not use fluid that has been standing open for some time, as it absorbs moisture from the air. Excess moisture can cause a dangerous loss of braking effectiveness.*

1 The procedure is similar to that for the bleeding of the hydraulic system as described in Chapter 9, except that the brake fluid reservoir should be emptied by siphoning, using a clean poultry baster or similar before starting, and allowance should be made for the old fluid to be expelled when bleeding a section of the circuit.

2 Working as described in Chapter 9, open the first bleed screw in the sequence, and pump the brake pedal gently until nearly all the old fluid has been emptied from the master cylinder reservoir. Top-up to the "MAX" level with new fluid, and continue pumping until only the new fluid remains in the reservoir, and new fluid can be seen emerging from the bleed screw. Tighten the screw, and top the reservoir level up to the "MAX" level line.

3 Old hydraulic fluid is invariably much darker in colour than the new, making it easy to distinguish the two.

4 Work through all the remaining bleed screws in the sequence until new fluid can be seen at all of them. Be careful to keep the master cylinder reservoir topped-up to above the "MIN" level at all times, or air may enter the system and greatly increase the length of the task.

5 When the operation is complete, check that all bleed screws are securely tightened, and that their dust caps are refitted. Wash off all traces of spilt fluid, and recheck the master cylinder reservoir fluid level.

6 Check the operation of the brakes before taking the car on the road.

Chapter 2 Part A:
OHV and HCS engines

Contents

Degrees of difficulty

Easy, suitable for novice with little experience	**Fairly easy,** suitable for beginner with some experience	**Fairly difficult,** suitable for competent DIY mechanic	**Difficult,** suitable for experienced DIY mechanic	**Very difficult,** suitable for expert DIY or professional

Specifications

General

Engine type	Four-cylinder, in-line overhead valve
Capacity:	
1.1 litre:	
OHV engines	1117 cc
HCS engines	1118 cc
1.3 litre	1297 cc
Bore:	
All except 1.1 litre HCS engine	73.96 mm
1.1 litre HCS engine	68.68 mm
Stroke:	
All except 1.1 litre OHV engine	75.48 mm
1.1 litre OHV engine	64.98 mm
Compression ratio:	
1.1 litre OHV engines (pre-1986)	9.15:1
1.1 litre OHV engines (1986 onwards)	9.5:1
1.1 litre HCS engines	9.5:1
1.3 litre OHV engines	9.3:1
1.3 litre HCS engines	9.5:1
Firing order	1-2-4-3 (No 1 at timing cover end)

Cylinder block

Material	Cast iron
Number of main bearings:	
1.1 litre	3
1.3 litre	5
Cylinder bore diameter:	
All except 1.1 litre HCS engines:	
Standard (1)	73.940 to 73.950 mm
Standard (2)	73.950 to 73.960 mm
Standard (3)	73.960 to 73.970 mm
Standard (4) - all except HCS engines	73.970 to 73.980 mm
Oversize 0.5 mm	74.500 to 74.510 mm
Oversize 1.0 mm	75.000 to 75.010 mm

Cylinder bore diameter (continued):
  1.1 litre HCS engine:
    Standard (1) . . . . 68.680 to 68.690 mm
    Standard (2) . . . . 68.690 to 68.700 mm
    Standard (3) . . . . 68.700 to 68.710 mm
    Oversize 0.5 mm . . . . 69.200 to 69.210 mm
    Oversize 1.0 mm . . . . 69.700 to 69.710 mm
Main bearing shell inner diameter:
  Standard . . . . 57.009 to 57.036 mm
  0.254 mm undersize . . . . 56.755 to 56.782 mm
  0.508 mm undersize . . . . 56.501 to 56.528 mm
  0.762 mm undersize . . . . 56.247 to 56.274 mm
Camshaft bearing inner diameter . . . . 39.662 to 39.682 mm

Crankshaft

Main bearing journal diameter:
  Standard . . . . 56.990 to 57.000 mm
  Standard with yellow dot (1.1 litre only) . . . . 56.980 to 56.990 mm
  0.254 mm undersize . . . . 56.726 to 56.746 mm
  0.508 mm undersize . . . . 56.472 to 56.492 mm
  0.762 mm undersize . . . . 56.218 to 56.238 mm
Main bearing running clearance:
  All except 1.3 litre HCS engine . . . . 0.009 to 0.046 mm
  1.3 litre HCS engine . . . . 0.009 to 0.056 mm
Crankpin (big-end) diameter:
  OHV engines:
    Standard . . . . 42.99 to 43.01 mm
    0.254 mm undersize . . . . 42.74 to 42.76 mm
    0.508 mm undersize . . . . 42.49 to 42.51 mm
    0.762 mm undersize . . . . 42.24 to 42.26 mm
  HCS engines:
    Standard . . . . 40.99 to 41.01 mm
    0.254 mm undersize . . . . 40.74 to 40.76 mm
    0.508 mm undersize . . . . 40.49 to 40.51 mm
    0.762 mm undersize . . . . 40.24 to 40.26 mm
Thrustwasher thickness:
  Standard . . . . 2.80 to 2.85 mm
  Oversize . . . . 2.99 to 3.04 mm
Crankshaft endfloat:
  OHV engines . . . . 0.079 to 0.279 mm
  HCS engines . . . . 0.075 to 0.285 mm
Maximum permissible journal and crankpin ovality and taper . . . . 0.0254 mm

Camshaft

Number of bearings 3
Drive . . . . Single chain
Thrust plate thickness . . . . 4.457 to 4.508 mm
Camshaft bearing diameter . . . . 39.615 to 39.636 mm
Camshaft bearing bush internal diameter . . . . 39.662 to 39.682 mm
Camshaft endfloat . . . . 0.02 to 0.19 mm
Number of links/Length of drive chain . . . . 46/438.15 mm

Piston and piston rings

Diameter:
  All except 1.1 litre HCS engines:
    Standard (1) . . . . 73.910 to 73.920 mm
    Standard (2) . . . . 73.920 to 73.930 mm
    Standard (3) . . . . 73.930 to 73.940 mm
    Standard (4) . . . . 73.940 to 73.950 mm
    0.5 mm oversize . . . . 74.460 to 74.485 mm
    1.0 mm oversize . . . . 74.960 to 74.985 mm
  1.1 litre HCS engines:
    Standard (1) . . . . 68.65 to 68.66 mm
    Standard (2) . . . . 68.66 to 68.67 mm
    Standard (3) . . . . 68.67 to 68.68 mm
    0.5 mm oversize . . . . 69.20 to 69.21 mm
    1.0 mm oversize . . . . 69.70 to 69.71 mm
Piston-to-bore clearance . . . . 0.015 to 0.050 mm
Piston ring end gap:
  Compression . . . . 0.25 to 0.45 mm
  Oil control . . . . 0.20 to 0.40 mm

Cylinder head

Material .... Cast iron
Maximum permissible cylinder head distortion measured over
   entire length .... 0.15 mm
Minimum combustion chamber depth after skimming:
   OHV engines .... 9.07 mm
   HCS engines .... 14.4 ± 0.15 mm
Valve seat angle .... 45°
Valve seat width:
   OHV engines:
     Inlet .... 1.20 to 1.75 mm
     Exhaust .... 1.20 to 1.70 mm
   HCS engines (inlet and exhaust) .... 1.18 to 1.75 mm
Seat cutter correction angle:
   Upper .... 30°
   Lower .... 75°
Valve guide bore (standard) .... 7.907 to 7.938 mm

Valves - general

Operation .... Cam followers and pushrods
Valve timing:
   Pre-1986 OHV engines:
     Inlet valve opens .... 21° BTDC
     Inlet valve closes .... 55° ABDC
     Exhaust valve opens .... 70° BBDC
     Exhaust valve closes .... 22° ATDC
   1986 onwards OHV engines:
     Inlet valve opens .... 14° BTDC
     Inlet valve closes .... 46° ABDC
     Exhaust valve opens .... 65° BBDC
     Exhaust valve closes .... 11° ATDC
   1.1 litre HCS engines:
     Inlet opens .... 14° BTDC
     Inlet closes .... 46° ABDC
     Exhaust opens .... 49° BBDC
     Exhaust closes .... 11° ATDC
   1.3 litre HCS engines:
     Inlet opens .... 16° BTDC
     Inlet closes .... 44° ABDC
     Exhaust opens .... 51° BBDC
     Exhaust closes .... 9° ATDC
Valve clearance (cold):
   Inlet .... 0.22 mm
   Exhaust:
     OHV engines .... 0.59 mm
     HCS engines .... 0.32 mm
Cam follower diameter .... 13.081 to 13.094 mm
Cam follower clearance in bore .... 0.016 to 0.062 mm
Valve spring free length:
   OHV engines:
     Pre-1986 .... 42.0 mm
     1986 onwards:
       1.1 litre .... 41.2 mm
       1.3 litre .... 42.4 mm
   HCS engines .... 41.0 mm

Inlet valve

Length:
   OHV engines .... 105.45 to 106.45 mm
   HCS engines .... 103.70 to 104.40 mm
Head diameter:
   OHV engines:
     Pre-1986 .... 38.02 to 38.28 mm
     1986 onwards:
       1.1 litre .... 32.89 to 33.15 mm
       1.3 litre .... 38.02 to 38.28 mm
   HCS engines:
     1.1 litre .... 32.90 to 33.10 mm
     1.3 litre .... 34.40 to 34.60 mm

Inlet valve (continued)

Stem diameter:
  OHV engines:
    Standard . . . . 7.866 to 7.868 mm
    0.076 mm oversize . . . . 7.944 to 7.962 mm
    0.38 mm oversize . . . . 8.249 to 8.267 mm
  HCS engines:
    Standard . . . . 7.025 to 7.043 mm
    0.076 mm oversize . . . . 7.225 to 7.243 mm
    0.381 mm oversize . . . . 7.425 to 7.443 mm
Valve stem clearance in guide . . . . 0.021 to 0.070 mm

Exhaust valve

Length:
  OHV engines:
    Pre-1986 . . . . 105.15 to 106.15 mm
    1986 onwards . . . . 106.04 to 107.04 mm
  HCS engines . . . . 104.02 to 104.72 mm
Head diameter:
  OHV engines . . . . 29.01 to 29.27 mm
  HCS engines . . . . 28.90 to 29.10 mm
Stem diameter:
  OHV engines:
    Standard . . . . 7.846 to 7.864 mm
    0.076 mm oversize . . . . 7.922 to 7.940 mm
    0.38 mm oversize . . . . 8.227 to 8.245 mm
  HCS engines:
    Standard . . . . 6.999 to 7.017 mm
    0.076 mm oversize . . . . 7.199 to 7.217 mm
    0.381 mm oversize . . . . 7.399 to 7.417 mm
Valve stem clearance in guide . . . . 0.043 to 0.092 mm

Lubrication system

Oil pump type . . . . Rotor, external driven by gear on camshaft
Minimum oil pressure at 80° C (175° F):
  Engine speed 750 rpm . . . . 0.6 bar (8.5 lbf/in^2)
  Engine speed 2000 rpm . . . . 1.5 bar (21.3 lbf/in^2)
Oil pressure warning lamp operates . . . . 0.32 to 0.53 bar (4.5 to 7.5 lbf/in^2)
Relief valve opens . . . . 2.41 to 2.75 bar (34.3 to 39.1 lbf/in^2)
Oil pump clearances:
  Outer rotor-to-body . . . . 0.14 to 0.26 mm
  Inner-to-outer rotor . . . . 0.051 to 0.127 mm
  Rotor endfloat . . . . 0.025 to 0.06 mm

Torque wrench settings

	Nm	lbf ft
Main bearing cap bolts	88 to 102	65 to 75
Connecting rod (big-end bearing cap) bolts:		
OHV engines	29 to 36	21 to 27
HCS engines:		
Stage 1	4	3
Stage 2	Tighten by a further 90°	Tighten by a further 90°
Rear oil seal retainer bolts	16 to 20	12 to 15
Flywheel bolts	64 to 70	47 to 52
Timing chain tensioner	7 to 9	5 to 7
Camshaft thrust plate	4 to 5	3 to 4
Camshaft sprocket bolt	16 to 20	12 to 15
Timing cover bolts	7 to 10	5 to 8
Crankshaft pulley bolt:		
OHV engines	54 to 59	40 to 44
HCS engines	100 to 120	74 to 89
Oil pump to crankcase	16 to 20	12 to 15
Oil pump cover bolts	8 to 12	6 to 9
Sump bolts:		
Stage 1	6 to 8	4 to 6
Stage 2	8 to 11	6 to 8
Stage 3	8 to 11	6 to 8
Sump drain plug	21 to 28	15 to 21
Oil pressure switch	13 to 15	10 to 11

Torque wrench settings (continued)

	Nm	lbf ft
Rocker shaft pedestal bolts	40 to 46	30 to 34
Cylinder head bolts:		
OHV engines:		
Stage 1	10 to 15	8 to 11
Stage 2	40 to 50	30 to 37
Stage 3	80 to 90	59 to 66
Stage 4 (after 10 to 20 minutes)	100 to 110	74 to 81
HCS engines:		
Stage 1	30	22
Stage 2	Tighten by a further 90°	Tighten by a further 90°
Stage 3	Tighten by a further 90°	Tighten by a further 90°
Rocker cover	4 to 5	3 to 4
Engine to transmission	35 to 45	26 to 33
Right-hand engine mounting to body	41 to 58	30 to 43
Right-hand engine mounting bracket to engine	54 to 72	40 to 53
Right-hand engine mounting rubber insulator to brackets	70 to 95	52 to 70
Front transmission mounting bracket to transmission (pre-1986)	41 to 51	30 to 38
Front and rear transmission mounting bolts (pre-1986)	52 to 64	38 to 47
Transmission mountings to transmission (1986 onwards)	80 to 100	59 to 74
Transmission support crossmember to body (1986 onwards)	52	38

1 General information

OHV engines

The 1.1 litre and 1.3 litre OHV engines are of four-cylinder, in-line overhead valve type (hence OHV), mounted transversely together with the transmission, at the front of the car.

The crankshaft on 1.1 litre engines is supported in three shell type main bearings, whereas the 1.3 litre unit features a five main bearing crankshaft. Apart from this difference and other minor alterations, the two engines are virtually the same in design and construction.

The connecting rods are attached to the crankshaft by horizontally split shell type big-end bearings and to the pistons by interference fit gudgeon pins. The aluminium alloy pistons are of the slipper type and are fitted with three piston rings; two compression and one oil control.

The camshaft is chain driven from the crankshaft and operates the valves via pushrods and rocker arms. The inlet and exhaust valves are each closed by a single valve spring and operate in guides integral with the cylinder head. The oil pump and distributor are driven by a skew gear on the camshaft while an eccentric cam operates the fuel pump lever.

The oil pump is mounted externally on the cylinder block just below the distributor, and the full flow type oil filter is screwed directly into the oil pump. Engine oil contained in the sump is drawn through a strainer and pick-up tube by an externally mounted oil pump of twin rotor design. The oil is then forced through the full-flow, throw-away type oil filter. Oil pressure is regulated by a relief valve integral in the oil pump. The pressurised oil is directed through the various galleries and passages to all bearing surfaces. A drilling in the big-end provides lubrication for the gudgeon pins and cylinder bores. The timing chain and sprockets are lubricated by an oil ejection nozzle.

HCS engines

The 1.1 and 1.3 litre High Compression Swirl (HCS) engines were introduced at the beginning of 1989 and fitted to certain 1.1 Escort models and all 1.3 Escort models, including the Van and Combi, replacing the previous OHV engine.

A further development of the Ford "lean burn" principle, the HCS engine is basically similar to the previous OHV engine, being of four cylinder, in-line OHV construction, but nearly every aspect of the engine has been re-designed. The major differences are in the cylinder head, where the inlet valve ports and combustion chambers are designed to impart a high level of "swirl" to the incoming fuel/air mixture. The valve arrangement is also different, being of "mirror" design, where the inlet valves of the centre cylinders are next to each other. Combined with the DIS fully

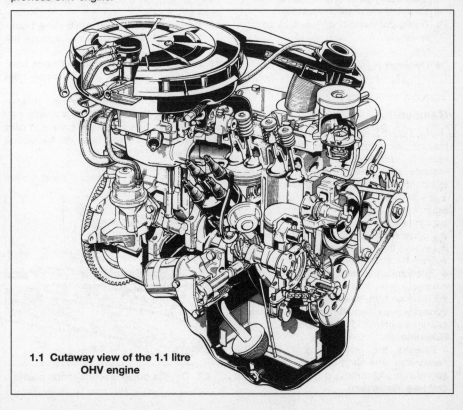

1.1 Cutaway view of the 1.1 litre OHV engine

2A

electronic ignition system which has no moving parts, the result is an economical engine with cleaner exhaust emissions which can run on leaded or unleaded fuel without adjustment to the ignition system.

Although most components of the HCS engine have been redesigned, for the most part the servicing and overhaul procedures remain unchanged, unless otherwise stated.

2 Major operations possible with the engine in the car

The following work can be carried out without having to remove the engine:
a) Cylinder head - removal and refitting.
b) Valve clearances - adjustment (see Chapter 1).
c) Sump - removal and refitting.
d) Rocker gear - overhaul.
e) Crankshaft front oil seal - renewal .
f) Pistons/connecting rods - removal and refitting.
g) Engine mountings - renewal.
h) Oil filter - removal and refitting.
i) Oil pump - removal and refitting.

3 Major operations requiring engine removal

The following work can only be carried out after removal of the engine from the car:
a) Crankshaft main bearings - renewal .
b) Crankshaft - removal and refitting.
c) Flywheel - removal and refitting.
d) Crankshaft rear oil seal - renewal.
e) Camshaft - removal and refitting.
f) Timing gears and chain - removal and refitting.

4 Cylinder head - removal and refitting

Removal

Note: *On HCS engines, cylinder head bolts may be used a total of three times (including initial fit) and must be suitably marked to indicate each removal operation. A new cylinder head gasket must be used on refitting.*
1 If the engine is in the car carry out the preliminary operations described in paragraphs 2 to 16.
2 Disconnect the battery negative terminal.
3 Remove the air cleaner (Chapter 4, Part A).
4 Drain the cooling system (Chapter 1).
5 Disconnect the hoses from the thermostat housing.
6 Disconnect the heater hose from the upper connection on the automatic choke housing, or inlet manifold as applicable **(see illustrations)**.
7 Release the throttle cable from the carburettor operating lever by moving the spring clip and removing the bracket fixing bolt **(see illustration)**.

4.6a Heater hose connection on choke housing

8 On manual choke models disconnect the choke cable from the linkage lever and support bracket.
9 Disconnect the fuel and vacuum pipes from the carburettor.
10 Disconnect the breather hose from the inlet manifold.
11 On vehicles with servo-assisted brakes, disconnect the vacuum hose from the inlet manifold.
12 Disconnect the HT leads from the spark plugs.
13 Disconnect the electrical leads from the temperature sender unit, the anti-run-on solenoid valve at the carburettor, and the radiator fan thermal switch.
14 Unbolt and remove the hot air box from the exhaust manifold.
15 Disconnect the exhaust downpipe from the manifold by unbolting the connecting flanges. Support the exhaust system at the front end.
16 Remove the oil filler cap with breather hose.
17 Extract the four screws and remove the rocker cover.
18 Unscrew and remove the four fixing bolts and lift away the rocker shaft assembly from the cylinder head.
19 Withdraw the pushrods, keeping them in their originally fitted sequence. A simple way to do this is to punch holes in a piece of card and number them 1 to 8 from the thermostat housing end of the cylinder head.
20 Remove the spark plugs.
21 Unscrew the cylinder head bolts

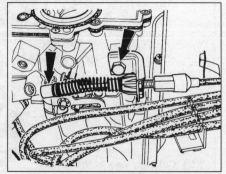

4.7 Throttle cable disconnection points

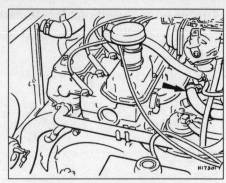

4.6b Heater hose connection at inlet manifold

progressively in the reverse order to that given for tightening **(see illustration 4.27)**. Remove the cylinder head.
22 To dismantle the cylinder head, refer to Section 13.

Refitting

23 Before refitting the cylinder head, remove every particle of carbon, old gasket and dirt from the mating surfaces of the cylinder head and block. Do not let the removed material drop into the cylinder bores or waterways, if it does, remove it. Normally, when a cylinder head is removed, the head is decarbonised and the valves ground in as described in Section 14 to remove all trace of carbon. Clean the threads of the cylinder head bolts and mop out oil from the bolt holes in the cylinder block. In extreme cases, screwing a bolt into an oil-filled hole can cause the block to fracture due to hydraulic pressure.
24 If there is any doubt about the condition of the inlet or exhaust gaskets, unbolt the manifolds and fit new ones to perfectly clean mating surfaces.
25 Locate a new cylinder head gasket on the cylinder block, making quite sure that the bolt holes, coolant passages and lubrication holes are correctly aligned.
26 Lower the cylinder head carefully into position on the block.
27 Screw in all the bolts finger tight and then tighten them in the stages given (see Specifications), and in the sequence shown to the specified torque **(see illustration)**. Note that

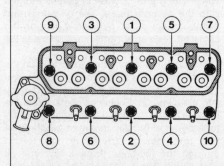

4.27 Cylinder head bolt tightening sequence

on all except HCS engines with M11 necked-shank (a reduced diameter section between the bolt head and the threaded portion) cylinder head bolts there are four tightening stages. On HCS engines with M11 necked-shank cylinder head bolts there are three tightening stages.

28 Refit the pushrods in their original order.

29 Lower the rocker shaft assembly into position, making sure that the rocker adjusting screws engage in the sockets at the ends of the pushrods.

30 Screw in the rocker pedestal bolts finger tight. At this stage, some of the rocker arms will be applying pressure to the ends of the valve stems and some of the rocker pedestals will not be in contact with the cylinder head. The pedestals will be pulled down however when the bolts are tightened to the specified torque, which should now be done.

31 Adjust the valve clearances as described in Chapter 1.

32 Refit the rocker cover, using a new gasket. Do not exceed the specified torque for the securing screws; this may result in oil leaks at the rocker cover/cylinder head mating face.

33 Fit the oil filler cap and breather hose and the spark plugs. Tighten these to the specified torque. They are of tapered seat type, no sealing washers being used.

34 Connect the exhaust downpipe and fit the hot air box.

35 Reconnect all electrical leads, vacuum and coolant hoses.

36 Reconnect the throttle and choke cables as described in Chapter 4, Part A.

37 Refit the air cleaner as described in Chapter 4, Part A and fill the cooling system as described in Chapter 1.

38 Reconnect the battery negative terminal.

5 Sump - removal and refitting

Note: *New gaskets and sealing strips must be used on refitting.*

Removal

1 Disconnect the battery negative lead and drain the engine oil (see Chapter 1).

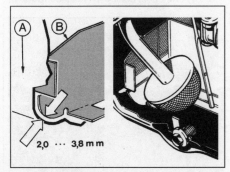

5.7 Sump and oil baffle clearance details

A Sump *B Baffle*

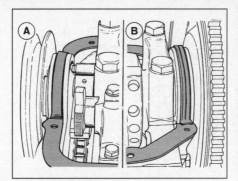

5.6a Sump gasket fitting details at timing cover end (A) and flywheel end (B)

2 Refer to Chapter 5, Part A and remove the starter motor.

3 Unbolt and remove the clutch cover plate.

4 Extract the sump securing bolts and remove the sump. If it is stuck, prise it gently with a screwdriver but do not use excessive leverage. If it is very tight, cut round the gasket joint using a sharp knife.

Refitting

5 Before refitting the sump, remove the front and rear sealing strips and gaskets. Clean the mating surfaces of the sump and cylinder block.

6 Stick new gaskets into position on the block using thick grease to retain them, then install new sealing strips into their grooves so that they overlap the gaskets **(see illustrations)**.

7 Before offering up the sump, check that the gap between the sump and the oil baffle is between 2.0 and 3.8 mm **(see illustration)**.

8 Screw in the sump bolts and tighten in three stages to the specified torque in the sequence shown **(see illustration)**.

   a) Stage 1- in alphabetical order
   b) Stage 2 - in numerical order
   c) Stage 3 - in alphabetical order

9 It is important to follow this procedure in order to provide positive sealing against oil leakage.

10 Refit the clutch cover plate and the starter motor and reconnect the battery.

11 Refill the engine with the correct grade and quantity of oil.

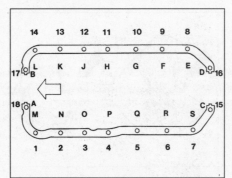

5.8 Sump bolt tightening sequence

5.6b Fitting the sump gasket sealing strips to overlap the tabs on the gasket

6 Rocker gear - dismantling and reassembly

Dismantling

1 With the rocker assembly removed as described in Section 4, extract the split pin from one end of the rocker shaft **(see illustration)**.

2 Take off the spring and plain washers from the end of the shaft.

3 Slide off the rocker arms, support pedestals and coil springs, keeping them in their originally fitted order. Clean out the oil holes in the shaft.

Reassembly

4 Apply engine oil to the rocker shaft before reassembling and make sure that the flat on the end of the shaft is to the same side as the rocker arm adjuster screws. This is essential for proper lubrication of the components.

7 Crankshaft front oil seal - renewal

1 Disconnect the battery negative lead.

2 Slacken the alternator mounting and adjuster bolts and after pushing the alternator in towards the engine, slip off the drivebelt.

3 Unscrew and remove the crankshaft pulley bolt. To prevent the crankshaft turning while the bolt is being released, jam the teeth of the

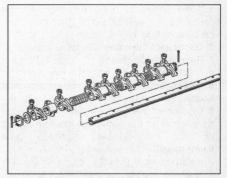

6.1 Rocker shaft assembly components

starter ring gear on the flywheel after removing the clutch cover plate or starter motor (Chapter 5, Part A) for access.
4 Remove the crankshaft pulley. This should come out using the hands but if it is tight, prise it carefully with two levers placed at opposite sides under the pulley flange.
5 Using a suitable claw tool, prise out the defective seal and wipe out the seat.
6 Install the new seal using a suitable distance piece, the pulley and its bolt to draw it into position. If it is tapped into position, the seal may be distorted or the timing cover fractured.
7 When the seal is fully seated, remove the pulley and bolt, apply grease to the seal rubbing surface of the pulley, install it and tighten the securing bolt to the specified torque.
8 Refit the clutch cover or starter motor.
9 Fit and tension the drivebelt as described in Chapter 1, and reconnect the battery.

8 Piston/connecting rod assemblies - removal and refitting

Note: *A piston ring compressor tool will be required for this operation.*

Removal

1 Remove the cylinder head and the sump as described in Sections 4 and 5 respectively. Do not remove the oil pick-up filter or pipe, which is an interference fit.
2 Note the location numbers stamped on the connecting rod big-ends and caps, and to which side they face. No 1 assembly is nearest the timing cover and the assembly numbers are towards the camshaft side of the engine **(see illustration)**.
3 Turn the crankshaft by means of the pulley bolt until the big-end cap bolts for No 1 connecting rod are in their most accessible position. Unscrew and remove the bolts and the big-end cap complete with bearing shell. If the cap is difficult to remove, tap it off with a plastic-faced hammer.
4 If the bearing shells are to be used again (Section 13), keep the shell taped to its cap.
5 Feel the top of the cylinder bore for a wear ridge. If one is detected, it should be scraped

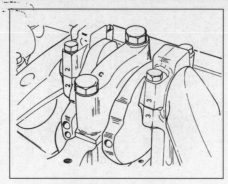

8.2 Connecting rod and big-end cap identification numbers

off before the piston/rod is pushed out of the top of the cylinder block. Take care when doing this not to score the cylinder bore surfaces.
6 Push the piston/connecting rod out of the block, retaining the bearing shell with the rod if it is to be used again.
7 Dismantling the piston/rod is covered in Section 13.
8 Repeat the operations on the remaining piston/rod assemblies.

Refitting

9 To install a piston/rod assembly, have the piston ring gaps staggered as shown, oil the rings and apply a piston ring compressor **(see illustration)**. Compress the piston rings.
10 Oil the cylinder bores.
11 Wipe out the bearing shell seat in the connecting rod and insert the shell.
12 Lower the piston/rod assembly into the cylinder bore until the base of the piston ring compressor stands squarely on the top of the block **(see illustration)**.
13 Check that the directional arrow on the piston crown faces towards the timing cover end of the engine and then apply the wooden handle of a hammer to the piston crown **(see illustrations)**. Strike the head of the hammer sharply to drive the piston into the cylinder bore.
14 Oil the crankpin and draw the connecting rod down to engage with the crankshaft. Check that the bearing shell is still in position in the connecting rod.

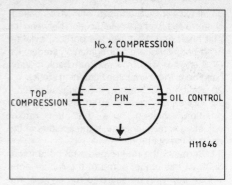

8.9 Piston ring end gap positioning diagram

15 Wipe the bearing shell seat in the big-end cap clean and insert the bearing shell.
16 Fit the cap, screw in the bolts and tighten to the specified torque.
17 Repeat the operations on the remaining pistons/connecting rods.
18 Refit the sump (Section 5) and the cylinder head (Section 4). Refill with oil and coolant.

9 Engine/transmission mountings - removal and refitting

Pre-1986 models

1 The engine mountings can be removed if the weight of the engine/transmission is first taken by one of the three following methods.
2 Either support the engine under the sump using a jack and a block of wood, or attach a hoist to the engine lifting lugs. A third method is to make up a bar with end pieces which will engage in the water channels at the sides of the bonnet lid aperture. Using an adjustable hook and chain connected to the engine lifting lugs, the weight of the engine can be taken off the mountings.

Rear mountings

Removal

3 Unbolt the mounting, according to type from the body member or panel, also from the engine or transmission. With the mounting withdrawn, the centre bolt can be unscrewed and the flexible component detached **(see illustrations)**.

8.12 Fitting a piston/connecting rod assembly with ring compressor in position

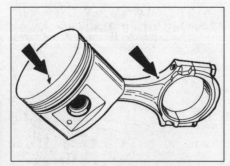

8.13a Relative positions of piston directional arrow and oil squirt hole in connecting rod

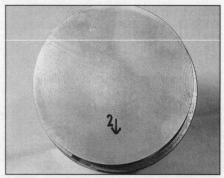

8.13b Arrow on piston crown must face the timing cover when installed

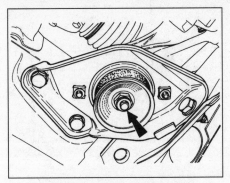

9.3a Transmission left-hand rear mounting-to-bracket attachment - pre-1986 models

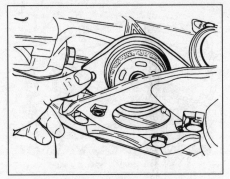

9.3b Removing transmission left-hand rear mounting - pre-1986 models

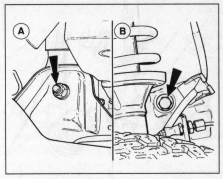

9.3c Right-hand rear engine mounting attachments - pre-1986 models
A Mounting to side member
B Mounting to inner wheel arch

Refitting

4 Refitting is a reversal of removal. Make sure that the original sequence of assembly of washers and plates is maintained.

Front left-hand mounting

Removal

5 Removal of the front mounting on the transmission requires a different removal procedure. Remove the centre bolt from the mounting and then using one of the methods described, raise the transmission just enough to be able to unbolt and remove the two insulator bolts and withdraw the insulator (see illustration).

Refitting

6 Refitting is a reversal of removal. Make sure that the original sequence of assembly of washers and plates is maintained.

1986 models onwards

Removal

7 From 1986 onwards a longitudinal crossmember is mounted beneath the transmission, and the front and rear left-hand mountings are attached to it. Removal of the rear right-hand mounting is as previously described, but removal of the front and rear left-hand mountings is as follows.

8 Support the engine; see paragraphs 1 and 2.

9 Undo the nuts securing the mountings to the transmission support crossmember and to the brackets on the transmission.

10 Unbolt the transmission support

crossmember at the front and rear and remove it from under the car. Remove the relevant mounting.

Refitting

11 Refitting is the reversal of removal. Make sure that the original sequence of assembly of washers and plates is maintained.

10 Oil pump - removal and refitting

Note: *A new gasket must be used on refitting.*

Removal

1 The oil pump is externally mounted on the rear facing side of the crankcase.

2 Using a strap wrench or similar, unscrew and remove the oil filter cartridge and discard it.

3 Unscrew the three mounting bolts and withdraw the oil pump from the engine (see illustration).

4 Clean away the old gasket.

Refitting

5 If a new pump is being fitted. it should be primed with engine oil before installation. Do this by turning its shaft while filling it with clean engine oil.

6 Locate a new gasket on the pump mounting flange, insert the pump shaft and bolt the pump into position.

7 Grease the rubber sealing ring of a new filter and screw it into position on the pump, using hand pressure only, not the removal tool.

8 Top-up the engine oil to replenish any lost during the operations.

11 Engine/transmission - removal and separation

Note: *Suitable lifting tackle will be required for this operation.*

OHV engines

Removal

1 The engine is removed complete with the transmission in a downward direction and then withdrawn from under the front of the car.

2 Disconnect the battery negative lead.

3 Place the transmission in fourth gear on four-speed versions, or reverse gear on the five-speed unit to aid adjustment of the gearchange linkage when refitting. On models produced from February 1987 onwards, place the transmission in second gear on four-speed versions, or fourth gear on five-speed versions.

4 Remove the bonnet (Chapter 11).

5 Remove the air cleaner (Chapter 4, Part A).

6 Drain the cooling system (Chapter 1).

7 Disconnect both the radiator hoses and the expansion tank hose at the thermostat housing.

8 Disconnect the heater hoses from the stub on the lateral coolant pipe, automatic choke housing or inlet manifold as applicable (see illustration).

2A

9.5 Transmission left-hand front mounting attachments - pre-1986 models

10.3 Removing the oil pump

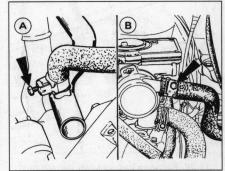

11.8 Heater hose attachments at lateral coolant pipe (A) and choke housing (B)

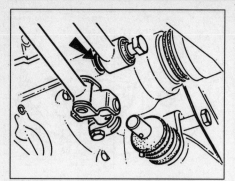

11.22 Gearchange rod and stabiliser disconnection points - washer fitted behind stabiliser arrowed

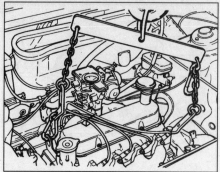

11.24 Typical lifting gear connection to engine

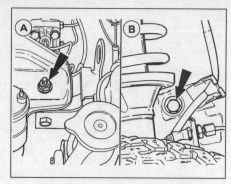

11.26 Engine right-hand mounting attachment at side member (A) and inner wing panel (B)

9 Disconnect the choke cable (where fitted) and the throttle cable from the carburettor throttle lever. Unbolt the cable support bracket and tie the cable assembly to one side of the engine compartment.

10 Disconnect the fuel pipe from the fuel pump and plug the pipe.

11 On vehicles equipped with power-assisted brakes, disconnect the vacuum pipe from the inlet manifold.

12 Disconnect the leads from the following electrical components:
   a) Alternator and electric fan temperature switch.
   b) Oil pressure sender.
   c) Coolant temperature sender.
   d) Reversing lamp switch.
   e) Anti-run on solenoid valve.

13 Disconnect the HT and LT (distributor) wires from the coil terminals.

14 Unscrew the speedometer drive cable from the transmission and release the breather hose.

15 Disconnect the clutch cable from the release lever and from its transmission support.

16 Unbolt and remove the hot air box from the exhaust manifold.

17 Disconnect the exhaust downpipe from the manifold by extracting the two flange bolts. Support the exhaust pipe to avoid straining it.

18 The vehicle should now be jacked up and safety stands fitted to provide sufficient clearance beneath it to be able to remove the engine/transmission from below. A distance of 686 mm (27.0 in) is recommended between the floor and the bottom edge of the front panel.

19 Disconnect the exhaust system from its flexible mountings and remove the system complete.

20 Disconnect the starter motor leads and the engine earth strap.

21 Disconnect the gearchange rod from the transmission selector shaft by releasing the clamp bolt and withdrawing the rod. Tie the rod to the stabiliser and then where fitted, unhook the tension spring.

22 Unscrew the single bolt and disconnect the stabiliser from the transmission housing, noting the washer fitted between the stabiliser trunnion and the transmission **(see illustration)**.

23 Remove the driveshafts from the transmission using the procedure described in the manual transmission removal procedure in Chapter 7, Part A. Note that on pre-1986 models equipped with an anti-roll bar the right-hand mounting clamp should also be undone and the bar lowered together with the suspension arms.

24 Connect a suitable hoist to the engine using chains and brackets **(see illustration)**.

25 Just take the weight of the engine/transmission assembly so that the tension is relieved from the mountings.

26 Unbolt the rear right-hand engine mounting (complete with coolant hose support on early models) from the side member and from the inner wing panel **(see illustration)**.

27 On pre-1986 models unbolt the front and rear transmission mountings from their brackets, and remove the front mounting and anti-roll bar support plates from the body on both sides **(see illustration)**.

28 On 1986 models onwards undo the nuts and bolts securing the transmission support crossmember to the body **(see illustrations)**. The crossmember is removed with the engine/transmission assembly.

29 Carefully lower the engine/transmission and withdraw it from under the car.

> **HAYNES HiNT** *To ease the withdrawal operation, lower the engine/transmission onto a crawler board or a sheet of substantial chipboard placed on rollers or lengths of pipe.*

Separation

30 Unscrew and remove the starter motor bolts and remove the starter.

31 Unbolt and remove the clutch cover plate from the lower part of the clutch bellhousing.

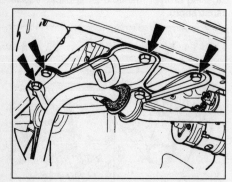

11.27 Remove the anti-roll bar support plates on both sides - pre-1986 models

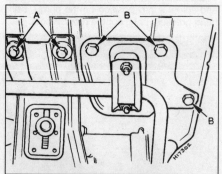

11.28a Transmission support crossmember front mounting bolts (A) and anti-roll bar support plate bolts (B) - 1986 models onwards

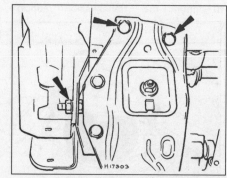

11.28b Transmission support crossmember rear mounting bolts - 1986 models onwards

**11.35 A locally made-up lifting eye -
HCS engine**

11.41a Radiator lower mounting bolt . . .

**11.41b . . . and upper locating peg -
HCS engine**

32 Unscrew and remove the bolts from the clutch bellhousing-to-engine mating flange.

33 Withdraw the transmission from the engine. Support its weight so that the clutch assembly is not distorted while the input shaft is still in engagement with the splined hub of the clutch driven plate.

HCS engines

Removal

34 The engine can be lifted from the engine bay provided the radiator and certain other ancillary components are removed first to give room for manoeuvring. These are detailed in the removal procedure.

35 Before commencing work it will be necessary to make up two lifting eyes from ¼"

mild steel bar, approximately 3" long and 1½" wide, with two ½" holes drilled in them **(see illustration)**.

36 Remove the bonnet (Chapter 11).

37 Disconnect the battery negative lead.

38 Remove the air cleaner (Chapter 4, Part A).

39 Drain the engine oil (Chapter 1).

40 Drain the coolant (Chapter 1).

41 Remove the radiator (Chapter 3) **(see illustrations)**.

42 Disconnect the heater hoses from the inlet manifold and the water pump.

43 Disconnect the lead at the anti-run-on valve solenoid on the carburettor.

44 Disconnect the throttle cable (Chapter 4, Part A).

45 Disconnect the choke cable (Chapter 4, Part A).

46 Disconnect the fuel inlet (blue clip) and outlet (green clip) pipes from the fuel pump (see Chapter 4, Part A).

47 Disconnect the brake servo vacuum hose from the inlet manifold. On later models depress the flanged collar towards the manifold, and pull out the hose **(see illustration)**. Do not pull the hose at an angle, or use excessive force, or the hose may lock in position.

48 Disconnect the earth lead from the inlet manifold.

49 Disconnect the following electrical connections:

a) *Cooling fan thermal switch on thermostat housing* **(see illustration)**.

b) *Coolant temperature sender* **(see illustration)**.

c) *Alternator.*

d) *Ignition (DIS) coil (Chapter 5, Part B).*

e) *Oil pressure switch.*

f) *Engine coolant temperature sensor (Chapter 5, Part B).*

g) *Engine speed sensor (Chapter 5, Part B).*

h) *Reversing light switch (Chapter 7, Part A).*

l) *Transmission housing earth lead.*

50 Disconnect the speedometer cable **(see illustration)**.

51 Disconnect the exhaust downpipe from the exhaust manifold flange. The nuts are easier to reach from underneath the vehicle. Once undone, support the exhaust on wire.

52 Disconnect the starter motor and engine earth lead which is under one of the starter motor bolts (Chapter 5, Part A).

2A

**11.41c Lifting out the radiator -
HCS engine**

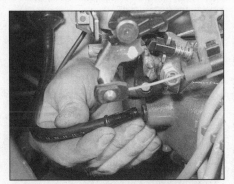

**11.47 Disconnecting the brake vacuum
servo hose - HCS engine**

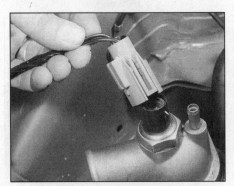

**11.49a Disconnecting the cooling fan
thermal switch . . .**

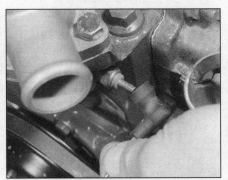

**11.49b . . . and coolant temperature
sender - HCS engine**

**11.50 Disconnecting the speedometer
cable - HCS engine**

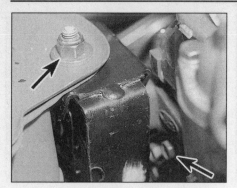

11.57a Right-hand engine mounting nuts/bolts (arrowed) - HCS engine

11.57b One bolt (arrowed) is accessible from within the wheelarch - HCS engine

11.58 Torx headed bolt (arrowed) securing the mounting to the bracket - HCS engine

53 Remove the starter lead support bracket from the transmission housing.
54 Disconnect the gearchange mechanism (Chapter 7, Part A).
55 Remove the driveshafts (Chapter 8). **Note:** *On removal of the driveshafts, push a length of wooden dowel into the hole vacated by the driveshaft in the transmission housing to prevent the sun gears of the differential becoming misaligned. A piece of broom handle is ideal, but will have to be turned down somewhat.*
56 Support the right-hand side of the engine on a trolley jack; just take the weight of the engine.
57 Remove the right-hand engine mounting by undoing the top nut on the wing panel, removing the bolt accessible from inside the wheelarch, and the three bolts securing the mounting bracket to the engine (see illustrations).

58 Once removed, undo the Torx headed bolt securing the mounting to the bracket (see illustration).
59 Refit the bracket to the cylinder block and bolt one of the made-up lifting eyes to the bracket using one of the spare bolts (see illustration).
60 Fit the other lifting eye to the transmission housing (see illustration).
61 Secure suitable lifting gear to the engine and just begin to take the weight. **Note:** *If the carburettor is likely to be damaged because of the angle of the lifting sling/chain, remove the carburettor as described in Chapter 4, Part A.*
62 Remove the alternator (Chapter 5, Part A) to give more room for manoeuvring the engine out.
63 Pull the transmission breather hose from inside the wing panel.

64 Remove the nut from the left-hand front engine mounting.
65 Remove the nut from the left-hand rear mounting. Remove the nuts securing the mounting bracket to the transmission housing and remove the bracket (see illustrations).
66 Commence lifting the engine slowly, checking all round that everything has been disconnected and that the engine does not foul other components as it is lifted. Swing the engine and tilt it as necessary to clear obstacles (see illustrations).
67 Once out of the engine bay, swing the engine clear and lower it onto a suitable work surface.

Separation

68 Proceed as described previously in this Section for OHV engines

11.59 Lifting eye (arrowed) bolted to right-hand mounting position on cylinder block . . .

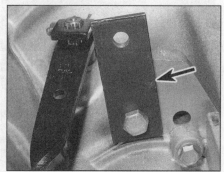

11.60 . . . and on transmission housing - HCS engine

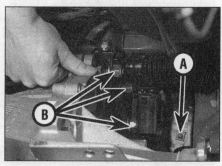

11.65a Mounting nut location (A) and bracket-to-transmission housing nuts (B) - HCS engine

11.65b Removing the mounting bracket - HCS engine

11.66a Lifting the engine and transmission upwards . . .

11.66b . . . and out of the engine compartment

12.13 Keep the pushrods in strict order after removal

12.28 Removing the timing chain tensioner

12.31 Camshaft thrust plate removal

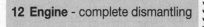

12 Engine - complete dismantling

OHV engines

1 The need for dismantling will have been dictated by wear or noise in most cases. Although there is no reason why only partial dismantling cannot be carried out to renew such items as the timing chain or crankshaft rear oil seal, when the main bearings or big-end bearings have been knocking and especially if the vehicle has covered a high mileage, then it is recommended that a complete strip down is carried out and every engine component examined (Section 13).

2 Position the engine so that it is upright on a bench or other convenient working surface. If the exterior is very dirty it should be cleaned before dismantling using paraffin and a stiff brush or a water-soluble solvent.

3 Remove the coolant pipe from the side of the engine by disconnecting the hose clips and the securing bolt.

4 If not already done, drain the engine oil.

5 Remove the dipstick and unscrew and discard the oil filter.

6 Disconnect the HT leads from the spark plugs, release the distributor cap and lift it away complete with leads.

7 Unscrew and remove the spark plugs.

8 Disconnect the breather hose from the inlet manifold and remove it with the oil filler cap.

9 Disconnect the fuel and vacuum pipes from the carburettor and unbolt and remove the carburettor (refer to Chapter 4, Part A).

10 Unbolt the thermostat housing cover and remove it together with the thermostat (refer to Chapter 3).

11 Remove the rocker cover.

12 Remove the rocker shaft assembly (four bolts).

13 Withdraw the pushrods, keeping them in their originally fitted order **(see illustration)**.

14 Remove the cylinder head complete with manifolds as described in Section 4.

15 Remove the distributor as described in Chapter 5, Part B.

16 Unbolt and remove the fuel pump.

17 Remove the oil pump (Section 10).

18 Pinch the two runs of the water pump drivebelt together at the pump pulley to prevent the pulley rotating and release the pulley bolts.

19 Release the alternator mounting and adjuster link bolts, push the alternator in towards the engine and remove the drivebelt.

20 Unbolt the alternator bracket and remove the alternator.

21 Unbolt and remove the water pump.

22 Unscrew the crankshaft pulley bolt. To do this, the flywheel starter ring gear will have to be jammed to prevent the crankshaft from turning.

23 Remove the crankshaft pulley. If this does not pull off by hand, carefully use two levers behind it placed at opposite points.

24 Place the engine on its side and remove the sump. Do not invert the engine at this stage, or sludge and swarf may enter the oilways.

25 Unbolt and remove the timing chain cover.

26 Take off the oil slinger from the front face

of the crankshaft sprocket.

27 Slide the chain tensioner arm from its pivot pin on the front main bearing cap.

28 Unbolt and remove the chain tensioner **(see illustration)**.

29 Bend back the lockplate tabs from the camshaft sprocket bolts and unscrew and remove the bolts.

30 Withdraw the sprocket complete with timing chain.

31 Unbolt and remove the camshaft thrust plate **(see illustration)**.

32 Rotate the camshaft until each cam follower (tappet) has been pushed fully into its hole by its cam lobe.

33 Withdraw the camshaft, taking care not to damage the camshaft bearings **(see illustration)**.

34 Withdraw each of the cam followers, keeping them in their originally fitted sequence by marking them with a piece of numbered tape or using a box with divisions **(see illustration)**.

35 From the front end of the crankshaft, draw off the sprocket using a two-legged extractor.

36 Check that the main bearing caps are marked F (Front), C (Centre) and R (Rear). The caps are also marked with an arrow which indicates the timing cover end of the engine, a point to remember when refitting the caps.

37 Check that the big-end caps and connecting rods have adjacent matching numbers facing towards the camshaft side of the engine. Number 1 assembly is nearest the timing chain end of the engine. If any markings are missing or indistinct, make some of your own with quick-drying paint **(see illustration)**.

2A

12.33 Withdrawing the camshaft from the front of the engine

12.34 Using a valve grinding tool suction cup to withdraw the cam followers

12.37 Connecting rod and big-end cap markings

38 Unbolt and remove the big-end bearing caps. If the bearing shell is to be used again, tape the shell to the cap.

39 Now check the top of the cylinder bore for a wear ring. If one can be felt, it should be removed with a scraper before the piston/rod is pushed out of the cylinder.

40 Remove the piston/rod by pushing it out of the top of the block. Tape the bearing shell to the connecting rod.

41 Remove the remaining three piston/rod assemblies in a similar way.

42 Unbolt the clutch pressure plate cover from the flywheel. Unscrew the bolts evenly and progressively until spring pressure is relieved, before removing the bolts. Be prepared to catch the clutch friction plate as the cover is withdrawn.

43 Unbolt and remove the flywheel. It is heavy, do not drop it. If necessary, the starter ring gear can be jammed to prevent the flywheel rotating. There is no need to mark the fitted position of the flywheel to its mounting flange as it can only be fitted one way. Take off the adapter plate (engine backplate).

44 Unbolt and remove the crankshaft rear oil seal retainer.

45 Unbolt the main bearing caps. Remove the caps, tapping them off if necessary with a plastic-faced hammer. Retain the bearing shells with their respective caps if the shells are to be used again, although unless the engine is of low mileage this is not recommended (see Section 13). To improve access to the No 2 main bearing bolt on 1.3 litre engines the oil pick-up tube can be removed by drifting it out. A new pick-up tube must be obtained for reassembly together with suitable adhesive to secure it in position.

46 Lift the crankshaft from the crankcase and lift out the upper bearing shells, noting the thrustwashers either side of the centre bearing. Keep these shells with their respective caps, identifying them for refitting to the crankcase if they are to be used again.

47 With the engine now completely dismantled, each component should be examined as described in Section 13 before reassembling.

HCS engines

48 The procedure is as described previously in this Section for OHV engines, noting the following differences.

a) *There is no coolant transfer pipe along the front of the engine.*

b) *Disconnect and remove the HT leads with reference to Chapter 5, Part B.*

c) *There is no distributor to remove. The procedure for removal of the DIS coil is given in Chapter 5, Part B.*

d) *big-end cap bolts are Torx type bolts.*

e) *Remove the engine speed sensor as described in Chapter 5, Part B before removing the flywheel to prevent damage to the sensor.*

f) *There are three main bearings on 1.1 engines and five on 1.3 engines. From the*

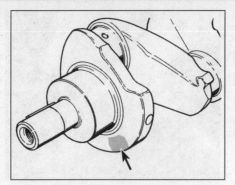

13.7a Crankshaft main bearing journal size identification mark on balance web (arrowed)

timing chain end, the main bearing caps are numbered 1 to 3 or 1 to 5 as applicable, and have an arrow on them which must point towards the timing chain end of the engine.

g) *The crankshaft thrust bearings are still fitted either side of the centre main bearing.*

h) *rear oil seal carrier is secured in place by Torx type bolts.*

13 Examination and renovation

1 Clean all components using paraffin and a stiff brush, except the crankshaft, which should be wiped clean and the oil passages cleaned out with a length of wire.

2 Never assume that a component is unworn simply because it looks all right. After all the effort which has gone into dismantling the engine, refitting worn components will make the overhaul a waste of time and money. Depending on the degree of wear, the overhauler's budget and the anticipated life of the vehicle, components which are only slightly worn may be refitted, but if in doubt it is always best to renew.

Crankshaft, main and big-end bearings

3 The need to renew the main bearing shells or to have the crankshaft reground will usually have been determined during the last few miles of operation when perhaps a heavy knocking has developed from within the crankcase or the oil pressure warning lamp has stayed on denoting a low oil pressure probably caused by excessive wear in the bearings.

4 Even without these symptoms, the journals and crankpins on a high mileage engine should be checked for out-of-round (ovality) and taper. For this a micrometer will be needed to check the diameter of the journals and crankpins at several different points around them. A motor factor or engineer can do this for you. If the average of the readings shows that either out-of-round or taper is outside permitted tolerance (see

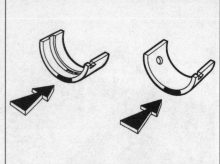

13.7b Bearing shell colour identification markings (arrowed)

Specifications), then the crankshaft should be reground by your dealer or engine reconditioning company to accept the undersize main and big-end shell bearings which are available. Normally, the company doing the regrinding will supply the necessary undersize shells.

5 If the crankshaft is in good condition, it is wise to renew the bearing shells as it is almost certain that the original ones will have worn. This is often indicated by scoring of the bearing surface or by the top layer of the bearing metal having worn through to expose the metal underneath.

6 Each shell is marked on its back with the part number. Undersize shells will have the undersize stamped additionally on their backs.

7 Standard size crankshafts having main bearing journal diameters at the lower end of the tolerance range are marked with a yellow spot on the front balance weight. You will find that with this type of crankshaft, a standard shell is fitted to the seat in the crankcase but a yellow colour-coded shell to the main bearing cap **(see illustrations)**.

8 If a green spot is seen on the crankshaft then this indicates that 0.25 mm (0.0098 in) undersize big-end bearings are used **(see illustration)**.

Cylinder bores, pistons, rings and connecting rods

9 Cylinder bore wear will usually have been evident from the smoke emitted from the

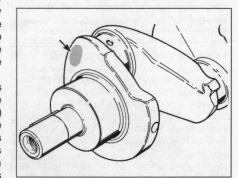

13.8 Crankshaft big-end journal size identification mark on crank throw web

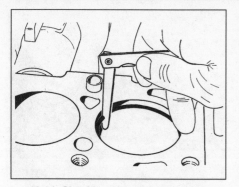

13.14 Checking piston ring end gap

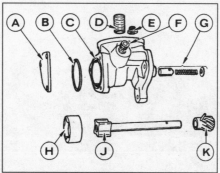

13.24a Exploded view of the oil pump

A Pump cover
B O-ring
C Pump body
D Oil filter
   attachment stud
E Filter relief valve

F Blind plug
G Oil pressure relief
   valve
H Outer rotor
J Inner rotor
K Drive gear

13.24b Lift off the oil pump cover and remove the O-ring

exhaust during recent operation of the vehicle on the road, coupled with excessive oil consumption and fouling of spark plugs.

10 Engine life can be extended by fitting special oil control rings to the pistons. These are widely advertised and will give many more thousands of useful mileage without the need for a rebore, although this will be inevitable eventually. If this remedy is decided upon, remove the piston/connecting rods (Section 8) and fit the proprietary rings in accordance with the manufacturer's instructions.

11 Where a more permanent solution is decided upon, the cylinder block can be rebored by your dealer or engineering works, or by one of the mobile workshops which now undertake such work. The cylinder bore will be measured both for out-of-round and for taper to decide how much the bores should be bored out. A set of matching pistons will be supplied in a suitable oversize to suit the new bores.

12 Due to the need for special heating and installing equipment for removal and refitting of the interference type gudgeon pin, the removal and refitting of pistons to the connecting rods is definitely a specialist job, preferably for your Ford dealer.

13 The removal and refitting of piston rings is however well within the scope of the home mechanic. Do this by sliding two or three old feeler blades round behind the top compression ring so that they are at equidistant points. The ring can now be slid up the blades and removed. Repeat the removal operations on the second compression ring and then the oil control ring. This method will not only prevent the rings dropping onto empty grooves as they are withdrawn, but it will also avoid ring breakage.

14 Even when new piston rings have been supplied to match the pistons, always check that they are not tight in their grooves and also check their end gaps by pushing them squarely down their particular cylinder bore and measuring with a feeler blade **(see illustration)**. Adjustment of the end gap can be made by careful grinding to bring it within the specified tolerance.

15 If new rings are being fitted to an old piston, always remove any carbon from the grooves beforehand. The best tool for this job is the end of a broken piston ring. Take care

not to cut your fingers, piston rings are sharp. The cylinder bores should be roughened with fine glass paper to assist the bedding-in of the new rings.

Timing sprockets and chain

16 The teeth on the timing sprockets rarely wear, but still check for broken or hooked teeth.

17 The timing chain should always be renewed at time of major engine overhaul. A worn chain is evident if when supported horizontally at both ends it takes on a deeply bowed appearance.

18 Finally check the rubber cushion on the tensioner spring leaf. If grooved or chewed up, renew it.

Flywheel

19 Inspect the starter ring gear on the flywheel for wear or broken teeth. If evident, the ring gear should be renewed in the following way. Drill the ring gear with two holes, approximately 7 or 8 mm (0.3 in) diameter and offset slightly. Make sure that you do not drill too deeply or you will damage the flywheel.

20 Tap the ring gear downward off its register and remove it.

13.25 Check the oil pump rotor-to-body clearance (A) and the inner-to-outer rotor clearance (B)

21 Place the flywheel in the household refrigerator for about an hour and then heat the new ring gear to between 260 and 280°C (500 and 536°F) in a domestic oven. Do not heat it above 290°C (554°F) or its hardness will be lost.

22 Slip the ring onto the flywheel and gently tap it into position against its register. Allow it to cool without quenching.

23 The clutch friction surface on the flywheel should be checked for grooving or tiny hair cracks, the latter being caused by overheating. If these conditions are evident, it may be possible to surface grind the flywheel provided its balance is not upset. Otherwise, a new flywheel will have to be fitted consult your dealer about this.

Oil pump

24 The oil pump should be checked for wear by unbolting and removing the cover plate and O-ring and checking the following tolerances **(see illustrations)**:
   a) Outer rotor to pump body gap.
   b) Inner rotor to outer rotor gap.
   c) Rotor endfloat (use a feeler blade and straight-edge across pump body).

25 Use feeler blades to check the tolerances and if they are outside the specified values, renew the pump **(see illustration)**.

Oil seals and gaskets

26 Renew the oil seals on the timing cover and the crankshaft rear retainer as a matter of routine at time of major overhaul. Oil seals are cheap, oil is not! Use a piece of tubing as a removal and installing tool. Apply some grease to the oil seal lips and check that the small tensioner spring in the oil seal has not been displaced by the vibration caused during fitting of the seal.

27 Renew all the gaskets by purchasing the appropriate "de-coke", short or full engine set. Oil seals may be included in the gasket sets.

Crankcase

28 Clean out the oilways with a length of wire or by using compressed air. Similarly clean the coolant passages. This is best done by flushing through with a cold water hose. Examine the crankcase and block for stripped threads in bolt holes; if evident, thread inserts can be fitted.

2A

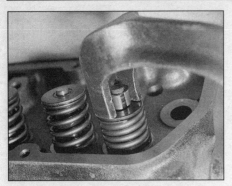

13.38 Compress the valve spring to remove the collets

13.39 Remove the valve spring retainer and spring . . .

13.40 . . . followed by the valve

29 Renew any core plugs which appear to be leaking or which are excessively rusty.

30 Cracks in the casting may be rectified by specialist welding, or by one of the cold metal key interlocking processes available.

Camshaft and bearings

31 Examine the camshaft gear and lobes for damage or wear. If evident a new camshaft must be purchased, or one which has been "built-up" such as are advertised by firms specialising in exchange components.

32 The bearing internal diameters should be checked against the specifications if a suitable gauge is available; otherwise, check for movement between the camshaft journal and the bearing. Worn bearings should be renewed by your dealer.

33 Check the camshaft endfloat by temporarily refitting the camshaft and the thrust plate. If the endfloat exceeds the specified tolerance, renew the thrust plate.

Cam followers

34 It is seldom that the cam followers wear in their bores, but it is likely that after a high mileage, the cam lobe contact surface will show signs of a depression or grooving.

35 Where this condition is evident, renew the cam followers. Grinding out the wear marks will only reduce the thickness of the hardened metal of the cam follower and accelerate further wear.

Cylinder head and rocker gear

36 The usual reason for dismantling the cylinder head is to de-carbonise and to grind in the valves. Reference should therefore be made to Section 14, in addition to the dismantling operations described here. First remove the manifolds.

37 Using a standard valve spring compressor, compress the spring on No 1 valve (valve nearest the timing cover). Do not over compress the spring or the valve stem may bend. If it is found that when screwing down the compressor tool, the spring retainer does not release from the collets, remove the compressor and place a piece of tubing on the retainer so that it does not impinge on the collets and strike the end of the tubing a sharp

blow with a hammer. Refit the compressor and compress the spring.

38 Extract the split collets and then gently release the compressor and remove it **(see illustration)**.

39 Remove the valve spring retainer, the spring and the oil seal **(see illustration)**.

40 Withdraw the valve **(see illustration)**.

41 Repeat the removal operations on the remaining seven valves. Keep the valves in their originally fitted sequence by placing them in a piece of card which has holes punched in it and numbered 1 to 8 (from the timing cover end).

42 Place each valve in turn in its guide so that approximately one third of its length enters the guide. Rock the valve from side to side. If there is any more than an imperceptible movement, the guides will have to be reamed (working from the valve seat end) and oversize stemmed valves fitted. If you do not have the necessary reamer (tool No 21-242), leave this work to your Ford dealer.

43 Examine the valve seats. Normally, the seats do not deteriorate but the valve heads are more likely to burn away in which case, new valves can be ground in as described in the next Section. If the seats require re-cutting, use a standard cutter available from most accessory or tool stores or consult your motor engineering works.

44 Renewal of any valve seat which is cracked or beyond recutting is definitely a job for your dealer or motor engineering works.

45 If the cylinder head mating surface is suspected of being distorted due to persistent leakage of coolant at the gasket joint, then it can be checked and surface ground by your dealer or motor engineering works. Distortion is unlikely under normal circumstances with a cast iron head.

46 Check the rocker shaft and rocker arms pads which bear on the valve stem end faces for wear or scoring, also for any broken coil springs. Renew components as necessary after dismantling as described in Section 6. If the springs have been in use for 50 000 miles (80 000 km) or more, they should be renewed.

47 Reassemble the cylinder head by fitting new valve stem oil seals. Install No 1 valve (lubricated) into its guide and fit the valve

spring with the closer coils to the cylinder head, followed by the spring retainer. Compress the spring and engage the split collets in the cutout in the valve stem. Hold them in position while the compressor is gently released and removed.

48 Repeat the operations on the remaining valves, making sure that each valve is returned to its original guide or if new valves have been fitted, into the seat into which it was ground.

49 On completion, support the ends of the cylinder head on two wooden blocks and strike the end of the valve stem with a plastic or copper-faced hammer, just a light blow to settle the components.

14 Cylinder head and pistons - decarbonising

OHV engines

1 With the cylinder head removed (Section 4), the carbon deposits should be removed from the combustion spaces using a scraper and a wire brush fitted into an electric drill. Take care not to damage the valve heads, otherwise no special precautions need be taken as the cylinder head is of cast iron construction.

2 Where a more thorough job is to be carried out, the cylinder head should be dismantled (Section 13), so that the valves may be ground in and the ports and combustion spaces cleaned, brushed and blown out after the manifolds have been removed.

3 Before grinding in a valve, remove the carbon and deposits completely from its head and stem. With an inlet valve, this is usually quite easy, simply scraping off the soft carbon with a blunt knife and finishing with a wire brush. With an exhaust valve the deposits are much harder and those on the head may need a rub on coarse emery cloth to remove them.

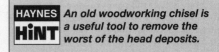

HAYNES HiNT *An old woodworking chisel is a useful tool to remove the worst of the head deposits.*

4 Ensure that the valve heads are really clean, otherwise the suction cup of the grinding tool will not stick during the grinding-in operations.

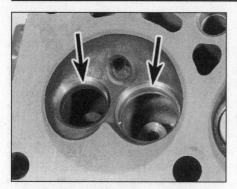

14.14a View of the swirl chamber in the cylinder head showing the valve seats (arrowed) - HCS engine

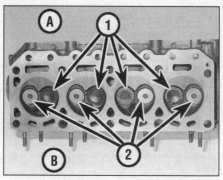

14.14b View of the cylinder head with valves fitted - HCS engine

A Inlet side   1 Inlet valves
B Exhaust side   2 Exhaust valves

HCS engines

14 The procedure is as described previously in this Section for OHV engines, noting the following.

a) *When cleaning out the swirl ports, great care must be exercised not to damage the valve seats, especially if using power tools (see illustration).*

b) *The valve arrangement is different, being of mirror effect, where the inlet valves for number 2 and 3 cylinders are next to each other (see illustration).*

c) *When refitting the valve stem oil seals, tape the end of the stem to prevent damage to the seal as it is fitted, and use a long reach socket or length of tube to push the seals fully down (see illustrations). Remove the tape on completion.*

d) *The valve seats cannot be re-worked using conventional tools.*

15 Engine - reassembly

Note: *Ensure that all necessary new oil seals and gaskets have been obtained before starting the reassembly procedure.*

OHV engines

1 With everything clean, commence reassembly by oiling the bores for the cam

14.14c Tape the end of the valve stem before fitting the valve stem seal - HCS engine

14.14d Using a long reach socket to push the seal fully home - HCS engine

followers and inserting them fully in their original sequence.

2 Lubricate the camshaft bearings and insert the camshaft from the timing cover end of the engine.

3 Fit the thrust plate and tighten the fixing bolts to the specified torque. The endfloat will already have been checked as described in Section 13. Secure the bolts with the locktabs **(see illustration)**.

4 Wipe clean the main bearing shell seats in the crankcase and fit the shells. Using a little grease, stick the semi-circular thrustwashers on either side of the centre bearing so that the oil grooves are visible when the washers are installed **(see illustration)**.

5 Check that the Woodruff key is in position on the front end of the crankshaft and tap the

5 Before starting to grind in a valve, support the cylinder head so that there is sufficient clearance under for the valve stem to project fully without being obstructed.

6 Take the first valve and apply a little coarse grinding paste to the bevelled edge of the valve head. Insert the valve into its guide and apply the suction grinding tool to its head. Rotate the tool between the palms of the hands in a back-and-forth rotary movement until the gritty action of the grinding-in process disappears. Repeat the operation with fine paste and then wipe away all traces of grinding paste and examine the seat and bevelled edge of the valve. A matt silver mating band should be observed on both components, without any sign of black spots. If some spots do remain, repeat the grinding-in-process until they have disappeared. A drop or two of paraffin applied to the contact surfaces will increase the speed of grinding-in, but do not allow any paste to run down into the valve guide. On completion, wipe away every trace of grinding paste using a paraffin-moistened cloth.

7 Repeat the operations on the remaining valves, taking care not to mix up their originally fitted sequence.

8 The valves are refitted as described in Section 13.

9 An important part of the decarbonising operation is to remove the carbon deposits from the piston crowns. To do this, turn the crankshaft so that two pistons are at the top of their stroke and press some grease between these pistons and the cylinder walls. This will prevent carbon particles falling down into the piston ring grooves. Stuff rags into the other two bores.

10 Cover the oilways and coolant passages with masking tape and then using a blunt scraper remove all the carbon from the piston crowns. Take care not to score the soft alloy of the crown or the surface of the cylinder bore.

11 Rotate the crankshaft to bring the other two pistons to TDC and repeat the operations.

12 Wipe away the circle of grease and carbon from the cylinder bores.

13 Clean the top surface of the cylinder block by careful scraping.

15.3 Secure the camshaft thrust plate bolts with the locktabs

15.4 Fit the upper main bearing shell and thrustwashers (arrowed) to the centre bearing

2A

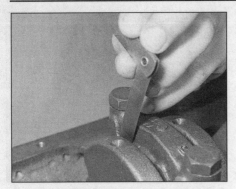

15.9 Using feeler blades to check crankshaft endfloat

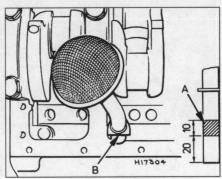

15.10 Oil pick-up tube details - 1.3 litre engine
A Area for application of adhesive
B Edge must be parallel with engine longitudinal axis

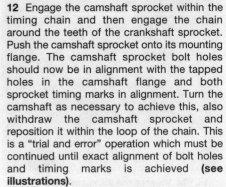

crankshaft sprocket into place using a piece of tubing.

6 Oil the bearing shells and lower the crankshaft into the crankcase.

7 Wipe the seats in the main bearing caps and fit the bearing shells into them. Install the caps so that their markings are correctly positioned as explained at dismantling in Section 12.

8 Screw in the cap bolts and tighten evenly to the specified torque.

9 Now check the crankshaft endfloat. Ideally a dial gauge should be used, but feeler blades are an alternative if inserted between the face of the thrustwasher and the machined surface of the crankshaft balance weight after having prised the crankshaft first in one direction and then the other **(see illustration)**. Provided the thrustwashers at the centre bearing have been renewed, the endfloat should be within the specified tolerance. If it is not, oversize thrustwashers are available (see Specifications).

10 If the oil pick-up tube was previously removed on 1.3 litre engines a new tube should now be fitted. Apply a suitable adhesive (available from Ford dealers) to the area shown, and fit the tube with the flat edge of the mounting flange parallel with the longitudinal axis of the engine **(see illustration)**.

11 Rotate the crankshaft so that the timing mark on its sprocket is directly in line with the centre of the camshaft sprocket mounting flange.

12 Engage the camshaft sprocket within the timing chain and then engage the chain around the teeth of the crankshaft sprocket. Push the camshaft sprocket onto its mounting flange. The camshaft sprocket bolt holes should now be in alignment with the tapped holes in the camshaft flange and both sprocket timing marks in alignment. Turn the camshaft as necessary to achieve this, also withdraw the camshaft sprocket and reposition it within the loop of the chain. This is a "trial and error" operation which must be continued until exact alignment of bolt holes and timing marks is achieved **(see illustrations)**.

13 Screw in the sprocket bolts to the specified torque and bend up the tabs of a new lockplate **(see illustration)**.

14 Bolt the timing chain tensioner into position, retract the tensioner cam spring and then slide the tensioner arm onto its pivot pin. Release the cam tensioner so that it bears upon the arm **(see illustration)**.

15 Fit the oil slinger to the front of the crankshaft sprocket so that its convex side is against the sprocket **(see illustration)**.

16 Using a new gasket, fit the timing cover, which will already have been fitted with a new oil seal (see Section 13) **(see illustration)**. One fixing bolt should be left out at this stage as it also holds the water pump. Grease the oil seal lips and fit the crankshaft pulley. Tighten the pulley bolt to the specified torque.

17 Using a new gasket, bolt the crankshaft rear oil seal retainer into position. Tighten the

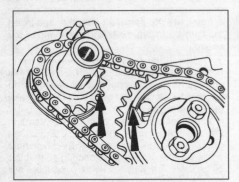

15.12a Crankshaft and camshaft sprocket timing mark locations

15.12b Fit the timing chain and camshaft sprocket . . .

15.12c . . . with the sprocket timing marks aligned with the shaft centres

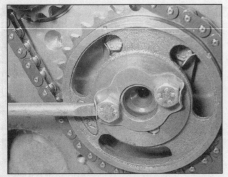

15.13 Secure the camshaft sprocket bolts with the locktabs

15.14 Refit the timing chain tensioner and arm

15.15 Fit the oil slinger with its convex side against the sprocket

15.16 Fitting the timing cover

15.17 Fitting the crankshaft rear oil seal retainer

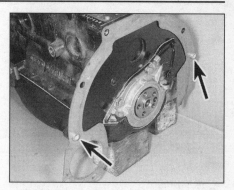

15.18a Locate the engine adapter plate over the dowels (arrowed) . . .

15.18b . . . then refit and secure the flywheel

bolts to the specified torque **(see illustration)**.
18 Locate the engine adapter (back) plate on its dowels and then fit the flywheel **(see illustrations)**.
19 Screw in and tighten the flywheel bolts to the specified torque. To prevent the flywheel turning, the starter ring gear can be jammed or a piece of wood placed between a crankshaft balance weight and the inside of the crankcase.
20 Install and centralise the clutch as described in Chapter 6.
21 The pistons/connecting rods should now be installed. Although new pistons may have been fitted to the rods by your dealer or supplier (see Section 13), it is worth checking to ensure that with the piston crown arrow pointing to the timing cover end of the engine,

the oil hole in the connecting rod is on the left **(see illustration 8.13a)**. Oil the cylinder bores.
22 Install the pistons/connecting rods as described in Section 8.
23 Fit the sump as described in Section 5.
24 Fit the oil pressure sender unit, if removed.
25 Turn the crankshaft until No 1 piston is at TDC (crankshaft pulley 3rd timing cover marks aligned) and fit the oil pump complete with a new gasket and a new oil filter as described in Section 10.
26 Using a new gasket, fit the fuel pump. If the insulating block became detached from the crankcase during removal, make sure that a new gasket is fitted to each side of the block.
27 Fit the water pump using a new gasket.
28 Fit the cylinder head as described in Section 4.
29 Refit the pushrods in their original sequence and the rocker shaft, also as described in Section 4.
30 Adjust the valve clearances (Chapter 1) and refit the rocker cover using a new gasket.
31 Fit the inlet and exhaust manifolds using new gaskets and tightening the nuts and bolts to the specified torque (Chapter 4, Part E).
32 Refit the carburettor using a new flange gasket and connect the fuel pipe from the pump (Chapter 4, Part A).
33 Screw in the spark plugs and the coolant temperature switch (if removed).
34 Refit the thermostat and the thermostat housing cover.

35 Fit the pulley to the water pump pulley flange.
36 Fit the alternator and the drivebelt and tension the belt as described in Chapter 1.
37 Refit the distributor as described in Chapter 5, Part B.
38 Refit the distributor cap and reconnect the spark plug HT leads.
39 Bolt on and connect the coolant pipe to the side of the cylinder block.
40 Fit the breather pipe from the oil filler cap to the inlet manifold and fit the cap.
41 Check the sump drain plug for tightness. A new seal should be fitted at regular intervals to prevent leakage. Refit the dipstick.
42 Refilling with oil should be left until the engine is installed in the vehicle.

15.43a Line up the flange using a spanner - HCS engine

15.43b Fitting the flywheel to the crankshaft (dowel arrowed) - HCS engine

15.43c Using the correct tool . . .

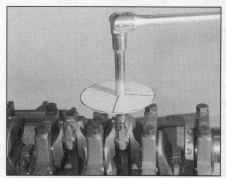

15.43d . . . and using a card template to angle-tighten the big-end cap bolts - HCS engine

2A

HCS engines

43 The procedure is as described previously in this Section for OHV engines, noting the following points.

a) *Tighten the main bearing cap bolts to the specified torque before fitting the oil pick-up tube.*

b) *When fitting the oil pick-up tube, use a spanner on the flats of the flange to line it up* **(see illustration)**.

c) *The flywheel is dowelled to the crankshaft and cannot be fitted off-centre* **(see illustration)**.

d) *The big-end bearing cap bolts are angle-tightened after an initial torque load (see Specifications). Use the correct tool if it is available or make up a card template with the specified angle marked on it* **(see illustrations)**.

e) *Apart from lining up the camshaft and crankshaft sprocket timing marks (for valve timing), there is no ignition timing mark to worry about.*

f) *Fit the rocker cover using a new gasket. Do not exceed the specified torque for the securing screws; this may result in oil leaks at the rocker cover/cylinder head mating face.*

16 Engine/transmission - reconnection and installation

1 This is a direct reversal of removal and separation from the transmission. Take care not to damage the radiator or front wings during installation.

Reconnection

2 Reconnection of the engine and transmission is a reversal of separation, but if the clutch has been dismantled, check that the friction plate has been centralised as described in Chapter 6.

Installation

OHV engines

3 First check that the engine sump drain plug is tight and then, where applicable refit the selector shaft cap nut (removed to drain the transmission oil) together with its spring and interlock pin. Apply sealer to the cap nut threads when refitting (see Specifications Chapter 7, Part A).

4 Manoeuvre the engine/transmission under the vehicle and attach the lifting hoist. Raise the engine/transmission carefully until the right-hand rear mounting can be engaged. Refit the mounting nut and bolt loosely only at this stage.

5 On pre-1986 models refit the front mounting and anti-roll bar support plates, then refit the left-hand front and rear mountings loosely only.

6 On 1986 models onwards refit the transmission support crossmember.

7 Lower the hoist and let the power unit rest on its mountings. Ensure that none of the mountings are under strain, then tighten all the mounting nuts and bolts and remove the hoist.

8 The driveshafts and suspension arms should now be refitted using the procedure described in the manual transmission refitting procedure in Chapter 7, Part A.

9 Reconnect and adjust the gearchange linkage using the procedure described in Chapter 7, Part A.

10 Fit the starter motor leads to their terminals.

11 Connect the engine earth leads.

12 Refit the exhaust system and bolt the downpipe to the manifold. Refit the hot air box which connects with the air cleaner.

13 Reconnect the clutch operating cable.

14 Reconnect the electrical leads, the fuel pipe, the brake vacuum hose and the speedometer cable.

15 Reconnect the throttle cable and the choke cable (where applicable) as described in Chapter 4, Part A.

16 Reconnect the radiator coolant hoses, and heater hoses.

17 Fill up with engine oil, transmission oil and coolant, then reconnect the battery (photo).

18 Refit the bonnet, bolting the hinges to their originally marked positions. Reconnect the screen washer pipe.

19 Fit the air cleaner and reconnect the hoses and the air cleaner inlet spout.

20 Once the engine is running, check the dwell angle, timing, idle speed and mixture adjustment as applicable (refer to Chapter 1).

21 If a number of new internal components have been installed, run the vehicle at restricted speed for the first few hundred miles to allow time for the new components to bed in. It is also recommended that with a new or rebuilt engine, the engine oil and filter are changed at the end of the running-in period.

HCS engines

22 Refitting is a reversal of the removal procedure described in Section 11.

Chapter 2 Part B:
CVH engines

Contents

Degrees of difficulty

Easy, suitable for novice with little experience 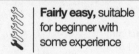	Fairly easy, suitable for beginner with some experience	Fairly difficult, suitable for competent DIY mechanic	Difficult, suitable for experienced DIY mechanic	Very difficult, suitable for expert DIY or professional

Specifications

General

Engine type	Four-cylinder, in-line overhead camshaft
Capacity:	
1.1 litre	1117 cc
1.3 litre	1296 cc
1.4 litre	1392 cc
1.6 litre	1597 cc
Bore:	
1.1 litre	73.96 mm
1.3 and 1.6 litre	79.96 mm
1.4 litre	77.24 mm
Stroke:	
1.1 litre	64.98 mm
1.3 litre	64.52 mm
1.4 litre	74.30 mm
1.6 litre	79.52 mm
Compression ratio:	
All except 1.6 litre Turbo	9.5:1
1.6 litre Turbo	8.3:1
Firing order	1-3-4-2 (No 1 at timing belt end)

Cylinder block

Material	Cast iron
Number of main bearings	5
Cylinder bore (diameter):	
1.1 litre:	
Standard (1)	73.94 to 73.95 mm
Standard (2)	73.95 to 73.96 mm
Standard (3)	73.96 to 73.97 mm
Standard (4)	73.97 to 73.98 mm
Oversize (A)	74.23 to 74.24 mm
Oversize (B)	74.24 to 74.25 mm
Oversize (C)	74.25 to 74.26 mm

Cylinder bore (diameter) (continued):

1.3 and 1.6 litre:

Standard (1)	79.94 to 79.95 mm
Standard (2)	79.95 to 79.96 mm
Standard (3)	79.96 to 79.97 mm
Standard (4)	79.97 to 79.98 mm
Oversize (A)	80.23 to 80.24 mm
Oversize (B)	80.24 to 80.25 mm
Oversize (C)	80.25 to 80.26 mm

1.4 litre:

Standard (1)	77.22 to 77.23 mm
Standard (2)	77.23 to 77.24 mm
Standard (3)	77.24 to 77.25 mm
Standard (4)	77.25 to 77.26 mm
Oversize (A)	77.51 to 77.52 mm
Oversize (B)	77.52 to 77.53 mm
Oversize (C)	77.53 to 77.54 mm

Main bearing shell inner diameter:

Standard	58.011 to 58.038 mm
Undersize 0.25 mm	57.761 to 57.788 mm
Undersize 0.50 mm	57.511 to 57.538 mm
Undersize 0.75 mm	57.261 to 57.288 mm

Crankshaft

Main bearing journal diameter:

Standard	57.98 to 58.00 mm
Undersize 0.25 mm	57.73 to 57.75 mm
Undersize 0.50 mm	57.48 to 57.50 mm
Undersize 0.75 mm	57.23 to 57.25 mm
Main bearing running clearance	0.011 to 0.058 mm

Thrustwasher thickness:

Standard	2.301 to 2.351 mm
Oversize	2.491 to 2.541 mm
Crankshaft endfloat	0.09 to 0.30 mm

Crankpin (big-end) diameter:

1.1 engines:

Standard	42.99 to 43.01 mm
Undersize 0.25 mm	42.74 to 42.76 mm
Undersize 0.50 mm	42.49 to 42.51 mm
Undersize 0.75 mm	42.24 to 42.26 mm
Undersize 1.00 mm	41.99 to 42.01 mm

1.3, 1.4 and 1.6 engines:

Standard	47.89 to 47.91 mm
Undersize 0.25 mm	47.64 to 47.66 mm
Undersize 0.50 mm	47.39 to 47.41 mm
Undersize 0.75 mm	47.14 to 47.16 mm
Undersize 1.00 mm	46.89 to 46.91 mm
Big-end bearing running clearance	0.006 to 0.060 mm

Camshaft

Number of bearings	5
Drive	Toothed belt
Thrust plate thickness	4.99 to 5.01 mm

Camshaft bearing diameter:

1	44.75 mm
2	45.00 mm
3	45.25 mm
4	45.50 mm
5	45.75 mm
Camshaft endfloat	0.05 to 0.15 mm

Pistons and piston rings

Diameter 1.1 litre:

Standard 1	73.910 to 73.920 mm
Standard 2	73.920 to 73.930 mm
Standard 3	73.930 to 73.940 mm
Standard 4	73.940 to 73.950 mm
Standard service	73.930 to 73.955 mm
Oversize 0.29 mm	74.210 to 74.235 mm
Oversize 0.50 mm	74.460 to 74.485 mm

Pistons and piston rings (continued)

Diameter - 1.3 and 1.6 litre:
Standard 1	79.910 to 79.920 mm
Standard 2	79.920 to 79.930 mm
Standard 3	79.930 to 79.940 mm
Standard 4	79.940 to 79.950 mm
Standard service	79.930 to 79.955 mm
Oversize 0.29 mm	80.210 to 80.235 mm
Oversize 0.50 mm	80.430 to 80.455 mm

Diameter - 1.4 litre:
Standard 1	77.190 to 77.200 mm
Standard 2	77.200 to 77.210 mm
Standard 3	77.210 to 77.220 mm
Standard 4	77.220 to 77.230 mm
Standard service	77.210 to 77.235 mm
Oversize 0.29 mm	77.490 to 77.515 mm
Oversize 0.50 mm	77.710 to 77.735 mm
Piston-to-bore clearance	0.010 to 0.045 mm

Piston ring end gap:
1.1 litre:
Compression rings	0.25 to 0.45 mm
Oil control ring	0.20 to 0.40 mm

1.3, 1.4 and 1.6 litre:
Compression rings	0.30 to 0.50 mm
Oil control ring	0.40 to 1.40 mm

Connecting rod

Big-end bore diameter:
1.1 litre	46.685 to 46.705 mm
1.3, 1.4 and 1.6 litre	50.890 to 50.910 mm
Small-end bore diameter	20.589 to 20.609 mm

Big-end bearing shell inside diameter:
1.1 litre:
Standard	43.016 to 43.050 mm
Undersize 0.25 mm	42.766 to 42.800 mm
Undersize 0.50 mm	42.516 to 42.550 mm
Undersize 0.75 mm	42.266 to 42.300 mm
Undersize 1.00 mm	42.016 to 42.050 mm

1.3, 1.4 and 1.6 litre:
Standard	47.916 to 47.950 mm
Undersize 0.25 mm	47.666 to 47.700 mm
Undersize 0.50 mm	47.416 to 47.450 mm
Undersize 0.75 mm	47.166 to 47.200 mm
Undersize 1.00 mm	46.916 to 46.950 mm
Big-end bearing running clearance	0.006 to 0.060 mm

Cylinder head

Material	Light alloy
Maximum permissible cylinder head distortion (over entire length)	0.15 mm

Minimum combustion chamber depth after skimming:
1.1 litre	18.22 mm
1.3 and 1.6 litre	19.60 mm
1.4 litre	17.40 mm
Valve seat angle	45°
Valve seat width	1.75 to 2.32 mm

Seat cutter:
Upper correction angle	18°

Lower correction angle:
1.1 litre	80° (inlet), 70° (exhaust)
1.3, 1.4 and 1.6 litre	75° (inlet), 70° (exhaust)

Valve guide bore:
Standard	8.063 to 8.094 mm
Oversize 0.2 mm	8.263 to 8.294 mm
Oversize 0.4 mm	8.463 to 8.494 mm

Valves - general

Operation	Rocker arms and hydraulic cam followers

Valve timing:
1.1 litre and 1.3 litre:
Inlet valve opens	13° ATDC
Inlet valve closes	28° ABDC

Valve timing (1.1 litre and 1.3 litre) (continued):

Exhaust valve opens	30° BBDC
Exhaust valve closes	15° BTDC
1.4 litre:	
Inlet valve opens	15° ATDC
Inlet valve closes	30° ABDC
Exhaust valve opens	28° BBDC
Exhaust valve closes	13° BTDC
1.6 litre (except carburettor versions 1986 onwards):	
Inlet valve opens	8° ATDC
Inlet valve closes	36° ABDC
Exhaust valve opens	34° BBDC
Exhaust valve closes	6° BTDC
1.6 litre (carburettor versions - 1986 onwards):	
Inlet valve opens	4° ATDC
Inlet valve closes	32° ABDC
Exhaust valve opens	38° BBDC
Exhaust valve closes	10° BTDC
Valve lift:	
Inlet:	
1.1, 1.3 and 1.4 litre	9.56 mm
1.6 litre	10.09 mm
Exhaust:	
1.1, 1.3 and 1.4 litre	9.52 mm
1.6 litre	10.06 mm
Valve spring free length	47.2 mm

Inlet valve

Length:	
1.1 litre	135.74 to 136.20 mm
1.3 and 1.6 litre	134.54 to 135.0 mm
1.4 litre	136.29 to 136.75 mm
Head diameter:	
1.1 litre	37.9 to 38.1 mm
1.3 and 1.6 litre	41.9 to 42.1 mm
1.4 litre	39.9 to 40.1 mm
Stem diameter:	
Standard	8.025 to 8.043 mm
0.20 mm oversize	8.225 to 8.243 mm
0.40 mm oversize	8.425 to 8.443 mm
Valve stem clearance in guide	0.020 to 0.063 mm

Exhaust valve

Length:	
1.1 litre	132.62 to 133.08 mm
1.3 litre	131.17 to 131.63 mm
1.4 litre	132.97 to 133.43 mm
1.6 litre	131.57 to 132.03 mm
Head diameter:	
1.1 litre	32.1 to 32.3 mm
1.3 litre	33.9 to 34.1 mm
1.4 litre	33.9 to 34.1 mm
1.6 litre	36.9 to 37.1 mm
Valve stem diameter:	
Standard	7.999 to 8.017 mm
0.20 mm oversize	8.199 to 8.217 mm
0.40 mm oversize	8.399 to 8.417 mm
Valve stem clearance in guide	0.046 to 0.089 mm

Lubrication

Oil filter	Champion C104
Oil pump type:	
Pre-1986	Gear type driven by crankshaft
1986 onwards	Rotor type driven by crankshaft
Minimum oil pressure at 80°C (176°F):	
At 750 rpm	1.0 bar (14.5 lbf/in^2)
At 2000 rpm	2.8 bar (40.6 lbf/in^2)
Oil pressure warning lamp operates	0.3 to 0.5 bar (4.3 to 7.2 lbf/in^2)

Lubrication (continued)

Relief valve opens	4.0 bar (58 lbf/in^2)
Oil pump clearances (rotor type pump only):	
Outer rotor to body	0.060 to 0.190 mm
Inner to outer rotor	0.050 to 0.180 mm
Rotor endfloat	0.014 to 0.100 mm

Torque wrench settings

	Nm	lbf ft
Main bearing caps	90 to 100	66 to 74
Connecting rod bolts	30 to 36	22 to 26
Oil pump to crankcase	8 to 11	6 to 8
Oil pump cover bolts	8 to 11	6 to 8
Oil pump pick-up tube to block	17 to 23	12 to 17
Oil pump pick-up tube to pump	8 to 11	6 to 8
Oil cooler threaded sleeve to block	55 to 60	40 to 44
Rear oil seal carrier bolts	8 to 11	6 to 8
Sump with multi-piece gasket:		
Stage 1	8 to 11	6 to 8
Stage 2	8 to 11	6 to 8
Sump with one-piece gasket:		
Stage 1	5 to 8	4 to 6
Stage 2	5 to 8	4 to 6
Flywheel to crankshaft	82 to 92	60 to 68
Torque converter drive plate to crankshaft	80 to 88	59 to 65
Crankshaft pulley bolt	100 to 115	74 to 85
Cylinder head bolts:		
Stage 1	25	18
Stage 2	55	40
Stage 3	Tighten by a further 90°	Tighten by a further 90°
Stage 4	Tighten by a further 90°	Tighten by a further 90°
Camshaft thrust plate	9 to 13	7 to 10
Camshaft sprocket bolt	54 to 59	40 to 43
Timing belt tensioner bolts	16 to 20	12 to 15
Rocker arm studs in head:		
Plain stud	10 to 15	7 to 11
Stud with nylon insert	18 to 23	13 to 17
Rocker arm nut	25 to 29	18 to 21
Rocker cover screws	6 to 8	4 to 6
Timing belt cover bolts	9 to 11	7 to 8
Sump drain plug	21 to 28	15 to 21
Engine to manual transmission	35 to 45	26 to 33
Engine to automatic transmission	30 to 50	22 to 37
Right-hand engine mounting to body	41 to 58	30 to 43
Right-hand engine mounting bracket to engine	76 to 104	56 to 77
Right-hand engine mounting rubber insulator to brackets	41 to 58	30 to 43
Front transmission mounting bracket to transmission (pre-1986 models)	41 to 51	30 to 38
Front and rear transmission mounting bolts (pre-1986 models)	52 to 64	38 to 47
Transmission mountings to transmission (1986 models onwards)	80 to 100	59 to 74
Transmission support crossmember to body (1986 models onwards)	52	38
Oil pressure switch	18 to 22	13 to 16

1 General information

The 1.1 litre, 1.3 litre, 1.4 litre and 1.6 litre CVH (Compound Valve angle, Hemispherical combustion chambers) engines are of four cylinder in-line overhead camshaft type, mounted transversely, together with the transmission, at the front of the car (see illustrations).

The crankshaft is supported in five main bearings within a cast iron crankcase.

The cylinder head is of light alloy construction, supporting the overhead camshaft in five bearings. Camshaft drive is by a toothed composite rubber belt, driven from a sprocket on the crankshaft.

The distributor (where applicable) is driven from the rear (flywheel) end of the camshaft by means of an offset dog.

The cam followers are of hydraulic type, which eliminates the need for valve clearance adjustment. If the engine has been standing idle for a period of time, or after overhaul, when the engine is started up, valve clatter may be heard. This is a normal condition and will gradually disappear within a few minutes of starting up as the cam followers are pressurised with oil.

The water pump is mounted on the timing belt end of the cylinder block and is driven by the toothed belt.

A gear or rotor type oil pump is mounted on the timing belt end of the cylinder block and is driven by a gear on the front end of the crankshaft.

A full-flow oil filter of throw-away type is located on the side of the crankcase.

An engine oil cooler is located under the oil filter on fuel-injection and automatic transmission models.

2 Major operations possible with the engine in the car

The following work can be carried out without having to remove the engine:

a) *Timing belt - renewal.*
b) *Camshaft oil seal - renewal.*
c) *Camshaft - removal and refitting.*
d) *Cylinder head - removal and refitting.*
e) *Crankshaft front oil seal - renewal.*
f) *Sump - removal and refitting.*
g) *Piston/connecting rod - removal and refitting.*
h) *Engine/transmission mountings - removal and refitting.*

3 Major operations requiring engine removal

The following work can only be carried out after removal of the engine from the car:

a) *Crankshaft main bearings - renewal.*
b) *Crankshaft - removal and refitting.*
c) *Flywheel - removal and refitting.*
d) *Crankshaft rear oil seal - renewal.*
e) *Oil pump - removal and refitting.*

1.1a Cutaway view of the CVH engine

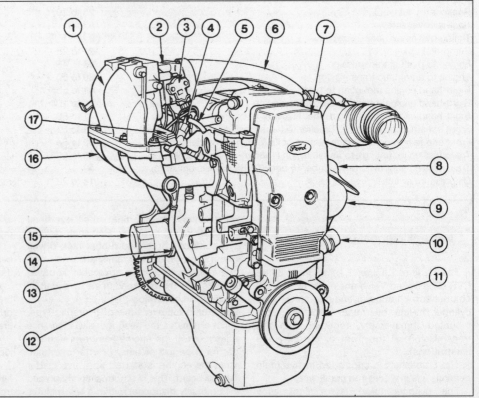

1.1b 1.6 litre EFI engine

1 *Inlet manifold (upper)*
2 *Throttle housing*
3 *Throttle position sensor*
4 *Fuel rail*
5 *Fuel hose*
6 *Air inlet duct*
7 *Timing belt cover*
8 *Exhaust heat shield*
9 *Exhaust manifold*
10 *Coolant inlet pipe*
11 *Crankshaft pulley*
12 *Flywheel ribs*
13 *Flywheel*
14 *Oil cooler*
15 *Oil filter*
16 *Inlet manifold (lower)*
17 *Fuel injection wiring harness*

4.3a Crankshaft pulley notch (arrowed) aligned with TDC (0) mark on belt cover scale

4.3b Camshaft sprocket at TDC position

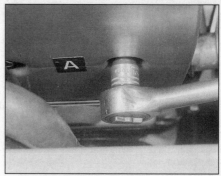

4.4a Where a two-piece timing belt cover is fitted, undo the bolts . . .

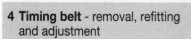

4 Timing belt - removal, refitting and adjustment

Removal

Note: *From April 1988 (build code JG) a modified timing belt tensioner incorporating a larger diameter tensioner roller was introduced, and from October 1988 an improved timing belt was used. When renewal of the timing belt becomes necessary, only the latest, improved timing belt must be used (the older type will no longer be available). On models produced before April 1988 this will also entail renewal of the tensioner roller.*

1 Disconnect the battery negative lead.

2 Release the alternator mounting and adjuster link bolts, push the alternator in towards the engine and slip the drivebelt off the pulleys.

3 Using a spanner on the crankshaft pulley bolt, turn the crankshaft until the notch on the pulley is aligned with the TDC (0) mark on the timing belt cover scale. On models with a distributor, now remove the distributor cap and check that the rotor arm is pointing towards the No 1 cylinder HT lead segment in the cap. If the rotor arm is pointing towards the No 4 cylinder segment, turn the crankshaft through another complete turn and realign the pulley notch with the TDC mark. On EFI engine models (see Chapter 4, Part D), check

that the timing mark on the camshaft sprocket is opposite the TDC mark on the cylinder head **(see illustrations)**.

4 On early models unscrew the four bolts and remove the one-piece timing belt cover. On later models fitted with a two-piece cover, unscrew the two upper bolts and remove the top half, then unscrew the two lower bolts. The lower half cannot be removed at this stage **(see illustrations)**.

5 Undo the bolts and remove the right-hand engine splash shield.

6 Using a ring spanner unscrew the crankshaft pulley retaining bolt. Remove the starter motor as described in Chapter 5, Part A and lock the flywheel ring gear with a cold chisel or similar tool to prevent the crankshaft rotating **(see illustration)**. Remove the pulley, followed by the timing belt cover lower half on later models.

7 Slacken the two bolts which secure the timing belt tensioner and, using a large screwdriver, prise the tensioner to one side to relieve the tautness of the belt **(see illustration)**. If the tensioner is spring-loaded, tighten one of the bolts to retain it in the slackened position.

8 If the original belt is to be refitted, mark it for direction of travel and also the exact tooth positions on all three sprockets.

9 Slip the timing belt off the camshaft, water pump and crankshaft sprockets.

Refitting

10 Before refitting the belt, check that the crankshaft is still at TDC (the small projection on the belt sprocket front flange in line with the TDC mark on the oil pump housing) and that the timing mark on the camshaft sprocket is opposite the TDC mark on the cylinder head **(see illustrations)**. Adjust the position of the sprockets slightly, but avoid any excessive movement of the sprockets while the belt is off, as the piston crowns and valve heads may make contact.

11 Engage the timing belt with the teeth of the crankshaft sprocket and then pull the belt vertically upright on its right-hand run. Keep it taut and engage it with the teeth of the camshaft sprocket. Check that the positions of the sprockets have not altered **(see illustration)**.

12 Wind the belt round the camshaft sprocket, around and under the tensioner and over the water pump sprocket.

13 Refit the crankshaft pulley and tighten the bolt, using the same procedure as used previously to stop the crankshaft turning. On later models make sure that the timing belt cover lower half is placed in position before refitting the pulley.

Adjustment

Note: *Accurate adjustment of the timing belt entails the use of Ford special tools. An approximate setting can be achieved using the*

2B

4.4b . . . and remove the upper half

4.6 Using a stout bar to lock the flywheel ring gear

4.7 Timing belt tensioner retaining bolts (arrowed)

4.10a Crankshaft sprocket projection (arrowed) aligned with TDC mark on oil pump housing

4.10b . . . and camshaft sprocket timing mark aligned with TDC mark on cylinder head

4.11 Place the timing belt in position

method described in this Section, but the tension should be checked by a dealer on completion.

14 To adjust the belt tension, slacken the tensioner and move it towards the front of the car to apply an initial tension to the belt. Secure the tensioner in this position.

15 Rotate the crankshaft clockwise through two complete revolutions, then return to the TDC position. Check that the camshaft sprocket is also at TDC as previously described.

16 Grasp the belt between thumb and forefinger at a point midway between the crankshaft and camshaft sprocket on the straight side of the belt. When the tension is correct it should just be possible to twist the belt through 90° at this point. Slacken the tensioner and using a large screwdriver as a lever, move it as necessary until the tension is correct. Tighten the tensioner bolts, rotate the camshaft to settle the belt, then recheck the tension. It will probably take two or three attempts to achieve success.

17 It must be emphasised that this is an approximate setting only and should be rechecked by a Ford dealer at the earliest opportunity.

18 Refit the starter motor, engine splash shield, distributor cap and timing belt cover/s.

19 Refit the alternator drivebelt and adjust its tension as described in Chapter 1.

20 Reconnect the battery.

5 Oil seals - renewal

Camshaft oil seal

Note: Thread locking compound will be required to coat the camshaft sprocket bolt on refitting.

1 Disconnect the battery negative lead.

2 Release the timing belt from the camshaft sprocket, as described in Section 4.

3 Pass a bar through one of the holes in the camshaft sprocket to anchor the sprocket while the retaining bolt is unscrewed. Remove the sprocket.

4 Using a suitable tool, hooked at its end, prise out the oil seal **(see illustration)**.

5 Apply a little grease to the lips of the new seal and draw it into position using the sprocket bolt and a suitable distance piece.

6 Refit the sprocket, tightening the bolt to the specified torque wrench setting. Thread locking compound should be applied to the threads of the bolt.

7 Refit and tension the timing belt (Section 4).

8 Reconnect the battery.

Crankshaft front oil seal

9 Disconnect the battery negative lead.

10 Release the alternator mounting and adjuster link bolts, push the alternator in towards the engine and slip the drivebelt from the pulleys.

11 Unbolt and remove the timing belt cover. On models with a two-piece cover only the upper half can be removed at this stage.

12 Locate a spanner onto the crankshaft pulley bolt and turn the crankshaft over in its normal direction of travel until the timing marks of the crankshaft sprocket and cylinder head are in alignment.

13 You will now need to remove the crankshaft pulley. To prevent the crankshaft turning, place the vehicle in gear and have an assistant apply the brakes or unbolt and remove the starter motor so that the flywheel ring gear can be jammed with a cold chisel or suitable implement. Unbolt the crankshaft pulley and remove it with its thrustwasher. Where a two-piece timing belt cover is fitted, remove the lower half.

14 Slacken the belt tensioner bolts, lever the tensioner to one side and retighten the bolts. With the belt slack, it can now be slipped from the sprockets. Before removing the belt note its original position on the sprockets (mark the teeth with quick-drying paint), also its direction of travel.

15 Withdraw the crankshaft sprocket. If it is tight you will need to use a special extractor, but due to the confined space available you may need to lower the engine from its mounting on that side. Before resorting to this, try levering the sprocket free using screwdrivers. If the mounting is to be disconnected refer to Part A of this Chapter.

16 Remove the dished washer from the crankshaft, noting that the concave side is against the oil seal.

17 Using a suitably hooked tool, prise out the oil seal from the oil pump housing.

18 Grease the lips of the new seal and press it into position using the pulley bolt and suitable distance piece made from a piece of tubing.

19 Fit the thrustwasher (concave side to oil seal), the belt sprocket and the pulley to the crankshaft. On models with a two-piece timing belt cover, place the lower half in position before refitting the pulley.

20 Fit and tension the timing belt by the method described in Section 4.

21 Fit the timing belt cover.

22 Refit and tension the alternator drivebelt (Chapter 1).

23 Remove the starter ring gear jamming device (if fitted), refit the starter motor and reconnect the battery.

6 Camshaft - removal and refitting

Carburettor engines

Note: Thread locking compound will be required to coat the camshaft sprocket bolt on refitting.

Removal

1 Disconnect the battery negative lead.

2 Refer to the relevant Part of Chapter 4 and remove the air cleaner and the fuel pump.

3 Disconnect the throttle and where fitted the

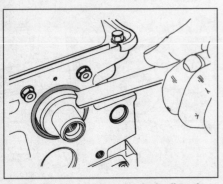

5.4 Removing the camshaft oil seal

6.12 Removing the camshaft sprocket

6.13a Unscrew the camshaft thrust plate bolts . . .

6.13b . . . and withdraw the thrust plate

choke cable ends from the carburettor linkage, then undo the bolts and move the cable support bracket to one side.

4 Where applicable, refer to Chapter 5, Part B and remove the distributor.

5 Remove the timing belt cover-to-cylinder head attachment bolts.

6 Disconnect the crankcase ventilation hoses at the rocker cover, undo and remove the bolts and washers and remove the rocker cover.

7 Unscrew the securing nuts and remove the rocker arms and guides. Keep the components in their originally installed sequence by marking them with a piece of numbered tape or by using a suitably sub-divided box.

8 Withdraw the hydraulic cam followers, again keeping them in their originally fitted sequence.

9 Slacken the alternator mounting and adjuster link bolts, push the alternator in towards the engine and slip the drivebelt from the pulleys.

10 Unbolt and remove the timing belt cover (top half only on later models with two-piece cover) and turn the crankshaft to align the timing mark on the camshaft sprocket with the one on the cylinder head.

11 Slacken the bolts on the timing belt tensioner, lever the tensioner against the tension of its coil spring (if fitted) and retighten the bolts. With the belt now slack, slip it from the camshaft sprocket.

12 Pass a rod or large screwdriver through one of the holes in the camshaft sprocket to lock it and unscrew the sprocket bolt. Remove the sprocket **(see illustration)**.

6.14 Withdrawing the camshaft

13 Extract the two bolts and pull out the camshaft thrustplate **(see illustrations)**.

14 Carefully withdraw the camshaft from the distributor end of the cylinder head **(see illustration)**.

Refitting

15 Refitting the camshaft is a reversal of removal, but observe the following points.

16 Lubricate the camshaft bearings before inserting the camshaft into the cylinder head.

17 It is recommended that a new oil seal is always fitted after the camshaft has been installed (see preceding Section). Apply thread locking compound to the sprocket bolt threads. Tighten the bolt to the specified torque.

18 Fit and tension the timing belt, as described in Section 4.

19 Oil the hydraulic cam followers with hypoid type transmission oil before inserting them into their original bores.

20 Refit the rocker arms and guides in their original sequence, use new nuts and tighten to the specified torque. It is essential that before each rocker arm is installed and its nut tightened, the respective cam follower is positioned at its lowest point (in contact with cam base circle). Turn the camshaft (by means of the crankshaft pulley bolt) as necessary to achieve this.

21 Use a new rocker cover gasket, and to ensure that a good seal is made, check that its location groove is clear of oil, grease and any portions of the old gasket. A length of sealant should be applied to the gasket recess where the cover engages under the timing belt cover.

7.4 Disconnecting the hose from the thermostat housing - carburettor engine

When in position tighten the cover retaining screws to the specified torque setting.

22 Refit the remainder of the components with reference to their relevant Chapters. Do not forget the timing belt cover bolts.

Fuel injection engines

Note: *Thread locking compound will be required to coat the camshaft sprocket bolt on refitting.*

Removal

23 Disconnect the battery negative lead.

24 Where necessary, disconnect any hoses and wiring restricting access to the timing belt cover and/or the rocker cover. If necessary, refer to the relevant Part(s) of Chapters 4 and 5 for details.

25 On XR3i and Cabriolet models with mechanical (Bosch K-Jetronic) fuel injection, disconnect the inlet air hose between the fuel distributor and throttle housing and position it out of the way.

26 On RS Turbo models disconnect the inlet air hose and the small connecting hose at the inlet air duct, then undo the two bolts and remove the air duct from the rocker cover.

27 Proceed as described in paragraphs 4 to 14 inclusive.

Refitting

28 Proceed as described in paragraphs 15 to 22 inclusive.

7 Cylinder head - removal and refitting

Carburettor engines

Removal

Note: *The cylinder head must only be removed when the engine is cold. New cylinder head bolts and a new gasket must be used on refitting.*

1 Disconnect the battery earth lead.

2 Remove the air cleaner (Chapter 4, Part A).

3 Drain the cooling system (Chapter 1).

4 Disconnect the coolant hoses from the thermostat housing, automatic choke and inlet manifold as applicable **(see illustration)**.

7.5 Disconnect the choke cable from the linkage clamp (arrowed) - carburettor engine

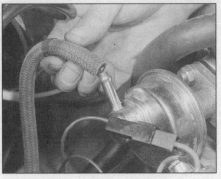

7.6 Disconnect the fuel feed pipe at the pump - carburettor engine

7.7 Disconnect the brake servo vacuum hose (arrowed) - 1.4 litre carburettor engine

5 Disconnect the throttle and where fitted the choke cable ends from the carburettor linkage, then undo the bolts and move the cable support bracket to one side **(see illustration)**.

6 Disconnect the fuel pipe from the fuel pump **(see illustration)**.

7 Disconnect the vacuum servo hose (where fitted) from the inlet manifold **(see illustration)**.

8 Where fitted, disconnect the fuel return pipe from the carburettor **(see illustration)**.

9 Disconnect the remaining vacuum hoses at the carburettor and inlet manifold, noting their locations **(see illustration)**.

10 Disconnect the leads from the temperature sender unit, ignition coil, anti-run-on valve solenoid and where applicable, carburettor electric choke and back bleed solenoid **(see illustrations)**.

11 Unbolt the exhaust downpipe from the manifold by unscrewing the flange bolts. Support the exhaust pipe by tying it up with wire.

12 Release the alternator mounting and adjuster link bolts, push the alternator in towards the engine and slip the drivebelt from the pulleys.

13 Unbolt and remove the timing belt cover (upper cover only on later models).

14 Slacken the belt tensioner bolts, lever the tensioner to one side against the pressure of the coil spring (if fitted) and retighten the bolts.

15 With the timing belt now slack, slip it from the camshaft sprocket.

16 Disconnect the leads from the spark plugs and unscrew and remove the spark plugs.

17 Remove the rocker cover.

18 Unscrew the cylinder head bolts, progressively and in the sequence shown **(see illustration)**. Discard the bolts, as new ones must be used at reassembly.

19 Remove the cylinder head and manifolds.

> **HAYNES HINT** *Use the manifolds if necessary as levers to rock the head from the block. Do not attempt to tap the head sideways off the block as it is located on dowels, and do not attempt to lever between the head and the block or damage will result.*

Refitting

20 Before installing the cylinder head, make sure that the mating surfaces of head and block are perfectly clean with the head locating dowels in position. Clean the bolt holes free from oil. In extreme cases it is possible for oil left in the holes to crack the block due to hydraulic pressure.

21 Turn the crankshaft to position No 1 piston about 20 mm (0.8 in) before it reaches TDC.

22 Place a new gasket on the cylinder block and then locate the cylinder head on its dowels. The upper surface of the gasket is marked OBEN-TOP **(see illustration)**.

23 Install and tighten the new cylinder head bolts, tightening them in four stages (see Specifications). After the first two stages, the bolt heads should be marked with a spot of quick-drying paint so that the paint spots all face the same direction. Now tighten the bolts

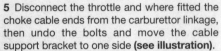

7.8 Fuel return pipe location (arrowed) - 1.4 litre carburettor engine

7.9 Vacuum hose attachments at the inlet manifold - 1.4 litre carburettor engine

7.10a Disconnect the lead at the temperature sender . . .

7.10b . . . anti-run-on valve and back bleed solenoid (if fitted) - 1.4 litre carburettor engine

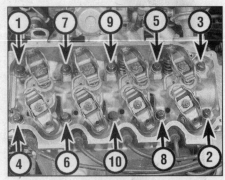

7.18 Cylinder head bolt removal sequence

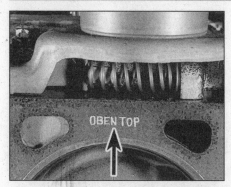

7.22 The upper surface of the cylinder head gasket is marked OBEN-TOP (arrowed)

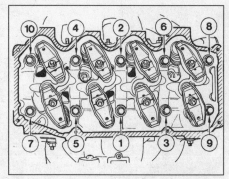

7.23a Cylinder head bolt tightening sequence

7.23b Tightening the cylinder head bolts

(Stage 3) through 90° (quarter turn) followed by a further 90° (Stage 4). Tighten the bolts at each stage only in the sequence shown before going on to the next stage. If all the bolts have been tightened equally, the paint spots should now all be pointing in the same direction **(see illustrations)**.

24 Fit the timing belt (Section 4).

25 Refitting and reconnection of all other components is a reversal of dismantling, with reference to the relevant Chapter.

26 Refill the cooling system (Chapter 1).

Fuel injection engines

Note: *The cylinder head must only be removed when the engine is cold. New cylinder head bolts and a new gasket must be used on refitting.*

XR3i and Cabriolet models with mechanical (Bosch K-Jetronic) fuel injection

27 Disconnect the battery negative lead.

28 Disconnect the inlet air hose at the throttle housing.

29 Drain the cooling system (Chapter 1).

30 Disconnect the crankcase ventilation hoses from the inlet manifold and rocker cover.

31 Disconnect the coolant hoses from the thermostat housing, inlet manifold and inlet manifold intermediate flange.

32 Disconnect the throttle cable from the throttle housing.

33 Relieve the fuel system pressure by *slowly* loosening the fuel feed pipe union at the warm-up regulator **(see illustration)**. Absorb fuel leakage in a cloth. Reference to the fuel-injection system layout in Chapter 4, Part B, or D, as applicable will assist in identification of the relevant components where necessary.

34 Disconnect the vacuum servo hose from the inlet manifold.

35 Disconnect the two fuel pipe unions at the warm-up regulator, the single pipe to the cold start valve and the four injector feed pipes at the fuel distributor **(see illustration)**. Recover the sealing washers located on each side of the banjo unions and seal all disconnected pipes and orifices to prevent dirt ingress.

36 Disconnect the vacuum hoses at the throttle housing after marking their locations to aid refitting.

37 Disconnect the wiring multi plugs at the cold start valve, warm-up regulator, and auxiliary air device, then disconnect the throttle valve stop earth cable **(see illustration)**.

38 Disconnect the leads from the spark plugs and remove the distributor cap. Disconnect the distributor multi plug.

39 The remainder of the removal and the refitting sequence is the same as described for carburettor engines in paragraphs 11 to 26 inclusive.

1.4 CFI (Central Fuel Injection) and 1.6 EFI (Electronic Fuel Injection) engines

40 Disconnect the battery negative lead.

41 Disconnect all relevant hoses, pipes and

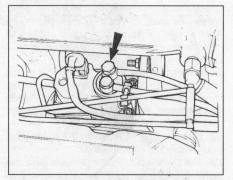

7.33 Fuel feed pipe union at the warm-up regulator - XR3i and Cabriolet

wiring to facilitate cylinder head removal, with reference to the appropriate Sections of Chapters 4 and 5.

42 Disconnect the throttle cable as described in Chapter 4, Part C or Part D, as applicable.

43 The remainder of the removal and the refitting sequence is the same as described for carburettor engines in paragraphs 11 to 26 inclusive.

RS Turbo models

44 Disconnect the battery negative lead.

45 Drain the cooling system as described in Chapter 1.

46 Disconnect the inlet air hose and the connecting hose at the inlet air duct, then undo the two bolts and remove the air duct

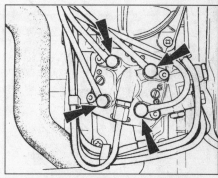

7.35 Injector pipe unions at the fuel distributor - XR3i and Cabriolet

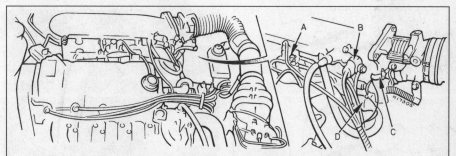

7.37 Wiring connections on the fuel-injection system - XR3i and Cabriolet

A Warm-up regulator
B Cold start valve

C Throttle valve stop earth cable
D Auxiliary air device

2B

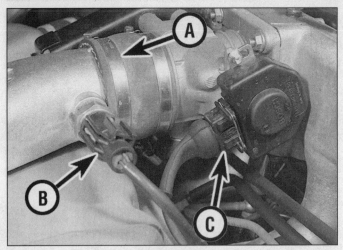

7.46 Air inlet duct connecting hose clip (A) charge air temperature sensor multi-plug (B) and throttle position sensor multi-plug (C) on RS Turbo models

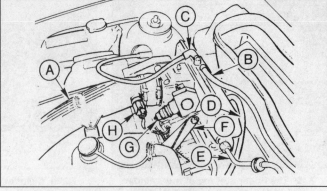

7.49 Wiring connections and hose attachments on the fuel-injection system - RS Turbo

A Inlet air duct
B Vacuum hose
C Crankcase ventilation valve hose
D Auxiliary air device hose
E Vacuum servo hose
F Mounting bracket
G Throttle position sensor multi-plug
H Charge air temperature sensor multi-plug

from the rocker cover. Disconnect the sensor multi plugs **(see illustration)**.

47 Disconnect the coolant hoses from the thermostat housing, inlet manifold and inlet manifold intermediate flange.

48 Disconnect the crankcase ventilation hose at the rocker cover and the two vacuum hoses from the inlet manifold. Release the hoses from their clips.

49 Disconnect the brake servo vacuum hose at the inlet manifold **(see illustration)**.

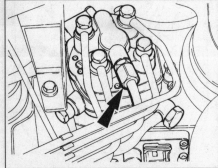

7.52 Cold start valve union on fuel distributor - RS Turbo

50 Disconnect the throttle cable from the throttle housing.

51 Remove the turbocharger (Chapter 4, Part B).

52 Relieve the fuel system pressure by slowly loosening the cold start valve union on the top of the fuel distributor **(see illustration)**. Absorb fuel leakage in a cloth. Reference to the fuel-injection system layout in Chapter 4, Part B will assist in identification of the relevant components where necessary.

53 Disconnect the fuel pipes at the fuel injectors and at the cold start valve **(see illustration)**. Recover the sealing washers located on each side of the banjo unions and seal all disconnected pipes and orifices to prevent dirt ingress. Move the fuel pipes clear of the cylinder head.

54 Disconnect the wiring multi plugs at the temperature gauge sender unit, ignition coil, throttle position sensor, solenoid control valve, coolant temperature sensor, thermo-time switch, cold start valve and auxiliary air device.

55 Disconnect the leads from the spark plugs and remove the distributor cap.

56 The remainder of the removal and the refitting sequence is the same as described for carburettor engines in paragraphs 12 to 26 inclusive.

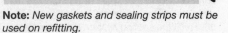
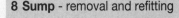

8 Sump - removal and refitting

Note: *New gaskets and sealing strips must be used on refitting.*

Removal

1 Disconnect the battery negative lead.

2 Drain the engine oil.

3 Remove the starter motor as described in Chapter 5, Part A.

4 Apply the handbrake, jack up the front of the car and support it on stands (see "*Jacking and Vehicle Support*").

5 Unbolt and remove the cover plate from the clutch housing **(see illustration)**.

6 Unbolt and remove the engine splash shield at the crankshaft pulley end **(see illustration)**.

7 Unscrew the sump securing bolts progressively and remove them.

8 Remove the sump and peel away the gaskets and sealing strips.

Refitting

9 Make sure that the mating surfaces of the sump and block are clean, then fit new end sealing strips into their grooves and stick new

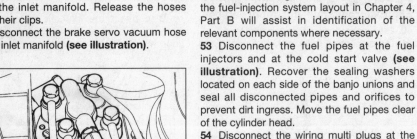

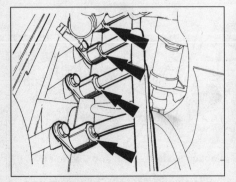

7.53 Fuel pipe connections at the fuel injectors - RS Turbo

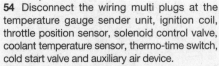

8.5 Remove the clutch housing cover plate

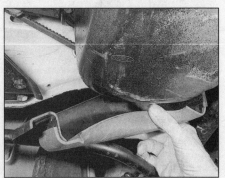

8.6 And the right-hand engine splash shield

8.9a Fitting the sump sealing strips . . .

8.9b . . . followed by the side gaskets with their ends overlapped

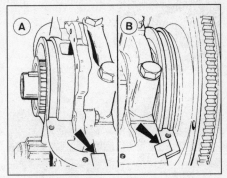

8.9c Apply sealer to the areas shown when fitting a one piece sump gasket
A Oil pump housing-to-block joint
B Rear oil seal carrier-to-block joint

side gaskets into position using thick grease. The ends of the side gaskets should overlap the seals. On later models a one-piece sump gasket is used. Before fitting, apply sealer to the joints of the cylinder block and rear oil seal carrier, and cylinder block and oil pump housing (four locations). Without applying any further sealer, locate the gasket into the grooves of the oil seal carrier and oil pump housing **(see illustrations)**. To retain the gasket insert two or three studs into the cylinder block if necessary and remove them once the sump is in place.

10 Offer up the sump, taking care not to displace the gaskets and insert the securing bolts. Tighten the bolts in two stages to the final torque given in the Specifications.

11 Refit the cover plate to the clutch housing and refit the engine splash shield.

12 Refit the starter motor.

13 Fill the engine with oil and reconnect the battery.

9 Pistons/connecting rods - removal and refitting

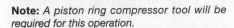

Note: *A piston ring compressor tool will be required for this operation.*

Removal

1 Remove the sump, as described in Section 8, and the cylinder head, as described in Section 7.

2 Check that the connecting rod and cap have adjacent numbers at their big-end to indicate their position in the cylinder block (No 1 nearest timing cover end of engine) **(see illustration)**.

3 Bring the first piston to the lowest point of its throw by turning the crankshaft pulley bolt and then check if there is a wear ring at the top of the bore. If there is, it should be removed using a scraper, but do not damage the cylinder bore.

4 Unscrew the big-end bolts and remove them.

5 Tap off the big-end cap. If the bearing shell is to be used again, make sure that it is retained with the cap. Note the two cap positioning roll pins.

6 Push the piston/rod out of the top of the block, again keeping the bearing shell with the rod if the shell is to be used again.

7 Repeat the removal operations on the remaining piston/rod assemblies.

8 Dismantling a piston/connecting rod is covered in Section 13.

Refitting

9 To refit a piston/rod assembly, have the piston ring gaps staggered as shown **(see illustrations)**. Oil the rings and apply a piston ring compressor. Compress the piston rings.

10 Oil the cylinder bores.

11 Wipe clean the bearing shell seat in the connecting rod and insert the shell **(see illustration)**.

12 Insert the piston/rod assembly into the cylinder bore until the base of the piston ring compressor stands squarely on the top of the block.

13 Check that the directional arrow on the piston crown faces towards the timing cover end of the engine, then apply the wooden handle of a hammer to the piston crown. Strike the head of the hammer sharply to drive the piston into the cylinder bore and release the ring compressor **(see illustrations)**.

14 Oil the crankpin and draw the connecting rod down to engage with the crankshaft. Make sure the bearing shell is still in position.

2B

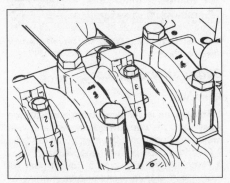

9.2 Connecting rod and main bearing identification numbers

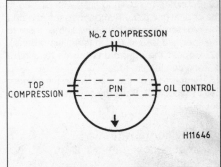

9.9a Piston ring end gap positioning diagram - all except 1.6 EFI engines

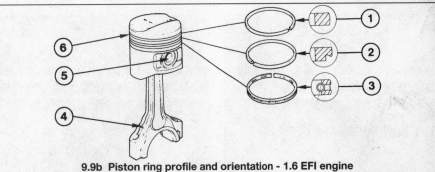

9.9b Piston ring profile and orientation - 1.6 EFI engine

1 Top compression ring   *3 Oil control rings*   *5 Gudgeon pin*
2 Second compression ring   *4 Oil squirt hole*   *6 Piston ring grooves*

9.11 Fitting the bearing shell in the connecting rod

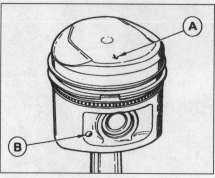

9.13a Arrow (A) or cast nipple (B) faces the timing belt end of the engine when installed

9.13b Installing a piston/connecting rod assembly

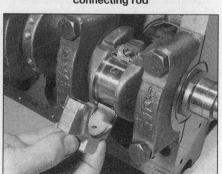

9.16a Fitting the big-end cap to the connecting rod

9.16b Tightening the big-end cap bolts to the specified torque

15 Wipe the bearing shell seat in the big-end cap clean and insert the bearing shell .

16 Lubricate the bearing shell with oil then fit the cap, aligning the numbers on the cap and the rod, screw in the bolts and tighten them to the specified torque setting **(see illustrations)**.

17 Repeat the operations on the remaining pistons/connecting rods.

18 Refit the sump (Section 8) and the cylinder head (Section 7). Refill the engine with oil and coolant.

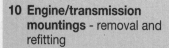

10 Engine/transmission mountings - removal and refitting

Refer to Part A, Section 11.

11 Engine/transmission - removal and separation

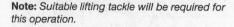

Note: *Suitable lifting tackle will be required for this operation.*

Carburettor engines

Removal

1 The engine is removed complete with the transmission in a downward direction and then withdrawn from under the front of the car.

2 Disconnect the battery negative lead.

3 Place the transmission in fourth gear on four-speed manual transmission models or reverse gear on the five-speed unit, to aid adjustment of the gearchange linkage when

refitting. On models produced from February 1987 onwards, place the transmission in second gear on four-speed versions, or fourth gear on five-speed versions.

4 Refer to Chapter 11 and remove the bonnet.

5 Refer to Chapter 4, Part B and remove the air cleaner.

6 Refer to Chapter 1 and drain the cooling system.

7 Disconnect the radiator top and bottom hoses and the expansion tank hose at the thermostat housing.

8 Disconnect the heater hoses from the automatic choke, thermostat housing and inlet manifold as applicable.

9 Disconnect the throttle cable and where fitted the choke cable ends from the carburettor throttle levers **(see illustration)**. Unbolt the cable support bracket and move the bracket and cable(s) to one side.

10 Disconnect the fuel feed pipe from the fuel pump and plug the pipe. Where fitted disconnect the fuel return hose at the carburettor.

11 Disconnect the brake servo vacuum hose from the inlet manifold.

12 Disconnect the leads from the following electrical components:

a) Alternator **(see illustration)**.

b) Cooling fan temperature switch and temperature sender **(see illustrations)**.

c) Oil pressure switch **(see illustration)**.

d) Reversing lamp switch **(see illustration)**.

e) Anti-run-on valve solenoid **(see illustration)** and back bleed solenoid (where applicable).

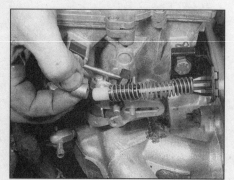

11.9 Disconnecting the throttle cable end (1.3 litre carburettor engine)

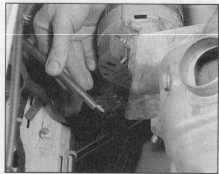

11.12a Disconnecting the alternator multi-plug . . .

11.12b . . . cooling fan switch . . .

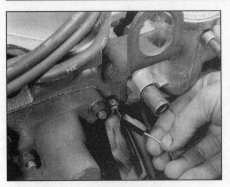

11.12c . . . temperature sender . . .

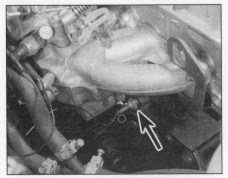

11.12d . . . oil pressure switch . . .

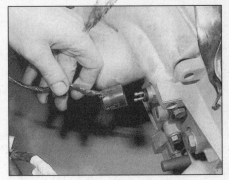

11.12e . . . reversing lamp switch . .

f) *Electric choke (where applicable).*
g) *Ignition coil.*
h) *Distributor* **(see illustration).**
l) *Starter motor solenoid* **(see illustration).**

13 Unscrew the speedometer drive cable from the transmission and release the breather hose **(see illustration)**.
14 Disconnect the transmission earth strap.
15 On manual transmission models disconnect the clutch cable from the release lever and from the transmission support.
16 Disconnect the exhaust downpipe from the manifold flange and support the system to avoid undue strain.
17 Apply the handbrake, jack up the front of the car and support it on stands to provide sufficient clearance beneath it to remove the engine/transmission from below. A distance of

686 mm (27.0 in) is recommended between the floor and the bottom edge of the front panel.
18 Disconnect the exhaust system from its flexible mountings and remove the system complete.
19 On manual transmission models disconnect the gearchange rod from the transmission selector shaft by releasing the clamp bolt and withdrawing the rod **(see illustration)**. Tie the rod to the stabiliser and then where fitted, unhook the tension spring. Unscrew the single bolt and disconnect the stabiliser from the transmission housing, noting the washer fitted between the stabiliser trunnion and the transmission.
20 On automatic transmission models refer to Chapter 7, Part B, and disconnect the starter inhibitor switch wiring, the selector

cable and the downshift linkage.
21 Remove the driveshafts from the transmission using the procedure described in Chapter 8 for each driveshaft.
22 On pre-1986 models equipped with an anti-roll bar, undo the two bolts each side securing the anti-roll bar mounting clamps and remove the clamps.
23 On 1986 models onwards, undo the three bolts each side securing the anti-roll bar mounting plates to the body **(see illustration)**.
24 On automatic transmission models undo the transmission fluid cooler pipes and withdraw the pipes. Plug the unions to prevent dirt Ingress.
25 Unbolt the right-hand and left-hand engine splash shields and remove them from under the car **(see illustrations)**.

2B

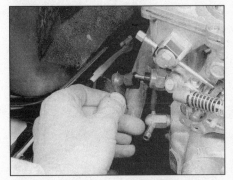

11.12f . . . anti-run-on valve solenoid . . .

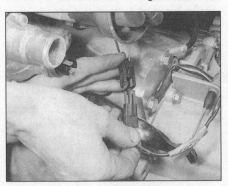

11.12g . . . distributor . . .

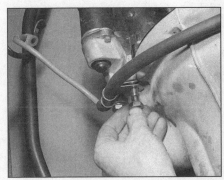

11.12h . . . and starter motor connections on the 1.3 litre carburettor engine

11.13 Disconnect the speedometer cable (arrowed) at the transmission

11.19 Disconnect the gearchange rod at the selector shaft clamp

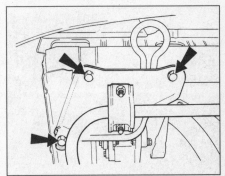

11.23 Anti-roll bar mounting plate attachments - 1986 models onwards

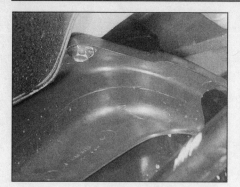

11.25a Remove the right-hand splash shield . . .

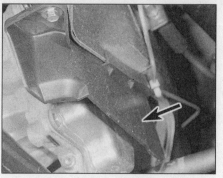

11.25b . . . and left-hand splash shield (arrowed)

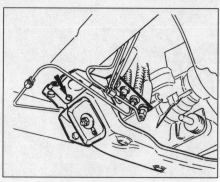

11.26 Anti-lock Braking System (ABS) pipe bracket retaining bolt location (arrowed)

26 On cars equipped with an Anti-lock Braking System (ABS) undo the hydraulic pipe mounting bracket bolt (see illustration). Remove the modulator clamp bolt and pivot bolt each side and tie the modulator to the underbody (see Chapter 9).

27 Connect a suitable hoist to the engine using chains and the lifting brackets on the cylinder head.

28 Just take the weight of the engine/transmission assembly so that the tension is relieved from the mountings.

29 Unbolt the rear right-hand engine mounting (complete with coolant hose support on early models) from the side member and from the inner wing panel (see illustrations).

30 On pre-1986 models unbolt the left-hand front and rear transmission mountings from

their brackets and remove the front mounting and anti-roll bar support plates from the body on both sides (see illustrations).

31 On 1986 models onwards undo the nuts and bolts securing the transmission support crossmember to the body (see illustration). The crossmember is removed with the engine/transmission assembly.

32 Carefully lower the engine/transmission and withdraw it from under the car. To ease the withdrawal operation, lower the engine/transmission onto a crawler board or a sheet of substantial chipboard placed on rollers or lengths of pipe (see illustration).

Separation (manual transmission models)

33 Unscrew and remove the starter motor

bolts and remove the starter.

34 Unbolt and remove the clutch cover plate from the lower part of the clutch bellhousing.

35 Unscrew and remove the bolts from the clutch bellhousing-to-engine mating flange.

36 Withdraw the transmission from the engine. Support its weight so that the clutch assembly is not distorted while the input shaft is still in engagement with the splined hub of the clutch driven plate.

Separation (automatic transmission models)

37 Unscrew and remove the starter motor bolts and remove the starter motor.

38 Undo the two bolts and remove the torque converter cover plate.

39 Working through the cover plate aperture,

11.29a Rear right-hand engine mounting attachment (arrowed) at side member . . .

11.29b . . . and at the inner wing panel

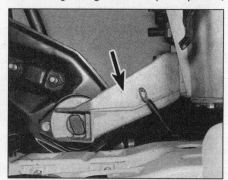

11.30a Detach the left-hand front (arrowed) . . .

11.30b . . . and left-hand rear transmission mountings on pre-1986 models

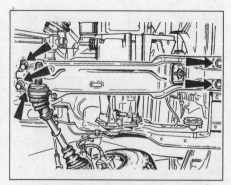

11.31 Transmission support crossmember bolt locations - 1986 models onwards

11.32 Removing the engine/transmission assembly from under the car

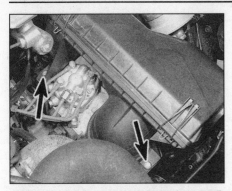

11.66 Air cleaner retaining bolts (arrowed) on RS Turbo models

unscrew and remove the four nuts securing the driveplate to the torque converter. For this to be accomplished it will be necessary to progressively turn the crankshaft for access to each nut in turn. Unscrew the nuts in a progressive manner, one turn at a time until removed.

40 Unscrew and remove the engine-to-transmission flange bolts and then separate the two units, but take care not to catch the torque converter studs on the driveplate. The torque converter is only loosely attached, so keep it in position in the transmission housing during and after removal of the transmission.

Fuel injection engines

Removal

XR3i and Cabriolet models with mechanical (Bosch K-Jetronic) fuel injection

41 The engine is removed complete with the transmission in a downward direction and then withdrawn from under the front of the car.
42 Disconnect the battery negative lead.
43 Place the transmission in fourth gear on four-speed models or reverse gear on the five-speed unit to aid adjustment of the gearchange linkage when refitting. On models produced from February 1987 onwards, place the transmission in second gear on four-speed versions, or fourth gear on five-speed versions.
44 Remove the bonnet (Chapter 11).
45 Drain the cooling system (Chapter 1).
46 Remove the air inlet hose between the fuel distributor and throttle housing.
47 Disconnect the radiator top and bottom hoses and the expansion tank hose at the thermostat housing.
48 Disconnect the heater hoses from the thermostat housing, and the three-way connection fitting on the oil cooler.
49 Disconnect the throttle cable end from the throttle lever and unbolt the cable bracket from the throttle housing.
50 Relieve the fuel system pressure by *slowly* loosening the fuel feed pipe union at the warm-up regulator. Absorb fuel leakage in a cloth. Reference to the fuel-injection system layout in Chapter 4, Part B will assist in identification of the relevant components where necessary.
51 Disconnect the vacuum servo hose from the inlet manifold.

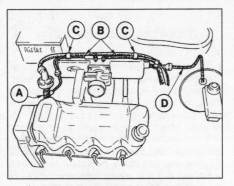

11.70 Vacuum and breather hose connections - RS Turbo

A *Crankcase ventilation hose at rocker cover*
B *Vacuum hoses at inlet manifold*
C *Retaining clips*
D *Vacuum servo hose*

52 Disconnect the two fuel pipe unions at the warm-up regulator, the single pipe to the cold start valve and the four injector feed pipes at the fuel distributor. Recover the sealing washers located on each side of the banjo unions and seal all disconnected pipes and orifices to prevent dirt ingress.
53 Disconnect the leads from the following electrical components:
 a) Alternator.
 b) Cooling fan temperature switch.
 c) Oil pressure sender.
 d) Reversing lamp switch.
 e) Ignition coil.
 f) Distributor.
 g) Starter motor solenoid.
 h) Cold start valve.
 j) Warm-up regulator.
 k) Auxiliary air device.
 l) Throttle valve stop earth cable.
54 Unscrew the speedometer drive cable from the transmission and release the breather hose.
55 Disconnect the transmission earth strap.
56 Disconnect the clutch cable from the release lever and from the transmission support.
57 The remainder of the removal procedure is the same as described previously for carburettor engines in paragraphs 16 to 32 inclusive.

1.4 CFI (Central Fuel Injection) and 1.6 EFI (Electronic Fuel Injection) engines

58 Proceed as described in paragraphs 41 to 49 inclusive, ignoring the reference to the fuel distributor.
59 Disconnect all relevant hoses, pipes and wiring to facilitate engine removal, with reference to the relevant Parts of Chapters 4 and 5.
60 Proceed as described in paragraphs 54 to 57 inclusive.

RS Turbo models

61 Disconnect the battery negative lead.
62 Place the transmission in reverse gear to aid adjustment of the gearchange linkage when refitting. On models produced from February 1987 onwards, place the transmission in fourth gear.
63 Remove the bonnet (Chapter 11).

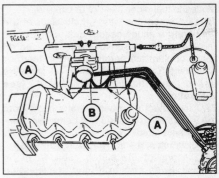

11.74 Fuel pipe connections - RS Turbo

A *Fuel injectors*   B *Cold start valve*

64 Drain the cooling system (Chapter 1).
65 Disconnect the air inlet hose and connecting hose at the inlet air duct. Disconnect the charge air temperature sensor multi plug, undo the two bolts securing the air duct to the rocker cover and remove the duct.
66 Undo the two bolts and remove the air cleaner assembly from the fuel distributor **(see illustration)**.
67 Disconnect the radiator top and bottom hoses at the thermostat housing, radiator and turbocharger return pipe as applicable.
68 Disconnect the heater hoses from the thermostat housing, three-way connector piece and inlet manifold as applicable.
69 Remove the turbocharger (Chapter 4, Part B).
70 Disconnect the crankcase ventilation hose at the rocker cover and the two vacuum hoses from the top of the inlet manifold **(see illustration)**. Release the hoses from their clips.
71 Disconnect the vacuum servo hose from the inlet manifold.
72 Disconnect the hose at the solenoid control valve.
73 Disconnect the throttle cable at the throttle housing.
74 Relieve the fuel system pressure by *slowly* loosening the cold start valve union on the top of the fuel distributor. Absorb fuel leakage in a cloth **(see illustration)**.
75 Disconnect the fuel pipes at the fuel injectors and at the cold start valve. Recover the sealing washers located on each side of the banjo unions and seal all disconnected pipes and orifices to prevent dirt ingress.

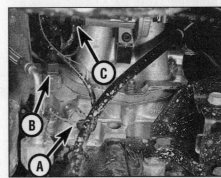

11.76 Coolant temperature sensor (A) thermo-time switch (B) and auxiliary air device (C) multi-plugs on RS Turbo models

Move the fuel pipes clear of the engine.

76 Disconnect the wiring multi plugs at the temperature gauge sender unit, ignition coil, throttle position sensor, solenoid control valve, coolant temperature sensor, thermo-time switch, cold start valve, oil pressure switch and auxiliary air device **(see illustration)**.

77 Disconnect the speedometer cable from the transmission and the fuel computer multi-plug (where fitted).

78 Disconnect the transmission earth strap.

79 Disconnect the clutch cable from the release lever and from the transmission support.

80 The remainder of the removal procedure is the same as described previously for carburettor engines in paragraphs 17 to 32 inclusive.

Separation (all models)

81 Separation from the manual or automatic transmission is as described previously for carburettor engines.

12 Engine - complete dismantling

1 The need for dismantling will have been dictated by wear or noise in most cases. Although there is no reason why only partial dismantling cannot be carried out to renew such items as the oil pump or crankshaft rear oil seal, when the main bearings or big-end bearings have been knocking and especially if the vehicle has covered a high mileage, then it is recommended that a complete strip-down is carried out and every engine component examined as described in Section 13.

2 Position the engine so that it is upright and safely chocked on a bench or other convenient working surface. If the exterior of the engine is very dirty it should be cleaned before dismantling, using paraffin and a stiff brush or a water-soluble solvent.

3 Remove the alternator, the mounting bracket and exhaust heat shield, and the adjuster link **(see illustration)**.

12.3 Removing the alternator heat shield

4 Disconnect the heater hose from the water pump.

5 Drain the engine oil and remove the filter and oil cooler where applicable.

6 Jam the flywheel starter ring gear to prevent the crankshaft turning and unscrew the crankshaft pulley bolt. Remove the pulley.

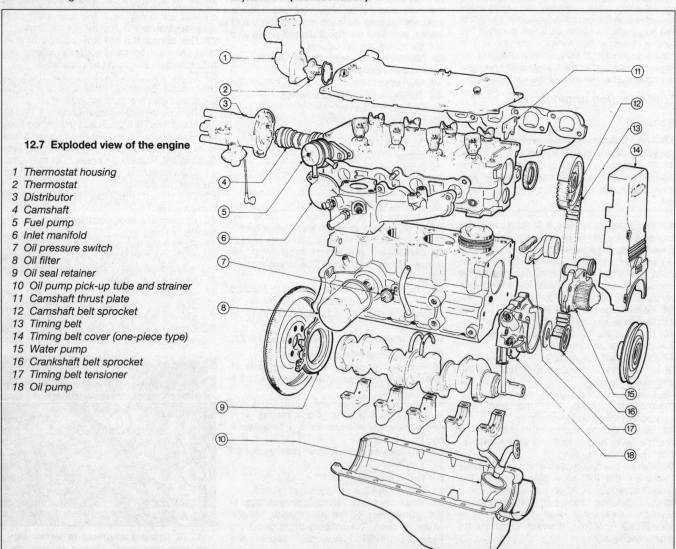

12.7 Exploded view of the engine

1 Thermostat housing
2 Thermostat
3 Distributor
4 Camshaft
5 Fuel pump
6 Inlet manifold
7 Oil pressure switch
8 Oil filter
9 Oil seal retainer
10 Oil pump pick-up tube and strainer
11 Camshaft thrust plate
12 Camshaft belt sprocket
13 Timing belt
14 Timing belt cover (one-piece type)
15 Water pump
16 Crankshaft belt sprocket
17 Timing belt tensioner
18 Oil pump

12.13 Remove the rocker cover

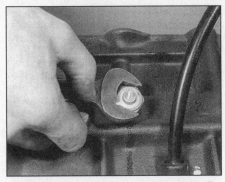

12.25 Unscrew the oil pressure switch

7 Unbolt and remove the timing belt cover (4 bolts) **(see illustration)**. Note that the cover is in two halves on later models.

8 Slacken the two bolts on the timing belt tensioner, lever the tensioner against its spring pressure where applicable and tighten the bolts to lock it in position.

9 With the belt now slack, note its running direction and mark the mating belt and sprocket teeth with a spot of quick-drying paint. This is not necessary if the belt is being renewed.

10 Disconnect the spark plug leads and, where applicable, remove the distributor cap complete with HT leads (if not already done).

11 Unscrew and remove the spark plugs.

12 Disconnect the crankcase ventilation hose from its connector on the crankcase.

13 Remove the rocker cover **(see illustration)**.

14 Unscrew the cylinder head bolts in the sequence shown in **illustration 7.18** and discard them. New bolts must be used at reassembly.

15 Remove the cylinder head complete with manifolds.

16 Turn the engine on its side. Do not invert it as sludge in the sump may enter the oilways. Remove the sump bolts, withdraw the sump and peel off the gaskets and sealing strips.

17 Remove the bolts from the clutch pressure plate in a progressive manner until the pressure of the assembly is relieved and then remove the cover, taking care not to allow the friction plate to fall to the floor.

18 Unbolt and remove the flywheel. The bolt holes are offset so it will only fit one way.

19 Remove the engine adapter plate.

20 Unbolt and remove the crankshaft rear oil seal retainer.

21 Unbolt and remove the timing belt tensioner and take out the coil spring. (This spring is not used on all models).

22 Unbolt and remove the water pump.

23 Remove the belt sprocket from the crankshaft using the hands or if tight, a two-legged puller. Take off the thrustwasher.

24 Unbolt the oil pump and pick-up tube and remove them as an assembly.

25 Unscrew and remove the oil pressure switch **(see illustration)**.

26 Turn the crankshaft so that all the pistons are half-way down the bores, and feel if a wear ridge exists at the top of the bores. If so, scrape the ridge away, taking care not to damage the bores.

27 Inspect the big-end and main bearing caps for markings. The main bearings should be marked 1 to 5 with a directional arrow pointing to the timing belt end. The big-end caps and connecting rods should have adjacent matching numbers. Number 1 is at the timing belt end of the engine. Make your own marks if necessary.

28 Unscrew the bolts from the first big-end cap and remove the cap. The cap is located on two roll pins, so if the cap requires tapping off make sure that it is not tapped in a sideways direction.

29 Retain the bearing shell with the cap if the shell is to be used again.

30 Push the piston/connecting rod out of the top of the cylinder block, again retaining the bearing shell with the rod if the shell is to be used again.

31 Remove the remaining pistons/rods in a similar way.

32 Remove the main bearing caps, keeping the shells with their respective caps if the shells are to be used again. Lift out the crankshaft.

33 Take out the bearing shells from the crankcase, noting the semi-circular thrustwashers on either side of the centre bearing. Keep the shells identified as to position in the crankcase if they are to be used again.

34 Prise down the spring arms of the crankcase ventilation baffle and remove it from inside the crankcase just below the ventilation hose connection.

35 The engine is now completely dismantled and each component should be examined as described in Section 13 before reassembling.

13 Examination and renovation

Crankshaft, bearings, cylinder bores and pistons

1 Refer to Section 13 in Part A of this Chapter. The information applies equally to the CVH engine, except that standard sized crankshafts are unmarked and the following differences in the piston rings should be noted.

2 The top rings are coated with molybdenum. Avoid damaging the coating when fitting the rings to the pistons.

3 The lower (oil control) ring must be fitted so that the manufacturer's mark is towards the piston crown, or the groove towards the gudgeon pin. Take care that the rails of the oil control ring abut without overlapping.

Timing sprockets and belt

4 It is very rare for the teeth of the sprockets to wear, but attention should be given to the tensioner idler pulley. It must turn freely and smoothly, be ungrooved and without any shake in its bearing. Otherwise renew it.

5 Always renew the coil spring (if fitted) in the tensioner. If the engine has covered 36 000 miles (60 000 km) then it is essential that a new belt is fitted, even if the original one appears in good condition.

Flywheel

6 Refer to Section 13 in Part A of this Chapter.

Oil pump

7 The oil pump on pre-1986 models is of gear type incorporating a crescent shape spacer. From 1986 onwards a low friction rotor type is fitted. Although no wear limit tolerances are specified for the gear type pump, if on inspection there is obvious wear between the gears, or signs of scoring or wear ridges, the pump should be renewed **(see illustrations)**. Similarly if a high mileage engine is being reconditioned it is recommended that a new pump is fitted. Inspection of the rotor type pump is covered in Section 13, in Part A of this Chapter.

2B

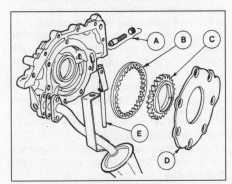

13.7a Gear type oil pump

A Pressure relief valve   D Oil pump cover
B Driven gear   E Return pipe
C Driving gear

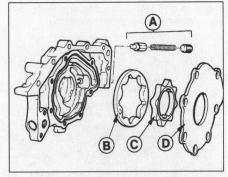

13.7b Rotor type oil pump

A Pressure relief valve   C Inner rotor
B Outer rotor   D Oil pump cover

Oil seals and gaskets

8 Renew the oil seals in the oil pump and in the crankshaft rear oil seal retainer as a matter of routine at time of major overhaul. It is recommended that the new seals are drawn into these components using a nut and bolt and distance pieces, rather than tapping them into position, to avoid distortion of the light alloy castings.

9 Renew the camshaft oil seal after the camshaft has been installed.

10 Always smear the lips of a new oil seal with grease, and check that the small tensioner spring in the oil seal has not been displaced during installation.

11 Renew all gaskets by purchasing the appropriate engine set, which usually includes the necessary oil seals.

Crankcase

12 Refer to Section 13 in Part A of this Chapter.

Camshaft and bearings

13 Examine the camshaft gear and lobes for damage or wear. If evident, a new camshaft must be purchased, or one which has been built-up, such as are advertised by firms specialising in exchange components.

14 The bearing internal diameters in the cylinder head should be checked against the Specifications if a suitable gauge is available, otherwise check for movement between the camshaft journal and the bearing. If the bearings are proved to be worn, then a new cylinder head is the only answer as the bearings are machined directly in the cylinder head.

15 Check the camshaft endfloat by temporarily refitting the camshaft and thrust plate. If the endfloat exceeds the specified tolerance, renew the thrust plate.

Cam followers

16 It is seldom that the hydraulic type cam followers (tappets) wear in their cylinder head bores. If the bores are worn then a new cylinder head is called for.

17 If the cam lobe contact surface shows signs of a depression or grooving, grinding out the wear surface will not only remove the hardened surface of the follower but may also reduce its overall length to a point where the self-adjusting capability of the cam follower is exceeded and valve clearances are not taken up, with consequent noisy operation.

18 Cam followers cannot be dismantled so if they become worn after high mileage, they must be renewed. On refitting, it is only necessary to smear the outside surfaces with clean engine oil, as they are self priming and will fill with engine oil once the engine is running, although initial operation may be noisy until primed.

Cylinder head and rocker arms

19 The usual reason for dismantling the cylinder head is to decarbonise and to grind in the valves. Reference should therefore be made to Section 14 in addition to the dismantling operations described here.

20 Remove the inlet and exhaust manifolds and their gaskets (Chapter 4, Part E) also the thermostat housing (Chapter 3).

21 Unscrew the nuts from the rocker arms and discard the nuts. New ones must be fitted at reassembly.

22 Remove the rocker arms and the hydraulic cam followers, keeping them in their originally fitted sequence. Keep the rocker guide and spacer plates in order.

23 The camshaft need not be withdrawn but if it is wished to do so, first remove the thrust plate and take the camshaft out from the rear of the cylinder head.

24 The valve springs should now be compressed. A standard type of compressor will normally do the job, but a forked tool (Part No 21-097) can be purchased or made up to engage on the rocker stud using a nut and distance piece to compress it.

25 Compress the valve spring and extract the split collets. Do not overcompress the spring, or the valve stem may bend. If it is found when screwing down the compressor tool that the spring retainer does not release from the collets, remove the compressor and place a piece of tubing on the retainer so that it does not impinge on the collets and place a small block of wood under the head of the valve. With the cylinder head resting flat down on the bench, strike the end of the tubing a sharp blow with a hammer. Refit the compressor and compress the spring.

26 Extract the split collets and then gently release the compressor and remove it.

27 Remove the valve spring retainer, the spring and the valve stem oil seal. Withdraw the valve.

28 Valve removal should commence with No 1 valve (nearest timing belt end). Keep the valves and their components in their originally installed order by placing them in a piece of card which has holes punched in it and numbered 1 to 8.

29 To check for wear in the valve guides, place each valve in turn in its guide so that approximately one third of its length enters the guide. Rock the valve from side to side. If any more than the slightest movement is possible, the guides will have to be reamed (working from the valve seat end) and oversize stemmed valves fitted. If you do not have the necessary reamer (Tool No 21-071 to 21-074), leave this work to your Ford dealer.

30 Examine the valve seats. Normally the seats do not deteriorate, but the valve heads are more likely to burn away, in which case new valves can be ground in as described in the next Section. If the seats require recutting, use a standard cutter, available from most accessory or tool stores.

31 Renewal of any valve seat which is cracked or beyond recutting is definitely a job for your dealer or motor engineering works.

32 If the rocker arm studs must be removed for any reason, a special procedure is necessary. Warm the upper ends of the studs with a blow-lamp flame (not a welder) before unscrewing them. Clean out the cylinder head threads with an M10 tap and clean the threads of oil or grease. Discard the old studs and fit new ones, which will be coated with adhesive compound on their threaded portion or will have a nylon locking insert. Screw in the studs without pausing, otherwise the adhesive will start to set and prevent the stud seating.

33 If the cylinder head mating surface is suspected of being distorted, it can be checked and surface ground by your dealer or motor engineering works. Distortion is possible with this type of light alloy head if the bolt tightening method is not followed exactly, or if severe overheating has taken place.

34 Check the rocker arm contact surfaces for wear. Renew the valve springs if they have been in service for 50 000 miles (80 000 km) or more.

35 Commence reassembly of the cylinder head by fitting new valve stem oil seals **(see illustration)**.

36 Oil No 1 valve stem and insert the valve into its guide **(see illustration)**.

37 Fit the valve spring (closer coils to cylinder head), then the spring retainer **(see illustrations)**.

38 Compress the spring and engage the split collets in the cut-out in the valve stem. Hold them in position while the compressor is gently released and removed **(see illustration)**.

13.35 Using a socket to install a valve stem oil seal

13.36 Inserting a valve into its guide

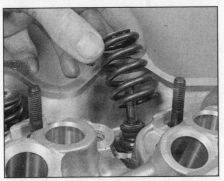

13.37a Fit the valve spring . . .

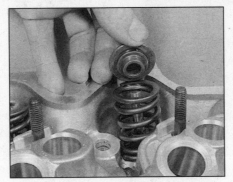

13.37b . . . and spring retainer

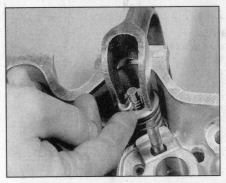

13.38 Compress the spring and fit the collets

39 Repeat the operations on the remaining valves, making sure that each valve is returned to its original guide or new valves have been fitted, into the seat into which it was ground.

40 Once all the valves have been fitted, support the ends of the cylinder head on two wooden blocks and strike the end of each valve stem with a plastic or copper-faced hammer, just a light blow to settle the components.

41 Fit the camshaft (if removed) and a new oil seal as described in Section 6.

42 Smear the hydraulic cam followers with hypoid type transmission oil and insert them into their original bores **(see illustration)**.

43 Fit the rocker arms with their guides and spacer plates, use new nuts and tighten to the specified torque. It is important that each rocker arm is installed only when its particular cam follower is at its lowest point (in contact with the cam base circle) **(see illustrations)**.

44 Refit the exhaust and inlet manifolds and the thermostat housing, using all new gaskets.

14 Cylinder head and pistons - decarbonising

1 With the cylinder head removed as described in Section 7, the carbon deposits should be removed from the combustion surfaces using a blunt scraper. Take great care as the head is of light alloy construction and avoid the use of a rotary (power-driven) wire brush.

2 Where a more thorough job is to be carried out, the cylinder head should be dismantled as described in Section 13 so that the valves may be ground in, and the ports and combustion spaces cleaned and blown out after the manifolds have been removed.

3 Before grinding in a valve, remove the carbon and deposits completely from its head and stem. With an inlet valve this is usually quite easy, simply a case of scraping off the soft carbon with a blunt knife and finishing with a wire brush. With an exhaust valve, the deposits are very much harder and those on the valve head may need a rub on coarse emery cloth to remove them. An old woodworking chisel is a useful tool to remove the worst of the valve head deposits.

4 Make sure that the valve heads are really clean, otherwise the rubber suction cup grinding tool will not stick during the grinding-in operations.

5 Before starting to grind in a valve, support the cylinder head so that there is sufficient clearance under it for the valve stem to project fully without being obstructed, otherwise the valve will not seat properly during grinding.

6 Take the first valve and apply a little coarse grinding paste to the bevelled edge of the valve head. Insert the valve into its guide and apply the suction grinding tool to its head. Rotate the tool between the palms of the hands in a back-and-forth rotary movement until the gritty action of the grinding-in process disappears. Repeat the operation with fine paste and then wipe away all trace of grinding

paste and examine the seat and bevelled edge of the valve. A matt silver mating band should be observed on both components, without any sign of black spots. If some spots do remain, repeat the grinding-in process until they have disappeared. A drop or two of paraffin applied to the contact surfaces will speed the grinding process, but do not allow any paste to run down into the valve guide. On completion, wipe away every trace of grinding paste using a paraffin-moistened cloth.

7 Repeat the operations on the remaining valves, taking care not to mix up their originally fitted sequence.

8 An important part of the decarbonising operation is to remove the carbon deposits from the piston crowns. To do this (engine in vehicle), turn the crankshaft so that two pistons are at the top of their stroke and press some grease between the pistons and the cylinder walls. This will prevent carbon particles falling down into the piston ring grooves. Plug the other two bores with rag.

9 Cover the oilways and coolant passages with masking tape and then using a blunt scraper, remove all the carbon from the piston crowns. Take great care not to score the soft alloy of the crown or the surface of the cylinder bore.

10 Rotate the crankshaft to bring the other two pistons to TDC and repeat the operations.

11 Wipe away the circles of grease and carbon from the cylinder bores.

12 Clean the top surfaces of the cylinder block by careful scraping.

13.42 Fitting a cam follower to its bore

13.43a Fit the rocker arm spacer plate . . .

13.43b . . . followed by the rocker arm and guide

2B

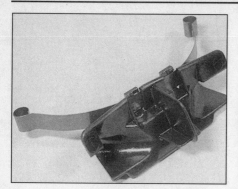

15.1 Crankcase ventilation baffle

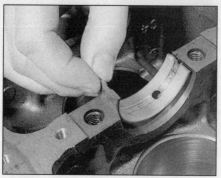

15.2 Inserting a main bearing shell into the crankcase

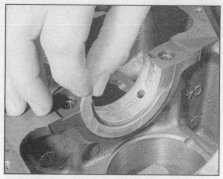

15.3 Locating the crankshaft thrustwashers on the centre main bearing

15 Engine - reassembly

Note: *Ensure that all necessary new oil seals and gaskets have been obtained before starting the reassembly procedure.*

1 With everything clean and parts renewed where necessary, commence reassembly by inserting the ventilation baffle into the crankcase. Make sure that the spring arms engage securely **(see illustration)**.

2 Insert the bearing half shells into their seats in the crankcase, making sure that the seats are perfectly clean **(see illustration)**.

3 Stick the semi-circular thrustwashers on either side of the centre bearing with thick grease. Make sure that the oil channels face outwards **(see illustration)**.

4 Oil the bearing shells and carefully lower the crankshaft into position.

5 Insert the bearings shells into the main bearing caps, making sure that their seats are perfectly clean. Oil the bearings and install the caps in their correct numbered location and with the directional arrow pointing towards the timing belt end of the engine **(see illustrations)**.

6 Tighten the main bearing cap bolts to the specified torque.

7 Check the crankshaft endfloat. Ideally a dial gauge should be used, but feeler blades are an alternative if inserted between the face of the thrustwasher and the machined surface of the crankshaft balance web, having first prised the crankshaft in one direction and then the other

(see illustration). Provided the thrustwashers at the centre bearing have been renewed, the endfloat should be within specified tolerance. If it is not, oversize thrustwashers are available (see Specifications).

8 The pistons/connecting rods should now be installed. Although new pistons may have been fitted to the rods by your dealer or supplier due to the special tools needed, it is worth checking to ensure that with the piston crown arrow or cast nipple in the piston oil cut-out pointing towards the timing belt end of the engine, the F mark on the connecting rod or the oil ejection hole in the rod big-end is as shown **(see illustration)**.

9 Oil the cylinder bores and install the pistons/connecting rods (Section 9).

10 Fit the oil pressure switch.

11 Before fitting the oil pump, action must be taken to prevent damage to the pump oil seal from the step on the front end of the crankshaft. First remove the Woodruff key and then build up the front end of the crankshaft using adhesive tape to form a smooth inclined surface to permit the pump seal to slide over the step without its lip turning back or the seal spring being displaced during installation **(see illustration)**.

12 If the oil pump is new, pour some oil into it before installation in order to prime it and rotate its driving gear a few turns **(see illustration)**.

13 Align the pump gear flats with those on the crankshaft and install the oil pump complete with new gasket. Tighten the bolts to the specified torque.

15.5a Fit the caps to their correct numbered locations . . .

15.5b . . . with the arrows on the caps pointing toward the timing belt end

15.7 Checking crankshaft endfloat with a feeler blade

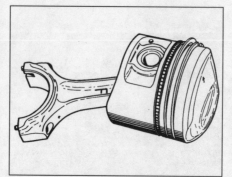

15.8 Piston/connecting rod orientation

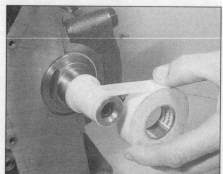

15.11 Using masking tape to eliminate the step on the crankshaft

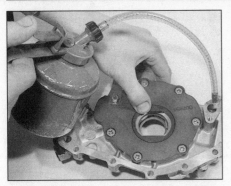

15.12 Priming the oil pump prior to fitting

15.15 Fitting the oil pump pick-up tube

15.16 Fit the timing belt guide with its concave side towards the pump

14 Remove the adhesive tape and tap the Woodruff key into its groove.

15 Bolt the oil pump pick-up tube into position **(see illustration)**.

16 To the front end of the crankshaft, fit the thrustwasher (belt guide) so that its concave side is towards the pump **(see illustration)**.

17 Fit the crankshaft belt sprocket. If it is tight, draw it into position using the pulley bolt and a distance piece. Make sure that the belt retaining flange on the sprocket is towards the front of the crankshaft and the nose of the shaft has been smeared with a little grease before fitting **(see illustration)**.

18 Install the water pump using a new gasket and tightening the bolts to the specified torque **(see illustration)**.

19 Fit the timing belt tensioner and its coil spring (where fitted). Lever the tensioner fully against spring pressure and temporarily tighten the bolts.

20 Using a new gasket, bolt on the rear oil seal retainer, which will have been fitted with a new oil seal and the seal lips greased **(see illustration)**.

21 Engage the engine adapter plate on its locating dowels and then offer up the flywheel. It will only go on in one position as it has offset holes. Insert new bolts and tighten to the specified torque **(see illustrations)**. The bolts should be pre-coated with thread sealant.

22 Fit the clutch and centralise it (refer to Chapter 6).

23 With the engine resting on its side (not inverted unless you are quite sure that the pistons are not projecting from the block), fit the sump, gaskets and sealing strips as described in Section 8.

24 Fit the cylinder head as described in Section 7, using new bolts. Refit the manifolds **(see illustrations)**.

25 Install and tension the timing belt as described in Section 4.

26 Using a new gasket, fit the rocker cover.

27 Reconnect the crankcase ventilation hoses between the rocker cover and the crankcase **(see illustrations)**.

28 Screw in a new set of spark plugs, correctly gapped, and tighten to the specified torque - this is important. If the specified torque is exceeded, the plugs may be impossible to remove (see Chapter 1).

29 Fit the timing belt cover.

2B

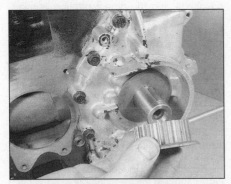

15.17 Fitting the crankshaft sprocket with the flange outward

15.18 Fitting the water pump

15.20 Crankshaft rear oil seal retainer with new seal prior to fitting

15.21a Locate the adapter plate on the dowels . . .

15.21b . . . fit the flywheel to the crankshaft

15.24a Fit the inlet manifold gasket . . .

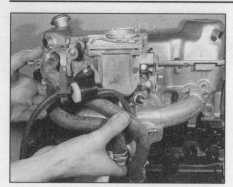

15.24b . . . and manifold

15.27a Connecting the crankcase rear ventilation hose . . .

15.27b . . . and the front hose

15.32 Fitting the right-hand engine mounting

15.33 Fitting the alternator mounting bracket

30 Fit the crankshaft pulley and tighten the bolt to the specified torque while the flywheel ring gear is locked to prevent it turning.

31 Smear the sealing ring of a new oil filter with a little grease, and screw it into position using hand pressure only. Where applicable, refit the oil cooler at the same time.

32 Install the engine mounting brackets, if removed (see illustration).

33 Refit the ancillaries. The alternator bracket and alternator (Chapter 5, Part A), the fuel pump, where applicable (Chapter 4, Part A), the thermostat housing (Chapter 3), and the distributor (Chapter 5, Part B) (see illustration).

34 Fit the distributor cap and reconnect the HT leads.

35 Check the tightness of the oil drain plug and insert the dipstick.

16 Engine/transmission - reconnection and installation

1 This is a direct reversal of removal and separation from the transmission. Take care not to damage the radiator or front wings during installation.

Reconnection

2 Make sure that the engine adapter plate is correctly located on its dowels.

3 On manual transmission models check that the clutch driven plate has been centralised as described in Chapter 6. Smear the splines of the transmission input shaft with molybdenum disulphide grease and then, supporting the weight of the transmission, connect it to the engine by passing the input shaft through the splined hub of the clutch plate until the transmission locates on the dowels. Screw in the bolts and tighten to the specified torque. Refit the clutch cover plate and the starter motor.

4 On automatic transmission models ensure that the torque converter is fully seated on the transmission, then locate the transmission on the engine dowels while at the same time guiding the torque converter studs through the holes in the driveplate. Screw in the engine-to-transmission bolts and tighten to the specified torque. Turn the crankshaft to provide access to each of the torque converter studs in turn, then fit and tighten the nuts. Refit the cover plate and the starter motor.

Installation

5 First check that the engine sump drain plug is tight and then, where applicable refit the selector shaft cap nut (removed to drain the manual transmission oil) together with its spring and interlock pin (see illustration). Apply sealer to the cap nut threads when refitting (see Specifications Chapter 7, Part A).

6 Manoeuvre the engine/transmission under the vehicle and attach the lifting hoist. Raise the engine/transmission carefully until the right-hand rear mounting can be engaged. Refit the mounting nut and bolt but loosely only at this stage.

7 On pre-1986 models refit the front mounting and anti-roll bar support plates, then refit the left-hand front and rear mountings loosely only.

8 On 1986 models onwards, refit the transmission support crossmember.

9 Lower the hoist and let the power unit rest on its mountings. Ensure that none of the mountings are under strain, then tighten all the mounting nuts and bolts to the specified torque and remove the hoist.

10 The driveshafts and suspension arms should now be refitted using the procedure described in Chapter 8.

11 Refit the anti-roll bar clamps and mounting plates as applicable.

12 On cars equipped with an Anti-lock Braking System (ABS), refit the modulators, drivebelts and the pipe mounting bracket, then adjust the modulator drivebelt tension as described in Chapter 9.

13 Refit the engine splash shields.

14 On automatic transmission models reconnect the fluid cooler pipes, then reconnect and adjust the selector cable and downshift linkage as described in Chapter 7, Part B.

15 On manual transmission models reconnect and adjust the gearchange linkage using the procedure described in Chapter 7, Part A.

16 On RS Turbo models refer to Chapter 4, Part B and refit the turbocharger.

17 Refit the exhaust system and bolt the downpipe to the manifold.

16.5 Fitting the selector shaft cap nut, spring and interlock pin

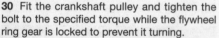
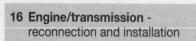
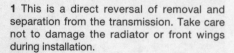

18 Check that everything has been reconnected underneath, then lower the car to the ground.

19 Where applicable reconnect the clutch operating cable.

20 Reconnect the transmission earth strap and speedometer cable.

21 Reconnect the coolant and heater hoses.

22 Reconnect the accelerator cable and where fitted the choke cable and adjust as described in Chapter 4, Part A.

23 Reconnect all fuel and vacuum hoses and pipes with reference to the relevant Part of Chapter 4 where necessary. Use screw type hose clips to secure any hoses originally retained with crimped clips. On fuel-injection models use new sealing washers on each side of the banjo unions.

24 Reconnect all electrical wiring with reference to Chapters 3, 4, 5 and 12 and to any notes made during removal.

25 Fill up with engine oil, transmission oil or fluid and coolant, then reconnect the battery.

26 Refit the bonnet and the air cleaner or on RS Turbo models the inlet air duct.

27 Once the engine is running check the dwell angle, timing, idle speed and mixture as described in Chapter 1.

28 If a number of new internal components have been installed, run the vehicle at a restricted speed for the first few hundred miles to allow time for the new components to bed in. It is also recommended that with a new or rebuilt engine, the engine oil and filter are changed at the end of the running-in period.

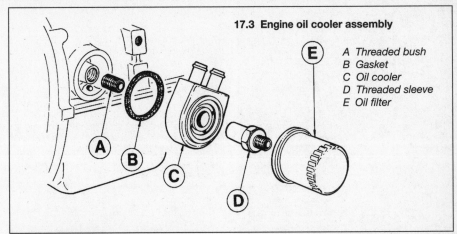

17.3 Engine oil cooler assembly

A Threaded bush
B Gasket
C Oil cooler
D Threaded sleeve
E Oil filter

17 Engine oil cooler - removal and refitting

Note: *Suitable sealant will be required on refitting - see text.*

Removal

1 Remove the engine oil filter (Chapter 1).

2 Note the angle at which the coolant hoses are set, then disconnect the hoses and plug their ends to minimise coolant loss. If necessary, drain the coolant (Chapter 1).

3 Using a ring spanner or socket, undo and remove the threaded sleeve **(see illustration)**.

4 Remove the oil cooler and its gasket.

5 Should the threaded bush come out with the threaded sleeve, or if it is removed for other reasons, it should be renewed.

Refitting

6 Clean the threads of the female connection in the cylinder block, then commence refitting by screwing a new threaded bush into the cylinder block.

7 Apply Omnifit Activator "Rapid" (to Ford Specification SSM-998-9000-AA) to the exposed threads of the bush and to the internal threads of the threaded sleeve.

8 Apply **one drop** of Omnifit Sealant "300 Rapid" (to Ford Specification SSM-4G-9003-AA) to the threads of the bush. **Do not** use more than one drop, as there is risk of contaminating the oil system.

9 Fit the oil cooler over the threaded bush using a new gasket, and secure it in position (remember the angle of the coolant pipes) with the threaded sleeve, tightening it to the specified torque.

10 Fit the new oil filter (Chapter 1).

11 Reconnect the coolant hoses, top-up the oil and coolant to their correct levels, and then run the engine to normal operating temperature and check for leaks. On completion, allow the engine to cool and recheck oil and coolant levels.

2B

Chapter 3
Cooling, heating and ventilation systems

Contents

Degrees of difficulty

Easy, suitable for novice with little experience	Fairly easy, suitable for beginner with some experience	Fairly difficult, suitable for competent DIY mechanic	Difficult, suitable for experienced DIY mechanic	Very difficult, suitable for expert DIY or professional

Specifications

System type . . . . Pressurised, pump-assisted thermo-syphon with front mounted radiator and electric cooling fan

Pressure cap rating
Up to 1986:
  1.1 litre OHV engine . . . . 0.9 bar (13.0 lbf/in^2)
  1.3 and 1.6 litre CVH engine . . . . 0.85 to 1.1 bar (12.0 to 15.7 lbf/in^2)
1986 onwards . . . . 0.98 to 1.2 bar (14.2 to 17.0 lbf/in^2)

Thermostat
Type . . . . Wax
Start to open temperature . . . . 85° to 89°C (189° to 192°F)
Fully open temperature . . . . 102°C (223°F) (±3°C/5°F for used thermostats)

Torque wrench settings

	Nm	lbf ft
Radiator mounting bolts:		
Pre-1986 models	7 to 10	5 to 7
1986 models onwards	20 to 27	15 to 20
Thermostat housing bolts:		
OHV engines	17 to 21	13 to 16
CVH engines	9 to 12	7 to 9
Water pump bolts:		
OHV engines	7 to 10	5 to 7
CVH engines	7 to 10	5 to 7
Water pump pulley (OHV engines)	9 to 11	6 to 8
Fan shroud to radiator:		
Pre-1986 models	7 to 10	5 to 7
1986 models onwards	3 to 5	2 to 4
Fan motor to shroud	9 to 12	7 to 9

1 General description

The cooling system is of the pressurised pump-assisted thermo-syphon type. The system consists of the radiator, water pump, thermostat, electric cooling fan, expansion tank and associated hoses.

The system functions as follows. When the coolant is cold the thermostat is shut and coolant flow is restricted to the cylinder block, cylinder head, inlet manifold and the vehicle interior heater matrix. As the temperature of the coolant rises, the thermostat opens allowing the coolant to pass into the radiator. The coolant now circulates through the radiator where it is cooled by the inrush of air when the car is in forward motion, supplemented by the operation of the radiator cooling fan. Coolant is then circulated from the base of the radiator, up through the water pump, and into the cylinder block to complete the circuit.

On OHV engines, the water pump is driven by a vee-belt from the crankshaft pulley. On CVH engines, the water pump is driven by the timing belt.

When the engine is at normal operating temperature the coolant expands, and some of it is displaced into the expansion tank. The coolant collects in the tank and is returned to the radiator when the system cools. On 1.1 litre engines the system pressure cap is fitted to the thermostat housing and the expansion tank acts as a simple overflow bottle. On all other engines the pressure cap is fitted to the expansion tank which is pressurised with the rest of the system.

On all engines except 1.1 litre CVH versions the radiator cooling fan is controlled by a thermal switch located in the thermostat housing. When the coolant reaches a predetermined temperature the switch contacts close thus actuating the fan. On 1.1 litre CVH engines with standard equipment the cooling fan operates continuously whenever the ignition is switched on.

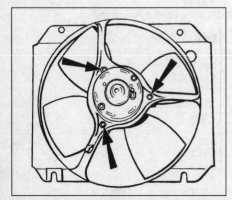

2.7 Fan motor retaining nuts - pre-1986 models

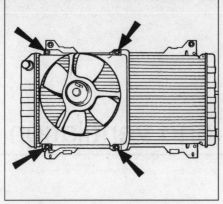

2.3 Radiator fan shroud retaining bolts - pre-1986 models

2 Radiator fan - removal and refitting

All models except RS Turbo

Removal

1 Disconnect the battery negative terminal.
2 Disconnect the wiring plug at the fan motor and unclip the wiring from the shroud.
3 On pre-1986 models the fan shroud is secured to the radiator with four bolts. Unscrew the two upper bolts and slacken the two lower bolts **(see illustration)**.
4 For 1986 models onwards the shroud is retained by two bolts at the top and two clips at the bottom. Unscrew the two upper bolts **(see illustration)**.
5 On all models carefully lift the fan and shroud assembly upwards and out of the engine compartment, taking care not to damage the radiator.
6 Extract the retaining clip and remove the fan from the motor shaft.
7 Unscrew the three nuts and separate the motor from the shroud **(see illustration)**.

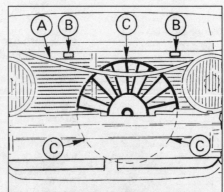

2.10 Radiator fan removal details - 1985 RS Turbo
A Transverse cooling hose
B Transverse cooling hose clips
C Fan shroud retaining bolts

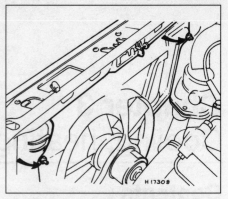

2.4 Radiator fan shroud retaining bolts - 1986 models onwards

Refitting

8 Reassembly and refitting are reversals of the removal and dismantling operations.

RS Turbo models

1985 models

Removal

9 Disconnect the battery negative terminal.
10 Detach the transverse coolant hose from the two clips above the radiator **(see illustration)**.
11 Unscrew the three fan shroud retaining bolts.
12 Disconnect the upper and lower air hoses at the turbo intercooler mounted alongside the radiator.
13 Undo the two air cleaner retaining bolts and remove the air cleaner assembly **(see illustration)**.
14 Undo the single upper retaining screw and lift the intercooler to disengage the lower retaining peg **(see illustration)**. Remove the intercooler.
15 Undo the two upper radiator retaining bolts, disengage the lower guides and move the radiator towards the engine taking care not to stretch the hoses.
16 Disconnect the fan wiring multi-plug, release the cable-tie and separate the fan wiring from the harness.

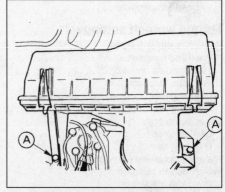

2.13 Air cleaner retaining bolts (A) - 1985 RS Turbo

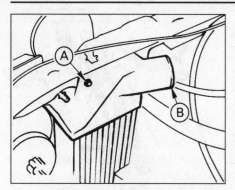

2.14 Intercooler retaining bolt (A) and upper air hose connection (B) - 1985 RS Turbo

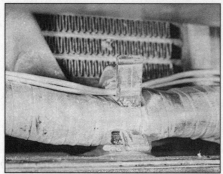

2.20a Release the wiring harness clips . . .

2.20b . . . to gain access to the fan shroud bolts on 1986 RS Turbo models

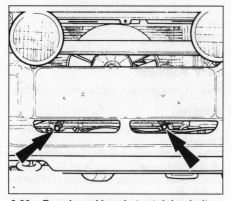

2.20c Fan shroud bracket retaining bolts - RS Turbo from 1986 onwards

17 Carefully lift the fan up and out of its location. The fan, motor and shroud are serviced as an assembly on these models and further dismantling is not recommended.

Refitting

18 Refitting is the reverse sequence to removal.

1986 models onwards

Removal

19 Disconnect the battery negative terminal.

20 Working through the aperture below the front bumper, release the wiring harness clips and unscrew the two shroud bracket retaining bolts **(see illustrations)**.

21 Unhook the shroud from the top of the radiator, disconnect the wiring at the harness connector and remove the fan and shroud assembly from the front of the radiator.

22 Remove the fan guard from the shroud.

23 Extract the retaining circlip and washer, then withdraw the fan from the motor shaft.

24 Unscrew the three nuts, unclip the wiring and remove the motor from the shroud.

Refitting

25 Reassembly and refitting are the reversals of the removal and dismantling operations.

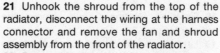

3 Radiator - removal, inspection and refitting

All models except RS Turbo

Pre-1986 models

Removal

1 Drain the cooling system as described in Chapter 1.

2 Disconnect the battery negative terminal.

3 Release the retaining clips and disconnect all the hoses from the radiator, and on vehicles with automatic transmission, disconnect and plug the oil cooler pipelines.

4 Disconnect the wiring plug at the fan motor and unclip the wiring from the shroud **(see illustration)**.

5 Unscrew the two upper mounting bolts and carefully lift the radiator, complete with fan and cowl from the engine compartment. Note

that the base of the radiator is held in place by two lugs **(see illustrations)**.

Inspection

6 If the purpose of removal was to thoroughly clean the radiator, first reverse flush it with a cold water hose. The normal coolant flow is from left to right (from the thermostat housing to the radiator) through the matrix and out of the opposite side.

7 If the radiator fins are clogged with flies or dirt, remove them with a soft brush or blow compressed air from the rear face of the radiator. It is recommended that the fan assembly is first removed as described in the preceding Section (if not already done). In the absence of a compressed air line, a strong jet from a water hose may provide an alternative method of cleaning.

8 If the radiator is leaking, it is recommended that a reconditioned or new one is obtained from specialists. In an emergency, minor leaks can be cured by using a radiator sealant. If the radiator, due to neglect, requires the application of chemical cleaners, then these are best used when the engine is hot and the radiator is in the vehicle. Follow the manufacturer's instructions precisely and appreciate that there is an element of risk in the use of most de-scaling products, especially in a system which incorporates alloy and plastic materials.

Refitting

9 Refit the radiator by reversing the removal operations, but ensure that the rubber lug

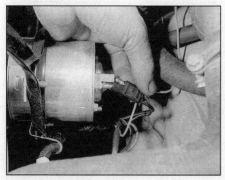

3.4 Disconnecting radiator fan wiring plug

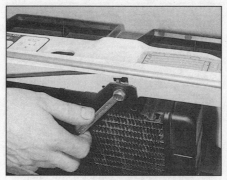

3.5a Undo the radiator upper bolts . . .

3.5b . . . and lift out the unit complete with fan - pre-1986 models (except RS Turbo)

3

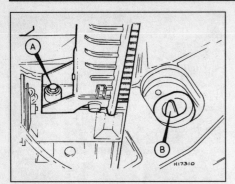

3.12 Radiator lower retaining bolts (A) and upper lugs (B) - 1986 models onwards (except RS Turbo)

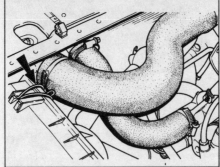

3.23 Intercooler upper air hose attachment - RS Turbo from 1986 onwards

3.25 Radiator and intercooler retaining bolts - RS Turbo from 1986 onwards (one lower bolt not shown)

insulators are in position. Fill the cooling system as described in Chapter 1 and on later models adjust the alternator drivebelt as described in Chapter 1.

1986 models onwards

Removal

10 Refer to Section 2 and remove the radiator fan.
11 To provide greater clearance for radiator removal, slacken the alternator mounting and adjustment arm bolts and push the alternator in towards the engine as far as it will go.
12 Unscrew the two radiator lower retaining bolts (**see illustration**).
13 Move the bottom of the radiator in towards the engine, then lower it to disengage the two upper retaining lugs. Carefully lift the radiator from the engine compartment.

Inspection and refitting

14 Proceed as described previously in this Section for pre-1986 models.

RS Turbo models

1985 models

Removal

15 Drain the cooling system as described in Chapter 1.
16 Disconnect the battery negative terminal.
17 Release the retaining clips and disconnect all the coolant hoses from the radiator.

18 Refer to Section 2 and remove the radiator fan.
19 Lift the radiator up and out of the engine compartment.

Inspection and refitting

20 Proceed as described previously in this Section for all models except RS Turbo.

1986 models onwards

Removal

21 Drain the cooling system as described in Chapter 1.
22 Disconnect the battery negative terminal.
23 Release the retaining clips and disconnect the coolant hoses at the radiator and the air hoses at the turbo intercooler (**see illustration**).
24 Refer to Section 2 and remove the radiator fan.
25 Undo the two radiator and intercooler lower retaining bolts (**see illustration**).
26 Undo the four bolts securing the intercooler to the radiator and remove the intercooler from the front.
27 Manipulate the radiator up and out of its location from the front (**see illustration**).

Inspection and refitting

28 Proceed as described previously in this Section for all models except RS Turbo.

4 Thermostat - removal, testing and refitting

OHV engines

Note: *A new gasket must be used on refitting.*

Removal

1 Drain the cooling system as described in Chapter 1.
2 Slacken the clips and disconnect the hoses at the thermostat housing (**see illustration**). Disconnect the radiator fan thermal switch wiring plug.
3 Unscrew the two bolts and remove the thermostat housing cover. If it is tight carefully tap it with a soft-faced mallet.
4 Extract the thermostat (**see illustration**). If it is stuck tight in its seat, do not lever it out by its bridge piece, but cut round it with a very sharp knife.

Testing

5 To test the thermostat, first check that in a cold condition its valve plate is closed. Suspend it on a string in a pan of cold water together with a thermometer (**see illustration**). Heat the water and check that the thermostat starts to open at the temperature given in the Specifications. It is difficult to check that the thermostat opens fully, as this occurs at a temperature above the boiling point of water.

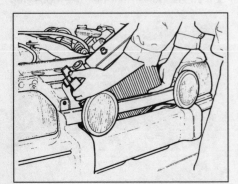

3.27 Radiator removal - RS Turbo from 1986 onwards

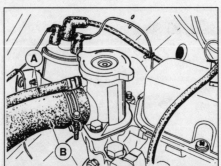

4.2 Expansion tank hose (A) and radiator top hose (B) connections at thermostat housing - OHV engine

4.4 Thermostat location in cylinder head - OHV engine

4.5 Testing the thermostat

4.10 Disconnect the expansion tank hose at the thermostat housing - CVH engine

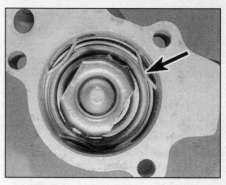

4.13a Extract the retaining spring clip (arrowed) . . .

6 Remove the thermostat from the water and check that the valve closes as the unit cools. If the thermostat does not operate as described, obtain a new thermostat.

Refitting

7 Refitting is the reverse sequence to removal, but ensure that all traces of old gasket are removed from the housing mating faces and use a new gasket lightly smeared with jointing compound. Tighten the retaining bolts to the specified torque.

8 On completion, refill the cooling system as described in Chapter 1.

CVH engines

Note: *A new gasket must be used on refitting.*

Removal

9 Drain the cooling system as described in Chapter 1.

10 Slacken the clips and disconnect the expansion tank hose, radiator hose and heater hose at the thermostat housing **(see illustration)**.

11 Disconnect the radiator fan thermal switch wiring plug.

12 Unscrew the three bolts and remove the thermostat housing from the cylinder head. If it is stuck, tap it off carefully with a soft-faced mallet.

13 Extract the retaining spring clip and withdraw the thermostat from the housing followed by the sealing ring **(see illustrations)**.

Testing and refitting

14 Proceed as described previously in this Section for OHV engines.

> ## 5 Water pump - removal and refitting

OHV engines

Note: *A new gasket and suitable jointing compound must be used on refitting.*

Removal

1 Drain the cooling system as described in Chapter 1.

2 Slacken the three water pump pulley retaining bolts. Any tendency for the pulley to turn as the bolts are undone can be restrained by depressing the top run of the drivebelt.

3 Release the alternator mounting and adjustment arm bolts, push the alternator in towards the engine and slip the drivebelt off the pulleys.

4 Unscrew the previously slackened pulley bolts and remove the pulley.

5 Release the clip and disconnect the hose at the pump outlet.

6 Unscrew the three retaining bolts and remove the pump from the cylinder block **(see illustration)**.

7 Peel away the old gasket from the cylinder block and thoroughly clean the mating face.

8 No provision is made for repair of the water

pump and if the unit is leaking, noisy, or in any way unserviceable, renewal will be necessary.

Refitting

9 Refitting is the reverse sequence to removal. Use a new gasket lightly smeared with jointing compound and tighten the retaining bolts to the specified torque.

10 Refill the cooling system, and adjust the drivebelt tension as described in Chapter 1.

CVH engines

Note: *The following procedure entails the use of special tools to tension the timing belt after refitting the water pump. Read through the entire Section to familiarise yourself with the procedure and refer also to Chapter 2. A new gasket and suitable jointing compound must be used on refitting.*

Removal

11 Drain the cooling system as described in Chapter 1.

12 On carburettor engines refer to Chapter 4 and remove the air cleaner to improve access.

13 Slacken the alternator mounting and adjustment arm bolts, push the alternator in towards the engine and slip the drivebelt off the pulleys.

14 Using a spanner on the crankshaft pulley bolt, turn the crankshaft until the notch on the

4.13b . . . withdraw the thermostat . . .

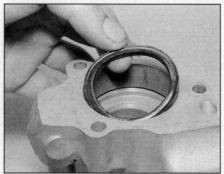

4.13c . . . and remove the sealing ring

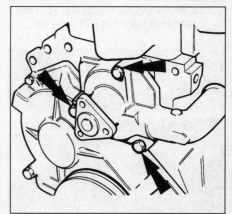

5.6 Water pump retaining bolts - OHV engines

3

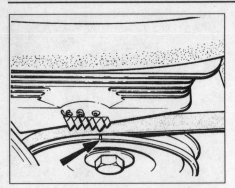

5.14 Crankshaft pulley notch aligned with TDC (O) mark on timing belt cover scale - CVH engines

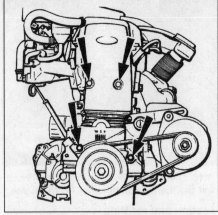

5.15 Timing belt cover retaining bolts - early CVH engine models with one-piece cover

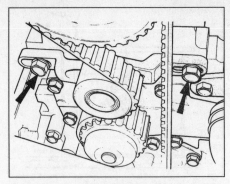

5.17 Timing belt tensioner retaining bolts - CVH engines

pulley is aligned with TDC (O) mark on the timing belt cover scale **(see illustration)**. Now remove the distributor cap and check that the rotor arm is pointing towards the No 1 cylinder HT lead segment in the cap. If the rotor arm is pointing towards No 4 cylinder segment, turn the crankshaft through another complete turn and realign the pulley notch with the TDC mark.
15 On early models unscrew the four bolts and remove the one-piece timing belt cover **(see illustration)**. On later models fitted with a two-piece cover, unscrew the two upper bolts and remove the top half, then unscrew the two lower bolts. The lower half cannot be removed at this stage.
16 Using a dab of quick drying paint, mark the teeth of the timing belt and their notches

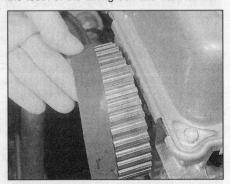

5.18 Removing the timing belt from the camshaft sprocket - CVH engine

on the sprockets so that the belt can be engaged in its original position on reassembly.
17 Slacken the two timing belt tensioner retaining bolts and slide the tensioner sideways to relieve the tautness of the belt **(see illustration)**. If the tensioner is spring-loaded, tighten one of the bolts to retain it in the slackened position.
18 Slip the timing belt off the camshaft, tensioner and water pump sprockets **(see illustration)**.
19 Remove the bolts and lift off the tensioner and, where fitted, the tensioning spring **(see illustration)**.
20 Slacken the clips and disconnect the hoses at the water pump.
21 Undo the four bolts and remove the pump from the cylinder block face **(see illustrations)**.
22 Renewal of the pump will be necessary if there are signs of water leakage, roughness of the bearings, or excessive side play or endfloat at the sprocket. From 1983 onwards a revised water pump was introduced in conjunction with a two-piece timing belt cover. If a water pump is being renewed on an early model with one-piece belt cover, then it will also be necessary to obtain a replacement kit. This kit contains a modified belt cover and related parts to suit the later type pump which is now the only type supplied.

Refitting

23 Scrape away all traces of old gasket and ensure that the mating faces are clean and dry.
24 Lightly smear jointing compound on both sides of a new gasket and locate the gasket on the cylinder block face.
25 Place the pump in position, then fit and tighten the bolts to the specified torque.
26 Fit the timing belt tensioners (and spring where applicable), but only tighten the bolts finger tight at this stage.
27 Refer to Chapter 2, and refit and tension the timing belt.
28 Refit the hoses to the water pump.
29 Refit the timing belt cover(s).
30 Refit the alternator drivebelt and adjust its tension as described in Chapter 1.
31 On carburettor engines, refit the air cleaner.
32 Refill the cooling system as described in Chapter 1.

6 Radiator fan thermal switch - testing, removal and refitting

Testing

1 The thermal switch is located on the side of the thermostat housing on early OHV engine models and in the thermostat housing cover on later OHV versions. On all CVH engines, the switch is located in the thermostat housing. If

5.19 Removing the timing belt tensioner - CVH engine

5.21a Undo the four bolts . . .

5.21b . . . and remove the water pump - CVH engine

the operation of the radiator fan is suspect, the thermal switch may be tested as follows.

2 Disconnect the wiring plug and bridge the two plug terminals with a length of wire or suitable metal object. The fan should now operate with the ignition switched on. If it does, the thermal switch is proved faulty and must be renewed. If the fan still does not operate, check the appropriate fuses, wiring and connections. If these are satisfactory it is likely that the fan motor itself is faulty.

Removal

Note: A new sealing washer will be required on refitting.

3 To renew the thermal switch wait until the engine is cold, then remove the pressure cap on the thermostat housing or expansion tank as applicable.

4 Place a container beneath the thermostat housing to collect the small amount of coolant that will be released when the switch is removed.

5 Disconnect the wiring plug and unscrew the switch from its location.

Refitting

6 Using a new sealing washer, refit and tighten the switch securely. Fit the wiring plug and top-up the system as described in Chapter 1.

7 Temperature gauge sender unit - removal and refitting

Note: Suitable jointing compound will be required on refitting.

Removal

1 With the engine cold unscrew the pressure cap on the thermostat housing or expansion tank as applicable, then refit it. This will release any residual pressure in the system and minimise coolant loss when the sender unit is removed.

2 Disconnect the wiring and unscrew the sender unit located on the forward facing side of the cylinder head, below the thermostat housing on OHV engines, or adjacent to the thermostat housing on CVH engines **(see illustrations)**.

Refitting

3 To refit, smear the threads of the sender unit with jointing compound and screw it into the cylinder head securely.

4 Reconnect the wiring and top-up the cooling system as described in Chapter 1.

8 Heating and ventilation system - description

The heater is of the type which utilises waste heat from the engine coolant. The coolant is pumped through the matrix in the heater casing where air, force-fed by a duplex radial fan, disperses the heat into the vehicle interior.

Fresh air enters the heater or the ventilator ducts through the grille at the rear of the bonnet lid. Air is extracted from the interior of the vehicle through outlets at the rear edges of the doors.

There are differences between the heater used on Base models and other versions in the Escort range. On Base models, a two-speed fan switch is used instead of the three-position switch used on other versions. On all models except the Base version, central and side window vents are incorporated in the facia panel.

The heater/ventilator controls are of lever type or rotary type on later models, operating through cables to flap valves which deflect the air flowing through the heater both to vary the temperature and to distribute the air between the footwell and demister outlets.

9 Heater controls - adjustment

1 On heaters with lever control, set both control levers approximately 2.0 mm up from their lowest setting. On heaters with rotary controls set the controls just off the COLD and CLOSED positions.

2 Release the securing bolts on the cable clamps and pull the temperature control and air direction flap valve arms to the COLD and CLOSED positions respectively **(see illustration)**. Check to see that the setting of the levers or rotary knobs on the control panel has not changed and retighten the cable clamps.

10 Heater controls - removal and refitting

Pre-1986 models

Removal

1 Working inside the vehicle, remove the dash lower trim panel from the right-hand side. The panel is secured by two metal tags and two clips.

2 Detach the air ducts from the right-hand side of the heater casing and swivel them to clear the control cables.

3 Disconnect the control cables from the heater casing.

4 Giving a sharp jerk, pull the knobs from the control levers on the facia panel, then press the control indicator plate downwards and remove it.

5 Unscrew and remove the two screws which are now exposed and which hold the control lever assembly in position.

6 Carefully withdraw the control unit with the cables from the facia and disconnect the wire from the illumination lamp.

1986 models onwards

Removal

7 Pull the air ducts off the heater on the right-hand side and move them clear.

8 Detach the right-hand cable from the heater casing and temperature control flap lever.

9 Pull the cover off the left-hand actuating lever and detach the cable from the heater casing and air distribution flap lever.

10 Pull off the heater control knobs and undo the two screws, one located under each outer control knob, then remove the control panel bezel. Remove the centre vents.

11 Undo the two control panel screws and withdraw the panel with cables, through the aperture.

Refitting (all models)

12 Refitting is a reversal of removal. On completion adjust as described in the preceding Section.

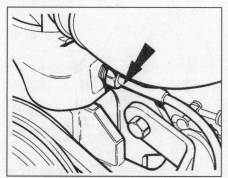

7.2a Temperature gauge sender unit location in cylinder head - OHV engines

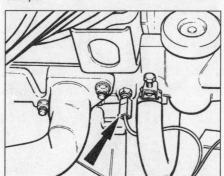

7.2b Temperature gauge sender unit location in cylinder head - CVH engines

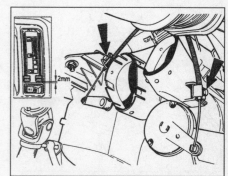

9.2 Heater control cable connections (arrowed) - pre-1986 models

3

11 Heater - removal and refitting

Removal

1 Disconnect the battery negative lead.

2 Refer to Chapter 11 and remove the centre console.

3 Working within the engine compartment, disconnect the coolant hoses from the heater pipe stubs at the rear bulkhead **(see illustration)**. Raise the ends of the hoses to minimise loss of coolant.

4 The heater matrix will still contain coolant and should be drained by blowing into the upper heater pipe stub and catching the coolant which will be ejected from the lower one.

5 Remove the cover plate and gasket from around the heater pipe stubs. This is held to the bulkhead by two self-tapping screws.

6 Working inside the vehicle, remove the dash lower trim panels from both sides. The panels are held in position by clips and tags.

7 Pull the air distribution ducts from the heater casing and swivel them as necessary to clear the control cables.

8 Disconnect the control cables from the heater casing and the flap arms.

9 Remove the two heater mounting nuts and lift the heater assembly out of the vehicle, taking care not to spill any remaining coolant on the carpet **(see illustration)**.

Refitting

10 Refitting is a reversal of removal. Check that the heater casing seal to the cowl is in good order, otherwise renew it. Adjust the heater controls on completion as described in Section 9.

11 Top-up the cooling system (see "*Weekly checks*") and reconnect the battery.

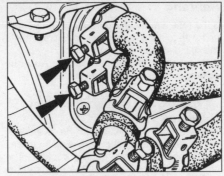

11.3 Coolant hose connections at heater pipe stubs

12 Heater matrix - removal and refitting

Removal

1 With the heater removed from the vehicle as previously described, extract the two securing screws and slide the matrix out of the heater casing.

2 If further dismantling is necessary, cut the casing seal at the casing joint, prise off any securing clips and separate the two halves of the casing.

3 Remove the air flap valves. It should be noted that the lever for the air distribution valve can only be removed when the mark on the lever is in alignment with the one on the gearwheel **(see illustration)**.

4 If the heater matrix is leaking, it is best to obtain a new or reconditioned unit. Home repairs are seldom successful. A blocked matrix can sometimes be cleared using a cold water hose and reverse flushing, but avoid the use of searching chemical cleaners.

Refitting

5 Reassembly is a reversal of removal. Take care not to damage the fins or tubes of the matrix when inserting it into the casing. Refit the heater with reference to Section 11.

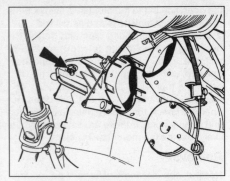

11.9 Heater mounting nut location - left-hand side

13 Heater motor/fan - removal and refitting

Removal

1 Open the bonnet, disconnect the battery and pull off the rubber seal which seals the air inlet duct to the bonnet lid when the lid is closed.

2 Prise off the five spring clips from the plenum chamber cover and detach the cover at the front.

3 Disconnect the wiring harness multi-plug, and the earth lead at its body connection adjacent to the heater pipe stub cover plate on the engine compartment bulkhead.

4 Unscrew and remove the fan housing mounting nuts and lift the housing from the engine compartment **(see illustration)**.

5 Insert the blade of a screwdriver and prise off the securing clips so that the fan covers can be removed **(see illustration)**.

6 Remove the resistor and lift out the motor/fan assembly.

Refitting

7 Reassembly and refitting are reversals of dismantling and removal.

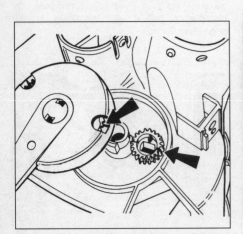

12.3 Air distribution valve lever and gear marks (arrowed)

13.4 Heater motor/fan assembly - viewed with cover removed

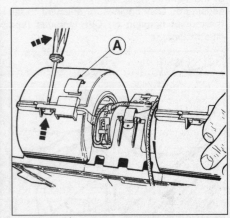

13.5 Prising off a heater fan cover clip

Chapter 4 Part A:
Carburettor fuel system

Contents

Degrees of difficulty

| **Easy,** suitable for novice with little experience | **Fairly easy,** suitable for beginner with some experience | **Fairly difficult,** suitable for competent DIY mechanic | **Difficult,** suitable for experienced DIY mechanic | **Very difficult,** suitable for expert DIY or professional |

4A

Specifications

Fuel pump

Type . . . . Mechanically-operated by eccentric on camshaft
Delivery pressure . . . . 0.24 to 0.38 bar (3.5 to 5.5 lbf/in^2)

Carburettor

Type . . . . Ford variable venturi (VV) or Weber 2V
Application:
  1.1 litre OHV engine . . . . Ford VV
  1.1 litre CVH engine . . . . Ford VV
  1.1 litre HCS engine . . . . Weber 2V TLDM
  1.3 litre OHV engine . . . . Ford VV
  1.3 litre HCS engine . . . . Weber 2V TLDM
  1.3 litre CVH engine . . . . Ford VV
  1.4 litre CVH engine . . . . Weber 2V DFTM
  1.6 litre CVH engine (except XR3 models):
    Up to 1986 . . . . Ford VV
    1986 on . . . . Weber VV TLD
  1.6 litre CVH engine (XR3 models) . . . . Weber 2V DFT
Choke type:
  All models up to 1984 . . . . Automatic
  1.1 and 1.3 litre engines, 1984 on . . . . Manual
  1.4 and 1.6 litre engines, 1984 on . . . . Automatic

Ford carburettor specification

Idle speed (Cooling fan on):
  Manual transmission . . . . 750 to 850 rpm
  Automatic transmission . . . . 850 to 950 rpm
Idle mixture CO content . . . . 1.0 to 2.0%

Weber carburettor specification

Weber 2V DFTM:

Idle speed (cooling fan on)	750 to 850 rpm	
Idle mixture CO content	1.25 to 1.75%	
Throttle kicker speed	1250 to 1350 rpm	
Fast idle speed	2600 to 2800 rpm	
Choke pull-down	2.7 to 3.2 mm	
Float height	7.5 to 8.5 mm	

	Primary	Secondary
Venturi diameter	21 mm	23 mm
Air correction jet	200	165
Emulsion tube	F22	F60
Idle jet	42	60
Main jet	102	125

Weber 2V TLD:

Idle speed (cooling fan on):		
Manual transmission	750 to 850 rpm	
Automatic transmission	850 to 950 rpm	
Idle mixture CO content	1.0 to 2.0%	
Throttle kicker speed	1050 to 1150 rpm	
Fast idle speed:		
Manual transmission	1850 to 1950 rpm	
Automatic transmission	1950 to 2050 rpm	
Choke pull-down:		
Manual transmission	4.0 to 5.0 mm	
Automatic transmission	3.5 to 4.5 mm	
Float height	28.5 to 29.5 mm	

	Primary	Secondary
Venturi diameter	21 mm	23 mm
Air correction jet	185	125
Emulsion tube	F105	F71
Main jet:		
Manual transmission	117	127
Automatic transmission	115	130

Weber 2V DFT:

Idle speed (cooling fan on)	750 to 850 rpm	
Idle mixture CO content	1.0 to 1.5%	
Fast idle speed	2600 to 2800 rpm	
Choke pull-down	5.2 to 5.8 mm	
Choke phasing	1.5 to 2.5 mm	
Float height	34.5 to 35.5 mm	

	Primary	Secondary
Venturi diameter	24	25
Air correction jet	160	150
Emulsion tube	F30	F30
Idle jet	50	60
Main jet	115	125

Weber 2V TLDM:

Idle speed (fan on)	700 to 800 rpm	
Idle mixture (CO content)	0.5 to 1.5%	
Fast idle speed:		
1.1 litre	2800 rpm	
1.3 litre	2500 rpm	
Float height	28.0 to 30.0 mm	

	Primary	Secondary
Venturi diameter	26	28
Main jet:		
1.1 litre	92	122
1.3 litre	90	122
Emulsion tube	F113	F75
Air correction jet:		
1.1 litre	195	155
1.3 litre	185	130

Fuel requirement

Fuel octane rating:
All except HCS engines . . . . 97 RON (four-star)
HCS engines . . . . 97 RON (four-star) or 95 RON (unleaded)

Torque wrench settings

	Nm	lbf ft
Carburettor to manifold	17 to 21	12 to 15
Fuel pump	16 to 20	11 to 14
Inlet manifold	16 to 20	11 to 14
Exhaust manifold	14 to 17	10 to 12
Exhaust downpipe to manifold	35 to 40	25 to 29
U-bolt clamps	35 to 40	25 to 29
Downpipe to front section connecting flange	35 to 47	25 to 34

1 General information and precautions

The fuel system on all models with carburettor induction is composed of a centrally mounted fuel tank, a fuel pump, a carburettor and an air cleaner.

The fuel tank is mounted under the floor pan beneath the rear seats. The tank is ventilated, has a simple filler pipe and a fuel gauge sender unit.

The fuel pump is a mechanical diaphragm type actuated by means of a pushrod bearing on an eccentric cam on the camshaft. The pump is a sealed unit and cannot be dismantled.

The carburettor may be either a Ford variable venturi (VV) type or one of four versions of the Weber 2V type, depending on model.

The air cleaner has a thermostatically or waxstat-controlled air inlet, supplying either hot air from the exhaust manifold heat box or cold air from the front of the engine compartment. On the thermostatically-controlled type, a flap valve within the air cleaner unit regulates the air inlet temperature according to operating conditions in conjunction with a vacuum diaphragm unit and a heat sensor unit. On the waxstat air cleaner, being progressively introduced from 1986 onwards the air cleaner operates in the same way as the thermostatically-controlled type, but the flap valve is controlled by a wax capsule. The capsule is mounted in the inlet spout and operates the flap valve by expansion and contraction of the wax which varies according to temperature.

Warning: Many of the procedures in this Chapter entail the removal of fuel pipes and connections which may result in some fuel spillage. Before carrying out any operation on the fuel system refer to the precautions given in Safety First! at the beginning of this manual and follow them implicitly. Petrol is a highly dangerous and volatile liquid and the precautions necessary when handling it cannot be overstressed

2 Air cleaner assembly - removal and refitting

Removal

1 Disconnect the battery negative terminal.
2 Disconnect the crankcase ventilation hoses which are accessible from above, from the air cleaner body **(see illustration)**.
3 Disconnect the cold air inlet hose from the end of the air cleaner spout where applicable **(see illustration)**.
4 Where fitted, on CVH engines, pull out the crankcase emission valve from the underside of the air cleaner body.
5 Undo the retaining screws or bolts on the air cleaner lid and lift the unit off the carburettor.
6 On 1.1 and 1.3 litre HCS engines, unclip the fuel trap from the side of the air cleaner casing.
7 According to model, disconnect the vacuum hose and the remaining crankcase ventilation hose(s) as applicable, then remove the air cleaner from the engine.

Refitting

8 Refitting is a reversal of removal.

3 Air cleaner air temperature control - description and testing

Thermostatically-controlled air cleaner

1 On all pre-1986 models and certain models from 1986 onwards, the air cleaner is thermostatically-controlled by a vacuum operated system to provide air at the most suitable temperature for combustion with minimum emission levels.
2 This is accomplished by drawing in cold air from an inlet at the front of the car, and hot air from a collector box on the exhaust manifold and blending them. The proportion of hot and cold air is varied by the position of a flap valve in the inlet spout which itself is controlled by a vacuum diaphragm. The vacuum pressure is regulated by a heat sensor located within the air cleaner body to ensure that the appropriate degree of inlet manifold vacuum is applied to the flap valve, thus maintaining the air temperature within the preset limits.
3 To check the thermostatic control of the air cleaner the engine must be cold. First observe the position of the flap valve which should be fully closed prior to starting the engine **(see illustration)**. The flap valve can be observed using a mirror after disconnecting the inlet hose.

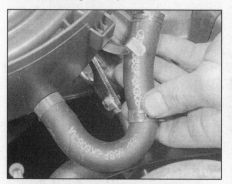

2.2 Disconnecting the crankcase ventilation hose at the air cleaner body

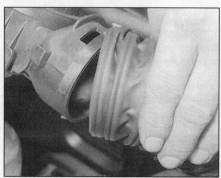

2.3 Cold air inlet hose removal from air cleaner spout

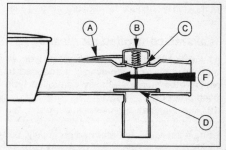

3.3 Thermostatically controlled air cleaner operation under low vacuum conditions
A *Vacuum hose to heat sensor*
B *Vacuum diaphragm*
C *Diaphragm*
D *Flap valve closed*
F *Cold air inlet*

4A

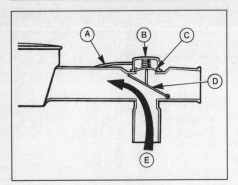

3.4 Thermostatically-controlled air cleaner operation under high vacuum conditions

A Vacuum hose to heat sensor
B Vacuum diaphragm
C Diaphragm
D Flap valve open
E Hot air inlet

4 Start the engine and check that the flap valve opens fully at idle speed to allow only hot air from the manifold to enter the air cleaner **(see illustration)**.

5 Should the flap valve remain in the closed position once the engine is started, then the diaphragm unit or the heat sensor is at fault and should be tested to isolate the defective unit.

6 Make sure that all vacuum lines are secure and free from leaks as a final check.

7 To check the operation of these components a vacuum pump is required. If one is available proceed as follows, if not, have the tests carried out by a dealer.

8 Detach the diaphragm-to-heat sensor vacuum line at the sensor end and connect a vacuum pump to the diaphragm unit. Apply a vacuum up to 100 mm (4.0 in) of mercury and retain this whilst checking the flap valve.

9 If the flap valve is now open, then the heat sensor is faulty and must be renewed. If the valve remains shut, the diaphragm unit is faulty and a new air cleaner will have to be obtained, as the diaphragm unit is not available separately.

10 After the checks, disconnect the vacuum pump and reconnect the vacuum line and inlet hose.

Waxstat-controlled air cleaner

11 From 1986 onwards the waxstat type air cleaner is being progressively introduced to replace the thermostatically-controlled type used previously.

12 The waxstat air cleaner performs the same hot and cold air blending operation using a flap valve as described previously, but the flap valve is controlled by a wax capsule and is not dependent on manifold vacuum.

13 When the engine is cold the wax in the capsule contracts and the flap valve is pulled back to shut off the cold air inlet. As engine ambient temperature rises the wax expands and the flap is opened to admit only cold air into the air cleaner.

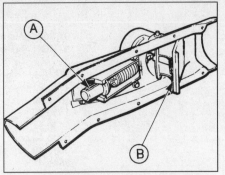

3.15 Waxstat type air cleaner components in air cleaner spout

A Wax capsule   *B Flap valve*

14 To test the unit the engine must initially be cold.

15 Remove the manifold-to-air cleaner hot air hose and observe the position of the flap valve which should be open to allow only hot air to enter **(see illustration)**.

16 Refit the hose and warm up the engine to normal operating temperature.

17 Remove the hot air hose again and check the position of the flap valve. With the engine at normal operating temperature the flap should be closed to admit only cold air into the air cleaner.

18 If this is not the case the waxstat is defective and the air cleaner must be renewed as the waxstat is not available separately.

19 Refit the hot air hose on completion of the checks.

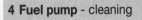

4 Fuel pump - cleaning

Note: *Refer to the warning at the end of Section 1 before proceeding.*

1 On certain early models the fuel pump has a detachable cover allowing access to the internal filter for cleaning. If this type of pump is fitted (identified by a raised cover secured with a screw) the filter can be cleaned as follows.

2 Place a piece of rag around the pump body to catch the fuel which will drain out when the cover is removed.

3 Unscrew and remove the single cover screw and lift off the cover **(see illustration)**.

4 Take out the rubber sealing ring and the filter screen from inside the cover.

5 Clean the screen by brushing it in clean fuel, then fit it into the cover, noting the projections on some screens which centralise it.

6 Fit the sealing ring. If it is not in good order, renew it.

7 Locate the cover on the pump body. On some pumps, the cover is correctly installed when the notch in the cover engages in the groove in the pump body.

8 Screw in the retaining screw, but do not overtighten it provided it is making a good seal.

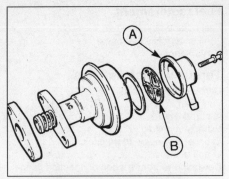

4.3 CVH engine fuel pump filter components

A Pump cover   *B Filter*

5 Fuel pump - testing, removal and refitting

Note: *Refer to the warning at the end of Section 1 before proceeding.*

Testing

1 The fuel pump may be quite simply tested by disconnecting the fuel inlet pipe from the carburettor and placing its open end in a container.

2 Disconnect the LT lead from the negative terminal of the ignition coil to prevent the engine firing.

3 Actuate the starter motor. Regular well-defined spurts of fuel should be seen being ejected from the open end of the fuel inlet pipe.

4 Where this is not evident and yet there is fuel in the tank, the pump is in need of renewal. The pump is a sealed unit and cannot be dismantled or repaired.

Removal

5 On OHV and HCS engines, the fuel pump is mounted on the cylinder block and is actuated by a lever which is in direct contact with an eccentric cam on the camshaft.

6 On CVH engines, the fuel pump is mounted on the cylinder head and is actuated by a pushrod from an eccentric cam on the camshaft.

5.7 CVH engine fuel pump removal

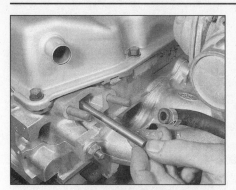

5.9 Removing the fuel pump push-rod

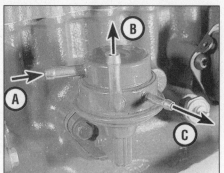

5.10 Fuel pump connections on 1.1 and 1.3 litre HCS engines
A Inlet from tank
B Outlet to carburettor
C Return to tank

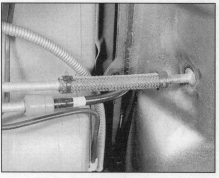

6.3 Fuel tank flexible hose connections at front of tank

7 To remove the pump, disconnect and plug the fuel inlet and outlet hoses (and on HCS engines, the fuel return hose) at the pump and then unbolt it from the engine **(see illustration)**. Note the fuel hose connections to ensure correct reconnection on refitting.

8 Retain any insulating spacers and remove and discard the flange gaskets.

9 On CVH engines, withdraw the push-rod **(see illustration)**.

Refitting

10 Refitting is a reversal of removal, but use new flange gaskets. If crimped type hose clips were used originally, these will have been destroyed when disconnecting the fuel hoses. Renew them with conventional nut and screw type clips. Ensure that the fuel hoses are correctly reconnected as noted before removal **(see illustration)**.

6 Fuel tank - removal and refitting

Note: *Refer to the warning at the end of Section 1 before proceeding.*

Removal

1 The fuel tank will normally only need to be removed if it is severely contaminated with sediment or other substance, or requires repair.

2 As there is no drain plug incorporated in the tank, the best time to remove it is when it is nearly empty. If this is not possible, syphon as much fuel as possible from the tank into a container which can be sealed, but before doing so, observe the following precautions:
 a) Disconnect the battery, negative lead first.
 b) Do not smoke or bring naked lights near.
 c) Avoid placing the vehicle over an inspection pit as the fuel vapour is heavier than air.

3 With the rear of the vehicle raised and supported securely, disconnect the flexible hose connection between the sections of rigid fuel line at the front face of the tank **(see illustration)**. On some models dual pipelines are used, the second one being a fuel return line which returns excess fuel from the carburettor.

4 Disconnect the electrical leads from the tank sender unit.

5 Brush away all adhering dirt and disconnect the tank filler pipe and vent pipes from the tank pipe stubs **(see illustration)**. Additionally, on 1986 models onwards, disconnect the filler vent pipe.

6 Support the tank and unscrew the bolts from the support straps **(see illustration)**.

7 Lower the tank until the fuel hoses can be detached from the sender unit and from their retaining clips. On 1986 models onwards disconnect the small bore vent pipe located on the top face of the tank **(see illustration)**. Lower the tank fully and remove it from under the car.

Refitting

8 If the tank is to be cleaned out, repaired or renewed, remove the sender unit. To do this, unscrew the unit in an anti-clockwise direction using the special tool (23-014) or a suitable lever engaged behind the tabs.

9 If the tank contains sediment or water, clean it out by shaking vigorously using paraffin as a solvent. After several changes, rinse out finally with petrol.

10 If the tank is leaking, leave repair to a specialist company. Attempting to weld or solder the tank without it first having been steamed out for several hours is extremely dangerous.

11 Refit the sender unit using a new sealing ring.

12 Refit the tank into the vehicle by reversing the removal operations. Check all connections for leaks after the tank has been partly filled with fuel.

4A

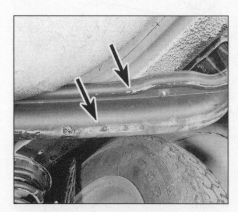

6.5 Fuel tank filler and vent pipe locations (arrowed)

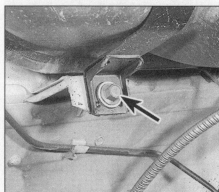

6.6 Fuel tank support strap bolt (arrowed)

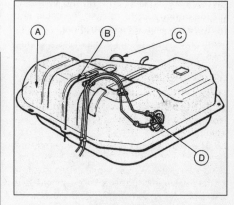

6.7 Fuel tank assembly
A Fuel tank
B Vent pipe
C Fuel filler stub
D Fuel gauge sender unit

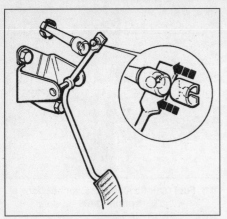

7.8 Throttle cable attachment at pedal end

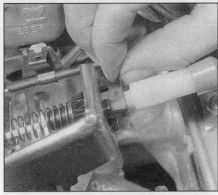

7.11a Prise out the throttle cable retaining clip . . .

7.11b . . . then release the cable retainer (arrowed)

7 Throttle cable - adjustment, removal and refitting

Adjustment

1 Disconnect the battery earth lead.
2 On manual transmission models remove the air cleaner unit, as given in Section 2.
3 Get an assistant to sit in the driving seat and fully depress the accelerator pedal, then whilst it is depressed turn the cable adjuster at the carburettor or throttle cable mounting bracket connection to the point at which the linkage is just fully open.
4 Release the accelerator pedal then fully depress and release it again and check that when depressed the throttle is fully opened. Readjust if necessary.
5 On completion refit the air cleaner and reconnect the battery earth lead.

Removal

6 Disconnect the battery earth lead.
7 Working within the vehicle, remove the facia lower insulation panel.
8 Disconnect the cable from the upper end of the accelerator pedal arm. Do this by sliding off the spring clip to release the cable end from the ball-stud **(see illustration)**.

9 Working under the bonnet, release the cable from the bulkhead.

> **HAYNES HiNT** *It is easier to release the cable if an assistant can punch the cable grommet out from inside the vehicle.*

10 Remove the air cleaner (manual transmission models only).
11 The cable must now be detached from its bracket on the carburettor or, on automatic transmission models, from the throttle cable mounting bracket on the right-hand side of the engine. Prise out the clip then depress the four lugs on the retainer simultaneously so that the retainer can be slid out of its bracket. Take care not to damage the outer cable. On 1.1 and 1.3 litre HCS engine models, pull the securing clip from the support assembly, and release the cable from the bracket **(see illustrations)**.
12 Disconnect the end of the cable from the ball-stud by sliding back the spring retaining clip **(see illustration)**.

Refitting

13 Fit the new cable by reversing the removal procedure, then adjust as described previously in this Section.

8 Accelerator pedal - removal and refitting

Removal

1 The pedal can be removed once the throttle cable has been disconnected from it as described in Section 7.
2 Undo the two pedal support bracket retaining bolts and remove the pedal.

Refitting

3 Refitting is the reversal of removal but on completion check the throttle cable adjustment as described in Section 7.

9 Choke control cable - removal, refitting and adjustment

Pre-1986 models

Removal

1 Disconnect the battery earth lead.
2 For improved access, remove the air cleaner unit (Section 2).

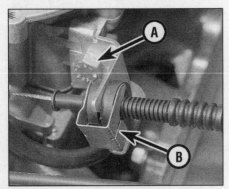

7.11c Throttle cable support bracket on 1.3 litre HCS engine

A Securing bolt   *B Securing clip*

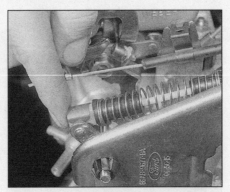

7.12 Release the cable end fitting spring retaining clip

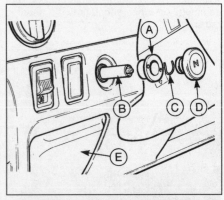

9.4 Choke cable attachments at facia - pre-1986 models

A Bezel   *D Knob*
B Switch lever   *E Coin box*
C Knob retaining clip

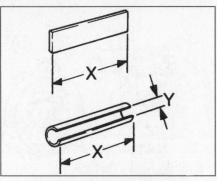

9.9 Choke cable adjustment spacer dimensions - pre-1986 models
X = 37.0 to 37.5 mm
Y = 12.0 mm minimum

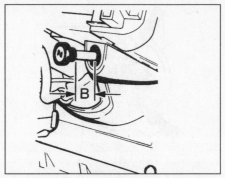

9.10 Choke knob pulled out for adjustment with spacer (B) in position - pre-1986 models

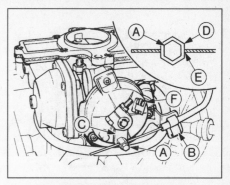

9.11 Choke cable adjustment at carburettor - pre-1986 models
A Cable clamp bolt
B Outer cable retaining clip
C Operating lever
D Cable clamp
E Point 22 mm from cable end
F Full choke stop

3 At the carburettor end of the cable, loosen the cable clamp bolt, detach the outer cable securing clip at the choke control bracket and disconnect the cable.
4 Working inside the car, remove the coin box from the lower facia panel (beneath the choke control knob) **(see illustration)**.
5 Remove the clip retaining the cable control knob and withdraw the knob from the switch lever.
6 Remove the control switch bezel and then, reaching up underneath the facia withdraw the switch from the underside of the panel (through the coin box aperture).
7 The choke cable can now be pulled through the engine bulkhead and the switch removed.

Refitting

8 Refitting is the reversal of removal, but in conjunction with the following adjustment procedure.

Adjustment

9 From either a flat strip of metal or preferably metal tubing make up a spacer as shown **(see illustration)**.
10 Pull out the choke and locate the spacer behind the choke knob. Ensure that the spacer remains in position throughout the procedure **(see illustration)**.
11 At the carburettor end, mark the inner cable at a point 22 mm (0.86 in) from the end using pencil or tape **(see illustration)**. On some cables the cable may be kinked for reference at this point or a ferrule may be fitted.
12 Insert the cable in the cable clamp until the mark or ferrule is against the edge of the clamp. Tighten the clamp bolt.
13 Pull the outer cable so that the operating lever on the choke is against the "full choke" stop on the housing. Secure the outer cable to its bracket, in this position, using the retaining clip.
14 Remove the spacer and check that the operating lever contacts the "choke off" stop and "full choke" stop on the housing when the choke knob is pushed in and pulled out respectively. On completion of the adjustment

ensure that there is a small clearance between the lever and the "off stop" when the choke knob is pushed in.

1986 models onwards

Removal

15 Disconnect the battery earth lead.
16 Remove the air cleaner as described in Section 2.
17 At the carburettor end of the cable, loosen the cable clamp bolt, detach the outer cable securing clip at the choke control bracket and disconnect the cable. On 1.1 and 1.3 litre HCS engine models, release the outer cable securing clamp and unhook the cable end fitting from the choke lever **(see illustrations)**.
18 Working inside the car remove the steering column shrouds for access to the cable.
19 From behind the facia disconnect the warning light wire from the choke control assembly **(see illustration)**.
20 Using a small probe, depress the locking pin on the underside of the choke knob collar and remove the knob **(see illustration)**.
21 Unscrew the choke control retaining collar and withdraw the cable from under the facia.

9.17a Releasing the choke cable clamp bolt (arrowed)

9.17b Choke cable outer cable clamp (A) and end fitting (B) on 1.3 litre HCS engine

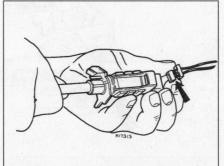

9.19 Removing choke assembly warning light wire - 1986 models onwards

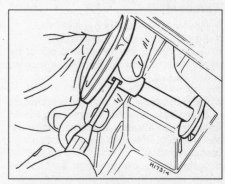

9.20 Using a small probe to release choke knob locking pin - 1986 models onwards

4A

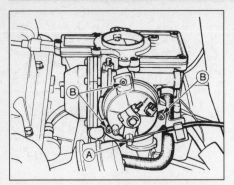

10.4 Choke cable clamp bolt (A) and lever housing retaining screws (B) - Ford VV carburettor

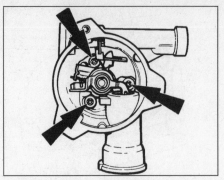

10.5 Choke unit retaining screw locations - Ford VV carburettor

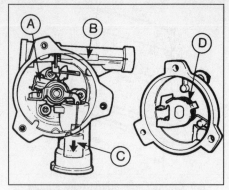

10.7 Manual choke and lever assembly - Ford VV carburettor

  A Choke linkage
  B Tapered needle (metering rod)
  C Pull-down piston
  D Spring-loaded lever

Pull the cable through the bulkhead and remove it from inside the car.

Refitting

22 Refitting is the reversal of removal, but in conjunction with the following adjustment procedure.

Adjustment

23 With the cable in position in the facia and routed through the bulkhead, push the choke knob fully in and engage the inner cable end with the clamp at the carburettor.
24 Pull the cable through the clamp up to the cable ferrule, then tighten the clamp bolt.
25 Pull out the choke knob to the full choke position and also hold the choke lever on the carburettor in the full choke position. Secure the cable to the bracket with the clip.
26 Check that with the knob pulled fully out the choke lever contacts the full choke stop on the carburettor and returns fully to the choke off position when the knob is pushed in. On models fitted with the Ford VV carburettor, ensure that there is a small clearance between the choke lever and the choke off stop when the choke knob is pushed fully in.

10 Ford VV carburettor manual choke unit - removal, checking and refitting

Note: *A new gasket will be required on refitting.*

Removal

1 Disconnect the battery negative lead.
2 Remove the air cleaner (Section 2).
3 Slacken the choke cable clamp bolt at the choke lever, detach the outer cable securing clip at the bracket and remove the cable from the carburettor.
4 Using a suitable Torx type key or socket bit, undo the three lever housing retaining screws and withdraw the lever housing, together with the choke cable bracket from the carburettor **(see illustration)**.
5 Carefully unscrew the three Torx screws which secure the main choke unit to the carburettor and withdraw the choke unit together with the gasket **(see illustration)**.

Checking

6 With the choke removed clean the unit inside by gently blowing out dust and any dirt with an air line or foot pump.
7 Using a small screwdriver or thin rod, raise the pull-down piston and allow it to drop under its own weight, checking that it falls smoothly to the lower limit of its travel **(see illustration)**.
8 Repeat this check but with the choke linkage lever held in various positions. If the piston binds in any position throughout its total travel, try cleaning the unit once more with an air line, nothing else, then repeat the checks. Under no circumstances attempt to ease a sticking piston with lubrication of any kind otherwise the calibration of the piston will be affected and its operating characteristics radically altered. Check also that the choke control spring leg is seated in its slot in the choke lever **(see illustration)**. If not, carefully slip it back into place. Check the operation of the piston once more and if it still sticks, renew the choke unit and lever housing as an assembly.
9 Check the choke metering rod by carefully moving the needle bracket through its full range of travel using a small screwdriver **(see illustration)**. As with the pull-down piston, the check should be made with the linkage lever held in various positions. Ensure that the rod

does not bind in any position throughout its total travel. If binding does occur it may be lightly lubricated with "Ballistol Spray" which should be available from main Ford dealers. Do not use any other lubricant otherwise a sludge build-up may occur, and do not allow overspray to contact the pull-down piston or linkage. If the metering rod is partially or completely seized, lubrication will not help and the choke unit and lever housing should be renewed as an assembly.
10 If both the metering rod and the pull-down piston are satisfactory but binding was noticed when moving the linkage lever, then the central shaft should be lightly lubricated from the rear of the choke unit using the "Ballistol Spray".

Refitting

11 To refit the choke unit first position a new gasket onto the carburettor mating face, locate the choke unit and fit the retaining screws.
12 When refitting the lever housing, align the new gasket with the screw holes and with the tab of the gasket positioned as shown. With

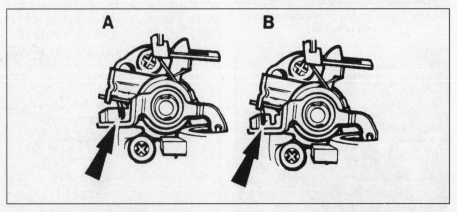

10.8 Correct position of choke control spring leg - Ford VV carburettor

  A Correctly located   *B Incorrectly located*

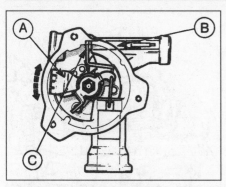

10.9 Checking choke operation - Ford VV carburettor

A Linkage lever   C Needle
B Metering rod   bracket

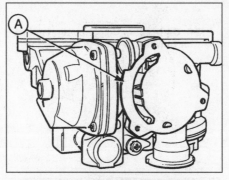

10.12a Correct location of choke lever housing gasket with tab (A) positioned as shown - Ford VV carburettor

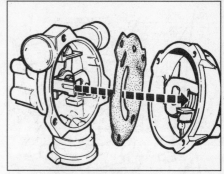

10.12b Fitting lever housing to choke unit - Ford VV carburettor

the linkage lever at its mid travel position, fit the lever housing ensuring that the linkage lever engages with the springloaded arm in the lever housing **(see illustrations)**.

13 Secure the lever housing and choke cable bracket with the three retaining screws.

14 Reconnect the choke cable and adjust it as described in Section 9.

15 Refit the air cleaner (Section 2), reconnect the battery, then adjust the idle speed and mixture settings (Chapter 1).

11 Ford VV carburettor automatic choke components - removal, checking and refitting

Bi-metal housing

Note: *A new gasket will be required on refitting.*

Removal

1 Disconnect the battery negative lead.

2 Remove the air cleaner as described in Section 2.

3 Release any pressure in the cooling system by loosening the pressure cap (see Chapter 1), then detach the inlet and outlet hoses at the automatic choke unit. Clamp the hoses or position them with their ends facing upwards to minimise coolant leakage.

4 Mark the bi-metal housing-to-choke body joint with quick-drying paint to ensure correct realignment on reassembly.

5 Unscrew and remove the three bi-metal housing retaining screws and withdraw the housing and gasket **(see illustration)**.

Refitting

6 Refitting is a reversal of the removal procedure.

7 Use a new gasket between the main body and the bi-metal housing.

8 When fitting the bi-metal housing, engage the bi-metal coil with the linkage lever centre slot, then loosely fit the three retaining screws, starting with the lower one **(see illustration)**.

9 Before tightening the retaining screws, align the paint mark on the bi-metal body with the choke body marking **(see illustration)**.

10 Refit the air cleaner as described in Section 2 and top-up the cooling system as described in Chapter 1.

Automatic choke unit

Note: *A new gasket will be required on refitting.*

Removal

11 Remove the bi-metal housing as described previously in this Section.

12 Carefully remove the three screws within the choke housing body and withdraw the unit from the carburettor together with the gasket.

Checking

13 Carry out the checks described for the manual choke unit in Section 10.

Refitting

14 If a new choke unit is to be fitted, it will first be necessary to tap out the securing screw holes for the bi-metal housing. The thread can be tapped out using the retaining screws which are of the thread-cutting type. **Do not** cut the threads with a standard tap.

15 Refit the choke housing body to the carburettor using a new gasket, then refit the bi-metal housing as described previously in this Section.

12 Ford VV carburettor - removal and refitting

Note: *Refer to the warning at the end of Section 1 before proceeding. A new gasket must be used on refitting.*

Removal

1 Disconnect the battery negative lead.

2 Remove the air cleaner (Section 2).

3 On automatic choke carburettors, if the engine is still hot, depressurise the cooling system by carefully releasing the pressure cap (see Chapter 1). Disconnect the coolant hoses from the automatic choke housing and clamp or plug them to prevent coolant loss.

4A

11.5 Removing the automatic choke bi-metal housing

11.8 Automatic choke linkage lever centre slot (arrowed)

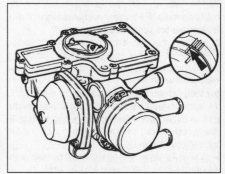

11.9 Alignment marks on choke unit and bi-metal housing Ford VV carburettor

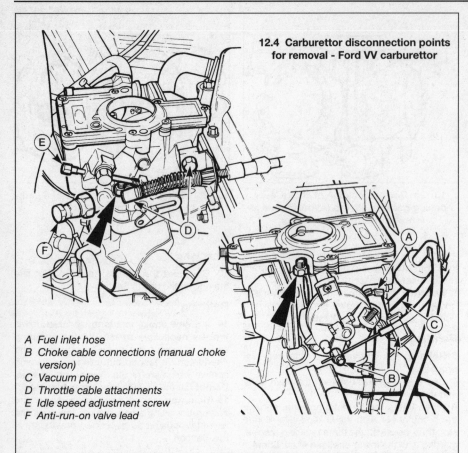

12.4 Carburettor disconnection points for removal - Ford VV carburettor

A Fuel inlet hose
B Choke cable connections (manual choke version)
C Vacuum pipe
D Throttle cable attachments
E Idle speed adjustment screw
F Anti-run-on valve lead

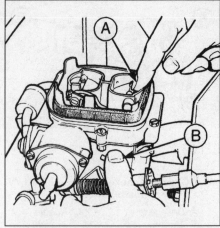

13.4 Weber 2V carburettor choke linkage position for fast idle adjustment - XR3 models
A Choke plates held closed
B Throttle held partially open

4 Detach the anti-run-on valve lead at the carburettor end **(see illustration)**.

5 On manual choke models disconnect the choke cable from the lever and the outer cable from its clamp on the support bracket.

6 Disconnect the distributor vacuum pipe.

7 Disconnect the throttle cable by pulling the spring clip to release the end fitting from the ball-stud and then unscrewing the cable bracket fixing bolt.

8 Disconnect and plug the fuel inlet and, where fitted, the return hose from the carburettor. If crimped type hose clips are used, cut them off and fit screw type clips at reassembly.

9 Unscrew the two carburettor mounting flange nuts and lift the carburettor from the inlet manifold. Remove the idle speed screw if necessary for access to the nuts.

Refitting

10 Refitting is a reversal of removal, but make sure that a new flange gasket is used on perfectly clean mating surfaces.

11 On manual choke models readjust the choke cable on reconnection, as described in Section 9.

12 When reconnecting the vacuum pipe make sure that the fuel trap is correctly positioned.

13 When refitting the fuel inlet hose ensure that it is positioned in such a way that no part

of the hose is closer than 11 mm (0.4 in) to the automatic choke coolant hoses. If this is not done fuel vaporisation can occur under certain conditions.

14 On automatic choke models recheck the coolant level.

15 On completion restart the engine and check the idle speed and mixture adjustments, as given in Chapter 1.

13 Weber 2V carburettor - adjustment

Idle speed and mixture adjustment

1 Refer to Chapter 1.

Fast idle speed (XR3 models)

2 Remove the air cleaner as described in Section 2.

3 Have the engine at normal operating temperature, with a tachometer connected in accordance with the manufacturer's instructions.

4 With the engine switched off, partially open the throttle by moving the cable at the carburettor. Close the choke plates with the fingers and hold them closed while the throttle is released. This has the effect of setting the choke mechanism in the high cam/fast idle position **(see illustration)**.

5 Release the choke valve plates and without touching the accelerator pedal, start the engine by just turning the key. Record the engine speed shown on the tachometer and compare the figure with that specified.

6 Where necessary turn the fast idle screw in or out to adjust the fast idle speed **(see illustration)**.

7 Refit the air cleaner.

Fast idle speed (1.4 litre models)

8 Adjust the engine idle speed and mixture settings as previously described, then switch off the engine. Leave the tachometer connected from the previous operation.

9 Undo the four bolts securing the air cleaner to the carburettor, disconnect the hot and cold air inlet hoses and lift off the air cleaner. Position the air cleaner clear of the carburettor, but leave the crankcase breather hoses and the vacuum supply hose connected.

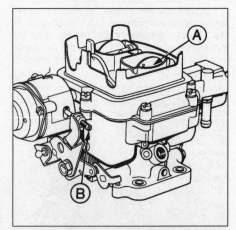

13.6 Weber 2V carburettor fast idle adjustment - XR3 models
A Choke plates in open position
B Fast idle adjustment screw

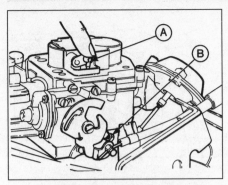
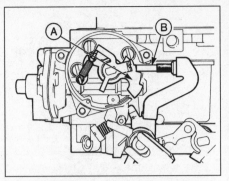

13.11 Weber 2V carburettor fast idle adjustment - 1.4 litre models
A Choke plates held open
B Fast idle adjustment screw

13.16 Weber 2V carburettor fast idle adjustment - 1.6 litre models
A Fast idle cam
B Fast idle adjustment screw positioned on third step of cam

13.23 Weber 2V carburettor fast idle adjustment screw (arrowed) - 1.1 and 1.3 litre HCS engine models

10 Pull the choke knob fully out and start the engine.

11 Using a finger on the linkage lever as shown, hold the choke plate open and note the fast idle speed (see illustration).

12 If adjustment is necessary turn the fast idle adjusting screw until the specified speed is obtained.

13 On completion refit the air cleaner and disconnect the tachometer.

Fast idle speed (1.6 litre models - 1986 onwards)

14 Remove the air cleaner as described in Section 2.

15 Have the engine at normal operating temperature with a tachometer connected in accordance with the manufacturer's instructions.

16 With the engine stopped, open the throttle linkage slightly by hand and close the choke plate until the fast idle adjusting screw lines up with the third (middle) step of the fast idle cam (see illustration). Release the throttle so that the fast idle screw rests on the cam. Release the choke plate.

17 Without touching the accelerator pedal, start the engine by just turning the key.

18 Note the fast idle speed and if adjustment is necessary, turn the fast idle adjusting screw until the specified speed is obtained.

19 On completion refit the air cleaner and disconnect the tachometer.

Fast idle speed (1.1 and 1.3 litre HCS engine models)

20 Adjust the engine idle speed and mixture settings as previously described, then switch off the engine. Leave the tachometer connected from the previous operation.

21 Remove the air cleaner assembly as described in Section 2.

22 Hold the choke valve fully open, start the engine and check the engine speed.

23 Adjust as necessary on the fast idle speed screw (see illustration).

24 Turning the screw anti-clockwise increases the fast idle speed, turning it

clockwise decreases the speed.

25 On completion, stop the engine, remove the test equipment and refit the air cleaner.

Throttle kicker (1.4 litre models)

26 Remove the air cleaner as described in Section 2. Plug the vacuum supply from the manifold.

27 Have the engine at normal operating temperature with a tachometer connected in accordance with the manufacturer's instructions.

28 With the engine running and the idle speed and mixture correctly adjusted, manually operate the throttle kicker by lifting the operating lever upwards. Note the increase in engine speed.

29 If the increased speed is outside the figure given in the Specifications, remove the tamperproof plug from the top of the kicker body and adjust the unit to give the specified speed.

30 Remove the tachometer and refit the air cleaner on completion.

Throttle kicker (1.6 litre models - 1986 onwards)

31 The throttle kicker is only fitted to models with automatic transmission.

32 Have the engine at normal operating temperature, with the idle speed and mixture correctly adjusted and with a tachometer connected.

33 Disconnect the wiring multi-plug from the radiator cooling fan thermostatic switch in the thermostat housing, and bridge the two contacts in the plug using a suitable length of wire. This is necessary so that the cooling fan runs continuously during adjustment.

34 Disconnect the vacuum supply at the throttle kicker and also disconnect the vacuum supply to the throttle kicker electrically-operated vacuum switch, at the manifold take-off. Using a new hose connect the kicker directly to the manifold.

35 Start the engine and record the rpm.

36 If the engine speed is outside the figure given in the Specifications, remove the

tamperproof plug from the top of the kicker body and adjust the unit to give the specified speed.

37 On completion refit the vacuum connections in their original positions, reconnect the fan motor multi-plug and refit the air cleaner.

14 Weber 2V carburettor automatic choke unit - adjustment

XR3 models

1 Remove the air cleaner as described in Section 2.

2 Disconnect the electrical lead to the automatic choke.

3 Unscrew and remove the three screws which hold the automatic choke housing cover in position (see illustration). Withdraw the cover and bi-metal coil, followed by the internal heat shield.

4 The choke plate vacuum pull-down should now be adjusted. To do this, fit a rubber band to the choke plate lever, open the throttle to allow the choke plates to close and then secure the band to keep the plates closed (see illustration).

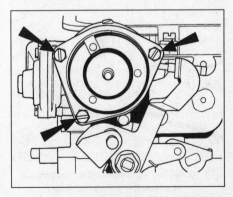

14.3 Weber 2V carburettor automatic choke housing cover screw locations - XR3 models

4A

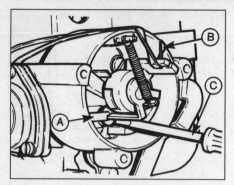

14.4 Weber 2V carburettor vacuum pull-down check - XR3 models

A *Diaphragm connecting push-rod*
B *Rubber band holding choke plates closed*
C *Screwdriver*

5 Using a screwdriver, push the diaphragm open to its stop and measure the clearance between the lower edge of the primary choke plate and the air horn using a twist drill or other gauge rod. Where the clearance is outside that specified, remove the plug from the diaphragm housing and turn the screw, now exposed, in or out as necessary (**see illustration**).

6 Refit the plug and remove the rubber band.

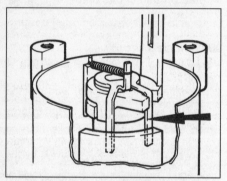

14.9 Weber 2V carburettor choke phasing adjustment - XR3 models

Bend tag (arrowed) to achieve specified clearance

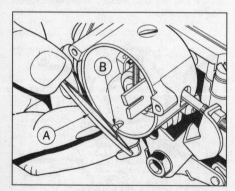

14.10 Weber 2V carburettor heat shield reassembly - XR3 models

A *Heat shield*
B *Locating peg engaged with housing notch*

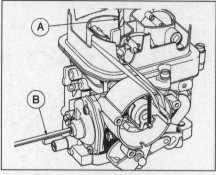

14.5 Weber 2V carburettor vacuum pull-down adjustment - XR3 models

A *Twist drill*
B *Adjusting the pull-down setting*

7 The choke phasing must now be checked and adjusted. Hold the throttle partially open and set the fast idle cam so that the fast idle screw is located on the centre step of the cam. Release the throttle so that the cam is held in this position (**see illustration**).

8 Push the choke plates downward until the step on the cam jams against the fast idle screw. Now measure the clearance between the lower edge of the primary choke plate and the air horn using a twist drill or gauge rod of suitable diameter.

9 Where necessary, bend the tag to adjust the clearance (**see illustration**).

10 Refit the heat shield, making sure that the locating peg is correctly engaged in the notch in the housing (**see illustration**).

11 Offer up the cover and engage the bi-metal coil with the slot in the choke lever which projects through the cut-out in the heat shield.

12 Screw in the retaining screws finger tight and then rotate the cover to set the cover mark opposite the centre index line (**see illustration**).

13 Reconnect the lead to the choke.

14 Refit the air cleaner.

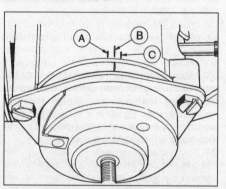

14.12 Weber 2V carburettor choke housing alignment marks - XR3 models

A *Rich position*
B *Index mark*
C *Weak position*

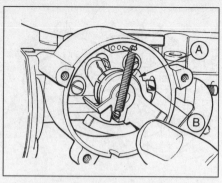

14.7 Weber 2V carburettor choke phasing check - XR3 models

A *Fast idle cam*
B *Fast idle adjustment screw positioned on centre step of cam*

1.6 litre models - 1986 onwards

15 Remove the air cleaner (Section 2).

16 Release any pressure in the cooling system by loosening the pressure cap (see Chapter 1), then detach the water inlet and outlet hoses at the automatic choke unit. Clamp the hoses or position them with their ends facing upwards to minimise coolant leakage.

17 Undo the three screws and detach the choke bi-metal coil housing followed by the internal heat shield.

18 Fit a rubber band to the choke plate lever, open the throttle to allow the choke plate to close, and then secure the band to keep the plate closed (**see illustration**).

19 Using a screwdriver, push the diaphragm open to its stop and measure the clearance between the lower edge of the choke plate and the air horn using a twist drill or other gauge rod. Where the clearance is outside that specified, remove the plug from the diaphragm housing and turn the screw, now exposed, in or out as necessary.

20 Fit a new diaphragm housing plug and remove the rubber band.

21 Refit the heat shield, making sure that the locating peg is correctly engaged in the notch in the housing.

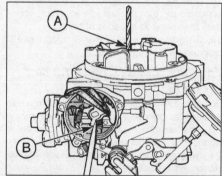

14.18 Weber 2V carburettor vacuum pull-down adjustment - 1.6 litre models

A *Twist drill*
B *Diaphragm pushed fully open with rubber band holding choke plate closed*

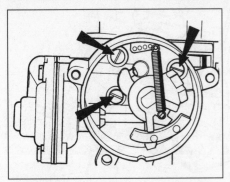

15.5 Weber 2V carburettor choke housing retaining screw locations - XR3 models

22 Place the bi-metal coil housing in position with the coil engaged with the slot in the choke lever which projects through the cut-out in the heat shield.
23 Screw in the retaining screws finger tight and then rotate the housing to set the mark opposite the dot punch mark on the choke body. Secure the housing.
24 Reconnect the hoses and refit the air cleaner.
25 Check and if necessary top-up the cooling system as described in Chapter 1.

15 Weber 2V carburettor automatic choke unit - removal, checking and refitting

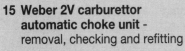

XR3 models

Removal

1 Remove the air cleaner (Section 2).
2 Disconnect the electrical lead to the automatic choke.
3 Undo the three choke housing cover retaining screws, withdraw the cover and bi-metal coil, followed by the internal heat shield.
4 Undo the six carburettor upper body retaining screws, hold the fast idle operating lever clear of the choke housing and lift off the upper body.
5 Undo the three screws securing the choke housing to the upper body, disconnect the link rod and remove the choke housing (see illustration).
6 Undo the three screws and remove the vacuum pull-down housing cover, then withdraw the spring, diaphragm and operating rod assembly (see illustration).
7 Extract the circlip on the end of the vacuum pull-down operating rod and slide off the rod components.
8 Make a note of the exact position of the choke mechanism return and tension springs then undo the shaft nut, withdraw the shaft from the choke housing and remove the linkages and cams.

Checking

9 Clean and inspect all the parts for wear, damage, cracking, or distortion. Pay particular attention to the condition of the pull-down diaphragm and the choke housing O-ring seal. Renew any parts as necessary.

Refitting

10 Reassemble the choke mechanism shaft, linkages, cams and tension springs with reference to illustration 15.6 and the notes made during removal. Secure the shaft with the retaining nut.
11 Assemble the components to the vacuum pull-down operating rod and secure with the circlip.
12 Locate the vacuum pull-down diaphragm and operating rod to the choke housing and with the diaphragm laying flat on the housing face refit the cover and secure with the three screws.
13 Place the O-ring seal on the choke housing, then connect the housing to the link rod.
14 Position the housing on the carburettor upper body and secure with the three screws.
15 Refit the upper body to the carburettor.
16 Before refitting the housing cover and bi-metal coil, refer to Section 14 and adjust the vacuum pull-down and choke phasing, then fit the cover and bi-metal coil as described.

1.6 litre models - 1986 onwards

Removal

17 Remove the air cleaner as described in Section 2.
18 Release any pressure in the cooling system by loosening the filler cap, then detach the water inlet and outlet hoses at the automatic choke unit. Clamp the hoses or position them with their ends facing upwards to minimise coolant leakage.
19 Disconnect the lead at the anti-run-on valve solenoid.
20 Disconnect the fuel supply and return hoses at the carburettor. If crimped type hose clips are used, cut them off and use screw type clips at reassembly.
21 Undo the six carburettor upper body retaining screws and remove the upper body. Note that four of the screws are of the Torx type and a suitable key or socket bit will be needed for removal.
22 With the upper body removed, undo the three screws and remove the choke bi-metal coil housing followed by the internal heat shield.

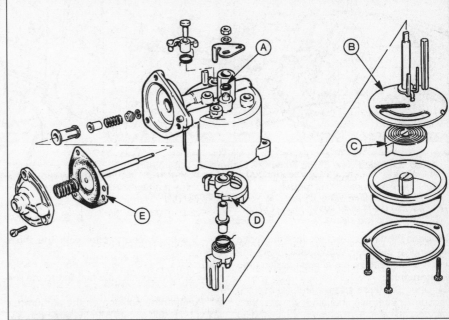

15.6 Exploded view of the Weber 2V carburettor automatic choke unit - XR3 models

A Housing O-ring   C Bi-metal coil   E Pull-down diaphragm
B Heat shield   D Fast idle cam

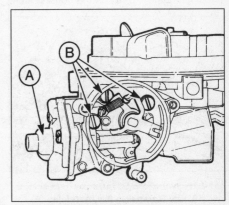

15.23 Weber 2V carburettor pull-down housing cover (A) and choke housing retaining screws (B) - 1.6 litre models

4A

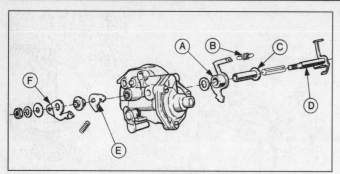

15.25 Exploded view of the Weber 2V carburettor automatic choke unit - 1.6 litre models

A Upper choke operating link
B Fast idle cam return spring
C Connecting rod sleeve
D Connecting rod and lever
E Pull-down link
F Actuating lever

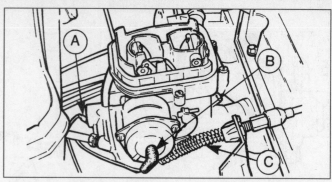

16.3 Weber 2V carburettor disconnection points - XR3 models

A Anti-run-on valve lead
B Electric choke lead
C Throttle cable

23 Undo the three screws securing the choke housing to the upper body, disconnect the link rod and remove the choke housing **(see illustration)**.

24 Undo the three screws and remove the vacuum pull-down housing cover, then withdraw the spring, diaphragm and operating rod assembly.

25 Make a note of the exact position of the choke mechanism return and tension springs, then undo the nut and remove the connecting rod, levers and link from the choke housing **(see illustration)**.

Checking

26 Clean and inspect all the parts for wear, damage, cracking or distortion. Pay particular attention to the condition of the pull-down diaphragm and the choke housing O-ring seal. Renew any parts as necessary.

Refitting

27 Reassemble the choke mechanism connecting rod, levers, link and springs with reference to illustration 15.25 and the notes made during removal. Secure the assembly with the retaining nut.

28 Locate the vacuum pull-down diaphragm and operating rod in the choke housing. With the diaphragm lying flat on the housing face,

refit the cover and secure with the three screws.

29 Locate the O-ring seal on the choke housing, then connect the housing to the link rod.

30 Position the housing on the carburettor upper body and secure with the three screws.

31 Refit the upper body to the carburettor.

32 Before refitting the bi-metal coil housing refer to Section 14 and adjust the vacuum pull-down, then fit the coil housing as described.

16 Weber 2V carburettor - removal and refitting

Note: *Refer to the warning at the end of Section 1 before proceeding.*

XR3 models

Removal

1 Disconnect the battery negative lead.

2 Remove the air cleaner as described in Section 2.

3 Disconnect the electrical leads at the electric choke and anti-run-on valve **(see illustration)**.

4 Disconnect the vacuum pipe at the carburettor outlet.

5 Disconnect the throttle cable by releasing the spring clip securing the end fitting to the ball-stud, and unscrew the cable bracket fixing bolts.

6 Disconnect the fuel inlet and return hoses, noting their respective positions, and plug them after removal. If crimped type clips are used, cut them off and use screw type clips when refitting.

7 Undo the four mounting flange nuts and washers and withdraw the carburettor from the inlet manifold.

Refitting

8 Refitting is the reverse sequence to removal, but use a new flange gasket and ensure that the mating surfaces are perfectly clean. Make sure that the vacuum pipe fuel trap is correctly positioned, and on completion check the idle speed and mixture settings as described in Chapter 1.

1.4 litre models

9 The procedure is identical to that just described for XR3 models except that a manual choke is fitted and the choke inner cable must be released by slackening the linkage clamp bolt.

10 Additionally when refitting, observe the following points.

a) *Adjust the choke cable as described in Section 9.*

b) *Where applicable, the lead for the anti-run-on valve should be removed from the metal clip which secures it to the carburettor body, re-routed as shown, and taped to the vacuum hose **(see illustrations)**. The metal clip should be discarded, and the securing screw refitted to the carburettor body, ensuring it is fully tightened.*

1.6 litre models - 1986 onwards

Removal

11 Disconnect the battery negative lead.

12 Remove the air cleaner as described in Section 2.

13 If the engine is still hot, depressurise the cooling system by carefully releasing the pressure cap (see Chapter 1).

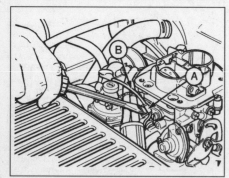

16.10a Removing the metal clip (A) securing the anti-run-on valve lead (B) - 1.4 litre models

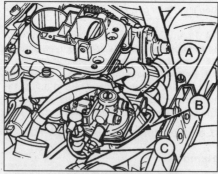

16.10b Correct routing of the anti-run-on valve lead - 1.4 litre models

A Anti-run-on valve
B Lead
C Lead taped to vacuum hose

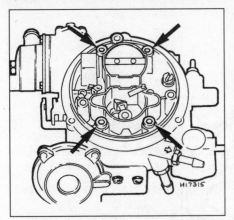

16.19 Weber 2V carburettor mounting through-bolt locations - 1.6 litre models

14 Disconnect the coolant inlet and outlet hoses at the automatic choke and clamp or plug their ends to prevent coolant loss.

15 Disconnect the throttle cable by releasing the spring clip securing the end fitting to the ball-stud, then unscrewing the cable bracket fixing bolts.

16 Disconnect the fuel inlet and return hoses, noting their respective positions, and plug them after removal. If crimped type clips are used, cut them off and use screw type clips when refitting.

17 Disconnect the distributor vacuum pipe and the throttle kicker vacuum pipe on automatic transmission models.

18 Disconnect the electrical lead at the anti-run-on valve solenoid.

19 Using a suitable Torx type key or socket bit, unscrew the four mounting through-bolts from the top of the carburettor and remove the unit from the manifold **(see illustration)**.

Refitting

20 Refitting is the reverse sequence to removal, but use a new flange gasket and ensure that the mating faces are perfectly clean. On completion top-up the cooling system as described in "*Weekly checks*" and check the idle speed and mixture settings as described in Chapter 1.

16.27 Lifting off the carburettor - 1.1 and 1.3 litre HCS engines

16.25 Anti-run-on valve solenoid (arrowed) - 1.1 and 1.3 litre HCS engines

1.1 and 1.3 litre HCS engine models

Removal

21 Disconnect the battery negative terminal.

22 Remove the air cleaner as described earlier.

23 Disconnect the throttle and choke cables as described in the relevant Sections.

24 Disconnect the fuel inlet hose. If crimped connections are used cut them off and renew them with screw type clips.

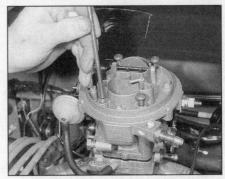

16.26 Removing a Torx through-bolt - 1.1 and 1.3 litre HCS engines

25 Disconnect the lead at the anti-run-on valve solenoid **(see illustration)**.

26 Remove the four Torx type through-bolts securing the carburettor to the inlet manifold **(see illustration)**.

27 Lift off the carburettor **(see illustration)**.

Refitting

28 Refit in reverse order using a new flange gasket.

29 On completion check the idle speed and mixture settings as described earlier.

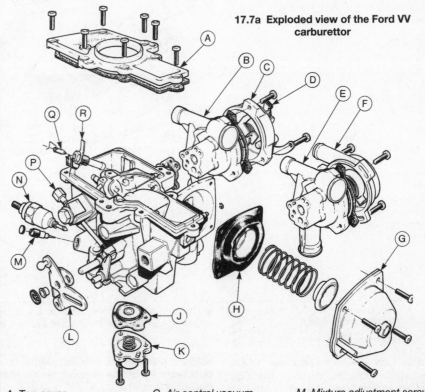

17.7a Exploded view of the Ford VV carburettor

A Top cover
B Manual choke unit
C Lever housing
D Choke cable bracket
E Automatic choke unit
F Bi-metal housing
G Air control vacuum diaphragm housing
H Air control diaphragm
J Accelerator pump diaphragm
K Accelerator pump cover
L Throttle linkage
M Mixture adjustment screw
N Anti-run-on valve solenoid
P Idle speed adjustment screw
Q Fuel needle valve
R Float bracket

4A

17.7b Exploded view of Weber 2V DFT carburettor - XR3 models

1 Choke housing cover
2 Vacuum pull-down assembly
3 Upper body
4 Fuel filter
5 Accelerator pump discharge tube
6 Anti-run-on valve solenoid
7 Mixture adjustment screw
8 Accelerator pump assembly
9 Power valve assembly
10 Throttle valve plates
11 Secondary throttle spindle
12 Fast idle adjustment screw
13 Fuel return connection
14 Fuel inlet needle valve
15 Needle valve housing
16 O-ring
17 Idle jets
18 Combined emulsion tube, air
     correction and main jets
19 Idle speed adjustment screw
20 Float

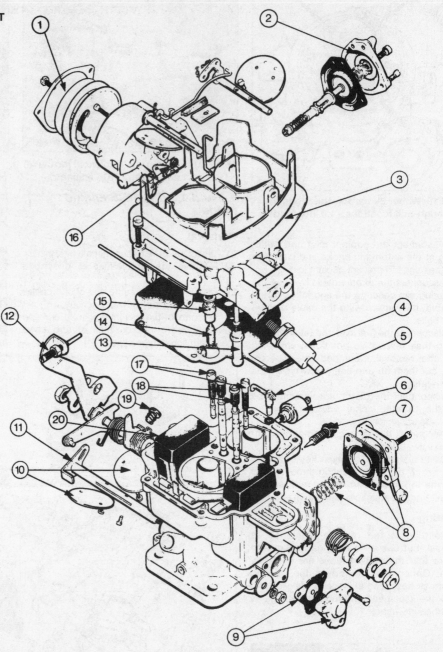

17 Carburettor overhaul - general information

Faults with the carburettor are usually associated with dirt entering the float chamber and blocking the jets, causing a weak mixture or power failure within a certain engine speed range. If this is the case, then a thorough clean will normally cure the problem.

If a carburettor fault is suspected, always check first (where possible) that the ignition timing is correct, and that the spark plugs are in good condition and correctly gapped. Also

check that the throttle cable is correctly adjusted, and that the air cleaner element is clean.

If careful checking of all the preceding points produces no improvement, the carburettor should be removed for cleaning and possible overhaul.

Complete overhaul of a carburettor is seldom required. It will usually be found sufficient to use a suitable carburettor cleaning agent to remove any fuel deposits and/or dirt. Follow the instructions supplied with the cleaning agent - most products can be used without removing the carburettor from the vehicle.

Blocked jets or internal passages can be cleaned using an air line.

If the carburettor is worn or damaged, it should either be renewed or overhauled by a specialist, who will be able to restore the carburettor to its original calibration.

Carburettor overhaul kits are available from a Ford dealer, but it is worth checking on the cost of a reconditioned or new unit before contemplating overhaul. Exploded views of the carburettors are provided as a guide for those wishing to carry out overhaul **(see illustrations)**.

17.7c Exploded view of Weber 2V DFTM carburettor - 1.4 litre models

4A

A	Manual choke assembly	F	Mixture adjustment screw	L	Primary emulsion tube
B	Vacuum pull-down unit	G	Accelerator pump assembly	M	Primary idle jet
C	Secondary idle jet	H	Throttle kicker	N	Needle valve
D	Secondary venturi vacuum unit	J	Power valve diaphragm	P	Fuel inlet filter
E	Idle speed adjustment screw	K	Float	Q	Secondary emulsion tube

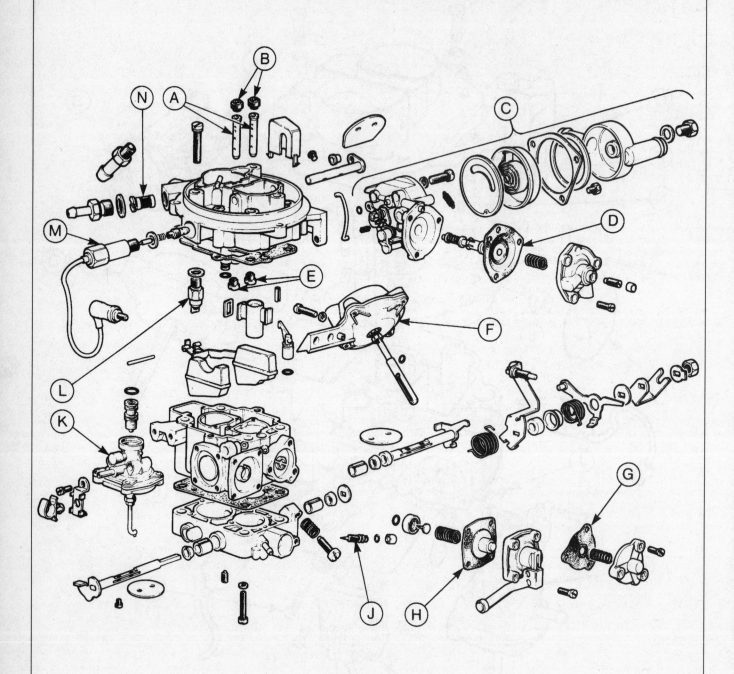

17.7d Exploded view of Weber 2V TLD carburettor - 1.6 litre models

A Emulsion tubes
B Air correction jets
C Automatic choke assembly
D Vacuum pull-down diaphragm
E Main jets

F Secondary venturi vacuum unit
G Power valve diaphragm
H Accelerator pump diaphragm
J Mixture adjustment screw

K Throttle kicker (automatic transmission
   models)
L Needle valve
M Anti-run-on valve solenoid
N Fuel inlet filter

Chapter 4 Part B:
Bosch K-Jetronic and KE-Jetronic mechanical fuel injection systems

Contents

Degrees of difficulty

Easy, suitable for novice with little experience	Fairly easy, suitable for beginner with some experience	Fairly difficult, suitable for competent DIY mechanic	Difficult, suitable for experienced DIY mechanic	Very difficult, suitable for expert DIY or professional

4B

Specifications

General

System type . . . .   Bosch mechanical continuous injection system
Application:
   XR3i and XR3i Cabriolet models up to 1990 . . . .   Bosch K-Jetronic
   RS Turbo models . . . .   Bosch KE-Jetronic

K-Jetronic system specification

Fuel pump type . . . .   12 volt electric roller cell type
Fuel pump delivery quantity (minimum) . . . .   0.7 litre (1.32 pints) in 30 seconds
Idle speed (cooling fan on) . . . .   750 to 850 rpm
Idle mixture CO content . . . .   1.0 to 1.5%
Main system pressure . . . .   4.7 to 5.5 bar (68 to 80 lbf/in^2)
Control pressure (warm engine) . . . .   3.4 to 3.8 bar (39 to 45 lbf/in^2)
Injector valve opening pressure . . . .   3.2 to 4.0 bar (46.4 to 51.5 lbf/in^2)

KE-Jetronic system specification

Fuel pump type . . . .   12 volt electric roller cell type
Fuel pump delivery quantity (minimum):
   1985 models . . . .   1.1 litres (1.9 pints) in 60 seconds
   1986 models onwards . . . .   2.5 litres (4.4 pints) in 60 seconds
Idle speed (cooling fan on):
   1985 models . . . .   800 to 900 rpm
   1986 models onwards . . . .   920 to 960 rpm
Idle mixture CO content:
   1985 models . . . .   0.25 to 0.75%
   1986 models onwards . . . .   0.5 to 1.1%
Main system pressure . . . .   5.6 to 6.0 bar (82 to 87 lbf/in^2)
Injector valve opening pressure . . . .   3.0 to 4.1 bar (43.5 to 59.5 lbf/in^2)

Turbocharger

Type	Garrett AiResearch T3
Maximum boost pressure	0.45 to 0.55 bar (6.5 to 7.9 lbf/in^2)
Solenoid control valve operating range	2500 to 6000 rpm (approximately)

Fuel requirement

Fuel octane rating	97 RON (four-star)

Torque wrench settings

	Nm	lbf ft
K-Jetronic system		
Air cleaner retaining bolts	4 to 5	3 to 4
Fuel distributor-to-sensor plate screws	32 to 38	24 to 28
Sensor plate-to-air cleaner screws	8 to 11	6 to 8
Warm-up regulator bolts	3 to 5	2 to 4
Cold start valve bolts	3 to 5	2 to 4
Auxiliary air device bolts	3 to 5	2 to 4
Inlet manifold nuts	16 to 20	12 to 15
Throttle housing nuts	8 to 11	6 to 8
Exhaust manifold nuts	14 to 17	10 to 13
Exhaust downpipe to manifold	35 to 40	25 to 29
Banjo union bolts:		
Fuel distributor inlet and return	16 to 20	11 to 15
Fuel distributor injector pipes	5 to 8	4 to 6
Fuel distributor cold start valve feed pipe	5 to 8	4 to 6
Fuel distributor warm-up regulator feed and return pipes	5 to 8	4 to 6
Warm-up regulator inlet (M10)	11 to 15	8 to 11
Warm-up regulator outlet (M8)	5 to 8	4 to 6
Fuel pump, filter and accumulator	16 to 20	11 to 15
KE-Jetronic system		
Air cleaner bolts	8 to 11	6 to 8
Fuel distributor-to-sensor plate screws	32 to 38	24 to 28
Cold start valve bolts	8 to 11	6 to 8
Auxiliary air device bolts	8 to 11	6 to 8
Inlet manifold nuts	16 to 20	11 to 15
Throttle housing nuts	8 to 11	6 to 8
Thermo-time switch	20 to 25	15 to 18
Charge air temperature sensor	20 to 25	15 to 18
Air inlet duct to rocker cover	14 to 18	10 to 13
Cold start valve fuel supply pipe	5 to 8	4 to 6
Auxiliary air valve vacuum connection	4	3
Fuel pressure regulator unions	14 to 20	10 to 15
Fuel distributor unions	11 to 15	8 to 11
Fuel pump, filter and accumulator unions	16 to 20	11 to 15
Fuel injector pipe unions	10 to 12	7 to 9
Exhaust manifold to cylinder head	14 to 17	10 to 13
Turbocharger to exhaust manifold	21 to 26	15 to 19
Exhaust downpipe to turbocharger	35 to 40	25 to 29

1 General information and precautions

General information

The fuel system comprises a centrally mounted fuel tank, electrically-operated fuel pump and Bosch K-Jetronic or KE-Jetronic continuous injection system according to model. The system is used in conjunction with a turbocharger on RS Turbo models.

A more detailed description of the various system components is given in the following paragraphs.

Bosch K-Jetronic system

The Bosch K-Jetronic fuel-injection system is of the continuous injection type and supplies a precisely controlled quantity of atomised fuel to each cylinder under all operating conditions.

This system, when compared with conventional carburettor arrangements, achieves a more accurate control of the air/fuel mixture resulting in reduced emission levels and improved performance.

The main components of the fuel injection system are as follows (see illustration).

a) Fuel tank
b) Fuel pump
c) Fuel accumulator
d) Fuel filter
e) Fuel distributor/mixture control assembly
f) Throttle valve (plate)
g) Injector valves
h) Air box (plenum chamber)
l) Warm-up regulator
j) Auxiliary air device
k) Cold start valve
l) Thermo-time switch
m) Safety module
n) Fuel shut-off valve
o) Speed sensor module

The fuel pump is of electrically-operated, roller cell type.

1.5 K-Jetronic system main component locations

A *Warm-up regulator*
B *Speed sensing module*
C *Fuel accumulator (early model location)*
D *Fuel pump*
E *Throttle housing*
F *Cold start valve*
G *Fuel distributor*
H *Fuel filter*

4B

The fuel accumulator has two functions, (i) to dampen the pulsation of the fuel flow, generated by the pump and (ii) to maintain fuel pressure after the engine has been switched off. This prevents a vapour lock developing with consequent hot starting problems.

The fuel filter incorporates two paper filter elements to ensure that the fuel reaching the injection system components is completely free from dirt.

The fuel distributor/mixture control assembly. The fuel distributor controls the quantity of fuel being delivered to the engine, ensuring that each cylinder receives the same amount. The mixture control assembly incorporates an air sensor plate and control plunger. The air sensor plate is located in the main airstream between the air cleaner and the throttle butterfly. During idling, the airflow lifts the sensor plate which in turn raises a control plunger which allows fuel to flow past the plunger and out of the metering slits to the injector valves. Increases in engine speed cause increased airflow which raises the control plunger and so admits more fuel.

The throttle valve assembly is mounted in the main air inlet between the mixture control assembly and the air box.

The injector valves are located in the inlet manifold.

The air box is mounted on the top of the engine and functions as an auxiliary inlet manifold directing air from the sensor plate to each individual cylinder.

The warm-up regulator is located on the inlet manifold and incorporates two coil springs, a bi-metal strip and a control pressure valve. The regulator controls the fuel supplied to the control circuit which provides pressure variations to the fuel distributor control plunger. When the coil springs are pushing against the control pressure valve there is a high control pressure and this gives a weak mixture. The coil spring pressure application is controlled by the bi-metal strip which in turn is activated in accordance with engine temperature and an electrical heat coil.

The auxiliary air device is located on the inlet manifold. It consists of a pivoted plate, bi-metal strip and heater coil. The purpose of this device is to supply an increased volume of fuel/air mixture during cold idling.

The start valve system consists of an electrical injector and a **thermo-time switch**. Its purpose is to spray fuel into the air box to assist cold starting, the thermo-time switch regulating the amount of fuel injected.

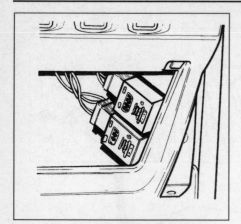

1.16 K-Jetronic system speed sensing module and fuel pump safety module locations

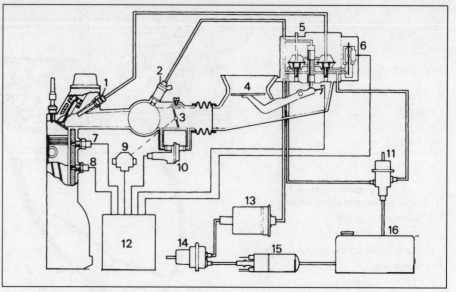

1.19 KE-Jetronic fuel-injection system layout and components

1 Injector	9 Throttle position switch
2 Cold start valve	10 Auxiliary air device
3 Throttle plate	11 Pressure regulator
4 Sensor plate	12 Control module
5 Fuel distributor	13 Fuel filter
6 Electro-magnetic pressure actuator	14 Fuel accumulator
7 Thermo-time switch	15 Fuel pump
8 Temperature sensor	16 Fuel tank

The **safety module** is located under the facia panel on the driver's side and is coloured purple **(see illustration)**. Its purpose is to shut off the power supply to the fuel pump should the engine stall or the vehicle be involved in an accident. The module senses ignition pulses, and cuts the fuel supply if the ignition pulses stop.

The **fuel shut-off valve** system is an economy device whereby air is drawn from within the air cleaner unit through the shut-off valve and directed into the ducting chamber above the air sensor plate causing a depression. This then causes the sensor plate to drop which, in turn, shuts off the fuel supply. The valve is operated by signals from a coolant temperature sensor and a throttle position sensor. The shut-off valve will only operate under the following circumstances:

a) When the engine coolant temperature is at or above 35°C (95°F)

b) When the throttle is closed and with the engine speed decelerating from speeds above 1600 rpm

The engine speed is sensed by a speed sensing module which is coloured black and located beneath the facia panel on the driver's side.

Bosch KE-Jetronic system

The Bosch KE-Jetronic fuel-injection system is fitted to Escort RS Turbo models and is a further development of the K-Jetronic system.

Apart from minor alterations the basic principles of the hydraulics and mechanics used on the K-Jetronic system are unchanged on the KE-Jetronic system. The main difference between the two types is that on the KE-Jetronic system all mixture corrections are controlled electronically by an electromagnetic pressure actuator incorporated in the fuel distributor. The pressure actuator is directly controlled by a variable electric current delivered by the fuel-injection control module.

This module receiver inputs from the various engine sensors concerning engine temperature, engine load, throttle shift, throttle position and starter actuation. This information modifies a program stored in the module memory so that the electromagnetic pressure actuator, on receiving the signal from the module, can alter the mixture to suit all engine operating conditions. This renders the control pressure circuit and warm-up regulator of the K-Jetronic system unnecessary, and also undertakes the functions of the fuel shut-off valve, safety module and speed sensing module **(see illustration)**.

Precautions

Due to the complexity of the fuel-injection system, and the need for special tools and test equipment, any work should be limited to the operations described in this Chapter. Other adjustments and system checks are beyond the scope of most readers and should be left to a Ford dealer.

Before disconnecting any fuel lines, unions or components thoroughly clean the component or connection and the adjacent area.

Place any removed components on a clean surface and cover them with plastic sheet or paper. Do not use fluffy rags for cleaning.

The system operates under pressure at all times and care must be taken when disconnecting fuel lines. Relieve the system pressure as described in the relevant Section before disconnecting any fuel lines under pressure. Refer to the warning note at the end of this Section, and always work with the battery negative lead disconnected and in a well ventilated area.

When working on the KE-Jetronic system the following additional precautions must be observed:

a) Never start the engine when the battery is not firmly connected.

b) Never disconnect the battery when the engine is running.

c) If the battery is to be rapid charged from an external source it should be completely disconnected from the vehicle electrical system.

d) The KE-Jetronic control unit must be removed from the car if temperatures are likely to exceed 80°C (176°F) as would be experienced, for example, in a paint spray oven or if any electric welding is being carried out on the car.

e) The ignition must be switched off when removing the control unit.

⚠️ **Warning: Many of the procedures in this Chapter entail the removal of fuel pipes and connections which may result in some fuel spillage. Before carrying out any operation on the fuel system refer to the precautions given in Safety First! at the beginning of this manual and follow them implicitly. Petrol is a highly dangerous and volatile liquid and the precautions necessary when handling it cannot be overstressed**

2 Air cleaner - removal and refitting

K-Jetronic system

Removal

1 Remove the air cleaner element as described in Chapter 1.
2 Detach the fuel filter from the side of the cleaner casing (leave the fuel lines attached to the filter) and the air inlet hose from the front end of the case.
3 Unscrew and remove the casing retaining nuts from the inner wing panel and lift out the casing.

Refitting

4 Refitting is the reversal of the removal procedure. Refit the air cleaner element as described in Chapter 1.

KE-Jetronic system

Removal

5 Undo the two bolts securing the air cleaner assembly to the air sensor plate unit and remove the air cleaner assembly **(see illustration)**.

Refitting

6 Refit the unit to the air sensor plate and secure with the two bolts.

3 Fuel tank - removal and refitting

The procedures are the same as described in Part A of this Chapter for carburettor engines, but in addition disconnect the fuel tank-to-fuel pump hose from the rear face of the tank.

4 Throttle cable - adjustment, removal and refitting

Adjustment

The procedure is the same as described in Part A of this Chapter for carburettor engines, except that the cable adjuster is situated in a bracket alongside the throttle housing.

Removal and refitting

The procedure is the same as described in Part A of this Chapter for carburettor engines, except that it is not necessary to remove the air cleaner, and the location of the mounting bracket is alongside the throttle housing.

5 Accelerator pedal - removal and refitting

The procedure is the same as described in Part A of this Chapter for carburettor models.

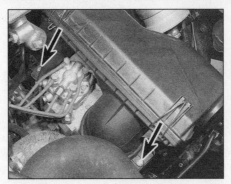

2.5 KE-Jetronic air cleaner retaining bolts (arrowed)

6 Fuel pump - removal and refitting

Note: *Refer to the precautions at the end of Section 1 before proceeding.*

Removal

1 The fuel pump is bolted to the underside of the car just to the rear of the fuel tank. For access raise and support the car securely at the rear.
2 Disconnect the battery earth lead.
3 On the K-Jetronic system relieve the system pressure by slowly loosening the fuel feed pipe union at the warm-up regulator **(see illustration)**. Absorb the fuel leakage in a cloth.
4 On the KE-Jetronic system relieve the system pressure by slowly loosening the cold start valve union on the top of the fuel distributor **(see illustration)**. Absorb fuel leakage in a cloth.
5 Clamp the fuel inlet hose midway between the tank and the pump using a brake hose clamp, self-locking grips or similar. If the fuel level in the tank is low you may prefer to drain the fuel from the tank into a suitable container once the inlet hose is disconnected.
6 Disconnect the fuel inlet and outlet pipes from the pump, catching fuel spillage in a suitable container **(see illustration)**. Once disconnected do not allow dirt to enter the

6.4 KE-Jetronic system cold start valve pipe union (arrowed) on fuel distributor

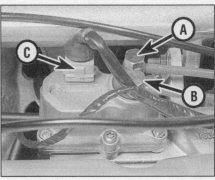

6.3 Warm-up regulator fuel feed pipe (A), outlet pipe (B) and wiring multi-plug (C)

pipes, temporarily plug or seal them if necessary.
7 Note the electrical connections to the pump and disconnect them.
8 Loosen the pump bracket retaining bolt and then withdraw the pump unit with rubber protector sleeve.

Refitting

9 Refitting of the fuel pump is a reversal of the removal procedure. Renew the feed pipe from the tank if it is damaged or defective.
10 Check that the rubber protector sleeve is correctly positioned round the pump before tightening the clamp nut.
11 On completion, tighten the warm-up regulator or cold start valve fuel unions, reconnect the battery earth lead, start the engine and check for any fuel leaks.

7 Fuel accumulator - removal and refitting

Note: *Refer to the precautions at the end of Section 1 before proceeding.*

Pre-1986 models

Removal

1 The fuel accumulator is mounted adjacent to the fuel pump, above the rear left-hand suspension arm.
2 Disconnect the battery negative lead.

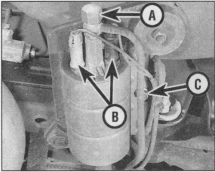

6.6 Fuel pump outlet pipe (A), electrical connections (B) and pump bracket retaining bolt (C)

4B

7.5 Fuel pipe connections (arrowed) at the underbody mounted fuel accumulator

7.12 Fuel inlet pipe (A) and outlet pipe (B) at the engine compartment mounted fuel accumulator

3 Raise the rear of the car and support it on axle-stands (see *"Jacking and Vehicle Support"*).

4 Relieve the system pressure by slowly loosening the fuel feed pipe at the warm-up regulator. Absorb fuel leakage in a cloth.

5 Disconnect the fuel pipes from the fuel accumulator and catch the small quantity of fuel which will be released **(see illustration)**.

6 Remove the clamp screw and remove the accumulator.

Refitting

7 Refitting is a reversal of removal. Check for leaks on completion (with the engine restarted).

1986 models onwards

Removal

8 On later models with K-Jetronic and KE-Jetronic systems the fuel accumulator is located in the engine compartment behind the fuel distributor.

9 Disconnect the battery negative lead.

10 For access remove the air cleaner as described in Section 2.

11 Relieve the system pressure by slowly loosening the cold start valve union on the top of the fuel distributor **(see illustration 6.4)**. Absorb fuel leakage in a cloth.

12 Disconnect the fuel pipes from the

accumulator and catch the small quantity of fuel which will be released **(see illustration)**.

13 Remove the clamp screw and remove the accumulator.

Refitting

14 Refitting is a reversal of removal. Check for leaks on completion (with the engine restarted).

8 Fuel injectors and injector delivery pipes - removal and refitting

Note: *Refer to the precautions at the end of Section 1 before proceeding. It is important to note that each injection supply pipe connection in the distributor head has a screw adjacent to it. These four screws are not for adjustment and must not be removed or have their settings altered. New O-ring seals must be used on refitting.*

Removal

1 Disconnect the battery earth lead.

2 Detach the four supply pipes from the injectors, and use a rag to collect any spilled fuel.

3 Unscrew and remove the respective injector retaining bracket bolts, then withdraw the injectors and their O-ring seals **(see illustration)**.

4 The injector fuel delivery pipes can be removed by unscrewing and removing the four banjo bolts at the distributor head. Note the respective pipe connections as they are detached and remove the pipes complete with the plastic hoses and the injector harness. **Do not** separate the pipes or hoses from the injector harness.

5 Before reassembling the fuel delivery pipes, or the injectors, clean all pipe connections thoroughly and use new O-ring seals on the injectors. Use new seal washers on the banjo connections fitting two washers (one each side) per union. Do not overtighten the banjo bolts, or the washers may fracture.

Refitting

6 Refitting of the injectors and the fuel delivery pipes is otherwise a reversal of the removal procedure. On completion check that the pipes and hoses are not distorted and when the engine is restarted check for any signs of leaks.

9 Cold start valve - removal and refitting

Note: *Refer to the precautions at the end of Section 1 before proceeding.*

K-Jetronic system

Removal

1 Disconnect the battery earth lead.

2 Detach the electrical wiring multi-plug from the valve **(see illustration)**.

3 Slowly unscrew and remove the fuel supply pipe banjo bolt. Take care on removal, as the system will be under pressure. Soak up fuel spillage with a cloth.

4 Unscrew and remove the two socket-head mounting bolts using an Allen key or Torx type key or socket bit on later models, and remove the valve.

Refitting

5 Refitting is a reversal of the removal procedure. Do not overtighten the banjo bolt or the washers may fracture (use a new one each side of the union).

6 On completion restart the engine and check for signs of fuel leakage.

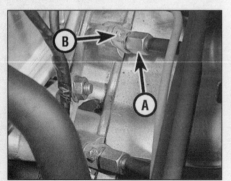

8.3 Injector fuel pipe union (A) and retaining bracket bolt (B)

9.2 Disconnecting the cold start valve wiring multi-plug

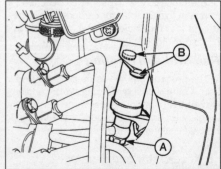

9.8 KE-Jetronic system cold start valve location

A Fuel pipe union   *B Retaining bolts*

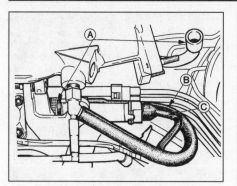

10.2 K-Jetronic system auxiliary air device connections
- A Throttle housing hose
- B Cold start valve hose
- C Wiring multi-plug

KE-Jetronic system

Removal

7 Disconnect the battery earth lead.
8 Disconnect the wiring multi-plug from the valve which is located underneath the throttle housing **(see illustration)**.
9 Slowly unscrew and remove the fuel supply pipe banjo union. Take care on removal, as the system will be under pressure. Soak up fuel spillage with a cloth.
10 Unscrew and remove the two Torx type mounting bolts using a Torx key or socket bit. Remove the valve from under the throttle housing.

Refitting

11 Refitting is a reversal of removal. Do not overtighten the banjo bolt or the washers may fracture (use a new one each side of the union).
12 On completion restart the engine and check for leaks.

10 Auxiliary air device - removal and refitting

K-Jetronic system

Removal

1 Disconnect the battery earth lead.
2 Disconnect the wiring multi-plug and the two air hoses from the device which is located beneath the cold start valve **(see illustration)**.
3 Undo the two Torx type retaining bolts using a Torx key or socket bit and lift the unit away **(see illustration)**.

Refitting

4 Refitting is a reversal of removal.

KE-Jetronic system

Removal

5 Apply the handbrake, jack up the front of the car and support it on axle stands (see "Jacking and Vehicle Support").

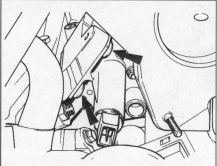

10.3 K-Jetronic system auxiliary air device retaining bolt locations

6 Disconnect the battery negative lead.
7 Disconnect the auxiliary air device wiring multi-plug and the two air hoses.
8 Undo the two Torx type retaining bolts using a Torx key or socket bit and remove the unit from under the inlet manifold **(see illustration)**.

Refitting

9 Refitting is a reversal of removal.

11 Fuel distributor - removal and refitting

Note: *Refer to the precautions at the end of Section 1 before proceeding. It is important to note that each injection supply pipe connection in the distributor head has a screw adjacent to it. These four screws are not for adjustment and must not be removed or have their settings altered. A new O-ring and new banjo union sealing washers will be required on refitting.*

K-Jetronic system

Removal

1 Disconnect the battery negative lead.
2 Relieve the system pressure by slowly loosening the fuel feed pipe union at the

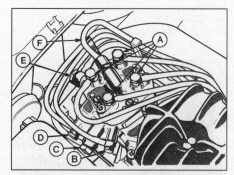

11.3 K-Jetronic fuel distributor pipe connections

- A To injectors
- B To cold start valve
- C Fuel return
- D From warm-up regulator
- E Fuel inlet
- F To warm-up regulator

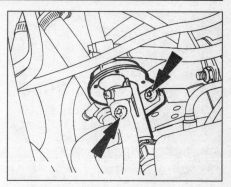

10.8 KE-Jetronic system auxiliary air device retaining bolts

warm-up regulator **(see illustration 6.3)**. Absorb the fuel leakage in a cloth.
3 Disconnect the four injector feed pipes, the fuel inlet and return pipes, and the warm-up regulator feed and return pipe banjo unions at the fuel distributor **(see illustration)**. Note the sealing washers on each side of the banjo unions which must be renewed on reconnection of the pipes. Take care not to allow dirt to enter the pipes or their connection ports.
4 Unscrew the three retaining screws from the fuel distributor top face and remove the unit from the car **(see illustration)**. Recover the sealing O-ring.

Refitting

5 Refitting is a reversal of removal, but ensure perfectly clean mating faces and use a new sealing O-ring and new washers for the banjo unions. Check for any signs of leaks on completion and adjust the idle speed and mixture settings as described in Chapter 1.
6 The main system fuel pressure should be checked and if necessary adjusted by a Ford dealer to ensure satisfactory running of the system.

KE-Jetronic system

Removal

7 Disconnect the battery negative lead.
8 Relieve the system pressure by slowly loosening the cold start valve union on the top of the fuel distributor **(see illustration 6.4)**. Absorb fuel leakage in a cloth.

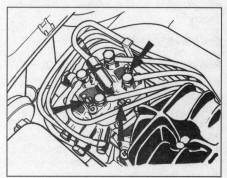

11.4 K-Jetronic system fuel distributor retaining screws (arrowed)

4B

11.11 KE-Jetronic fuel distributor retaining screws (arrowed)

12.9 Component attachments at the KE-Jetronic throttle housing

A Charge air temperature sensor multi-plug
B Throttle position sensor wiring multi-plug
C Throttle cable bracket
D Connecting hose retaining clip

12.11 Air inlet duct retaining bolts (arrowed)

9 Disconnect the four injector feed pipes, the cold start valve pipe and union adapter, the fuel inlet pipe and pressure regulator return pipe from the fuel distributor. Note the sealing washers on each side of the banjo unions which must be renewed on reconnection of the pipes. Take care not to allow dirt to enter the pipes or their connection parts.

10 Disconnect the wiring multi-plug from the pressure actuator on the side of the fuel distributor.

11 Undo the retaining screws and remove the fuel distributor **(see illustration)**. Recover the sealing O-ring.

Refitting

12 Refitting is a reversal of removal, but ensure perfectly clean mating faces and use a new sealing O-ring and new washers for the banjo unions. Check for any signs of leaks on completion and adjust the idle speed and mixture settings as described in Chapter 1.

12 Throttle housing - removal and refitting

Note: *During manufacture the throttle plate is adjusted so that it is fractionally open, to avoid the possibility of it jamming shut, and it* **must not** *be repositioned. Idle speed adjustment is provided for by means of a screw which, according to its setting, restricts the airflow through the air bypass channel in the throttle housing.*

K-Jetronic system

Removal

1 Disconnect the battery negative lead.
2 Slacken the retaining screw and detach the inlet air hose from the throttle housing.
3 Disconnect the accelerator cable at the housing linkage with reference to Section 4.
4 Disconnect the distributor vacuum hose and auxiliary air hose from the underside of the throttle housing.
5 Undo the four nuts and carefully withdraw the throttle housing from the manifold studs.

Refitting

6 Refitting is a reversal of removal, but ensure that the mating faces are perfectly clean. Renew the gaskets, one on each side of the insulator block, if necessary.
7 On completion adjust the idle speed as described in Chapter 1.

KE-Jetronic system

Removal

8 Disconnect the battery negative terminal.
9 Disconnect the charge air temperature sensor and throttle position sensor wiring multi-plugs **(see illustration)**.
10 Slacken the hose clip and detach the air inlet hose from the inlet duct.
11 Undo the two bolts securing the inlet duct to the rocker cover slacken the throttle housing connecting hose clip and remove the inlet duct **(see illustration)**.
12 Extract the retaining clip and disconnect the throttle cable end from the linkage ball-stud.
13 Undo the two bolts and remove the throttle cable bracket from the throttle housing.
14 Disconnect the auxiliary air hose, then undo the four nuts and remove the throttle housing.

13.1 KE-Jetronic fuel pressure regulator location (arrowed) behind fuel distributor

15 Do not remove the throttle position sensor from the throttle housing unless absolutely necessary. If it must be removed, mark its position for refitting and then have it accurately adjusted by a Ford dealer on completion. This will also be necessary if the sensor or throttle housing are renewed.

Refitting

16 Refitting is the reversal of removal, but use a new gasket and ensure clean mating faces. After refitting adjust the idle speed as described in Chapter 1.

13 Fuel pressure regulator - removal and refitting

Note: *Refer to the precautions at the end of Section 1 before proceeding.*

Removal

1 The fuel pressure regulator is only used on KE-Jetronic systems and is located behind the fuel distributor **(see illustration)**.
2 Disconnect the battery negative lead.
3 Relieve the system pressure by slowly loosening the cold start valve union on the top of the fuel distributor **(see illustration 6.4)**. Absorb fuel leakage in a cloth.
4 Place absorbent cloth beneath the regulator and undo the two fuel feed unions and the fuel return union. Note the pipe locations to ensure correct refitting.

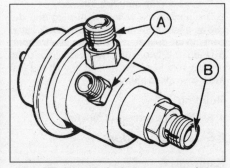

13.6 KE-Jetronic fuel pressure regulator pipe connections

A Fuel feed   *B Fuel return*

5 Remove the securing tie and withdraw the regulator from its bracket.

Refitting

6 Refitting is a reversal of removal. Ensure that all unions are correctly reconnected and secure, and on completion check for fuel leaks with the engine running **(see illustration)**.

14 Warm-up regulator - removal and refitting

Note: *Refer to the precautions at the end of Section 1 before proceeding. New banjo union sealing washers must be used on refitting.*

Removal

1 The warm-up regulator is only used on K-Jetronic systems and is situated on the inlet manifold just to the rear of the rocker cover.
2 Disconnect the battery negative lead.
3 Relieve the system pressure by slowly loosening the fuel feed pipe union at the warm-up regulator **(see illustration 6.3)**. Absorb the fuel leakage in a cloth.
4 After relieving the system pressure disconnect the fuel feed union completely, followed by the outlet union. Recover the sealing washers used on each side of the unions.
5 Disconnect the regulator wiring multi-plug.
6 Undo the two Torx type screws using a suitable Torx key or socket bit and remove the regulator from its location **(see illustration)**.

Refitting

7 Refitting is a reversal of removal, but use new sealing washers on each side of the banjo unions and apply a thread-locking compound to the Torx retaining bolts. On completion check for leaks with the engine running.

15 Electro-magnetic pressure actuator - removal and refitting

Note: *Refer to the precautions at the end of Section 1 before proceeding. New O-rings must be used on refitting.*

Removal

1 The electro-magnetic pressure actuator is only used on KE-Jetronic systems and is located on the side of the fuel distributor.
2 Disconnect the battery negative lead.
3 Remove the air cleaner as described in Section 2.
4 Relieve the system pressure by slowly loosening the cold start valve union on the top of the fuel distributor **(see illustration 6.4)**. Absorb fuel leakage in a cloth.
5 Disconnect the wiring multi-plug, then undo the two screws securing the actuator to the fuel distributor **(see illustration)**. Remove the unit and the sealing O-rings.

Refitting

6 Refitting is the reverse sequence to removal, but ensure both mating faces are clean. New O-rings must be used and care taken not to displace them when fitting. On completion check for fuel leaks with the engine running.

16 Fuel-injection control module - removal and refitting

Removal

1 The fuel-injection control module is only used on KE-Jetronic systems and is located in the engine compartment behind the heater plenum chamber and fan motor.
2 Disconnect the battery negative lead.
3 Remove the plenum chamber top cover rubber seal **(see illustration)**.
4 Release the five retaining clips and lift off the plenum chamber top cover **(see illustrations)**.
5 Undo the two nuts securing the heater fan motor assembly to the bulkhead. Lift the unit off the studs and place it on the engine, but avoid straining the wiring **(see illustrations)**.
6 Disconnect the module wiring multi-plug, then undo the three screws and remove the unit from its location **(see illustration)**.

Refitting

7 Refitting is the reversal of removal. Take care not to trap the motor wiring when refitting the fan motor assembly and ensure that it is engaged in the slot provided in the housing **(see illustration)**.

4B

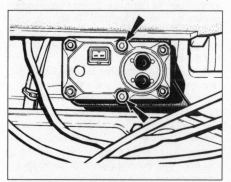

14.6 K-Jetronic system warm-up regulator retaining screws

15.5 Pressure actuator wiring multi-plug (arrowed)

16.3 Remove the plenum chamber rubber seal

16.4a Release the retaining clips . . .

16.4b . . . and lift off the plenum chamber top cover

16.5a Heater fan motor retaining nut

16.5b Removing the heater fan motor assembly . . .

16.6 . . . for access to the fuel-injection control module

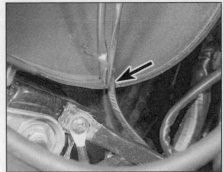

16.7 Fan motor wiring engaged in housing slot (arrowed)

17 Charge air temperature sensor - removal and refitting

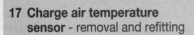

Removal

1 The charge air temperature sensor is only used on KE-Jetronic systems and is located in the air inlet duct (see illustration).
2 Disconnect the battery negative lead.
3 Disconnect the wiring multi-plug and unscrew the sensor from its location.

Refitting

4 Refitting is the reversal of removal.

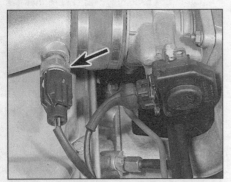

17.1 Charge air temperature sensor location (arrowed)

18 Thermo-time switch - removal and refitting

Removal

1 Disconnect the battery negative lead.
2 Drain the cooling system as described in Chapter 1.
3 Raise the front of the car and support it on axle stands (see *"Jacking and Vehicle Support"*).
4 Disconnect the wiring multi-plug from the thermo-time switch located on the inlet manifold intermediate flange and accessible from under the car (see illustration).
5 Unscrew the unit and remove it from its location.

Refitting

6 Refitting is a reversal of removal. Refill the cooling system as described in Chapter 1.

19 Idle speed compensator - removal and refitting

Removal

1 The idle speed compensator is only fitted to K-Jetronic systems from 1986 onwards and is located in the centre of the engine compartment bulkhead (see illustration).

2 Disconnect the battery negative lead.
3 Disconnect the electrical lead, undo the two screws and withdraw the unit. Detach the air hoses from each end and remove the compensator.

Refitting

4 Refitting is a reversal of removal. The air hoses can be connected to either end and the arrows on the unit can be ignored.

20 Turbocharger - general description

Escort RS Turbo models are equipped with an exhaust driven turbocharger, which is a device designed to increase the engine's power output without increasing exhaust emissions or adversely affecting fuel economy. It does so by utilising the heat energy present in the exhaust gases as they exit the engine.

Basically the turbocharger consists of two fans mounted on a common shaft. One fan is driven by the hot exhaust gases as they rush through the exhaust manifold and expand. The other draws in fresh air and compresses it before it enters the inlet manifold. By compressing the air, a larger charge can be let into each cylinder and greater power output is achieved.

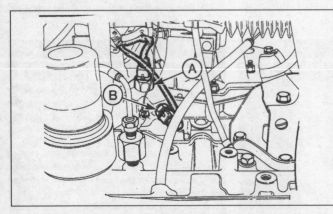

18.4 Thermo-time switch (A) and temperature sensor (B) on the KE-Jetronic system (viewed from under the car)

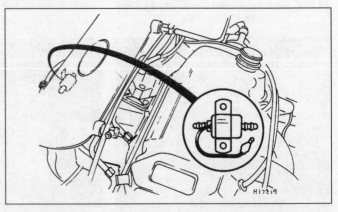

19.1 K-Jetronic system idle speed compensator location

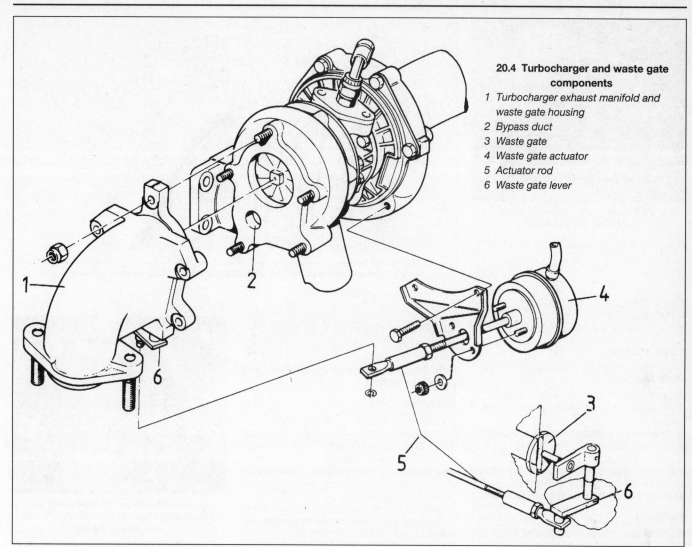

20.4 Turbocharger and waste gate components

1 Turbocharger exhaust manifold and waste gate housing
2 Bypass duct
3 Waste gate
4 Waste gate actuator
5 Actuator rod
6 Waste gate lever

4B

The temperature of the inlet air is reduced, thus increasing its density, by passing it through an intercooler, mounted alongside the radiator, prior to it entering the manifold.

The boost pressure generated by the turbocharger is controlled by a waste gate which when open allows a high proportion of the exhaust gases to bypass the turbocharger and directly enter the exhaust system **(see illustration)**. The turbocharger therefore loses speed and boost pressure is reduced.

The waste gate is opened and closed by the waste gate actuator through an actuator rod. The waste gate actuator is in turn controlled by the solenoid control valve which receives signals in the form of a pulsed voltage from the ignition system. Electronic Spark Control module (see Chapter 5, Part B). The Electronic Spark Control module receives data from various engine sensors, particularly the charge air temperature sensor in the inlet air duct, which modify the module program to suit all operating conditions. he module then signals the solenoid control valve to open or close the waste gate via the waste gate actuator.

Lubrication oil for the turbocharger is taken from the engine lubricating circuit via a special branch line. The turbocharger shaft rotates in plain bearings through which a relatively large amount of oil is allowed to pass. Therefore when rotating, the shaft floats on a thick film of lubricating oil.

The turbocharger is a close tolerance,

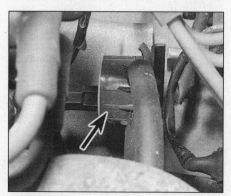

21.1 Waste gate solenoid control valve location (arrowed)

expensive component and servicing or repairs should be left to a dealer service department or specialist with turbocharger repair experience. Apart from the information in the following Sections, any other work on the turbocharger or its related components is beyond the scope of the average reader.

21 Waste gate solenoid control valve - removal and refitting

Removal

1 The solenoid control valve is mounted on a bracket located underneath the ignition distributor **(see illustration)**.
2 Disconnect the battery negative lead.
3 Disconnect the solenoid wiring multi-plug.
4 Identify and mark the hose locations at the solenoid connections, then remove the hoses.
5 Undo the retaining screws and remove the unit from its location.

Refitting

6 Refitting is a reversal of removal.

22.3 Intercooler upper air hose attachment (arrowed)

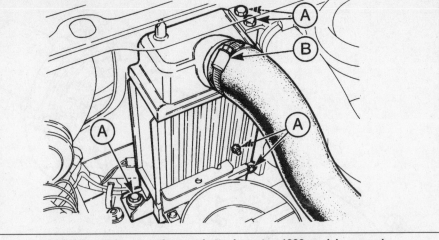

22.7 Intercooler mountings and attachments - 1986 models onwards

A Retaining bolts   *B Upper air hose*

22 Intercooler - removal and refitting

1985 models

Removal

1 Disconnect the battery negative lead.
2 Remove the air cleaner as described in Section 2.
3 Remove the intercooler upper and lower air hoses **(see illustration)**.
4 Undo the upper retaining bolt, tilt the intercooler towards the engine at the top and lift up to disengage the lower retaining pins. Remove the unit from the engine compartment.

Refitting

5 Refitting is a reversal of removal.

1986 models onwards

Removal

6 Proceed as described in paragraphs 1 to 3.
7 Undo the two radiator and intercooler lower retaining bolts **(see illustration)**.
8 Move the radiator and intercooler assembly towards the engine and undo the four bolts securing the intercooler to the radiator.
9 Undo the retaining bolt and move the horn nearest to the intercooler to one side.
10 Withdraw the intercooler from the engine compartment.

Refitting

11 Refitting is a reversal of removal.

23 Turbocharger- removal and refitting

Note: *New gaskets and new tabwashers must be used on refitting.*

Removal

1 Disconnect the battery negative lead.
2 Disconnect the turbocharger inlet and outlet air hoses and the hoses from the waste gate actuator and solenoid control valve at their turbocharger connections. Tape over all the disconnected unions and outlets to prevent dirt ingress.
3 Support the exhaust system and disconnect it from the turbocharger exhaust manifold .
4 Disconnect the oil feed union on the top of the turbocharger and the oil return line from underneath the unit **(see illustration)**. Tape over all disconnected pipes and unions.
5 Bend up the tabwashers, then unscrew the nuts securing the turbocharger to the exhaust manifold. Remove the unit and store it in a clean plastic bag while removed from the car.

Refitting

6 Before refitting the turbocharger ensure that all mating faces are clean and obtain new gaskets and a set of new tabwashers. It is also advisable to renew the engine oil and filter, particularly if a new turbocharger is being fitted or if there was any sign of previous oil contamination.

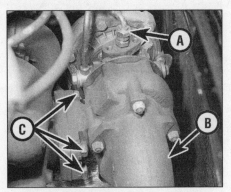

23.4 Turbocharger oil feed union (A), turbocharger exhaust manifold (B) and retaining nuts (C)

7 Refitting is a reversal of removal, but bearing in mind the following points:
a) Tighten all retaining nuts to the specified torque and secure with the tabwashers.
b) Before connecting the oil feed union, prime the turbocharger bearings by injecting clean engine oil into the union orifice.
c) Crank the engine over on the starter with the ignition LT lead at the coil disconnected until the oil pressure warning light goes out.

Chapter 4 Part C:
Central (single-point)
Fuel Injection (CFI) system

Contents

4C

Degrees of difficulty

Easy, suitable for novice with little experience	**Fairly easy,** suitable for beginner with some experience	**Fairly difficult,** suitable for competent DIY mechanic	**Difficult,** suitable for experienced DIY mechanic	**Very difficult,** suitable for expert DIY or professional

---

Specifications

General

System type	Single-point electronic fuel injection
Application	1.4 litre engines from 1990

Fuel requirement

Fuel octane rating	95 RON (unleaded)

Torque wrench settings

	Nm	lbf ft
HEGO sensor	50 to 70	37 to 52
Fuel filter unions	14 to 20	11 to 15

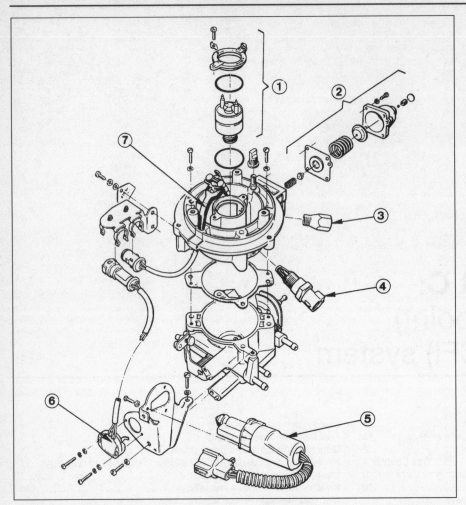

1.2 Exploded view of the Central Fuel Injection (CFI) unit - 1.4 CFI engine
1 Fuel injector assembly
2 Fuel pressure regulator components
3 Fuel inlet connector
4 Air charge temperature (ACT) sensor
5 Throttle valve control motor
6 Throttle position sensor (TPS)
7 Fuel injector wiring

The CFI unit, resembling a carburettor, houses the throttle valve, throttle valve control motor, TPS (Throttle Position Sensor), ACT sensor, electronic injector unit, and pressure regulator.

Engine management and emission system

The EEC IV (Electronic Engine Control IV) module is a microprocessor-based system containing within its memory the necessary strategy and calibration data. It provides control signals to the output actuators according to the input signals received from the various engine condition sensors. In addition to the sensors mentioned previously, the module also receives data from an engine coolant temperature sensor (ECT), and a speed sender unit (mounted on the speedometer take-off point on the gearbox). The EEC IV module will calculate the necessary requirements against data stored or programmed into its memory. Accurate control of the engine is thus maintained.

Ignition system

The ignition system consists of a distributor, TFI IV module, ignition coil and HT wiring. These components are more fully described in Chapter 5, Part B.

A knock sensor detects engine detonation, which may occur when using low octane fuel. Screwed into the cylinder block in such a position as to detect detonation in any of the four cylinders, it passes a signal based on vibration to the EEC IV module. The module analyses the signal and adjusts the ignition timing accordingly.

Catalytic converter

The function of the catalytic converter is to control and reduce exhaust gas emissions, keeping oxides of nitrogen (NOx), hydrocarbons (HC) and carbon monoxide (CO) to an acceptable level.

The catalyst consists of a ceramic honeycomb coated with platinum and rhodium, housed in a metal exhaust box. The honeycomb design presents a large surface area to the exhaust gas promoting maximum conversion. A HEGO (Heated Exhaust Gas Oxygen) sensor screwed into the exhaust downpipe allows the engine management system to control the air/fuel ratio at the ideal ratio of 14.7:1, which is required for the catalyst to function most effectively.

1 General information and precautions

General information

The system is best described by dividing it into four separate sub-systems: air, fuel, engine management (EEC IV system), and ignition.

Air system

The air system consists of an air cleaner, connecting air inlet duct, CFI unit, MAP (Manifold Absolute Pressure) sensor, and inlet manifold.

Air is drawn through the air cleaner and inlet duct to the CFI unit. The CFI unit contains an ACT (Air Charge Temperature) sensor and a throttle valve **(see illustration)**. The ACT sensor passes information to the EEC IV module, which uses the information to determine the engine's fuel requirement. The inlet air then passes the throttle valve into the inlet manifold. Below the throttle valve is a take-off point for the MAP sensor which measures pressure in the manifold, passing this information to the EEC IV module. The EEC IV module uses this information as

another factor in determining fuel requirements and ignition timing at full throttle or during ignition key "on" engine "off" conditions. Using the information from the ACT and MAP sensors, the EEC IV module can calculate the mass of air entering the engine and adjust the fuelling and ignition timing accordingly.

Fuel system

The fuel system consists of a fuel pump, fuel filter, and the CFI unit. Power to the system is supplied by the power relay, which has a built-in timer which allows the throttle valve motor to continue to operate after the engine is switched off, preventing the engine from "running on".

The fuel pump is electric, of roller cell design, and delivers fuel under pressure to the engine. Electric power to the pump is supplied via a relay which is controlled directly by the EEC IV module. The pump contains a non-return valve which maintains pressure in the system after the ignition is switched off, to assist starting.

From the fuel pump, the fuel passes through an in-line filter to the CFI unit. A fuel pressure regulator, mounted on the CFI unit maintains fuel pressure to the injector at 1 bar. Excess fuel is returned to the fuel tank.

Precautions

Note: *Following disconnection of the battery, all Keep Alive Memory (KAM) values will be erased from the EEC IV system module memory, which may result in erratic idle, engine surge, hesitation and a general deterioration of driving characteristics.*

⚠️ **Warning: Many of the procedures in this Chapter entail the removal of fuel pipes and connections which may result in some fuel spillage. Before carrying out any operation on the fuel system refer to the precautions given in Safety First! at the beginning of this manual and follow them implicitly. Petrol is a highly dangerous and volatile liquid and the precautions necessary when handling it cannot be overstressed**

Refer to the precautions given in Part B of this Chapter for models with mechanical fuel injection.

2 Air cleaner - removal and refitting

The procedure is similar to that described in Part A of this Chapter for carburettor engines.

3 Fuel tank - removal and refitting

The procedure is as described in Part A of this Chapter for carburettor engines.

4 Throttle cable - adjustment, removal and refitting

The procedure is similar to that described in Part A of this Chapter for carburettor engines.

5 Accelerator pedal - removal and refitting

The procedure is the same as described in Part A of this Chapter for carburettor models.

6 Fuel system - depressurising

⚠️ **Warning: The fuel system will remain pressurised after the engine is switched off. Comply with all relevant safety precautions during this operation and refer to the "Safety first!" Section at the beginning of this manual before proceeding.**

1 Disconnect the battery negative lead.
2 Remove the air cleaner assembly.
3 Position a suitable container or a sufficient quantity of absorbent cloth beneath the fuel inlet connection on the CFI unit.
4 Use an open-ended spanner on the flats of the inlet union screwed into the CFI unit to

prevent it from turning while the inlet pipe union is loosened. Allow all pressure/fuel seepage to dissipate before fully unscrewing the union if it is to be disconnected, or tightened if another part of the system is to be worked on.
5 The system will remain depressurised until the fuel pump is primed prior to starting the engine. Remove the container or cloth, as applicable, on completion.

7 Fuel pump - removal and refitting

Removal

1 The fuel pump is integral with the fuel level sender unit in the fuel tank **(see illustration)**.
2 Chock the front wheels, then jack up the rear of the vehicle and support it securely on axle stands (see "*Jacking and Vehicle Support*").
3 Disconnect the battery negative lead.
4 Depressurise the fuel system (Section 6).
5 Remove the fuel tank, then proceed as described for fuel level sender unit removal and refitting. This is described as part of the fuel tank removal and refitting procedure in Part A of this Chapter.

Refitting

6 Refitting is a reversal of removal.

8 Central Fuel Injection (CFI) unit - removal and refitting

Note: *Refer to the precautions at the end of Section 1 before proceeding.*

Removal

1 Disconnect the battery negative lead.
2 Remove the air cleaner assembly.
3 Depressurise the fuel system as described in Section 6, and disconnect the fuel inlet pipe from the CFI unit.
4 Disconnect the fuel return pipe from the CFI unit.
5 Disconnect the throttle cable from the linkage on the CFI unit.

8.9 Unscrewing the CFI unit securing bolts (arrowed)

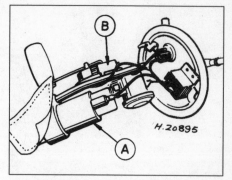

7.1 Integral fuel level sender unit/fuel pump - 1.4 CFI engine

A Fuel pump   *B Sender unit*

6 Either drain the cooling system as described in Chapter 1, or clamp the coolant hoses as close as possible to the CFI unit to minimise coolant loss, then disconnect the hoses from the unit.
7 Disconnect the air charge temperature sensor, throttle position sensor, and throttle valve control motor wiring plugs.
8 Disconnect the vacuum pipe from the CFI unit.
9 Unscrew the four securing bolts, and lift the CFI unit from the inlet manifold **(see illustration)**.

Refitting

10 Refitting is a reversal of removal, but on completion, refill or top-up the cooling system (as applicable) as described in Chapter 1, and check for fuel leaks with the engine running.

9 Fuel pressure regulator - removal and refitting

Removal

1 Remove the CFI unit as described in Section 8.
2 Remove the four screws securing the regulator housing to the CFI unit, then carefully lift off the housing and recover the ball, cup, large spring, diaphragm, valve, and small spring, noting the position and orientation of all components **(see illustration)**. Do not

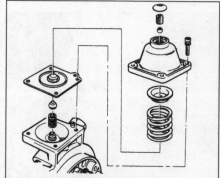

9.2 Exploded view of fuel pressure regulator - 1.4 CFI engine

4C

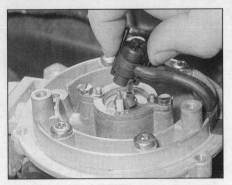

10.4 Disconnecting the fuel injector wiring plug - 1.4 CFI engine

10.5a Removing an injector retaining collar securing bolt and locktab - 1.4 CFI engine

10.5b Removing the injector retaining collar - 1.4 CFI engine

attempt to prise the plug from the regulator housing, or adjust the Allen screw (if no plug is fitted); this will alter the fuel system pressure.

3 Examine all components and renew any defective items as necessary

Refitting

4 Commence reassembly by supporting the CFI unit on its side so that the regulator components can be fitted from above.

5 Fit the small spring, valve, diaphragm (ensuring that it locates correctly), large spring, and the spring cup.

6 Carefully place the ball into position on the spring cup, and ensure that it locates correctly.

7 Refit the regulator housing, taking great care to avoid disturbing the ball, and once

10.6 Withdrawing the injector from the CFI unit

10.7 Removing the seal from the injector retaining collar - 1.4 CFI engine

correctly in position, tighten the screws evenly to avoid distorting the diaphragm.

8 Refit the CFI unit as described in Section 8.

9 On completion, the fuel system pressure should be checked by a Ford dealer at the earliest opportunity.

10 Fuel injector - removal and refitting

Note: *Refer to the precautions at the end of Section 1 before proceeding. New injector seals will be required on refitting.*

Removal

1 Disconnect the battery negative lead.

2 Remove the air cleaner assembly.

3 Depressurise the fuel system as described in Section 6.

4 Disconnect the fuel injector wiring plug **(see illustration)**.

5 Bend back the injector retaining collar securing bolt locktabs, then unscrew the bolts. Remove the injector retaining collar **(see illustrations)**.

6 Withdraw the injector from the CFI unit, noting its orientation, then withdraw the injector seals **(see illustration)**.

7 Remove the seal from the injector retaining collar **(see illustration)**.

Refitting

8 Refitting is a reversal of removal, bearing in mind the following points.

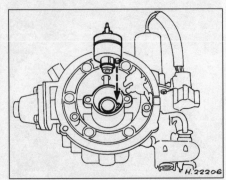

10.10 Align locating peg on injector with slot in CFI unit when refitting

9 Use new injector seals, and coat them with silicon grease (to Ford specification ESEM-1C171A or equivalent).

10 Ensure that the locating peg on the injector is correctly positioned **(see illustration)**.

11 Throttle Position Sensor (TPS) - removal and refitting

Removal

1 Disconnect the battery negative lead.

2 Unclip and disconnect the sensor wiring plug.

3 Remove the two securing screws, and withdraw the sensor from the throttle valve shaft **(see illustration)**.

Refitting

4 Refitting is a reversal of removal, but ensure that the sensor actuating arm is correctly located.

12 Throttle valve control motor - removal and refitting

Removal

1 Disconnect the battery negative lead.

2 Remove the air cleaner assembly.

3 Disconnect the wiring plugs from the motor and the throttle position sensor.

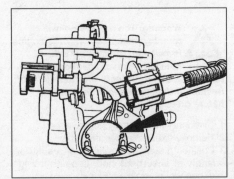

11.3 Throttle position sensor (TPS) location (arrowed) on side of CFI unit

13.4 Disconnecting the ACT sensor wiring plug - 1.4 CFI engine

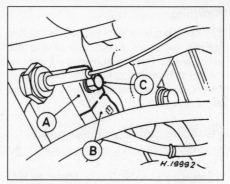

15.1 Knock sensor location - 1.4 CFI engine

A Knock sensor   *C Securing bolt*
B Wiring plug

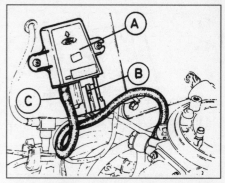

16.2 Manifold absolute pressure (MAP) sensor - 1.4 CFI engine

A MAP sensor   *C Vacuum hose*
B Wiring plug

4 Remove the screws securing the motor and throttle position sensor assembly mounting bracket to the CFI unit, and withdraw the assembly.
5 Remove the motor securing screws and withdraw the motor from the bracket.

Refitting

6 Refitting is a reversal of removal, bearing in mind the following points.
7 Ensure that the throttle position sensor locates correctly on the throttle valve spindle, and that the mounting bracket aligns with its locating pegs.
8 On completion, the idle speed should be checked by a Ford dealer at the earliest opportunity.

13 Air Charge Temperature (ACT) sensor - removal and refitting

Removal

1 The ACT sensor is screwed into the CFI unit.
2 Disconnect the battery negative lead.
3 Remove the air cleaner assembly.
4 Disconnect the ACT sensor wiring plug **(see illustration)**.
5 Unscrew the sensor from the CFI unit.

Refitting

6 Refitting is a reversal of removal.

14 Engine Coolant Temperature (ECT) sensor - removal and refitting

Removal

1 The ECT sensor is screwed into the inlet manifold.
2 Disconnect the battery negative lead.
3 Partially drain the cooling system as described in Chapter 1.
4 Disconnect the sensor wiring plug.
5 Unscrew the sensor from the inlet manifold.

Refitting

6 Refitting is a reversal of removal, but on completion top-up the cooling system as described in *"Weekly checks"*.

15 Knock sensor - removal and refitting

Removal

1 The knock sensor is screwed into the cylinder block, near the oil filter **(see illustration)**.
2 Disconnect the battery negative lead.
3 Disconnect the sensor wiring plug by depressing the plug locking lugs and pulling the plug from the sensor. Do not pull on the wiring.
4 Unscrew the securing bolt and withdraw the sensor from the cylinder block.

Refitting

5 Refitting is a reversal of removal, but ensure that the mating faces of the sensor and cylinder block are clean.

16 Manifold Absolute Pressure (MAP) sensor - removal and refitting

Removal

1 Disconnect the battery negative lead.
2 Disconnect the sensor wiring plug **(see illustration)**. Do not pull on the wiring.
3 Disconnect the vacuum pipe from the sensor.
4 Remove the two securing screws, and withdraw the sensor from the engine compartment bulkhead.

Refitting

5 Refitting is a reversal of removal.

17 Heated Exhaust Gas Oxygen (HEGO) sensor - removal and refitting

Note: *A new sealing ring will be required on refitting.*

Removal

1 Apply the handbrake, then jack up the front of the vehicle and support it on axle stands (see *"Jacking and Vehicle Support"*).
2 Disconnect the battery negative lead.
3 Unclip the wiring and disconnect the sensor wiring plug **(see illustration)**.
4 Remove the sensor heat shield, then unscrew the sensor from the exhaust downpipe, and carefully remove it complete with sealing ring.

> ⚠ **Warning: Do not touch the tip of the HEGO sensor.**

Refitting

5 Refitting is a reversal of removal, bearing in mind the following points.
6 Clean the sensor threads, and take care not to touch the tip of the sensor during the refitting procedure.

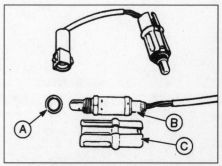

17.3 Heated exhaust gas oxygen (HEGO) sensor - 1.4 CFI engine

A Sealing ring   *C Sensor shield*
B HEGO sensor

4C

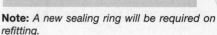

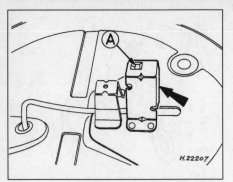

18.1 Fuel cut-off (inertia) switch location (arrowed) - 1.4 CFI engine
A Reset button

7 Use a new sensor sealing ring.
8 Tighten the sensor to the specified torque.
9 On completion, start the engine and check for leaks between the sensor and the exhaust downpipe.

18 Fuel cut-off (inertia) switch - removal and refitting

Removal

1 The fuel cut-off switch is located in the luggage compartment, under the spare wheel **(see illustration)**.
2 Disconnect the battery negative lead.
3 Remove the spare wheel and its cover to gain access to the switch.
4 Disconnect the switch wiring plug.
5 Remove the two screws securing the switch to its bracket, then withdraw the switch.

Refitting

6 Refitting is a reversal of removal, but before refitting the spare wheel, ensure that the switch is reset by pushing down the button on the top of the switch, and on completion start the engine and check that the switch operates correctly.

19 Speed sender unit - removal and refitting

The speed sender unit is similar to that used with the fuel computer described in Chapter 12.

20 EEC IV module - removal and refitting

Removal

1 The EEC IV module is located behind the centre console, beneath the trim panel **(see illustration)**.
2 Disconnect the battery negative lead.
3 Remove the trim panel to expose the module, then pull the module from its bracket behind the centre console.
4 Loosen the screw securing the wiring plug, then disconnect the plug and withdraw the module.

Refitting

5 Refitting is a reversal of removal.

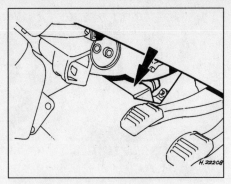

20.1 EEC IV module location (arrowed) - 1.4 CFI engine

Chapter 4 Part D:
Electronic Fuel Injection (EFI) system

Contents

Degrees of difficulty

Easy, suitable for novice with little experience	**Fairly easy,** suitable for beginner with some experience	**Fairly difficult,** suitable for competent DIY mechanic	**Difficult,** suitable for experienced DIY mechanic	**Very difficult,** suitable for expert DIY or professional

Specifications

General

System type	Multi-point electronic fuel injection
Application	1.6 litre engines from 1990
Control pressure (engine running)	2.3 to 2.5 bar (33 to 36 lbf/in^2)

Fuel requirement

Fuel octane rating	95 RON (unleaded) or 97 RON (leaded)

Torque wrench setting

	Nm	lbf ft
Fuel filter unions	14 to 20	11 to 15

1 General information and precautions

General information

From the 1990 model year, an Electronic Fuel Injection (EFI) system controlled by the Electronic Engine Control IV (EEC IV) system, and incorporating an Electronic Distributorless Ignition system (E-DIS 4) is used on all 1.6 litre fuel injection models. The system is designed to meet the requirements of the European 15.04 exhaust emission control laws.

Those components more easily related to the ignition system are described in Chapter 5, Part B. Those relating to the fuel system are described in this Section.

The engine management and fuel systems are best described by dividing them into two separate sub-systems the air inlet system, and the fuel system.

Air inlet system

The volume of air drawn into the system depends on air pressure and density, throttle valve position, engine speed and the cleanliness of the air cleaner element.

The EEC IV module evaluates these factors through the Air Charge Temperature (ACT) sensor, Manifold Absolute Pressure (MAP) sensor and Throttle Position Sensor (TPS), and controls the engine idle speed via the Idle Speed Control Valve (ISCV).

The air cleaner is similar to that used on earlier fuel injection models. A flexible hose connected to the valve cover acts as a cylinder head and crankcase breather. A further connection leads to the idle speed control valve. The valve is controlled by the EEC IV module, and operates by varying the size and opening duration of an auxiliary air passage, which by-passes the throttle valve. A throttle housing bolted to the upper section of the inlet manifold houses the throttle valve and TPS. The TPS measures throttle opening.

The MAP sensor, mounted on the engine bulkhead and connected to the inlet manifold by a vacuum pipe and electrically to the EEC IV module, measures the vacuum in the inlet manifold. If the MAP sensor fails in service, the EEC IV module uses the TPS to provide one of three values:

a) Idle
b) Part load
c) Full load

Inlet air temperature is measured by an electrically resistive element in the air charge temperature sensor (ACT) screwed into the upper half of the inlet manifold. This supplies information to the EEC IV module.

Fuel system

The fuel pump and fuel level sender unit are contained in an integral unit in the fuel tank.

The fuel pump is electric, and its electrical supply is provided via a relay controlled by the EEC IV module. When the ignition is switched on, the fuel pump is given a lead-in time of approximately one second in order to build up pressure in the system. The pump also incorporates a non-return valve which prevents system pressure dropping after the ignition is switched off, to improve the warm start characteristics.

An inertia switch (located under the spare wheel in the luggage compartment), installed between the fuel pump relay and the fuel pump will break the supply to the pump in the event of sudden impact, thus switching off the pump. If the switch has been activated, the reset button will be in the raised position.

A fuel rail is bolted to the lower section of the inlet manifold. The fuel rail acts as a fuel reservoir for the four fuel injectors, and locates the injectors in the inlet manifold.

A fuel filter is installed between the fuel pump and the fuel rail.

A fuel pressure regulator, mounted on the return end of the fuel rail and connected by a pipe to the inlet manifold to sense manifold pressure, controls fuel pressure in the fuel rail. Excess fuel is returned to the fuel tank.

The fuel injectors are electro-magnetically operated, and the volume of fuel injected is regulated by varying the electrical pulse duration which is computed by the EEC IV module.

A "limited operation strategy" (LOS) means that the vehicle is still driveable (albeit at reduced power and efficiency) in the event of a failure in the EEC IV module or its sensors.

Precautions

Note: *Following disconnection of the battery, all Keep Alive Memory (KAM) values will be erased from the EEC IV system module memory, which may result in erratic idle, engine surge, hesitation and a general deterioration of driving characteristics.*

 Warning: Many of the procedures in this Chapter entail the removal of fuel pipes and connections which may result in some fuel spillage. Before carrying out any operation on the fuel system refer to the precautions given in Safety First! at the beginning of this manual and follow them implicitly. Petrol is a highly dangerous and volatile liquid and the precautions necessary when handling it cannot be overstressed

Refer to the precautions given in Part B of this Chapter for models with mechanical fuel injection.

2 Air cleaner - removal and refitting

The procedure is similar to that described in Part B of this Chapter for models with mechanical fuel injection.

3 Fuel tank - removal and refitting

The procedure is as described in Part A of this Chapter for carburettor engines.

4 Throttle cable - adjustment, removal and refitting

The procedure is similar to that described in Part A of this Chapter for carburettor engines.

5 Accelerator pedal - removal and refitting

The procedure is the same as described in Part A of this Chapter for carburettor models.

6 Fuel system - depressurising

 Warning: The fuel system will remain pressurised after the engine is switched off. Comply with relevant safety precautions during this operation and refer to the "Safety First" Section at the beginning of this manual before proceeding

1 Disconnect the battery negative lead.
2 Position a suitable container beneath the fuel filter.
3 Cover the outlet union on the filter with a wad of absorbent cloth to minimise the risk of fuel spray, then slowly loosen the outlet union and allow the pressure to dissipate.
4 Tighten the union on completion unless the filter is to be renewed.
5 The system will remain depressurised until the fuel pump is primed prior to starting the engine. Remove the container and cloth on completion.

7 Fuel pump - removal and refitting

The fuel pump is integral with the fuel level sender unit in the fuel tank. Removal and refitting are as described in Part C of this Chapter for models with the CFI system.

8 Fuel pressure regulator - removal and refitting

Note: *Refer to the precautions at the end of Section 1 before proceeding. A new sealing ring will be required on refitting.*

Removal

1 Disconnect the battery negative lead.
2 Depressurise the fuel system as described in Section 6.
3 Disconnect the fuel return hose from the regulator. Be prepared for fuel spillage and

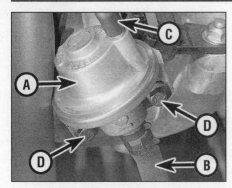

8.3 Fuel pressure regulator assembly - 1.6 EFI engine

A Regulator
B Fuel return hose (to tank)
C Vacuum hose
D Securing bolts

take adequate fire precautions **(see illustration))**.

4 Disconnect the vacuum hose from the regulator.

5 Unscrew the two securing bolts and withdraw the regulator from the fuel rail.

6 Recover the sealing ring.

Refitting

7 Refitting is a reversal of removal, but use a new sealing ring, and on completion, switch the ignition on and off five times without cranking the engine and check for fuel leaks.

9 Throttle housing - removal and refitting

Note: *A new gasket must be used on refitting.*

Removal

1 Disconnect the battery negative lead.

2 Depressurise the fuel system as described in Section 6.

3 Remove the air inlet pipe **(see illustration)**.

4 Disconnect the throttle cable from the throttle valve linkage, then unbolt the cable bracket from the housing.

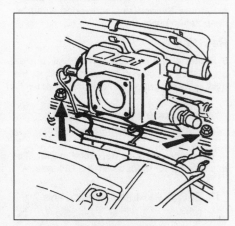

10.5 Fuel injection wiring harness securing nuts (arrowed) - 1.6 EFI engine

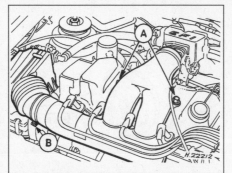

9.3 Air inlet pipe securing screws (A) and hose securing clip (B) - 1.6 EFI engine

5 Disconnect the throttle position sensor wiring plug.

6 Unscrew the four securing nuts, and withdraw the throttle housing from the inlet manifold. Recover the gasket.

Refitting

7 Refitting is a reversal of removal, but use a new gasket between the throttle housing and the inlet manifold.

10 Fuel injectors - removal and refitting

Note: *Refer to the precautions at the end of Section 1 before proceeding. New injector seals will be required on refitting.*

Removal

1 Disconnect the battery negative lead.

2 Depressurise the fuel system as described in Section 6.

3 Remove the throttle housing as described in Section 9.

4 Disconnect the wiring plugs from the fuel injectors, air charge temperature sensor, and engine coolant temperature sensor.

5 Remove the two fuel injection wiring harness securing nuts, and position the wiring harness clear of the fuel rail **(see illustration)**.

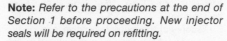

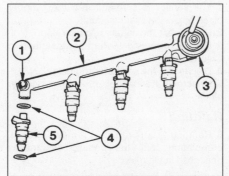

10.8 Fuel rail and injector assembly - 1.6 EFI engine

1 Fuel inlet
2 Fuel rail
3 Pressure regulator
4 Seals
5 Injector

6 Disconnect the fuel supply hose from the fuel rail, and disconnect the fuel return hose and the vacuum hose from the pressure regulator.

7 Unscrew the two fuel rail securing bolts, and remove the fuel rail, complete with injectors.

8 To remove the injectors, simply pull them from the fuel rail. Recover the O-ring seals **(see illustration)**.

Refitting

9 Refitting is a reversal of removal, but note that new seals must be fitted to all injectors even if only one injector has been renewed, and all the seals must be lubricated with clean engine oil before fitting to the injectors.

11 Throttle Position Sensor (TPS) - removal and refitting

Removal

Note: *During this procedure, ensure that the sensor wiper is not rotated beyond its normal operating arc*

1 Disconnect the battery negative lead.

2 Disconnect the wiring plug from the sensor **(see illustration)**.

3 Remove the two securing screws, and withdraw the sensor from the throttle valve shaft.

Refitting

4 Refitting is a reversal of removal, ensuring that the moulded side of the sensor faces the throttle housing, and that the flat on the sensor wiper engages with the flat on the throttle shaft.

12 Idle Speed Control Valve (ISCV) - removal, cleaning and refitting

Removal

1 Disconnect the battery negative lead.

4D

11.2 Throttle position sensor - 1.6 EFI engine

A Wiring plug
B Securing screws

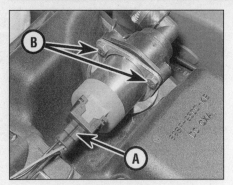

**12.2 Idle speed control valve -
1.6 EFI engine**

A Wiring plug *B Securing bolts*

2 Disconnect the valve wiring plug **(see illustration)**.

3 Unscrew the two securing bolts, and withdraw the valve from the air cleaner housing.

Cleaning

4 Remove the valve as described earlier in this Section.

5 Immerse the valve in a container of clean petrol and allow it to soak for approximately three minutes.

6 Use a clean paint brush to clean the bore, slots and piston of the valve.

7 Using a small screwdriver, carefully move the piston up and down in the bore (do not use the slots to do this), then rinse the valve with petrol and dry it, preferably using compressed air **(see illustration)**.

8 Refit the valve as described in the following paragraphs.

Refitting

9 Refitting is a reversal of removal, ensuring that the mating faces of the valve and air cleaner are clean.

10 On completion, start the engine and check that the idle speed is stable, and that there are no air leaks. Warm the engine up to normal operating temperature, then switch on all available electrical loads and check that the idle speed is maintained.

13 Manifold Absolute Pressure (MAP) sensor - removal and refitting

Removal

1 Disconnect the battery negative lead.

2 Disconnect the sensor wiring plug. Do not pull on the wiring.

3 Disconnect the vacuum hose from the sensor.

4 Remove the two securing screws and withdraw the sensor from the engine compartment bulkhead.

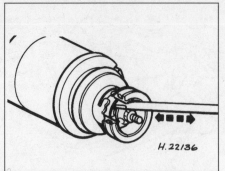

12.7 Using a screwdriver to move the idle speed control valve piston - 1.6 EFI engine

Refitting

5 Refitting is a reversal of removal, but note that the fuel trap in the vacuum line between the inlet manifold and the sensor should be fitted with the white end towards the sensor.

14 Air Charge Temperature (ACT) sensor - removal and refitting

Removal

1 The air charge temperature sensor is screwed into the inlet manifold **(see illustration)**.

2 Disconnect the battery negative lead.

3 Disconnect the sensor wiring plug. Do not pull on the wiring.

4 Unscrew the sensor from the inlet manifold.

Refitting

5 Refitting is a reversal of removal, but apply suitable sealer to the sensor threads.

15 Engine Coolant Temperature (ECT) sensor - removal and refitting

Removal

1 The sensor is screwed into the cylinder block below the inlet manifold.

2 Disconnect the battery negative lead.

3 Drain the cooling system as described in Chapter 1.

4 Disconnect the sensor wiring plug.

5 Unscrew the sensor from the cylinder block.

Refitting

6 Refitting is a reversal of removal, but on completion refill the cooling system as described in Chapter 1.

16 Speed sender unit - removal and refitting

The sender unit is similar to that used with the fuel computer described in Chapter 12.

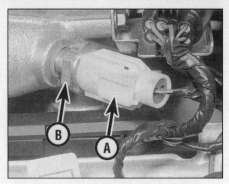

**14.1 Air charge temperature sensor -
1.6 EFI engine**

A Wiring plug *B Sensor*

**17.1 Mixture (CO) adjustment
potentiometer (arrowed) - 1.6 EFI engine**

17 Mixture (CO) adjustment potentiometer - removal and refitting

Removal

1 The potentiometer is located on the side of the left-hand suspension turret **(see illustration)**.

2 Disconnect the battery negative lead.

3 Disconnect the potentiometer wiring plug.

4 Remove the securing screw and withdraw the potentiometer.

Refitting

5 Refitting is a reversal of removal, but on completion check and if necessary adjust the mixture as described earlier in this Chapter 1.

18 Fuel cut-off (inertia) switch - removal and refitting

The procedure is as described in Part C of this Chapter for models with the CFI system.

19 EEC IV module - removal and refitting

The procedure is as described in Part C of this Chapter for models with the CFI system.

Chapter 4 Part E:
Manifolds, exhaust and emission control systems

Contents

Degrees of difficulty

| Easy, suitable for novice with little experience | | Fairly easy, suitable for beginner with some experience | | Fairly difficult, suitable for competent DIY mechanic | | Difficult, suitable for experienced DIY mechanic | | Very difficult, suitable for expert DIY or professional | |

Specifications

Fuel evaporative emission control system - carburettor engines

Ported vacuum switch operating temperature:

Two-port valve	52 to 55°C (125 to 131°F)
Three-port valve	52 to 55°C (125 to 131°F)

1 General information

All models utilise a light alloy inlet manifold which on carburettor models is coolant heated to improve the atomisation of the fuel/air mixture.

The exhaust manifold is of cast iron construction and incorporates a heated air box as part of the air inlet system on carburettor models.

The exhaust system fitted as original equipment is of single or two section type incorporating a silencer and expansion box and suspended on rubber mountings under the car.

Emission control consists of reducing the emission of noxious gases and vapours, which are by products of combustion, into the atmosphere. The system can be divided into three categories; fuel evaporative emission control, crankcase emission control and exhaust emission control. The components and system operation for Escort models operating in the United Kingdom are as follows.

Fuel evaporative emission control

Carburettor engines

Fuel evaporative emission control simply consists of internal venting of the carburettor float chamber and closed circuit fuel tank ventilation.

Central Fuel Injection (CFI) engine models

To minimise the escape of unburned hydrocarbons, the fuel tank filler cap is sealed, and a charcoal canister collects the petrol vapours generated in the fuel tank when the car is parked. The canister stores them until they can be cleared from the canister (under the control of the fuel injection/ignition system electronic control unit) via the canister purge solenoid valve. When the valve is opened, the fuel vapours pass into the inlet tract, to be burned by the engine during normal combustion.

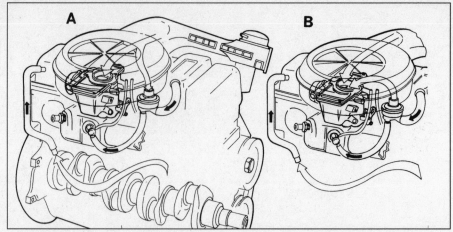

1.9 Typical crankcase ventilation system as used on CVH engines with carburettor

A Ventilation at idle with part-closed throttle

B Ventilation at full throttle position

Crankcase emission control

OHV engines

On OHV engines a closed circuit crankcase ventilation system is used ensuring that blow-by gases which pass the piston rings and collect in the crankcase, as well as oil vapour, are drawn into the combustion chambers to be burnt.

The system consists of a vented engine oil filler cap connected by one hose to the inlet manifold and by another to the air cleaner. The gas flow is controlled by a calibrated port in the oil filler cap and by manifold vacuum according to throttle position.

CVH engines

On CVH engines a closed circuit crankcase ventilation system is also used **(see illustration)**.

At light throttle openings, the emissions are drawn out of the rocker cover, through a control orifice in the crankcase ventilation filter (where fitted), and into the inlet manifold. Under full throttle conditions the gas flow

routing is still as just described, but in addition the gases are drawn through a filter and pass into the air cleaner.

This arrangement offsets any tendency for the fuel/air ratio to be adversely affected at full throttle.

Exhaust emission control

Carburettor engine models

On carburettor engine models an exhaust emission control system is used of which the exact components fitted can vary according to model. In general the system operates as follows.

To improve driveability during warm-up conditions and to keep exhaust emission levels to a minimum, a vacuum-operated, temperature-sensitive emission control system is fitted to OHV and CVH engines covered by this manual. The system is designed to ensure that the rate of distributor vacuum advance is compatible with the change in fuel/air mixture flow under all throttle conditions, thus resulting in more complete combustion and reduced exhaust emissions.

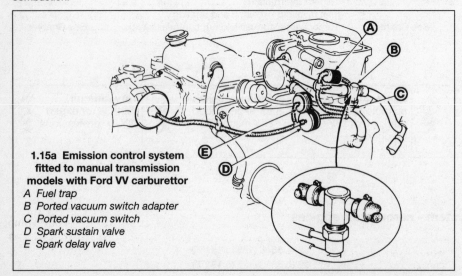

1.15a Emission control system fitted to manual transmission models with Ford VV carburettor

A Fuel trap
B Ported vacuum switch adapter
C Ported vacuum switch
D Spark sustain valve
E Spark delay valve

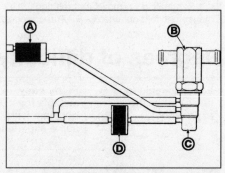

1.15b Alternative emission control system layout for manual transmission models with Ford VV carburettor

A Fuel trap
B Ported vacuum switch adapter
C Ported vacuum switch
D Spark sustain valve

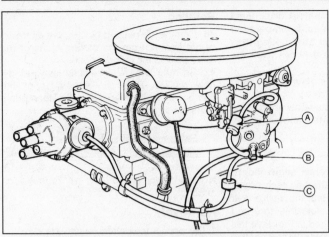

1.15c Emission control system layout for manual transmission models with Weber 2V carburettor

A *Fuel trap*   C *Spark sustain valve*
B *Ported vacuum switch*

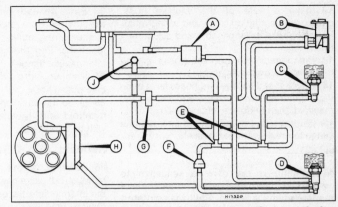

1.15d Emission control system layout for automatic transmission models with Ford VV carburettor

A *Fuel trap*   F *Check valve*
B *Two-way solenoid*   G *Restrictor*
C *Ported vacuum switch (blue)* H *Dual diaphragm distributor*
D *Ported vacuum switch (green)* J *Inlet manifold connection*
E *T-connectors*

Under part throttle cruising conditions, distributor vacuum advance is required to allow time for the fuel/air mixture in the cylinders to burn. When returning to a part throttle opening after accelerating or decelerating, the distributor vacuum increases before the fuel/air mixture has stabilised. On certain engines this can lead to short periods of incomplete combustion and increased exhaust emission. To reduce this condition a spark delay valve is incorporated in the vacuum line between the carburettor and distributor to reduce the rate at which the distributor advances. Under certain conditions, particularly during the period of

engine warm-up, some models may suffer from a lack of throttle response. To overcome this problem a spark sustain valve may be fitted in the vacuum line either individually or in conjunction with the spark delay valve. This valve is used to maintain distributor vacuum under transient throttle conditions, thus stabilising the combustion process.

The operation of the valves is controlled by a ported vacuum switch (PVS) which has the vacuum lines connected to it. The PVS is actuated by the engine cooling water and is sensitive to changes in engine operating temperature. A fuel trap prevents fuel or fuel vapour from being drawn into the distributor vacuum unit **(see illustrations)**.

The carburettor speed control system is an integral part of the emission control system on some UK models as well as for some overseas market models **(see illustration)**.

The system's function is to improve the air and fuel mixture when the engine is cold in low ambient temperatures. It achieves this by increasing the air volume to the inlet manifold in order to weaken the mixture ratio which has been enriched by choke operation.

The carburettor speed control valve is fitted to a vacuum hose which is located between the air cleaner unit and the inlet manifold on UK models.

Central Fuel Injection (CFI) engine models

To minimise the amount of pollutants which escape into the atmosphere, a catalytic converter is fitted in the exhaust system of CFI engine models.

The system is of a closed loop type. A Heated Exhaust Gas Oxygen (HEGO) sensor located in the exhaust system provides the fuel injection/ignition electronic control unit with constant feedback, enabling the control unit to adjust the mixture to provide the best possible conditions for the converter to operate.

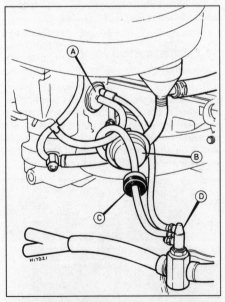

1.16 Carburettor speed control system layout

A *Temperature vacuum switch*
B *Carburettor speed control valve*
C *Spark delay valve*
D *Ported vacuum switch and adapter*

2 Inlet manifold - removal and refitting

Note: *A new gasket will be required on refitting.*

Carburettor models

Removal

1 Disconnect the battery negative lead.
2 Remove the air cleaner as described in Part A of this Chapter.
3 Refer to Chapter 1 and drain the cooling system.
4 Remove the carburettor as described in Part A of this Chapter according to type.
5 Disconnect the manifold coolant hoses.
6 Make a careful note of all vacuum connections at the vacuum switches and solenoids and disconnect them.
7 Where applicable disconnect the switch wiring multi-plugs after noting their locations.
8 Undo the manifold retaining nuts and withdraw the manifold from the cylinder head studs. Recover the gasket.

Refitting

9 Refitting is the reverse sequence to removal but use a new gasket and ensure that the mating faces are clean. On completion refill the cooling system as described in Chapter 1.

XR3i and XR3i Cabriolet models with mechanical (Bosch K- and KE-Jetronic) fuel injection

Removal

10 Disconnect the battery negative lead.
11 Remove the warm-up regulator, throttle housing, fuel injectors and cold start valve as described in Part B of this Chapter.
12 Drain the cooling system (Chapter 1).

4E

13 Make a note of the vacuum hose, crankcase ventilation hose and wiring multi-plug locations as applicable and disconnect them.
14 Disconnect the coolant hoses at the manifold intermediate flange.
15 Check that all wiring and hoses have been disconnected from above and below the manifold, then undo the retaining nuts.
16 Withdraw the manifold and intermediate flange together with their gaskets.

Refitting

17 Refitting is the reverse sequence to removal, but use a new gasket on each side of the intermediate flange. Refit the cold start valve, fuel injectors, throttle housing and warm-up regulator as described in Part B of this Chapter, and on completion refill the cooling system as described in Chapter 1.

RS Turbo models (1985 to May 1986)

Removal

18 Disconnect the battery negative lead.
19 Remove the throttle housing, fuel injectors and cold start valve as described in Part B of this Chapter.
20 Drain the cooling system (Chapter 1).
21 Disconnect the crankcase ventilation hose and vacuum hose from the top of the plenum chamber.
22 Disconnect the vacuum servo hose from the side of the plenum chamber.
23 From below the inlet manifold remove the auxiliary air device as described in Part B of this Chapter, then disconnect the thermo-time switch and temperature sensor wiring multi-plugs after noting their locations.
24 Remove the oil cooler-to-inlet manifold connecting hose.
25 From above, undo the bolts and remove the plenum chamber support bracket.
26 Undo the nuts and remove the inlet manifold and plenum chamber from the cylinder head. Recover the gasket.
27 If required undo the nuts and separate the plenum chamber from the inlet manifold. Recover the gaskets.

Refitting

28 Refitting is the reverse sequence to removal, but use new gaskets on all flange joints. Refit the auxiliary air device, cold start valve, fuel injectors and throttle housing as described in Part B of this Chapter, and refill the cooling system as described in Chapter 1.

RS Turbo models (May 1986-on)

Removal

29 Disconnect the battery negative lead.
30 Remove the throttle housing, fuel injectors, cold start valve and auxiliary air device as described in Part B of this Chapter.
31 Drain the cooling system (Chapter 1).
32 Disconnect the crankcase ventilation hose and vacuum hose from the top of the manifold and the vacuum servo hose from the side.

33 From beneath the manifold disconnect the thermo-time switch and temperature sensor wiring multi-plugs after noting their locations, and the coolant hoses from the intermediate flange.
34 Remove the oil cooler-to-manifold connecting hose.
35 Undo the retaining nuts and withdraw the manifold and intermediate flange together with their gaskets.

Refitting

36 Refitting is the reverse sequence to removal, but use a new gasket on each side of the intermediate flange. Refit the auxiliary air device, cold start valve, fuel injectors and throttle housing as described in Part B of this Chapter and on completion refill the cooling system as described in Chapter 1.

Central Fuel Injection (CFI) engine models

37 Remove the CFI unit as described in Part C of this Chapter.
38 The remainder of the procedure is similar to that described previously in this Section for carburettor engine models.

Electronic Fuel Injection (EFI) engine models

Removal

39 Depressurise the fuel system as described in Part D of this Chapter.
40 Disconnect the battery negative lead.
41 Remove the air inlet ducting, and disconnect the throttle cable from the throttle linkage (see Part A of this Chapter).
42 Remove the fuel rail and fuel injectors as described in Part D of this Chapter.
43 Noting their locations, disconnect the coolant, vacuum and breather hoses from the manifold.
44 Disconnect the wiring multi-plugs from the engine sensors at the inlet manifold.
45 Undo the retaining bolts, and withdraw the manifold from the cylinder head. Where applicable, note the location of the engine lifting bracket and/or earth lead. Remove the gasket.

Refitting

46 Commence refitting by cleaning all traces of old gasket from the mating faces of the manifold and the cylinder head.
47 Refitting is the reversal of removal, using a new gasket. Refit the remainder of the components with reference to the appropriate Parts of this Chapter.

3 Exhaust manifold - removal and refitting

Note: *A new gasket will be required on refitting.*

Removal

1 Disconnect the battery negative lead.
2 On carburettor and CFI engine models remove the air cleaner as described in the appropriate Part of this Chapter.
3 Remove the turbocharger on RS Turbo models as described in Part B of this Chapter.
4 On EFI engines, unbolt the air inlet pipe and move it to one side.
5 Where applicable, unbolt the hot air shroud for access to the manifold securing nuts.
6 Support the exhaust system on a jack or blocks, then disconnect the downpipe at the manifold. On models with CFI engines, take care not to strain the HEGO sensor wiring (see Part C of this Chapter).
7 Undo the nuts securing the manifold to the cylinder head and remove it from the engine. Recover the manifold gasket.

Refitting

8 Refitting is the reverse sequence to removal, but refit the turbocharger on RS Turbo models as described in Part B of this Chapter.

4 Exhaust system - renewal

1 The layout of the exhaust system varies considerably according to model and engine. All except the RS Turbo versions can be renewed in sections; coupling sleeves are supplied, enabling an old section to be cut out and a new one inserted without the need to renew the entire system all at once.

4.2a Exhaust silencer mounting . . .

4.2b . . . and expansion box mounting

2 It is recommended when working on an exhaust system that the complete assembly be removed from under the vehicle by releasing the downpipe from the manifold and unhooking the flexible suspension hangers (see illustrations).

3 Assemble the complete system, but do not fully tighten the joint clips until the system is back in the vehicle. Use a new exhaust manifold/flange gasket and check that the flexible mountings are in good order, also check the connecting flange joint.

4 Set the silencer and expansion box in their correct attitudes in relation to the rest of the system before finally tightening the joint clips.

5 Check that with reasonable deflection in either direction, the exhaust does not knock against any adjacent components.

5 Fuel evaporative emission control system components (Central Fuel Injection/CFI engines) - removal and refitting

Carbon canister

Removal

1 The carbon canister is located behind the bumper, under the front right-hand wheelarch (see illustration).

2 Disconnect the battery negative lead.

3 Remove the wheelarch liner.

4 Disconnect the pipe from the carbon canister.

5 Remove the screw securing the canister to the mounting bracket, and withdraw the canister.

Refitting

6 Refitting is a reversal of removal.

Carbon canister purge solenoid

Removal

7 The solenoid is located near the bulkhead on the right-hand side of the engine compartment (see illustration).

5.1 Carbon canister location (wheelarch liner removed) - CFI engine

8 Disconnect the battery negative lead.

9 Disconnect the solenoid wiring plug.

10 Disconnect both hoses from the solenoid, noting their locations, then withdraw the solenoid from the vehicle.

Refitting

11 Refitting is a reversal of removal.

6 Crankcase emission control system components - removal and refitting

Carburettor and Central Fuel Injection (CFI) engines

1 On OHV and HCS engines renewal of the vented oil filler cap and crankcase ventilation hoses is simply a matter of removing them from their locations and fitting new parts as required.

2 On CVH engines the crankcase ventilation filter (where fitted) can be renewed by pulling it out of the air cleaner after disconnecting the hoses (see illustration). Ensure that the sealing grommet is in position in the air cleaner before pushing a new filter into place.

Mechanical (Bosch K- and KE-Jetronic) fuel injection engines

3 On fuel-injection engines the crankcase ventilation filter is located on the right-hand

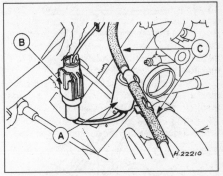

5.7 Carbon canister purge solenoid location - CFI engine

A Canister purge solenoid
B Wiring plug
C Hose

side of the engine and can be removed after disconnecting the hoses (see illustration). On early versions detach the filter from its support bracket also. Refitting is a reversal of removal.

4 During the course of production modifications have been made to the crankcase ventilation system on K-Jetronic fuel-injected engines to eliminate stalling and rough idling caused by oil from the crankcase venting system contaminating the throttle housing.

5 Three versions of the system may be encountered. If the stalling and rough idling problems are encountered on cars equipped with the Mk 1 or Mk 2 system, then they should be uprated to Mk 3 specification as described in the following paragraphs. It should be noted that even the latest (Mk 3) level system failed to cure the problem completely and at the beginning of 1986 a revised throttle housing was introduced. These can be identified by having their idle speed adjustment screw located on the top of the housing under a tamperproof cap, rather than underneath the housing as on early versions. The latest version of throttle housing can be fitted to early cars but the work should

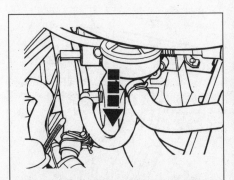

6.2 Crankcase ventilation filter renewal on CVH engines with carburettor - pull valve in direction of arrow

6.3 Crankcase ventilation filter location (arrowed) on KE-Jetronic fuel-injected engines

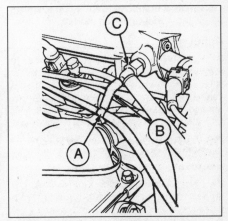

6.9 Components of Mk 1 crankcase ventilation system - fuel-injection models

A T-connector
B Short hose
C Plenum chamber connector

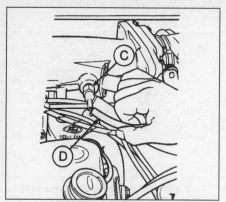

6.10 Fuel shut-off valve hose (D) and plenum chamber connector (C) on Mk 1 type crankcase ventilation system - fuel-injection models

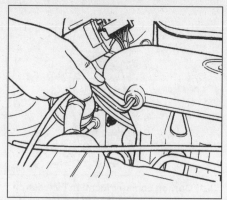

6.15a Unscrewing the plenum chamber plug - fuel-injection models

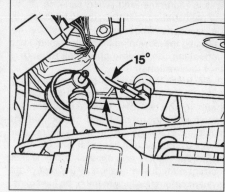

6.15b Correct setting of plenum chamber angled connector - fuel-injection models

be carried out by a dealer, as numerous modifications are involved. The latest version of crankcase ventilation system should always be fitted first however, as follows.

6 As a preliminary operation, remove the idle speed adjustment screw and blow out the idle passage in the throttle housing using air pressure.

7 Refit the screw.

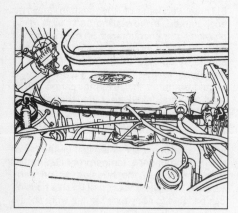

6.19 Mk 2 crankcase ventilation system - fuel-injection models

Cars with earliest type (Mk 1) crankcase ventilation system

8 Remove and discard the crankcase ventilation filter vacuum hose.

9 Remove and discard the T-connector and also the short hose (see illustration).

10 Fit the overrun fuel shut off valve hose to the plenum chamber connector (see illustration).

11 Remove and discard the crankcase ventilation filter bracket.

12 Remove and discard the hose which runs between the ventilation filter and the rocker cover.

13 Turn the filter and its hose, which is connected to the air cleaner, so that the small spigot on the filter is uppermost.

14 Fit a new hose between the filter and rocker cover, secure it with the hose clips.

15 Remove and discard the plug from the plenum chamber and in its place screw in the angled connectors. Set the connector as shown (see illustrations).

16 Connect the ventilation filter to the angled connector using a new hose.

17 Seat the idle speed screw gently and then unscrew it two complete turns.

18 Bring the engine to normal working temperature and adjust the idle speed and mixture as described in Chapter 1.

Cars with Mk 2 crankcase ventilation system

19 Remove and discard the crankcase ventilation filter vacuum hose and fit a blanking cap to the hose connector on the throttle housing end of the plenum chamber (see illustration).

20 Remove and discard the plug from the plenum chamber and substitute the new angled connector as described in paragraph 15.

21 Fit the new hose between the ventilation filter and the angled connector.

22 Repeat the operations described in paragraphs 17 and 18.

23 Later model cars have the crankcase ventilation filter hose connections as shown (see illustration).

Electronic Fuel Injection (EFI) engines

24 A crankcase ventilation filter is fitted in the hose run to the air cleaner. During the course of production, modifications have been made to the crankcase ventilation system, and two versions of the system may be encountered (see illustrations).

25 Removal and refitting of the filter is simply a matter of disconnecting the relevant hoses.

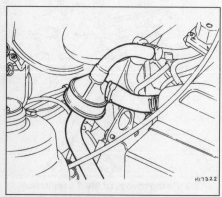

6.23 Mk 3 crankcase ventilation system - fuel-injection models

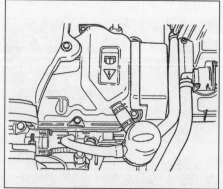

6.24a Early type crankcase ventilation system - 1.6 EFI engine

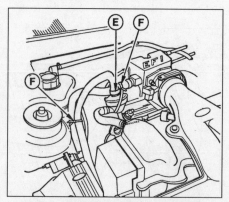

6.24b Later type crankcase ventilation system - 1.6 EFI engine

E Hose clip   F Cable-ties

7 Exhaust emission control system components - removal and refitting

Carburettor engines

Spark delay/sustain valve

Removal

1 Disconnect the vacuum lines at the valve and remove the valve from the engine.

Refitting

2 When refitting a spark delay valve it must be positioned with the black side (marked CARB) towards the carburettor and the coloured side (marked DIST) towards the distributor. When refitting a spark sustain valve the side marked VAC must be towards the carburettor and the side marked DIST towards the distributor.

Ported vacuum switch

Removal

3 Remove the filler cap from the expansion tank to reduce pressure in the cooling system. If the engine is hot, remove the cap slowly using a rag to prevent scalding.

4 Disconnect the vacuum lines and the water hoses, then unscrew the valve.

Refitting

5 When refitting the valve, note that the vacuum line from the carburettor is connected to the middle outlet on the PVS, the vacuum line from the spark delay valve (where fitted) is connected to the outlet nearest to the threaded end of the PVS, and the vacuum line from the spark sustain valve is connected to the outlet furthest from the threaded end of the PVS.

6 Reconnect the water hoses and if necessary top-up the cooling system.

Fuel trap

Removal

7 Disconnect the vacuum lines and remove the fuel trap from the engine.

Refitting

8 When refitting, make sure that the fuel trap is positioned with the black side (marked CARB) towards the carburettor and the white side (marked DIST) towards the PVS **(see illustration)**.

Central Fuel Injection (CFI) engines

Catalytic converter

Removal

Note: *Handle the catalyst with care. Any sudden knocks can cause damage to the internal substrates*

9 Disconnect the battery negative lead.

10 Apply the handbrake, then jack up the front of the vehicle and support it securely on axle stands (see *"Jacking and Vehicle Support"*).

11 Remove the bolts from the exhaust downpipe-to-catalytic converter flanged joint.

12 Unscrew the nuts, and remove the clamp securing the rear of the catalytic converter to the exhaust system.

13 Unhook the catalytic converter from the rubber mountings, and carefully manipulate the converter from under the vehicle. If necessary, unhook the front end of the exhaust system from the rubber mountings to ease the procedure.

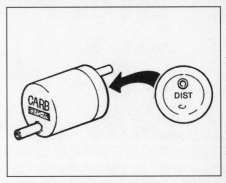

7.8 Fuel trap marked for direction of fitting

Refitting

14 Commence refitting by ensuring that the mating faces of the catalytic converter, downpipe, and exhaust system are clean.

15 Examine the mounting rubbers, and renew if necessary, noting that the rubbers used are of a special high temperature type due to the high operating temperature of the catalyst.

16 Loosely fit the catalytic converter in position, but do not tighten the fixings yet. Use a new gasket at the converter-to-downpipe flanged joint.

17 Carefully align the downpipe, converter and exhaust system, then tighten the fixings.

18 Lower the vehicle and reconnect the battery negative lead, then start the engine and check the exhaust system for leaks.

Heater Exhaust Gas Oxygen (HEGO) sensor

19 Refer to Part C of this Chapter.

4E

Chapter 5 Part A:
Starting and charging systems

Contents

Degrees of difficulty

Easy, suitable for novice with little experience	**Fairly easy,** suitable for beginner with some experience	**Fairly difficult,** suitable for competent DIY mechanic	**Difficult,** suitable for experienced DIY mechanic	**Very difficult,** suitable for expert DIY or professional

5A

Specifications

Battery
Type . . . . 12 volt lead-acid, 35 to 52 Ah depending on model
Charge condition:
  Poor . . . . 12.4 volts or less
  Normal . . . . 12.6 volts
  Good . . . . 12.7 volts or over

Alternator
Minimum brush length:
  Bosch, Lucas and Mitsubishi . . . . 5.0 mm
  Motorola . . . . 4.0 mm
Regulator voltage at 4000 rpm with 3 to 7A load (all models) . . . . 13.7 to 14.6 volts

Starter motor
Type . . . . Pre-engaged
Make:
  Bosch . . . . 0.8 kW, 0.85 kW, 0.9 kW, 0.95 kW
  Lucas . . . . 8M 90, 9M 90, M 79
  Nippondenso . . . . 0.6 kW, 0.9 kW
Minimum brush length:
  Bosch . . . . 10.0 mm
  Lucas . . . . 8.0 mm
  Nippondenso 0.6 kW . . . . 10.0 mm
  Nippondenso 0.9 kW . . . . 9.0 mm

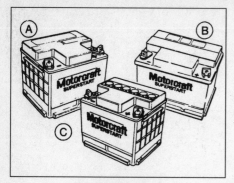

1.3 Battery types
A Maintenance-free sealed cell type
B Maintenance-free removable cell top type
C Low maintenance type

1 General information and precautions

General information

The engine electrical system includes all charging, starting and ignition system components and the engine oil pressure sensor. Because of their engine-related functions, these components are covered separately from the body electrical devices such as the lights, instruments, etc (which are covered in Chapter 12). Refer to Part B of this Chapter for information on the ignition system.

The electrical system is of the 12-volt negative earth type.

The battery is of the low maintenance or maintenance-free type and is charged by the alternator, which is belt-driven from a crankshaft-mounted pulley **(see illustration)**.

The starter motor is of the pre-engaged type, incorporating an integral solenoid. On starting, the solenoid moves the drive pinion into engagement with the flywheel ring gear before the starter motor is energised. Once the engine has started, a one-way clutch prevents the motor armature being driven by the engine until the pinion disengages from the flywheel.

Further details of the various systems are given in the relevant Sections of this Chapter. While some repair procedures are given, the usual course of action is to renew the component concerned. The owner whose interest extends beyond mere component renewal should obtain a copy of the "Automobile Electrical & Electronic Systems Manual", available from the publishers of this manual.

Precautions

It is necessary to take extra care when working on the electrical system to avoid damage to semi-conductor devices (diodes and transistors), and to avoid the risk of personal injury. In addition to the precautions given in "Safety First!" at the beginning of this manual, observe the following items when working on the system.

Always remove rings watches, etc before working on the electrical system. Even with the battery disconnected, capacitive discharge could occur if a component live terminal is earthed through a metal object. This could cause a shock or nasty burn.

Do not reverse the battery connections. Components such as the alternator, or any other having semi-conductor, could be irreparably damaged.

If the engine is being started using jump leads and a slave battery, connect the batteries positive to positive and negative to negative. This also applies when connecting a battery charger.

Never disconnect the battery terminals, or alternator multi-plug connector, when the engine is running.

The battery leads and alternator multi-plug must be disconnected before carrying out any electric welding on the car.

Never use an ohmmeter of the type incorporating a hand cranked generator for circuit or continuity testing.

2 Electrical fault finding - general information

Refer to Chapter 12.

3 Battery - testing and charging

Note: Refer to the precautions at the end of Section 1 before proceeding.

Standard and low maintenance battery - testing

1 If the car covers a small annual mileage it is worthwhile checking the specific gravity of the electrolyte every three months to determine the state of charge of the battery. Use a hydrometer to make the check and compare the results with the following table.

Ambient temperature:

	Above 25ºC	Below 25ºC
Fully charged	1.210 to 1.230	1.270 to 1.290
70% charged	1.170 to 1.190	1.230 to 1.250
discharged	1.050 to 1.070	1.110 to 1.130

Note that the specific gravity readings assume an electrolyte temperature of 15°C (60°F); for every 10°C (50°F) below 15°C (60°F) subtract 0.007. For every 10°C (50°F) above 15°C (60°F) add 0.007.

2 If the battery condition is suspect first check the specific gravity of electrolyte in each cell. A variation of 0.040 or more between any cells indicates loss of electrolyte or deterioration of the internal plates.

3 If the specific gravity variation is 0.040 or more, the battery should be renewed. If the cell variation is satisfactory but the battery is discharged, it should be charged as described later in this Section.

Maintenance-free battery - testing

4 In cases where a "sealed for life" maintenance-free battery is fitted, topping-up and testing of the electrolyte in each cell is not possible. The condition of the battery type can therefore only be tested using a battery condition indicator or a voltmeter.

5 If testing the battery using a voltmeter, connect it across the battery and compare the result with those given in the Specifications under "charge condition". The test is only accurate if the battery has not been subject to any kind of charge for the previous six hours. If this is not the case switch on the headlights for 30 seconds then wait four to five minutes before testing the battery after switching off the headlights. All other electrical components must be switched off, so check that the doors and tailgate are fully shut when making the test.

6 If the voltage reading is less than the 12.2 volts then the battery is discharged, whilst a reading of 12.2 to 12.4 volts indicates a partially discharged condition.

7 If the battery is to be charged, remove it from the vehicle (Section 4) and charge it as described later in this Section.

Standard and low maintenance battery - charging

8 Charge the battery at a rate of 3.5 to 4 amps and continue to charge the battery at this rate until no further rise in specific gravity is noted over a four hour period.

9 Alternatively, a trickle charger charging at the rate of 1.5 amps can be safely used overnight.

10 Specially rapid "boost" charges which are claimed to restore the power of the battery in 1 to 2 hours are not recommended as they can cause serious damage to the battery plates through overheating.

11 While charging the battery note that the temperature of the electrolyte should never exceed 37.8°C (100°F).

Maintenance-free battery - charging

12 This battery type takes considerably longer to fully recharge than the standard type, the time taken being dependent on the extent of discharge, but it can take anything up to three days.

13 A constant voltage type charger is required, set to 13.9 to 14.9 volts with a charger current below 25 amps. Using this method the battery should be usable within three hours, giving a voltage reading of 12.5 volts, but this is for a partially discharged battery and, as mentioned, full charging can take considerably longer.

14 If the battery is to be charged from a fully discharged state (condition reading less than 12.2 volts) have it recharged by your Ford dealer or local automotive electrician as the charge rate is higher and constant supervision during charging is necessary.

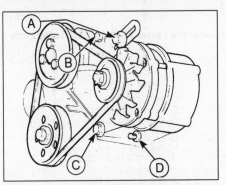

5.4 Alternator mounting and adjuster link bolts

A Adjuster link-to-alternator bolt
B Adjuster link-to-engine bolt
C and D Alternator mounting bolts

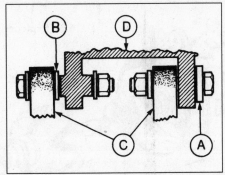

5.6a Correct fitting of alternator mounting components - early models

A Large washer
B Small washer (pre-1985 CVH engines only)
C Mounting bracket
D Alternator

5.6b Alternator mounting bolt arrangement - later models

4 Battery - removal and refitting

Note: Refer to the precautions at the end of Section 1 before proceeding.

Removal

1 The battery is located on the left-hand side of the engine compartment on a bulkhead platform.
2 Disconnect the leads at the negative (earth) terminal by undoing the retaining nut and removing the bolt. Disconnect the positive terminal leads in the same way.
3 Undo the bolts securing the two battery clamps and remove the clamps.
4 Lift the battery from its location, keeping it in an upright position to avoid spilling electrolyte on the paintwork.

Refitting

5 Refitting is the reverse sequence to removal. Smear petroleum jelly on the terminals when refitting and always connect the positive lead first and the negative lead last.

5 Alternator - removal and refitting

Note: Refer to the precautions at the end of Section 1 before proceeding.

Removal

1 The operations are similar for all makes of alternator.
2 Disconnect the battery negative terminal, then disconnect the multiplug or leads from the rear of the alternator.
3 On certain CVH engine models it may be necessary to remove the air cleaner hose, and disconnect the radiator bottom hose to give sufficient clearance to enable removal of the alternator, in which case the cooling system must be drained with reference to Chapter 1.
4 Release the mounting and adjuster link bolts, push the alternator in towards the engine and remove the drivebelt **(see**

illustration)**. It may be necessary to remove the adjuster link-to-alternator bolt to facilitate removal of the drivebelt.
5 Undo and remove the mounting nuts and bolts and adjuster link bolt, if not already removed, and withdraw the alternator from the engine.

Refitting

6 Refitting is the reverse sequence to removal, bearing in mind the following points.
  a) Ensure that the mounting bolts and washers are assembled as shown **(see illustrations)**.
  b) Adjust the drivebelt tension as described in Chapter 1.
  c) On completion, where applicable, refill the cooling system as described in Chapter 1.

6 Alternator brushes and regulator - renewal

Bosch alternator

1 With the alternator removed from the engine, clean the external surfaces free from dirt.
2 Extract the brush box/regulator screws from the rear cover and withdraw the brush box/regulator **(see illustration)**. Check the brush length and, if less than the specified minimum, renew them.
3 Unsolder the brush wiring connectors and remove the brushes and the springs.
4 Refit by reversing the removal operations.

5A

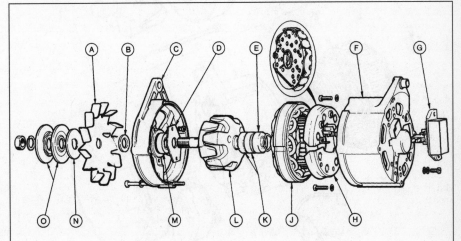

6.2 Exploded view of the Bosch G1 and K1 series alternators

A Fan
B Spacer
C Drive end housing
D Drive end bearing retaining plate
E Slip ring end bearing
F Slip ring end housing
G Brush box/regulator
H Rectifier diode pack
J Stator
K Slip rings
L Rotor
M Drive end bearing
N Spacer
O Pulley

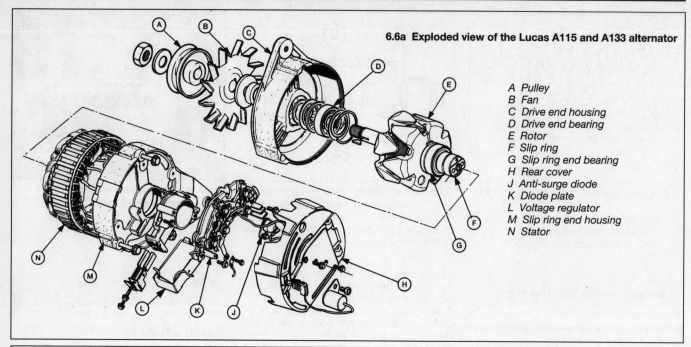

6.6a Exploded view of the Lucas A115 and A133 alternator

A Pulley
B Fan
C Drive end housing
D Drive end bearing
E Rotor
F Slip ring
G Slip ring end bearing
H Rear cover
J Anti-surge diode
K Diode plate
L Voltage regulator
M Slip ring end housing
N Stator

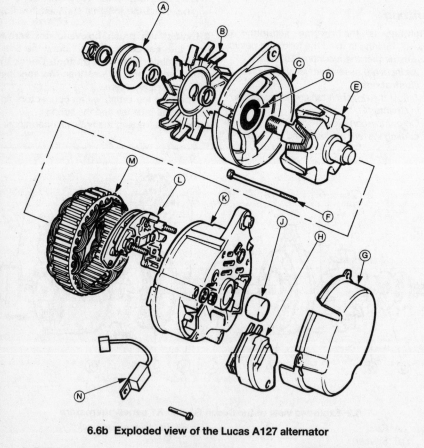

6.6b Exploded view of the Lucas A127 alternator

A Pulley
B Fan
C Drive end housing
D Drive end bearing
E Rotor
F Through-bolt
G Rear cover
H Brush box and regulator
J Slip ring end bearing
K Slip ring end housing
L Rectifier pack
M Stator
N Suppressor

Lucas alternator

5 Proceed as described in paragraph 1.
6 Remove the alternator rear cover **(see illustrations)**.
7 Extract the brush box retaining screws and withdraw the brush assemblies from the brush box.
8 If the length of the brushes is less than the specified minimum, renew them. Refit by reversing the removal operations.
9 To remove the regulator, disconnect the wires from the unit and unscrew the retaining screw (A115 and A133 units only - three screws on A127 type).
10 Refit by reversing the removal operations, but check that the small plastic spacer and the connecting link are correctly located.

Motorola alternator

11 Proceed as described in paragraph 1.
12 Extract the two regulator securing screws, disconnect the two regulator leads and withdraw the unit **(see illustration)**.
13 Extract the brush box retaining screw and pull and tilt the brush box from its location, taking care not to damage the brushes during the process.
14 If necessary, unsolder the brush connections.
15 Fit the new brushes by reversing the removal operations.

Mitsubishi alternator

16 Proceed as described in paragraph 1.
17 Undo the three housing through-bolts and remove the slip ring end housing. It may be necessary to apply heat from a high-power (200 watt) soldering iron to the centre of the end housing for a few minutes if the housing refuses to free from the rotor **(see illustrations)**.

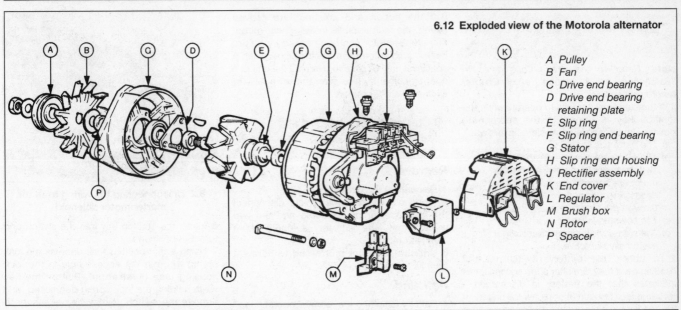

6.12 Exploded view of the Motorola alternator

A Pulley
B Fan
C Drive end bearing
D Drive end bearing
    retaining plate
E Slip ring
F Slip ring end bearing
G Stator
H Slip ring end housing
J Rectifier assembly
K End cover
L Regulator
M Brush box
N Rotor
P Spacer

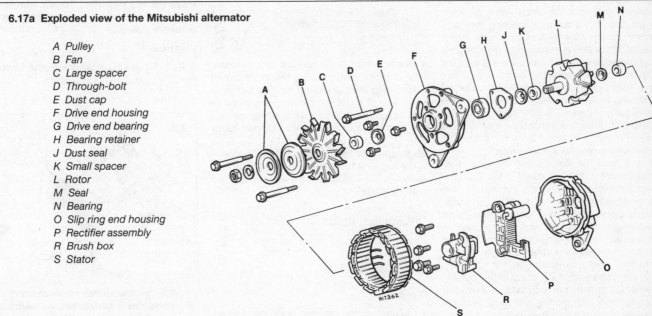

6.17a Exploded view of the Mitsubishi alternator

A Pulley
B Fan
C Large spacer
D Through-bolt
E Dust cap
F Drive end housing
G Drive end bearing
H Bearing retainer
J Dust seal
K Small spacer
L Rotor
M Seal
N Bearing
O Slip ring end housing
P Rectifier assembly
R Brush box
S Stator

5A

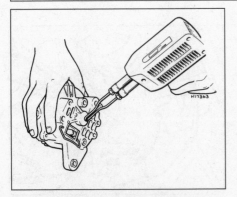

6.17b Using a soldering iron to heat the slip ring end housing - Mitsubishi alternator

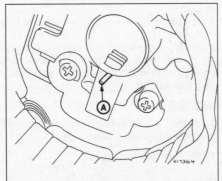

6.21 Using a length of wire (A) to hold brushes in the retracted position - Mitsubishi alternator

18 Undo the four bolts and remove the stator and rectifier assembly from the slip ring end housing.
19 Unsolder the brush box-to-rectifier assembly terminal and remove the brush box.
20 Renew the brush box and brushes if they are worn below the specified minimum.
21 Fit the new brushes by reversing the removal operations.

 Insert a suitable piece of wire through the access hole in the housing to keep the brushes retracted as the housing is fitted (see illustration). After fitting the housing release the brushes by removing the wire.

7 Starter motor - testing in the car

Note: *Refer to the precautions given in "Safety first!" and in Section 1 of this Chapter before proceeding.*

1 If the starter motor fails to operate when the ignition key is turned to the appropriate position, the possible causes are as follows.
   a) *The battery is faulty.*
   b) *The electrical connections between the switch, solenoid, battery and starter motor are somewhere failing to pass the necessary current from the battery through the starter to earth.*
   c) *The solenoid is faulty.*
   d) *The starter motor is mechanically or electrically defective.*

2 To check the battery, switch on the headlamps. If they dim after a few seconds, this indicates that the battery is discharged - recharge (see Section 3) or renew the battery. If the headlamps glow brightly, operate the starter switch and observe the lamps. If they dim, then this indicates that current is reaching the starter motor, therefore the fault must lie in the starter motor. If the lamps continue to glow brightly (and no clicking sound can be heard from the starter motor solenoid), this indicates that there is a fault in the circuit or solenoid - see the following paragraphs. If the starter motor turns slowly when operated, but the battery is in good condition, then this indicates either that the starter motor is faulty, or there is considerable resistance somewhere in the circuit.

3 If a fault in the circuit is suspected, disconnect the battery leads, the starter/solenoid wiring and the engine/transmission earth strap(s). Thoroughly clean the connections, and reconnect the leads and wiring. Use a voltmeter or test lamp to check that full battery voltage is available at the battery positive lead connection to the solenoid. Smear petroleum jelly around the battery terminals to prevent corrosion - corroded connections are among the most frequent causes of electrical system faults.

4 If the battery and all connections are in good condition, check the circuit by disconnecting the wire from the solenoid blade terminal. Connect a voltmeter or test lamp between the wire end and a good earth (such as the battery negative terminal), and check that the wire is live when the ignition switch is turned to the "start" position. If it is, then the circuit is sound - if not, there is a fault in the ignition/starter switch or wiring.

5 The solenoid contacts can be checked by connecting a voltmeter or test lamp between the battery positive feed connection on the starter side of the solenoid, and earth. When the ignition switch is turned to the "start" position, there should be a reading or lighted bulb, as applicable. If there is no reading or lighted bulb, the solenoid is faulty and should be renewed.

6 If the circuit and solenoid are proved sound, the fault must lie in the starter motor. The starter motor can be checked by a Ford dealer or an automotive electrical specialist. A specialist may be able to overhaul the unit at a cost significantly less than that of a new or exchange starter motor.

8 Starter motor - removal and refitting

Removal

1 Disconnect the battery.
2 Working from under the vehicle, disconnect the main starter motor cable and the two wires from the starter solenoid **(see illustration)**.
3 Unbolt the starter motor and withdraw it from its location.

Refitting

4 Refit by reversing the removal operations.

9 Starter motor brushes - renewal

1 Starter motor brush renewal is a relatively difficult procedure, requiring skill in the use of a soldering iron. It should also be borne in mind that if the starter motor has been in service long enough to wear the brushes out, the rest of the unit is likely to be well worn also. In such a case the best course is to obtain a new or reconditioned starter motor.
2 For further advice on brush renewal and on starter motor overhaul in general, consult an auto electrical specialist.

10 Ignition switch - removal and refitting

Pre-1986 models

Removal

1 Disconnect the battery, undo the screws and remove the steering column lower shroud.
2 Insert the ignition key into the lock and turn it to position I.
3 Using a flat-bladed screwdriver, depress the switch retaining clip, at the same time pulling out the switch using the ignition key **(see illustration)**.

Refitting

4 Refitting is a reversal of removal, ensuring that the ignition key is in position I.

1986 models onwards

Removal

5 Disconnect the battery, undo the screws and remove the steering column lower shroud.

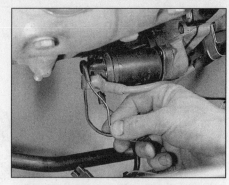

8.2 Disconnecting the wiring from the starter motor solenoid

6 Insert the ignition key into the switch and turn it to position I.
7 Using a thin pointed tool, depress the lock spring through the access hole in the lock housing **(see illustration)**. Pull on the key while holding the lock spring depressed, and remove the switch. It may be necessary to move the key slightly to the left and right to align the key barrel and lock housing cam, so permitting removal.

Refitting

8 Refitting is a reversal of removal, ensuring that the ignition key is in position I.

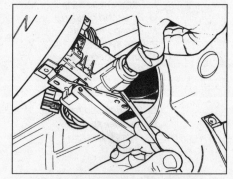

10.3 Ignition switch removal using a screwdriver to depress the switch retaining clip - pre-1986 models

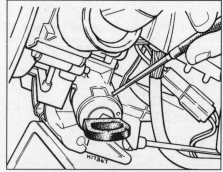

10.7 Ignition switch removal using a pointed tool to depress the lock spring - 1986 models onwards

Chapter 5 Part B:
Ignition systems

Contents

Degrees of difficulty

Easy, suitable for novice with little experience	**Fairly easy,** suitable for beginner with some experience	**Fairly difficult,** suitable for competent DIY mechanic	**Difficult,** suitable for experienced DIY mechanic	**Very difficult,** suitable for expert DIY or professional

Specifications

General

System type:

1.1 litre OHV engines	Mechanical contact breaker and coil
1.1 litre CVH engines up to 1986	Mechanical contact breaker and coil
1.1 litre CVH engines from 1986	Electronic breakerless ignition
1.1 litre HCS engines	Distributorless ignition system (DIS/ESC)
1.3 litre OHV engines	Electronic breakerless ignition
1.3 litre CVH engines	Electronic breakerless ignition
1.3 litre HCS engines	Distributorless ignition system (DIS/ESC)
1.4 litre carburettor engines	Electronic breakerless ignition
1.4 litre fuel injection engines	Programmed electronic ignition (EEC IV)
1.6 litre carburettor engines	Electronic breakerless ignition
1.6 litre K-Jetronic fuel injection engines	Electronic breakerless ignition
1.6 litre Electronic Fuel Injection (EFI) engines	Distributorless ignition system (DIS/EEC IV)
1.6 litre RS Turbo engines	Programmed electronic ignition (ESC II)
Location of number No 1 cylinder	Crankshaft pulley end

Firing order:

OHV and HCS engines	1-2-4-3
CVH engines	1-3-4-2

Spark plugs

Type ....   See Chapter 1 Specifications

Distributor

Direction of rotor arm rotation (all engines)	Anti-clockwise viewed from cap

Contact breaker points gap:

Bosch distributor	0.40 to 0.50 mm (0.016 to 0.020 in)
Lucas distributor	0.40 to 0.59 mm (0.016 to 0.023 in)
Dwell angle (contact breaker system)	48° to 52°

Ignition coil - contact breaker ignition system

Type	Low voltage for use with 1.5 ohm ballast resistance
Output:	
OHV engines	23.0 k volt (minimum)
CVH engines	25.0 k volt (minimum)
Primary resistance	1.2 to 1.4 ohms
Secondary resistance	5000 to 9000 ohms

Ignition coil - electronic ignition systems (except DIS)

Type	Oil filled high output
Output	25.0 to 30.0 k volt according to application
Primary resistance:	
All models except RS Turbo 1986 onwards	0.72 to 0.88 ohms
RS Turbo from 1986 onwards	1.0 to 1.2 ohms
Secondary resistance	4500 to 7000 ohms

Ignition coil - DIS

Output	37 k volt (minimum) open circuit
Primary resistance (measured at coil):	
1.1 and 1.3 litre HCS engines	0.50 to 1.00 ohm
1.6 litre Electronic Fuel Injection engines	4.5 to 5.0 ohms

HT leads

Resistance	30 000 ohms maximum per lead (typical value)
Type:	
OHV engines	Champion CLS 8
CVH engines	Champion CLS 9

Torque wrench settings

	Nm	lbf ft
Spark plugs:		
OHV and HCS engines	13 to 20	10 to 15
CVH engines	25 to 38	18 to 28
Distributor clamp pinch bolt (OHV engines)	4	3
Distributor clamp plate bolt (OHV engines)	10	7
Distributor mounting bolts (CVH engines)	7	5

1 General information and precautions

Contact breaker ignition system

The ignition system is divided into two circuits, low tension (primary) and high tension (secondary). The low tension circuit consists of the battery, ignition switch, primary coil windings and the contact breaker points and condenser. The high tension circuit consists of the secondary coil windings, the heavy ignition lead from the centre of the distributor cap to the coil, the rotor arm and the spark plug leads and spark plugs.

When the system is in operation, low tension voltage is changed in the coil into high tension voltage by the opening and closing of the contact breaker points in the low tension circuit. High tension voltage is then fed, via the carbon brush in the centre of the distributor cap, to the rotor arm of the distributor. The rotor arm revolves inside the distributor and each time it comes in line with one of the four metal segments in the distributor cap, which are connected to the spark plug leads, the opening and closing of the contact breaker points causes the high tension voltage to build up and jump the gap from the rotor arm to the appropriate metal segment. The voltage then passes via the spark plug lead to the spark plug, where it finally jumps the spark plug gap before going to earth.

The distributor is driven by a skew gear from the camshaft on the OHV engine and by an offset dog on the end of the camshaft on CVH engines.

The ignition advance is a function of the distributor and is controlled both mechanically and by a vacuum-operated system.

A ballast resistor is incorporated in the low tension circuit between the ignition switch and the coil primary windings. The ballast resistor consists of a grey coloured resistive wire running externally to the main loom between the ignition switch and coil. During starting this resistor is bypassed allowing full available battery voltage to be fed to the coil which is of a low voltage type. This ensures that during starting when there is a heavy drain on the battery, sufficient voltage is still available at the coil to produce a powerful spark. During normal running, battery voltage is directed through the ballast resistor to limit the voltage supplied to the coil to seven volts.

Electronic breakerless ignition

The fundamentals of operation of the electronic breakerless ignition system are similar to those described previously for the contact breaker system, however in the breakerless electronic ignition system, the action of the contact breaker points is simulated electronically within the distributor. Control of ignition advance characteristics is still carried out in the conventional way using mechanical and vacuum systems.

Programmed electronic ignition (RS Turbo models)

The two main components of the system are the electronic control module designated Electronic Spark Control II (ESC II), and a Hall effect electronic ignition distributor.

The distributor is mounted on the flywheel end of the cylinder head, and is driven directly off the camshaft by an offset dog coupling. Contained within the distributor is a trigger vane, permanent magnet and position sensor. The trigger vane is a cylindrical disc attached to the distributor shaft and having four slots on its vertical surface, one for each cylinder. The permanent magnet and position sensor are secured to the distributor baseplate in such a way that the vertical surface of the trigger vane passes between them. As the trigger vane rotates, the magnetic field between the magnet and position sensor is interrupted and a series of square wave electronic pulses are produced. This output wave form is sent to the ESC II module and from this, engine speed, ignition advance and idle speed are calculated.

A small bore hose connecting the inlet manifold to a vacuum transducer within the module supplies the unit with information on engine load, and a charge air temperature sensor, which is a temperature sensitive resistor located in the air intake duct, provides information on engine intake air temperature. From this constantly changing data the ESC II module selects a particular advance setting from a range of ignition characteristics stored in its memory.

With the firing point established, the module switches off the ignition coil primary circuit, the magnetic field in the coil collapses and the high tension voltage is created. At precisely the right instant the ESC II module switches the coil primary circuit back on and the cycle is repeated for each cylinder in turn.

Additionally the ESC II module operates in conjunction with the fuel-injection and turbo systems to provide data on engine rpm to the fuel-injection control module, and to provide an overriding control of turbo boost pressure.

Programmed electronic ignition (1.4 litre fuel injection engines)

The ignition system consists of a Hall effect distributor (as described previously for RS Turbo models), TFI IV ignition module, coil and EEC IV module.

The distributor is similar to that used on earlier CVH engine models, but has no centrifugal or vacuum advance mechanisms, the advance functions being carried out by the EEC IV module. The distributor acts as a trigger and provides a pulse signal to the EEC IV module.

The distributor performs the following functions:

a) *Sends signals to the EEC IV module to trigger the ignition firing process.*
b) *Enables the EEC IV module to calculate engine speed from the pulse signals.*
c) *Distributes HT voltage to the spark plugs.*

The TFI (Thick Film Integration) IV module functions as a high current switch by controlling the ignition coil primary LT circuit. The module is controlled by one of two input signals, either from the Hall effect sensor in the distributor, or from the EEC IV module.

The signal from the distributor passes via the TFI IV module to the EEC IV module. The EEC IV module modifies the signal to provide ignition timing advance relative to engine speed, load and temperature, before returning it to the TFI IV module.

The EEC IV module provides total engine management via the ignition and fuel systems. From signals received from the various sensors, the module controls the following functions:

a) *Ignition timing.*
b) *Fuel delivery.*
c) *Deceleration fuelling.*

d) *Idle speed.*
e) *Engine overspeed protection.*

If the module should fail, the ignition timing will be switched by the TFI IV module (there will be no ignition advance) and fuel will be delivered at a constant rate. This state is known as the Limited Operation Strategy (LOS) and allows the vehicle to be driven, albeit with greatly reduced engine performance and fuel economy.

Should any of the system sensors fail, the EEC IV module will sense this and substitute a single predetermined value for the failed input. Again, this will allow continued engine operation, with reduced performance and driveability. Under these conditions a self-test code will be stored in the module memory to aid subsequent fault diagnosis by a Ford dealer.

Distributorless ignition system (DIS)

1.4 litre fuel injection engines

The mechanical distribution of high tension voltage (by a rotating distributor) is replaced by "static" solid-state electronic components.

The system selects the most appropriate ignition advance setting for the prevailing engine operating conditions from a three-dimensional map of values stored in the Electronic Spark Control (ESC) module memory. The module selects the appropriate advance value according to information supplied on engine load, speed, and operating temperature by various sensors.

Engine speed is monitored by a sensor mounted in the cylinder block, which is activated by 35 equally-spaced teeth on the flywheel. A gap occupies the position of the 36th tooth, which denotes 90° BTDC for No 1 cylinder. As the engine speed increases, so does the frequency and amplitude of the signal sent to the ESC module (photos).

Engine load information is provided by a pressure sensor which is integral with the ESC module. The sensor monitors vacuum in the inlet manifold via a hose.

Engine temperature is monitored by an Engine Coolant Temperature (ECT) sensor screwed into the bottom of the inlet manifold.

A DIS coil assembly is mounted on the cylinder block next to No 1 cylinder. The coil has two primary and two secondary windings.

One secondary winding supplies current to numbers 1 and 4 cylinders simultaneously, while the other supplies current to numbers 2 and 3 cylinders. Whenever either of the coils is energised, two sparks are generated. For example, one spark is produced in No 1 cylinder on its compression stroke, while the other spark is produced in No 4 cylinder on its exhaust stroke. The spark in No 4 cylinder is "redundant" and has no detrimental effect on engine performance.

1.6 litre Electronic Fuel Injection engines

The ignition system is under the overall control of the EEC IV engine management module. The module compares the signals provided by the various sensors with engine operating parameters stored in its memory, and varies the engine operating settings directly according to engine load and the prevailing operating conditions.

Ignition is via a Distributorless Ignition System (DIS), similar to that described previously for 1.4 litre fuel injection engines. The DIS is controlled by the E-DIS 4 module.

Precautions

 Warning: The DIS system carries much higher voltages than conventional systems, and adequate precautions must be taken to avoid personal injury. Refer to the "Safety first!" Section at the beginning of this manual before proceeding, and always disconnect the battery negative lead before working on the system

It is necessary to take extra care when working on the ignition system, both to avoid damage to semi-conductor devices and to avoid personal injury. Refer to the precautions given in "Safety First!" at the beginning of this manual, with particular reference to the warning concerning ignition HT voltage. Also refer to the precautions at the beginning of Chapter 5A.

5B

2 Ignition system - testing

Note: *Refer to the precautions given in Section 1 before proceeding.*

Contact breaker ignition system

1 By far the majority of breakdown and running troubles are caused by faults in the ignition system either in the low tension or high tension circuits.

2 There are two main symptoms indicating faults. Either the engine will not start or fire, or the engine is difficult to start and misfires. If it is a regular misfire (ie the engine is running on only two or three cylinders), the fault is almost sure to be in the secondary or high tension circuit. If the misfiring is intermittent the fault could be in either the high or low tension circuits. If the car stops suddenly, or will not start at all, it is likely that the fault is in the low tension circuit. Loss of power and overheating, apart from faulty carburation settings, are normally due to faults in the distributor or to incorrect ignition timing.

Engine fails to start

3 If the engine fails to start and the car was running normally when it was last used, first check there is fuel in the petrol tank. If the engine turns over normally on the starter motor and the battery is evidently well charged, then the fault may be in either the high or low tension circuits. First check the HT circuit.

4 One of the commonest reasons for bad starting is wet or damp spark plug leads and distributor. Remove the distributor cap. If condensation is visible internally dry the cap with a rag and also wipe over the leads. Refit the cap. A moisture dispersant can be very effective in these situations.

5 If the engine still fails to start, check the voltage is reaching the plugs by disconnecting each plug lead in turn at the spark plug end, and holding the end of the cable about ³⁄₁₆ inch (5 mm) away from the cylinder block. Spin the engine on the starter motor.

6 Sparking between the end of the cable and the block should be fairly strong with a strong regular blue spark. (Hold the lead with rubber to avoid electric shocks). If voltage is reaching the plugs, then remove them and clean and regap them. The engine should now start.

7 If there is no spark at the plug leads, take off the HT lead from the centre of the distributor cap and hold it to the block as before. Spin the engine on the starter once more. A rapid succession of blue sparks between the end of the lead and the block indicate that the coil is in order and that the distributor cap is cracked, the rotor arm is faulty, or the carbon brush in the top of the distributor cap is not making good contact with the rotor arm.

8 If there are no sparks from the end of the lead from the coil, check the connections at the coil end of the lead. If it is in order start checking the low tension circuit.

9 Use a 12v voltmeter or a 12v bulb and two lengths of wire. With the ignition switched on and the points open, test between the low tension wire to the coil and earth. No reading indicates a break in the supply from the ignition switch. Check the connections at the switch to see if any are loose. Refit them and the engine should run.

10 With the points still open take a reading between the moving point and earth. No reading here indicates a break in the wire or poor connections between the coil "-" terminal and distributor, or a faulty coil. Take a further reading between the coil "- " terminal and earth. No reading confirms a faulty coil. For these tests it is sufficient to separate the points with a piece of dry paper while testing with the points open.

Engine misfires

11 If the engine misfires regularly, run it at a fast idling speed. Pull off each of the plug caps in turn and listen to the note of the engine. Hold the plug cap in a dry cloth or with a rubber glove as additional protection against a shock from HT supply.

12 No difference in engine running will be noticed when the lead from the defective circuit is removed. Removing the lead from one of the good cylinders will accentuate the misfire.

13 Hold the lead about 3/16 inch (5 mm) away from the block. Re-start the engine. If the sparking is fairly strong and regular, the fault must lie in the spark plug.

14 The plug may be loose, the insulation may be cracked, or the points may have burnt away giving too wide a gap for the spark to jump. Worse still, one of the points may have broken off. Either renew the plug, or clean it, reset the gap and then test it.

15 If there is no spark at the end of the plug lead, or if it is weak and intermittent, check the ignition lead from the distributor to the plug. If the insulation is cracked or perished, renew the lead. Check the connections at the distributor cap.

16 If there is still no spark, examine the distributor cap carefully for tracking. This can be recognised by a very thin black line running between two or more electrodes, or between an electrode and some other part of the distributor. These lines are paths which now conduct electricity across the cap thus letting it run to earth. The only answer is a new distributor cap.

17 Apart from the ignition timing being incorrect, other causes of misfiring have already been dealt with under the Section dealing with the failure of the engine to start. To recap, these are that

a) *The coil may be faulty giving an intermittent misfire;*

b) *There may be a damaged wire or loose connection in the low tension circuit;*

c) *The condenser may be faulty; or*

d) *There may be a mechanical fault in the distributor (broken driving spindle or contact breaker spring).*

18 If the ignition timing is too far retarded, it should be noted that the engine will tend to overheat, and there will a quite noticeable drop in power. If the engine is overheating and the power is down, and the ignition timing is correct, then the carburettor should be checked, as it is likely that this is where the fault lies.

Electronic breakerless ignition

19 Testing of the electronic ignition system can only be accurately carried out using Ford dedicated test equipment and a systematic test procedure. For this reason any suspected faults in the system must be referred to a Ford dealer.

Programmed electronic ignition (RS Turbo models)

20 Refer to paragraph 19.

Programmed electronic ignition (1.4 litre fuel injection models)

21 Complete and accurate fault diagnosis is only possible using special test equipment available to a Ford dealer.

22 Where a component is obviously defective, it can be removed and a new component fitted in its place.

23 Although certain electrical checks can be

carried out to establish continuity or resistance, this is not recommended as the incorrect use of test probes between component connector pins can cause damage to the internal circuitry of some components.

24 Following the disconnection of the battery, all of the system Keep Alive Memory (KAM) values will be erased from the EEC IV module memory, which may result in erratic idle, engine surge, hesitation and a general deterioration of driving characteristics.

25 After reconnecting the battery, start the engine and allow it to idle for at least three minutes. After normal operating temperature is reached, increase the engine speed to 1200 rpm and maintain this speed for at least two minutes.

26 This procedure will allow the module to "re-learn" its reference values. It may be necessary to drive the vehicle for approximately five miles of varied driving to complete the learning process.

Distributorless ignition system (DIS)

All engines

27 Refer to paragraphs 21 to 23.

1.6 litre Electronic Fuel Injection engines

28 Refer to paragraphs 24 to 26.

3 Condenser (contact breaker system) - testing, removal and refitting

Note: *Refer to the precautions given in Section 1 before proceeding.*

Testing

1 The purpose of the condenser is to prevent excessive arcing of the contact breaker points, and to ensure that a rapid collapse of the magnetic field, created in the coil, and necessary if a healthy spark is to be produced at the plugs, is allowed to occur.

2 The condenser is fitted in parallel with the contact breaker points. If it becomes faulty it will lead to ignition failure, as the points will be prevented from cleanly interrupting the low tension circuit.

3 If the engine becomes very difficult to start, or begins to miss after several miles of running, and the contact breaker points show signs of excessive burning, then the condition of the condenser must be suspect. A further test can be made by separating the contact breaker points by hand, with the ignition switched on. If this is accompanied by an excessively strong flash, it indicates that the condenser has failed.

4 Without special test equipment, the only reliable way to diagnose condenser trouble is to renew the suspect unit and note if there is any improvement in performance. To do this proceed as follows according to engine type.

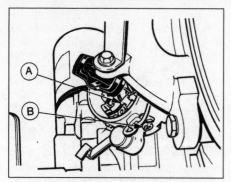

3.7 Distributor turned through 120° for condenser renewal - Bosch distributor, OHV engines

A LT lead connector
B Condenser retaining screw

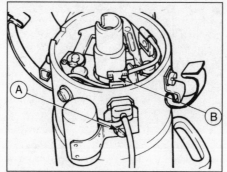

3.13 Bosch distributor condenser renewal - CVH engines

A Condenser retaining screw
B LT lead connector

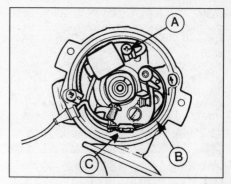

3.14 Lucas distributor condenser renewal - CVH engines

A Condenser retaining screw
B Contact breaker spring arm
C Hooked end of spring arm

Removal

OHV engines

5 Spring back the retaining clips and lift off the distributor cap. Withdraw the rotor arm from the distributor shaft.
6 Accurately mark the position of the distributor body in relation to the clamp plate, then slacken the clamp plate pinch bolt.
7 Turn the distributor body approximately 120° in a clockwise direction to expose the externally mounted condenser **(see illustration)**.
8 Disconnect the contact breaker points LT lead from the spade terminal, and the ignition LT lead at the coil.
9 Undo the retaining screw and withdraw the condenser from the side of the distributor body.
10 Place the new condenser in position and secure with the retaining screw.
11 Reconnect the LT leads, then turn the distributor back to its original position and align the marks made during removal. Tighten the clamp plate pinch bolt.

CVH engines

12 Spring back the retaining clips or undo

the screws as appropriate and lift off the distributor cap.
13 On the Bosch distributor disconnect the contact breaker points LT lead from the spade terminal, undo the retaining screw and withdraw the condenser from the side of the distributor body. Disconnect the ignition LT lead at the coil and remove the condenser **(see illustration)**.
14 On the Lucas distributor ease the contact breaker spring arm out of the plastic insulator and slide the combined LT and condenser lead out of the hooked end of the spring arm. Undo the condenser retaining screw and earth lead, disconnect the ignition LT lead at the coil, and withdraw the condenser and wiring from the distributor **(see illustration)**.

Refitting

OHV engines

15 Refit the rotor arm and distributor cap. If in any doubt about the distributor position, check the ignition timing as described in Chapter 1.

CVH engines

16 On all distributors refitting is the reverse sequence to removal.

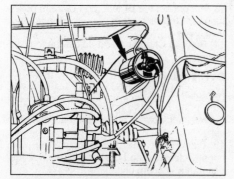

4.2a Ignition coil location (arrowed) - CVH engines with contact breaker ignition system

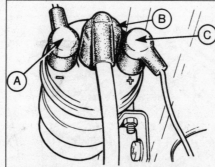

4.2b Ignition coil terminal identification - contact breaker ignition system

A Negative LT terminal to distributor
B HT terminal to distributor cap
C Positive LT feed terminal

4 Ignition HT coil - testing, removal and refitting

Note: *Refer to the precautions given in Section 1 before proceeding.*

All except models with DIS ignition system

Testing

1 Accurate checking of the coil output requires the use of special test equipment and should be left to a dealer or suitably equipped automotive electrician. It is however possible to check the primary and secondary winding resistance using an ohmmeter as follows.
2 To check the primary resistance disconnect the LT and HT wiring at the coil and connect the ohmmeter across the coil positive and negative terminals **(see illustrations)**. The resistance should be as given in the Specifications at the beginning of this Chapter.
3 To check the secondary resistance, connect one lead from the ohmmeter to the coil negative terminal, and the other lead to the centre HT terminal. Again the resistance should be as given in the Specifications.
4 If any of the measured valves vary significantly from the figures given in the Specifications, the coil should be renewed.
5 If a new coil is to be fitted, ensure that it is of the correct low voltage type suitable for use in conventional ignition systems equipped with ballast resistance.

Removal

6 The ignition coil is mounted on the engine compartment right-hand inner valance on OHV engine models, and on the left-hand inner valance on CVH engine versions.
7 To remove the coil, disconnect the LT leads at the coil positive and negative terminals and the HT lead at the centre terminal.
8 Undo the mounting bracket retaining bolts and remove the coil.

5B

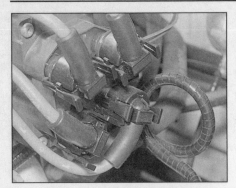

4.12 DIS coil location (plastic cover removed) - 1.6 litre Electronic Fuel Injection engine

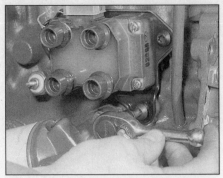

4.17 Removing a DIS coil securing screw - 1.3 litre HCS engine

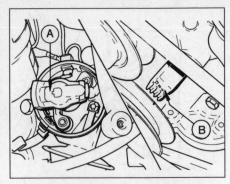

5.5 Distributor removal - OHV engines (contact breaker system)

A Rotor arm facing distributor cap No 1 spark plug lead segment
B Pulley notch aligned with TDC mark on timing scale

Refitting

9 Refitting is the reverse sequence to removal.

DIS ignition system

Testing

10 Testing of the DIS type ignition coil requires the use of specialist equipment, and should be entrusted to a Ford dealer.

Removal

11 On 1.1 and 1.3 litre HCS engines, the coil is mounted on the cylinder block, above the oil filter.
12 On 1.6 litre Electronic Fuel Injection (EFI) engines, the coil is mounted on the left-hand side of the cylinder head **(see illustration)**.
13 Disconnect the battery negative lead.
14 If applicable, remove the securing screw(s) and withdraw the plastic cover from the coil.
15 Release the retaining clip, and disconnect the coil wiring plug.
16 Compress the retaining clips on each side of the HT lead connectors, and disconnect the HT leads from the coil. Note the location of each lead to ensure correct refitting.
17 Remove the securing screws, and withdraw the coil **(see illustration)**.

Refitting

18 Refitting is a reversal of removal, ensuring that the HT leads are correctly reconnected.

---

5 Distributor - removal and refitting

Contact breaker ignition system

OHV engines

Removal

1 Disconnect the leads from the spark plugs, spring back the retaining clips and lift off the distributor cap.
2 Disconnect the LT lead at the coil negative terminal and the vacuum hose at the distributor vacuum unit.
3 Remove No 1 spark plug (nearest the crankshaft pulley).
4 Place a finger over the plug hole and turn the crankshaft in the normal direction of rotation (clockwise viewed from the crankshaft pulley end) until pressure is felt in No 1 cylinder. This indicates that the piston is commencing its compression stroke. The crankshaft can be turned with a spanner on the pulley bolt.
5 Continue turning the crankshaft until the notch in the pulley is aligned with the "O" mark on the timing scale just above the pulley. In this position No 1 piston is at Top Dead Centre (TDC) on compression **(see illustration)**.
6 Using a dab of quick drying paint, mark the position of the rotor arm on the rim of the distributor body. Make a further mark on the

distributor body and a corresponding mark on the cylinder block.
7 Undo the bolt securing the distributor clamp plate to the cylinder block. Do not remove the distributor by releasing the clamp plate pinch bolt.
8 Withdraw the distributor from the cylinder block. As the distributor is removed, the rotor arm will move a few degrees clockwise. Note the new position of the rotor arm and make a second mark on the distributor body rim **(see illustration)**.

Refitting

9 Before installing the distributor make sure that the crankshaft is still positioned at TDC as previously described. If a new distributor is being fitted, transfer the markings made during removal to the new unit.
10 Hold the distributor over its hole in the cylinder block with the mark made on the distributor body aligned with the mark on the cylinder block.
11 Position the rotor arm so that it points toward the mark made on the distributor rim after removal and push the distributor fully home. As the skew gears mesh the rotor arm will move anti-clockwise and should align with the first mark made on the distributor rim.
12 With all the marks aligned, refit and tighten the distributor clamp plate retaining bolt.
13 Reconnect the LT lead and vacuum hose, then refit the distributor cap, spark plug and plug leads.
14 Refer to Chapter 1 and adjust the ignition timing.

CVH engines

Removal

15 Spring back the retaining clips, or undo the retaining screws and lift off the distributor cap.
16 Disconnect the LT lead at the coil negative terminal and the vacuum hose at the distributor vacuum unit.
17 Undo the three distributor flange retaining bolts and withdraw the distributor from the cylinder head **(see illustration)**.

Refitting

18 Before refitting, check the condition of the

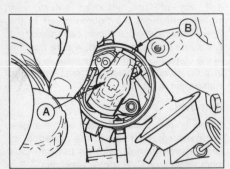

5.8 Rotor arm position marked on distributor body after removal - OHV engines (contact breaker system)

A Rotor arm
B Mark made on distributor body rim

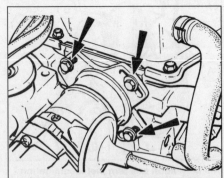

5.17 Distributor flange retaining bolt locations - CVH engines (contact breaker system)

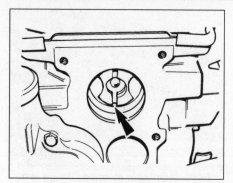

5.19 Align distributor shaft drive dog with slots in camshaft - CVH engines (contact breaker system)

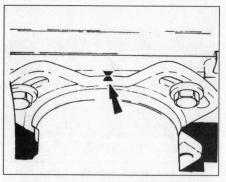

5.21 Distributor mounting flange and cylinder head punch mark locations - CVH engines (contact breaker system)

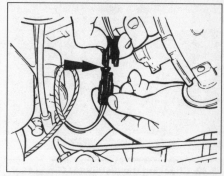

5.25 Disconnecting the distributor LT wiring multi-plug - CVH engines (electronic breakerless system)

O-ring oil seal at the base of the distributor and renew it if necessary.

19 Hold the distributor with the vacuum unit towards the inlet manifold side of the engine. Align the distributor shaft drive dog with slots in the end of the camshaft (see illustration).

20 Insert the distributor and turn the rotor arm slightly so that the drive dogs engage and the distributor moves fully home. Refit but do not tighten the three retaining bolts.

21 During production the distributor is precisely positioned for optimum ignition timing and marked accordingly with a punch mark on the distributor mounting flange and the cylinder head (see illustration).

22 If the original distributor is being refitted, align the punch marks, tighten the distributor flange mounting bolts and refit the distributor cap, LT lead and vacuum hose.

23 If a new distributor is being fitted, turn the distributor body so that the mounting bolts are positioned centrally in their elongated slots, then tighten the bolts just over finger tight. Refit the distributor cap, LT lead and vacuum hose, then adjust the ignition timing as described in Chapter 1.

Electronic breakerless ignition

OHV engines

Removal

24 Disconnect the leads from the spark

plugs, spring back the retaining clips and lift off the distributor cap.

25 Disconnect the distributor LT wiring multi-plug and the vacuum hose at the distributor vacuum unit (see illustration).

26 Proceed as described in paragraphs 3 and 4.

27 Refer to Chapter 1 and look up the ignition timing setting for the engine being worked on.

28 Continue turning the crankshaft until the notch in the pulley is aligned with the correct setting on the scale located just above and to the right of the pulley. The "O" mark on the scale represents Top Dead Centre (TDC) and the raised projections to the left of TDC are in increments of 4° BTDC (see illustration 5.5).

29 Check that the rotor arm is pointing to the notch on the rim of the distributor body (see illustration).

30 Make a mark on the distributor body and a corresponding mark on the cylinder block to aid refitting.

31 Undo the bolt securing the distributor clamp plate to the cylinder block, then withdraw the distributor from its location. As the distributor is removed, the rotor arm will move a few degrees clockwise. Note the new position of the rotor arm and make an alignment mark on the distributor body rim.

Refitting

32 Before installing the distributor, make sure that the crankshaft is still positioned at TDC as previously described. If a new distributor is

being fitted, transfer the markings made during removal to the new unit.

33 Hold the distributor over its hole in the cylinder block with the mark made on the distributor body aligned with the mark made on the cylinder block.

34 Position the rotor arm so that it points to the mark made on the distributor rim after removal, and push the distributor fully home (see illustration). As the skew gears mesh, the rotor arm will move anti-clockwise and should align with the manufacturer's mark on the distributor rim.

35 With the distributor in place, turn the body slightly, if necessary so that the arms of the trigger wheel and stator are aligned, then refit and tighten the clamp plate bolt.

36 Reconnect the LT wiring multi-plug and vacuum hose, then refit the distributor cap, spark plug and plug leads.

37 Refer to Chapter 1 and adjust the ignition timing.

CVH engines

Removal

38 Spring back the retaining clips or undo the retaining screws and lift off the distributor cap.

39 Disconnect the LT wiring multi-plug and the vacuum hose(s) at the distributor vacuum unit (where applicable).

40 Undo the distributor flange retaining bolts and withdraw the distributor from the cylinder head (see illustration).

5B

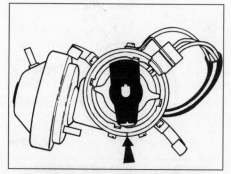

5.29 Rotor arm aligned with manufacturer's mark on distributor body rim - OHV engines (electronic breakerless system)

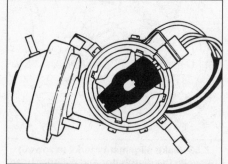

5.34 Rotor arm position prior to refitting - OHV engines (electronic breakerless system)

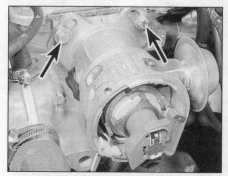

5.40 Distributor flange upper retaining bolts (arrowed) - CVH engines (electronic breakerless system)

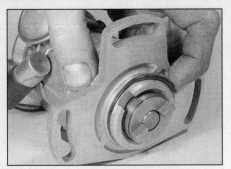

5.42 Checking the distributor O-ring seal condition - CVH engines (electronic breakerless system)

5.45a Distributor mounting flange and cylinder head punch marks (arrowed) - CVH engines (electronic breakerless system - early type distributor shown)

5.45b Distributor mounting flange and cylinder head punch marks (arrowed) - CVH engines (electronic breakerless system - later type distributor shown)

Refitting

41 At the beginning of 1985 a modified distributor of either Bosch or Lucas manufacture was introduced for all CVH engines equipped with electronic ignition. The modified unit is identifiable from the earlier type by only having no retaining bolt flanges instead of the three used previously. If an early type distributor is being renewed, only the modified type will be supplied by Ford parts dealers and it will therefore also be necessary to obtain an LT wire assembly (part No. 84AG-12045-BA) to adapt the existing wiring on the car to suit the modified distributor. It is also recommended by the manufacturers that a complete new set of HT leads to the latest Ford specification is obtained at the same time. Apart from connecting the new LT wire assembly which is described later in this Section, fitting the new distributor is the same as for earlier units, as follows.

42 Before refitting check the condition of the O-ring seal at the base of the distributor and renew it if necessary **(see illustration)**.

43 Hold the distributor with the vacuum unit (where fitted) towards the inlet manifold side of the engine and align the distributor shaft drive dog with the slot in the end of the camshaft.

44 Insert the distributor and turn the rotor arm slightly so that the drive dogs engage and the distributor moves fully home. Refit but do not tighten the retaining bolts.

45 During production the distributor is precisely positioned for optimum ignition timing and marked accordingly with punch marks on the distributor mounting flange and the cylinder head **(see illustrations)**.

46 If the original distributor is being refitted, align the punch marks, tighten the distributor flange retaining bolts and refit the distributor cap, wiring multi-plug and vacuum hose(s) as applicable.

47 If a new distributor is being fitted, turn the distributor body so that the retaining bolts are positioned centrally in their elongated slots, then tighten the bolts just over finger tight.

48 Refit the distributor cap, wiring multi-plug and vacuum hose(s) (as applicable). If an early type distributor is being replaced with the modified type, connect the green wire of the new LT wire assembly to the coil negative terminal, the black wire to the positive terminal and the brown wire to a suitable earth. Join the existing coil wires to the stud terminals of the new wiring assembly, green to green and black to black **(see illustration)**.

49 Adjust the ignition timing (Chapter 1).

Programmed electronic ignition (EEC IV) - 1.4 litre fuel injection engines

Removal

Note: *During production, engines are timed to*

an accuracy of half a degree using a microwave timing system. Subsequent timing requires the use of special test equipment. Unless absolutely necessary do not remove the distributor

50 Disconnect the battery negative lead.

51 Disconnect the HT lead from the coil, then remove the distributor cap and position it to one side.

52 Disconnect the distributor wiring plug.

53 Ensure that there are suitable alignment marks between the base of the distributor and the cylinder head. If necessary, make suitable marks using a scribe or a centre punch **(see illustration)**.

54 Remove the distributor retaining bolts and withdraw the distributor from the cylinder head.

Refitting

55 Commence refitting by checking the condition of the distributor oil seal, renewing it if necessary. Lubricate the seal with clean engine oil.

56 Align the distributor drive dog with the slot in the camshaft. The dog will only fit one way, as the slot is offset.

57 Loosely secure the distributor to the cylinder head with the retaining bolts, then turn the distributor body until the marks on the base of the distributor and the cylinder head are aligned. If a new distributor or cylinder

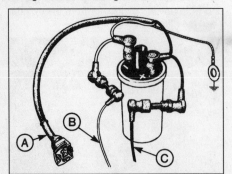

5.48 LT wire assembly to suit modified distributor - CVH engines (electronic breakerless system)

A Wiring multi-plug to amplifier module
B Green wire
C Black wire

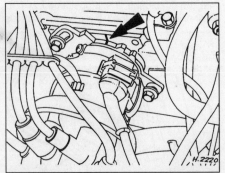

5.53 Make alignment marks (arrowed) between the distributor and cylinder head to assist alignment on refitting - 1.4 litre fuel injection engine

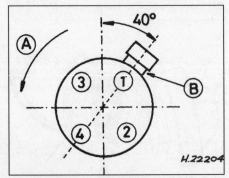

5.57 Correct alignment of distributor wiring plug - 1.4 litre fuel injection engine

A Direction of rotation
B Centreline through distributor wiring plug (40° to the vertical)

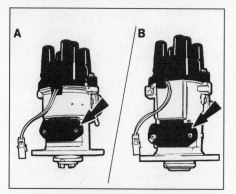

6.1 Electronic amplifier module locations
A *Early type Bosch distributor*
B *Early type Lucas distributor*

6.3a Electronic amplifier securing screw (arrowed) - later type Bosch distributor

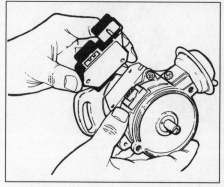

6.3b Removing the electronic amplifier module - later type Lucas distributor

6.10a Release the retaining clips . . .

6.10b . . . and remove the plenum chamber top cover

head has been fitted, position the wiring plug as shown **(see illustration)**. Tighten the retaining bolts.

58 Reconnect the distributor wiring plug, then fit the distributor cap and reconnect the coil HT lead.

59 Reconnect the battery negative lead.

60 Take the vehicle to a Ford dealer at the earliest opportunity to have the ignition timing accurately adjusted.

6 Ignition system electronic modules - removal and refitting

Amplifier module - electronic breakerless system

Removal

1 The amplifier module is located on the side of the distributor **(see illustration)**.

2 If necessary, to improve access remove the distributor as described in Section 5.

3 Remove the two securing screws, and withdraw the module from the side of the distributor **(see illustrations)**.

Refitting

4 Start refitting by cleaning all traces of old heat sink compound from the distributor body.

5 Apply fresh heat sink compound (supplied with new amplifier modules) to the back of the amplifier before fitting.

6 Refit the module and tighten the securing screws.

7 Where applicable, refit the distributor as described in Section 5.

RS Turbo engines (ESC II)

Electronic Spark Control (ESC II) module

Removal

8 Disconnect the battery negative terminal.

9 Remove the heater plenum chamber top cover rubber seal,

10 Release the five retaining clips and lift off the plenum chamber top cover **(see illustrations)**.

11 Undo the two nuts securing the heater fan

6.11 Undo the fan motor retaining nuts (arrowed)

motor assembly to the bulkhead. Lift the unit off the studs and place it on the engine. Avoid straining the wiring **(see illustration)**.

12 Unclip and detach the wiring multi-plug from the spark control module **(see illustration)**.

13 Undo the retaining screws and remove the module from the bulkhead. Detach the module vacuum hose.

Refitting

14 Refitting is the reverse sequence to removal. Take care not to trap the motor wiring when refitting the fan motor assembly, and ensure that it is engaged in the slot provided in the housing.

1.1 and 1.3 litre HCS engines (DIS/ESC)

⚠️ *Warning: The DIS system carries much higher voltages than conventional systems, and adequate precautions must be taken to avoid personal injury. Refer to the "Safety first!" Section at the beginning of this manual before proceeding, and always disconnect the battery negative lead before working on the system*

ESC module

Removal

15 The module is located on the front left-hand inner wing panel.

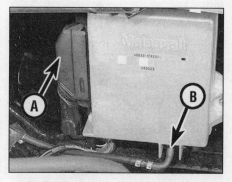

6.12 Spark control module wiring multi-plug (A) and vacuum hose (B)

5B

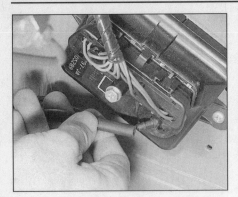

6.17 Disconnecting the vacuum hose from the ESC module

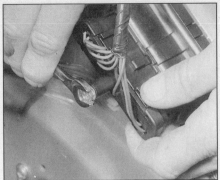

6.18 Unscrewing the ESC module wiring plug securing screw

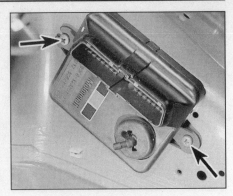

6.19 ESC module securing screws (arrowed)

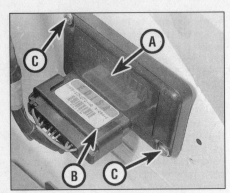

6.29 E-DIS-4 module location

A Module
B Wiring plug
C Securing screws

16 Disconnect the battery negative lead.
17 Disconnect the vacuum hose from the module **(see illustration)**.
18 Unscrew the central securing screw, and disconnect the wiring plug **(see illustration)**.
19 Remove the two screws securing the module to the wing panel, and withdraw the module **(see illustration)**.
Refitting
20 Refitting is a reversal of removal.

Fuel trap

21 A fuel trap is fitted in the vacuum line between the inlet manifold and the ESC module.

22 When refitting the fuel trap, the side marked "DIST" must face the ESC module, and the side marked "CARB" must face the inlet manifold.

1.4 litre fuel injection engines (EEC IV)

TFI IV module

Removal
23 The TFI IV module is located on the front left-hand inner wing panel.
24 Disconnect the battery negative lead.
25 Depress the locking tabs and disconnect the module wiring plug.
26 Remove the retaining screws, and withdraw the module.
Refitting
27 Refitting is a reversal of removal.

EEC IV module

28 Refer to Chapter 4, Part C.

1.6 litre Electronic Fuel Injection engines (EEC IV)

E-DIS 4 module

Refitting
29 The module is located on the front left-hand inner wing panel in the engine compartment **(see illustration)**.
30 Disconnect the battery negative lead.
31 Disconnect the module wiring plug. Do not pull on the wiring.

32 Remove the two securing screws and withdraw the module.
Refitting
33 Refitting is a reversal of removal.

EEC IV module

34 Refer to Chapter 4, Part D.

7 Distributorless Ignition System (DIS) components - removal and refitting

Electronic modules

1 Refer to Section 6.

DIS coil

2 Refer to Section 4.

Engine speed sensor

Removal

3 Disconnect the battery negative lead.
4 Disconnect the sensor wiring plug **(see illustration)**.
5 Remove the securing screw and withdraw the sensor.

Refitting

6 Refitting is a reversal of removal.

Engine Coolant Temperature (ECT) sensor

Removal

7 The ECT sensor is screwed into the inlet manifold **(see illustration)**.
8 Disconnect the battery negative lead.
9 Partially drain the cooling system as described in Chapter 1.
10 Disconnect the sensor wiring plug.
11 Unscrew the sensor from the inlet manifold.

Refitting

12 Refitting is a reversal of removal, but on completion top up the cooling system as described in "Weekly checks".

7.4 Disconnecting the engine speed sensor wiring plug - DIS

7.7 Engine coolant temperature sensor location (arrowed) - DIS

Chapter 6
Clutch

Contents

Degrees of difficulty

Easy, suitable for novice with little experience 	Fairly easy, suitable for beginner with some experience	Fairly difficult, suitable for competent DIY mechanic	Difficult, suitable for experienced DIY mechanic	Very difficult, suitable for expert DIY or professional

6

Specifications

General

Type . . . .   Single dry plate operated by self-adjusting cable

Driven plate

Diameter:
  1.1 litre Saloon . . . .   165 mm
  1.1 litre Estate and Van . . . .   190 mm
  1.3 and 1.4 litre (all models) . . . .   190 mm
  1.6 litre up to 1986:
    All models except RS Turbo . . . .   200 mm
    RS Turbo models . . . .   220 mm
  1.6 litre, 1986 onwards:
    All models . . . .   220 mm
Lining thickness . . . .   3.23 mm nominal
Pedal stroke . . . .   155 mm nominal

Torque wrench settings

	Nm	lbf ft
Cover assembly to flywheel:		
All except OHV engine models - 1987-on:		
165 mm diameter clutch	9 to 11	7 to 8
190, 200 and 220 mm diameter clutches	16 to 20	12 to 15
All OHV engine models - 1987-on	24 to 35	18 to 26
Lever assembly-to-clutch fork bolt	31 to 38	23 to 28

1 General description

1 The clutch is of single dry plate diaphragm spring type, operated mechanically by a self-adjusting cable.

2 The clutch components comprise a steel cover assembly, clutch driven plate, release bearing and release mechanism. The cover assembly which is bolted and dowelled to the rear face of the flywheel contains the pressure plate and diaphragm spring **(see illustration)**.

3 The driven plate is free to slide along the transmission input shaft splines and is held in position between the flywheel and pressure plate by the pressure of the diaphragm spring.

4 Friction material is riveted to the driven plate which has a spring cushioned hub to absorb transmission shocks and to help ensure a smooth take-up of the drive.

5 Depressing the clutch pedal moves the release lever on the transmission by means of the cable. This movement is transmitted to the release bearing which moves inwards against the fingers of the diaphragm spring. The spring is sandwiched between two annular rings which act as fulcrum points. As the release bearing pushes the spring fingers in, the outer circumference pivots out, so moving the pressure plate away from the flywheel and releasing its grip on the driven plate.

6 When the pedal is released, the diaphragm spring forces the pressure plate into contact with the friction linings of the driven plate. The plate is now firmly sandwiched between the pressure plate and flywheel, thus transmitting engine power to the transmission.

7 The self-adjusting mechanism is incorporated in the clutch pedal and consists of a pawl, toothed segment and tension spring **(see illustration)**. When the pedal is released the tension spring pulls the quadrant through

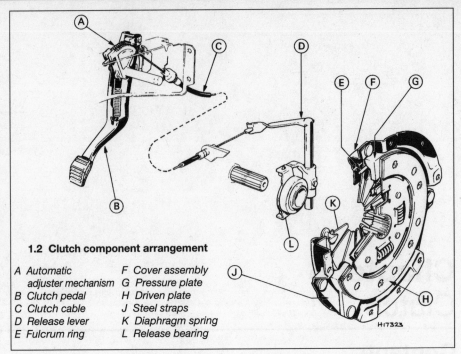

1.2 Clutch component arrangement

A Automatic	F Cover assembly
adjuster mechanism	G Pressure plate
B Clutch pedal	H Driven plate
C Clutch cable	J Steel straps
D Release lever	K Diaphragm spring
E Fulcrum ring	L Release bearing

the teeth of the pawl until all free play of the clutch cable is taken up. When the pedal is depressed the pawl teeth engage with the quadrant teeth thus locking the quadrant. The particular tooth engagement position will gradually change as the components move to compensate for wear in the clutch driven plate and stretch in the cable.

2 Clutch cable - removal and refitting

Removal

1 Bend back the two tabs, release the two clips and remove the insulating panel below the facia on the driver's side.

2 Using pliers, pull the cable forward and sideways to disengage it from the release lever on the transmission **(see illustration)**.

3 Release the plastic clip securing the cable to the steering rack housing.

4 Release the cable from the clutch pedal quadrant, pull it through the bulkhead into the

engine compartment and remove it from the car **(see illustration)**.

Refitting

5 Refitting is the reverse sequence to removal but align the white band on the cable with the paint spot on the steering rack housing before fitting the cable securing clip.

3 Clutch pedal - removal and refitting

Removal

1 Bend back the two tabs, release the two clips and remove the insulating panel below the facia on the driver's side.

2 Using pliers, pull the cable forward and sideways to disengage it from the release lever on the transmission.

3 Extract the retaining clip securing the brake pedal to the master cylinder or servo linkage pushrod.

4 Detach the clutch cable from the pedal.

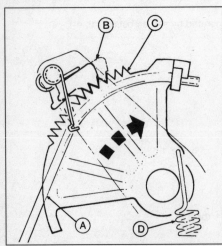

1.7 Clutch cable self-adjustment mechanism

A Clutch cable	C Toothed quadrant
B Pawl	D Tension spring

2.2 Disconnecting clutch cable at transmission release lever

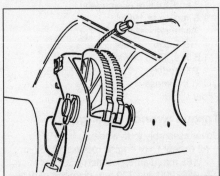

2.4 Disconnecting clutch cable from self-adjusting quadrant at pedal

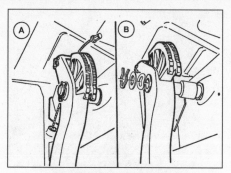

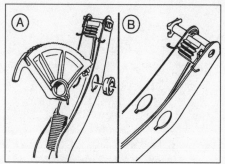

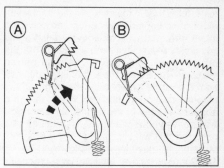

**3.5 Clutch pedal removal
(LHD shown, RHD similar)**
A Removing cable from pedal quadrant
B Removing pedal from pivot shaft

**3.6 Clutch pedal components
(LHD shown, RHD similar)**
A Toothed quadrant, tension spring and
   pivot bushes
B Pawl, pivot pin and clips

**3.7 Positioning of self-adjusting
mechanism prior to refitting pedal**
A Lift pawl and turn quadrant
B Pawl teeth resting on quadrant smooth
   face

5 Remove the retaining clip from the pedal cross-shaft. Note the position of the spacers and washers, then withdraw the cross-shaft towards the heater. Lift off the clutch and brake pedals **(see illustration)**.

6 The pedal can now be dismantled as necessary in order to renew the bushes, spring or adjustment mechanism **(see illustration)**.

Refitting

7 To refit, first set the pawl with its spring so that the pawl is in contact with the smooth part of the quadrant **(see illustration)**.

8 Position the pedals in the support bracket and refit the cross-shaft, which should have been greased with molybdenum disulphide grease. Ensure that the washers are refitted in the same position as noted during removal then refit the central retaining clip to the cross-shaft.

9 Refit the master cylinder or servo linkage pushrod-to-brake pedal retaining clip.

10 Connect the clutch cable to the pedal and, at the transmission end, to the release lever.

11 Operate the clutch pedal two or three times and refit the facia lower insulating panel.

4 Clutch assembly - removal, inspection and refitting

Removal

1 Remove the transmission as described in Chapter 7.

2 In a diagonal sequence, half a turn at a time, slacken the bolts securing the clutch cover assembly to the flywheel.

3 When all the bolts are slack, remove them and then ease the cover assembly off the locating dowels. Collect the driven plate which will drop out when the cover assembly is removed.

Inspection

Note: During the production life of the vehicle, various modifications were made to the clutch cover and driven plate components. Note all components are interchangeable, and it is therefore important to ensure that the correct replacement parts are obtained if components are renewed. Retain the old components for reference, and if necessary consult a Ford dealer for advice.

4 With the clutch assembly removed, clean off all traces of asbestos dust using a dry cloth. This is best done outside or in a well ventilated area; asbestos dust is harmful, and must not be inhaled.

5 Examine the linings of the driven plate for wear and loose rivets, distortion, cracks, broken torsion springs and worn splines. The surface of the friction linings may be highly glazed, but, as long as the friction material pattern can be clearly seen, this is satisfactory. If there is any sign of oil contamination, indicated by a continuous, or patchy, shiny black discolouration, the plate must be renewed and the source of the contamination traced and rectified. This will be either a

leaking crankshaft oil seal or transmission input shaft oil seal - or both. Renewal procedures are given in Chapter 2 and Chapter 7 respectively. The plate must also be renewed if the lining thickness has worn down to, or just above, the level of the rivet heads.

6 Check the machined faces of the flywheel and pressure plate. If either is grooved, or heavily scored, renewal is necessary. The pressure plate must also be renewed if any cracks are apparent, or if the diaphragm spring is damaged or its pressure suspect.

7 With the gearbox removed it is advisable to check the condition of the release bearing, as described in Section 5.

Refitting

8 To refit the clutch assembly, place the driven plate in position with the flat side marked "FLYWHEEL SIDE" or "SCHWUNGRADSEITE" towards the flywheel **(see illustrations)**.

9 Hold the plate in place and refit the cover assembly loosely on the dowels. Refit the retaining bolts and tighten them finger tight so that the driven plate is gripped, but can still be moved.

10 The clutch must now be centralised so that when the engine and gearbox are mated, the gearbox input shaft splines will pass through the splines in the centre of the hub.

11 Centralisation can be carried out quite easily by inserting a round bar or long screwdriver through the hole in the centre of the driven plate, so that the end of the bar

6

4.8a Fit the driven plate with the flat side towards the flywheel

4.8b Driven plate marking

4.12 Tightening the cover retaining bolts. Note clutch aligning tool in position

rests in the hole in the centre of the crankshaft. Moving the bar sideways or up and down will move the plate in whichever direction is necessary to achieve centralisation. With the bar removed, view the driven plate hub in relation to the hole in the end of the crankshaft and the circle created by the ends of the diaphragm spring fingers. When the hub appears exactly in the centre, all is correct. Alternatively, if a clutch aligning tool can be obtained this will eliminate all the guesswork obviating the need for visual alignment.

12 Tighten the cover retaining bolts gradually, in a diagonal sequence to the specified torque wrench setting **(see illustration)**.

13 Refit the transmission (Chapter 7).

5 Clutch release bearing - removal, inspection and refitting

Models with release fork bolted to shaft

Removal

1 Remove the transmission (Chapter 7).
2 Undo the bolt securing the release bearing fork to the release lever shaft **(see illustration)**.
3 Slide out the shaft and remove the bearing from the fork **(see illustrations)**.

Inspection

4 Check the bearing for smoothness of operation and renew it if there is any roughness or harshness as the bearing is spun. If this operation is being carried out in conjunction with renewal of the clutch

5.2 Removing release bearing fork retaining bolt

assembly, it is advisable to renew the release bearing as a matter of course.

Refitting

5 Refit in reverse order, using a little lithium-based grease on all pivot points.

Models with one-piece release fork/shaft

Removal

6 Remove the transmission (Chapter 7).
7 Undo and remove the pinch-bolt, and then lift off the release lever **(see illustrations)**.
8 Remove the rubber cover from the end of the shaft.
9 Remove the nylon bush **(see illustration)**.
10 Remove the release bearing **(see illustration)**.
11 Lift the fork/shaft assembly from the lower bearing, then lower it out of the bellhousing **(see illustration)**.

5.3a Slide out the release lever shaft . . .

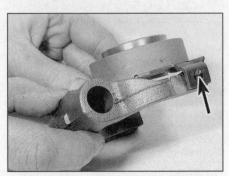

5.3b . . . then separate the bearing from the fork. Fork locating roll pin arrowed

Inspection

12 Refer to paragraph 4.

Refitting

13 Refit in reverse order, using a little lithium-based grease on all pivot points.

5.7a One-piece release fork/shaft in situ

5.7b Clutch release lever pinch-bolt

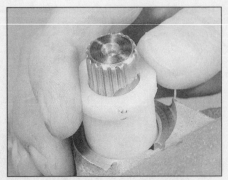

5.9 Removing the nylon bush

5.10 Removing the release bearing

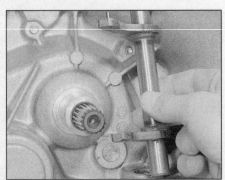

5.11 Lifting out the fork/shaft assembly

Chapter 7 Part A:
Manual transmission

Contents

Degrees of difficulty

| **Easy,** suitable for novice with little experience | **Fairly easy,** suitable for beginner with some experience | **Fairly difficult,** suitable for competent DIY mechanic | **Difficult,** suitable for experienced DIY mechanic | **Very difficult,** suitable for expert DIY or professional |

Specifications

Type . . . .   Four or five forward speeds and reverse. Synchromesh on all forward speeds

Gear ratios

Four-speed transmission:
   1.1 litre OHV engine with 3 + E transmission:

1st	3.58 : 1
2nd	2.04 : 1
3rd	1.30 : 1
4th (E)	0.88 : 1
Reverse	3.77 : 1

   1.1 and 1.3 litre OHV, and 1.1, 1.3 and 1.4 litre CVH engines:

1st	3.58 : 1
2nd	2.04 : 1
3rd	1.35 : 1
4th	0.95 : 1
Reverse	3.77 : 1

   1.6 litre CVH engines:

1st	3.15 : 1
2nd	1.91 : 1
3rd	1.28 : 1
4th	0.95 : 1
Reverse	3.62 : 1

Five-speed transmission:
   1.1 litre OHV, and 1.1, 1.3 and 1.4 litre CVH engines:

1st	3.58 : 1
2nd	2.04 : 1
3rd	1.35 : 1
4th	0.95 : 1
5th	0.76 : 1
Reverse	3.62 : 1

7A

Gear ratios (continued)

1.3 litre OHV, and 1.3 and 1.6 litre CVH engines:

1st	3.15 : 1
2nd	1.91 : 1
3rd	1.28 : 1
4th	0.95 : 1
5th	0.76 : 1
Reverse	3.62 : 1

Final drive ratios:

	Saloon and Estate	Van
Four-speed transmission:		
1.1 litre OHV engine with 3+ E transmission	3.58 : 1	3.58 : 1
1.1 litre OHV and CVH engines (up to 1986)	4.06 : 1	4.29 : 1
1.1 litre OHV engine (1986 onwards)	3.84 : 1	4.29 : 1
1.3 litre OHV, and 1.3 and 1.4 litre CVH engines	3.84 : 1	4.29 : 1
1.6 litre CVH engine (except XR3 models)	3.58 : 1	4.06 : 1
1.6 litre CVH engine (XR3 models)	3.84 : 1	-
Five-speed transmission:		
1.1 and 1.3 litre OHV engines, and 1.1, 1.3 and 1.4 litre		
CVH engines	3.84 : 1	-
1.6 litre CVH engine with carburettor (except XR3 models)	3.58 : 1	3.59 : 1
1.6 litre CVH engine with fuel injection	4.27 : 1	-
1.6 litre CVH engine (XR3 models)	3.84 : 1	-
1.6 litre CVH engine (XR3i models)	4.27 : 1	-
1.6 litre CVH engine (RS Turbo models)	3.82 : 1	-

General

Lubricant type/specification . . . . See *"Lubricants and Fluids"*

Torque wrench settings

	Nm	lbf ft
Transmission assembly to engine	35 to 45	26 to 33
Clutch housing cover plate	35 to 45	26 to 33
Front transmission mounting bracket to transmission (pre-1986		
models)	41 to 51	30 to 38
Front and rear transmission mounting bolts (pre-1986 models)	52 to 64	38 to 47
Transmission mountings to transmission (1986 models onwards)	80 to 100	59 to 74
Transmission support crossmember to body (1986 models onwards) .	52	38
Lower arm mounting pivot bolt	51 to 64	38 to 47
Lower arm balljoint pinch-bolt	48 to 60	35 to 44
Starter motor bolts	35 to 45	26 to 33
Anti-roll bar clamp bolts	45 to 56	33 to 41
Gearchange rod clamp bolt	14 to 17	10 to 13
Gearchange stabiliser to transmission	50 to 60	37 to 44
Selector shaft locking mechanism cap nut	30	22
Oil filler plug	23 to 30	17 to 22
Gearchange housing to floor (pre-1984 models)	13 to 17	10 to 12
Gearchange housing to floor (1984 models onwards)	5 to 7	4 to 5
Transmission housing cover bolts (four-speed)	12 to 15	9 to 11
Reversing light switch	23 to 30	17 to 22

---

1 General description

1 The manual transmission may be of four or five-speed type depending on model, year of manufacture and/or options fitted. Both transmission types are basically the same except that the five-speed version incorporates a modified selector mechanism, and an additional gear and synchro-hub contained in a housing attached to the side of the main transmission casing. Both transmission types use synchromesh gear engagement on all forward gears **(see illustrations)**.

2 The mainshaft and input shaft carry the constant mesh gear cluster assemblies and are supported on ball and roller bearings. The short v-splined end of the input shaft eliminates the need for additional support from a crankshaft spigot bearing.

3 The synchromesh gear engagement is by sliding keys which act against baulk rings under the movement of the synchroniser sleeves. Gear selection is by means of a floor-mounted lever connected by a remote control housing and gearchange rod to the selector shaft in the gearbox. Selector shaft movement is transmitted to the selector forks via the guide shaft and guide levers.

4 The final drive (differential) unit is integral with the transmission and is located between the two transmission housings. On RS Turbo models a viscous coupling type limited slip differential is fitted as standard equipment.

2 Gearchange mechanism - removal, refitting and adjustment

Pre-1984 models

Removal

1 If working on the four-speed transmission engage 4th gear. If working on the five-speed transmission engage reverse gear.

2 Unscrew the gear lever knob, slide the rubber gaiter up the lever and remove it.

3 Jack up the front of the car and support it on axle stands (see *"Jacking and Vehicle Support"*).

4 To provide working clearance, release the exhaust system from its rubber mountings at

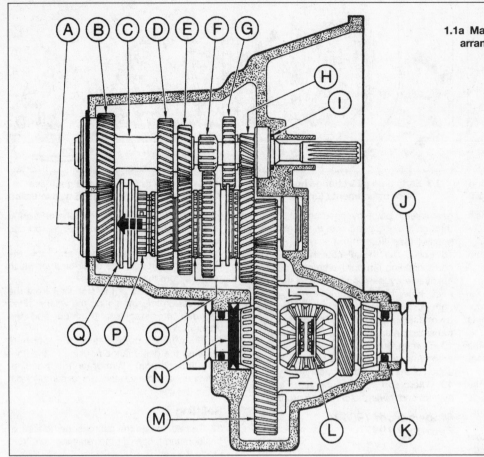

1.1a Manual transmission and final drive gear arrangement - four-speed transmission

A Mainshaft
B 4th gear
C Input shaft
D 3rd gear
E 2nd gear
F Reverse gear
G Reverse idler gear
H 1st gear
I Input shaft oil seal
J Driveshaft joint
K Driveshaft oil seal
L Driveshaft snap-ring
M Differential
N Diaphragm springs
O 1st/2nd synchro
P 3rd/4th synchro
Q 3rd/4th synchro ring
  (4th gear engaged)

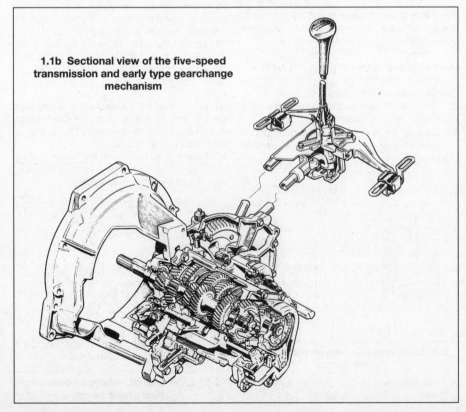

1.1b Sectional view of the five-speed transmission and early type gearchange mechanism

the rear, lower the system slightly and support it on blocks.

5 Where fitted unhook the tension spring which runs between the gearchange rod and the chassis side-member.

6 Slacken the clamp bolt and pull the gearchange rod from the selector shaft which projects from the transmission **(see illustration)**.

7 Unbolt the end of the stabiliser from the transmission housing noting the washer fitted between the stabiliser trunnion and the transmission **(see illustration)**.

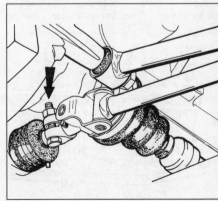

2.6 Gearchange rod-to-selector shaft clamp bolt (arrowed)

7A

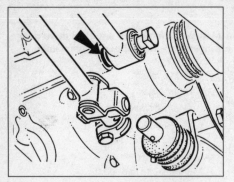

2.7 Gearchange stabiliser-to-transmission attachment with spacing washer arrowed

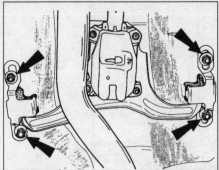

2.8 Early type gearchange housing-to-floor attachments (arrowed)

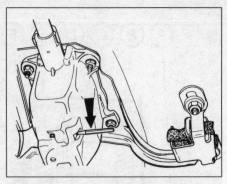

2.15 Using a drift to lock the gear lever in 4th gear position - four-speed transmission

8 Undo the four nuts and recover the washers securing the gearchange housing to the floor **(see illustration)**. Withdraw the housing, gearchange rod and stabiliser assembly from under the car.

Refitting

9 To refit, locate the housing over the four studs in the floorpan and loosely fit the nuts with their washers.

10 Reconnect the stabiliser ensuring that the washer is fitted between the stabiliser trunnion and the transmission.

11 Tighten the stabiliser retaining bolt to the specified torque then tighten the gearchange housing nuts, also to the specified torque. Refit the gaiter and gear lever knob.

12 Ensure that the selector shaft is free from grease and oil then engage the gearchange rod over the selector shaft end. Do not tighten the clamp bolt at this stage.

13 Where fitted reconnect the tension spring to the gearchange rod and chassis member, then adjust the linkage as follows.

Adjustment

Note: *A 3.5 mm twist drill will be required for this operation.*

14 With the gearchange rod-to-selector shaft clamp bolt loosened, proceed as follows.

15 Have an assistant move the gear lever into 4th gear position (four-speed transmission) or reverse gear position (five-speed transmission). From under the car lock the

gear lever in place by inserting a 3.5 mm drift through the alignment hole in the gearchange housing **(see illustration)**.

16 Ensure that the selector shaft is also in the corresponding 4th or reverse gear position as applicable by inserting a rod into the selector shaft hole, turning clockwise and pushing right in. Take up any play in the selector shaft by attaching an elastic band to the rod and transmission as shown **(see illustration)**.

17 Tighten the gearchange rod clamp bolt then remove the drift and rod and check the action of the gearchange mechanism.

18 Where applicable, reconnect the exhaust system and lower the car to the ground.

Models from 1984 to February 1987

Removal

19 If working on the four-speed transmission, engage 4th gear. If working on the five-speed transmission, engage the reverse gear.

20 Unscrew the gear lever knob then disengage the outer rubber gaiter from the centre console. Slide the gaiter up and off the gear lever **(see illustration)**.

21 Release the inner rubber gaiter and slide it up and off the gear lever.

22 Jack up the front of the car and support it on axle stands (see *"Jacking and Vehicle Support"*).

23 Where fitted unhook the tension spring which runs between the gearchange rod and the chassis side-member.

24 Slacken the clamp bolt and pull the gearchange rod from the selector shaft which projects from the transmission.

25 Unbolt the end of the stabiliser from the transmission housing noting the washer fitted between the stabiliser trunnion and the transmission.

26 From inside the car undo the four nuts securing the gearchange housing to the floor **(see illustration)**. Withdraw the housing, gearchange rod and stabiliser assembly from under the car.

Refitting

27 To refit, locate the gearchange housing in position and loosely fit the retaining nuts from inside the car.

28 From below reconnect the stabiliser ensuring that the washer is fitted between the stabiliser trunnion and the transmission.

29 Tighten the stabiliser retaining bolt to the specified torque then tighten the gearchange housing nuts, also to the specified torque.

30 Refit the rubber gaiters and the gear lever knob.

31 Ensure that the selector shaft is free from grease and oil then engage the gearchange rod over the selector shaft end. Do not tighten the clamp bolt at this stage.

32 Where fitted reconnect the tension spring to the gearchange rod and chassis member, then adjust the linkage as follows.

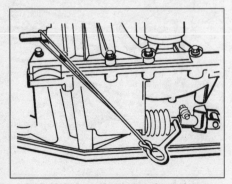

2.16 Using an elastic band to take up selector shaft free play

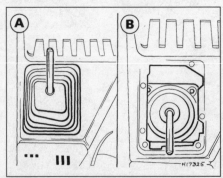

2.20 Later type gearchange mechanism rubber gaiters

A Gear lever outer gaiter *B Gear lever inner gaiter*

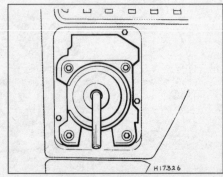

2.26 Later type gearchange housing-to-floor attachments

3.5 Levering out an old differential side gear oil seal

3.8 Driving a new differential side gear oil seal into position using a socket

Adjustment

33 With the gearchange rod-to-selector shaft clamp bolt loosened, proceed as described in paragraphs 14 to 17 inclusive then lower the car to the ground.

Models from February 1987 on

34 The procedure is the same as that for 1984 to February 1987 models except that the 2nd gear should be selected for four-speed transmissions, and the 4th gear should be selected for five-speed transmissions.

3 Oil seals - renewal

1 Oil leaks frequently occur due to wear or deterioration of the differential side gear seals and/or the gearchange selector shaft oil seal and speedometer drive pinion O-ring. Renewal of these seals is relatively easy, since repairs can be performed without removing the transmission from the vehicle.

Differential side gear oil seals

2 The differential side gear oil seals are located at the sides of the transmission. If leakage at the seal is suspected, raise the vehicle and support it securely on axle stands (see "Jacking and Vehicle Support"). If the seal is leaking, oil will be found on the side of the transmission below the driveshaft.
3 Refer to Chapter 8, and remove the appropriate driveshaft.
4 Wipe clean the old oil seal and then note the seal orientation and fitted depth below the edge of the casing. This is necessary to determine the correct fitted position of the new oil seal.
5 Using a large screwdriver or lever, carefully prise the oil seal out of the transmission casing, taking care not to damage the casing **(see illustration)**. If the oil seal is reluctant to move, it is sometimes helpful to carefully drive it into the transmission a little way applying the force at one point only. This will have the effect of swivelling the seal out of the casing,

and it can then be pulled out. If the oil seal is particularly difficult to remove, an oil seal removal tool may be obtained from a garage or accessory shop.
6 Wipe clean the oil seal seating in the transmission casing.
7 Dip the new oil seal in clean oil, then press it a little way into the casing by hand, making sure that it is square to its seating.
8 Using a suitable piece of tubing or a large socket, carefully drive the oil seal fully into the casing up to its previously-noted fitted depth **(see illustration)**.
9 Refit the driveshaft with reference to Chapter 8.

Gearchange selector shaft oil seal

10 Apply the handbrake, then jack up the front of the vehicle and support it on axle stands (see "Jacking and Vehicle Support").
11 Unscrew the clamp bolt securing the gearchange rod to the selector shaft. Pull off the gearchange rod, and remove the rubber boot.
12 Using a suitable tool or grips, pull the oil seal out of the transmission casing. Ford technicians use a slide hammer, with an end fitting which locates over the oil seal extension. In the absence of this tool, if the oil seal is particularly tight, drill one or two small holes in the oil seal, and screw in self-tapping

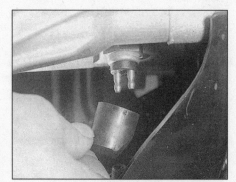

4.4 Disconnecting the wiring from the reversing light switch

screws. The oil seal can then be removed from the casing by pulling on the screws.
13 Wipe clean the oil seal seating in the transmission.
14 Dip the new oil seal in clean oil, then press it a little way into the casing by hand, making sure that it is square to its seating.
15 Using a suitable tube or a large socket, carefully drive the oil seal fully into the casing.
16 Locate the rubber boot over the selector shaft.
17 Refit the gearchange rod to the linkage and adjust with reference to Section 2, then tighten the clamp bolt.

Speedometer drive pinion O-ring

18 The procedure is described in Section 5 of this Chapter.

4 Reversing light switch - testing, removal and refitting

Testing

1 The reversing light circuit is controlled by a plunger-type switch screwed into the forward facing side of the transmission housing, beneath the clutch release lever.
2 If a fault develops in the circuit, first ensure that the fuse has not blown.
3 To test the switch, disconnect the switch wiring, and use a test meter (set to the resistance function), or a battery-and-bulb test circuit to check that there is continuity between the switch terminals only when the reverse gear is selected. If this is not the case, and there are no obvious breaks or other damage to the wires, the switch is faulty and must be renewed.

Removal

4 Disconnect the battery negative lead, then disconnect the wiring from the switch **(see illustration)**.
5 Unscrew the switch from the transmission.

Refitting

6 Refitting is a reversal of removal.

7A

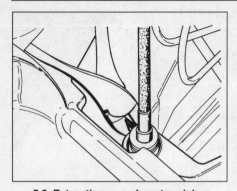

5.2 Extracting speedometer pinion retaining roll pin

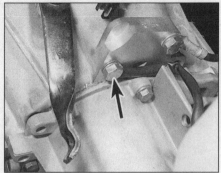

6.3 Transmission earth strap (arrowed)

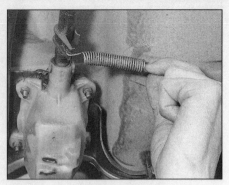

6.13 Gearchange rod tension spring

5 Speedometer driven gear - removal and refitting

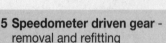

Removal

Note: *A new pinion bearing O-ring must be used on refitting.*

1 This work may be done without having to remove the transmission from the vehicle.

2 Using a pair of side cutting pliers, lever out the roll pin which secures the speedometer drive pinion bearing in the transmission housing **(see illustration)**.

3 Withdraw the pinion bearing, together with the speedometer drive cable. Separate the cable from the pinion by unscrewing the knurled ring or nut.

4 Slide the pinion out of the bearing.

Refitting

5 Always renew the O-ring on the pinion bearing before fitting.

6 Insert the pinion and bearing into the transmission housing using a back-and-forth twisting motion to mesh the pinion teeth with those of the drivegear. Secure with the roll pin.

 HAYNES HINT *Do not fit the pin flush with the casing, as this makes possible future removal difficult.*

7 Reconnect the speedometer cable.

6 Manual transmission assembly - removal and refitting

Removal

1 Disconnect the battery negative terminal.

2 To ensure correct connection and adjustment of the gearchange mechanism when refitting the transmission on pre-February 1987 models, select 4th gear on four-speed models or reverse gear on five-speed models. On cars produced from February 1987 select 2nd gear on four-speed models or 4th gear on five-speed models.

3 Disconnect the earth strap from the top of the transmission housing **(see illustration)**.

4 Undo the retaining nut and disconnect the speedometer cable at the transmission.

5 Pull the transmission breather hose out of the opening in the side-member.

6 Using pliers, pull the clutch cable forwards and sideways to disengage it from the release lever then withdraw it from the support bracket on the transmission.

7 Where applicable, tie the heater hose, which runs from the thermostat housing to the heater, to one side to provide greater access.

8 Jack up the front of the car and support it on axle stands (see *"Jacking and Vehicle Support"*).

9 Support the engine using a jack and suitable block of wood positioned under the sump.

10 Disconnect the wiring at the starter

solenoid then undo the three nuts and bolts and remove the starter motor.

11 Undo the two bolts and remove the cover plate from the lower face of the clutch housing.

12 Disconnect the reversing light switch wires.

13 Where fitted, unhook the tension spring which runs between the gearchange rod and the chassis side-member **(see illustration)**.

14 Slacken the clamp bolt and pull the gearchange rod from the selector shaft which projects from the transmission **(see illustration)**.

15 Unbolt the end of the gearchange stabiliser from the transmission housing and recover the spacer washer **(see illustration)**.

16 On cars equipped with an anti-lock braking system refer to Chapter 9 and remove the modulator drivebelt.

17 On pre-1986 models place a suitable container beneath the selector shaft locking mechanism cap nut **(see illustration)**. Unscrew the cap nut, remove the spring and interlock pin and allow the transmission oil to drain.

Caution: *Take care when unscrewing the cap nut as the tension of the spring may cause the pin to fly out when the cap nut is released. Apply sealer to the cap nut threads when refitting (see "Specifications"). From 1986 onwards there is insufficient clearance to allow removal of the cap nut and the oil cannot be drained until the transmission has been removed.*

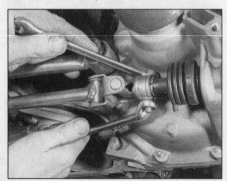

6.14 Removing the gearchange rod from the selector shaft

6.15 Removing the gearchange stabiliser

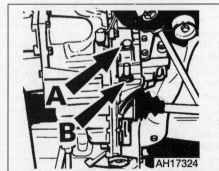

6.17 Transmission oil filler plug (A) and selector shaft locking mechanism cap nut (B)

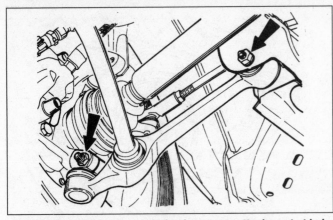

6.19 Right-hand front suspension lower arm attachment at hub carrier and body (arrowed)

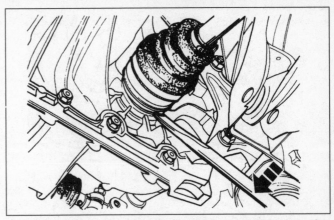

6.20 Using a lever to release the constant velocity joint from the transmission

18 Disconnect the right-hand front suspension lower arm balljoint from the hub carrier by removing the nut and pinch-bolt. Note that the pinch-bolt is of the socket-headed (Torx) type and a special key or socket bit, available from most accessory shops, will be required for removal.

19 Disconnect the lower suspension arm from the body at its inner end by removing the mounting pivot bolt (see illustration).

20 Insert a lever between the inner constant velocity joint and the transmission. Firmly strike the lever while pulling outwards on the

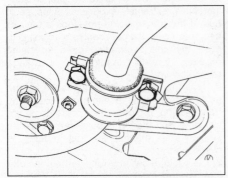

6.22a Anti-roll bar left-hand mounting clamp bolts - pre-1986 models

roadwheel to release the constant velocity joint from the differential (see illustration). Withdraw the joint completely from the differential and suspend the driveshaft so that it does not hang down by more than 45°. If the transmission oil has not been drained, be prepared for some spillage when the driveshaft is removed.

21 Repeat paragraphs 18, 19 and 20 for the left-hand driveshaft. After removal, retain the differential sun gears in alignment by inserting a dowel or similar, of suitable diameter into the differential so that it engages the sun gear on one side.

22 On pre-1986 models equipped with an anti-roll bar, undo the two bolts securing the left-hand mounting clamp and remove the clamp. Additionally, on 1985 RS Turbo models, disconnect the left-hand suspension tie-bar front mounting (see illustrations).

23 On 1986 models onwards undo the three bolts each side securing the anti-roll bar mounting plates to the body (see illustration).

24 Where fitted remove the engine splash shields on the left and right-hand sides (see illustration).

25 Support the transmission assembly using a suitable jack.

26 Undo all the bolts securing the clutch housing flange to the engine.

27 On pre-1986 models undo the four bolts securing the front mounting bracket to the transmission and the nut securing the mounting to the body bracket. Also undo the bolts securing the rear mounting body bracket to the body (see illustrations).

28 On 1986 models onwards, undo the two front bolts, two rear bolts and additional side nut and bolt securing the transmission support crossmember to the body (see illustration).

29 Lower the engine and transmission assembly as far as possible and withdraw the transmission squarely off the engine. Lower the unit to the ground and withdraw it from under the car.

Refitting

30 Before refitting, lightly smear the splined end of the input shaft with molybdenum disulphide grease.

31 Check that the engine adapter plate is correctly located on its dowels.

32 Offer the transmission up to the engine and engage the input shaft with the splined hub of the clutch driven plate.

33 Push the transmission into full engagement with the engine and check that the unit sits on its locating dowels and that the adapter plate has not been displaced. Any reluctance for the transmission to mate with

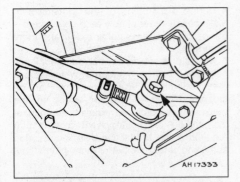

6.22b Left-hand suspension tie-bar front mounting (arrowed) - 1985 RS Turbo models

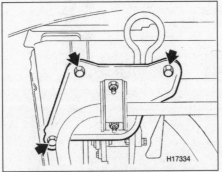

6.23 Anti-roll bar mounting plate attachments (arrowed) - 1986 models onwards

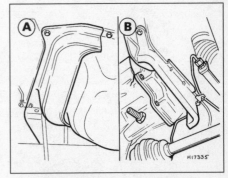

6.24 Engine splash shield details

A Right-hand side   B Left-hand side

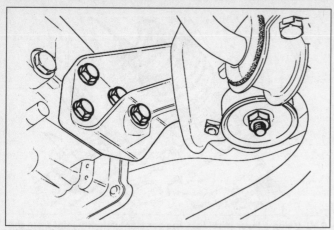

6.27a Transmission front mounting and bracket attachments - pre-1986 models

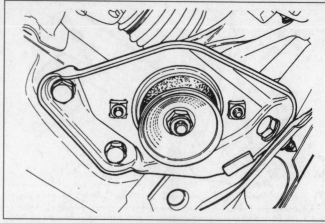

6.27b Transmission rear mounting body bracket attachments - pre-1986 models

the engine may be due to the splines of the input shaft and clutch driven plate not engaging. Try swivelling the transmission slightly, or have an assistant rotate the crankshaft by applying a spanner to the crankshaft pulley bolt.

34 Once the transmission is fully engaged, screw in the two lower retaining bolts to hold it to the engine.

35 Refit the transmission mountings and/or support crossmember as applicable.

36 Refit all the clutch housing flange to engine retaining bolts then remove the engine and transmission support jacks.

37 Reconnect the anti-roll bar mountings and, on RS Turbo models the tie-bar mounting.

38 Fit a new snap-ring to the splines of the left-hand driveshaft constant velocity joint and, after removing the dowel used to maintain the sun gears in alignment, engage the joint with the differential. Firmly push the roadwheel inwards to force the joint home.

39 Reconnect the suspension lower arm to the body and hub carrier noting that the Torx

bolt is positioned with its head to the rear. Tighten the mountings to the specified torque.

40 Repeat the foregoing operations on the right-hand driveshaft.

41 Reconnect the gearchange stabiliser to the transmission with the washer fitted between the stabiliser trunnion and the transmission housing.

42 Engage the gearchange rod with the selector shaft then adjust the mechanism as described in Section 2.

43 Where fitted reconnect the gearchange rod tension spring.

44 Refit the clutch housing cover plate, starter motor and reversing light wires.

45 Lower the car to the ground and reconnect the clutch cable and speedometer cable.

46 Reconnect the transmission earth strap and locate the breather hose in the side member opening.

47 Refill the transmission with the specified type and quantity of oil with reference to Chapter 1.

7 Manual transmission overhaul - general information

1 Overhauling a manual transmission is a difficult and involved job for the DIY home mechanic. In addition to dismantling and reassembling many small parts, clearances must be precisely measured and, if necessary, changed by selecting shims and spacers. Internal transmission components are also often difficult to obtain and, in many instances, extremely expensive. Because of this, if the transmission develops a fault or becomes noisy, the best course of action is to have the unit overhauled by a specialist repairer, or to obtain an exchange reconditioned unit.

2 Nevertheless, it is not impossible for the more experienced mechanic to overhaul the transmission, provided the special tools are available, and the job is done in a deliberate step-by-step manner so that nothing is overlooked.

3 The tools necessary for overhaul include internal and external circlip pliers, bearing pullers, a slide hammer, a set of pin punches, a dial test indicator, and (possibly) a hydraulic press. In addition, a large, sturdy workbench and a vice will be required.

4 During dismantling of the transmission, make careful notes of how each component is fitted, to make reassembly easier and more accurate.

5 Before dismantling the transmission, it will help if you have some idea of which area is malfunctioning. Certain problems can be closely related to specific areas in the transmission, which can reduce the amount of dismantling and component examination required. Refer to the *"Fault finding"* Section at the end of this manual for more information.

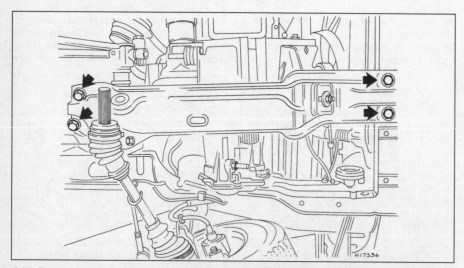

6.28 Transmission support crossmember attachments (arrowed) - 1986 models onwards

Chapter 7 Part B:
Automatic transmission

Contents

Degrees of difficulty

Easy, suitable for novice with little experience	Fairly easy, suitable for beginner with some experience	Fairly difficult, suitable for competent DIY mechanic	Difficult, suitable for experienced DIY mechanic	Very difficult, suitable for expert DIY or professional

Specifications

General

Transmission type	Ford ATX (automatic transaxle) with three forward speeds and reverse
Converter ratio	2.35 : 1
Transmission ratios:	
1st	2.79 : 1
2nd	1.61 : 1
3rd	1.00 : 1
Reverse	1.97 : 1
Final drive ratio	3.31 : 1
Oil cooler type	Twin tube in coolant radiator

Torque wrench settings

	Nm	lbf ft
Downshift/throttle valve shaft nut	13 to 15	10 to 11
Starter inhibitor switch	9 to 12	6 to 9
Oil cooler fluid pipes to transmission	22 to 24	16 to 18
Oil cooler fluid pipes to cooler	18 to 22	13 to 16
Transmission-to-engine retaining bolts	30 to 50	22 to 37
Torque converter-to-driveplate bolts	35 to 40	26 to 30
Driveplate to crankshaft	80 to 88	59 to 65
Torque converter cover plate bolts	7 to 10	5 to 7
Transmission mounting bolts	52 to 64	38 to 47
Selector cable bracket to engine	40 to 45	30 to 33
Throttle cable mounting bracket bolts	20 to 25	15 to 18
Downshift linkage control lever clamp bolt	5 to 7	4 to 5
Downshift linkage damper locknut	5 to 8	3 to 6
Gear selector housing bolts	9 to 10	6 to 7
Gear selector lever nut	20 to 23	15 to 17

7B

1.1 Automatic transmission internal components

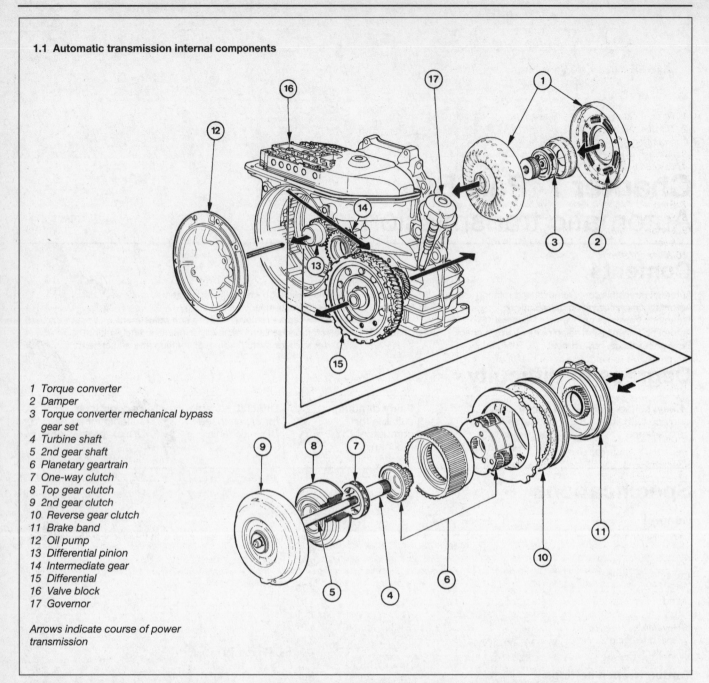

1 Torque converter
2 Damper
3 Torque converter mechanical bypass gear set
4 Turbine shaft
5 2nd gear shaft
6 Planetary geartrain
7 One-way clutch
8 Top gear clutch
9 2nd gear clutch
10 Reverse gear clutch
11 Brake band
12 Oil pump
13 Differential pinion
14 Intermediate gear
15 Differential
16 Valve block
17 Governor

Arrows indicate course of power transmission

1 General description

1 The automatic transmission used on Escort models is the Ford ATX (automatic transaxle) unit equipped with three forward speeds and reverse, and incorporating the final drive differential **(see illustration)**. The transmission is mounted transversely in line with the engine crankshaft.

2 The ATX transmission is a split torque type, whereby engine torque is transmitted to the geartrain by mechanical or hydraulic means in accordance with the gear selected and the roadspeed. This is achieved by using a torque converter with a bypass allowing the transmission a proportion of engine torque mechanically. This eliminates the hydraulic slip within the torque converter at high engine speeds resulting in greater efficiency and improved fuel economy.

3 The planetary geartrain provides one of the three forward or single reverse gear ratios according to which of its component parts are held stationary or allowed to turn. The geartrain components are held or released by three clutches and one brake band which are activated by hydraulic valves. An oil pump within the transmission provides the necessary hydraulic pressure to operate the clutches and brake.

4 Driver control of the transmission is by a six position selector lever which allows fully automatic operation with a hold facility on the first and second gear ratios.

5 Due to the complexity of the automatic transmission, any repair or overhaul work must be left to a Ford dealer or automatic transmission specialist with the necessary equipment for fault diagnosis and repair. The contents of this Chapter are therefore confined to supplying general information and any service information and instructions that can be used by the owner.

2.2a Exploded view of the downshift linkage

1 Throttle cable
2 Throttle cable mounting bracket
3 Downshift linkage
4 Throttle linkage
5 Clip
6 Bush
7 Stepped washer
8 Damper
9 Linkage control lever
10 Throttle valve shaft lever
11 Return spring
12 Bolt
13 Bolt
14 Linkage control lever clamp bolt
15 Clamp bolt nut
16 Downshift/throttle valve shaft lever retaining nut
17 Washer
18 Washer
19 Spire nut

2 Downshift linkage - adjustment

1 Before making any adjustments the engine and transmission must be at normal operating temperature, with the correct transmission fluid level and with fuel and ignition system adjustments as specified (Chapters 4 and 5).
2 Slacken the adjuster screw on the throttle valve shaft lever to give a clearance of 2 to 3 mm (0.079 to 0.118 in) between the stop end face and the adjuster screw (see illustrations). Use a feeler blade to set this clearance.
3 With the handbrake fully applied, start the engine and check that the idle speed is correct then tighten the adjuster screw to reduce the stop end face-to-adjuster screw clearance to 0.1 to 0.3 mm (0.004 to 0.012 in).
4 The following additional adjustment should be carried out if the downshift linkage has been removed and refitted, or if the position of

the damper has been disturbed.
5 Slacken the locknut and screw in the damper to give a clearance of 1 mm (0.04 in) between the damper body and the bracket (see illustration). Use a feeler blade or drill bit of suitable diameter to check this.
6 Slacken the linkage control lever clamp bolt, move the lever so that it just contacts the

plastic cap of the damper rod and tighten the clamp bolt.
7 Make a reference mark on the damper body then turn the damper so that the damper body-to-bracket dimension is now 7 mm (0.28 in) (see illustration).
8 Hold the damper in this position and tighten the locknut.

7B

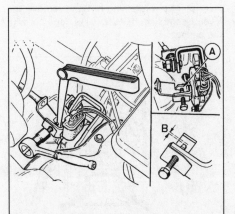

2.2b Downshift linkage adjustment

A Adjuster screw
B Adjuster screw clearance

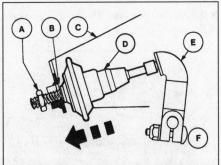

2.5 Damper unit initial adjustment

A Locknut
B Damper body-to-bracket clearance = 1 mm (0.4 in)
C Damper bracket
D Damper
E Linkage control lever
F Linkage control lever clamp bolt

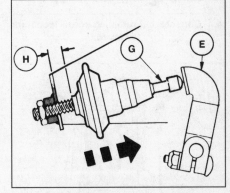

2.7 Damper unit final adjustment

E Linkage control lever
G Damper rod
H Damper body-to-bracket clearance = 7 mm (0.28 in)

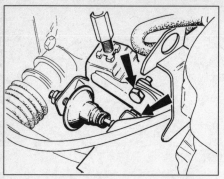

3.3 Throttle cable mounting bracket retaining bolt locations (arrowed)

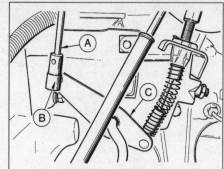

3.4 Disconnecting throttle linkage from linkage pivot lever
A Throttle linkage
B Retaining clip
C Downshift linkage pivot lever

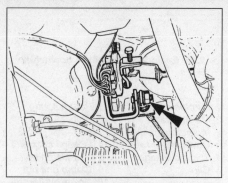

4.2 Selector cable-to-selector shaft cable retaining nut (arrowed)

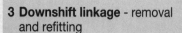

3 Downshift linkage - removal and refitting

Removal

1 Disconnect the downshift linkage from the transmission downshift/throttle valve shaft.
2 Disconnect the throttle linkage from the linkage pivot lever beneath the inlet manifold by removing the securing clip.
3 Unscrew and remove the two nuts which secure the throttle cable mounting bracket (on the right-hand side of the engine) **(see illustration)**. Withdraw the linkage and bracket.

4.4 Console unit retaining screw locations (arrowed)

4 Disconnect the throttle cable from the downshift linkage pivot lever by extracting the clip, then remove the clamp bolt and nut to separate the downshift linkage from the control lever **(see illustration)**. Remove the downshift linkage.

Refitting

5 To refit, insert the linkage into the bracket and tighten the clamping bolt nut. Check that lever movement is possible.
6 Reattach the throttle cable to the pivot lever, then refit the downshift linkage and bracket. Slide the linkage onto the downshift/throttle shaft of the transmission, fitting the stepped washer between the lever and linkage on the valve shaft. The bracket securing screws should be tightened to the specified torque setting.
7 Secure the throttle linkage to the downshift linkage pivot lever by refitting the retaining clip. Refit the downshift/throttle valve shaft nut.
8 Adjust the downshift linkage as described in Section 2.

4 Selector mechanism - removal and refitting

Removal

1 Move the selector lever to the D position.
2 At the transmission, slacken the nut securing the selector cable to the selector shaft lever **(see illustration)**.
3 Unscrew and remove the gear selector lever knob, then carefully prise up and remove the selector gate cover from the console.
4 Remove the console unit which is secured in position by two screws at the rear and screws on each side at the front **(see illustration)**.
5 Remove the selector gate and stop plate which are secured by two screws, one on each corner at the front **(see illustration)**.
6 Disconnect the selector cable from the selector lever and housing by removing the securing clips, and, where applicable, the ball and socket joint **(see illustration)**.
7 Disconnect the escutcheon light holder from the lever housing, then unscrew and remove the four housing retaining screws **(see illustration)**. Lift the housing clear.
8 To dismantle the selector unit, unscrew the lever pivot pin retaining nut and remove the lever assembly from its housing, together with the bushes.

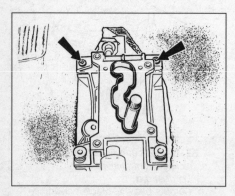

4.5 Selector gate and stop plate retaining screw locations (arrowed)

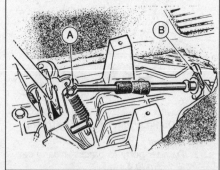

4.6 Selector cable attachments
A Cable-to-selector lever securing clip (ball and socket joint on later models)
B Cable-to-housing securing clip

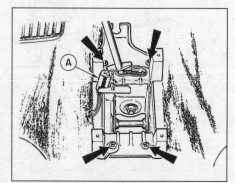

4.7 Selector lever housing retaining screw locations (arrowed)
A Escutcheon light holder

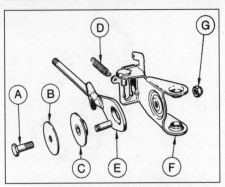

4.9 Exploded view of the selector lever components

A *Lever pivot pin* E *Lever*
B *Washer* F *Bush*
C *Plastic spacer* G *Nut*
D *Spring*

9 The lever can be removed from the guide by unhooking the spring, unscrewing the retaining pin nut and withdrawing the pin, washers and lever **(see illustration)**.

Refitting

10 Reassembly of the selector unit is a reversal of the removal procedure. Tighten the selector lever nut to the specified torque wrench setting. The pivot pin nut must be tightened to provide a lever movement effort of 0.5 to 2.5 Nm (0.4 to 1.8 lbf ft).

11 Refitting of the gear selector unit is a reversal of the removal procedure. Tighten the retaining screws of the lever housing to the specified torque.

12 On completion, adjust the selector cable by moving the selector lever to the D position, check that the selector shaft lever is in the corresponding D position then retighten the cable nut. To prevent the threaded pin rotating as the nut is tightened, press the cable slot onto the thread.

5 Selector cable - removal, refitting and adjustment

Removal

1 Move the selector lever to the D position.
2 At the transmission, undo the nut securing the selector cable to the selector shaft lever **(see illustration 4.2)**.
3 Unscrew and remove the selector lever knob, then carefully prise up and remove the selector gate cover from the console.
4 Remove the console unit which is secured in position by two screws at the rear and screws on each side at the front.
5 Remove the selector gate and stop plate which are secured by two screws, one at each front corner.
6 Disconnect the selector cable from the selector lever and housing by removing the securing clips and, where applicable, the ball and socket joint.

7 Jack up the front of the car and support it on axle stands (see *"Jacking and Vehicle Support"*).
8 From under the car undo the two bolts securing the selector cable bracket to the transmission **(see illustration)**.
9 Release the rubber grommet from the floorpan and pull the cable through the hole. Withdraw the cable from under the car.

Refitting and adjustment

10 Refitting is the reverse sequence to removal but ensure that the selector lever is in D and the linkage is in the corresponding D position before tightening the cable-to-selector shaft lever retaining nut. To prevent the threaded pin rotating as the nut is tightened, press the cable slot onto the thread.

6 Starter inhibitor switch - removal, refitting and adjustment

Removal

1 Disconnect the multi-plug connector from the switch.
2 Remove the retaining nut and disconnect the linkage from the throttle valve shaft lever on the transmission.
3 To remove the downshift linkage from the transmission, unscrew and remove the two securing screws to the location bracket on the right-hand side of the engine and pull the linkage free.
4 Remove the downshift/throttle valve shaft lever, together with the stepped washer and disconnect the return spring. Unscrew the two retaining screws and remove the starter inhibitor switch **(see illustration)**.
5 The switch must be renewed if it is known to be defective.

Refitting and adjustment

6 On refitting the starter inhibitor switch do not fully tighten the securing screws until it is adjusted for position. To do this, first move the selector lever to the D position, then using

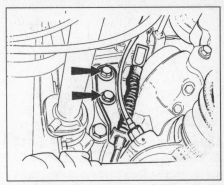

5.8 Selector cable bracket-to-transmission retaining bolt locations (arrowed)

a 2.3 mm (0.091 in) diameter drill shank as shown locate it into the hole in the switch body **(see illustration)**.
7 Move the switch whilst pushing on the drill so that the switch case aligns with the inner location hole in the switch and with the drill fully inserted so that the switch is immobilised, fully tighten the retaining screws to the specified torque.
8 With the switch in position, refitting of the downshift/throttle valve shaft lever and linkage is a reversal of the removal procedure, but readjust the downshift linkage as described in Section 2.

7 Automatic transmission - removal and refitting

Removal

1 Disconnect the battery negative terminal.
2 Refer to Chapter 4 and remove the air cleaner.
3 Disconnect the wiring multi-plug at the starter inhibitor switch.
4 Move the gear selector lever to position D then unscrew the nut securing the selector cable to the selector shaft lever **(see illustration 4.2)**. Press the cable slot onto the threaded pin to prevent the pin rotating as the nut is unscrewed.
5 Slacken the downshift linkage adjuster screw then disconnect the downshift linkage from the downshift/throttle valve shaft by

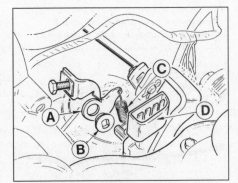

6.4 Starter inhibitor switch removal
  A *Throttle valve shaft lever*
  B *Stepped washer*
  C *Return spring*
  D *Starter inhibitor switch*

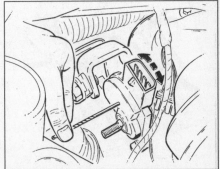

6.6 Starter inhibitor switch adjustment

7B

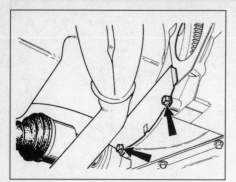

7.12 Torque converter cover plate retaining bolt locations (arrowed)

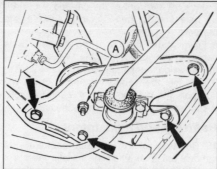

7.14 Front transmission mounting support plate bolt locations (arrowed) and mounting nut (A)

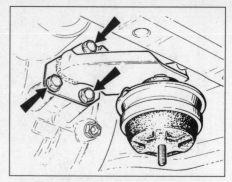

7.16 Front mounting bracket bolt locations (arrowed)

undoing the retaining nut. To facilitate removal and subsequent refitting of the downshift linkage, undo the two throttle cable mounting bracket bolts on the right-hand side of the engine **(see illustration 5.8)**.

6 Unscrew the two upper transmission-to-engine retaining bolts.

7 Jack up the front of the car and support it on axle stands (see *"Jacking and Vehicle Support"*). Ensure that the vehicle is high enough to allow removal of the transmission from below.

8 Support the engine under the sump using a jack and interposed block of wood. Alternatively support the engine from above using a crane or hoist.

9 Disconnect the speedometer drive cable and the reversing light switch leads.

10 Undo the two bolts and detach the selector cable bracket from the transmission assembly.

11 Refer to Chapter 5 and remove the starter motor.

12 Undo the two bolts and remove the torque converter cover plate **(see illustration)**.

13 Remove the driveshafts from the transmission as described in Chapter 8. After removal of the driveshafts retain the differential sun gears in alignment by inserting a dowel of suitable diameter into the differential so that it engages the sun gear on one side.

14 Undo the nut securing the front transmission mounting to the support plate and the four bolts securing the support plate to the body **(see illustration)**.

15 Undo the transmission oil cooler fluid pipe union nuts at the transmission and withdraw the pipes. Plug the transmission and the pipe ends to prevent dirt ingress.

16 Undo the three bolts and remove the front mounting bracket from the transmission **(see illustration)**.

17 Undo the bolts and nuts and remove the rear mounting complete with bracket from the transmission and body **(see illustration)**.

18 Turn the flywheel as necessary to bring each of the torque converter retaining nuts in turn into an accessible position through the cover plate aperture**(see illustration)**. Undo and remove the nuts.

19 Support the transmission beneath the oil pan using a jack and interposed block of wood.

20 Undo the remaining transmission-to-engine retaining bolts and carefully withdraw and lower the transmission from the engine. As the unit is removed, hold the torque converter firmly against the transmission taking care not to allow the studs to catch on the driveplate.

Refitting

21 Refitting is the reverse sequence to removal bearing in mind the following points:
a) *Tighten all nuts and bolts to the specified torque.*
b) *Connect the transmission oil cooler fluid pipes as shown* **(see illustration)**.
c) *Refit the driveshafts with reference to*

Chapter 8, and with new snap-rings on the end of the constant velocity joint splines.
d) *Refit the downshift linkage and selector cable with reference to the adjustment procedures contained in Sections 2 and 5 respectively. Note that final adjustment of the downshift linkage can only be carried out after refitting and running the transmission to normal operating temperature.*
e) *Refill the transmission with the specified type and quantity of fluid (see Chapter 1 regarding fluid types).*

8 Automatic transmission overhaul - general

In the event of a fault occurring in the transmission, it is first necessary to determine whether it is of an electrical, mechanical or hydraulic nature, and to do this, special test equipment is required. It is therefore essential to have the work carried out by a Ford dealer if a transmission fault is suspected.

Do not remove the transmission from the car for possible repair before professional fault diagnosis has been carried out, since most tests require the transmission to be in the vehicle.

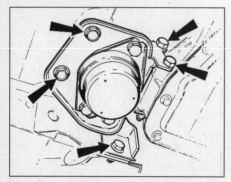

7.17 Rear transmission mounting bracket and support plate bolt locations (arrowed)

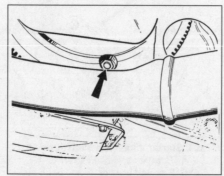

7.18 Torque converter nut accessible through the cover plate aperture (arrowed)

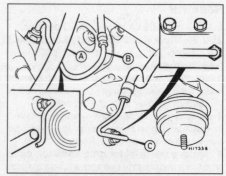

7.21 Oil cooler fluid pipe positioning details
A *Dipstick/filler tube*
B *Pipe feed to oil cooler*
C *Pipe return from oil cooler*

Chapter 8
Driveshafts

Contents

Degrees of difficulty

Easy, suitable for novice with little experience	**Fairly easy,** suitable for beginner with some experience	**Fairly difficult,** suitable for competent DIY mechanic	**Difficult,** suitable for experienced DIY mechanic	**Very difficult,** suitable for expert DIY or professional

Specifications

General

Type . . . . Unequal length solid (left-hand) or tubular (right-hand) shafts, splined to inner and outer constant velocity joints

Lubrication (overhaul only - see text)

Lubricant type:

   All joints except outer tripod type . . . . Lithium based molybdenum disulphide grease to Ford specification S-MIC-75-A/SQM-1C-9004-A

   Outer tripod type joint . . . . Lithium based grease to Ford specification A77SX 1C 9004 AA

Lubricant quantity:

   All joints except outer tripod type . . . . 40 g per joint

   Outer tripod type joint . . . . 95 g in joint housing, 20 g on spider (per joint)

Torque wrench settings

	Nm	lbf ft
Driveshaft retaining nut (threads lightly greased)	205 to 235	151 to 173
Lower arm mounting pivot bolt	51 to 64	38 to 47
Lower arm balljoint pinch-bolt	48 to 60	35 to 44
Brake caliper anchor bracket mounting bolts	50 to 66	37 to 49
Selector shaft locking mechanism cap nut	30	22
Roadwheel bolts	70 to 100	52 to 74

8

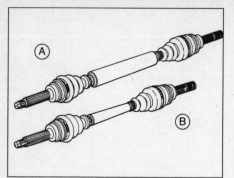

1.1 Driveshaft assemblies
A Right-hand driveshaft
B Left-hand driveshaft

1 General description

1 Drive is transmitted from the differential to the front wheels by means of two unequal length driveshaft assemblies. The left-hand driveshaft is solid whereas the longer right-hand driveshaft is tubular and of larger diameter to reduce harmonic vibrations and resonance **(see illustration)**.

2 Both driveshafts are fitted with ball and cage type constant velocity joints at each end except for certain later models which are equipped with a tripod type inner constant velocity joint **(see illustration)**. On all models the inner joints are of the sliding type allowing lateral movement of the driveshaft to cater for suspension travel. Both constant velocity joints incorporate an externally splined stub shaft which engages with the differential sun gears (inner joint) or wheel hub (outer joint). The constant velocity joint inner members are internally splined to accept the driveshaft. Circlips, snap-rings and the driveshaft retaining nut are used to secure the assemblies.

3 The driveshaft lengths and weights vary slightly to suit the different engine/torque characteristics of the cars in the range and are therefore not interchangeable from model to model.

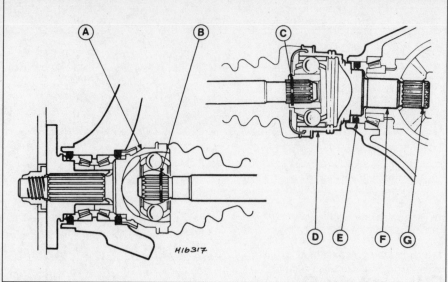

1.2 Sectional view of ball and cage type constant velocity joints

A Outer constant velocity joint
B Circlip
C Circlip
D Inner constant velocity joint

E Oil seal
F Inner joint stub shaft
G Snap-ring

2 Inner constant velocity joint bellows - renewal

1 Jack up the front of the car, support it on axle stands (see *"Jacking and Vehicle Support"*) and remove the roadwheel.

2 On cars equipped with an anti-lock braking system, refer to Chapter 9 and remove the modulator drivebelt cover.

3 Disconnect the front suspension lower arm balljoint from the hub carrier by removing the nut and pinch-bolt **(see illustrations)**. Note that the pinch-bolt is of the socket-headed (Torx) type and a special key or socket bit (available from accessory shops) will be required for this purpose.

4 On models fitted with an anti-roll bar, disconnect the lower arm from the body at its inner end by removing the mounting pivot bolt.

5 Release both retaining clips from the bellows on the inner constant velocity joint and slide the bellows off the joint and along the shaft.

6 If the joint is of the ball and cage type, wipe away enough grease to expose the circlip which secures it to the driveshaft. Extract the circlip and pull the driveshaft out of the joint **(see illustration)**.

7 If the joint is of the tripod type withdraw the driveshaft and spider from the joint outer member, extract the circlip and remove the spider from the driveshaft.

8 Slide the bellows off the end of the driveshaft.

9 Slide on the new bellows then connect the driveshaft to the constant velocity joint. On the ball and cage type joint, the circlip should be engaged in its groove in the joint and the shaft slid through it until it engages with the groove in the shaft **(see illustration)**.

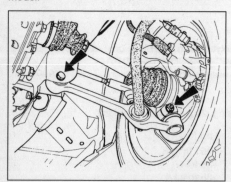

2.3a Lower suspension arm balljoint pinch-bolt and inner mounting pivot bolt - arrowed (models with anti-roll bar shown)

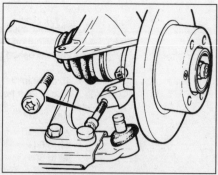

2.3b Lower arm balljoint pinch bolt removal

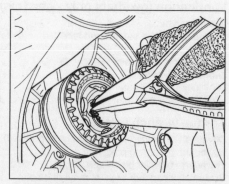

2.6 Extracting driveshaft retaining circlip from ball and cage type inner joint

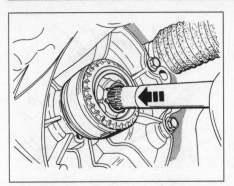

2.9 Refitting driveshaft to ball and cage type inner joint with circlip in position

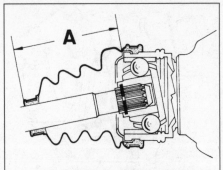

2.11 Constant velocity joint bellows setting diagram
A = setting dimension (see text)

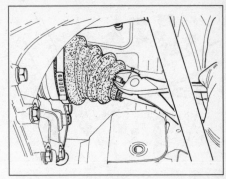

2.12 Crimping the bellows retaining clip to tighten

10 Replenish the joint with grease of the specified type then pull the bellows over the joint.

11 Set the length of the bellows according to model as follows (**see illustration**):

Pre-1986 models:

1.1 litre	127 mm
1.3 and 1.6 litre	132 mm

1986 models onwards:

All models	95 mm

12 Fit the new bellows retaining clips engaging the peg on the clip with the tightest possible hole. Now crimp the raised portion of the clip to tighten it securely (**see illustration**).

13 Reconnect the suspension lower arm to the body (where applicable) and tighten the mounting pivot bolt to the specified torque.

14 Reconnect the lower arm balljoint to the hub carrier and insert the Torx bolt with its head to the rear. Refit the nut and tighten to the specified torque.

15 On cars equipped with an anti-lock braking system, refit the modulator drivebelt cover.

16 Refit the roadwheel and lower the car.

3 Outer constant velocity joint bellows - renewal

Left-hand driveshaft bellows

1 Unless the driveshaft is to be removed completely for other repair work to be carried out (see Section 5), the following method of bellows renewal is recommended to avoid having to disconnect the driveshaft from the hub carrier.

2 Remove the inner joint bellows as described in Section 2, paragraphs 1 to 8 inclusive.

3 Release both retaining clips from the bellows on the outer constant velocity joint and slide the bellows off the joint and along the driveshaft until it can be removed from the inner end.

4 Thoroughly clean the driveshaft then slide on the new bellows.

5 Replenish the outer joint with the specified grease and pull the bellows over the joint.

6 Set the length of the bellows according to model as follows (**see illustration 2.11**):

Pre-1986 models:

1.1 litre	70 mm
1.3 and 1.6 litre	82 mm

1986 models onwards:

All models	95 mm

7 Fit the new bellows retaining clips engaging the peg on the clip with the tightest possible hole. Now crimp the raised portion of the clip to tighten it securely. Make sure that the crimped part of the clip nearest the hub carrier does not foul the carrier when the driveshaft is rotated.

8 Refit the inner bellows as described in Section 2, paragraphs 9 to 16 inclusive.

Right-hand driveshaft bellows

9 In order to remove the bellows, the driveshaft must be disconnected from the hub carrier. If desired, the driveshaft can be removed completely. In either case, refer to Section 4 - if the driveshaft is to be left in position, ignore the paragraphs describing disconnection of the driveshaft from the transmission, and ensure that the shaft is adequately supported to avoid straining the inner joint.

10 Release the outer bellows retaining clips,

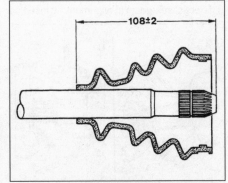

3.16 Correct position of bellows on driveshaft with tripod type outer constant velocity joint
Dimension given in mm

and slide the bellows toward the centre of the driveshaft.

11 If the outer joint is of the ball and cage type, wipe away enough grease to expose the joint retaining clip then, using circlip pliers, extract the circlip and withdraw the joint from the driveshaft. Remove the bellows.

12 If the outer joint is of the tripod type, withdraw the outer member from the driveshaft and spider, then extract the circlip and remove the spider from the driveshaft. Slide the bellows from the end of the driveshaft.

13 Thoroughly clean the driveshaft then slide on the new bellows.

14 Replenish the outer joint with grease of the specified type then pull the bellows over the joint.

15 On models with a ball and cage type outer joint, set the length of the bellows according to model, as described in paragraph 6.

16 On models with a tripod type outer joint, set the length of the bellows as shown (**see illustration**).

17 Fit the new bellows retaining clips engaging the peg on the clip with the tightest possible hole. Now crimp the raised portion of the clip to tighten it securely. Make sure that the crimped part of the clip nearest the hub carrier does not foul the carrier when the driveshaft is rotated.

18 Reconnect the driveshaft to the hub carrier, or refit the driveshaft, as applicable, as described in Section 4.

4 Driveshaft assembly - removal and refitting

Removal

Note: *A new driveshaft retaining nut and a new snap-ring must be used on refitting.*

1 Remove the wheel trim and release the staking on the driveshaft retaining nut using a suitable punch.

2 Slacken the driveshaft retaining nut and the wheel bolts.

3 Jack up the front of the car, support it on stands (see *"Jacking and Vehicle Support"*) and remove the roadwheel.

8

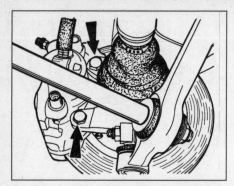

4.4 Brake caliper retaining bolts (arrowed)

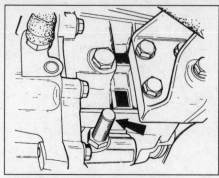

4.7 Selector shaft locking mechanism cap nut location (arrowed)

4.10 Using a lever to release the inner constant velocity joint

4 Undo the two bolts securing the brake caliper anchor bracket to the hub carrier **(see illustration)**.

5 Withdraw the anchor bracket and brake caliper, complete with disc pads, and suspend it from a convenient place under the wheel arch.

6 On cars equipped with an anti-lock braking system refer to Chapter 9 and remove the modulator drivebelt.

7 On pre-1986 manual transmission models, place a suitable container beneath the selector shaft locking mechanism cap nut **(see illustration)**. Unscrew the cap nut, remove the spring and interlock pin and allow the transmission oil to drain. **Caution:** *Take care when unscrewing the cap nut as the tension of the spring may cause the pin to fly out as the cap nut is released.* Note that due to the revised transmission support crossmember shrouding the cap nut on 1986 models onward, and on all cars equipped with automatic transmission, the oil/fluid cannot be drained with the unit in the car. This will result in a quantity of transmission oil or fluid spillage when the driveshaft is removed. Be prepared for this with a container at the ready.

8 Disconnect the front suspension lower arm balljoint from the hub carrier by removing the nut and pinch-bolt. Note that the pinch-bolt is of the socket-headed (Torx) type and a special key or socket bit will be required for this purpose. These are readily available from most accessory shops.

9 On models fitted with an anti-roll bar, disconnect the lower arm from the body at its inner end by removing the mounting pivot bolt.

10 Insert a lever between the inner constant velocity joint and the transmission casing **(see illustration)**. Firmly strike the lever to release the inner constant velocity joint from the differential. On automatic transmission models a groove is provided in the left-hand constant velocity joint for insertion of the lever, but on the right-hand side it will be necessary to use a small piece of wood to protect the oil pan when levering.

11 With the joint released, move the hub carrier outwards and pull the constant velocity joint out of the differential.

12 Suspend the driveshaft or support it in such a way as to avoid placing an angular strain on the constant velocity joints. The shaft must not hang down by more than 45° from the outer joint or 20° from the inner joint.

13 Remove the driveshaft retaining nut and washer.

14 Undo the retaining screw and withdraw the brake disc from the hub.

15 It should now be possible to pull the driveshaft out of the hub. If tight, use a two-legged puller to push it out **(see illustration)**.

16 Withdraw the driveshaft assembly from under the car. If both driveshafts are to be removed at the same time retain the differential sun gears in alignment by inserting

a dowel of suitable diameter into the differential so that it engages the sun gear on one side.

Refitting

17 To refit the driveshaft, first lubricate the splines of the outer constant velocity joint, engage the joint with the hub splines and push the joint firmly into the hub.

18 Using the original driveshaft retaining nut and packing pieces, draw the constant velocity joint fully into the hub.

19 Remove the old nut and packing and fit the washer and a new nut, but only tighten the nut finger tight at this stage.

20 Refit the brake disc and caliper anchor bracket, tightening the anchor bracket bolts to the specified torque.

21 On cars equipped with an anti-lock braking system, refit the modulator drivebelt as described in Chapter 9.

22 Fit a new snap-ring to the splines of the inner constant velocity joint and engage the joint with the differential sun gear splines. Firmly push the hub carrier inwards to force the joint home **(see illustration)**.

23 Reconnect the suspension lower arm to the body (where applicable) and tighten the mounting pivot bolt to the specified torque.

24 Reconnect the lower arm balljoint to the hub carrier and insert the Torx bolt with its head to the rear. Refit the nut and tighten to the specified torque.

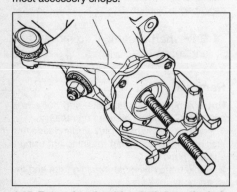

4.15 Removing the driveshaft from the hub using a puller

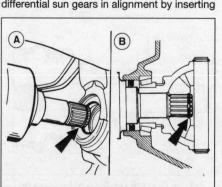

4.22 Refitting driveshaft inner joint
A Snap-ring in position on joint splines
B Snap-ring engaged with differential sun gear

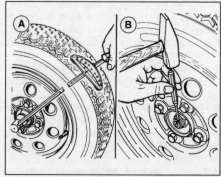

4.27 Tighten driveshaft retaining nut to specified torque (A) and stake into driveshaft groove (B)

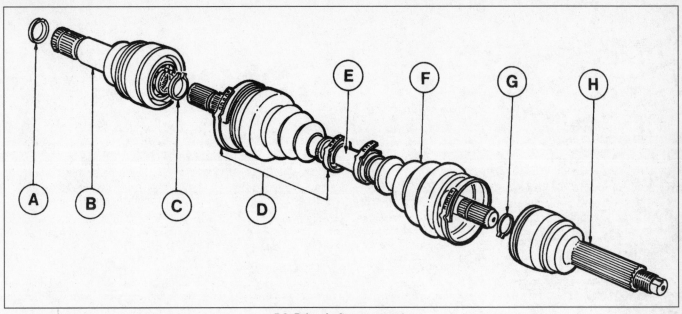

5.3 Driveshaft components

A Snap-ring
B Inner constant velocity joint

C Circlip
D Bellows retaining clips

E Driveshaft
F Bellows

G Circlip
H Outer constant velocity joint

25 On pre-1986 manual transmission models, refit the selector shaft locking mechanism pin, spring and cap nut using sealer on the cap nut threads then fill the transmission with oil as described in Chapter 1.

26 Refit the roadwheel and lower the car to the ground.

27 Tighten the driveshaft retaining nut to the specified torque then stake the nut into the driveshaft groove using a small punch **(see illustration)**.

28 Tighten the wheel bolts to the specified torque and refit the wheel trim.

29 On automatic transmission models refer to Chapter 1 and top-up the transmission with the specified fluid.

5 Driveshaft assembly - overhaul

1 Remove the driveshaft as described in Section 4.

2 Clean away external dirt and grease, release the bellows retaining clips and slide both bellows toward the centre of the driveshaft.

3 If the outer constant velocity joint is of the ball and cage type, wipe away enough grease to expose the retaining circlip. Using circlip pliers extract the circlip and withdraw the joint from the driveshaft. Remove the bellows **(see illustration)**.

4 If the outer constant velocity joint is of the tripod type, withdraw the outer member, then extract the circlip and withdraw the spider, complete with roller cups, from the driveshaft. Remove the bellows.

5 Remove the inner constant velocity joint, as described previously in paragraph 3 or 4, depending on the joint type **(see illustration)**.

6 With the driveshaft dismantled, wipe away as much of the old grease as possible using rags only. Do not use any solvents.

7 On the ball and cage type joints move the internal parts of the joint around and check for signs of scoring, pitting and wear ridges on the balls, ball tracks and ball cage. If wear is evident or if the components move with very little resistance and rattle, then a new joint should be obtained.

8 On the tripod type joints check for signs of scoring, pitting and wear ridges on the roller cups and tracks of the outer member. Also check the roller cups for smooth operation and check the fit of the cups in the outer member. Renew the joint if wear is evident.

9 Check for wear of the constant velocity joint

and driveshaft splines and check for side play with the joint temporarily assembled onto the driveshaft. Renew any parts as necessary.

10 Before reassembly obtain new rubber bellows and retaining clips for each dismantled joint along with the correct quantity of the specified grease.

11 Reassemble the driveshaft by reversing the dismantling operations. Use new circlips if necessary to retain the joints and pack the joints thoroughly with the specified grease. When refitting the bellows set their length and secure with the clips in accordance with the information contained in Section 2 or 3 depending on which joint (inner or outer) is being worked on.

12 Refit the driveshaft as described in Section 4. After fitting ensure that the crimped portion of the outer joint bellows clip does not foul the hub carrier as the driveshaft is rotated.

5.5 Tripod type inner constant velocity joint

8

Chapter 9
Braking system

Contents

Degrees of difficulty

Easy, suitable for novice with little experience	**Fairly easy,** suitable for beginner with some experience	**Fairly difficult,** suitable for competent DIY mechanic	**Difficult,** suitable for experienced DIY mechanic	**Very difficult,** suitable for expert DIY or professional

Specifications

System type ....   Diagonally split dual circuit, hydraulic with pressure regulating valve to rear brakes. Servo assistance and Anti-lock Braking System (ABS) as standard or optional equipment according to model. Cable-operated handbrake on rear brakes

Front brakes

Type ....   Solid or ventilated disc with single piston sliding calipers
Disc diameter ....   239.45 mm
Disc thickness:
  Solid disc ....   10.0 mm
  Ventilated disc ....   24.0 mm
Minimum disc thickness:
  Solid disc ....   8.7 mm
  Ventilated disc ....   22.7 mm
Maximum disc run-out ....   0.15 mm
Minimum disc pad thickness ....   1.5 mm

Rear brakes

Type ....   Self-adjusting single leading shoe drum
Drum diameter:
  Standard hub/drum ....   180.0 mm
  Van, XR3i, RS Turbo and certain 1.6 litre models ...   203.2 mm
Wheel cylinder diameter ....   17.78 mm, 19.05 mm or 22.2 mm according to model - see text
Minimum brake shoe lining thickness ....   1.0 mm

Torque wrench settings

	Nm	lbf ft
Caliper piston housing to anchor bracket	20 to 25	15 to 18
Caliper anchor bracket to hub carrier	50 to 66	37 to 49
Rear brake backplate bolts	45 to 55	33 to 40
Brake pressure regulating valve mounting bolts	20 to 25	15 to 18
Light laden valve to mounting bracket	20 to 25	15 to 18
Hydraulic unions	12 to 15	9 to 11
Master cylinder to servo	21 to 26	15 to 19
Modulator pivot bolt (ABS)	22 to 28	16 to 21
Modulator adjuster bolt (ABS)	22 to 28	16 to 21
Modulator drivebelt cover (ABS)	8 to 11	6 to 8
Load apportioning valve adjusting bracket nuts (ABS)	21 to 29	15 to 21
Load apportioning valve to mounting bracket (ABS)	21 to 29	15 to 21
Rear suspension arm inner mounting nuts	70 to 90	52 to 66
Front suspension lower arm balljoint pinch-bolt	48 to 60	35 to 44
Tie-rod balljoint nut	57 to 68	42 to 50

1 General description

The braking system is of the dual circuit hydraulic type with disc brakes at the front and drum brakes at the rear. A diagonally split dual circuit hydraulic system is employed in which each circuit operates one front and one diagonally opposite rear brake from a tandem master cylinder. Under normal conditions both circuits operate in unison; however, in the event of hydraulic failure in one circuit, full braking force will still be available at two wheels. A pressure regulating valve on Saloon and Estate models, and a light laden valve on Van models is incorporated in the rear brake hydraulic circuit. The valve regulates the pressure applied to each rear brake and reduces the possibility of the rear wheels locking under heavy braking.

The front brakes utilise solid or ventilated discs according to model and are operated by single piston sliding type calipers. At the rear, leading and trailing shoes are operated by twin piston wheel cylinders and are self-adjusting by footbrake application. A cable-operated handbrake provides an independent mechanical means of rear brake operation.

From 1986 onwards an anti-lock braking system is available as standard or optional equipment according to model. Further information on this system will be found in later Sections of this Chapter.

Note: *When servicing any part of the system, work carefully and methodically; also observe scrupulous cleanliness when overhauling any part of the hydraulic system. Always renew components (in axle sets, where applicable) if in doubt about their condition, and use only genuine Ford replacement parts, or at least those of known good quality. Note the warnings given in "Safety first" and at the relevant points in this Chapter concerning the dangers of asbestos dust and hydraulic fluid.*

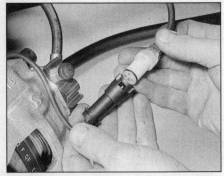

2.2 Disconnect the disc pad wear sensor lead at the connector

2 Front disc pads - renewal

Warning: Renew both sets of front brake pads at the same time - never renew the pads on only one wheel, as uneven braking may result. Note that the dust created by wear of the pads may contain asbestos, which is a health hazard. Never blow it out with compressed air, and don't inhale any of it. An approved filtering mask should be worn when working on the brakes. DO NOT use petrol or petroleum-based solvents to clean brake parts; use brake cleaner or methylated spirit only.

1 Slacken the roadwheel bolts, raise the front of the vehicle, support it with safety stands (see *"Jacking and Vehicle Support"*) and remove the roadwheel(s).
2 Where fitted, disengage the brake pad wear sensor from its retaining clip (beneath the bleed screw) and disconnect the lead connector **(see illustration)**.
3 Using a screwdriver, prise free the retaining clip from the caliper **(see illustration)**.
4 Using a 7 mm Allen key, unscrew the bolts until they can be withdrawn from the caliper anchor brackets **(see illustrations)**.
5 Withdraw the piston housing and tie it up

2.3 Disc pad retaining clip

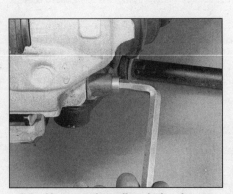

2.4a Unscrew the caliper bolt using an Allen key . . .

2.4b . . . and withdraw the bolt from the anchor bracket

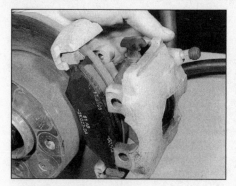

2.5 Withdraw the caliper piston housing

2.6 Removing the inboard pad from the piston housing . . .

2.7 . . . and the outboard pad from the anchor bracket

with a length of wire to prevent strain on the flexible hose **(see illustration)**.
6 Withdraw the inboard pad from the piston housing **(see illustration)**.
7 Withdraw the outboard pad from the anchor bracket **(see illustration)**.
8 Clean away all residual dust or dirt, **taking care not to inhale the dust** as, being asbestos based, it is injurious to health.
9 Using a piece of flat wood, a tyre lever or similar, push the piston squarely into its bore. This is necessary in order to accommodate the new thicker pads when they are fitted.
10 Depressing the piston will cause the fluid level in the master cylinder reservoir to rise, so anticipate this by siphoning out some fluid using an old hydrometer or poultry baster.

Take care not to drip hydraulic fluid onto the paintwork; it acts as an effective paint stripper.
11 Commence reassembly by fitting the inboard pad into the piston housing. Make sure that the spring on the back of the pad fits into the piston.
12 The wear sensor wire should be routed to ensure that it cannot chafe against any moving parts. Attach the wear sensor connector to the bleed screw clip (where applicable), and reconnect it.
13 Where the cable has become unwound, loosely coil the surplus wire so that slack is taken out, yet enough flexibility (25 mm) is still allowed for pad wear. The coiled wire must on no account be stretched.
14 Peel back the protective paper covering

from the surface of the new outboard pad and locate it in the jaws of the caliper anchor bracket.
15 Locate the caliper piston housing and screw in the Allen bolts to the specified torque.
16 Fit the retaining clip.
17 Repeat the operations on the opposite brake.
18 Apply the footbrake hard several times to position the pads against the disc and then check and top-up the fluid in the master cylinder reservoir.
19 Fit the roadwheel(s) and lower the vehicle.
20 Avoid heavy braking (if possible) for the first hundred miles or so when new pads have been fitted. This is to allow them to bed in and reach full efficiency.

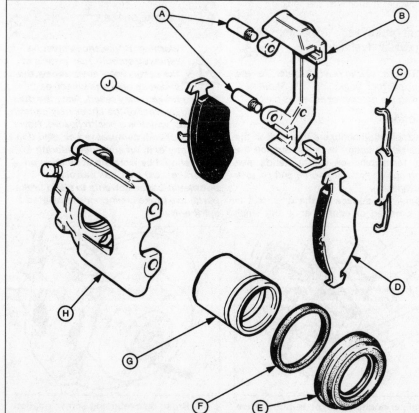

3.4 Exploded view of the front brake caliper

A Piston housing-to-anchor bracket bolts
B Anchor brackets
C Retaining clip
D Disc pad
E Dust excluder
F Piston seal
G Piston
H Piston housing
J Disc pad

9

3 Front brake caliper - removal, overhaul and refitting

⚠️ **Warning: Hydraulic fluid is poisonous; wash off immediately and thoroughly in the case of skin contact, and seek immediate medical advice if any fluid is swallowed or gets into the eyes. Certain types of hydraulic fluid are inflammable, and may ignite when allowed into contact with hot components; when servicing any hydraulic system, it is safest to assume that the fluid is inflammable, and to take precautions against the risk of fire as though it is petrol that is being handled. Hydraulic fluid is also an effective paint stripper, and will attack plastics; if any is spilt, it should be washed off immediately, using copious quantities of fresh water. Finally, it is hygroscopic (it absorbs moisture from the air) - old fluid may be contaminated and unfit for further use. When topping-up or renewing the fluid, use the recommended type, and ensure that it comes from a freshly-opened sealed container.**

Note: *Before starting work, refer to the warning at the beginning of Section 2 concerning the dangers of asbestos dust.*

Removal

1 Proceed as described in paragraphs 1 to 8 in the previous Section.
2 Disconnect the brake flexible hose from the caliper. This can be carried out in one of two ways. Either disconnect the flexible hose from the rigid hydraulic pipeline at the support bracket by unscrewing the union, or, once the caliper is detached, hold the end fitting of the hose in an open-ended spanner and unscrew the caliper from the hose. Do not allow the hose to twist, and plug its end after caliper removal.

Overhaul

3 Brush away all external dirt and pull off the piston dust-excluding cover.

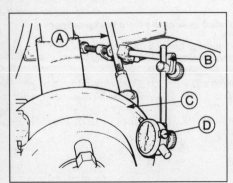

4.3 Checking brake disc run-out

A Steering tie-rod
B Dial gauge support fixture
C Brake disc
D Dial gauge

4 Apply air pressure to the fluid inlet hole and eject the piston **(see illustration)**. Only low air pressure is needed for this, such as is produced by a foot-operated tyre pump.
5 Using a sharp pointed instrument, pick out the piston seal from the groove in the cylinder bore. Do not scratch the surface of the bore.
6 Examine the surfaces of the piston and the cylinder bore. If they are scored or show evidence of metal-to-metal rubbing, then a new piston housing will be required. Where the components are in good condition, discard the seal and obtain a repair kit.
7 Wash the internal components in clean brake hydraulic fluid or methylated spirit only, nothing else.
8 Using the fingers, manipulate the new seal into its groove in the cylinder bore.
9 Dip the piston in clean hydraulic fluid and insert it squarely into its bore.
10 Connect the rubber dust excluder between the piston and the piston housing, and then depress the piston fully.

Refitting

11 Refit the caliper by reversing the removal operations, referring to paragraphs 11 to 16 in the previous Section.
12 Reconnect the brake hose to the caliper, taking care not to distort it. When secured it must not interfere with any of the adjacent steering or suspension components.
13 Bleed the brake hydraulic circuit as given in Section 11 or 23, as applicable, then refit the roadwheel(s) and lower the vehicle.

4 Front brake disc - inspection, removal and refitting

Note: *Before starting work, refer to the warning at the beginning of Section 2 concerning the dangers of asbestos dust.*

Inspection

1 Fully apply the handbrake then loosen the front roadwheel bolts. Raise and support the front of the vehicle on safety stands (see *"Jacking and Vehicle Support"*) and remove the roadwheel(s).
2 Examine the surface of the disc. If it is deeply grooved or scored or if any small

4.6 Caliper anchor bracket-to-hub carrier retaining bolts (arrowed)

cracks are evident, it must either be refinished or renewed. Any refinishing must not reduce the thickness of the disc to below a certain minimum (see *"Specifications"*). Light scoring on a brake disc is normal and should be ignored.
3 If disc distortion is suspected, the disc can be checked for run-out using a dial gauge or feeler blades located between its face and a fixed point as the disc is rotated **(see illustration)**.
4 Where the run-out exceeds the specified figure, renew the disc.

Removal

5 With the roadwheel removed (see paragraph 1), proceed as follows.
6 To remove a disc, unbolt the caliper anchor bracket, withdraw it and tie it up to the suspension strut to avoid strain on the flexible hose (if necessary, remove the brake pads as described in Section 2) **(see illustration)**.
7 Extract the small disc retaining screw and pull the disc from the hub **(see illustration)**.

Refitting

8 If a new disc is being installed, clean its surface free from preservative.
9 Fit the disc and tighten the retaining screw.
10 Refit the caliper anchor bracket (and where applicable the brake pads - see Section 2), and the roadwheel and lower the vehicle to the floor.

5 Rear brake shoes - renewal

⚠️ **Warning: Brake shoes must be renewed on both rear wheels at the same time - never renew the shoes on only one wheel, as uneven braking may result. Also, the dust created by wear of the shoes may contain asbestos, which is a health hazard. Never blow it out with compressed air, and don't inhale any of it. An approved filtering mask should be worn when working on the brakes. DO NOT use petrol or petroleum-based solvents to clean brake parts; use brake cleaner or methylated spirit only.**

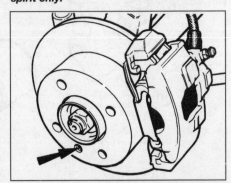

4.7 Brake disc retaining screw location (arrowed)

5.3a Remove the rear hub dust cap . . .

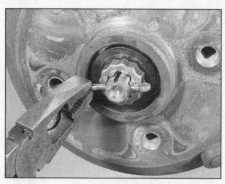

5.3b . . . extract the split pin and nut retainer . . .

5.3c . . . then unscrew the hub nut . . .

5.3d . . . and remove the thrustwasher

5.4 Remove the hub outer bearing . . .

5.5 . . . followed by the hub/drum assembly

Carburettor engine models except Van variants

1 Slacken the roadwheel bolts, raise the rear of the vehicle and support it securely (see *"Jacking and Vehicle Support"*). Remove the roadwheels.

2 Release the handbrake fully.

3 Tap off the hub dust cap, remove the split pin, nut retainer, nut and thrustwasher **(see illustrations)**.

4 Pull the hub/drum towards you and then push it back enough to be able to take the outer bearing from the spindle **(see illustration)**.

5 Remove the hub/drum and brush out any dust taking care not to inhale it **(see illustration)**.

6 Remove the shoe hold-down spring from the leading shoe **(see illustration)**. Do this by gripping the dished washer with a pair of pliers, depressing it and turning it through 90°. Remove the washer, spring and the hold-down post. Note the locations of the leading and trailing shoes and the cut-back of the linings at the leading ends.

7 Pull the leading shoe outwards and upwards away from the backplate **(see illustration)**.

8 Twist the shoe to disengage it from the return springs and adjuster strut. On models with the later type rear brake assembly it will be necessary to move the auto adjuster to maximum adjustment to disengage the shoe from the strut. Make a note of the return spring arrangement and hole locations if in any doubt **(see illustrations)**.

9 Remove the trailing shoe in a similar way, at the same time withdrawing the adjuster strut.

10 Release the end of the handbrake cable from the lever on the shoe **(see illustration)**.

11 Disconnect the trailing shoe from the adjuster strut by pulling the shoe outwards and twisting the shoe spring **(see illustration)**.

12 Before reassembly, sparingly lubricate the brake shoe contact areas on the backplate, fixed abutment and wheel cylinder pistons with a high melting-point brake grease.

13 Commence reassembly by installing the trailing shoe. Do this by engaging the handbrake lever return spring to the shoe. Hook the strut onto the spring and lever it into position. Set the strut self-adjusting

mechanism to its contracted position (early type) or maximum position (later type).

14 Locate the webs of the trailing shoe on the wheel cylinder and the fixed abutment, making sure that the lower end of the handbrake lever is correctly located on the face of the plastic plunger and not trapped behind it.

15 Fit the trailing shoe hold-down post and spring. Hold the leading shoe in position.

16 Connect the larger shoe return spring at the lower (abutment) position between both shoes.

17 Holding the leading shoe almost at right-angles to the backplate, connect the spring between it and the strut and then engage the bottom end of the shoe behind the abutment retainer plate.

5.6 Removing the brake shoe hold-down washer and spring

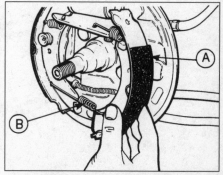

5.7 Removing the leading brake shoe
A Leading shoe   B Lower spring

9

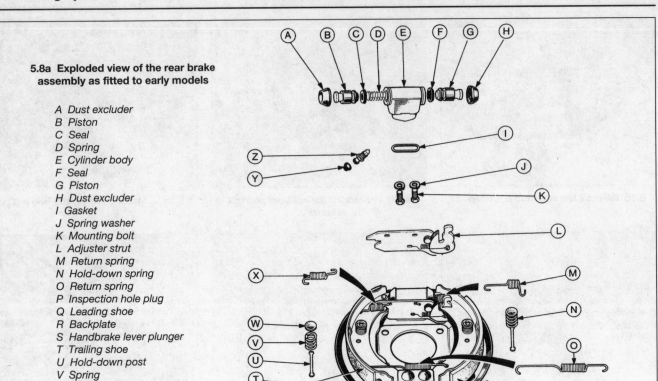

5.8a Exploded view of the rear brake assembly as fitted to early models

A Dust excluder
B Piston
C Seal
D Spring
E Cylinder body
F Seal
G Piston
H Dust excluder
I Gasket
J Spring washer
K Mounting bolt
L Adjuster strut
M Return spring
N Hold-down spring
O Return spring
P Inspection hole plug
Q Leading shoe
R Backplate
S Handbrake lever plunger
T Trailing shoe
U Hold-down post
V Spring
W Dished washer
X Return spring
Y Dust cover
Z Bleed screw

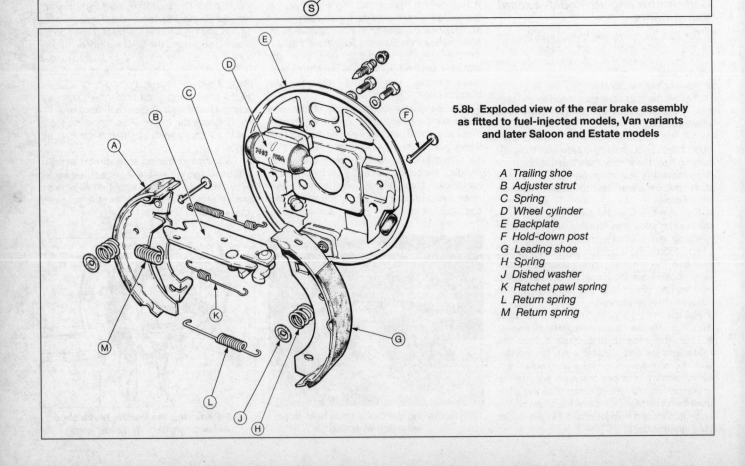

5.8b Exploded view of the rear brake assembly as fitted to fuel-injected models, Van variants and later Saloon and Estate models

A Trailing shoe
B Adjuster strut
C Spring
D Wheel cylinder
E Backplate
F Hold-down post
G Leading shoe
H Spring
J Dished washer
K Ratchet pawl spring
L Return spring
M Return spring

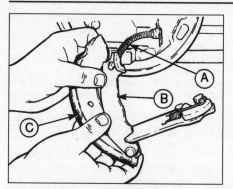

5.10 Removing the handbrake cable from the trailing brake shoe

A Handbrake cable C Trailing shoe
B Lever

18 Swivel the shoe towards the backplate so that the cut-out in its web passes over the quadrant lever. Fit the shoe hold-down post, spring and washer.
19 Centralise the shoes within the backplate by tapping them if necessary with the hand, then fit the hub/drum and slide the outer bearing onto the spindle.
20 Fit the thrustwasher and hub nut finger tight only.
21 Tighten the hub nut to a torque of between 20 and 25 Nm (15 and 18 lbf ft), at the same time rotating the roadwheel in an anti-clockwise direction.
22 Unscrew the nut one half a turn and then tighten it only finger tight.
23 Fit the nut retainer so that two of its slots line up with the split pin hole. Insert a new split pin, bending the end around the nut, not over the end of the stub axle.
24 Tap the dust cap into position.
25 Refit the roadwheel and check that a small amount of hub bearing free play can be felt when the wheel is rocked at the top and bottom.
26 Depress the brake pedal fully several times to operate the self-adjusting mechanism then lower the car to the ground.
27 Recheck the tightness of the wheel bolts.

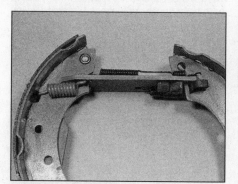

5.33a Brake shoe return spring and adjuster strut arrangement on Van, fuel-injected models and later Saloon and Estate models

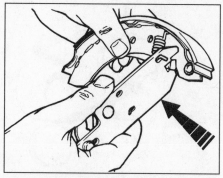

5.11 Separating the trailing brake shoe from the adjuster strut

Fuel-injection engine models and Van variants

28 On these vehicles the brake drum is separate from the hub and can be removed without the need to remove the hub as well. The bearings will therefore not need to be readjusted during reassembly.
29 The brake shoe inspection and removal procedure is very similar to that described previously but note the following differences.
30 Before removing the drum unscrew the drum retaining screw **(see illustration)**.
31 Disconnect the lower shoe return spring which bridges the shoes and then disconnect the handbrake cable from the lever.
32 Prise the shoes away from the lower pivot, twist them from the wheel cylinder and remove as an assembly.
33 With the shoes removed they can be separated from the strut. Note how the components are positioned before dismantling **(see illustrations)**.
34 Refitting is a reversal of the removal procedure.

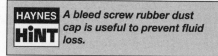

6 Rear wheel cylinder - removal, overhaul and refitting

Note: *Before starting work, refer to the warning at the beginning of Section 2 concerning the dangers of asbestos dust, and*

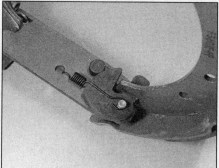

5.33b Automatic adjuster assembly on Van, fuel-injected models and later Saloon and Estate models

5.30 Removing the drum retaining screw on models with a separate brake drum

to the warning at the beginning of Section 3 concerning the dangers of hydraulic fluid.

Removal

1 Remove the rear brake shoes, as described in the preceding Section.
2 Disconnect the fluid pipeline from the wheel cylinder and cap the end of the pipe to prevent loss of fluid.

> **HAYNES HiNT** *A bleed screw rubber dust cap is useful to prevent fluid loss.*

3 Unscrew the two bolts which hold the wheel cylinder to the brake backplate and remove the cylinder with sealing gasket **(see illustration)**.

Overhaul

4 Clean away external dirt and then pull off the dust-excluding covers.
5 The pistons and seals will probably shake out. If they do not, apply air pressure (from a tyre pump) at the inlet hole to eject them **(see illustration)**.
6 Examine the surfaces of the pistons and the cylinder bores for scoring or metal-to-metal rubbing areas. If evident, renew the complete cylinder assembly.
7 If the cylinder is to be renewed note that any one of three different sizes may be fitted

9

6.3 Rear wheel cylinder retaining bolts (arrowed)

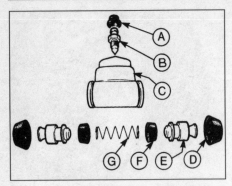

6.5 Exploded view of the rear wheel cylinder

A *Dust cap*   E *Piston*
B *Bleed screw*   F *Piston seal*
C *Wheel cylinder*   G *Spring*
D *Dust excluder*

according to model and year. The wheel cylinders are identified by a letter stamped on the rear face which corresponds to the following **(see illustration)**:

Letter "T" = 22.2 mm diameter cylinder
Letter "L" = 19.05 mm diameter cylinder
Letter "H" = 17.78 mm diameter cylinder

Ensure that the new cylinder obtained is the same as the one removed and more importantly, is the same as the cylinder on the other rear brake.

8 Where the components are in good condition, discard the rubber seals and dust excluders and obtain a repair kit.

9 Any cleaning should be done using hydraulic fluid or methylated spirit-nothing else.

10 Reassemble by dipping the first piston in clean hydraulic fluid and inserting it into the cylinder. Fit a dust excluder to it.

11 From the opposite end of the cylinder body, insert a new seal, spring, a second new seal, the second piston and the remaining dust excluder. Use only the fingers to manipulate the seals into position and make quite sure that the lips of the seals are the correct way round.

Refitting

12 Bolt the wheel cylinder to the backplate,

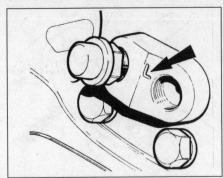

6.7 Wheel cylinder identification letter location (arrowed)

reconnect the fluid line and refit the shoes (Section 5).
13 Refit the brake drum and roadwheel and lower the vehicle to the floor.
14 Bleed the brake hydraulic system as described in Section 11 or 23 as applicable.

7 Brake drum - inspection and renewal

Note: *Before starting work, refer to the note at the beginning of Section 2 concerning the dangers of asbestos dust.*

1 Whenever a brake drum is removed, brush out dust from it, **taking care not to inhale it** as it contains asbestos and is injurious to health.

2 Examine the internal friction surface of the drum. If deeply scored, or so worn that the drum has become pocketed to the width of the shoes, then the drums must be renewed.

3 Regrinding is not recommended as the internal diameter will no longer be compatible with the shoe lining contact diameter.

8 Handbrake - adjustment

1 Adjustment of the handbrake is normally automatic by means of the self-adjusting mechanism working on the rear brake shoes.

2 However, due to cable stretch, occasional inspection of the handbrake adjusters is

recommended. Adjustment must be carried out if the movement of the control lever becomes excessive.

3 Chock the front wheels. Release the handbrake.

4 Raise and support the vehicle at the rear with safety stands (see *"Jacking and Vehicle Support"*).

5 Grip each adjustment plunger, one located on each rear brake backplate, and move it in and out **(see illustration)**.

6 If the total movement of both plungers added together is between 0.5 and 2.0 mm (0.02 and 0.08 in) then adjustment of the handbrake is satisfactory. If the plunger movement is not as specified proceed as follows.

7 Two cable types are used on Escort models according to year of manufacture and it is necessary to identify the type being worked on before proceeding.

8 Locate the cable adjuster which is located just forward of the fuel tank. If the cable adjuster nut has finger grips but the abutment sleeve is smooth, proceed as follows. If both the cable adjuster and abutment sleeve have finger grips, proceed to paragraph 14 **(see illustration)**.

Early type cable with smooth abutment sleeve

9 Make sure that the abutment sleeve on the cable is fully engaged in its bracket slot. Unlock the adjusting nut by levering between the shoulders of the nut and the sleeve.

10 Now turn the adjuster nut to eliminate slackness from the cable so that it is just possible to rotate the adjustment plungers on the brake backplates.

11 Apply the handbrake fully to seat the adjusting nut against its sleeve.

12 If adjustment of the cable does not alter the plunger movement then the handbrake cable is likely to be binding or seized or the brake mechanism is at fault.

13 On completion lower the car to the ground.

Later type cable with finger grip abutment sleeve

14 If the cable adjuster and abutment sleeve both have finger grips check to see if a nylon

8.5 Handbrake adjustment plunger location (arrowed) on backplate

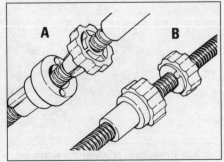

8.8 Handbrake cable identification
A *Early cable with smooth abutment sleeve*
B *Later cable with finger grip abutment sleeve*

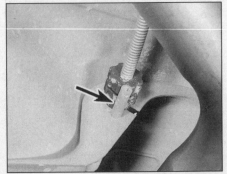

8.14 Handbrake cable adjuster nylon locking pin (arrowed)

locking pin is used to lock the adjusting nut in position (see illustration). If so remove the locking pin using pliers. Note that a new pin will be needed after adjustment.

15 Slacken the adjusting nut then apply the footbrake hard several times to ensure full self-adjustment of the brake shoes.

16 Turn the abutment sleeve as necessary until the total movement of both adjustment plungers added together is between 0.5 and 2.0 mm (0.02 and 0.08 in).

17 Tighten the adjusting nut against the abutment sleeve as tight as possible by hand (2 clicks) then tighten it by a further 2 clicks (maximum) using a suitable wrench.

18 Where applicable fit a new locking pin and tap it into place.

19 On completion lower the car to the ground.

9 Handbrake cables - renewal

1 Chock the front wheels, then fully release the handbrake.

2 Raise and support the vehicle at the rear with axle stands (see *"Jacking and Vehicle Support"*).

Primary cable

3 Extract the spring clip and clevis pin and disconnect the primary cable from the equaliser (see illustrations).

4 Working inside the vehicle, disconnect the cable from the hand-brake control lever, again by removal of clip and pin. Drift out the cable guide to the rear and withdraw the cable through the floorpan.

5 Refitting is a reversal of removal. Adjust the handbrake, if necessary, as described in Section 8.

Secondary cable

6 Using the procedure described in Section 8, slacken the cable adjusting nut so that the abutment sleeve can be disengaged from its body guide (see illustration).

7 Release the cable connector from its body guide by extracting the spring clip and passing the inner cable through the slit in the guide (see illustration).

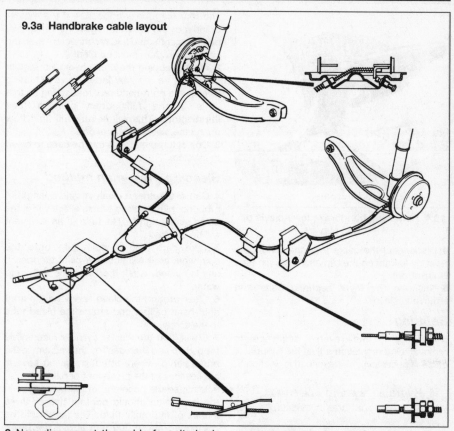

9.3a Handbrake cable layout

8 Now disconnect the cable from its body guide on the right-hand side of the vehicle.

9 Separate the cable assembly/equaliser from the primary cable by extracting the spring clip and clevis pin.

10 Release the cable from the body guides.

11 Remove the rear roadwheels and the brake drums.

12 Release the shoe hold-down spring so that the shoe can be swivelled and the handbrake lever unclipped from the relay lever.

13 Remove the cable ends through the brake backplate and withdraw the complete cable assembly from the vehicle.

14 Refitting is a reversal of removal. Grease the cable groove in the equaliser and adjust the handbrake, as described in Section 8.

10 Handbrake lever - removal and refitting

Removal

1 Chock the front wheels, raise and support the vehicle at the rear using stands (see *"Jacking and Vehicle Support"*) then release the handbrake.

2 Working underneath, extract the spring clip and clevis pin and disconnect the primary cable from the equaliser.

3 From inside the car detach the handbrake warning switch.

9

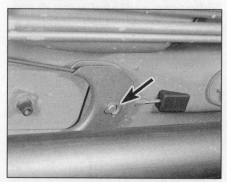

9.3b Primary cable-to-equaliser clevis pin and spring clip (arrowed)

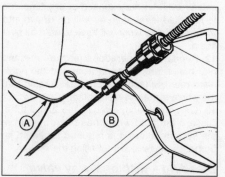

9.6 Removing handbrake cable abutment sleeve from the body guide

A Body guide   *B Secondary cable*

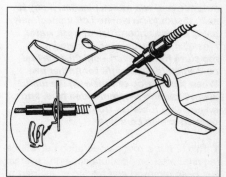

9.7 Handbrake cable connector spring clip removal

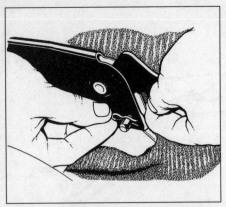

10.4 Removing handbrake lever clevis pin and clip

4 Disconnect the cable from the handbrake lever by extracting the clip and clevis pin **(see illustration)**.

5 Unscrew the lever securing bolts and remove the lever.

Refitting

6 Refitting is the reverse sequence to removal. On completion adjust the handbrake cable, if necessary, as described in Section 8.

11 Hydraulic system - bleeding (conventional braking system)

Note: *On cars equipped with the Anti-lock Braking System, refer to Section 23.*

⚠️ *Warning: Hydraulic fluid is poisonous; wash off immediately and thoroughly in the case of skin contact, and seek immediate medical advice if any fluid is swallowed or gets into the eyes. Certain types of hydraulic fluid are inflammable, and may ignite when allowed into contact with hot components; when servicing any hydraulic system, it is safest to assume that the fluid is inflammable, and to take precautions against the risk of fire as though it is petrol that is being handled. Hydraulic fluid is also an effective paint stripper, and will attack plastics; if any is spilt, it should be washed off immediately, using copious quantities of fresh water. Finally, it is hygroscopic (it absorbs moisture from the air) - old fluid may be contaminated and unfit for further use. When topping-up or renewing the fluid, always use the recommended type, and ensure that it comes from a freshly-opened sealed container.*

1 This is not a routine operation but will be required after any component in the system has been removed and refitted or any part of the hydraulic system has been opened. Where an operation has only affected one circuit of the hydraulic system, then bleeding will normally only be required to that circuit (front

and rear diagonally opposite). If the master cylinder or the pressure regulating valve have been disconnected and reconnected, then the complete system must be bled.

2 When bleeding the brake hydraulic system on a Van, tie the light laden valve actuating lever to the right-hand rear roadspring so that it is in the fully open position **(see illustration)**. This will ensure full fluid flow during the bleeding operations.

3 One of three methods can be used to bleed the system.

Bleeding - two-man method

4 Gather together a clean jar and a length of rubber or plastic bleed tubing which will fit the bleed screw tightly. The help of an assistant will be required.

5 Take care not to spill fluid onto the paintwork as it will act as a paint stripper. If any is spilled, wash if off at once with cold water.

6 Clean around the bleed screw on the front right-hand caliper and attach the bleed tube to the screw.

7 Check that the master cylinder reservoir is topped up and then destroy the vacuum in the brake servo (where fitted) by giving several applications of the brake foot pedal.

8 Immerse the open end of the bleed tube in the jar, which should contain two or three inches of hydraulic fluid. The jar should be positioned about 300 mm above the bleed nipple to prevent any possibility of air entering the system down the threads of the bleed screw when it is slackened.

9 Open the bleed screw half a turn and have your assistant depress the brake pedal slowly to the floor and then, after the bleed screw is retightened, quickly remove his foot to allow the pedal to return unimpeded. Repeat the procedure.

10 Observe the submerged end of the tube in the jar. When air bubbles cease to appear, tighten the bleed screw when the pedal is being held fully down by your assistant.

11 Top-up the fluid reservoir. It must be kept topped up throughout the bleeding operations. If the connecting holes to the master cylinder are exposed at any time due to low fluid level, then air will be drawn into the system and work will have to start all over again.

12 Repeat the operations on the left-hand rear brake, the left-hand front and the right-hand rear brake in that order (assuming that the whole system is being bled).

13 On completion, remove the bleed tube. Discard the fluid which has been bled from the system unless it is required for bleed jar purposes, never use it for filling the system.

Bleeding - with one-way valve

14 There are a number of one-man brake bleeding kits currently available from motor accessory shops. It is recommended that one of these kits should be used whenever

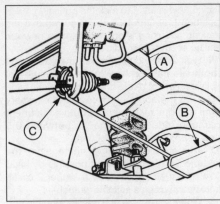

11.2 Light laden valve retained in open position - Van models

A Wire   C Actuating
B Roadspring   lever

possible as they greatly simplify the bleeding operation and also reduce the risk of expelled air or fluid being drawn back into the system.

15 Connect the outlet tube of the bleeder device to the bleed screw and then open the screw half a turn. Depress the brake pedal to the floor and slowly release it. The one-way valve in the device will prevent expelled air from returning to the system at the completion of each stroke. Repeat this operation until clean hydraulic fluid, free from air bubbles, can be seen coming through the tube. Tighten the bleed screw and remove the tube.

16 Repeat the procedure on the remaining bleed nipples in the order described in paragraph 12. Remember to keep the master cylinder reservoir full.

Bleeding - with pressure bleeding kit

17 These too are available from motor accessory shops and are usually operated by air pressure from the spare tyre.

18 By connecting a pressurised container to the master cylinder fluid reservoir, bleeding is then carried out by simply opening each bleed screw in turn and allowing the fluid to run out, rather like turning on a tap, until no air bubbles are visible in the fluid being expelled.

19 Using this system, the large reserve of fluid provides a safeguard against air being drawn into the master cylinder during the bleeding operations.

20 This method is particularly effective when bleeding "difficult" systems or when bleeding the entire system at time of routine fluid renewal.

All systems

21 On completion of bleeding, top-up the fluid level to the mark. Check the feel of the brake pedal, which should be firm and free from any "sponginess" which would indicate air still being present in the system.

22 On Van models release the light laden valve actuating lever.

12 Master cylinder - removal, overhaul and refitting

Note: *Before starting work, refer to the warning at the beginning of Section 3 concerning the dangers of hydraulic fluid.*

Removal

1 Disconnect the leads from the level warning switch in the reservoir cap. Remove the cap.
2 Syphon out as much fluid as possible from the master cylinder reservoir using an old battery hydrometer or a poultry baster. Do not drip the fluid onto the paintwork as it will act as an effective paint stripper.
3 Disconnect the pipelines from the master cylinder by unscrewing the unions. Additionally on models equipped with the anti-lock braking system, release the clips and disconnect the two modulator fluid return pipes.
4 On non-servo models release the retaining clip securing the master cylinder pushrod to the brake pedal **(see illustration)**.
5 Unbolt the master cylinder unit from the servo unit or bulkhead, as applicable, and withdraw it.

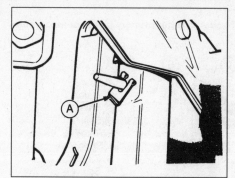

12.4 Master cylinder push rod-to-pedal retaining clip (A) - non-servo models

Overhaul

6 Clean away external dirt and then detach the fluid reservoir by tilting it sideways and gently pulling. Remove the two rubber seals **(see illustration)**.
7 Secure the master cylinder carefully in a vice fitted with jaw protectors.
8 Unscrew and remove the piston stop bolt.
9 Pull the dust excluder back and, using circlip pliers, extract the circlip which is now exposed **(see illustration)**.

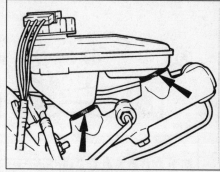

12.6 Master cylinder reservoir rubber seals (arrowed)

10 Remove the pushrod, dust excluder and washer.
11 Withdraw the primary piston assembly, which will already have been partially ejected.
12 Tap the end of the master cylinder on a block of wood and eject the secondary piston assembly.
13 Examine the piston and cylinder bore surface for scoring or signs of metal-to-metal rubbing. If evident, renew the cylinder complete.

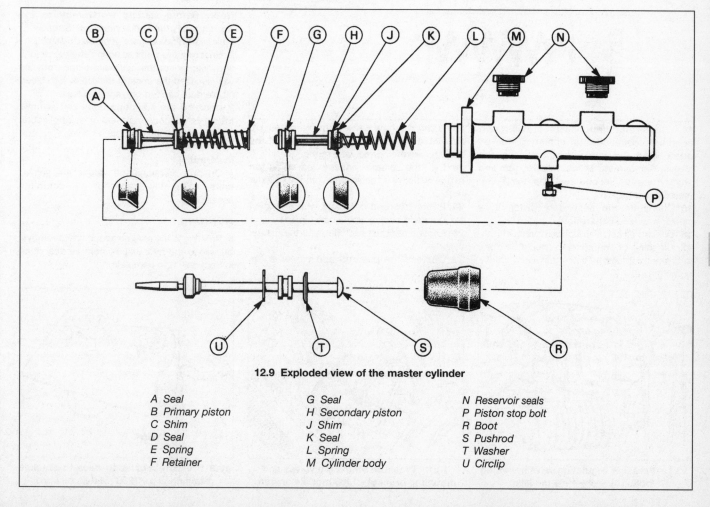

12.9 Exploded view of the master cylinder

A Seal	G Seal	N Reservoir seals
B Primary piston	H Secondary piston	P Piston stop bolt
C Shim	J Shim	R Boot
D Seal	K Seal	S Pushrod
E Spring	L Spring	T Washer
F Retainer	M Cylinder body	U Circlip

9

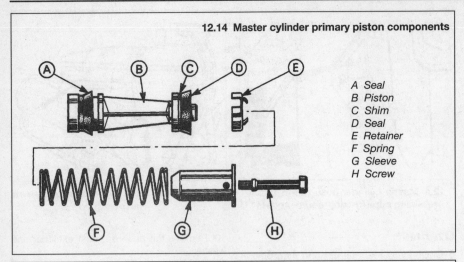

12.14 Master cylinder primary piston components

A Seal
B Piston
C Shim
D Seal
E Retainer
F Spring
G Sleeve
H Screw

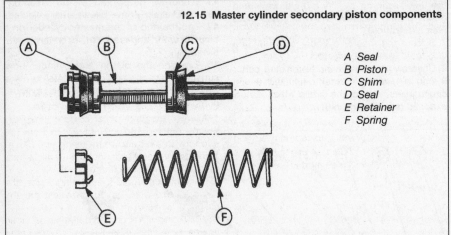

12.15 Master cylinder secondary piston components

A Seal
B Piston
C Shim
D Seal
E Retainer
F Spring

14 Where the components are in good condition, dismantle the primary piston by unscrewing the screw and removing the sleeve. Remove the spring, retainer, seal and shim. Prise the second seal from the piston **(see illustration)**.

15 Dismantle the secondary piston in a similar way **(see illustration)**.

16 Discard all seals and obtain a repair kit.

17 Cleaning of components should be done in brake hydraulic fluid or methylated spirit - nothing else.

18 Using the new seals from the repair kit, assemble the pistons, making sure that the seal lips are the correct way round.

19 Dip the piston assemblies in clean hydraulic fluid and enter them into the cylinder bore.

20 Fit the pushrod complete with new dust excluder and secure with a new circlip.

21 Engage the dust excluder with the master cylinder.

22 Depress the pushrod and screw in the stop bolt.

23 Locate the two rubber seals and push the fluid reservoir into position.

24 It is recommended that a small quantity of fluid is now poured into the reservoir and the pushrod operated several times to prime the unit.

Refitting

25 Refit the master cylinder by reversing the removal operations.

26 Bleed the complete hydraulic system on completion of work (see Section 11 or 23 as applicable).

13 Pressure regulating valve (Saloon and Estate models) - removal and refitting

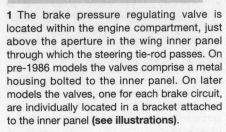

1 The brake pressure regulating valve is located within the engine compartment, just above the aperture in the wing inner panel through which the steering tie-rod passes. On pre-1986 models the valves comprise a metal housing bolted to the inner panel. On later models the valves, one for each brake circuit, are individually located in a bracket attached to the inner panel **(see illustrations)**.

Removal

Note: *Before starting work, refer to the warning at the beginning of Section 3 concerning the dangers of hydraulic fluid.*

2 Unscrew the unions, noting their locations and disconnect the hydraulic pipes from the valve(s). Cap the ends of the pipes with bleed nipple dust caps to prevent fluid loss.

3 Unscrew the mounting bolts and remove the valve or mounting bracket as applicable. On later models extract the retaining clips and remove the valves from the bracket **(see illustration)**.

4 On both versions the valves are sealed units and only serviced as complete assemblies.

Refitting

5 Refitting is the reverse sequence to removal but bleed the hydraulic system as described in Section 11 on completion.

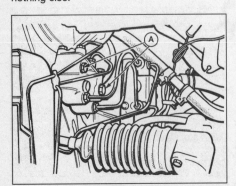

13.1a Pressure regulating valve mounting bolts (A) - pre-1986 models

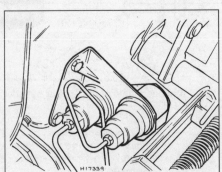

13.1b Pressure regulating valves and mounting bracket - 1986 models onward

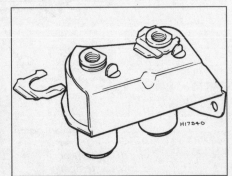

13.3 Pressure regulating valve-to-bracket retaining clip - 1986 models onward

14 Light laden valve (Van models) - adjustment, removal and refitting

1 The light laden valve used on Van models is a pressure regulating valve which reacts to suspension height according to vehicle load. The valve is mounted on the underside of the vehicle above the rear axle tube and is connected to the axle by a rod **(see illustration)**.

2 The valve should never be dismantled but it must be adjusted whenever the valve itself, the axle tube, spring or shock absorber have been removed, refitted or renewed.

Adjustment

3 Follow this adjustment procedure provided the original roadsprings have been refitted, but when new valve linkage has been installed. Measure the dimension "X" and if necessary adjust the position of the nut to make the dimension between 10 and 12 mm **(see illustration)**.

4 Rotate the spacer tube so that the dimension "C" is between 18.5 and 20.5 mm **(see illustration)**. Crimp the end of the spacer tube adjacent to the knurled section of the tube to prevent the tube from rotating.

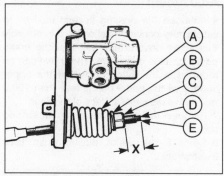

14.3 Light laden valve adjustment diagram - Van models

A Control spring
B Linkage retaining clip
C Adjuster nut
D Threaded rod
E Flats
X = 10 to 12 mm

14.1 Light laden valve components - Van models

A Valve body
B Fluid outlet
C Fluid inlet
D Actuating lever
E Adjuster nut
F Linkage retaining clip
G Control spring
H Adjuster rod
I Spacer tube
J Link rod
K Rear axle tube

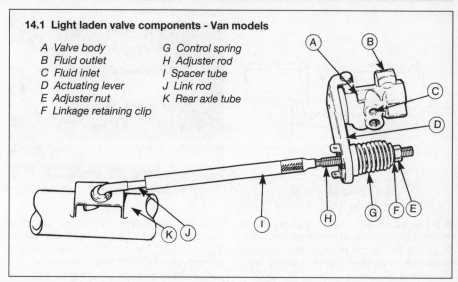

5 If the original roadsprings have been refitted and also the original valve linkage, hold the threaded adjustment rod by means of its flats and turn the adjusting nut in either direction until the correct dimensions are obtained.

6 If one or both rear roadsprings have been renewed, carry out the adjustment procedure described in paragraph 3, except that the end of the spacer tube should be aligned with the groove in the link rod **(see illustration)**.

Removal

Note: *Before starting work, refer to the warning at the beginning of Section 3 concerning the dangers of hydraulic fluid.*

7 If the pressure regulating valve must be removed, first disconnect the hydraulic pipelines from the valve and cap the pipes.

8 Unbolt the valve from its mounting bracket, lower the valve and slide the spacer tube assembly off the link rod. Remove the link rod.

Refitting

9 Refitting is a reversal of removal, but bleed the brakes (Section 11) and adjust the valve as described previously in this Section.

15 Hydraulic pipes and hoses - renewal

Note: *Before starting work, refer to the warning at the beginning of Section 3 concerning the dangers of hydraulic fluid.*

1 Always disconnect a flexible hose by prising out the spring anchor clip from the support bracket and then, using two close-fitting spanners, disconnect the rigid line from the flexible hose **(see illustration)**.

2 Once disconnected from the rigid pipe, the flexible hose may be unscrewed from the caliper or wheel cylinder.

3 When reconnecting pipelines, or hose fittings, remember that all union threads are to metric sizes. No copper washers are used at unions and the seal is made at the swaged end of the pipe, so do not try to wind a union in if it is tight yet still stands proud of the surface into which it is screwed.

4 A flexible hose must never be installed twisted, but a slight "set" is permissible to give it clearance from an adjacent component. Do this by turning the hose slightly before inserting the bracket spring clip.

5 Rigid pipelines can be made to pattern by factors supplying brake components.

9

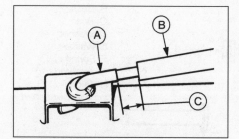

14.4 Light laden valve linkage adjustment diagram with original roadsprings - Van models

A Link rod
B Spacer tube
C = 18.5 to 20.5 mm

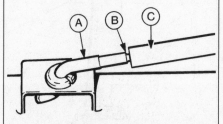

14.6 Light laden valve linkage adjustment diagram with new roadsprings - Van models

A Link rod
B Groove
C Spacer tube

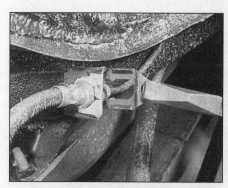

15.1 Removing a flexible hose spring anchor clip

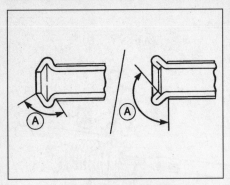

15.8 Brake pipe flare
A Protective coating removed before flaring

6 If you are making up a brake pipe yourself, observe the following essential requirements.
7 Before flaring the ends of the pipe, trim back the protective plastic coating by a distance of 5.0 mm.
8 Flare the end of the pipe as shown **(see illustration)**.
9 The minimum pipe bend radius is 12.0 mm, but bends of less than 20.0 mm should be avoided if possible.

16 Vacuum servo unit and linkage - removal and refitting

Removal

1 Refer to Section 12 and remove the master cylinder.
2 On fuel-injection models unclip and lift out the front section of the heater plenum chamber to provide access to the connecting linkage across the lower bulkhead **(see illustration)**.
3 Working inside the vehicle, remove the spring clip which attaches the pushrod to the arm of the brake pedal.
4 Unscrew the nuts which hold the servo to its mounting bracket, also the servo support brace to the body.
5 Disconnect the valve hose from the servo.
6 Detach the linkage arm spring at the rear of the servo and then pull the servo forward until the servo operating rod can be unclipped from the linkage.

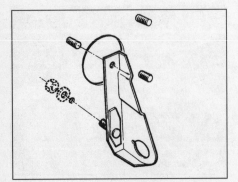

16.8b Vacuum servo unit connecting link bracket on driver's side

16.2 Heater plenum chamber removal

7 Remove the servo from the vehicle. It must be renewed if defective, no repair is possible.
8 If necessary, the rest of the servo operating linkage can be removed from under the instrument panel once the covering and cowl side trim have been removed from above the brake pedal inside the vehicle. Unbolt the connecting link bracket from the driver's side **(see illustrations)**.

Refitting

9 Refitting is the reverse sequence to removal. Refit the master cylinder as described in Section 12 and bleed the hydraulic system as described in Sections 11 or 23 as applicable.

17 Brake pedal - removal, refitting and adjustment

Removal

1 Working within the vehicle, remove the under-dash cover panel.
2 Extract the spring clip which connects the pushrod to the arm of the brake pedal.

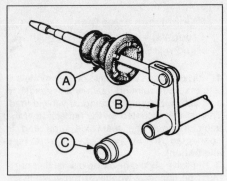

16.8a Vacuum servo unit connecting linkage

A Grommet   *C Bush*
B Connecting link

3 Extract the circlip from the end of the pedal pivot shaft and withdraw the shaft with clutch pedal and the flat and wave washers **(see illustration)**.
4 Renew the bushes as necessary.

Refitting

5 Reassembly and refitting are reversals of removal and dismantling. Apply a little grease to the bushes when installing.

Adjustment

6 Although the braking system may be in satisfactory condition generally, it is possible that some drivers may feel that the brake pedal travel is excessive. The travel can be reduced in the following way if the upper surface of the pedal pad is less than 200.0 mm above the metal surface of the floor.
7 Remove the brake pedal as described above.
8 Remove the white plastic bush **(see illustration)**.

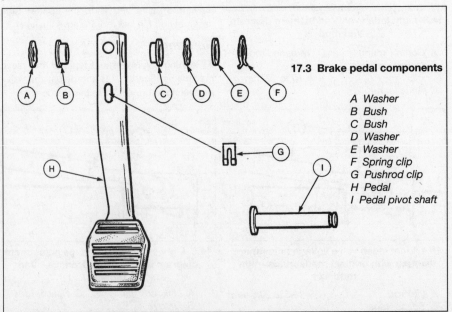

17.3 Brake pedal components

A Washer
B Bush
C Bush
D Washer
E Washer
F Spring clip
G Pushrod clip
H Pedal
I Pedal pivot shaft

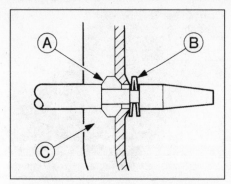

17.8 Sectional view of brake pedal and pushrod

A White plastic bush
B Pushrod clip
C Pedal arm

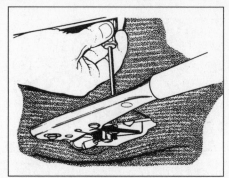

18.4 Removing handbrake warning switch

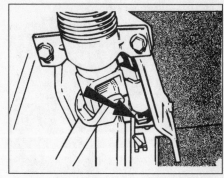

18.5 Brake stop-lamp switch locknut location (arrowed)

9 Fit a new bush which is red in colour and will increase the pedal height. Once this type of bush has been fitted it will not be possible to refit the anti-rattle retainer. This does not matter.

10 Adjust the stop-lamp switch (Section 18).

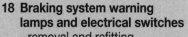

18 Braking system warning lamps and electrical switches - removal and refitting

General

1 All models are fitted with a low fluid level warning switch in the master cylinder reservoir cap and a brake pedal stop-lamp switch.

2 Some versions have front disc pad wear sensors and a handbrake "ON" warning switch.

3 Warning indicator lamps are mounted on the instrument panel. Their renewal is covered in Chapter 12.

Handbrake "ON" warning lamp switch

4 The handbrake "ON" warning switch is attached to the handbrake lever and can be removed after disconnecting the wiring and undoing the retaining screw **(see illustration)**.

Stop-lamp switch

5 The stop-lamp switch can be removed by disconnecting the leads and unscrewing the locknut which holds the switch to its bracket under the facia **(see illustration)**.

6 When fitting the switch, adjust its position by screwing it in or out so that it does not actuate during the first 5.0 mm of pedal travel.

19 Anti-lock Braking System - description

1 From 1986 onward an anti-lock braking system is available as standard or optional equipment on certain Escort models.

2 The system comprises four main components: two modulators, one for each brake circuit, and two rear axle load apportioning valves, again, one for each brake circuit. Apart from the additional hydraulic piping the remainder of the braking system is the same as for conventional models **(see illustration)**.

3 The modulators are located in the engine compartment with one mounted on each side of the transmission, directly above the driveshaft inner constant velocity joints. Each modulator contains a shaft which actuates a flywheel by means of a ball and ramp clutch. A rubber toothed belt is used to drive the modulator shaft from the driveshaft inner constant velocity joint.

4 During driving and under normal braking, the modulator shaft and the flywheel rotate together and at the same speed through the engagement of a ball and ramp clutch. In this condition, hydraulic pressure from the master cylinder passes to the modulators and then to each brake in the conventional way. In the event of a front wheel locking the modulator shaft rotation will be less than that of the flywheel and the flywheel will overrun the ball and ramp clutch. This causes the flywheel to slide on the modulator shaft, move inward and operate a lever which in turn opens a dump valve. Hydraulic pressure to the locked brake is released via a de-boost piston allowing the wheel to once again revolve. Fluid passed through the dump valve is returned to the master cylinder reservoir via the modulator return pipes. At the same time hydraulic pressure from the master cylinder causes a pump piston to contact an eccentric cam on the modulator shaft. The flywheel is then decelerated at a controlled rate by the flywheel friction clutch. When the speed of the modulator shaft and flywheel are once again equal the dump valve closes and the cycle repeats. This complete operation takes place many times a second until the vehicle stops or the brakes are released.

5 The load apportioning valves are mounted on the rear crossmember and connected to each rear suspension arm via a linkage. The valves regulate hydraulic pressure to the rear brakes in accordance with vehicle load and attitude in such a way that braking force at the front brakes will always be greater than that at the rear.

6 A belt break warning switch is fitted to the cover which surrounds each modulator drivebelt. The switch contains an arm which is in contact with the drivebelt at all times. If the belt should break, or if the adjustment of the belt is too slack, the arm will move out closing the switch contacts and informing the driver via an instrument panel warning light.

19.2 Anti-lock braking system hydraulic pipe arrangement and component layout

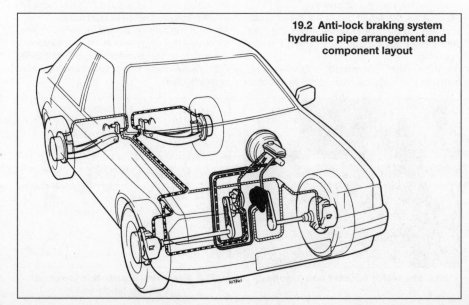

9

20.2 Removing the belt break switch from the modulator drivebelt cover

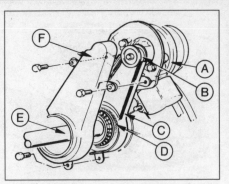

20.3a Modulator and drivebelt details

A Modulator   E Driveshaft
B Sprocket   F Drivebelt cover
C Drivebelt
D Constant
    velocity joint

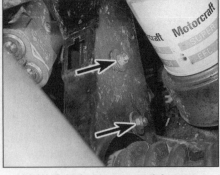

20.3b Drivebelt cover retaining nuts (arrowed) - models up to 1987

20 Modulator drivebelt (anti-lock braking system) - removal and refitting

Note: *Whenever an ABS modulator adjuster bolt is slackened or removed, the bolt threads should be lightly coated with grease to prevent the possibility of bolt seizure. Take care not to contaminate surrounding components when applying the grease.*

Right-hand side

Removal

Note: *A new driveshaft snap-ring and a new tie-rod balljoint split-pin will be required on refitting.*

1 Jack up the front of the car, support it on stands (see *"Jacking and Vehicle Support"*) and remove the roadwheel.
2 Remove the belt break switch from the drivebelt cover by pushing it upward and carefully levering out the bottom edge. Pull the switch down, withdraw the switch arm from the opening in the cover and place the switch to one side **(see illustration)**.
3 Undo the two drivebelt cover retaining nuts and washers, and on later models (1987-on), the retaining bolt **(see illustrations)**.

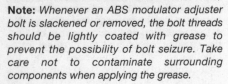

4 Withdraw the cover from the studs and remove it by moving it upwards to clear the oil filter.
5 Slacken the modulator adjuster bolt, move the modulator to relieve the tension on the drivebelt then slip the belt off the modulator sprocket **(see illustration)**.
6 Extract the split pin, undo the retaining nut and separate the tie-rod balljoint from the steering arm using a suitable balljoint separator tool.
7 Disconnect the front suspension lower arm balljoint from the hub carrier by removing the nut and pinch-bolt **(see illustration)**. Note that the pinch-bolt is of the socket-headed (Torx) type and a special key or socket bit will be required for this purpose. These are readily available from most accessory shops.
8 Place a suitable container beneath the driveshaft inner constant velocity joint.
9 Insert a lever between the inner constant velocity joint and the transmission housing. Firmly strike the lever to release the constant velocity joint from the differential.
10 Pull the driveshaft out of the transmission and slip the modulator drivebelt off the joint. Allow the transmission oil to drain into the container.
11 With the driveshaft disconnected, suspend it in such a way so as not to adopt an

angle of more than 45° from the outer constant velocity joint.

Refitting

12 Before refitting the drivebelt, renew the snap-ring fitted to the splines of the inner constant velocity joint.
13 Ensure that the modulator sprocket and constant velocity joint splines are clean and dry then slip the drivebelt over the joint.
14 Engage the joint splines with the differential and firmly push the hub carrier inwards to force the joint home.
15 Reconnect the lower arm balljoint to the hub carrier and insert the Torx bolt with its head to the rear. Refit the nut and tighten to the specified torque.
16 Reconnect the tie-rod balljoint to the steering arm, fit and tighten the nut to the specified torque and secure with a new split pin.
17 Slip the drivebelt over the modulator sprocket ensuring that it sits squarely in the sprocket teeth.
18 Move the modulator as necessary to tension the belt so that the belt deflection, under light finger pressure, is 5.0 mm. Check this using a ruler at a point midway between the two sprockets **(see illustration)**.
19 With the belt tensioned correctly, tighten the modulator adjuster bolt. Before tightening, the adjuster bolt threads should be coated with grease - refer to the note at the beginning of this Section.

20.3c Right-hand side ABS modulator drivebelt cover - 1987-on models

A Guard   C Bolt
B Support bracket   D Washer

20.5 Modulator adjuster bolt (arrowed)

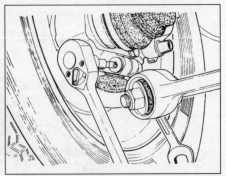

20.7 Removing suspension lower arm balljoint pinch-bolt

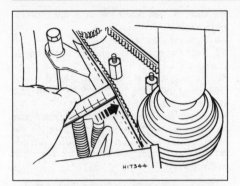

20.18 Using a ruler to check right-hand drivebelt adjustment

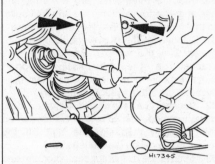

20.26 Left-hand drivebelt cover retaining bolt locations (arrowed)

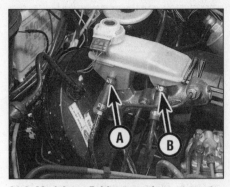

21.3 Modulator fluid return pipes at master cylinder reservoir
A To right-hand modulator
B To left-hand modulator

20 Refit the drivebelt cover and secure with the two nuts and washers, and the bolt (where applicable).

21 Engage the belt break switch arm upwards through the opening in the drivebelt cover then locate the switch in position. Pull the switch downward to secure.

22 Refit the roadwheel and lower the car to the ground.

23 Top-up the transmission oil as described in Chapter 1.

Left-hand side

24 The procedure is the same as for the right-hand side but note the following differences.

25 Remove the engine splash shield from the inner wheel arch.

26 When removing the drivebelt cover note that it is secured by three bolts, two at the top and one at the bottom **(see illustration)**.

27 To move the modulator for adjustment of the belt tension, use a suitable length of wood inserted through the steering tie-rod aperture in the inner wheel arch, to push on the modulator as necessary.

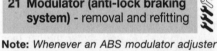

21 Modulator (anti-lock braking system) - removal and refitting

Note: Whenever an ABS modulator adjuster bolt is slackened or removed, the bolt threads should be lightly coated with grease to prevent the possibility of bolt seizure. Take care not to contaminate surrounding components when applying the grease.

Note: Before starting work, refer to the warning at the beginning of Section 3 concerning the dangers of hydraulic fluid.

Right-hand side

Removal

1 Disconnect the wiring plug from the level warning switch in the master cylinder reservoir filler cap. Remove the cap.

2 Syphon out as much fluid as possible from the reservoir using an old battery hydrometer. Do not drip the fluid onto the paintwork as it will act as an effective paint stripper.

3 Release the hose clip and disconnect the

right-hand modulator fluid return pipe at the master cylinder reservoir (nearest to the vacuum servo unit) **(see illustration)**.

4 Jack up the front of the car and support it on stands (see *"Jacking and Vehicle Support"*).

5 Remove the belt break switch from the drivebelt cover by pushing it upward and carefully levering out the bottom edge. Pull the switch down, withdraw the switch arm from the opening in the cover and place the switch to one side.

6 Undo the two drivebelt cover retaining nuts and washers, and on later models (1987-on), the retaining bolt.

7 Withdraw the cover from the studs and remove it by moving it upwards to clear the oil filter.

8 Disconnect the two hydraulic pipes and hoses with the yellow bands at the pipe bracket on the transmission support crossmember **(see illustration)**. Allow the remaining hydraulic fluid to drain into a suitable container.

9 Slacken the modulator adjuster bolt, move the modulator to relieve the tension on the drivebelt then slip the belt off the modulator sprocket **(see illustration)**.

10 Undo and remove the adjuster bolt and the modulator pivot bolt and withdraw the modulator from the engine compartment.

11 If required, disconnect the hydraulic hoses at the modulator after removal. Plug or tape over all pipe ends and orifices to prevent dirt ingress.

Refitting

12 If a new unit is being fitted check that it has a yellow arrow marked on its cover and a part number suffix "A" indicating a right-hand side modulator. Note that the units are not interchangeable from side to side.

13 Reconnect the modulator hydraulic hoses if applicable.

14 Locate the modulator on its mounting bracket, fit the pivot bolt and tighten it to the specified torque.

15 Slip the drivebelt over the modulator sprocket ensuring that it sits squarely in the sprocket teeth.

16 Move the modulator as necessary to tension the belt so that the belt deflection, under light finger pressure is 5.0 mm. Check this using a ruler at a point midway between the two sprockets.

17 With the belt tensioned correctly, tighten the modulator adjuster bolt. Before tightening, the adjuster bolt threads should be coated with grease - refer to the note at the beginning of this Section.

18 Reconnect the two modulator hydraulic pipes and hoses.

19 Refit the drivebelt cover and secure with the two nuts and washers, and the bolt (where applicable).

20 Engage the belt break switch arm upwards through the opening in the drivebelt

9

21.8 Hydraulic pipe and hose unions (arrowed) at the pipe bracket on the transmission support crossmember

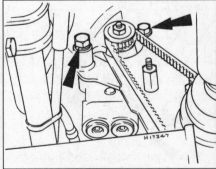

21.9 Right-hand modulator adjuster and pivot bolts (arrowed)

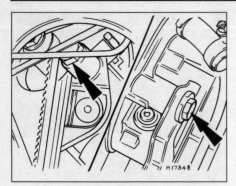

21.32 Left-hand modulator adjuster and pivot bolts (arrowed)

cover then locate the switch in position. Pull the switch downwards to secure.

21 Lower the car to the ground.

22 Reconnect the modulator fluid return pipe to the master cylinder reservoir then fill the reservoir with fresh fluid of the specified type.

23 Bleed the hydraulic system (Section 23).

Left-hand side

Removal

24 Disconnect the wiring plug from the level warning switch in the master cylinder reservoir filler cap. Remove the cap.

25 Syphon out as much fluid as possible from the reservoir using an old battery hydrometer or a poultry baster. Do not drip the fluid onto the paintwork as it will act as an effective paint stripper.

26 Release the hose clip and disconnect the left-hand modulator fluid return pipe at the master cylinder reservoir (the one furthest away from the vacuum servo unit).

27 Jack up the front of the car and support it on stands (see *"Jacking and Vehicle Support"*). Remove the left-hand roadwheel.

28 Remove the engine splash shield from the inner wheel arch.

29 Remove the belt break switch from the drivebelt cover by pushing it upwards and carefully levering out the bottom edge. Pull the switch down, withdraw the switch arm from the opening in the cover and place the switch to one side.

30 Undo the three bolts, two at the top and one at the bottom securing the drivebelt cover to the modulator bracket. Remove the cover.

31 Disconnect the two hydraulic pipes and hoses with the white bands at the pipe bracket on the transmission support crossmember. Allow the remaining hydraulic fluid to drain into a suitable container.

32 Slacken the modulator adjuster bolt, move the modulator to relieve the tension on the drivebelt then slip the belt off the modulator sprocket **(see illustration)**.

33 Remove the distributor cap, rotor arm and shield. Disconnect the left-hand belt break switch wiring at the multi-plug.

34 Undo and remove the adjuster bolt and the modulator pivot bolt and withdraw the modulator upwards out of the engine compartment.

35 If required, disconnect the hydraulic hoses at the modulator after removal. Plug or tape over all pipe ends and orifices to prevent dirt ingress.

Refitting

36 If a new unit is being fitted check that it has a white arrow marked on its cover and a part number suffix "C" indicating a left-hand side modulator. Note that the units are not interchangeable from side to side.

37 Reconnect the modulator hydraulic pipes if applicable.

38 Locate the modulator on its mounting bracket, fit the pivot bolt and tighten it to the specified torque.

39 Slip the drivebelt over the modulator sprocket ensuring that it sits squarely in the sprocket teeth.

40 Adjust the drivebelt tension as described in paragraphs 16 and 17, but use a suitable length of wood inserted through the steering tie-rod aperture in the inner wheel arch, to push on the modulator as necessary.

41 Reconnect the two modulator hydraulic pipes and hoses.

42 Refit the drivebelt cover and secure with the three bolts.

43 Refit the belt break switch as described in paragraph 20.

44 Refit the engine splash shield.

45 Refit the roadwheel and lower the car to the ground.

46 Reconnect the belt break switch wiring multi-plug then refit the shield, rotor arm and distributor cap.

47 Reconnect the modulator fluid return pipe to the master cylinder reservoir then fill the reservoir with fresh fluid of the specified type.

48 Bleed the hydraulic system as described in Section 23.

22 Load apportioning valve (anti-lock braking system) - removal and refitting

Note: *Before starting work, refer to the warning at the beginning of Section 3 concerning the dangers of hydraulic fluid.*

Removal

1 Raise the car on a hoist or drive the rear of the car up on ramps. The rear wheels must not hang free.

2 If removing the right-hand side load apportioning valve on fuel-injected models, undo the nut and bolt securing the fuel pump mounting bracket to the underbody. Move the fuel pump aside to gain access to the valve.

3 Disconnect the hydraulic pipes at the valve then plug the pipes and orifices to prevent loss of fluid and dirt ingress.

4 As an aid to reassembly, accurately mark the position of the valve adjusting bracket on the rear suspension arm. This will ensure that the valve adjustment is not lost when refitting.

5 Undo the nuts and remove the stud plate securing the adjusting bracket to the suspension arm **(see illustration)**.

6 Undo both rear suspension arm inner mounting nuts and remove the load apportioning valve mounting plate.

7 Undo the bolts securing the valve to the mounting plate and remove the valve and adjusting bracket from under the car **(see illustration)**.

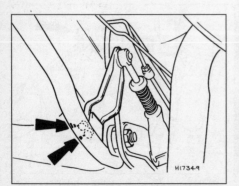

22.5 Load apportioning valve adjusting bracket retaining nut locations (arrowed)

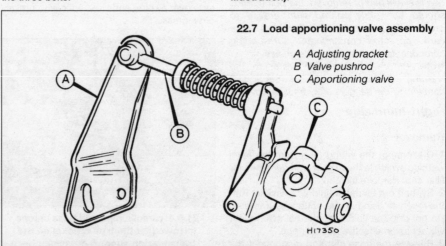

22.7 Load apportioning valve assembly

A *Adjusting bracket*
B *Valve pushrod*
C *Apportioning valve*

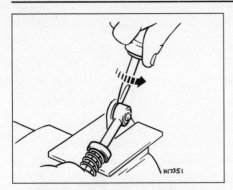

22.8 Separating apportioning valve pushrod from adjusting bracket

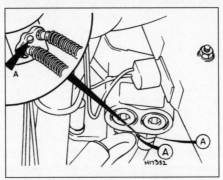

23.5 Modulator bypass valve (A) location

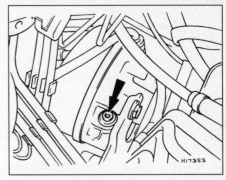

23.6 Modulator auto bleed plunger location (arrowed)

8 If required separate the valve pushrod from the adjusting bracket by levering off the pushrod trunnion with a screwdriver **(see illustration)**. Lubricate the trunnion rubber bush to aid removal.

Refitting

9 If a new valve is being fitted it will be supplied with nylon setting spacers and ties attached, to ensure correct adjustment of the valve. Leave these in position until the valve is installed.

10 Refit the pushrod trunnion to the adjusting bracket using a suitable socket and a vice.

11 Locate the valve on its mounting plate and secure with the retaining bolts.

12 Position the mounting plate over the suspension arm mounting bolts and secure with the nuts tightened to the specified torque.

13 Reconnect the hydraulic pipes to the valve.

14 Refit the stud plate and adjusting bracket to the suspension arm ensuring that the previously made marks are aligned if the original components are being refitted. Secure the adjusting bracket with the retaining nuts tightened to the specified torque.

15 If a new valve assembly is being fitted, remove the nylon setting spacers and ties.

16 Where applicable refit the fuel pump mounting bracket.

17 Lower the car to the ground.

18 Bleed the hydraulic system as described in Section 23.

19 It is recommended that the load apportioning valve adjustment be checked by a dealer if the original unit has been refitted. Special gauges are needed for this operation and it is not a DIY proposition.

23 Hydraulic system - bleeding (anti-lock braking system)

Note: *Before starting work, refer to the warning at the beginning of Section 11 concerning the dangers of hydraulic fluid.*

1 On cars equipped with the anti-lock braking system there are two bleed procedures possible according to which part of the hydraulic system has been disconnected.

2 If any one of the following conditions are present, bleed procedure A should be adopted:

a) *A modulator has been removed.*

b *A modulator-to-master cylinder return hose has been drained.*

c) *The two modulator hydraulic hoses have been removed.*

3 If any one of the following conditions are present, bleed procedure B should be adopted:

a) *Any condition where the master cylinder has been drained providing that the modulator fluid return pipe has not lost its head of fluid.*

b) *Removal of any of the basic braking system components ie brake caliper, flexible hose or pipe, wheel cylinder, load apportioning valve.*

Bleed procedure A

4 Top-up the master cylinder reservoir to the "MAX" mark using the specified type of fluid and keep it topped up throughout the bleed procedure.

5 Using a Torx type key or socket bit slacken the bypass valve on the relevant modulator by one to one and a half turns. The bypass valve is located between the two flexible hoses on the side of the modulator **(see illustration)**.

6 Fully depress and hold depressed the auto bleed plunger on the modulator so that the plunger circlip contacts the modulator body **(see illustration)**.

7 Have an assistant steadily pump the brake pedal at least twenty times while you observe the fluid returning to the master cylinder reservoir. Continue this operation until the returning fluid is free from air bubbles.

8 Release the auto bleed plunger ensuring that it has fully returned. Pull it out by hand if necessary.

9 Tighten the bypass valve on the modulator.

10 Now carry out bleed procedure B.

Bleed procedure B

11 This procedure is the same as for conventional braking systems and reference should be made to Section 11. Note, however, that all the weight of the car must be on the roadwheels, not suspended wheel free, otherwise the load apportioning valves will not bleed.

9

Chapter 10
Suspension and steering

Contents

Degrees of difficulty

Easy, suitable for novice with little experience	Fairly easy, suitable for beginner with some experience	Fairly difficult, suitable for competent DIY mechanic	Difficult, suitable for experienced DIY mechanic	Very difficult, suitable for expert DIY or professional

Specifications

Front suspension

Type . . . .   Independent by MacPherson struts with coil springs and integral telescopic shock absorbers. Anti-roll bar fitted to all models except pre-1983 1.1 litre versions

Rear suspension

Type:

  Saloon and Estate models . . . .   Independent with coil springs, telescopic shock absorbers and tie-bars

  Van models . . . .   Tubular axle located by semi-elliptic leaf springs and telescopic shock absorbers

Hub bearing grease . . . .   To Ford specification SAM-1C-9111A

Steering

Type . . . .   Rack and pinion
Steering gear lubricant:
  Type:
    Oil . . . .   To Ford specification SQM-2C9003-AA
    Semi-fluid grease . . . .   To Ford specification SAM1C-9106-AA
  Quantity:
    Pre-May 1983 models . . . .   95 cc of semi-fluid grease
    Post-May 1983 models . . . .   120 cc of oil, and 70 cc of semi-fluid grease (add grease to the rack ends)

10

Front wheel alignment

Toe setting:
  Pre-May 1983 models:
    Checking tolerance . . . . 1.5 mm toe-in to 5.5 mm toe-out
    Adjust to . . . . 1.0 mm toe-in to 3.0 mm toe-out
  May 1983 models onward:
    Checking tolerance . . . . 0.5 mm toe-in to 5.5 mm toe-out
    Adjust to . . . . 1.5 mm to 3.5 mm toe-out

Roadwheels

Wheel size:
  Steel wheels 13x4.50, 13x5, 14x6
  Alloy wheels 14x5.50, 14x6, 15x6

Tyres

Tyre size:
  Saloon and Estate models . . . . 145 SR 13,155 SR/TR 13, 175/70 SR/HR 13, 175/65 HR 14,
    185/60 HR 13, 185/60 HR 14, 195/50 VR 15
  Van models . . . . 155 SR 13, 165 RR 13

Torque wrench settings

	Nm	lbf ft
Front suspension		
Driveshaft retaining nut (threads lightly greased)	205 to 235	151 to 173
Lower arm mounting pivot bolt	51 to 64	38 to 47
Lower arm balljoint pinch-bolt	48 to 60	35 to 44
Brake caliper anchor bracket mounting bolts	50 to 66	37 to 49
Suspension strut to hub carrier	80 to 90	59 to 66
Tie-bar to lower arm (pre-1983 1.1 litre models)	75 to 90	55 to 66
Tie-bar to mounting bracket (pre-1983 1.1 litre models)	44 to 55	32 to 41
Anti-roll bar to lower arm	90 to 110	66 to 81
Anti-roll bar clamp nuts and bolts	45 to 56	33 to 41
Tie-bar to lower arm (1985 RS Turbo models)	90 to 110	66 to 81
Tie-bar-to-anti-roll bar clamp (1985 RS Turbo models)	22 to 26	16 to 19
Tie-bar front pivot nut (1985 RS Turbo models)	70 to 90	52 to 66
Suspension strut top mounting to body (pre-May 1983 models)	20 to 24	15 to 18
Suspension strut-to-body retaining nut (May 1983 models onward) . . .	40 to 52	30 to 38
Suspension strut top mounting piston rod nut	52 to 65	38 to 48
Rear suspension (Saloon and Estate models)		
Lower arm inboard pivot bolt	70 to 90	52 to 66
Lower arm-to-stub axle carrier through-bolt	60 to 70	44 to 52
Shock absorber top mounting nut	42 to 52	31 to 38
Shock absorber to stub axle carrier	70 to 90	52 to 66
Tie-bar front mounting pivot bolt	70 to 90	52 to 66
Tie-bar-to-stub axle carrier nut	70 to 90	52 to 66
Brake backplate to stub axle carrier	45 to 55	33 to 41
Rear suspension (Van models)		
Roadspring U-bolt nuts	36 to 45	27 to 33
Roadspring shackle nuts	40 to 50	30 to 37
Roadspring eye bolt nuts	70 to 90	52 to 66
Shock absorber top mounting bracket to body	20 to 25	15 to 18
Shock absorber to top mounting bracket	40 to 50	30 to 37
Brake backplate to stub axle	45 to 55	33 to 41
Steering		
Steering gear to bulkhead bolts	45 to 50	33 to 37
Tie-rod outer balljoint to steering arm	25 to 30	18 to 22
Tie-rod outer balljoint-to-tie-rod locknut	57 to 68	42 to 50
Steering column shaft coupling pinch-bolt	45 to 56	33 to 41
Steering wheel nut	27 to 34	20 to 25
Rack slipper cover plate bolts (pre-May 1983 models)	6 to 9	5 to 7
Pinion bearing cover plate bolts (pre-May 1983 models)	17 to 24	13 to 18
Rack slipper plug (post-May 1983 models)	4 to 5	3 to 4
Tie-rod inner balljoint to rack	68 to 90	50 to 66
Roadwheels		
Roadwheel bolts (all models)	70 to 100	52 to 74

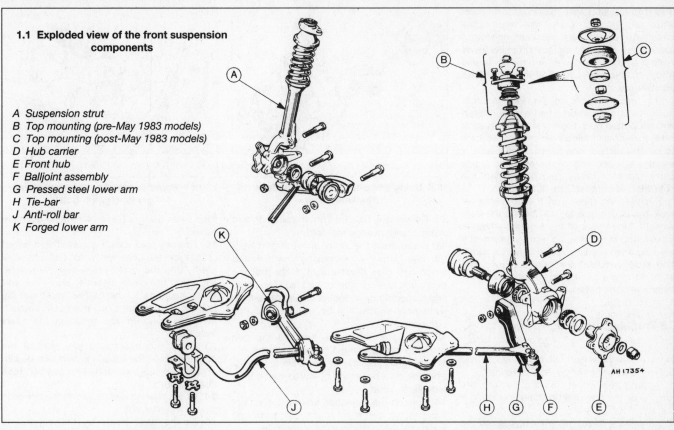

1.1 Exploded view of the front suspension components

A Suspension strut
B Top mounting (pre-May 1983 models)
C Top mounting (post-May 1983 models)
D Hub carrier
E Front hub
F Balljoint assembly
G Pressed steel lower arm
H Tie-bar
J Anti-roll bar
K Forged lower arm

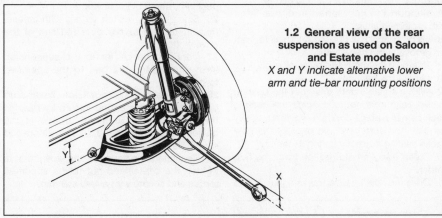

1.2 General view of the rear suspension as used on Saloon and Estate models
X and Y indicate alternative lower arm and tie-bar mounting positions

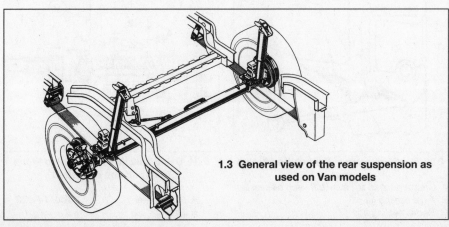

1.3 General view of the rear suspension as used on Van models

1 General description

The independent front suspension is of the MacPherson strut type, incorporating coil springs and integral telescopic shock absorbers. Lateral location of each strut assembly is by a forged or pressed steel lower suspension arm containing rubber inner mounting bushes and incorporating a balljoint at their outer ends. On pre-May 1983 1.1 litre models, fore and aft location of the pressed steel lower suspension arms is by a tie-bar. On post-May 1983 1.1 litre models and all other variants the forged steel lower arms are interconnected by an anti-roll bar which also provides fore and aft location of both suspension arms. Additional location is provided by an adjustable tie-bar on 1985 RS Turbo models. The hub carriers which contain the hub bearings, brake calipers and the hub/disc assemblies are bolted to the MacPherson struts and connected to the lower arms via the balljoints **(see illustration)**.

On Saloon and Estate models the rear suspension is also fully independent by means of pressed steel lower suspension arms, coil springs and separate telescopic shock absorbers. The suspension arms are attached to the underbody at their inner ends through rubber bushes and to the stub axle carrier at their outer ends, again through rubber bushes. The shock absorbers are

10

bolted to the stub axle carriers at their lower ends which also carry the rear brake backplate as well as the rear hub/drum assemblies. Fore and aft location of the lower arms is by a tie-bar and an anti-roll bar is also fitted to models with fuel-injection **(see illustration)**.

The rear suspension on Van variants consists of a transverse beam axle located and supported by a single leaf spring on each side, and utilising telescopic shock absorbers to control vertical movement. A stub axle is welded to each end of the axle and these carry the rear brake backplates and the hub/drum assemblies **(see illustration)**.

The steering gear is of the conventional rack and pinion type located behind the front wheels. Movement of the steering wheel is transmitted to the steering gear by means of a steering shaft containing two universal joints. The front wheels are connected to the steering gears by tie-rods each having an inner and outer balljoint.

2 Front hub bearings - renewal

Note: *A new driveshaft nut, and a new tie-rod balljoint split-pin must be used on refitting.*

1 Remove the wheel trim and release the staking on the driveshaft retaining nut using a suitable punch.
2 Slacken the driveshaft retaining nut and the wheel bolts.
3 Jack up the front of the car, support it on stands (see *"Jacking and Vehicle Support"*) and remove the roadwheel.
4 Undo the two bolts securing the brake caliper anchor bracket to the hub carrier.
5 Withdraw the anchor bracket and brake caliper complete with disc pads and suspend it from a convenient place under the wheel arch.
6 Remove the driveshaft retaining nut and washer.
7 Undo the retaining screw and withdraw the brake disc from the hub.
8 Using a two-legged puller draw off the hub **(see illustration)**.
9 Extract the split pin and unscrew the castellated nut from the steering tie-rod balljoint.

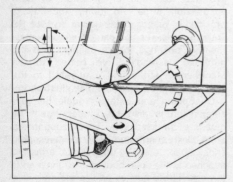

2.13 Using a lever to spread the hub carrier clamp jaws

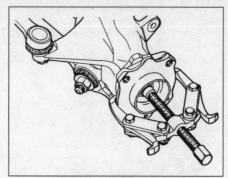

2.8 Using a two-legged puller to draw off the wheel hub

10 Release the balljoint from the steering arm using a balljoint separator tool.
11 Disconnect the lower arm balljoint from the hub carrier by removing the nut and pinch-bolt **(see illustration)**. Note that the pinch-bolt is of the socket-headed (Torx) type and a special key or socket bit (available from accessory shops) will be required for this purpose.
12 Undo the bolt which secures the hub carrier to the base of the suspension strut.
13 Using a suitable lever, separate the carrier from the strut by prising open the clamp jaws **(see illustration)**.
14 Support the driveshaft so that it does not hang down by more than 20° from the horizontal then withdraw the hub carrier.
15 Support the hub carrier in a vice fitted with protected jaws.
16 Using pliers, pull out the dust shield from the groove in the hub carrier.
17 Prise out the inner and outer oil seals.
18 Lift out the bearings.
19 With a suitable drift, drive out the bearing tracks. Take care not to damage the bearing track carrier surface during removal since any burrs on the surface could prevent the new tracks seating correctly during assembly.
20 Clean away all old grease from the hub carrier.
21 Drive the new bearing tracks squarely into

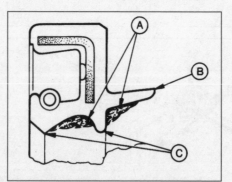

2.23 Sectional view of the hub bearing oil seal

A Grease applied to cavity between oil seal lips
B Axial sealing lip
C Radial sealing lips

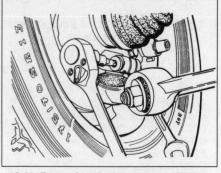

2.11 Removing the lower arm balljoint Torx type pinch-bolt

their seats using a piece of suitable diameter tubing.
22 Liberally pack a high quality lithium based grease into the bearings, making sure to work plenty into the spaces between the rollers. Note that the cavity between the inner and outer bearings in the carrier **must not** be packed with grease since this could cause a pressure build-up and result in the seals leaking.
23 Install the bearing to one side of the carrier, then fill the lips of the new oil seal with grease and tap it squarely into position **(see illustration)**.
24 Fit the bearing and its seal to the opposite side in a similar way.
25 Fit the dust shield by tapping it into position using a block of wood.
26 Smear the driveshaft splines with grease, then install the carrier over the end of the driveshaft.
27 Connect the carrier to the suspension strut and tighten the bolt to the specified torque.
28 Reconnect the suspension lower arm balljoint to the carrier and secure by passing the pinch-bolt through the groove in the balljoint stud. The head of the pinch-bolt should be to the rear.
29 Reconnect the tie-rod to the steering arm, tighten the castellated nut to the specified torque and secure with a new split pin.

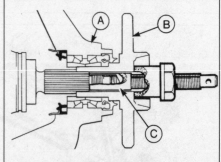

2.31 Using special tool 14-022 to fit the front hub and driveshaft

A Hub carrier   *C Tool 14-022*
B Hub

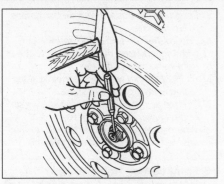

2.35 Staking the driveshaft retaining nut

30 Install the hub/disc and push it on to the driveshaft as far as it will go using hand pressure only.

31 The threaded end of the driveshaft joint should be protruding far enough through the hub to enable it to be drawn fully home using the old driveshaft nut and packing washers. If this is not the case it will be necessary to use Ford special tool 14-022 or a suitable alternative **(see illustration)**.

32 With the hub in place fit a new driveshaft retaining nut and the washer but only tighten the nut hand tight at this stage.

33 Refit the brake disc and caliper anchor bracket, tightening the anchor bracket bolts to the specified torque.

34 Refit the roadwheel and lower the car to the ground.

3.4a Removing the lower arm balljoint pinch-bolt nut

3.4b Separating the balljoint from the hub carrier

35 Tighten the driveshaft retaining nut to the specified torque then stake the nut into the driveshaft groove using a small punch **(see illustration)**.

36 Tighten the wheel bolts to the specified torque and refit the wheel trim.

3 Front suspension lower arm (forged type) - removal, overhaul and refitting

1 The forged type suspension arm is fitted to all models except pre-May 1983 1.1 litre versions.

Removal

2 Jack up the front of the car and support it on stands (see *"Jacking and Vehicle Support"*).

3 Undo the nut and remove the pivot bolt securing the lower arm at its inboard end **(see illustration)**.

4 Disconnect the lower arm balljoint from the hub carrier by removing the nut and pinch-bolt. Note that the pinch-bolt is of the socket-headed (Torx) type and a special key or socket bit (available from accessory shops) will be required for this purpose **(see illustrations)**.

5 Unscrew and remove the nut, washer and bush from the end of the anti-roll bar as described in Section 5 (or tie-bar on 1985 RS Turbo models) **(see illustration)**. Withdraw the arm from under the car.

Overhaul

6 Renewal of the pivot bush at the inboard end of the arm is possible using a vice and small tubes of suitable diameter **(see illustration)**. Lubricate the new bush thoroughly with rubber grease to ease installation.

7 If the balljoint is worn it will be necessary to renew the arm complete as the balljoint cannot be removed separately.

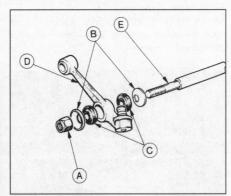

3.5 Anti-roll bar-to-lower arm mounting

A Nut
B Dished washer
C Bushes
D Lower arm
E Anti-roll bar

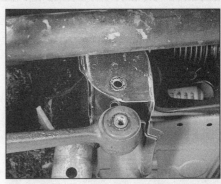

3.3 Suspension lower arm disconnected at inboard end

Refitting

8 Refitting is the reverse sequence to removal. Tighten all nuts and bolts to the specified torque with the weight of the car on its roadwheels. When refitting the Torx pinch-bolt, note that the head of the bolt must face the rear of the car.

4 Front suspension lower arm (pressed steel type) - removal, overhaul and refitting

1 The pressed steel type suspension is only fitted to pre-May 1983 1.1 litre models **(see illustration)**.

Removal

2 Jack up the front of the car and support it on stands (see *"Jacking and Vehicle Support"*).

3 Undo the nut and remove the pivot bolt securing the lower arm at its inboard end.

4 Undo the two nuts which secure the tie-bar and lower arm balljoint to the lower arm. Separate the arm from the tie-bar and remove it from under the car.

Overhaul

5 Renewal of the pivot bush is carried out in the same way as described in Section 3.

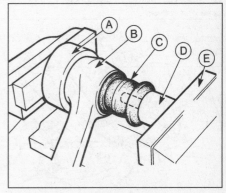

3.6 Method of fitting lower arm inboard pivot bush

A Tubular spacer
B Lower arm
C Bush
D Tube or socket
E Vice

10

6 If the balljoint is worn it can be renewed after removing it from the hub carrier as described in Section 3.

Refitting

7 Refitting is the reverse sequence to removal. Tighten all nuts and bolts to the specified torque with the weight of the car on its roadwheels. If the balljoint has been removed, refit the Torx pinch-bolt with its head towards the rear of the car.

5 Front anti-roll bar - removal and refitting

Removal

1 The anti-roll bar is used in conjunction with the forged type suspension lower arm.
2 Jack up the front of the car and support it on stands (see *"Jacking and Vehicle Support"*).
3 Where fitted flatten the lockplate tabs and unscrew the two bolts or two nuts each side securing the anti-roll bar clamps to the underbody **(see illustrations)**.
4 Disconnect the ends of the anti-roll bar by unscrewing the nuts and removing the

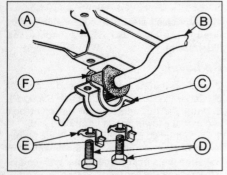

5.3a Anti-roll bar front mounting clamp details - pre-1986 models

A Body bracket   D Retaining bolts
B Anti-roll bar   E Lockplates
C Clamp   F Bush

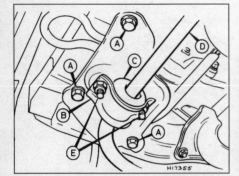

5.3b Anti-roll bar front mounting clamp details - post-1986 models

A Body bracket   C Bush
   bolts   D Anti-roll bar
B Clamp   E Retaining nuts

4.1 Pressed steel type lower arm components

A Lower arm   D Balljoint
B Tie-bar   E Retaining nuts
C Retaining bolt

washers and the bushes **(see illustration)**. Note that the nut on the right-hand side of the anti-roll bar has a left-hand thread and is unscrewed by turning it clockwise.
5 On 1985 RS Turbo models separate the ends of the anti-roll bar from the tie-bars by releasing the clamp nuts and bolts **(see illustration 6.12)**.
6 On all models except 1985 RS Turbo undo the nut and remove the pivot bolt securing one of the suspension lower arms at its inboard end.
7 Withdraw the anti-roll bar from the lower arms and remove it from under the car.
8 Remove the remaining rubber bush and washer from each end of the anti-roll bar. Smear the bar with rubber grease to aid bush removal.

Refitting

9 Inspect the bushes carefully and renew them if they show any signs of cracking, splitting or deformation. Bushes of different material have been introduced on Escort models during the course of production and it is therefore essential that the bushes are always renewed in sets of four to ensure that all are of the same type.
10 Refitting is the reverse sequence to removal but bearing in mind the following points:

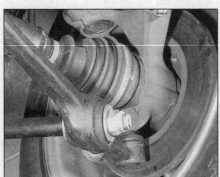

5.4 Anti-roll to lower arm retaining nut

a) Lubricate the bushes with rubber grease to aid refitting.
b) Ensure that the end of the anti-roll bar with the left-hand thread is fitted to the right-hand side of the car.
c) Fit the washers with their concave sides facing away from the bushes.
d) Tighten all nuts and bolts with the weight of the car on its roadwheels.
e) Where lockplates are used, bend up the tabs to lock the bolts after tightening.

6 Front tie-bar - removal and refitting

Pre-May 1983 1.1 litre models

Removal

1 Jack up the front of the car and support it on stands (see *"Jacking and Vehicle Support"*).
2 Unscrew and remove the nut which holds the tie-bar to the large pressed steel mounting bracket **(see illustration)**. Take off the dished washer and the rubber insulator.
3 Disconnect the lower arm balljoint from the hub carrier by removing the nut and pinch-bolt. Note that the pinch-bolt is of the socket-headed (Torx) type and a special key or socket bit (available from accessory shops) will be required for this purpose.
4 Unbolt the opposite end of the tie-bar from the suspension arm.
5 Withdraw the tie-bar from its pressed steel bracket and take off the remaining washer, insulator and steel sleeve.

Refitting

6 Where necessary the bush in the pressed steel mounting bracket can be renewed if the old bush is drawn out using a bolt, nut and suitable distance pieces.
7 Refitting the tie-bar is a reversal of removal. Finally tighten all nuts and bolts to the specified torque only when the weight of the vehicle is again on its roadwheels. When refitting the Torx pinch-bolt note that the head of the bolt must face the rear of the car.

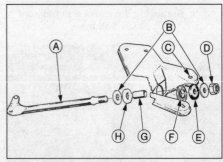

6.2 Front tie-bar mountings - pre-May 1983 1.1 litre models

A Tie-bar   E Front insulator
B Flat washers   F Bush
C Mounting bracket   G Steel sleeve
D Retaining nut   H Rear insulator

6.12 Front tie-bar mountings - 1985 RS Turbo models

A Retaining nut
B Anti-roll bar clamp
C Adjustment clamp
D Front mounting bolt
E Basic setting length
   = 565 ± 1.5 mm
   (22.24 ± 0.6 in)

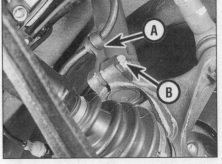

7.3 Brake hose and grommet location in strut (A) and strut-to-hub carrier pinch-bolt (B)

1985 RS Turbo models

Removal

8 Jack up the front of the vehicle and support it on stands (see *"Jacking and Vehicle Support"*).
9 Undo the nut and remove the washer and bush securing the end of the tie-bar to the suspension arm.
10 Undo the nut and bolt and remove the tie-bar-to-anti-roll bar clamp.
11 Undo the tie-bar front nut and pivot bolt and remove the bar from under the car.

Refitting

12 Do not alter the length of the tie-rod otherwise the steering castor angle will have to be reset. If the length has been altered or if a new tie-bar is being fitted, set the length to the basic setting as shown **(see illustration)**. The length can be adjusted by slackening the forward clamp bolt and turning the threaded portion as necessary. Tighten the clamp after adjustment.
13 Refitting is the reverse sequence to removal but tighten all nuts and bolts to the specified torque with the weight of the car on its roadwheels.

7 Front suspension strut - removal, overhaul and refitting

Removal

1 Slacken the roadwheel bolts, raise the front of the vehicle and support it securely on stands (see *"Jacking and Vehicle Support"*), then remove the roadwheel.
2 Support the underside of the driveshaft on blocks or by tying it up to the rack-and-pinion steering housing.
3 Where fitted, detach the brake hose and location grommet from the strut location bracket, then unscrew and remove the pinch-bolt which holds the base of the suspension strut to the hub carrier **(see illustration)**. Using a suitable tool, lever the sides of the slot in the carrier apart until it is free from the strut.
4 On pre-May 1983 models undo the two bolts securing the strut to the inner wing turret. On post-May 1983 models lift off the cover then unscrew the strut retaining nut. Prevent the piston rod from turning using a 6 mm Allen key **(see illustrations)**.
5 Withdraw the complete strut assembly from under the front wing.

Overhaul

Note: *Spring compressor tools will be required for this operation.*
6 Clean away external dirt and mud.
7 If the strut has been removed due to oil leakage or to lack of damping, then it should be renewed with a new or factory reconditioned unit. Dismantling of the original strut is not recommended and internal components are not generally available.
8 Before the strut is exchanged, the coil spring will have to be removed. To do this, a spring compressor or compressors will be needed. These are generally available from tool hire centres or they can be purchased at most motor accessory shops.
9 Engage the compressor over four coils of the spring and compress the spring sufficiently to release spring tension from the top mounting **(see illustration)**.
10 Once the spring is compressed, unscrew and remove the nut from the end of the piston rod which retains the top mounting. As there will be a tendency for the piston rod to turn while the nut is unscrewed, insert a 6 mm Allen key to hold the rod still.
11 Remove the top mounting and lift off the spring and compressor.
12 The compressor need not be released if the spring is to be fitted immediately to a new strut. If the compressor is to be released from the spring, make sure that you do it slowly and progressively.

10

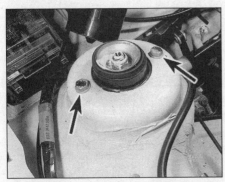

7.4a Suspension strut-to-turret mounting bolts on pre-1983 models

7.4b Removing the nut cover . . .

7.4c . . . and strut retaining nut on post-1983 models
Note Allen key to prevent piston rod turning

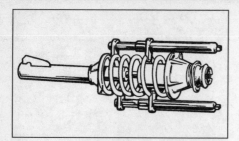

7.9 Coil spring retained with spring compressors

13 The top mounting can be dismantled by sliding off the thrust bearing and withdrawing the spring upper seat, gaiter spring and, where fitted, insulator. Also, if fitted, slide the bump stop from the piston rod **(see illustration)**.

14 Renew any worn or damaged components. If the front strut and/or coil spring is to be removed then it is advisable also to renew the equivalent assembly on the other side.

15 Fit the spring to the strut, making sure that the ends of the coils locate correctly in the shaped parts of the spring seats.

16 Fit the top mounting components, being very careful to maintain the correct order of assembly of the individual components.

17 Gently release and remove the spring compressor. Check that the ends of the spring are correctly located in the shaped sections of the spring seatings.

Refitting

18 Refit the strut using the reverse of the removal procedure. Lower the vehicle so that it is standing on its roadwheels before tightening the top mounting bolts or nut to the specified torque.

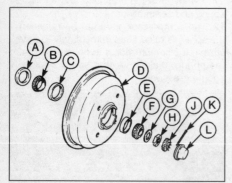

9.3 Exploded view of the rear hub bearings

A Oil seal
B Inboard bearing
C Bearing outer track
D Hub and drum
E Bearing outer track
F Outboard bearing
G Thrustwasher
H Retaining nut
J Nut retainer
K Split pin
L Dust cap

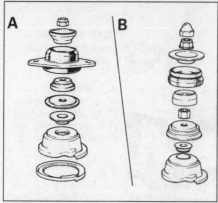

7.13 Exploded view of the suspension strut upper mounting components
A Pre-May 1983 models
B Post-May 1983 models

8 Rear hub bearings - adjustment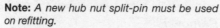

Note: *A new hub nut split-pin must be used on refitting.*

1 Raise and support the rear of the vehicle on stands. Release the handbrake.

2 This adjustment will normally only be required if, when the top and bottom of the roadwheel are gripped and "rocked" excessive movement can be detected in the bearings. Slight movement is essential.

3 Remove the roadwheel. Using a hammer and cold chisel, tap off the dust cap from the end of the hub.

4 Extract the split pin and take off the nut retainer.

5 Tighten the hub nut to a torque of between 20 and 25 Nm (15 and 18 lbf ft), at the same time rotating the brake drum in an anti-clockwise direction.

6 Unscrew the nut one half a turn and then tighten it only finger tight.

7 Fit the nut retainer so that two of its slots line up with the split pin hole. Insert a new split pin, bending the end around the nut, not over the end of the stub axle.

8 Tap the dust cap into position.

9 Recheck the play as described in paragraph 2.

9.6 Rear hub outboard bearing removal

A fractional amount of wheel movement must be present.

10 Repeat the operations on the opposite hub, refit the roadwheels and lower the vehicle to the floor.

9 Rear hub bearings - renewal

1 Raise and support the rear of the vehicle on stands (see *"Jacking and Vehicle Support"*). Remove the roadwheel and release the handbrake.

2 On fuel-injected models and Van versions undo the retaining screw and withdraw the brake drum from the hub.

3 Tap off the dust cap from the end of the hub **(see illustration)**.

4 Extract the split pin and remove the nut retainer.

5 Unscrew and remove the nut and take off the thrustwasher.

6 Pull the hub/drum off the stub axle slightly then push it back. This will now leave the outboard bearing ready to be taken off the stub axle **(see illustration)**.

7 Withdraw the hub/drum.

8 Prise the oil seal from the hub and take out the inboard taper roller bearing **(see illustration)**.

9 Using a punch, drive out the bearing outer tracks, taking care not to burr the bearing seats.

10 If new bearings are being fitted to both hubs, do not mix up the bearing components but keep them in their individual packs until required.

11 Drive the new bearing tracks squarely into their hub recesses.

12 Pack both bearings with the specified grease, working plenty into the rollers. Be generous, but there is no need to fill the cavity between the inner and outer bearings.

13 Locate the inboard bearing and then grease the lips of a new oil seal and tap it into position.

14 Fit the hub onto the stub axle, taking care not to catch the oil seal lips.

15 Fit the outboard bearing and the thrustwasher and screw on the nut.

16 Adjust the bearings (Section 8).

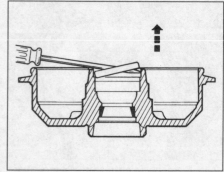

9.8 Removing the hub bearing oil seal

10.3 Rear shock absorber top mounting

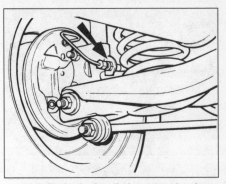

10.4 Removing the shock absorber top mounting nut - Saloon and Estate models

10.6 Brake hydraulic hose-to-shock absorber attachment (arrowed) - Saloon and Estate models

17 On fuel-injected models and Van versions refit the brake drum and secure with the retaining screw.
18 Refit the roadwheel and lower the car to the ground.

10 Rear shock absorber (Saloon and Estate models) - removal, testing and refitting

Removal

1 Slacken the roadwheel bolts, raise the rear of the vehicle, support it on stands (see *"Jacking and Vehicle Support"*) and remove the roadwheel.
2 Support the suspension lower arm with a jack.
3 Open the tailgate and lift the parcel tray to expose the shock absorber top mounting **(see illustration)**.
4 Remove the cap and then unscrew the nut from the shock absorber spindle. To prevent the spindle turning, use an Allen key in the socket provided **(see illustration)**.
5 Take off the cap and insulator.
6 Separate the brake hydraulic hose from the shock absorber by slackening the centre locking nut and easing the hose and pipe down and out of the slot in the bracket **(see illustration)**. On the right-hand side there is very little clearance for a spanner and it may be easier if the roadspring is removed as described in Section 13.

11.3 Removing the rear shock absorber top mounting bracket - Van models

7 Undo the two bolts securing the shock absorber to the stub axle carrier and withdraw the unit, together with cup and bump rubber, from under the wheel arch.

Testing

8 To test the shock absorber, grip its lower mounting in a vice so that the unit is vertical.
9 Fully extend and retract the shock absorber ten or twelve times. Any lack of resistance in either direction will indicate the need for renewal, as will evidence of leakage of fluid.

Refitting

10 Refitting is a reversal of removal, but if a new unit is being installed, prime it first in a similar way to that described for testing.

11 Rear shock absorbers (Van models) - removal, testing and refitting

Removal

1 Raise and support the rear of the vehicle on stands (see *"Jacking and Vehicle Support"*). Place a jack beneath the rear axle tube and just raise it slightly.
2 Disconnect the shock absorber lower mounting by unscrewing the nut and pivot bolt.

3 Unbolt the top mounting bracket from the body and withdraw the unit **(see illustration)**.
4 Undo the nut and pivot bolt to separate the mounting bracket from the shock absorber.

Testing

5 Proceed as described in Section 10.

Refitting

6 Refitting is a reversal of removal, but if a new unit is being installed, prime it first in a similar way to that described for testing.

12 Rear tie-bar (Saloon and Estate models) - removal and refitting

Removal

1 Before attempting to remove a tie-bar, note the location of all washers and bushes. These control the rear wheel alignment and they must be returned to their original locations.
2 Raise the rear of the vehicle and support it with stands (see *"Jacking and Vehicle Support"*).
3 Unscrew and remove the pivot bolt from the eye at the front end of the tie-bar **(see illustration)**.

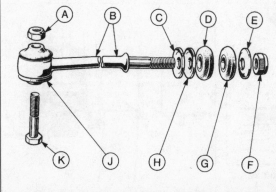

12.3 Exploded view of the rear tie-bar mountings - Saloon and Estate models

A Nut
B Tie-bar
C Washer (additional washers may be fitted)
D Bush
E Washer
F Nut
G Bush
H Washer (additional washers may be fitted)
J Bush
K Pivot bolt

10

12.4 Tie-bar-to-stub axle carrier retaining nut (arrowed) - Saloon and Estate models

13.3 Anti-roll bar-to-lower arm shackle attachment (arrowed)

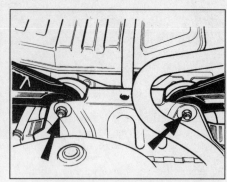

13.4 Lower arm inboard pivot nuts and bolts (arrowed) - Saloon and Estate models

4 Unscrew the nut from the rear end of the tie-bar, take off the washers and bushes as the tie-bar is withdrawn and keep them in strict sequence for refitting (see illustration).

Refitting

5 Renewal of the tie-bar flexible bush is quite easily carried out using sockets or distance pieces and applying pressure in the jaws of a vice.
6 Refit the tie-bar by reversing the removal operations.

13 Rear roadspring (Saloon and Estate models) - removal and refitting

Removal

1 Raise the rear of the car and support it on stands (see "Jacking and Vehicle Support"). Remove the roadwheel.
2 Support the suspension lower arm by placing a jack beneath the spring seating.
3 On models equipped with a rear anti-roll bar disconnect the bar from the shackles by levering them apart with a screwdriver (see illustration).
4 Undo the nut and remove the lower arm inboard pivot bolt (see illustration).
5 Slowly lower the jack beneath the arm and remove the spring and insulator pad.

Refitting

6 Refitting is the reverse sequence to

removal. If applicable the plastic sleeved end of the coil spring must be at the upper end when fitted. Tighten all nuts and bolts to the specified torque with the car standing on its roadwheels.

14 Rear roadspring (Van models) - removal and refitting

Removal

1 To remove the single leaf type rear roadspring from the Van, raise the rear of the vehicle and support it securely under the body members (see "Jacking and Vehicle Support"). Support the axle tube using a jack or stands.
2 Unscrew the spring U-bolt nuts and withdraw the bump rubber plate complete with shock absorber lower attachment (see illustration).
3 Disconnect the shackle from the rear end of the roadspring and pull the spring downward.
4 Unscrew and remove the spring front eye bolt and nut (see illustration).
5 Remove the spring from under the vehicle.

Refitting

6 Refit by reversing the removal operations, but do not tighten the nuts to the specified torque until the weight of the vehicle has been lowered onto the wheels.
7 On completion adjust the braking system light laden valve as described in Chapter 9.

15 Rear suspension lower arm (Saloon and Estate models) - removal and refitting

Removal

1 Raise the rear of the car and support it on stands (see "Jacking and Vehicle Support").
2 On cars equipped with the anti-lock braking system, refer to Chapter 9 and remove the load apportioning valve adjusting bracket from the lower arm.
3 If an anti-roll bar is fitted, disconnect the shackles from the lower arm by levering them apart with a screwdriver (see illustration 13.3).
4 Support the lower arm using a jack located beneath the roadspring.
5 Undo the nut and remove the arm inboard pivot bolt.
6 Undo the nut, remove the outboard pivot through-bolt then lower the jack and remove the spring and insulator pad.
7 Withdraw the lower arm from the car.

Refitting

8 Refitting is the reverse sequence to removal, bearing in mind the following points:
   a) If applicable the plastic sleeved end of the coil spring must be at the upper end when fitted.
   b) Tighten all nuts and bolts to the specified torque with the car standing on its roadwheels.
   c) On cars equipped with the anti-lock braking system, refit the load apportioning valve adjusting bracket as described in Chapter 9.

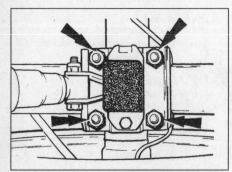

14.2 Rear roadspring U-bolt nuts (arrowed) - Van models

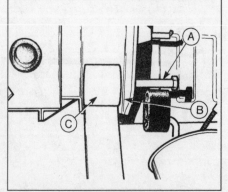

14.4 Rear roadspring front eye bolt - Van models

A Pivot bolt
B Mounting bracket
C Spring eye

16 Rear stub axle carrier (Saloon and Estate models) - removal and refitting

Removal

1 Raise and support the rear of the car on stands (see *"Jacking and Vehicle Support"*). Remove the roadwheel.

2 Remove the rear hub as described in Section 9.

3 Remove the rear brake shoe assembly, as described in Chapter 9. You will also need to disconnect the brake fluid pipe at its connection to the wheel cylinder. Plug the pipe and cylinder connections to prevent fluid loss and the ingress of dirt.

4 Extract the handbrake cable through the backplate, then unscrew the four backplate retaining bolts and withdraw the backplate.

5 Position a jack under the lower arm and support it.

6 Undo the two nuts and remove the bolts securing the shock absorber to the stub axle carrier **(see illustration)**.

7 Undo the nut and remove the lower arm outboard pivot through-bolt.

8 Accurately record the location and number of washers at the tie-bar attachment then undo the nut and withdraw the stub axle carrier.

Refitting

9 If the stub axle is damaged or worn excessively then it must be renewed.

10 Refitting is a reversal of the removal procedure, but note the following:

a) *When reassembling the tie-bar to the stub axle ensure that the spacers, washers and bushes are correctly located (as noted during removal).*

b) *Do not fully tighten the suspension retaining nuts and bolts to their specified torque settings until the vehicle is lowered and standing on its roadwheels.*

c) *Refit and connect the brake assembly components, as given in Chapter 9. Leave*

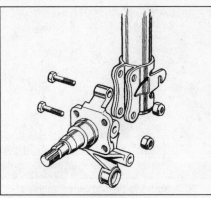

16.6 Rear stub axle and shock absorber attachment - Saloon and Estate models

bleeding the hydraulic circuit until after the hub and brake drum are refitted.

d) *Adjust the hub bearings, as detailed in Section 8.*

17 Rear axle tube (Van models) - removal and refitting

Removal

1 Raise the rear of the vehicle and support it on stands (see *"Jacking and Vehicle Support"*). Remove the rear roadwheels.

2 Support the axle tube on a jack preferably of trolley type.

3 Remove the rear hub as described in Section 9.

4 Disconnect the brake hydraulic pipes and hoses at the axle tube bracket. Plug the pipe and hose ends after removal.

5 Disconnect the brake pipe unions at the rear wheel cylinders then undo the four bolts each side and remove both rear brake backplates.

6 Undo the axle-to-roadspring retaining U-bolt nuts and remove the U-bolts.

7 Lower the axle tube to the ground while at the same time sliding the light laden valve link rod from its spacer tube. Remove the link rod and bush from the axle tube.

8 Withdraw the axle from under the vehicle.

Refitting

9 Refitting is the reverse sequence to removal bearing in mind the following:

a) *Adjust the hub bearings as described in Section 8.*

b) *Tighten the U-bolt nuts to the specified torque with the weight of the vehicle on its roadwheels.*

c) *Bleed the brake hydraulic system and adjust the light laden valve as described in Chapter 9.*

18 Rear anti-roll bar (Saloon and Estate models) - removal and refitting

Removal

1 Slacken the left-hand roadwheel bolts, raise and support the rear of the car on stands (see *"Jacking and Vehicle Support"*). Remove the roadwheel.

2 Lever the shackles from the right and left-hand suspension lower arms **(see illustration)**.

3 Unbolt the anti-roll bar from the underbody, carefully noting the relative fixing locations.

4 Release the fuel lines from their securing clips. Support the fuel tank and remove the three tank mounting bolts. Carefully lower the tank on its support **(see illustration)**.

5 Withdraw the anti-roll bar from the left-hand side of the vehicle.

6 To remove the rubber bushes from the anti-roll bar simply prise open the bush retainers with a screwdriver. Press the retainers together so that the fixing holes are in line when refitting.

Refitting

7 Refitting is a reversal of removal. The fuel tank must be bolted in position before securing the anti-roll bar. Ensure that the underbody fixings are refitted in their original locations.

8 Lubricate the shackle bushes with soap solution before reconnecting them to the lower arms.

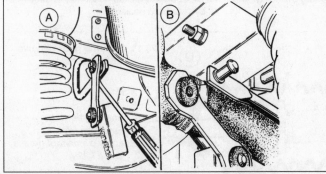

18.2 Disconnecting the rear anti-roll bar shackles - Saloon and Estate models

A Left-hand side   B Right-hand side

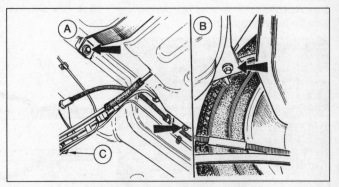

18.4 Fuel tank attachment details

A Mounting bolts (arrowed)   C Fuel line clips
B Mounting bolt (arrowed)

10

19 Rear suspension angles - general

The rear wheel toe and camber angles are set in production and do not require checking under normal service conditions. Of the two, only the toe setting can be adjusted, the camber angle being fixed by production sizes and tolerances.

The only time that angles will need to be checked will be after an accident in which the rear of the car has suffered damage or where a rear end skid has caused a side impact on a rear roadwheel.

Severely worn components of the rear suspension can also cause the angles to be misaligned, in which case renewal of the defective components should rectify the suspension angles and alignment.

The actual settings have been revised a number of times as a result of component changes during the course of production and also to improve directional stability. The settings also vary according to model year, engine size and optional equipment, and to list all the settings would be beyond the scope of this manual. If in any doubt about the rear suspension angles, or if the rear tyre wear appears excessive it is recommended that the car be taken to a Ford dealer for accurate checking on optical alignment equipment.

20 Steering gear bellows - renewal

1 At the first indication of a split or grease leakage from the bellows, renew them.
2 Loosen off the roadwheel bolts, raise the front of the vehicle and support it on stands (see *"Jacking and Vehicle Support"*). Remove the roadwheels.
3 Measure and take note of the amount of thread on the tie-rod which is exposed **(see illustration)**. This will ensure correct toe-setting on reassembly.
4 Loosen off the tie-rod outer ball-joint locknut.
5 Extract the split pin and remove the nut from the balljoint taper pin.

20.3 Steering tie-rod outer balljoint showing exposed threads (A) on tie-rod

6 Using a suitable balljoint extractor, separate the balljoint taper pin from the eye of the steering arm **(see illustration)**.
7 Unscrew the balljoint from the end of the tie-rod, also the locknut. As a double check for correct repositioning of the tie-rod balljoint when reassembling, note the number of turns required to remove it.
8 Release the clip from the end of the damaged bellow and slide it from the rack and the tie-rod **(see illustration)**.
9 When ordering the new bellows and retaining clips also specify the diameter of the tie-rod which will vary according to manufacture and can be checked with a ruler or calipers. This is important since if the wrong size bellows are fitted they will not seal or possibly be damaged on fitting.
10 If a damaged bellow has caused steering lubricant loss it will be necessary to drain any remaining lubricant and renew it. To do this turn the steering wheel gently to expel as much lubricant as possible from the rack housing. If the opposing bellow is not being renewed it is recommended that it is released from the rack housing to allow the old lubricant to be removed from that end, too.
11 Smear the narrow neck of the new bellows with grease and slide into position over the tie-rod, ensuring that the bellows are correctly located in the tie-rod groove on the outer bellow end (where applicable) **(see illustration)**.
12 If new bellows are being fitted to the pinion

20.6 Releasing tie-rod balljoint using separator tool

end of the rack, leave the bellows unclamped at this stage.
13 If the bellows are being fitted to the rack support bush end of the rack housing, clamp the inner end of the bellows.
14 Always use new screw-type clamps, never re-use the old factory-fitted wire type when securing the bellows.
15 Screw the locknut into position on the tie-rod, followed by the outer tie-rod balljoint. Screw the joint the exact number of turns noted during removal.
16 Connect the balljoint to the steering arm, tighten the nut to the specified torque and insert a new split pin to secure.
17 If applicable, add the correct quantity of the specified lubricant to the end of the steering rack (insert the grease into the bellows), then move the rack from lock-to-lock to assist the entry of the lubricant into the steering gear.
18 Where applicable, ensure that the fresh lubricant has worked its way into the steering gear, then tighten the bellow retaining clamp(s).
19 Refit the roadwheels and lower the vehicle to the ground. Settle the suspension by bouncing the front end.
20 Tighten the balljoint locknut and check the amount of tie-rod thread exposed. It should be as noted when dismantling and therefore provide the correct toe-setting, but in any case the alignment should really be checked at the earliest opportunity, as described in Section 27 or by your Ford dealer.

20.8 Bellows-to-rack and pinion housing wire type retaining clip (arrowed)

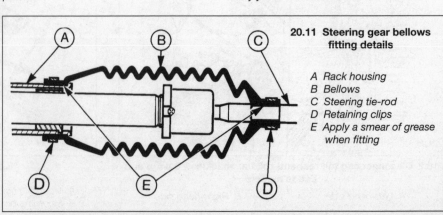

20.11 Steering gear bellows fitting details

A Rack housing
B Bellows
C Steering tie-rod
D Retaining clips
E Apply a smear of grease when fitting

22.1a Steering wheel trim removal

22.1b Prising up the steering wheel horn push . . .

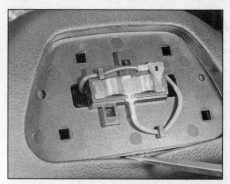

22.1c . . . followed by the contact plate

21 Steering tie-rod outer balljoint - renewal

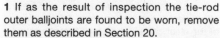

1 If as the result of inspection the tie-rod outer balljoints are found to be worn, remove them as described in Section 20.

2 When the balljoint nuts are unscrewed, it is sometimes found that the balljoint taper pin turns in the eye of the steering arm to prevent the nut from unscrewing. Should this happen, apply pressure to the top of the balljoint using a length of wood as a lever to seat the taper pin while the nut is unscrewed. When this condition is met with, a balljoint extractor is unlikely to be required to free the taper pin from the steering arm.

3 With the tie-rod removed, wire brush the threads of the tie-rod and apply grease to them.

4 Screw on the new balljoint to take up a position similar to the original. Due to manufacturing differences, the fitting of a new component will almost certainly mean that the front wheel alignment will require some adjustment. Check this as described in Section 27.

5 Connect the balljoint to the steering arm, as described in Section 20.

22 Steering wheel - removal and refitting

Removal

1 According to model, either pull off the steering wheel trim, prise out the insert which carries the Ford motif at the centre, or carefully prise up and lift off the horn push followed by the contact plate **(see illustrations)**.

2 Insert the ignition key and turn it to position I.

3 Hold the steering wheel from turning and have the front roadwheels in the straight-ahead attitude. Unscrew the steering wheel retaining nut using a socket and extension.

4 Withdraw the steering wheel from the shaft. No great effort should be necessary, as the wheel is located on a hexagonal-section shaft, which does not normally cause the binding associated with splined shafts. However, if difficulty is experienced, a puller may be used

to withdraw the wheel - take adequate precautions to avoid damage to the finish.

5 Where applicable note the steering shaft direction indicator cam which has its peg uppermost.

Refitting

6 Refitting is the reverse sequence to removal. Ensure that the direction indicator switch is in the neutral position (this will avoid the possibility of damage to the self-cancelling mechanism). Check that the roadwheels are still in the straight-ahead position and locate the steering wheel with the larger section between the spokes uppermost. Tighten the steering wheel retaining nut to the specified torque.

23 Steering wheel - alignment

1 Owing to the fact that the steering wheel is located on a hexagon shaped steering shaft, it may be difficult to obtain perfect steering wheel alignment due to lack of fine adjustment.

2 It is therefore acceptable to adjust the tie-rods to give unequal lengths.

3 Check that the front roadwheels are in the straight-ahead position and that the toe setting is as specified.

4 If the steering wheel is more than 30° out of alignment, remove it and centralise it as much as possible on its shaft.

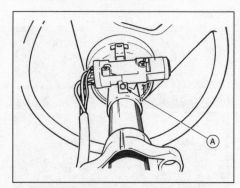

24.6a Steering column lock assembly shear bolt (A)
Pre-1986 version shown

5 To adjust the steering wheel through a small angle, carry out the following operations.

6 Release the tie-rod balljoint locknuts.

7 Turn one tie-rod clockwise and the opposite one anti-clockwise by the identical amount. For every 1° of steering wheel angular error, turn each tie-rod through 30°.

8 Once the steering wheel has been centralised (front wheels in straight-ahead position), retighten the tie-rod balljoint locknuts.

9 Although the toe setting should not have altered, check the front wheel alignment as described in Section 27.

24 Steering column lock - removal and refitting

Note: *For ignition switch removal see Chapter 5. A new shear-bolt will be required on refitting.*

Removal

1 To remove the ignition switch/column lock, the shear-head bolt must be drilled out.

2 Access for drilling can only be obtained if the steering column is lowered. To do this, remove the shrouds from the upper end of the column by extracting the fixing screws. Disconnect the battery earth lead.

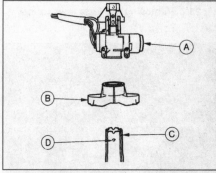

24.6b Steering column lock components - pre-1986 models

A Lock housing	D Shear bolt
B Upper clamp	indentation
C Column tube	

10

25.6a Removing the steering column upper . . .

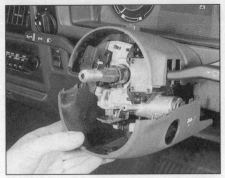

25.6b . . . and lower shrouds on a pre-1986 model . . .

25.6c . . . and on a post-1986 version

3 Unscrew the bonnet release lever mounting screw and position the lever to one side.
4 Disconnect the steering column clamps. The lower one is of bolt and nut type, while the upper one is of stud and nut design.
5 Lower the shaft/column carefully until the steering wheel rests on the seat cushion.
6 Centre-punch the end of the shear-bolt which secures the steering column lock and then drill it out. Remove the ignition switch/column lock (see illustrations).

Refitting

7 When refitting the lock, check for correct operation and then tighten the new shear-bolt securing bolt until its head breaks off.
8 Raise the steering column and reconnect the clamps.

9 Refit the bonnet release lever and the column shrouds.
10 Reconnect the battery.

25 Steering column - removal, overhaul and refitting

Removal

1 Disconnect the battery negative terminal.
2 Turn the ignition key and rotate the steering wheel to bring the front roadwheels to the straight-ahead position.
3 Working within the engine compartment, unscrew and remove the pinch-bolt which holds the steering shaft to the splined pinion shaft of the rack-and-pinion steering gear.

4 Remove the steering wheel, as described in Section 22.
5 Remove the direction indicator cam from the top end of the steering shaft (where fitted).
6 Extract the fixing screws and remove the upper and lower shrouds from the upper end of the steering column (see illustrations).
7 Remove the insulation panel from the lower part of the facia (see illustration).
8 Extract the screw, remove the bonnet release lever mounting and place it to one side (see illustration).
9 Take out the fixing screws and remove the switches from the steering column (see illustrations).
10 Disconnect the wiring harness multi-plug at the side of the column.
11 Unbolt the upper and lower clamps from the steering column and then withdraw the column/shaft into the vehicle. If any difficulty is experienced in separating the lower shaft from the pinion gear, prise the coupling open very slightly with a screwdriver. Note that on certain models (including all Cabriolets), an additional bracing bracket may be fitted between the column support bracket and the body (see illustrations).

Overhaul

12 Wear in the column bearings can be rectified by renewing them. Access to them is obtained by extracting the tolerance ring from the upper end of the column and then withdrawing the shaft from the lower end of the column. The lower bearing and spring will

25.7 Removing the facia lower panel

25.8 Removing the bonnet release lever

25.9a Steering column switch removal on a pre-1986 model . . .

25.9b . . . and switch retaining screw locations (arrowed) on post-1986 versions

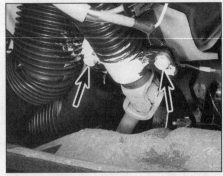

25.11a Steering column lower mounting clamp bolts (arrowed)

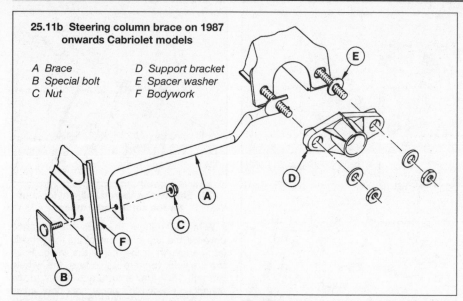

25.11b Steering column brace on 1987 onwards Cabriolet models

A Brace
B Special bolt
C Nut
D Support bracket
E Spacer washer
F Bodywork

come with it. Make sure that the steering column lock is unlocked before withdrawing the shaft.

13 If the upper bearing is to be renewed, first remove the lock assembly by drilling out the shear-head bolt. The upper bearing may now be levered out of its seat.

14 Commence reassembly by tapping the new upper bearing into its seat in the lock housing. Refit the column upper clamp and bush.

15 Locate the column lock on the column tube and screw in a new shear-head bolt until its head breaks off.

16 Insert the conical spring into the column tube so that the larger diameter end of the spring is against the lowest convolution of the collapsible section of the column tube.

17 Slide the lower bearing onto the shaft so that its chamfered edge will mate with the corresponding one in the column lower bearing seat when the shaft is installed.

18 Insert the shaft into the lower end of the steering column. Make sure that the lock is unbolted and pass the shaft up carefully through the upper bearing.

19 Fit the bearing tolerance ring and waved washer.

Refitting

20 Fit the direction indicator cancelling cam to the top of the shaft, making sure that the peg will be uppermost when the column is in the in-car attitude (where fitted).

21 Fit the steering wheel to the shaft, screwing on the nut sufficiently tightly to be able to pull the lower bearing into the column tube with the bearing slots correctly aligned with the pegs on the tube.

22 Refit the column, making sure to engage the coupling at its lower end with the splined pinion shaft.

23 Bolt up the column upper and lower clamps.

24 Reconnect the wiring harness multi-plug.

25 Refit the combination switches to the steering column.

26 Reconnect the bonnet release lever.

27 Fit the column shrouds.

28 Check that the steering wheel is correctly aligned (wheels in the straight-ahead position). If not, remove the steering wheel and realign it (see also Section 23).

29 Tighten the steering wheel nut to the specified torque and then insert the motif or horn push into the centre of the steering wheel.

30 Refit the insulation panel to the lower facia.

31 Tighten the coupling pinch-bolt at the base of the steering shaft.

32 Reconnect the battery negative terminal.

26 Steering gear - removal, overhaul and refitting

Removal

Note: New tie-rod balljoint split-pins must be used on refitting.

1 Set the front roadwheels in the straight-ahead position.

2 Raise the front of the vehicle and fit stands (see "Jacking and Vehicle Support"). Remove the front roadwheels.

3 Working under the bonnet, remove the pinch-bolt from the coupling at the base of the steering column shaft.

4 Extract the split pins from the tie-rod balljoint taper pin nuts, unscrew the nuts and remove them.

5 Separate the balljoints from the steering arms using a suitable separator tool.

6 Flatten the locktabs on the steering gear securing bolts and unscrew and remove the bolts. Withdraw the steering gear downwards to separate the coupling from the steering shaft and then take it out from under the front wing (see illustrations).

Overhaul

7 Examine the steering gear assembly for signs of wear or damage, and check that the rack moves freely throughout the full length of its travel, with no signs of roughness or excessive free play between the steering gear pinion and rack. It is possible to overhaul the steering gear assembly housing components, but this task should be entrusted to a Ford dealer. It is likely to be cheaper to obtain an exchange reconditioned steering gear assembly (which will be supplied complete with tie-rods) than to overhaul a worn or damaged assembly. The only components which can be renewed easily by the home mechanic are the steering gear bellows, and the tie-rod outer balljoints. Renewal procedures for the bellows and tie-rod outer balljoints are given in Sections 20 and 21 respectively.

Refitting

8 If a new steering gear assembly is being installed, the tie-rods balljoints may have to be removed from the original unit and screwed onto the new tie-rods to approximately the same setting. If a note was not made of the position of the original tie-rod balljoints on their rods, inspection of the threads will probably indicate their original location. In any event it is important that the new balljoints are screwed on an equal amount at this stage.

10

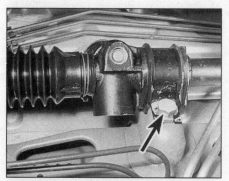

26.6a Steering gear-to-bulkhead mounting retaining bolt and locktab (arrowed)

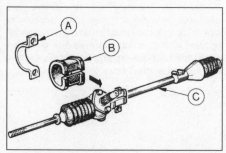

26.6b Steering gear mounting details

A Clamp
B Bush
C Steering gear

9 Make sure that the steering gear is centred. Do this by turning the pinion shaft to full lock in one direction and then count the number of turns required to rotate it to the opposite lock. Now turn the splined pinion shaft through half the number of turns just counted.

10 Check that the roadwheels and the steering wheel are in the straight-ahead attitude, offer up the steering gear and connect the shaft coupling without inserting the pinch-bolt.

11 Bolt up the gear housing and lock the bolts with their lockplate tabs.

12 Reconnect the tie-rod balljoints to the steering arms. Tighten the securing nuts to the specified torque setting and fit new split pins to secure.

13 Tighten the coupling pinch-bolt to the specified torque. Refit the roadwheels and lower the vehicle to the floor.

14 If the tie-rods were disturbed or if a new assembly was installed, check and adjust the wheel alignment, as described in Section 27.

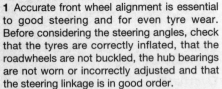

27 Steering angles and wheel alignment

1 Accurate front wheel alignment is essential to good steering and for even tyre wear. Before considering the steering angles, check that the tyres are correctly inflated, that the roadwheels are not buckled, the hub bearings are not worn or incorrectly adjusted and that the steering linkage is in good order.

2 Wheel alignment consists of four factors **(see illustration)**:

Camber is the angle at which the roadwheels are set from the vertical when viewed from the front or rear of the vehicle. Positive camber is the angle (in degrees) that the wheels are tilted outwards at the top from the vertical.

Castor is the angle between the steering axis and a vertical line when viewed from each side of the vehicle. Positive castor is indicated when the steering axis is inclined towards the rear of the vehicle at its upper end.

Steering axis inclination is the angle, when viewed from the front or rear of the vehicle, between the vertical and an imaginary line drawn between the upper and lower suspension swivel balljoints or upper and lower strut mountings.

Toe is the amount by which the distance between the front inside edges of the roadwheel rims differs from that between the rear inside edges. If the distance at the front is less than that at the rear, the wheels are said

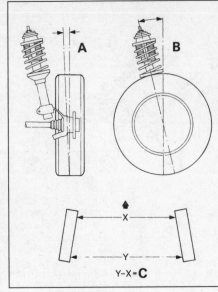

27.2 Wheel alignment diagram
A Camber
B Castor
C Toe setting

to toe-in. If the distance at the front inside edges is greater than that at the rear, the wheels toe-out.

3 Due to the need for precision gauges to measure the small angles of the steering and suspension settings, it is preferable to leave this work to your dealer. Camber and castor angles are set in production and are not adjustable. If these angles are ever checked and found to be outside specification then either the suspension components are damaged or distorted, or wear has occurred in the bushes at the attachment points.

4 If you wish to check the toe setting yourself, first make sure that the lengths of both tie-rods are equal when the steering is in the straight-ahead position. This can be measured reasonably accurately by counting the number of exposed threads on the tie-rod adjacent to the balljoint assembly (refer to Section 23).

5 Adjust, if necessary, by releasing the locknut from the balljoint assembly and the clamp at the small end of the bellows **(see illustration)**.

6 Obtain a tracking gauge. These are available in various forms from accessory stores, or one can be fabricated from a length of steel tubing, suitably cranked to clear the sump and bellhousing, and having a setscrew and locknut at one end.

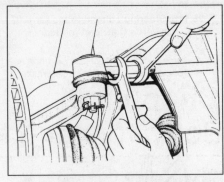

27.5 Slackening tie-rod balljoint locknut for toe setting adjustment

7 With the gauge, measure the distance between the two inner rims of the roadwheels (at hub height) at the rear of the wheel. Push the vehicle forward to rotate the wheel through 180° (half a turn) and measure the distance between the wheel inner rims, again at hub height, at the front of the wheel. This last measurement should differ from the first one by the specified toe-in/toe-out (see *"Specifications"*).

8 Where the toe setting is found to be incorrect, release the tie-rod balljoint locknuts and turn the tie-rods by an equal amount. Only turn them through a quarter turn at a time before re-checking the alignment. Do not grip the threaded part of the tie-rod during adjustment and make sure that the bellows outboard clip is released, otherwise the bellows will twist as the tie-rod is rotated. When each tie-rod is viewed from the rack housing, turning the rods clockwise will increase the toe-out. Always turn the tie-rods in the same direction when viewed from the centre of the vehicle, otherwise they will become unequal in length. This would cause the steering wheel spoke alignment to alter and also cause problems on turning with tyre scrubbing.

9 On completion of adjustment, tighten the tie-rod balljoint locknuts without altering the setting of the tie-rods. Hold the balljoint assembly at the mid-point of its arc of travel (flats are provided on it for a spanner) while the locknuts are tightened.

10 Finally, tighten the bellows clamps.

11 For rear wheel alignment refer to Section 19.

Chapter 11
Bodywork and fittings

Contents

Degrees of difficulty

Easy, suitable for novice with little experience	Fairly easy, suitable for beginner with some experience	Fairly difficult, suitable for competent DIY mechanic	Difficult, suitable for experienced DIY mechanic	Very difficult, suitable for expert DIY or professional

Specifications

Torque wrench setting	Nm	lbf ft
All seat belt anchor bolts	29 to 41	21 to 30

1 General description

The body is of welded steel construction available in 3 or 5-door Hatchback, 3 or 5-door Estate, soft-top Cabriolet, or Van configurations.

The body is of monocoque construction and is of energy-absorbing design.

Rust and corrosion protection is applied to all new vehicles and includes zinc phosphate dipping and wax injection of box sections and door interiors.

All body panels are welded, including the front wings, so it is recommended that major body damage repairs are left to your dealer.

2 Maintenance - bodywork and underframe

The general condition of a vehicle's bodywork is the one thing that significantly affects its value. Maintenance is easy but needs to be regular. Neglect, particularly after minor damage, can lead quickly to further deterioration and costly repair bills. It is important also to keep watch on those parts of the vehicle not immediately visible, for instance the underside, inside all the wheel arches and the lower part of the engine compartment.

The basic maintenance routine for the bodywork is washing preferably with a lot of water, from a hose. This will remove all the loose solids which may have stuck to the vehicle. It is important to flush these off in such a way as to prevent grit from scratching the finish. The wheel arches and underframe need washing in the same way to remove any accumulated mud which will retain moisture and tend to encourage rust. Paradoxically enough, the best time to clean the underframe and wheel arches is in wet weather when the mud is thoroughly wet and soft. In very wet weather the underframe is usually cleaned of large accumulations automatically and this is a good time for inspection.

Periodically, except on vehicles with a wax-based underbody protective coating, it is a good idea to have the whole of the underframe of the vehicle steam cleaned, engine compartment included, so that a thorough inspection can be carried out to see what minor

11

repairs and renovations are necessary. Steam cleaning is available at many garages and is necessary for removal of the accumulation of oily grime which sometimes is allowed to become thick in certain areas. If steam cleaning facilities are not available, there are one or two excellent grease solvents available which can be brush applied. The dirt can then be simply hosed off. Note that these methods should not be used on vehicles with wax-based underbody protective coating or the coating will be removed. Such vehicles should be inspected annually, preferably just prior to winter, when the underbody should be washed down and any damage to the wax coating repaired. Ideally, a completely fresh coat should be applied. It would also be worth considering the use of such wax-based protection for injection into door panels, sills, box sections, etc., as an additional safeguard against rust damage where such protection is not provided by the vehicle manufacturer.

After washing paintwork, wipe off with a chamois leather to give an unspotted clear finish. A coat of protective wax polish will give added protection against chemical pollutants in the air. If the paintwork sheen has dulled or oxidised, use a cleaner/polisher combination to restore the brilliance of the shine. This requires a little effort, but such dulling is usually caused because regular washing has been neglected. Care needs to be taken with metallic paintwork, as special non-abrasive cleaner/polisher is required to avoid damage to the finish. Always check that the door and ventilator opening drain holes and pipes are completely clear so that water can be drained out. Bright work should be treated in the same way as paint work. Windscreens and windows can be kept clear of the smeary film which often appears, by the use of a proprietary glass cleaner. Never use any form of wax or other body or chromium polish on glass.

3 Maintenance - upholstery and carpets

Mats and carpets should be brushed or vacuum cleaned regularly to keep them free of grit. If they are badly stained remove them from the vehicle for scrubbing or sponging and make quite sure they are dry before refitting. Seats and interior trim panels can be kept clean by wiping with a damp cloth and upholstery cleaner. If they do become stained (which can be more apparent on light coloured upholstery) use a little liquid detergent and a soft nail brush to scour the grime out of the grain of the material. Do not forget to keep the headlining clean in the same way as the upholstery. When using liquid cleaners inside the vehicle do not over-wet the surfaces being cleaned. Excessive damp could get into the seams and padded interior causing stains, offensive odours or even rot. If the inside of the vehicle gets wet accidentally it is worthwhile taking some trouble to dry it out properly, particularly where carpets are involved. Do not leave oil or electric heaters inside the vehicle for this purpose.

4 Minor body damage - repair

Note: *For more detailed information about bodywork repair, Haynes Publishing produce a book by Lindsay Porter called "The Car Bodywork Repair Manual". This incorporates information on such aspects as rust treatment painting and glass fibre repairs, as well as details on more ambitious repairs involving welding and panel beating.*

Repair of minor scratches in bodywork

If the scratch is very superficial, and does not penetrate to the metal of the bodywork, repair is very simple. Lightly rub the area of the scratch with a paintwork renovator, or a very fine cutting paste, to remove loose paint from the scratch and to clear the surrounding bodywork of wax polish. Rinse the area with clean water.

Apply touch-up paint to the scratch using a fine paint brush; continue to apply fine layers of paint until the surface of the paint in the scratch is level with the surrounding paintwork. Allow the new paint at least two weeks to harden: then blend it into the surrounding paintwork by rubbing the scratch area with a paintwork renovator or a very fine cutting paste. Finally, apply a coat of wax polish.

Where the scratch has penetrated right through to the metal of the bodywork, causing the metal to rust, a different repair technique is required. Remove any loose rust from the bottom of the scratch with a penknife, then apply rust inhibiting paint to prevent the formation of rust in the future. Using a rubber or nylon applicator, fill the scratch with bodystopper paste. If required, this paste can be mixed with cellulose thinners to provide a very thin paste which is ideal for filling narrow scratches. Before the stopper-paste in the scratch hardens, wrap a piece of smooth cotton rag around the top of a finger. Dip the finger in cellulose thinners, and then quickly sweep it across the surface of the stopper-paste in the scratch; this will ensure that the surface of the stopper-paste is slightly hollowed. The scratch can now be painted over as described earlier in this Section.

Repair of dents in bodywork

When deep denting of the vehicle's bodywork has taken place, the first task is to pull the dent out, until the affected bodywork almost attains its original shape. There is little point in trying to restore the original shape completely, as the metal in the damaged area will have stretched on impact and cannot be reshaped fully to its original contour. It is better to bring the level of the dent up to a point which is about 1/8 in (3 mm) below the level of the surrounding bodywork. In cases where the dent is very shallow anyway, it is not worth trying to pull it out at all. If the underside of the dent is accessible, it can be hammered out gently from behind, using a

mallet with a wooden or plastic head. Whilst doing this, hold a suitable block of wood firmly against the outside of the panel to absorb the impact from the hammer blows and thus prevent a large area of the bodywork from being "belled-out".

Should the dent be in a section of the bodywork which has a double skin or some other factor making it inaccessible from behind, a different technique is called for. Drill several small holes through the metal inside the area - particularly in the deeper section. Then screw long self-tapping screws into the holes just sufficiently for them to gain a good purchase in the metal. Now the dent can be pulled out by pulling on the protruding heads of the screws with a pair of pliers.

The next stage of the repair is the removal of the paint from the damaged area, and from an inch or so of the surrounding "sound" bodywork. This is accomplished most easily by using a wire brush or abrasive pad on a power drill, although it can be done just as effectively by hand using sheets of abrasive paper. To complete the preparation for filling, score the surface of the bare metal with a screwdriver or the tang of a file, or alternatively, drill small holes in the affected area. This will provide a really good "key" for the filler paste.

To complete the repair see the Section on filling and re-spraying.

Repair of rust holes or gashes in bodywork

Remove all paint from the affected area and from an inch or so of the surrounding "sound" bodywork, using an abrasive pad or a wire brush on a power drill. If these are not available a few sheets of abrasive paper will do the job just as effectively. With the paint removed you will be able to gauge the severity of the corrosion and therefore decide whether to renew the whole panel (if this is possible) or to repair the affected area. New body panels are not as expensive as most people think and it is often quicker and more satisfactory to fit a new panel than to attempt to repair large areas of corrosion.

Remove all fittings from the affected area except those which will act as a guide to the original shape of the damaged bodywork (eg headlamp shells etc). Then, using tin snips or a hacksaw blade, remove all loose metal and any other metal badly affected by corrosion. Hammer the edges of the hole inwards in order to create a slight depression for the filler paste.

Wire brush the affected area to remove the powdery rust from the surface of the remaining metal. Paint the affected area with rust inhibiting paint; if the back of the rusted area is accessible treat this also.

Before filling can take place it will be necessary to block the hole in some way. This can be achieved by the use of aluminium or plastic mesh, or aluminium tape.

Aluminium or plastic mesh or glass fibre matting is probably the best material to use for a large hole. Cut a piece to the approximate size and shape of the hole to be filled, then position it in the hole so that its edges are below the level of the surrounding bodywork. It can be retained in position by several blobs of filler paste around its periphery.

Aluminium tape should be used for small or very narrow holes. Pull a piece off the roll and trim it to the approximate size and shape required, then pull off the backing paper (if used) and stick the tape over the hole; it can be overlapped if the thickness of one piece is insufficient. Burnish down the edges of the tape with the handle of a screwdriver or similar, to ensure that the tape is securely attached to the metal underneath.

Bodywork repairs - filling and re-spraying

Before using this Section, see the Sections on dent, deep scratch, rust holes and gash repairs.

Many types of bodyfiller are available, but generally speaking those proprietary kits which contain a tin of filler paste and a tube of resin hardener are best for this type of repair. A wide, flexible plastic or nylon applicator will be found invaluable for imparting a smooth and well contoured finish to the surface of the filler.

Mix up a little filler on a clean piece of card or board - measure the hardener carefully (follow the maker's instructions on the pack) otherwise the filler will set too rapidly or too slowly. Using the applicator apply the filler paste to the prepared area; draw the applicator across the surface of the filler to achieve the correct contour and to level the filler surface. As soon as a contour that approximates to the correct one is achieved, stop working the paste - if you carry on too long the paste will become sticky and begin to "pick up" on the applicator. Continue to add thin layers of filler paste at twenty-minute intervals until the level of the filler is just proud of the surrounding bodywork.

Once the filler has hardened, excess can be removed using a metal plane or file. From then on, progressively finer grades of abrasive paper should be used, starting with a 40 grade production paper and finishing with 400 grade wet-and-dry paper. Always wrap the abrasive paper around a flat rubber, cork, or wooden block - otherwise the surface of the filler will not be completely flat. During the smoothing of the filler surface the wet-and-dry paper should be periodically rinsed in water. This will ensure that a very smooth finish is imparted to the filler at the final stage.

At this stage the "dent" should be surrounded by a ring of bare metal, which in turn should be encircled by the finely "feathered" edge of the good paintwork. Rinse the repair area with clean water, until all of the dust produced by the rubbing-down operation has gone.

Spray the whole repair area with a light coat of primer - this will show up any imperfections in the surface of the filler. Repair these imperfections with fresh filler paste or bodystopper, and once more smooth the surface with abrasive paper. If bodystopper is

used, it can be mixed with cellulose thinners to form a really thin paste which is ideal for filling small holes. Repeat this spray and repair procedure until you are satisfied that the surface of the filler, and the feathered edge of the paintwork are perfect. Clean the repair area with clean water and allow to dry fully.

The repair area is now ready for final spraying. Paint spraying must be carried out in a warm, dry, windless and dust free atmosphere. This condition can be created artificially if you have access to a large indoor working area, but if you are forced to work in the open, you will have to pick your day very carefully. If you are working indoors, dousing the floor in the work area with water will help to settle the dust which would otherwise be in the atmosphere. If the repair area is confined to one body panel, mask off the surrounding panels; this will help to minimise the effects of a slight mis-match in paint colours. Bodywork fittings (eg chrome strips, door handles etc) will also need to be masked off. Use genuine masking tape and several thicknesses of newspaper for the masking operations.

Before commencing to spray, agitate the aerosol can thoroughly, then spray a test area (an old tin, or similar) until the technique is mastered. Cover the repair area with a thick coat of primer; the thickness should be built up using several thin layers of paint rather than one thick one. Using 400 grade wet-and-dry paper, rub down the surface of the primer until it is really smooth. While doing this, the work area should be thoroughly doused with water, and the wet-and-dry paper periodically rinsed in water. Allow to dry before spraying on more paint.

Spray on the top coat, again building up the thickness by using several thin layers of paint. Start spraying in the centre of the repair area and then work outwards, with a side-to-side motion, until the whole repair area and about 2 inches of the surrounding original paintwork is covered. Remove all masking material 10 to 15 minutes after spraying on the final coat of paint.

Allow the new paint at least two weeks to harden, then, using a paintwork renovator or a very fine cutting paste, blend the edges of the paint into the existing paintwork. Finally, apply wax polish.

Plastic components

With the use of more and more plastic body components by the vehicle manufacturers (eg bumpers, spoilers, and in some cases major body panels), rectification of more serious damage to such items has become a matter of either entrusting repair work to a specialist in this field, or renewing complete components. Repair of such damage by the DIY owner is not really feasible owing to the cost of the equipment and materials required for effecting such repairs. The basic technique involves making a groove along the line of the crack in the plastic using a rotary burr in a

power drill. The damaged part is then welded back together by using a hot air gun to heat up and fuse a plastic filler rod into the groove. Any excess plastic is then removed and the area rubbed down to a smooth finish. It is important that a filler rod of the correct plastic is used, as body components can be made of a variety of different types (eg polycarbonate, ABS, polypropylene).

Damage of a less serious nature (abrasions, minor cracks etc) can be repaired by the DIY owner using a two-part epoxy filler repair material. Once mixed in equal proportions, this is used in similar fashion to the bodywork filler used on metal panels. The filler is usually cured in twenty to thirty minutes, ready for sanding and painting.

If the owner is renewing a complete component himself, or if he has repaired it with epoxy filler, he will be left with the problem of finding a suitable paint for finishing which is compatible with the type of plastic used. At one time the use of a universal paint was not possible owing to the complex range of plastics encountered in body component applications. Standard paints, generally speaking, will not bond to plastic or rubber satisfactorily, but paints to match any plastic or rubber finish can be obtained from dealers. However, it is now possible to obtain a plastic body parts finishing kit which consists of a pre-primer treatment, a primer and coloured top coat. Full instructions are normally supplied with a kit, but basically the method of use is to first apply the pre-primer to the component concerned and allow it to dry for up to 30 minutes. Then the primer is applied and left to dry for about an hour before finally applying the special coloured top coat. The result is a correctly coloured component where the paint will flex with the plastic or rubber, a property that standard paint does not normally possess.

5 Major body damage - repair

Where serious damage has occurred or large areas need renewal due to neglect, it means that completely new sections or panels will need welding in, and this is best left to professionals. If the damage is due to impact, it will also be necessary to completely check the alignment of the bodyshell structure. Due to the principle of construction, the strength and shape of the whole car can be affected by damage to one part. In such instances the service of a dealer with specialist checking jigs is essential. If a body is left misaligned, it is first of all dangerous, as the car will not handle properly, and secondly uneven stresses will be imposed on the steering, engine and transmission, causing abnormal wear or complete failure. Tyre wear may also be excessive.

11

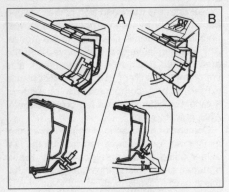

6.1 Bumper overrider details - pre-1986 models

A Without headlamp washer
B With headlamp washer

6 Bumper components - removal and refitting

Bumper overriders

Removal

1 On pre-1986 models the overrider is held to the bumper by a clamp screw. Find this screw on the underside of the bumper and release it - the overrider can then be withdrawn **(see illustration)**. If headlamp washers are fitted, disconnect the fluid hose as the overrider is withdrawn.
2 On models from 1986 onwards the bumper assembly must be removed for access. Once this is done undo the two nuts (or single screw on XR3i models) and remove the overrider.

Refitting

3 In all cases refitting is a reversal of removal.

Bumper moulding (pre-1986 models)

Removal

4 Where so equipped, remove the overriders as described previously in this Section.
5 Release the moulding from the bumper by compressing the jaws of the retaining clips inside the bumper.

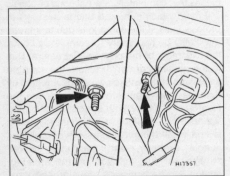

6.14 Front bumper retaining nuts in engine compartment - 1986 models onwards

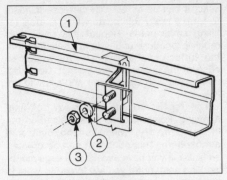

6.8 Front bumper attachments - pre-1986 models

1 Bumper bar   *3 Retaining nut*
2 Washer

6 Slide the moulding from the end retainers, noting that the front bumper moulding is in two parts.

Refitting

7 To refit, push the moulding into position and fully engage the clips.

Front bumper

Pre-1986 models

Removal

8 To remove the bumper complete, open the bonnet and unscrew the bumper securing nuts from each end of the bumper **(see illustration)**.
9 Withdraw the bumper from the vehicle.
10 Release the locking tangs using pliers, and pull or tap the quarter section free using a piece of soft wood to prevent damage. If required the quarter section end retaining clips can be removed from the body by twisting through 90° and pulling free.

Refitting

11 Reassembly and refitting are reversals of removal and dismantling.

Models from 1986 onwards

Removal

12 Undo the single screw each side securing the bumper to the edge of the wheel arch.

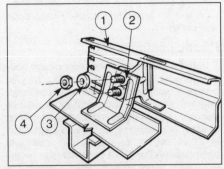

6.17 Rear bumper attachments - pre-1986 models

1 Bumper bar   *3 Washer*
2 Mounting bracket   *4 Fixing nut*

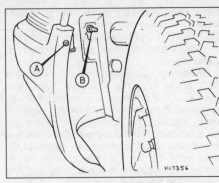

6.13 Front bumper-to-arch screw (A) and retaining nut (B) - 1986 models onwards

13 From under the wheel arch, undo the single bumper retaining nut on each side **(see illustration)**. On models with wheel arch liners, to improve access to the securing nuts, if desired the wheel arch liners and/or the windscreen washer reservoir can be removed.
14 From within the engine compartment undo the single nut each side securing the bumper to the front body panel **(see illustration)**.
15 Carefully withdraw the bumper from the front of the car.

Refitting

16 Refitting is the reversal of removal.

Rear bumper

Pre-1986 models except Van

Removal

17 To remove the bumper complete, open the tailgate and unscrew the bumper securing nuts from each end of the bumper **(see illustration)**.
18 Withdraw the bumper from the vehicle, and disconnect the number plate wiring plugs.
19 Release the locking tangs using pliers as shown, and pull or tap the quarter section free using a piece of soft wood to prevent damage **(see illustration)**. If required the quarter section end retaining clips can be removed from the body by twisting through 90° and pulling free.

Refitting

20 Reassembly and refitting are reversals of removal and dismantling.

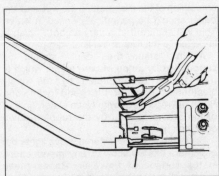

6.19 Removing rear quarter bumper retaining tangs - pre-1986 models

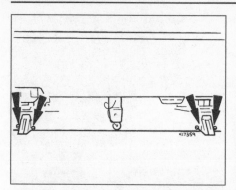

6.22 Rear bumper attachments in luggage compartment - 1986 models onwards

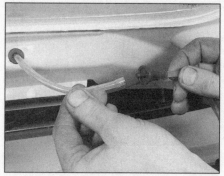

7.2 Disconnecting the windscreen washer fluid pipe

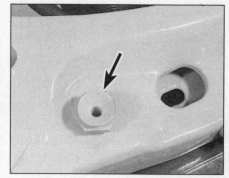

7.8 Bonnet bump stop (arrowed)

Models from 1986 onwards except Van

Removal

21 Undo the three screws each side securing the bumper to the edge of the wheel arch.

22 From inside the luggage compartment undo the two bumper retaining nuts each side **(see illustration)**.

23 Disconnect the number plate lamp wiring, ease the sides of the bumper outward and withdraw it from the car.

Refitting

24 Refitting is a reversal of removal.

Van models

25 To remove either rear quarter bumper, prise out the number plate lamp, disconnect the bulbholder and extract the two Torx screws. Refitting is a reversal of removal.

7 Bonnet - removal and refitting

Removal

1 Open the bonnet and support it on its stay.

2 Disconnect the screen washer pipe on the underside of the bonnet lid **(see illustration)**.

3 Where applicable, disconnect the earth lead from the bonnet.

4 Mark round the hinge plates on the underside of the bonnet lid as an aid to refitting.

5 With an assistant supporting one side of the

8.3 Bonnet cable attachment at latch and bracket (arrowed)

bonnet lid, unbolt the hinges and lift the lid from the vehicle.

Refitting

6 Refit by reversing the removal operations. If a new bonnet is being installed, position it so that an equal gap is provided at each side when it is being closed.

7 The bonnet should close smoothly and positively without excessive pressure. If it does not, carry out the following adjustment.

8 Screw in the bump stops which are located on the front upper cross rail **(see illustration)**. Close the bonnet and then readjust the bump stops until the bonnet is flush with the wing upper surfaces.

9 Adjust the striker centrally in relation to the latch. Release it by unscrewing its pressed steel locknut.

10 Screw the striker in or out until the bonnet fully closes under its own weight when allowed to drop from a point 300 mm (12 in) above its released position.

8 Bonnet release cable - removal and refitting

Removal

1 Working inside the vehicle, extract the three screws and remove the steering column shroud. Open the bonnet. If the cable is broken, the release latch must be operated using a suitably shaped bar through the grille aperture.

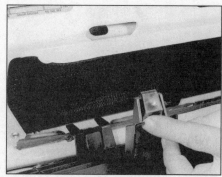

10.1 Radiator grille spring clip - pre-1988 models

2 Extract the single screw and remove the cable bracket from the steering column.

3 Working within the engine compartment, pull the cable grommet from the bonnet latch bracket and then disengage the cable end fitting from the latch **(see illustration)**.

4 Unclip the cable from the side of the engine compartment.

5 Withdraw the cable through the engine compartment rear bulkhead into the vehicle interior.

Refitting

6 Refitting is a reversal of removal.

9 Bonnet lock - removal and refitting

Removal

1 Extract the three securing screws from the lock and lower it until the cable can be disconnected.

2 Withdraw the lock from below the top rail.

Refitting

3 Refit by reversing the removal operations.

10 Radiator grille - removal and refitting

Pre-1988 models

Removal

1 The grille is held in position by four spring clips **(see illustration)**.

2 Once these clips are released, the grille can be removed from the body panel.

Refitting

3 Refit by reattaching the spring clips.

1988 models onwards

4 The radiator grille is integral with the bumper moulding, and is removed with the bumper.

11

11.2a Prise out the plastic insert . . .

11.2b . . . and unscrew the regulator handle

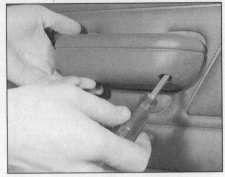

11.4 Unscrew the armrest

11 Door trim panel - removal and refitting

Pre-1986 models

Removal

1 On Ghia versions only, remove the panel capping by carefully prising out the retaining clips using a forked tool. This can easily be made from a piece of scrap metal.

2 Remove the door window regulator handle. Do this by prising out the plastic insert from the handle and extracting the screw which will now be exposed **(see illustrations)**.

3 On vehicles fitted with electrically operated front windows, pull out the switches and

11.5 Removing the remote control handle bezel

remove the door pocket finisher.

4 Remove the door pull/armrest. This is held by two screws **(see illustration)**. On Base models with a door pull only, the end caps will have to be prised up to reveal the screws.

5 Push the door lock remote control handle bezel towards the rear of the vehicle to release it from its retaining lugs **(see illustration)**.

6 Again using the forked tool, pass it round the edge of the panel between the panel and the door and release each of the panel clips in turn. Lift the panel from the door **(see illustration)**.

Refitting

7 Refitting is a reversal of removal.

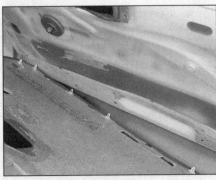

11.6 Removing the door trim panel

1986 models onwards

Removal

8 Remove the door window regulator handle. Do this by prising out the plastic insert from the handle and extracting the screw now exposed. Remove the washer from behind the handle.

9 Prise off the door pull handle capping, undo the three screws and remove the handle **(see illustrations)**. On vehicles with electrically operated windows, pull out the switches and disconnect the wiring.

10 Undo the door lock remote control handle bezel retaining screw and remove the bezel **(see illustrations)**.

11 Prise out the plastic trim cap and unscrew the lower front panel retaining screw. Unscrew the three remaining screws, one at the upper front and two at the rear of the panel **(see illustrations)**.

12 Carefully release the retaining clips at the top of the panel and lift upwards to disengage the lower brackets.

13 From 1989, a new foam watershield is fitted under the door trim panel, secured in position by a strip of butyl.

14 To remove the watershield, the butyl strip must not be touched with the hands or subsequent adhesion will be impaired.

15 If the foam watershield is damaged beyond re-use on removal, all traces of it, and the butyl, must be removed from the door inner skin. The butyl can be removed by "rolling" it up on itself to form a ball.

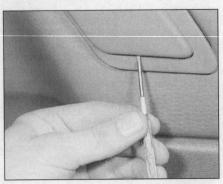

11.9a Prise out the door pull handle capping . . .

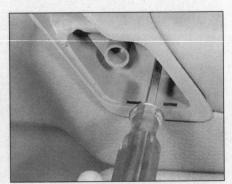

11.9b . . . undo the screws . . .

11.9c . . . and remove the handle

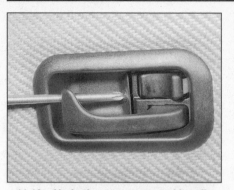

11.10a Undo the remote control handle bezel retaining screw . . .

11.10b . . . and remove the bezel

11.11a Release the trim cap and undo the screw . . .

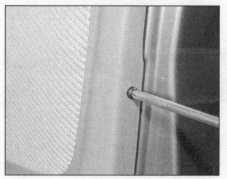

11.11b . . . followed by the side screws

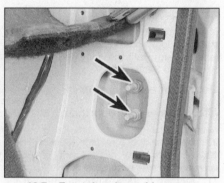

12.7a Front door lower hinge nuts (arrowed)

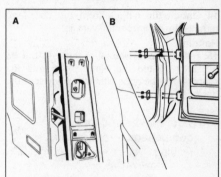

12.7b Door hinge assemblies - pre-1986 models

A Rear door   *B Front door*

16 New butyl strips can then be applied and a new watershield fitted. Use a roller to press the shield into contact with the butyl strip.

Refitting

17 Refitting is a reversal of removal.

12 Doors - removal and refitting

Front door

Pre-1986 models

Removal

1 Open the door fully and support its lower edge on a jack or blocks covered with a pad of cloth to prevent scratching.
2 Unscrew the two bolts which hold the check arm bracket to the body and disconnect the arm.
3 Remove the scuff plate from the sill at the bottom of the door aperture.
4 Unclip the lower cowl side trim panel, and where fitted remove the radio speaker (Chapter 12).
5 Remove the heater duct.
6 On cars with electrically operated windows, mirrors or central locking, disconnect the wiring multi-plug from inside the passenger compartment and feed the wires through the aperture in the pillar.
7 Unbolt the door lower hinge from the body pillar (see illustrations).
8 Unbolt the upper hinge from the body pillar, then lift the door from the vehicle.

Refitting

9 Refitting is a reversal of removal, but do not fully tighten the hinge bolts until the alignment of the door within the body aperture has been checked.

1986 models onwards

10 The procedure is as described previously in this Section for pre-1986 models, but it is necessary to extract the pin from the upper hinge rather than unbolting the hinge from the pillar. To do this, ideally special tool 41-018 is needed, but a suitable alternative can be made from a piece of metal with a U-shaped cut-out which will engage under the head of the pin (see illustrations). Strike the tool downward to remove the pin. When refitting, tap the pin upwards into place.

Rear door

Saloon and Estate models

11 The operations are similar to those described for the front door on pre-1986 models, except that the centre pillar trim panels must be removed for access to the hinge bolts.

Van models

Removal

12 Begin by opening the door to its full extent and supporting it on a jack or blocks, with a pad of cloth used to prevent scratching.
13 Disconnect the check strap from its lower edge.

12.10a Front door upper hinge pin (arrowed) on 1986 models onwards

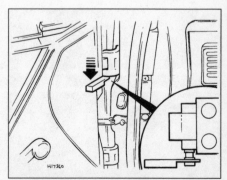

12.10b Front door upper hinge pin removal using special tool - 1986 models onwards

11

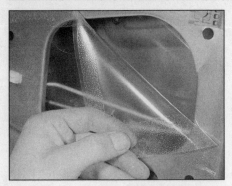

13.2 Peel back the waterproof sheet for access to the door handle

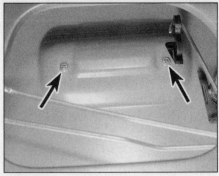

13.3 Door exterior handle retaining screws (arrowed)

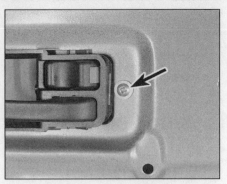

13.7 Remote control handle retaining screw (arrowed)

14 Unbolt the hinges from the door and remove the door from the vehicle.

Refitting

15 Refitting is a reversal of removal, but do not fully tighten the hinge bolts until the alignment of the door within the body aperture has been checked.

13 Door handle and lock components - removal and refitting

Door exterior handle

Removal

1 Remove the door trim panel (Section 11).
2 Peel back the waterproof sheet as necessary to gain access **(see illustration)**.
3 Undo the two screws and withdraw the handle from the door **(see illustration)**.
4 Disconnect the control rod and remove the handle.

Refitting

5 Refitting is a reversal of removal.

Door interior handle

Removal

6 Remove the door trim panel (Section 11).
7 Remove the interior handle securing screw, then manipulate the handle from the door and disconnect the lock operating rod **(see illustration)**.

Refitting

8 Refitting is a reversal of removal, but ensure that the lock operating rod is correctly reconnected. Refit the door trim panel with reference to Section 11.

Door lock and cylinder

All models except Cabriolet

Removal

9 Remove the door trim panel (Section 11).
10 Peel back the waterproof sheet as necessary to gain access.
11 On 1986 models onwards, remove the exterior handle as described previously in this Section.
12 Disconnect the control rods from the lock.
13 To remove the lock cylinder, pull out the retaining clip and seal and withdraw the cylinder **(see illustration)**.
14 Remove the lock by extracting the three securing screws and lowering the lock sufficiently to permit the cylinder lock rod to clear the lock housing **(see illustration)**. Turn the latch around the door frame and withdraw the assembly through the rear cut-out in the door.

Refitting

15 Refitting is a reversal of removal.

Cabriolet models

Removal

16 From late 1984, Cabriolet models were fitted with revised door locks. Due to it no longer being available, if an early type of lock

is to be renewed, the later type of lock must be fitted as follows.
17 On models with central locking, disconnect the battery negative lead.
18 Remove the door inner trim panel with reference to Section 11.
19 Peel back the waterproof sheet as necessary to gain access.
20 Disconnect the control rods from the lock.
21 To remove the lock cylinder, pull out the retaining clip and seal, and withdraw the cylinder.
22 On certain models, the lock is secured to the door with rivets. Drill out the rivets, or remove the securing screws, as applicable.
23 Withdraw the lock from the door, and where applicable remove the central locking solenoid from the lock.
24 Remove the plate from the inside edge of the door.

Refitting

25 If the lock was secured to the door with rivets, the door must be drilled as shown, in order to accept the securing screws for the new lock **(see illustration)**. Apply suitable corrosion protection and repaint the area around the holes.
26 Remove the shaded area of the new threaded plate, as shown **(see illustration)**.

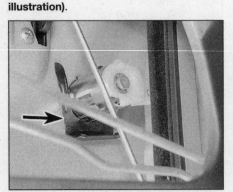

13.13 Door lock cylinder retaining clip (arrowed)

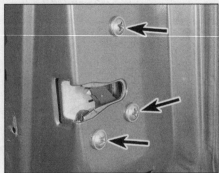

13.14 Door lock retaining screws (arrowed)

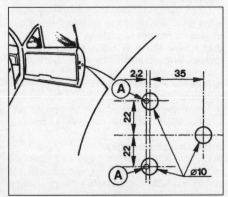

13.25 Drill the door at the points indicated when fitting a new lock to early Cabriolet models
A Existing holes
Note: dimensions given in millimetres

27 Where applicable, fit the central locking solenoid to the new lock, then fit the threaded plate in the door, and fit the lock. Tighten the securing screws finger-tight only at this stage.
28 Reconnect the control rods to the lock.
29 If a later type lock is being fitted to a model which was previously fitted with an early type lock, a revised lock striker plate must also be fitted. Where applicable, fit the new striker plate and tighten the securing screws finger-tight.
30 Close the door once to achieve correct alignment between the lock and striker, then open the door and tighten the lock and striker securing screws securely.
31 Refit the waterproof sheet and the door inner trim panel with reference to Section 11.
32 Where applicable, reconnect the battery negative lead.

14 Door window glass and regulator - removal and refitting

Front door window glass - models with manual windows

Saloon, Estate and Van models

Removal

1 Remove the door trim panel, as described in Section 11.
2 Carefully peel back the waterproof sheet from the door.
3 Prise off the inner and outer glass weatherstrips.
4 Lower the window so that the regulator connector is level with the door lower aperture.
5 Remove the single screw which retains the glass run extension (accessible through the small aperture at the lower corner of the door) **(see illustration)**.
6 Detach the window channel from the regulator ball and socket joints then raise and remove the window from the exterior side of the door **(see illustrations)**.

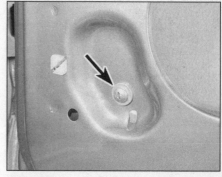

13.26 Remove the shaded area (A) when fitting a new door lock threaded plate to early Cabriolet models

Refitting

7 Refitting of the door glass is the reversal of the removal procedure. On completion check that the window operates freely before refitting the waterproof sheet and trim to the door.

Cabriolet models

Removal

8 Remove the door trim panel as described in Section 11.
9 Carefully peel back the waterproof sheet from the door.
10 Remove the door weatherstrip and rubber end block.
11 Lower the window and, working through the aperture, disconnect the linkage arms from the bottom rail.
12 Lift the glass upwards from the door.

Refitting

13 Refitting is a reversal of removal, but adjust the window stop as follows.
14 Loosen the adjustment bolt, then raise the window until the top edge of the glass touches the top guide seal **(see illustration)**. Now position the stop on the regulator mechanism and tighten the bolt. Check that, with the door shut and the window fully raised, the top front corner of the glass is

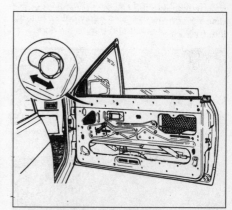

14.5 Glass run extension retaining screw (arrowed)

under the lip of the weatherstrip. Make any final adjustments as necessary.

Front door window glass - models with electric windows

Removal

15 Lower the window fully on the door that is being dismantled.
16 Disconnect the battery.
17 Remove the door trim panel as described in Section 11.
18 Disconnect the motor wiring multi-plugs and retaining clips.
19 Remove the mounting screws from the motor and the regulator - three screws each.
20 Extract the retaining screw from the door glass channel. Detach the channel from the door.
21 Remove the glass as described previously in this Section for models with manual windows.

Refitting

22 Refitting is a reversal of removal; ensure that the wiring is secured out of the way of the window regulating system, and check that the window operates freely before refitting the waterproof sheet and trim to the door.

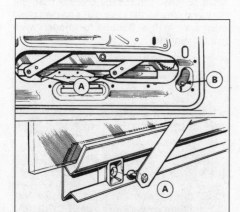

14.6a Window channel to regulator attachments (A) and glass run extension securing screw (B)

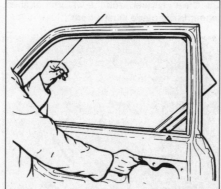

14.6b Removing the door window glass

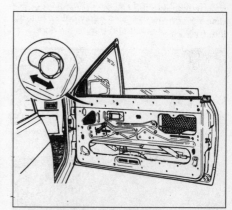

14.14 Window stop adjustment bolt - Cabriolet models

11

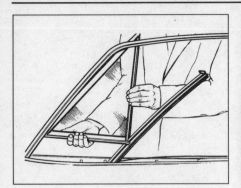

14.35 Removing the rear door quarter window

14.38 Peeling back the door waterproof sheet

39 Lower the glass so that the channel and regulator attachments are accessible through the door aperture. Detach the ball and socket joints (two for the front door, one for the rear door).

40 Lower the glass to the base of the door, then undo the seven screws, or drill out the seven rivets on later models, which secure the regulator in position. Note that on some models only five retaining rivets may be used **(see illustrations)**.

41 With the screws or rivets removed, the regulator unit can be withdrawn from the aperture in the door **(see illustration)**.

Rear door sliding window glass - models with manual windows

Removal

23 Proceed as described in paragraphs 1 to 4.
24 Remove the upper and lower screws which secure the divisional channel and quarter window in position. Remove the door quarter window.
25 Detach the window channel from the regulator ball and socket joints then raise and remove the window from the interior side of the door.

Refitting

26 Refitting of the door glass is the reversal of the removal procedure. On completion check that the window operates freely before refitting the waterproof sheet and trim to the door.

Rear door sliding window glass - models with electric windows

Removal

27 Proceed as described in paragraphs 15 to 20.
28 Remove the glass as described previously in this Section for models with manual windows.

Refitting

29 Refitting of the door glass is the reversal of the removal procedure. On completion check that the window operates freely before refitting the waterproof sheet and trim to the door.

Rear door fixed window glass

Removal

30 Remove the door trim panel, as described in Section 11.
31 Carefully peel back the waterproof sheet from the door.
32 Prise off the inner and outer glass weatherstrips.
33 Lower the sliding window so that the regulator connector is level with the door lower aperture.
34 Remove the upper and lower screws which secure the divisional channel and quarter window in position.
35 Remove the door quarter window **(see illustration)**.

Refitting

36 Refit in reverse order of removal. On completion check that the sliding window can be freely regulated before refitting the waterproof sheet and door trim.

Manual window regulator (all except Cabriolet rear quarter window regulator)

Note: *Seven M6 x 10 mm screws will be required to secure the regulator on refitting.*

Removal

37 Remove the door trim panel, as described in Section 11.
38 Carefully peel back the waterproof sheet from the door **(see illustration)**.

Refitting

42 Refitting is a reversal of the removal procedure. Align the regulator with the respective holes before screwing or pop riveting it to secure. The ball and socket joints are a push-fit to the glass channel, but support the channel when pushing on the joint.

43 Since the screw fixing regulator is no longer being manufactured, replacing the regulator on early models with the later type regulator necessitates drilling out the retaining holes to 7 mm (0.276 in). Special J-nuts must then be fitted to the regulator positioned in line with each of the seven securing holes. The regulator can then be attached to the door shell using seven M6 x 10 mm screws. Do not use any other screw type.

Electric window regulator

All models except Cabriolet

Removal
44 Lower the window fully.
45 Disconnect the battery.
46 Remove the door trim panel as described in Section 11.
47 Disconnect the motor wiring multi-plugs and retaining clips.
48 Remove the mounting screws from the motor and the regulator - three screws each **(see illustration)**.
49 Extract the retaining screw from the door glass channel. Detach the channel from the door and remove the door glass as described previously in this Section for models with manual windows.

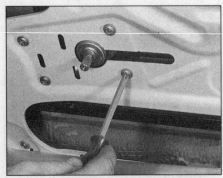

14.40a Removing the regulator retaining screws

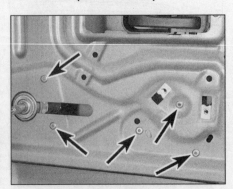

14.40b Regulator retaining rivet location (arrowed)

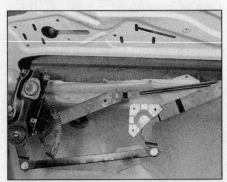

14.41 Withdrawing the window regulator

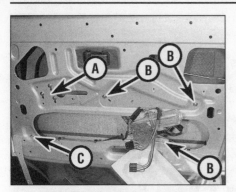

14.48 Electric window regulator mechanism

A *Regulator mounting screws*
B *Motor mounting screws*
C *Glass channel fixing screw*

50 Grip the motor mounting plate in one hand and the regulator in the other. Raise the regulator and at the same time pull the motor towards the hinge end of the door.

51 Slowly twist the motor in a clockwise direction and at the same time fold the regulator over the top of the motor so that it comes to rest on the lock side of the door **(see illustration)**.

52 Rotate the motor mounting in an anti-clockwise direction until a corner of the mounting comes into view in the cut-out of the door.

53 Move the assembly so that this corner projects through the cut-out and then turn the

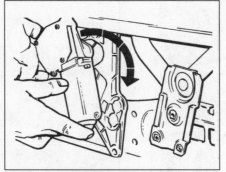

14.51 Twist the motor clockwise to clear the door aperture

whole assembly in a clockwise direction and guide it out of the cut-out **(see illustration)**.

54 Remove the two Allen screws from the regulator travel stop, and the single screw from the regulator gear guide **(see illustrations)**.

55 Extract the circlip from the motor driveshaft and remove the drivegear.

56 Move the regulator to expose the motor mounting bolts. Extract the bolts and separate the motor from the regulator **(see illustration)**.

Refitting

57 Reassembly and refitting is a reversal of the dismantling and removal procedures. Before refitting the door trim check that the wiring is secured out of the way of the window regulating system.

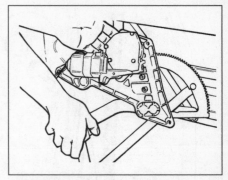

14.53 Withdrawing the window motor and regulator from the door

Cabriolet models

Removal

58 Proceed as described in paragraphs 44 to 47, then lower the window so that the window securing channel can be seen through the lower opening in the door. It may be necessary to temporarily connect the wiring to do this.

59 Remove the regulator securing bolts and nuts **(see illustration)**.

60 Release the regulator mechanism rollers from the window securing channels and remove the glass from the door (as described previously in this Section).

61 Release the wiring loom and remove the regulator mechanism from the door (refer to the previous sub-Section describing the procedure for non-Cabriolet models).

Refitting

62 Begin refitting by locating the regulator mechanism loosely in position in the door.

63 Refit the wiring loom.

64 Refit the window glass and insert the rollers of the regulator mechanism into the window securing channel.

65 Fit and tighten the regulator securing bolts and nuts.

66 Fit the inner and outer door weatherstrips.

67 Raise the window fully and check that the edge of the glass is in alignment with the roof seal.

68 Adjust the height and alignment of the glass using the screws indicated **(see illustration)**.

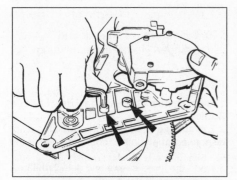

14.54a Removing the window motor regulator travel stop - Allen screws arrowed

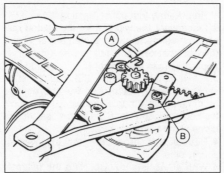

14.54b Window motor driveshaft circlip (A) and gear guide retaining screw (B)

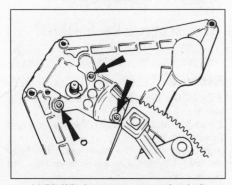

14.56 Window motor mounting bolt locations (arrowed)

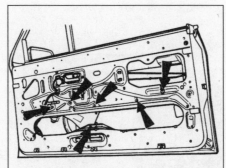

14.59 Electric window regulator securing bolts and nuts (arrowed) - Cabriolet models

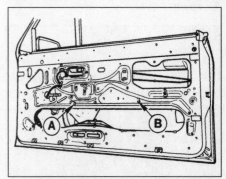

14.68 Adjusting screws (arrowed) for electric window glass on Cabriolet models

A *Glass height*   B *Glass alignment*

11

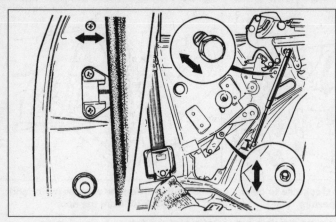

14.80 Rear quarter window adjustments - Cabriolet models

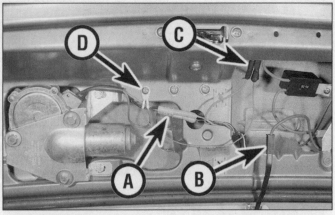

15.2 Electrical connections at the tailgate (1986 model shown)

A Wiper motor
B Radio aerial connection
C Feed and relay connectors
D Earthing point

69 The remainder of the refitting procedure is a reversal of removal.

Rear quarter window glass and regulator - Cabriolet models

Removal

70 Fully lower the roof and remove the weatherstrip and window channel from the centre pillar.

71 Extract the clip and pull back the trim to expose the upper seat belt anchorage. Unscrew the bolt and place the seat belt to one side.

72 Lower the window and remove the regulator handle.

73 Fold the rear seat cushion forwards.

74 Remove the inner and outer window weatherstrips and the quarter panel rubber end block.

75 Remove the front quarter trim panel.

76 Remove the roof lever knob and bezel, then remove the trim panel (3 screws) with the lever in the locked position and disconnect the speaker wires.

77 Peel off the waterproof sheet then, working through the aperture, unbolt the window rail from the regulator.

78 Move the window rearwards from the regulator then lift it from the car.

79 To remove the regulator, extract the six screws and withdraw it through the aperture.

Refitting

80 Refitting is a reversal of removal, but adjust the glass so that the upper and rear edges touch the weatherstrip using the screws shown **(see illustration)**.

15 Tailgate - removal and refitting

Removal

1 Remove the trim panel (Section 32).

2 Disconnect the wiring from the heated rear window element, radio aerial, wiper motor tailgate speakers and tailgate lock motor as applicable **(see illustration)**.

3 Tie a strong cord to the end of each separate wiring loom. Pull out the flexible grommets and withdraw the wiring looms until the cords appear. Untie the looms, leaving cords in the tailgate.

4 Repeat this procedure for the washer supply pipe.

5 With an assistant supporting the tailgate, prise off the stout clips or release the pegs and disconnect the support struts from the tailgate **(see illustration)**.

6 From the top edge of the tailgate aperture, remove the weatherstrip. Release the headlining clips from the flange.

7 Undo the screws and remove the pillar trim on each side, then pull the headlining down for access to the hinge bolts.

8 With the tailgate supported, undo the nuts from the hinge bolts and remove the tailgate.

Refitting

9 Refitting is a reversal of removal. Adjust the position of the tailgate in the aperture at the hinge bolts and the closing action at the striker plate.

16 Tailgate/boot lid lock and cylinder - removal and refitting

Removal

1 Remove the trim panel as described in Section 32.

2 Extract the lock cylinder retaining clip, disconnect the control rods and remove the cylinder.

3 Undo the three screws and detach the lock assembly **(see illustration)**.

Refitting

4 Refitting is a reversal of removal

17 Boot lid (Cabriolet models) - removal and refitting

Removal

1 Open the boot and prop it open using a length of wood.

2 Pull out the clips securing the gas strut and remove the strut.

3 Working inside the boot, undo the nuts securing the hinge assemblies to the framework.

4 Ease the lid rearwards to disengage the studs, and lift the lid away.

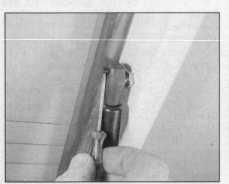

15.5 Releasing tailgate strut retaining clip

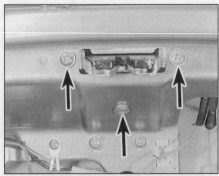

16.3 Tailgate lock retaining screws (arrowed)

5 The hinge assemblies can be removed from the lid by prising off the plastic covers and undoing the bolts securing the hinges to the lid. One is accessible from outside and one from inside.

Refitting

6 Refitting is a reversal of removal, but do not fully tighten the bolts until the lid has been lined up and closed properly.

18 Central door locking system components - removal and refitting

General

1 On pre-1986 models the locks, with the exception of the one on the driver's door, are actuated by solenoids **(see illustration)**. On 1986 models onwards, the locks are actuated by electric motors.

Switch (driver's door lock)

Removal

2 Raise the driver's door lock fully.
3 Disconnect the battery.
4 Remove the door trim panel (Section 11).
5 Disconnect the wiring plugs inside the door cavity and release the wires from their clips.
6 Release the lock control rods and remove the lock fixing screws.
7 Remove the lock from the door interior by guiding it round the glass guide channel.
8 Extract the two screws and remove the switch from the lock.

Refitting

9 Refitting is a reversal of removal, but before refitting the door trim panel check that the wires within the door cavity are out of the way of the window regulating mechanism and secured by strap clips.

Control relay

Removal

10 Disconnect the battery.
11 Remove the under-facia trim panel from the passenger side.

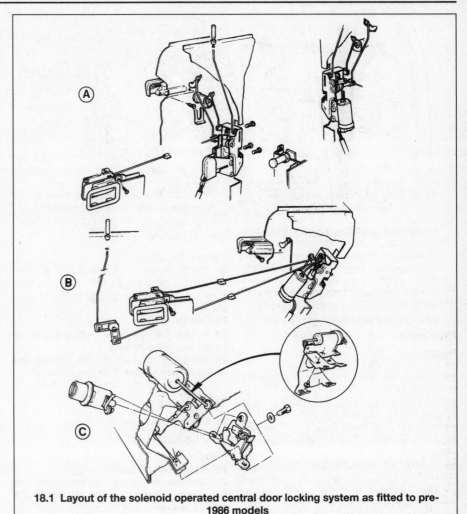

18.1 Layout of the solenoid operated central door locking system as fitted to pre-1986 models

A Front door components   B Rear door components   C Tailgate components

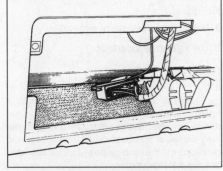

18.12 Central locking solenoid relay location behind glovebox - pre-1986 models

12 Pull the relay from its securing clips **(see illustration)**.
13 Disconnect the multi-plug and remove the relay.

Refitting

14 Refitting is a reversal of removal.

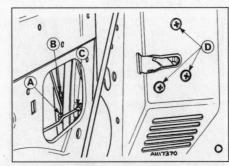

18.17 Door locking rod attachments - pre-1986 models

*A, B and C Control rods
D Lock retaining screws*

Solenoids - pre-1986 models

Front door

Removal

15 Disconnect the battery.
16 Remove the door trim panel as described in Section 11.
17 Disconnect the lock operating rods and extract the three lock fixing screws **(see illustration)**.
18 Release the wiring from the clips, manoeuvre the lock round the door glass guide channel and remove it through the cut-out in the door panel **(see illustration)**.
19 Separate the solenoid from the lock after extracting the fixing screws.
Refitting
20 Refitting is a reversal of removal, bearing in mind the following points.
a) When fitting the door lock solenoids, locate the guide lock assembly into position, but do not fully tighten the retaining screws until after the bellcrank and rubber operating rod guides, and the

11

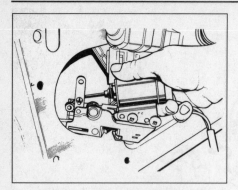

18.18 Door lock solenoid removal - pre-1986 models

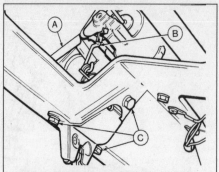

18.33 Tailgate lock and solenoid components - pre-1986 models

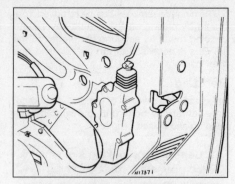

18.42 Door lock motor location - 1986 models onwards

internal lock operating lever are fitted.
b) *Check that, when the solenoid is in the unlocked position, the gaiter has an uncompressed length of 20 mm (0.78 in).*
c) *Before refitting the door trim panel check that the wires within the door cavity are out of the way of the window regulating mechanism and secured by strap clips.*

Rear door

Removal

21 Disconnect the battery.
22 Remove the door trim panel as described in Section 11.
23 Remove the bellcrank and operating lever by extracting the securing screws.
24 Release the operating rod rubber insulators from the door and disconnect the wiring.
25 Extract the lock securing screws, push the lock into the door cavity and then withdraw the lock with the operating rods through the cut-out in the door panel.
26 Extract the screws and disconnect the solenoid from the lock.
Refitting
27 Refer to paragraph 20.

Tailgate

Removal
28 Disconnect the battery.
29 Open the tailgate and remove the trim panel (see Section 32).
30 Remove the lock rod clip and then prise out the clip which retains the lock cylinder.

A Lock barrel clip   C Lock fixing bolts
B Lock rod clip

Remove the cylinder.
31 Slightly lower the tailgate and working through the lock cylinder hole, move the lock lever away from its spring until the lock engages.
32 Disconnect the solenoid wiring.
33 Extract the lock fixing bolts and remove the lock **(see illustration)**.
34 Insert a screwdriver through the aperture left by removal of the lock and unscrew the two solenoid fixing screws. Withdraw the solenoid.
Refitting
35 Refitting is a reversal of removal.

Boot lid (Cabriolet)

Removal
36 Disconnect the battery.
37 Remove the boot lid lock unit, as described in Section 16, and disconnect the solenoid wiring.
38 Unscrew and remove the two solenoid retaining screws, unhook the operating shaft and withdraw the solenoid.
Refitting
39 Refitting is a reversal of removal.

Motors - 1986 models onwards

Front and rear doors

Removal
40 Disconnect the battery.

41 Remove the door trim panel (Section 11).
42 Undo the two retaining screws, or drill out the bracket rivets, and withdraw the motor **(see illustration)**.
43 Disconnect the motor from the operating rod, disconnect the wiring multi-plug and remove the motor.
Refitting
44 Refitting is a reversal of removal.

Tailgate and boot lid

Removal
45 Disconnect the battery.
46 Open the tailgate or boot lid and remove the trim panel where applicable (see Section 32).
47 Disconnect the motor wiring multi-plug.
48 Undo the motor retaining bolts, disconnect the operating rod and remove the motor.
Refitting
49 Refitting is a reversal of removal.

19 Exterior mirror - removal and refitting

Without remote control

Removal

1 Using a screwdriver, prise off the triangular trim panel from inside the mirror mounting position.
2 Unscrew the three screws and withdraw the mirror.

Refitting

3 Refitting is a reversal of removal.

With remote control

Removal

4 Two types of remote control mirror are used on Escort models. On the original version, a special wrench is needed to unscrew the mirror actuator bezel, although a C-spanner may serve as a substitute. Once the bezel is removed the mirror is removed as for the non-remote control type.
5 On later versions extract the retaining circlip and pull off the remote control handle **(see illustrations)**.

19.5a Remote control mirror handle circlip

19.5b Removing the remote control handle

19.6a Extract the trim cover and undo the screw . . .

19.6b . . . then remove the trim panel

19.7 Removing the door mirror retaining screws

6 Extract the trim cover, undo the screw and remove the triangular trim panel **(see illustrations)**.

7 Undo the three screws and remove the mirror **(see illustration)**.

Refitting

8 Refitting is a reversal of removal.

Electrically-operated mirrors

Removal

9 Initially disconnect the battery earth lead or remove the heated window fuse from the fusebox.

10 Remove the door trim panel as described in Section 11 and disconnect the wiring multi-plug. The mirror is then removed in the same way as the non-remote control type.

Refitting

11 Refitting is a reversal of removal, but check the operation of the mirror before finally refitting the door trim panel.

Mirror glass renewal

Removal

12 On "high specification" models with fixed (ie not remote control) mirrors, lever the glass assembly outwards to disengage it from the balljoint on the mirror glass mounting.

13 On "low specification" models with fixed (ie not remote control) mirrors, unclip the cover, then remove the securing screw and withdraw the glass assembly.

14 On models with remote control mirrors, insert a thin screwdriver through the hole in the bottom of the mirror assembly, and whilst supporting the glass, move the tang in the direction of the door to release the locking ring.

Refitting

15 On "high specification" models with fixed mirrors, carefully push the glass into position, ensuring that the balljoint engages securely.

16 On "low specification" models with fixed mirrors, secure the glass with the screw, and refit the cover.

17 On models with remote control mirrors, ensure that the locking ring is in place, then carefully push the glass into position.

20 Windscreen and fixed window glass - removal and refitting

Windscreen

Note: *The average DIY mechanic is advised to leave windscreen removal and refitting to an expert. For the owner who insists on doing it himself, the following paragraphs are given.*

Removal

1 All models are fitted with a laminated glass screen and in consequence even if cracked, it will probably be removed as one piece.

2 Cover the bonnet in front of the windscreen with an old blanket to protect against scratching.

3 Remove the wiper arms and blades (see Chapter 12).

4 Working inside the vehicle, push the lip of the screen weather seal under the top and the sides of the body aperture flange.

5 With an assistant standing outside the car to restrain the screen, push the glass with weather seal out of the bodyframe.

6 Where fitted, extract the bright moulding from the groove in the weatherstrip and then pull the weatherstrip off the glass.

7 Unless the weatherstrip is in good condition, it should be renewed.

8 Although sealant it not normally used with these screens, check that the glass groove in the weatherstrip is free from sealant or glass chippings.

Refitting

9 Commence refitting by fitting the weatherstrip to the glass. Locate a length of nylon or terylene cord in the body flange groove of the weatherstrip so that the ends of the cord emerge at the bottom centre and cross over by a length of about 150 mm.

10 Offer the screen to the body and engage the lower lip of the weatherstrip on its flange. With an assistant applying gentle, even pressure on the glass from the outside, pull the ends of the cord simultaneously at right-angles to the glass. This will pull the lip of the weatherstrip over the body flange. Continue until the cord is released from the centre top

and the screen is fully fitted.

11 If a bright moulding was removed, refit it now. This can be one of the most difficult jobs to do without a special tool. The moulding should be pressed into its groove just after the groove lips have been prised open to receive it. Take care not to cut the weatherstrip if improvising with a made-up tool.

Tailgate glass

12 The operations are very similar to those described for windscreen renewal in the preceding sub-Section.

13 Disconnect the leads from the heated rear window/radio aerial and the wiper motor (where fitted).

14 The tailgate glass is of toughened type, not laminated, so if it has shattered, remove all granular glass with a small vacuum cleaner.

Rear window glass - Cabriolet models

Removal

15 Disconnect the heated rear window wiring and pull the wiring from the weatherstrip.

16 Have an assistant support the window frame from outside then push out the glass from the inside.

17 Remove the weatherstrip from the glass and clean away all traces of sealant.

Refitting

18 Refit in reverse order to removal using the method described previously in this Section for the windscreen, and finally apply suitable sealant beneath the outer lip of the weatherstrip.

Fixed rear quarter window

Removal

19 The glass is removed complete with weatherstrip by pushing it out from inside the vehicle.

20 The lip of the weatherstrip must be released from the top and sides of the window aperture using a suitable tool before exerting pressure to remove the assembly.

Refitting

21 Refit using a cord as described previously in this Section for the windscreen.

11

21 Sunroof components - removal, refitting and adjustment

Sunroof panel

Removal

1 To remove this type of glass panel, pull the sun blind into the open position and have the sliding roof closed.
2 Wind the sliding roof handle in an anti-clockwise direction for one complete turn.
3 Remove the three screws and clips which connect the lower frame and glass.
4 Turn the handle to close the sliding roof and remove the three screws from each side which hold the glass to the sliding gear.
5 Remove the glass panel by lifting it from the outside of the vehicle.

Refitting

6 To refit the panel, have the roof closed, locate the glass and secure with the three screws on each side. Once the screws are secure give the handle one complete turn in a clockwise direction.
7 Set the glass to align with the roof panel and locate the lower frame to glass brackets. Insert the clips through the brackets.
8 Insert the retaining screws in the sequence shown (**see illustration**).

Adjustment

9 The sunroof panel can be adjusted within its aperture and for flush fitting with the roof panel in the following way.
10 To correct the panel-to-aperture gap, bend the weatherstrip flange as necessary.
11 To adjust the panel height at its front edge, release the corner screws, raise or lower the panel as necessary and retighten the screws.
12 To adjust the panel height at its rear edge, release the two screws at each side on the link assemblies and push the links up or down within the limits of the elongated screw holes. Retighten the screws when alignment is correct.

Sunroof sliding gear

Removal

13 Remove the glass panel as described previously in this Section.
14 Turn the sliding roof regulator handle clockwise to the fully closed position. Extract the three screws and remove the regulator handle and the handle cup.
15 Extract the four screws from each side which hold the sliding gear to the roof (**see illustration**). Lift up the front of the gear and withdraw it from the front of the sliding roof aperture.

Refitting

16 Refitting is a reversal of removal, but if necessary adjust the sunroof panel as described previously in this Section.

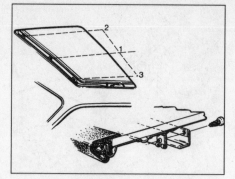

21.8 Fixing sequence for sunroof panel retaining screws

22 Folding roof (Cabriolet models) - removal and refitting

Removal

1 Remove the rear side, wheel arch and roof stowage compartment trim panels.
2 Disconnect the heated rear window wiring and pull it from the weatherstrip.
3 Release the roof front locking catches.
4 Unscrew the nuts and remove the rear window frame guides.
5 Remove the protection cover screw and the tensioning screw from each side (**see illustration**).
6 Unscrew the nuts at both tensioning cable blocks.
7 Pull the roof and cable from the rail and release the cable.
8 With the roof frame upright, unbolt the strap retaining brackets.
9 Remove the headlining wire screw and unhook the wire.
10 Disconnect the gas struts.
11 Lower the front of the roof then unscrew the three mounting bolts on each side.
12 Lift the complete folding roof from the car.

Refitting

13 Refitting is a reversal of removal, but do not tighten the mounting bolts or tensioning block nuts until the front of the roof is locked and the rear beading is in the rail (**see illustration**). It may be necessary to use a

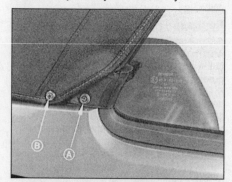

22.5 Protection cover screw (A) and tensioning screw (B) - Cabriolet models

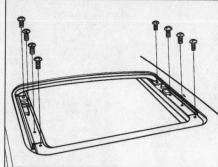

21.15 Sunroof sliding gear to roof screws

tamping tool to ensure that the tensioning cable is fully inserted in the rail. A little sealant should be applied at the points where the cable passes through the covering.

23 Power-operated folding roof - fluid level checking and bleeding

General

1 As from 1987, a power-operated folding roof is available as an option on Cabriolet models.
2 The roof is operated hydraulically from an electric pump located in the left-hand side of the boot. Hydraulic rams, mounted on each side of the vehicle by the rear wheel housings, actuate the roof folding mechanism. A control switch is mounted on the centre console. In the event of failure, the roof can be operated manually by opening a bypass valve on the side of the pump.
3 The system is sealed and requires no regular maintenance apart from periodic checking of the fluid level.

Fluid level checking

4 The level should be checked with the roof open. With the roof in the closed position, the level will be lower due to the displacement of the hydraulic rams.
5 Pull down the trim panel/pump cover on the left-hand side of the boot.

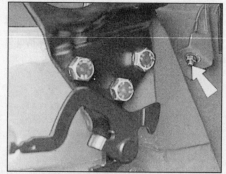

22.13 Cable tensioning block nut (arrowed) - Cabriolet models

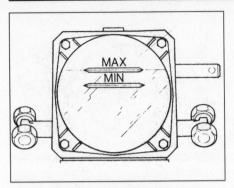

23.6 Fluid level sight glass for power-operated folding roof

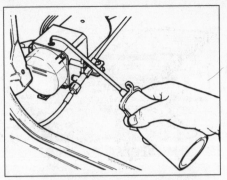

23.7 Filling the power-operated folding roof fluid pump reservoir

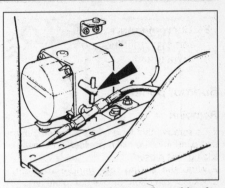

23.9 Bypass valve (arrowed) on side of power-operated folding roof fluid pump

6 Check that the fluid in the reservoir on the end of the pump is between the "MIN" and "MAX" marks on the sight glass **(see illustration)**.

7 If the level requires topping-up, remove the filler plug from the top of the pump reservoir and fill the reservoir with the specified fluid until the level reaches the "MAX" mark **(see illustration)**.

8 Refit the filler plug and trim panel.

Bleeding

9 Open the bypass valve on the side of the pump body **(see illustration)**.

10 Open, close and re-open the roof manually.

11 Fill the reservoir to the "MAX" mark, then fit the filler plug loosely and close the bypass valve on the side of the pump.

12 Open and close the roof several times using the power mode.

13 When all air has been bled from the system the roof will operate smoothly without

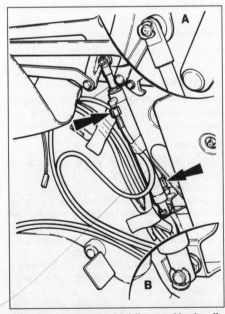

24.4 Power-operated folding roof hydraulic ram assembly - hydraulic unions (arrowed)
A and B Upper and lower clips

jerking, and the level of noise from the pump will be steady.

14 Top-up the system, tighten the filler plug and refit disturbed panels.

24 Power-operated folding roof components - removal and refitting

Hydraulic rams

Removal

1 Remove the rear wheelhouse covers with reference to Section 32.

2 Mark the two hoses connected to the ram as a guide to reassembly, then remove the circlips securing the ram to the two studs on the framework.

3 Release residual pressure in the system by opening the filler plug on the pump body.

4 Loosen the hydraulic unions on the ram, then remove the ram from the studs and lay it in a suitable container in the boot. Undo the unions and catch the hydraulic fluid in the container **(see illustration)**.

5 If the unions are to remain disconnected for any length of time, cover the ends to prevent dirt entering the system.

Refitting

6 Refitting the ram is a reversal of removal, noting that the large circlip is fitted to the lower stud.

7 On completion, fill and bleed the system as described in Section 23.

Hydraulic ram upper pivot stud

Removal

8 Should the hydraulic ram pivot stud break in service it can be renewed as follows.

9 Open the tap on the hydraulic pump, then manually open the roof halfway.

10 Using a mole wrench, remove the broken end of the pivot stud from the framework. If the remaining stud is too short it may be possible to remove it using a proprietary stud extractor kit.

Refitting

11 De-grease the threads on the new stud,

apply locking compound to them, then fit the stud and tighten it securely.

12 Refit the hydraulic rams as described previously in this Section.

Pump

Removal

13 Disconnect the battery, then pull down the pump cover in the boot and open the bypass valve by 90 to 180 degrees. Do not open it any further.

14 Open the roof manually.

15 Remove the floor panel and left-hand wheelhouse panel from the boot. This involves propping open the boot lid and disconnecting the supporting gas strut from the lower balljoint.

16 Release residual pressure in the system by opening the filler plug on the pump. Tighten the plug when the pressure has been released.

17 Disconnect the electrical lead to the pump.

18 Remove the nuts securing the pump to the boot floor, and place the pump in a suitable container to catch the fluid which will be spilt when the pump hoses are disconnected.

19 Mark the hoses as a guide to reassembly, then undo their connections **(see illustration)**. Cover the open ends if they are to remain disconnected for any length of time.

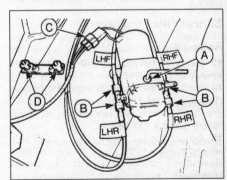

24.19 Power-operated folding roof fluid pump removed from mounting with hoses marked

A Filler plug *C Wiring plug*
B Hydraulic unions *D Pump mountings*

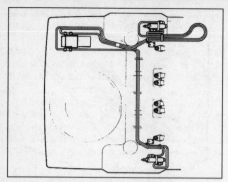

24.22 Routing of power-operated folding roof hydraulic hoses

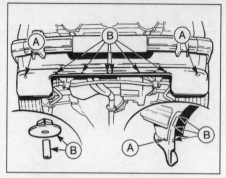

25.2a Front spoiler attachments - XR3 models

A Retaining screws   *B Retaining pegs*

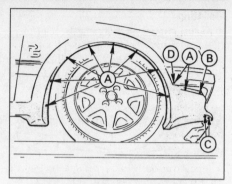

25.2b Front wheel arch extension attachments - RS Turbo models

A and B Rivets   *D Screw cap*
C Screws

Refitting

20 Refitting is a reversal of removal.
21 On completion, fill and bleed the system as described in Section 23.

Hydraulic hoses

Removal

22 Renewing the hydraulic hoses involves disconnecting the relevant hose connections from the pump or ram (see earlier paragraphs), noting its routing, and where it is clipped or taped to other components **(see illustration)**.

Refitting

23 Refit in the reverse order to removal.
24 On completion, fill and bleed the system as described in Section 23.

25 Body exterior fittings - removal and refitting

Spoilers and wheel arch deflectors

Removal

1 The spoilers and wheel arch deflectors fitted to XR3, XR3i, Cabriolet and RS Turbo models are secured by screws, rivets and clips, or a combination of all three.
2 The screw and rivet fasteners are concealed under blanking plugs which are prised out to gain access to the screw or rivet as applicable **(see illustrations)**. These can then be drilled out or unscrewed and the spoiler or wheel arch deflector withdrawn.

Refitting

3 Refitting is a reversal of removal.

Body adhesive emblems and mouldings

Removal

4 The radiator grille emblem, the front wing motif, the tailgate emblems and the body side mouldings are all of the self-adhesive type.
5 To remove these devices, it is recommended that a length of nylon cord is used to separate them from their mounting surfaces **(see illustration)**.

Refitting

6 New emblems have adhesive already applied and a protective backing. Before sticking them into position, clean off all the old adhesive from the mounting surface of the vehicle.

26 Seats - removal and refitting

Front seat

Removal

1 Slide the seat as far forward as it will go.
2 Unscrew and remove the bolts which retain the rear of the seat slides to the floor pan.
3 Slide the seat as far to the rear as it will go and remove the bolts which secure the front ends of the slides to the floor.
4 Remove the seat from the vehicle interior.
5 If the seat slides must be detached from the seat, invert the seat and remove the two bolts from each side. Detach the cross-rod and clips.

Refitting

6 Refitting is a reversal of removal. Tighten the front bolts before the rear ones to ensure that the seat is located evenly on the floorpan.

25.5 Removing tailgate adhesive badge

Rear seat cushion

Removal

7 Unscrew and remove the Torx (socket-headed) screws from the seat cushion hinges which are located on each side.
8 Lift the cushion from the floor and remove it from the vehicle.

Refitting

9 Refitting is a reversal of removal.

Rear seat backrest

Removal

10 Fold the seat cushion forward and then fold the seat back down to expose the hinges.
11 Extract the screws which hold the backrest to the hinges.
12 Remove the backrest from the vehicle.

Refitting

13 Refitting is a reversal of removal.

27 Seat belts - removal and refitting

Front belt - 3-door models

Note: *Note the fitted sequence of any plates, washers and spacers when unbolting the seat belt anchors.*

Removal

1 Slide the belt stalk cover upwards to expose the anchor bolt.
2 Unbolt the stalk.
3 Unbolt the lower anchor rail, pull the end of the rail away from the panel and slide the belt from it.
4 Prise the moulded cap from the centre pillar anchorage and remove the bolt.
5 Prise the belt guide runner from the rear quarter trim panel and slide the runner from the belt.
6 Remove the rear quarter trim panel (Section 32).
7 Unbolt the reel/belt assembly from the inner rear quarter body panel.

Refitting

8 Refitting is a reversal of removal, but ensure that any spacers, plates and washers are in correct sequence and tighten all bolts to the specified torque wrench settings.

Front belt - 5-door models

Note: *Note the fitted sequence of any plates, washers and spacers when unbolting the seat belt anchors.*

Removal

9 Proceed as described in paragraphs 1 and 2.
10 Prise the moulded cap from the centre pillar anchorage and remove the bolt.
11 Remove the pillar lower trim panel (see Section 32).
12 Unbolt the inertia reel and the anchor plate from the centre pillar.

Refitting

13 Refitting is a reversal of removal, but ensure that any spacers, plates and washers are in correct sequence and tighten all bolts to the specified torque wrench settings.

Front belt - Cabriolet

Note: *Note the fitted sequence of any plates, washers and spacers when unbolting the seat belt anchors.*

Removal

14 Unbolt the centre stalk.
15 Remove the clip and pull back the trim to expose the upper anchor. Unscrew the anchor bolt.
16 Unbolt and pull out the lower mounting rail. Slide the belt from the rail.
17 Remove the rear quarter trim panel then pull the belt through the slot in the panel and through the pillar guide.
18 Unbolt the inertia reel unit.

Refitting

19 Refitting is a reversal of removal, but ensure that any spacers, plates and washers are in correct sequence and tighten all bolts to the specified torque wrench settings.

Rear belt - Saloon models

Note: *Note the fitted sequence of any plates, washers and spacers when unbolting the seat belt anchors.*

Removal

20 Raise the rear seat cushion and remove the anchor bolt from the floor pan.
21 Unclip the elasticated strap from the lower belt buckle.
22 Unbolt the inertia reel anchor plate from the floor.
23 Unbolt the belt from the body pillar upper section.
24 Prise out the belt guide runner from the rear package tray support panel and slide the runner from the belt.
25 Raise the inertia reel cover, unscrew the reel mounting bolt and withdraw reel and spacer.

Refitting

26 Refitting is a reversal of removal, but ensure that any spacers, plates and washers are in correct sequence and tighten all bolts to the specified torque wrench settings.

Rear belt - Estate models

Note: *Note the fitted sequence of any plates, washers and spacers when unbolting the seat belt anchors.*

Removal

27 Proceed as described in paragraphs 20 to 22.
28 Raise the moulded cap from the support strap mounting, slide the mounting plate to one side until the large hole passes over the bolt head and the strap can be removed.
29 Unscrew the cap and bolt.
30 Raise the cover on the inertia reel to expose the bolt and unbolt the reel.

Refitting

31 Refitting is a reversal of removal, but ensure that any spacers, plates and washers are in correct sequence and tighten all bolts to the specified torque wrench settings.

Rear belt - Cabriolet

Note: *Note the fitted sequence of any plates, washers and spacers when unbolting the seat belt anchors.*

Removal

32 Raise the rear seat cushion.
33 Release the buckles from the elasticated straps.
34 Unbolt the seat belts from their floor mountings.

Refitting

35 Refitting is a reversal of removal, but ensure that any spacers, plates and washers are in correct sequence and tighten all bolts to the specified torque wrench settings.

28 Interior mirror - removal and refitting

Removal

1 The interior mirror is bonded to the windscreen glass. If it must be removed, grip the mirror firmly and push it forward to break the adhesive bond.
2 When refitting the mirror, the following preliminary work must first be carried out.
3 Remove existing adhesive from the windscreen glass using a suitable solvent. Allow the solvent to evaporate. The location of the mirror base is marked on the glass with a black patch, so that there should not be any chance of an error when fitting.

Refitting

4 If the original mirror is being refitted, clean all the old adhesive from the mirror mounting base, and apply a new adhesive patch to it.

5 If a new windscreen is being installed, peel off the protective layer from the black patch, which is pre-coated with adhesive.
6 Peel off the protective layer from the mirror adhesive patch and locate the mirror precisely onto the black patch on the screen. Hold it in position for at least two minutes.
7 For best results, the fitting of a bonded type mirror should be carried out in an ambient temperature of 70°C (158°F). The careful use of a blower heater on both the glass and mirror should achieve this temperature level.

29 Rear parcel shelf - removal and refitting

Removal

1 Open the tailgate fully and disengage the parcel shelf lifting strap loops from the tailgate retaining knobs.
2 Lift out the parcel shelf pivot pins from their notches in the support brackets and withdraw the shelf.
3 Pull each strap loop through its hole in the rear edge of the shelf by disengaging the upper and lower retaining collars.
4 The shelf brackets are secured with pop rivets which must be drilled out if the brackets are to be removed.

Refitting

5 Refitting is a reversal of removal.

30 Centre console - removal and refitting

Removal

1 Remove the gear lever knob.
2 Pull the rubber gaiter up the lever and remove it.
3 Undo the four screws and remove the console (**see illustrations**).

Refitting

4 Refitting is a reversal of removal.

30.3a Centre console lower retaining screws (arrowed)

11

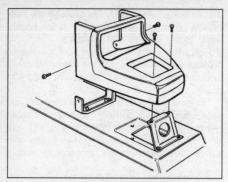

30.3b Centre console fixings

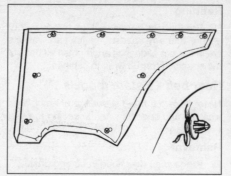

32.4 Rear quarter trim panel securing clip locations

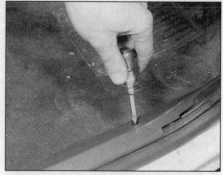

32.7 Removing a sill scuff plate securing screw

31 Glove compartment - removal and refitting

Pre-1986 models

Removal

1 Open the glovebox lid and extract the screws which hold the glovebox to the facia.
2 Remove the latch (two screws).
3 Remove the single screw inside the top of the glove compartment which holds it to the moulded bracket. Withdraw the glove compartment.

Refitting

4 Refitting is a reversal of removal.

1986 models onwards

Removal

5 Undo the two screws and remove the glove compartment lid.
6 Remove the latch (two screws) and disconnect the lamp wiring (where fitted).
7 Undo the three screws and remove the glove compartment.

Refitting

8 Refitting is a reversal of removal.

32 Interior trim panels - removal and refitting

Rear quarter trim panel

Removal

1 Unbolt the seat belt from its floor mounting.
2 Pass the belt buckle slide through the panel aperture.
3 Pull the seat cushion and backrest forward.
4 Extract the single screw from the quarter panel and then using a suitable forked tool, lever out the clips and remove the panel **(see illustration)**.
5 The clips and ashtray are detachable after the panel has been withdrawn.

Refitting

6 Refitting is a reversal of removal; tighten the seat belt anchor bolt to the specified torque.

Cowl side trim panel

Removal

7 Extract the two screws from the scuff plate **(see illustration)**.
8 Remove the two clips and detach the panel by pulling it from its two locating pegs **(see illustration)**.

Refitting

9 Refitting is a reversal of removal.

Windscreen pillar trim panel

Removal

10 Remove the windscreen as described in Section 20.
11 Pull off the door aperture weatherstrip.
12 Peel back the edges of the trim panel and remove it.

Refitting

13 Refitting is a reversal of removal, but refit the windscreen as described in Section 20.

Centre pillar trim panels

Removal

14 Remove the two seat belt anchorages from the pillar.
15 Pull off the weatherstrips from the door apertures.
16 Remove the upper trim panel from the pillar.

32.8 Removing cowl side trim panel

17 On three-door models, the rear quarter window will first have to be removed before the pillar trim panel can be withdrawn.
18 The lower trim panel can be removed from the pillar after the four screws have been extracted.

Refitting

19 Refitting is a reversal of removal, but tighten the seat belt anchor bolts to the specified torque.

Rear pillar trim panel

Removal

20 Remove the rear seat belt upper anchorage.
21 Fold down the rear seat back.
22 Extract the five securing screws and remove the trim panel **(see illustration)**.

Refitting

23 Refitting is a reversal of removal, but tighten the seat belt anchor bolts to the specified torque.

Tailgate trim panel

24 This comprises a flat panel secured with push-in type clips. If a rear wiper is fitted, this will have a moulded cover over the wiper motor secured by quarter-turn fasteners.
25 To remove the moulded cover, turn the heads of the fasteners through 90° to release them **(see illustration)**.

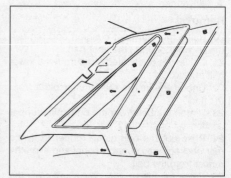

32.22 Rear pillar trim panel securing screw locations

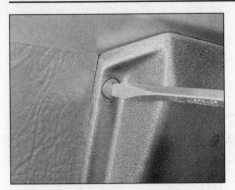

32.25 Releasing a tailgate moulded cover fastener

Rear wheelhouse covers

26 These are fitted to certain Base and L models and are of moulded type. On Ghia versions the covers are cloth covered while on 5-door versions, the covers have an upper finisher held by two screws.

Load space trim panel

27 These take the form of moulded panels on "high series" trim models and flat panels on Base and L versions. The panels are held in position by external clips.

Door trim panels

28 Refer to Section 11 of this Chapter.

33 Facia - removal and refitting

Pre-1986 models

Removal

1 Disconnect the battery negative lead.
2 Remove the under-dash cover panels.
3 Refer to Chapter 10 and remove the steering column assembly.
4 Refer to Chapter 12 and remove the instrument panel.
5 Where applicable, refer to Chapter 12 and remove the warning indicator control unit of the auxiliary warning system, and where fitted, the fuel computer.
6 Detach the heater controls, switches and wiring multi-plugs, with reference to Chapter 3.
7 Remove the ashtray and cigar lighter mounting panel.
8 Remove the radio and its mounting bracket (Chapter 12).
9 Disconnect the wire from the loudspeaker and remove the speaker (four screws).
10 Remove the glove compartment (Section 31).
11 Where fitted, remove the choke cable (Chapter 4).
12 Detach the vent ducts and demister hoses from the heater.
13 Extract the securing screws and clips and remove the facia panel complete with crash pad (see illustrations).

14 The crash padding can be detached by removing the glove compartment mounting bracket and lock bracket, withdrawing the side and centre face level vents and extracting all the securing clips.

Refitting

15 Refitting is a reversal of removal.

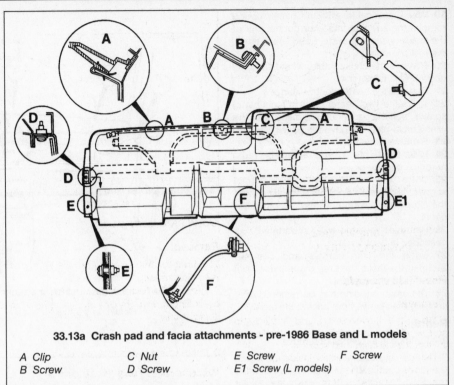

33.13a Crash pad and facia attachments - pre-1986 Base and L models

A Clip	C Nut	E Screw	F Screw
B Screw	D Screw	E1 Screw (L models)	

1986 models onwards

Removal

16 Disconnect the battery negative lead.
17 Refer to Chapter 10 and remove the steering column assembly.
18 Refer to Chapter 12 and remove the instrument panel.

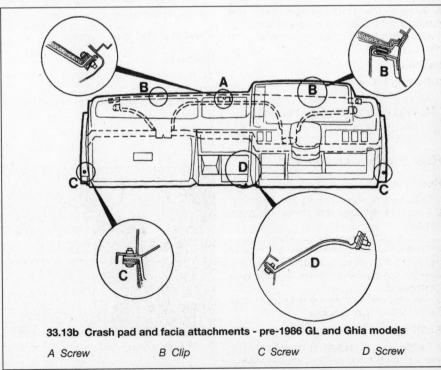

33.13b Crash pad and facia attachments - pre-1986 GL and Ghia models

A Screw	B Clip	C Screw	D Screw

11

19 Where applicable, refer to Chapter 12 and remove the warning indicator control unit of the auxiliary warning system and where fitted, the fuel computer.

20 Remove the choke cable, where fitted, as described in Chapter 4.

21 Remove the heater control knobs.

22 Undo the two heater control facia panel screws, pull the panel out and disconnect the wiring multi-plug. Remove the panel.

23 Remove the ashtray.

24 Refer to Chapter 12 and remove the radio or radio/cassette player.

25 Undo the radio/ashtray facia panel screws, withdraw the panel and disconnect the cigar lighter wiring, if fitted. Remove the panel.

26 Remove the glove compartment as described in Section 31.

27 Undo the nine screws and one nut securing the facia, then remove the unit from the car **(see illustration)**.

28 The crash padding can be removed after undoing the screws from behind the facia.

Refitting

29 Refitting is a reversal of removal.

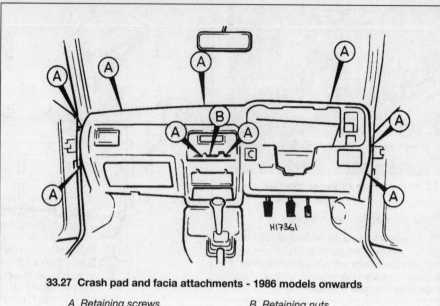

33.27 Crash pad and facia attachments - 1986 models onwards

A *Retaining screws*   B *Retaining nuts*

Chapter 12
Electrical system

Contents

Degrees of difficulty

Easy, suitable for novice with little experience	**Fairly easy,** suitable for beginner with some experience	**Fairly difficult,** suitable for competent DIY mechanic	**Difficult,** suitable for experienced DIY mechanic	**Very difficult,** suitable for expert DIY or professional

Specifications

System type . . . . 12 volt, negative earth

Bulbs   **Wattage**

Headlamp:
  Halogen 60/55
  Tungsten 50/45W
Front sidelamp 4W
Front indicator lamp 21W
Stop/tail lamp 21/5W
Reversing lamp 21W
Rear foglamp . . . . 21 W
Rear indicator lamp 21W
Rear number plate lamp 5W
Auxiliary lamp (Halogen) 55W
Foglamp (Halogen) 55W
Instrument cluster warning lamps 1.3W
Panel illumination 2.6W
Cigar lighter illumination 1.4W
Glove compartment lamp 2W
Luggage compartment lamp 10W
Interior lamp 10W

Windscreen wipers

Wiper blades:
  Front . . . . Champion X-4503
  Rear . . . . Champion X-5103
Wiper arms:
  Front . . . . Champion CCA6
  Rear . . . . Champion type not available

12

Torque wrench settings

	Nm	lbf ft
Horn to body	25 to 35	18 to 26
Windscreen wiper arm to pivot mounting	15 to 18	11 to 13
Rear wiper arm to pivot mounting	12 to 15	9 to 11
Reversing lamp switch to transmission	16 to 20	12 to 15
Door window motor mounting bolts	4 to 5	3 to 4
Window regulator bolts	4 to 5	3 to 4

1 General information and precautions

General information

The body electrical system consists of all lights, wash/wipe equipment, interior electrical equipment, and associated switches and wiring.

The electrical system is of the 12 volt negative earth type. Power to the system is provided by a 12-volt battery, which is charged by the alternator (see Chapter 5).

The engine electrical system (battery, alternator, starter motor, ignition system) is covered separately in Chapter 5.

Precautions

⚠️ *Warning: Before carrying out any work on the electrical system, read through the precautions given in "Safety first!" at the beginning of this manual, and in Chapter 5.*

Prior to working on any component in the electrical system, the battery negative lead should first be disconnected, to prevent the possibility of electrical short circuits and/or fires.

2 Electrical fault finding - general information

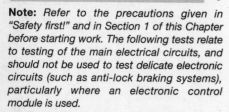

Note: *Refer to the precautions given in "Safety first!" and in Section 1 of this Chapter before starting work. The following tests relate to testing of the main electrical circuits, and should not be used to test delicate electronic circuits (such as anti-lock braking systems), particularly where an electronic control module is used.*

General

1 A typical electrical circuit consists of an electrical component, any switches, relays, motors, fuses, fusible links or circuit breakers related to that component, and the wiring and connectors which link the component to both the battery and the chassis. To help pinpoint a problem in a circuit, wiring diagrams are included at the end of this manual.

2 Before attempting to diagnose an electrical fault, first study the appropriate wiring diagram, to obtain a more complete understanding of the components included in the particular circuit concerned. The possible sources of a fault can be narrowed down by noting whether other components related to the circuit are operating properly. If several components or circuits fail at one time, the problem is likely to be related to a shared fuse or earth connection.

3 Electrical problems usually stem from simple causes, such as loose or corroded connections, a faulty earth connection, a blown fuse, a melted fusible link, or a faulty relay (refer to Section 3 for details of testing relays). Visually inspect the condition of all fuses, wires and connections in a problem circuit before testing the components. Use the wiring diagrams to determine which terminal connections will need to be checked, in order to pinpoint the trouble-spot.

4 The basic tools required for electrical fault-finding include a circuit tester or voltmeter (a 12-volt bulb with a set of test leads can also be used for certain tests); a self-powered test light (sometimes known as a continuity tester); an ohmmeter (to measure resistance); a battery and set of test leads; and a jumper wire, preferably with a circuit breaker or fuse incorporated, which can be used to bypass suspect wires or electrical components. Before attempting to locate a problem with test instruments, use the wiring diagram to determine where to make the connections.

5 To find the source of an intermittent wiring fault (usually due to a poor or dirty connection, or damaged wiring insulation), a "wiggle" test can be performed on the wiring. This involves wiggling the wiring by hand, to see if the fault occurs as the wiring is moved. It should be possible to narrow down the source of the fault to a particular section of wiring. This method of testing can be used in conjunction with any of the tests described in the following sub-Sections.

6 Apart from problems due to poor connections, two basic types of fault can occur in an electrical circuit - open-circuit or short-circuit.

7 Open-circuit faults are caused by a break somewhere in the circuit, which prevents current from flowing. An open-circuit fault will prevent a component from working, but will not cause the relevant circuit fuse to blow.

8 Short-circuit faults are caused by a "short" somewhere in the circuit, which allows the current flowing in the circuit to "escape" along an alternative route, usually to earth. Short-circuit faults are normally caused by a breakdown in wiring insulation, which allows a feed wire to touch either another wire, or an earthed component such as the bodyshell. A short-circuit fault will normally cause the relevant circuit fuse to blow.

Finding an open-circuit

9 To check for an open-circuit, connect one lead of a circuit tester or voltmeter to either the negative battery terminal or a known good earth.

10 Connect the other lead to a connector in the circuit being tested, preferably nearest to the battery or fuse.

11 Switch on the circuit, bearing in mind that some circuits are live only when the ignition switch is moved to a particular position.

12 If voltage is present (indicated either by the tester bulb lighting or a voltmeter reading, as applicable), this means that the section of the circuit between the relevant connector and the battery is problem-free.

13 Continue to check the remainder of the circuit in the same fashion.

14 When a point is reached at which no voltage is present, the problem must lie between that point and the previous test point with voltage. Most problems can be traced to a broken, corroded or loose connection.

Finding a short-circuit

15 To check for a short-circuit, first disconnect the load(s) from the circuit (loads are the components which draw current from a circuit, such as bulbs, motors, heating elements, etc).

16 Remove the relevant fuse from the circuit, and connect a circuit tester or voltmeter to the fuse connections.

17 Switch on the circuit, bearing in mind that some circuits are live only when the ignition switch is moved to a particular position.

18 If voltage is present (indicated either by the tester bulb lighting or a voltmeter reading, as applicable), this means that there is a short-circuit.

19 If no voltage is present, but the fuse still blows with the load(s) connected, this indicates an internal fault in the load(s).

Finding an earth fault

20 The battery negative terminal is connected to "earth" - the metal of the engine/transmission and the car body - and most systems are wired so that they only receive a positive feed, the current returning via the metal of the car body. This means that the component mounting and the body form part of that circuit. Loose or corroded mountings can therefore cause a range of electrical faults, ranging from total failure of a circuit, to a puzzling partial fault. In particular, lights may shine dimly (especially when another circuit sharing the same earth point is in operation), motors (eg wiper motors or the radiator cooling fan motor) may run slowly, and the operation of one circuit may have an apparently-unrelated effect on another. Note that on many vehicles, earth straps are used between certain components, such as the engine/transmission and the body, usually where there is no metal-to-metal contact between components, due to flexible rubber mountings, etc.

21 To check whether a component is properly earthed, disconnect the battery, and connect one lead of an ohmmeter to a known good earth point. Connect the other lead to the wire or earth connection being tested. The resistance reading should be zero; if not, check the connection as follows.

22 If an earth connection is thought to be faulty, dismantle the connection, and clean back to bare metal both the bodyshell and the wire terminal or the component earth connection mating surface. Be careful to remove all traces of dirt and corrosion, then use a knife to trim away any paint, so that a clean metal-to-metal joint is made. On reassembly, tighten the joint fasteners securely; if a wire terminal is being refitted, use serrated washers between the terminal and the bodyshell, to ensure a clean and secure connection. When the connection is remade, prevent the onset of corrosion in the future by applying a coat of petroleum jelly or silicone-based grease, or by spraying on (at regular intervals) a proprietary ignition sealer, or a water-dispersant lubricant.

3 Fuses, relays and circuit breakers - general information

Pre-1986 models

1 The fuses and most of the relays are located in a plastic box attached to the bulkhead on the driver's side of the engine compartment.

2 The fuses are numbered to identify the circuit which they protect and the circuits are represented by symbols on the plastic fusebox cover (see illustrations).

3 When an accessory or other electrical component or system fails, always check the fuse first. The fuses are coloured red (10A), blue (15A), yellow (20A), clear (25A) and green (30A). Always renew a fuse with one of an identical rating. Never renew a fuse more than once without finding the source of the trouble. Spare fuses are carried in the fusebox lid.

4 The radio, and where fitted, electrically operated aerial, have their own in-line circuit fuses, or are fused in the rear of the radio casing.

5 Relays are of the plug-in type and will be found within the fusebox with a symbol on the cover designating the relay circuit. Additional relays for the headlamp washers, fuel injection system and speed sensor (where fitted) are located below the facia on the driver's side,

3.2a Fuse and relay box showing plastic cover removal (2), fuse removal (3) and relays (4). Check if fuse has blown at point indicated in inset

H16318

and a relay for the central locking system is located under the instrument panel next to the glove compartment.

6 Circuit breakers are only fitted to vehicles equipped with electrically operated windows or a central locking system. The circuit breakers are also located in the fusebox.

1986 models onwards

7 The fusebox and its location are the same on later models but the fuse positions and circuits protected have been rearranged. Additional fuses are still used and located as for early models. A central locking system relay is no longer fitted following circuit modifications.

8 Relays located in the fusebox have their circuits designated by a symbol for identification. Up to six additional relays are located under the instrument panel on the driver's side. These are used in conjunction with the speed sensor, diode assembly, fuel-injection system, heated windscreen, and dim-dip lighting system. On certain RS Turbo models, a relay to prevent radio interference by the ignition system is fitted adjacent to the fuel-injection module behind the plenum chamber in the engine compartment.

9 The direction indicator/hazard flasher relay is located at the rear of the direction indicator multi-function switch on the steering column.

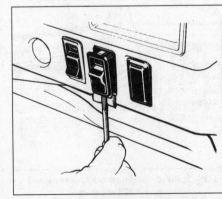

4.5 Rear window wash/wipe switch removal - pre-1986 models

3.2b Fusebox location (arrowed) on engine compartment bulkhead - cover removed to show fuses and relays

4 Switches - removal and refitting

General

1 Disconnect the battery negative terminal before removing any switches.

Pre-1986 models

Wiper delay switch

2 Remove the switch knob and the bezel nut.

3 Withdraw the switch through the parcel tray and disconnect it from the wiring harness.

4 Refitting is a reversal of removal.

Rear foglamp, heated rear window, rear window wash/wipe switches

5 Using a screwdriver carefully prise the switch from the facia panel (see illustration).

6 Disconnect the wiring multi-plug and remove the switch.

7 Refitting is a reversal of removal.

Steering column multi-function switches

8 Undo the screws and remove the upper and lower steering column shrouds.

12

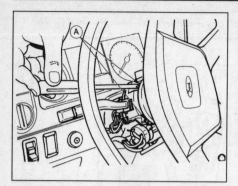

4.9 Steering column multi-function switch removal pre-1986 models
A Switch retaining screws

9 Undo the switch retaining screws, disconnect the wiring multiplug and remove the switch **(see illustration)**.
10 Refitting is a reversal of removal.

Load space lamp switch - all models except Cabriolet

11 Open the tailgate and release the four trim panel fasteners.
12 Disconnect the lead from the switch and remove the switch retaining screw.
13 Refitting is a reversal of removal.

Local space lamp switch - Cabriolet models

14 Open the boot lid and undo the switch retaining screw.
15 Withdraw the switch and disconnect the lead. Tape the lead to the rear panel to prevent it dropping in the hole.
16 Refitting is a reversal of removal.

Courtesy lamp switch

17 Extract the screw securing the switch to the door pillar.
18 Withdraw the switch from its rubber shroud and disconnect the lead. Tape the lead to the pillar to prevent it dropping in hole **(see illustration)**.
19 Refitting is a reversal of removal.

Ignition switch

20 Refer to Chapter 5, Part A.

4.18 Courtesy lamp switch removal from door pillar

Reversing lamp switch

Manual transmission

21 On manual transmission models the switch is located on the forward facing side of the transmission housing beneath the clutch release lever.
22 Working in the engine compartment disconnect the switch wiring and unscrew the switch.
23 Refitting is a reversal of removal.

Automatic transmission

24 On automatic transmission models the reversing lamp switch is combined with the starter inhibitor switch, and reference should be made to Chapter 7, Part B.

Stop-lamp switch/handbrake warning switch

25 Refer to Chapter 9.

Heater blower motor switch

26 Remove the switch knob by carefully pulling it off.
27 Depress the two tangs and withdraw the switch from the facia **(see illustration)**.
28 Disconnect the wiring and remove the switch.
29 Refitting is a reversal of removal.

Electric window switch

30 Carefully lever the switch from the armrest and disconnect the multi-plug connector.
31 Refit by reversing the removal operations.

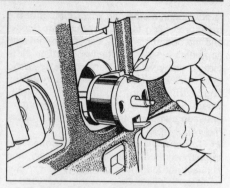

4.27 Removing the heater blower motor switch - pre-1986 models

Loudspeaker balance control joystick

32 Disconnect the battery.
33 Use a screwdriver and carefully prise free the balance control bezel **(see illustration)**.
34 Pull free the cassette stowage box from its aperture.
35 Rotate the securing clip anti-clockwise to remove it and the balance control from the box **(see illustration)**. Detach the wiring multi-plug.
36 Refit in the reverse order of removal.

1986 models onwards

Note: *With the exception of the switches listed in the following paragraphs, removal and refitting of all switches is as described previously in this Section for pre-1986 models.*

Heated windscreen/rear window, rear foglamp switches

37 Undo the two screws, carefully remove the instrument panel bezel then prise out the switch with a screwdriver **(see illustration)**.
38 Disconnect the wiring multi-plug and remove the switch.
39 Refitting is a reversal of removal.

Steering column multi-function switches

40 Remove the steering wheel (Chapter 10).
41 Undo the screws and remove the upper and lower steering column shroud **(see illustrations)**.

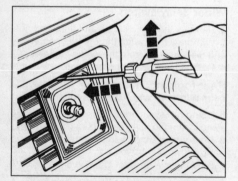

4.33 Removing the speaker balance control bezel - pre-1986 models

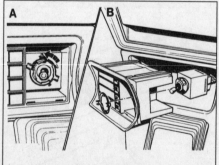

4.35 Speaker balance control removal - pre-1986 models
A Releasing the securing clip
B Balance control removal from stowage box

4.37 Rear foglamp switch removal - models from 1986 onwards

4.41a Unscrewing the steering column shroud upper . . .

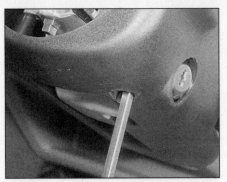

4.41b . . . and lower retaining screws

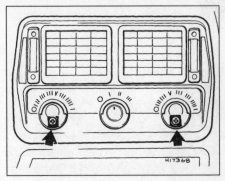

4.47 Heater control panel retaining screw locations - 1986 models onwards

42 Undo the retaining screws and remove the switch from the steering column.

43 Disconnect the switch wiring multi-plug.

44 If removing the direction indicator multi-function switch, remove the hazard flasher switch and relay if required.

45 Refitting is a reversal of removal, but refit the steering wheel with reference to Chapter 10.

Heater blower motor switch

46 Carefully pull off the three heater control knobs.

47 Undo the two retaining screws and remove the heater control panel **(see illustration)**.

48 Undo the two switch panel-to-facia securing screws and withdraw the panel.

49 Depress the two tabs on either side of the switch and remove the switch.

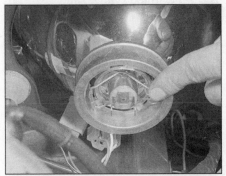

5.2 Releasing headlamp bulb spring clip arms

50 Disconnect the switch wiring multi-plug.

51 Refitting is a reversal of removal.

Door mirror control switch

52 Using a thin screwdriver carefully prise the switch out of its location in the facia.

53 Disconnect the wiring multi-plug and remove the switch.

54 Refitting is a reversal of removal.

Loudspeaker balance control joystick

55 Disconnect the battery then remove the instrument panel as described in Section 9.

56 Carefully prise off the trim bezel using a screwdriver.

57 Turn the retaining clip anti-clockwise and remove the clip.

58 From within the instrument panel aperture disconnect the wiring multi-plug and remove the unit.

59 Refit in the reverse order of removal.

5 Bulbs (exterior lamps) - renewal

Headlamp

1 From within the engine compartment pull the multi-plug from the rear of the headlamp.

2 Remove the rubber gaiter and rotate the bulb securing clip or release the spring clip arms according to type **(see illustration)**.

3 Withdraw the bulb, taking care not to touch the glass with your fingers **(see illustration)**. If the glass is touched, wipe the bulb with a rag

moistened with methylated spirit.

4 Fit the new bulb using a reversal of the removal procedure, taking care not to touch the glass.

Front sidelamp

5 The bulbholder is located on the side of the headlamp unit and is removed by twisting it anti-clockwise **(see illustration)**.

6 Withdraw the push-fit bulb from the holder.

7 Fit the new bulb using a reversal of the removal procedure.

Front direction indicator lamp

8 Working through the aperture in the inner wing panel in the engine compartment, turn the bulbholder anti-clockwise and withdraw it from the lens unit **(see illustration)**.

9 Depress and turn the bulb anti-clockwise to remove it from the holder.

10 Fit the new bulb using a reversal of the removal procedure.

Front direction indicator side repeater lamp

11 Reach up behind the front wheelarch and locate the back of the repeater lamp holder.

12 Depress the two clips on the holder body and push the assembly outwards and out of the wing.

13 Twist the bulbholder anti-clockwise to free it from the lens.

14 Pull the bulb from its socket.

15 Push in a new bulb and refit the assembly in the reverse order to removal.

5.3 Headlamp bulb removal

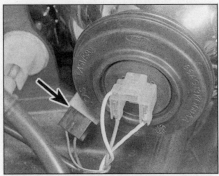

5.5 Sidelamp bulb location (arrowed) in side of headlamp

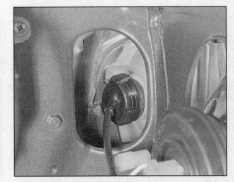

5.8 Front indicator bulbholder accessible through inner wing panel aperture

12

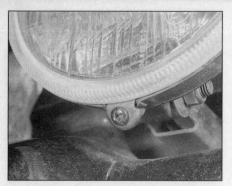

5.16 Front auxiliary lamp lens retaining screw

5.17 Disconnecting auxiliary lamp earth lead

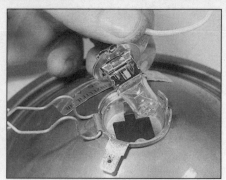

5.18 Removing the auxiliary lamp bulbholder

Front auxiliary lamp and foglamp

16 Undo the retaining screw at the bottom of the lens and withdraw the lens assembly **(see illustration)**.

17 Disconnect the earth lead and remove the lens **(see illustration)**.

18 Spring back the clip legs and remove the bulbholder, then withdraw the bulb **(see illustration)**. Avoid touching the bulb glass with your fingers. If the glass is touched, wipe it with a cloth moistened in methylated spirit.

19 Fit the new bulb using a reversal of the removal procedure, taking care not to touch the glass.

Rear lamps - Saloon

20 Open the tailgate, reach down and depress the retaining tab on the side of the bulbholder. Swing the bulbholder outward to release the locating tag at the other end **(see illustration)**.

21 Remove the relevant bulb by pushing down and turning anti-clockwise.

22 Fit the new bulb using a reversal of the removal procedure.

Rear lamp - Cabriolet

23 Open the boot and pull the bulb cover open.

24 Push the upper and lower retaining tabs apart and withdraw the bulbholder.

25 Remove the relevant bulb by pushing down and turning anti-clockwise.

26 Fit the new bulb using a reversal of the removal procedure.

Rear lamps - Estate

27 Open the tailgate and release the side trim panel by turning the four screws a quarter of a turn with a coin.

28 Push the upper and lower retaining tabs apart and withdraw the bulbholder.

29 Remove the relevant bulb by pushing down and turning anti-clockwise.

30 Fit the new bulb using a reversal of the removal procedure.

Rear lamp - Van

31 Open the rear doors and remove the rear trim panel to gain access to the bulbholders (where applicable).

32 Remove the individual bulbholders by turning anti-clockwise, then similarly remove the bulbs from the holders.

33 Fit the new bulb using a reversal of the removal procedure.

Rear number plate lamp

34 Using a small screwdriver carefully prise the lamp out of the bumper.

35 On pre-1986 models turn the bulbholder anti-clockwise and remove it from the lens. Withdraw the push-fit bulb **(see illustration)**.

36 On 1986 models onwards spread the retaining clips and withdraw the bulbholder. Remove the bulb by pushing and turning anti-clockwise.

37 Fit the new bulb using a reversal of the removal procedure.

6 Bulbs (interior lamps) - renewal

Pre-1986 models

Glove compartment lamp

1 This is simply a matter of gently pulling the bulb from its holder.

Heater control illumination lamp

2 Slide the heater control levers to the top of their travel.

3 Pull off the heater motor switch knob, then unclip the control trim panel from the facia.

4 Pull the bulb from the lamp socket.

5 Refitting is a reversal of removal.

Hazard warning switch lamp

6 Grip the switch cover and pull it off.

7 Gently pull the bulb from its socket **(see illustration)**.

8 Refitting is a reversal of removal.

Interior lamp

9 Carefully prise the lamp from its location and remove the bulb from its spring contact on the lamp body.

10 Fit the new bulb using a reversal of the removal procedure.

Load space lamp

11 Using a thin screwdriver, prise the lamp from its location **(see illustration)**.

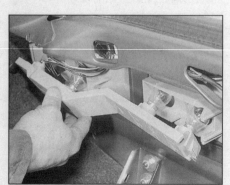

5.20 Removing the rear lamp bulbholder for access to the bulbs

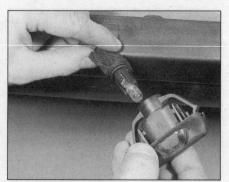

5.35 Removing the number plate lamp bulbholder from the lens

6.7 Hazard warning switch bulb renewal - pre-1986 models

6.11 Removing the load space lamp

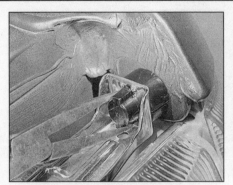

7.3a Releasing the headlamp side plastic retaining clip head

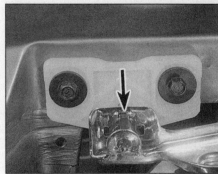

7.3b Headlamp upper plastic retaining clip head (arrowed)

12 Remove the bulb from its spring contact clip.
13 Fit the new bulb using a reversal of the removal procedure.

Load space lamp (Cabriolet)

14 Open the boot lid and prise out the lamp with a thin screwdriver.
15 Depress and twist the bulb from the holder.
16 Fit the new bulb using a reversal of the removal procedure.

Roof-mounted clock illumination lamp

17 Remove the clock (Section 13).
18 Remove the rear cover from the unit by depressing the two clips at the top outer corners of the cover.
19 The bulb is a bayonet fitting in its holder.
20 Refitting is a reversal of removal.

7.8a Removing the retaining clip . . .

1986 models onwards

Note: *With the exception of the bulbs listed in the following paragraphs, removal and refitting of all bulbs is as described previously in this Section for pre-1986 models.*

Glove compartment lamp

21 From inside the glove compartment undo the two switch assembly retaining screws and withdraw the assembly.
22 Using a thin screwdriver carefully prise out the switch and remove the bulb by pushing and turning anti-clockwise.
23 Refitting is a reversal of removal.

Heater control illumination lamp

24 Pull off the three heater control knobs.
25 Undo the two retaining screws and withdraw the heater control panel.
26 From the rear of the panel, push and turn the bulb anti-clockwise to remove.
27 Fit the new bulb using a reversal of the removal procedure.

Manual choke knob warning lamp

28 Remove the choke knob by depressing the pin located on the underside of the knob.
29 Withdraw the sleeve, then remove the bulb by pushing it down, then pushing down the bulb retainer using a thin screwdriver.
30 Refitting is a reversal of removal.

Fuel computer lamp

31 Remove the fuel computer (Section 14).
32 Using thin-nosed pliers, turn the bulbholder anti-clockwise to remove it then withdraw the push-fit bulb.

33 Refitting is a reversal of removal.

7 Exterior lamps - removal and refitting

Headlamp

Removal

1 On pre-1986 models, remove the radiator grille as described in Chapter 11.
2 Working in the engine compartment, disconnect the headlamp wiring multi-plug and remove the sidelamp bulbholder.
3 Rotate the side and upper plastic retaining clip heads through 90° to release the headlamp mountings **(see illustrations)**.
4 With the headlamp unit released, pull it sharply forward off its lower ballstud.

Refitting

5 Refitting is a reversal of removal.

Front direction indicator lamp

Removal

6 Working inside the engine compartment disconnect the indicator bulb holder from the lamp.
7 Remove the headlamp as described above.
8 Remove the headlamp upper plastic retaining clip then unscrew the ball-headed bolt **(see illustrations)**.
9 Remove the lower adjuster by turning the collar **(see illustrations)**.

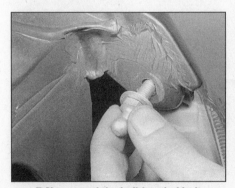

7.8b . . . and the ball-headed bolt

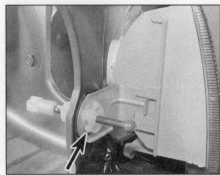

7.9a Release the adjuster by turning the collar (arrowed)

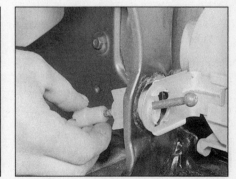

7.9b . . . then remove the adjuster

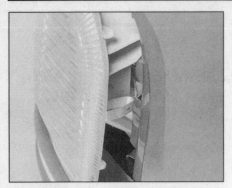

7.10 Release the direction indicator side spring clip

10 Release the side spring clip, then pull the lamp out at the bottom to disengage the upper tangs **(see illustration)**.

Refitting

11 Refitting is a reversal of removal.

Rear lamp

Removal

12 Remove the bulbholder(s) as described in Section 5.
13 Remove the lamp retaining screws or nuts as applicable, and remove the lamp.

Refitting

14 Refitting is a reversal of removal.

9.3 Removing an instrument panel retaining screw - pre-1986 model

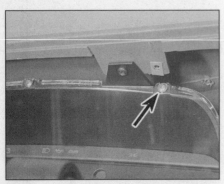

9.9a Instrument panel upper retaining screw (arrowed)

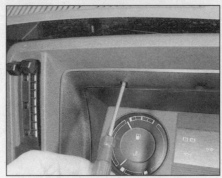

9.2a Extracting the instrument panel bezel screws - pre-1986 model

8 Headlamps and auxiliary lamps - beam alignment

The headlamps are adjustable individually for both horizontal and vertical alignment from within the engine compartment. The auxiliary lamp adjustment is carried out by slackening the lamp mounting and moving the lamp as necessary.

Accurate alignment can only be carried out using optical beam setting equipment, and this work should be entrusted to a Ford dealer.

9 Instrument panel - removal and refitting

Pre-1986 models

Removal

1 Disconnect the battery negative terminal.
2 Extract the screws and pull the instrument panel bezel from the panel. The two clips at the base of the bezel will release by the pulling action **(see illustrations)**.
3 Extract the two screws which hold the panel to the facia **(see illustration)**.
4 Remove the dash under-trim panel, reach up and disconnect the cable from the speedometer by depressing the serrated plastic ring.
5 Gently pull the cluster forwards and to one side so that the wiring multi-plug can be disconnected. Withdraw the panel.

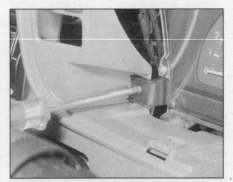

9.9b . . . and lower screw removal - 1986 models onwards

9.2b Removing the instrument panel bezel - pre-1986 model

Refitting

6 Refitting is a reversal of removal.

1986 models onwards

Removal

7 Refer to Chapter 10 and remove the steering wheel.
8 Extract the two screws and pull the instrument panel bezel from the panel. The two clips at the base will release by the pulling action **(see illustration)**.
9 Undo the four screws securing the panel to the facia **(see illustrations)**.
10 Pull the panel away from the facia and disconnect the wiring multi-plug and speedometer cable from the rear of the

9.8 Bezel lower retaining clip (arrowed) - 1986 models onwards

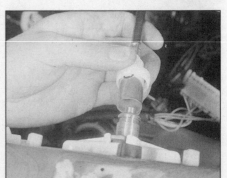

9.10 Disconnecting the speedometer cable

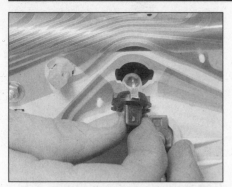

10.2 Instrument panel bulb renewal

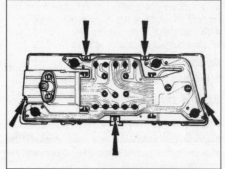

10.11a Instrument panel assembly upper retaining screws-pre-1986 models

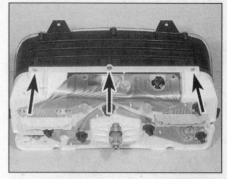

10.11b Instrument panel assembly upper retaining screws - 1986 models onwards

instrument panel. It may be necessary to feed the speedometer cable slack through the bulkhead from the engine compartment to facilitate removal. Withdraw the panel (see illustration).

Refitting

11 Refitting is a reversal of removal.

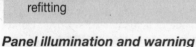

10 Instrument panel components - removal and refitting

Panel illumination and warning lamp bulbs

Removal

1 Remove the instrument panel as described in Section 9.
2 Turn the bulbholders anti-clockwise and remove them from the rear of the instrument panel (see illustration).
3 The bulbs and bulbholders are renewed complete, the bulbs cannot be removed from the holders separately.

Refitting

4 Refit by pushing down and turning clockwise.

Printed circuit

Removal

5 Remove the instrument panel (Section 9).

10.12a Extracting speedometer retaining screws

6 Remove all illumination and warning lamp bulbholders.
7 Undo all the nuts and remove the washers from the printed circuit terminals.
8 Remove the wiring multi-plug retainers and carefully pull the printed circuit off the pins on the rear of the panel.

Refitting

9 Refitting is the reverse sequence to removal.

Speedometer

Removal

10 Remove the instrument panel as described in Section 9.
11 Undo the retaining screws around the edge of the panel at the rear and separate the two panel halves (see illustrations).
12 Undo the two screws and remove the speedometer (see illustrations).

Refitting

13 Refitting is the reverse sequence to removal.

Tachometer

14 The procedure is the same as for the speedometer except that the unit is secured by three nuts.

Fuel and temperature gauges

15 Proceed as for the speedometer but remove the combined gauge assembly after undoing the four nuts.

10.12b Removing the speedometer

11 Cigar lighter - removal and refitting

Removal

1 Disconnect the battery negative terminal.
2 On pre-1986 models remove the ashtray then undo the screws and withdraw the ashtray housing. On 1986 models onwards, refer to Section 21 and remove the radio/cassette player.
3 Disconnect the wiring from the cigar lighter body.
4 Pull out the cigar lighter element.
5 Push the lighter body and illuminating ring out of their locations then separate the ring from the lighter body.

Refitting

6 Refitting is the reverse sequence to removal.

12 Speedometer cable - removal and refitting

Removal

1 Disconnect the battery and remove the instrument panel as described in Section 9.
2 Disconnect the cable from the transmission and release it from its clips and grommet.
3 Withdraw the cable through the bulkhead.

Refitting

4 Refitting is a reversal of removal. The inner and outer cables are supplied as a complete assembly.

13 Clock - removal and refitting

Facia mounted clock

Removal

1 Remove the instrument panel (Section 9).
2 Undo the screws around the edge of the instrument panel at the rear and separate the two panel halves.

12

3 Undo the nuts and remove the clock.

Refitting

4 Refitting is a reversal of removal.

Roof mounted clock

Removal

5 Disconnect the battery negative terminal.
6 Extract the two screws which hold the clock to the header panel.
7 Disconnect the clock and courtesy lamp wiring plug.
8 Detach the lamp from the clock.

Refitting

9 Refit by reversing the removal operations. Once the battery is reconnected, the time must be re-set.

14 Fuel computer components - removal and refitting

Computer unit

Removal

1 Disconnect the battery negative terminal.
2 Undo the two instrument panel bezel retaining screws and ease the bezel out to release the lower clips.

3 Withdraw the computer module from the facia to the right of the instrument panel.
4 Disconnect the wiring multi-plug and remove the computer.

Refitting

5 Refitting is a reversal of removal.

Speed sender unit

Removal

6 Undo the retaining nut and detach the speedometer cable from the speed sender unit **(see illustration)**.
7 Unclip and disconnect the wiring multi-plug.
8 Undo the retaining nut and withdraw the speed sender unit from the transmission.

Refitting

9 Refitting is a reversal of removal.

Fuel flow sensor

Removal

10 The fuel flow sensor is used in conjunction with the fuel computer on fuel-injected models and is located on the fuel distributor at the front left-hand side of the engine compartment.
11 Disconnect the wiring multi-plug then undo the two banjo unions on the side of the unit. Note the position of the sealing washers.

12 Undo the two retaining screws and remove the fuel flow sensor.

Refitting

13 Refitting is the reverse sequence to removal. Ensure that the sealing washers are correctly fitted.

15 Auxiliary warning system components - removal and refitting

General

1 This system monitors the fluid levels and front brake pads for excessive wear. In the event of a fluid level dropping below the specified level, or the brake pads wearing down to the minimum allowable thickness, the driver is warned of the particular malfunction by means of a warning lamp.

Low washer fluid warning switch

Removal

2 Drain or syphon out the reservoir fluid then disconnect the switch multi-plug. Lever the switch away from the seal grommet using the flat blade of a suitable screwdriver. Do not allow fluid to enter the connectors.

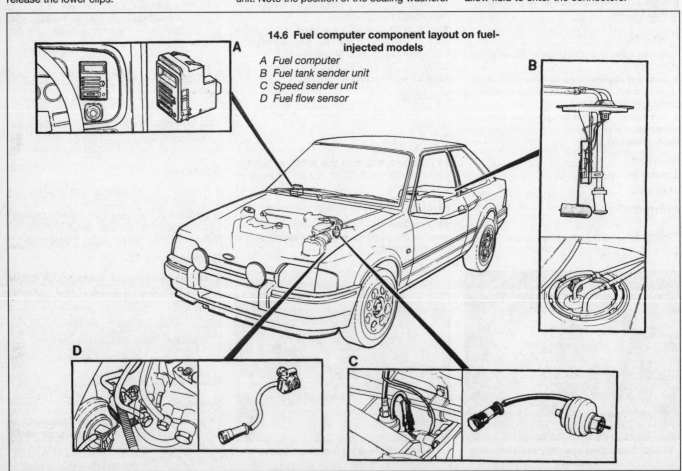

14.6 Fuel computer component layout on fuel-injected models

A Fuel computer
B Fuel tank sender unit
C Speed sender unit
D Fuel flow sensor

Refitting

3 Refit in reverse order of removal, checking that the grommet is correctly seated. On completion, check that the switch is operational and that there are no leaks around the grommet.

Low coolant warning switch

Removal

4 Drain the coolant from the expansion tank (see Chapter 1), having first depressurized the system if necessary.

5 Detach the switch multi-plug and then unscrew the threaded retainer. The switch can then be levered from the seal grommet using a flat-bladed screwdriver. Do not allow coolant to enter the connectors.

Refitting

6 Refit in reverse order, and, on completion, check the switch operation and, when the reservoir is refilled to the specified level, that there are no signs of leaks from the grommet/retainer.

Warning indicator control unit

Removal

7 Remove the radio speaker grille and speaker from the facia.

8 Disconnect the multi-plug from the warning indicator/control assembly and then remove the two nylon fixing nuts which hold the assembly in position on the facia panel. Take care when withdrawing and handling the unit not to knock it, as the integral micro-electronics could be damaged.

Refitting

9 Refit in the reverse order of removal. On completion check that the warning lights function for the initial period of five seconds after the ignition is switched on.

Low fuel sensor unit

10 This is integral with the fuel tank sender unit and is removed from the tank as described in Chapter 4.

Brake pad wear indicators

11 The sensors are integral with the brake

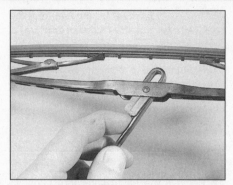
17.2 Disconnecting wiper blade from arm

pads. Refer to Chapter 9 for details of brake pad removal and refitting.

Auxiliary system warning light bulbs

12 The auxiliary warning light bulbs are integral with the instrument panel and are welded in position. They cannot be individually renewed. To remove the instrument panel refer to Section 9.

16 Horn - removal and refitting

Removal

1 The horn(s) are located in the left-hand front corner of the engine compartment. Before removing, disconnect the battery.

2 Disconnect the lead from the horn.

3 Unscrew the single bolt and remove the horn and bracket.

Refitting

4 Refitting is a reversal of removal.

17 Windscreen/tailgate wiper blades and arms - removal and refitting

Removal

1 Pull the wiper arm away from the glass until the arm locks.

2 Depress the small clip on the blade and slide the blade out of the hooked part of the arm **(see illustration)**.

3 Before removing the wiper arms it is worthwhile marking their parked position on the glass with a strip of masking tape as an aid to refitting. Raise the plastic nut cover.

4 Unscrew the nut which holds the arm to the pivot shaft and pull the arm from the splines.

Refitting

5 Refit by reversing the removal operations.

18 Windscreen wiper motor and linkage - removal and refitting

Removal

1 Remove the wiper arms and blades as described in Section 17.

2 Disconnect the battery negative terminal.

3 Remove the nut covers, the fixing nuts, washers and spacers from the pivot shafts.

4 Disconnect the wiper motor wiring at the multi-pin plugs.

5 Unscrew the two fixing bolts and withdraw the motor complete with linkage from the engine compartment **(see illustration)**.

6 Remove the spacers from the pivot shafts.

7 The motor can be separated from the linkage by removing the nut from the crankarm and then unbolting the motor from the mounting.

Refitting

8 Refitting is a reversal of removal, but connect the motor crankarm when the link is aligned with it as shown **(see illustration)**.

19 Tailgate wiper motor - removal and refitting

Removal

1 Disconnect the battery and remove the wiper arm/blade assembly.

2 Remove the pivot shaft nut, spacer and outer seals.

3 Open the tailgate and remove the trim panel (refer to Chapter 11).

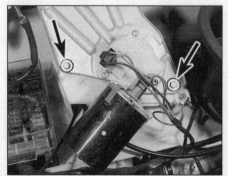
18.5 Windscreen wiper motor fixing bolts (arrowed)

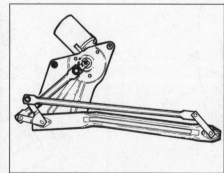
18.8 Windscreen wiper crankarm alignment for refitting

19.4 Tailgate wiper motor retaining bolts (arrowed)

12

4 Release the earth lead and unscrew the two, or on later models, three wiper motor mounting bolts **(see illustration)**.
5 Disconnect the multi-pin plug and remove the motor from the tailgate.
6 Take off the pivot shaft seal, spacer and bracket from the motor.

Refitting

7 Refit by reversing the removal operations.

20 Wash/wipe system components - removal and refitting

Windscreen washer pump

Engine compartment-mounted reservoir

Removal

1 Drain the washer fluid container.
2 Disconnect the lead and washer pipe.
3 Ease the top of the washer pump away from the fluid container and remove it.

Refitting

4 Refitting is a reversal of removal; check that the pump sealing grommet is a good fit.

Windscreen washer pump - wing-mounted reservoir

Removal

5 On some models the windscreen washer pump and fluid reservoir are mounted on the forward end of the underside of the left-hand front wing panel. It also incorporates the headlamp washer pump which also draws its fluid from this reservoir.
6 To remove the reservoir and pump units withdraw the level dipstick and syphon the fluid out of the reservoir through the filler neck.
7 Unscrew and remove the reservoir retaining bolts at its top end from inside the engine compartment.
8 Working under the wheel arch, unscrew and remove the two lower retaining bolts.
9 Withdraw the reservoir, carefully pulling its filler neck through the grommet on the inner wing panel. Disconnect the pump hoses.

10 The pump and fluid level sensor unit can be eased away from their location apertures in the reservoir.

Refitting

11 Refitting is a reversal of removal; check that the pump and fluid level sensor grommets are in good condition when reassembling, and check for leaks on completion.

Tailgate washer pump

Saloon models

Removal

12 Remove the load space trim panel as described in Chapter 11.
13 Disconnect the leads at the multi-plug.
14 Unscrew the three reservoir mounting screws, and remove the reservoir until the fluid pipe can be pulled from the pump.
15 With the reservoir removed, pull the pump from its reservoir seal.

Refitting

16 Refit by reversing the removal operations.

Estate models

Removal

17 Open the tailgate, raise the spare wheel cover and disconnect the electrical leads and fluid pipe from the pump.
18 Extract the two securing screws and remove the pump **(see illustration)**.

Refitting

19 Refitting is a reversal of removal.

Windscreen washer jets

Single jet system - pre-1986 models

Removal

20 Open the bonnet and disconnect the washer pipe from the jet.
21 If the pipe stub on the jet assembly is now pushed to one side, the jet retaining tang will be released and the jet can be removed from the bonnet grille slots.

Refitting

22 Refit by reversing the removal operations. The end of the plastic washer pipe should be warmed in very hot water to make it easier to push onto the jet pipe stub and so avoid breaking it.

23 Adjustment of the jet spray pattern can be done using a pin in the jet nozzle.

Twin jet system - pre-1986 models

24 Later models are fitted with a twin jet windscreen washer system instead of the single jet type used on earlier models.
25 The jets are located as shown, one each side on the bonnet inner panel **(see illustration)**. The washer supply hose is connected to a central T-piece connector which directs the fluid to each jet.
26 The twin jets can be adjusted in the same manner as the earlier single type. They should be set so that the fluid jets hit the windscreen about 250 mm (9.8 in) from the top edge of the windscreen.

Twin jet system - 1986 models onwards

27 1986 models onwards are fitted with a twin jet system but using the same jet type as the early single jet system.
28 Removal, refitting and adjustment procedures for this washer type are therefore the same as described previously.

Tailgate washer jet

Removal

29 Remove the tailgate wiper motor as described in Section 19.
30 Pull the washer jet off the tailgate wiper motor shaft, disconnect the hose and remove the jet.

Refitting

31 Refitting is the reverse of removal.

Headlamp washer pump

Removal

32 Drain the washer reservoir by siphoning, and disconnect the electrical leads from the pump.
33 Disconnect the fluid pipe from the pump.
34 Release the reservoir clamp screw.
35 Ease the top of the pump from the reservoir and remove it upwards.

Refitting

36 Refitting is a reversal of removal.

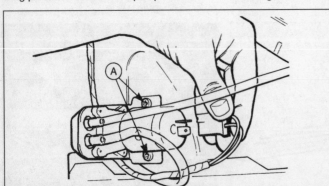

20.18 Tailgate washer pump retaining screws (A) - Estate models

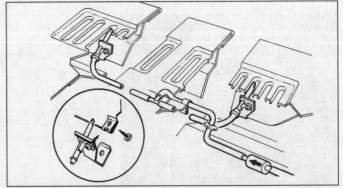

20.25 Twin jet windscreen washer layout - pre-1986 models

Headlamp washer jet

37 The headlamp washer jets are an integral part of the bumper overrider and cannot be removed separately. If a jet is to be renewed for any reason the complete overrider must be obtained (see Chapter 11).

38 Adjustment of the jets entails the use of special tool 32-004. If the tool is not available, have this work carried out by a Ford dealer.

21 Radio/cassette player and graphic equaliser - removal and refitting

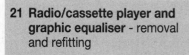

Note: *The information in this Section applies to Ford original equipment fitment components.*

Radio

Early models

Removal

1 Disconnect the battery.

2 Pull off the control knobs, the tuning knob spacer and the tone control lever. Remove the cover panel.

3 Extract the four fixing screws from the front of the radio.

4 Pull the radio far enough from the facia to be able to disconnect the aerial, power supply and earth leads and the speaker wires.

5 Unscrew the two nuts which hold the receiver to the mounting plate. Remove the mounting plate.

6 Take off the rear support bracket and locating plate.

Refitting

7 Refitting is a reversal of removal.

Later models

Removal

8 Disconnect the battery.

9 Remove the radio control knobs and withdraw the tuning knob spacer and the tone control lever.

10 Unscrew and remove the facia plate retaining nuts and washers, then withdraw the facia plate.

11 The radio retaining tangs can now be pulled inwards (towards the centre of the radio) and the radio withdrawn from its aperture. You may need to make a hook-ended rod (welding rod is ideal) to pull the tangs inwards to release the radio **(see illustration)**.

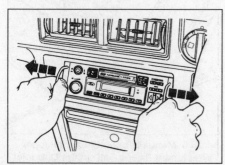

21.18 Radio/cassette player removal using the extractor tools

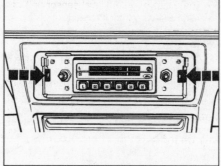

21.11 Later type radio retaining tang locations

12 With the radio withdrawn, disconnect the power lead, the speaker plug, earth lead, the aerial cable and feed.

13 From the rear of the radio remove the plastic support bracket and locating plate, then remove the radio from the front bracket.

Refitting

14 Refitting is the reversal of the removal procedure.

Radio/cassette player

Early models

15 Proceed as described previously in this Section for the radio fitted to early models.

Later models

Removal

16 Disconnect the battery.

17 To withdraw the radio/cassette unit from its aperture you will need to fabricate the U-shaped extractor tools from wire rod of suitable gauge to insert into the withdrawal slots on each side of the unit (in the front face) **(see illustration)**.

18 Insert the withdrawal tools as shown then, pushing each outwards simultaneously, pull them evenly to withdraw the radio/cassette unit **(see illustration)**. It is important that an equal pressure is applied to each tool as the unit is withdrawn.

19 Once withdrawn from its aperture disconnect the aerial cable, the power lead, the aerial feed, the speaker plugs, the earth lead and the light and memory feed (where applicable).

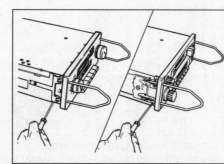

21.20 Releasing the extractor tool after removal

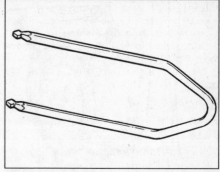

21.17 Radio/cassette player extractor tool

20 Push the retaining clips inwards to remove the removal tool from each side **(see illustration)**.

Refitting

21 Refit in the reverse order of removal. The withdrawal tools do not have to be used, simply push the unit into its aperture until the securing clips engage in their slots.

Graphic equaliser

22 The procedure is the same as for the radio/cassette player as fitted to later models and described previously in this Section.

22 Loudspeakers - removal and refitting

Facia mounted loudspeaker

Removal

1 Carefully prise up the speaker grille using a small screwdriver. Lift it from the facia.

2 Extract the speaker mounting screws which are now exposed.

3 Lift the speaker up until the connecting wires can be disconnected by pulling on their terminals. The wires have different connecting terminals to prevent incorrect connection.

Refitting

4 Refitting is a reversal of removal.

Cowl panel-mounted loudspeaker

Pre-1986 models (except Cabriolet)

Removal

5 Prise out the grille retaining clip.

6 Extract screws as necessary to be able to remove the cowl panel/grille.

7 Extract the four speaker mounting screws and withdraw the speaker until the leads can be disconnected at the rear of the speaker **(see illustration)**.

Refitting

8 Refitting is a reversal of removal.

1986 models onwards (except Cabriolet)

Removal

9 Extract sufficient screws from the scuff plate to facilitate cowl panel removal.

12

22.7 Cowl mounted loudspeaker retaining screw locations - pre-1986 models

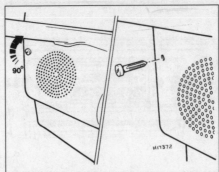

22.10 Cowl mounted loudspeaker panel retainer removal - 1986 models onwards

22.11 Cowl mounted loudspeaker retaining screw locations - 1986 models onwards

10 Insert a screwdriver into the captive plastic retainers and turn 90° anti-clockwise to remove them. Withdraw the cowl panel **(see illustration)**.

11 Undo the three speaker retaining screws, disconnect the leads and remove the speaker **(see illustration)**.

Refitting

12 Refitting is a reversal of removal.

Cabriolet models

Removal

13 Extract the screws from the scuff plate.

14 Extract the end screw from the facia panel.

15 Prise the door weatherseal from the cowl panel.

16 Remove the cowl panel and, if required, unclip the speaker grille.

17 Extract the four speaker mounting screws and withdraw the speaker until the leads can be disconnected.

Refitting

18 Refitting is a reversal of removal.

Rear parcel shelf-mounted loudspeaker

Removal

19 On pre-1986 models, prise the loudspeaker cover free by inserting a screwdriver blade into the slots on the side of the cover **(see illustration)**.

20 On all models undo the four speaker retaining screws, pull the speaker away from the shelf and disconnect the wires.

Refitting

21 Refitting is a reversal of removal.

Rear parcel tray-mounted loudspeaker

Removal

22 Unscrew the collar and pull the wiring plug from the loudspeaker.

23 Remove the rear parcel tray. Unscrew the four retaining screws and remove the speaker.

Refitting

24 Refit in the reverse order to removal.

Rear quarter panel-mounted loudspeaker - Cabriolet models

Removal

25 Fully open the roof and lock it.

26 Pull off the roof release lever knob and remove the window winder.

27 Pull back the rear quarter trim panel then remove the three screws and withdraw the trim panel with the speaker.

28 Disconnect the wiring then extract the screws and detach the speaker and grille from the panel. Note the location of the washers.

Refitting

29 Refitting is a reverse of removal. Position the speaker so that the terminals face forwards.

23 Aerial - removal and refitting

Manually-operated type - all models except Cabriolet

Removal

1 Withdraw the radio (Section 21) until the aerial lead can be pulled out of the receiver socket.

2 Working under the front wing, release the aerial inner wing bracket **(see illustration)**.

3 Prise out the grommet and pull the aerial lead through the hole in the inner wing.

4 Unscrew the aerial collar retaining nut.

5 Withdraw the aerial, spacers and seal **(see illustration)**.

Refitting

6 Refitting is a reversal of removal.

Manually-operated type - Cabriolet models

Removal

7 Open the boot lid and detach the support strut from the side panel.

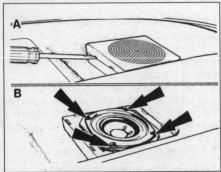

22.19 Rear parcel shelf-mounted loudspeaker removal - pre-1986 models
A Prising cover open
B Retaining screw locations

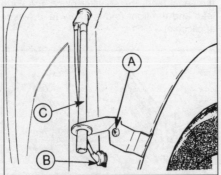

23.2 Manually operated aerial attachments - all except Cabriolet models
A Inner wing bracket screw
B Rubber grommet
C Aerial

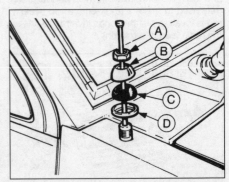

23.5 Manually operated aerial upper attachment fixings - all except Cabriolet
A Collar retaining nut
B Bezel
C Spacer
D Seal

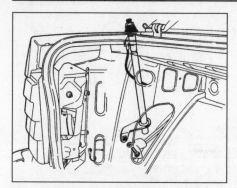

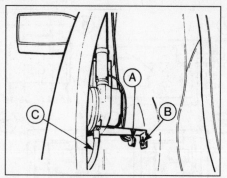

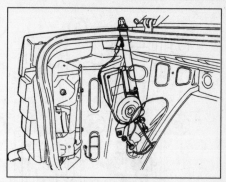

23.9 Manually operated aerial location on Cabriolet models

23.14 Power operated aerial attachments - all models except Cabriolet
A Grommet
B Lower bracket screw
C Aerial drain tube

23.18 Power operated aerial location on Cabriolet models

8 Release the tabs and remove the trim panel.
9 From under the rear panel undo the aerial bracket retaining screw **(see illustration)**.
10 Undo the aerial collar retaining nut and remove the spacers and seal. Withdraw the aerial after unscrewing the lead.

Refitting

11 Refitting is a reversal of removal.

Power-operated type - all models except Cabriolet

Removal

12 Carry out the operations described in paragraph 1.
13 Lower the bottom facia insulation panel and disconnect the red and white aerial feed cables.
14 Working under the front wing, extract the self-tapping screw which secures the aerial lower bracket **(see illustration)**.

15 Prise out the grommet and pull the aerial lead through the hole in the inner wing.
16 Unscrew the aerial upper retaining nut and lower the aerial from its location. Take off the seals and spacers.

Refitting

17 Refitting is a reversal of removal.

Power-operated type - Cabriolet models

18 The operations are the same as for the Cabriolet manually operated type described previously, but in addition disconnect the power feed multi-plug before unscrewing the aerial lead **(see illustration)**.

24 Heated rear window aerial amplifier - removal and refitting

Removal

1 On some 1986 models onwards the radio aerial is incorporated in the heated rear window element, and to assist reception an amplifier is fitted. This is located in the tailgate adjacent to the tailgate wiper motor. Removal and refitting is as follows.
2 Remove the tailgate wiper motor trim panel and the adjoining trim panel.
3 Undo the two screws and withdraw the amplifier.
4 Disconnect the wiring and remove the amplifier.

Refitting

5 Refitting is a reversal of removal.

Wiring diagrams commence overleaf

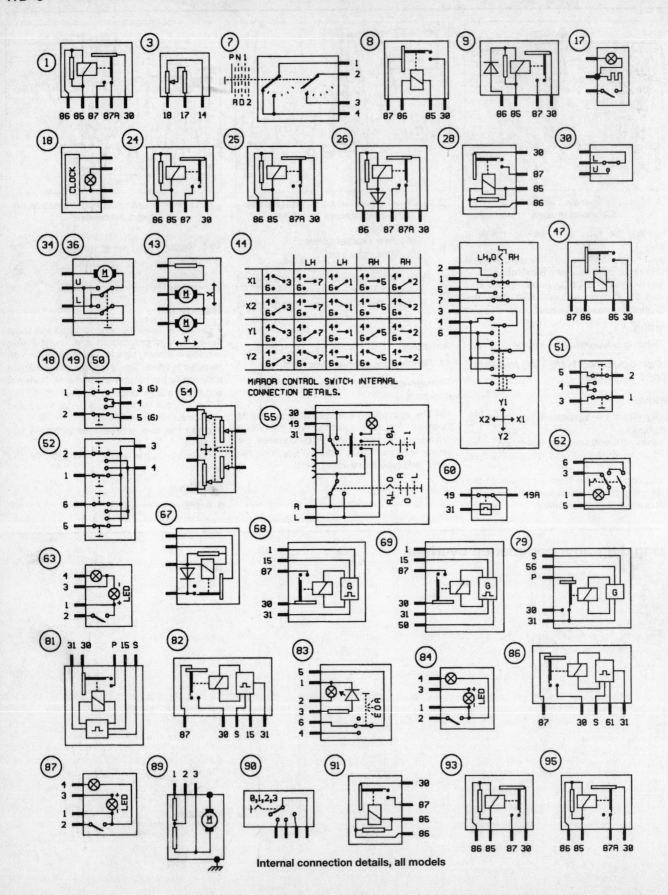

MIRROR CONTROL SWITCH INTERNAL CONNECTION DETAILS.

Internal connection details, all models

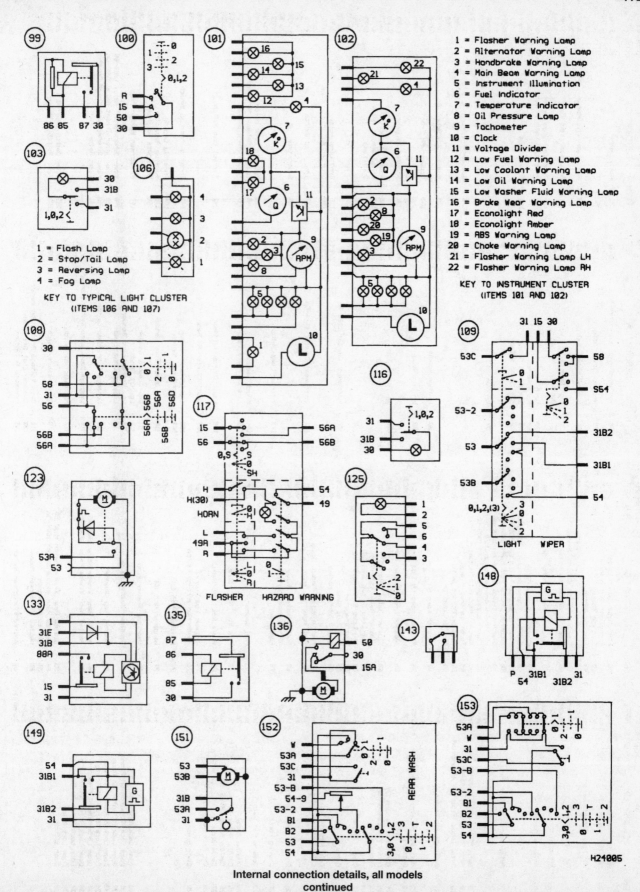

KEY TO INSTRUMENT CLUSTER (ITEMS 101 AND 102)

1 = Flasher Warning Lamp
2 = Alternator Warning Lamp
3 = Handbrake Warning Lamp
4 = Main Beam Warning Lamp
5 = Instrument Illumination
6 = Fuel Indicator
7 = Temperature Indicator
8 = Oil Pressure Lamp
9 = Tachometer
10 = Clock
11 = Voltage Divider
12 = Low Fuel Warning Lamp
13 = Low Coolant Warning Lamp
14 = Low Oil Warning Lamp
15 = Low Washer Fluid Warning Lamp
16 = Brake Wear Warning Lamp
17 = Econolight Red
18 = Econolight Amber
19 = ABS Warning Lamp
20 = Choke Warning Lamp
21 = Flasher Warning Lamp LH
22 = Flasher Warning Lamp RH

KEY TO TYPICAL LIGHT CLUSTER (ITEMS 106 AND 107)

1 = Flash Lamp
2 = Stop/Tail Lamp
3 = Reversing Lamp
4 = Fog Lamp

FLASHER   HAZARD WARNING

LIGHT   WIPER

REAR WASH

Internal connection details, all models continued

H24005

12

Key to wiring diagrams

ITEM	DESCRIPTION	DIAGRAM/GRID REF.
1	ABS Warning Relay	1a/C1
2	ABS Warning Switch	1a/B2
3	Air Flow Potentiometer	1a/B8, 4a/D7
4	Air Temp. Sensor	4a/D7, 4b/B7
5	Alternator	1/R3
6	Antenna Module	1a/R3, 3a/M2
7	Auto. Trans. Inhibitor Switch	5/F2, 5/F5, 5/F8, 1a/D7, 2a/B7
8	Auto. Trans. Relay 1988-86	1/E1
9	Auto. Trans. Relay 1986-On	1a/E1
10	Auto. Trans. Selector Illumination	2/J5
11	Auxiliary Air Device	4/F4, 4a/C7, 4b/C7
12	Auxiliary Warning System Module	1/K3
13	Battery	1/F8
14	Brake Pad Sender LH	1/C8
15	Brake Pad Sender RH	1/C1
16	Choke Switch	1a/K5
17	Cigar Lighter	2/K6
18	Clock	2/G5, 2a/G5
19	Cold Running Valve	1a/D6
20	Cold Starting Valve	4/F3, 4a/F3, 4b/F3
21	Coolant Temp. Sensor	1/B7
22	Cooling Fan	1a/F6, 1a/A6
23	Cooling Fan Switch	1a/A7, 1/R7
24	Dim/Dip Relay V	2a/D1
25	Dim/Dip Relay D	2a/E1
26	Dim/Dip Relay L4/L5	2a/F1
27	Diode Block	4/J6
28	Dip Beam Relay	2a/A5, 3a/R2
29	Distributor	1/D4, 1/D6
30	Door Lock RH Front	3/K6
31	Door Lock Actuator LH Front	3/J8
32	Door Lock Actuator LH Rear	3/L8
33	Door Lock Actuator RH Rear	3/L1
34	Door Lock Motor LH Front	3a/M8
35	Door Lock Motor LH Rear	3a/K8
36	Door Lock Motor LH Rear	3a/K1
37	Door Lock Motor RH Front	3/M1
38	Door Lock Relay	3/K6, 2/H1
39	Door Switch	2/H8, 2/K1, 2a/H1, 2a/M8

ITEM	DESCRIPTION	DIAGRAM/GRID REF.
40	Econolight Switch (amber)	1/F3
41	Econolight Switch (red)	1/F3
42	Electric Choke	1/F5
43	Electric Mirror Control Switch	3a/F1
44	Electric Mirror Motor LH	3a/F8, 3a/H2
45	Electric Window Motor RH	3/G8
46	Electric Window Relay	3/G1
47	Electric Window Switch LH 1988-86	3/A8
48	Electric Window Switch LH 1986-On	3/H8
49	Electric Window Switch RH 1988-86	3/H1
50	Electric Window Switch RH 1988-86 (LH window driver controlled)	3/K1
51	Electric Window driver Switch RH 1986-On	3a/H1
52	Fodar/Hydraulic Actuator	4a/E3
53	Fodar Control (4 way)	2a/K3
54	Flasher/Hazard Switch	2a/A8
55	Flasher Lamp LH	2/R1
56	Flasher Lamp RH	2/C8
57	Flasher Lamp LH Side Mark	2/C1
58	Flasher Lamp RH Side Mark	2a/C1
59	Flasher Relay 1988-86	2/D1
60	Flasher Relay 1986-On	2/J3
61	Fog Lamp Switch 1988-86	2/K6
62	Fog Lamp Switch 1986-On	2a/K6
63	Fuel Computer	2/G5
64	Fuel Flow Sensor	2a/G5
65	Fuel Injection Module	4/F3
66	Fuel Injection Module Relay	4a/F3
67	Fuel Injection Relay	4b/F3
68	Fuel Injection Relay (KE-Jetronic 1984-86)	1/B7
69	Fuel Pump	1a/A6, 1/R7
70	Fuel Sender	1a/A7
71	Fuel Shut Off Valve	1/L7, 1/C7
72	Glove Box Lamp/Switch	1a/C7
73	Graphic Equalizer	2/G7
74	Handbrake Warning Switch	2a/G7
75	Headlamp Unit LH	5/B7
76	Headlamp Unit RH	1/K7, 1a/K7
77	Headlamp Washer Pump	2/A7, 2/R2
78	Headlamp Washer Relay	3/A7
79	Heated Rear Window	3/C5
80	Heated Rear Window Relay 1988-86	3/B4, 3a/L1
81	Heated Rear Window Relay 1986-On	3/C3
82	Heated Windscreen	1a/B1
83	Heated Rear Window Switch 1988-86	3a/C1, 1/B1
84	Heated Rear Window Switch 1986-On	3/H3
85	Heated Windscreen Relay	3a/J6, 3a/F6
86	Heated Windscreen Switch	1a/H1, 3a/E1, 3a/J6

ITEM	DESCRIPTION	DIAGRAM/GRID REF.
88	Heater Blower Illumination	2/G6
89	Heater Blower Motor	2a/G6
90	Heater Blower Switch	3/G6
91	High Beam Relay	3/G5, 3a/G4
92	Horn	2a/R6
93	Horn Relay	3/R6
94	Horn Switch	3a/R6
95	Idle Speed Relay	3a/B1
96	Idle Speed Valve	1a/O1
97	Ignition Coil	1/F6, 1a/E4, 1/O6
98	Ignition Module	1a/C4
99	Ignition Relay	4b/C7, 1/O1
100	Ignition Switch	2a/C1, 2/C1, 2/O1
101	Instrument Cluster 1988-86	1a/L3, 1a/C8, 4b/J5, 4a/J3
102	Instrument Cluster 1986-On	4b/J2, 1a/O1, 2a/C1, 1/K4
103	Interior Lamp/Switch	2/F4, 4/K4, 4a/K4, 2a/F4
104	Knock Sensor	1/L3
105	Licence Plate Lamp	2/R4
106	Light Cluster LH Rear	4/L6, 4a/L6
107	Light Cluster RH Rear	4b/L6
108	Light/Dimmer Switch	1/L7
109	Light/Wiper Switch	1/C7
110	Low Brake Fluid Sender	2/G7, 2a/G7
111	Low Coolant Sender	5/B7
112	Low Oil Sender	1/K7, 1a/K7
113	Low Washer Fluid Sender	2/A7, 2/R2
114	Luggage Comp. Lamp	3/A7
115	Luggage Comp. Lamp Switch	3/C5
116	Luggage Comp. Lamp/Switch (cargo)	3/B4, 3a/L1
117	Multifunction Switch	3/C3, 1a/B1
118	Oil Pressure Switch	3/J4
119	Over Voltage Protection Device	1/F5
120	Overrun Shut Off Valve	1a/H1, 3a/E1
121	Pressure Actuator	3a/J6

ITEM	DESCRIPTION	DIAGRAM/GRID REF.
122	Radio Unit	3/H6
123	Rear Wash/Wipe Motor	5/D3
124	Rear Wash/Wipe Pump	5/D8
125	Rear Wash/Wipe Switch	5/D8
126	Reversing Lamp Switch	3a/M5
127	Spark Plugs	3/H6, 3/G4, 2a/C7, 2a/C7
128	Speaker LH Front	1/E4
129	Speaker LH Rear	1/E5
130	Speaker RH Front	1a/E4
131	Speaker RH Rear	1/O3, 1/O5, 4a/O5
132	Speed Sensor	1a/O5
133	Speed Sensor Relay	4/B3
134	Spot Lamp	5/R2
135	Spot Lamp Relay	5/R5
136	Starter Motor	5/R8
137	Stop Lamp Switch	5/F5
138	Suppressor	5/F8, 5/R1, 5/R4
139	Tailgate Lock Motor	5/R6, 5/F3
140	Tailgate Release Actuator	5/R1
141	Temperature Sensor	5/F6
142	Thermal Time Switch	4/J3, 2/R3, 2a/R6
143	Throttle Position Switch	2/E1
144	Throttle Switch	1/O5
145	Warm-Up Regulator	1a/O5
146	Wastegate Solenoid	2/C5
147	Windscreen Washer Pump	2a/C4
148	Wiper Intermittent Relay 1988-86	3a/B2
149	Wiper Intermittent Relay 1986-On	1/O2
150	Wiper Intermittent Speed Control	4b/H4
151	Wiper Motor	3a/M5, 4a/O6
152	Wiper Switch 1986-88	4b/C3, 4b/D6
153	Wiper Switch 1988-On	1a/C5, 4/O5

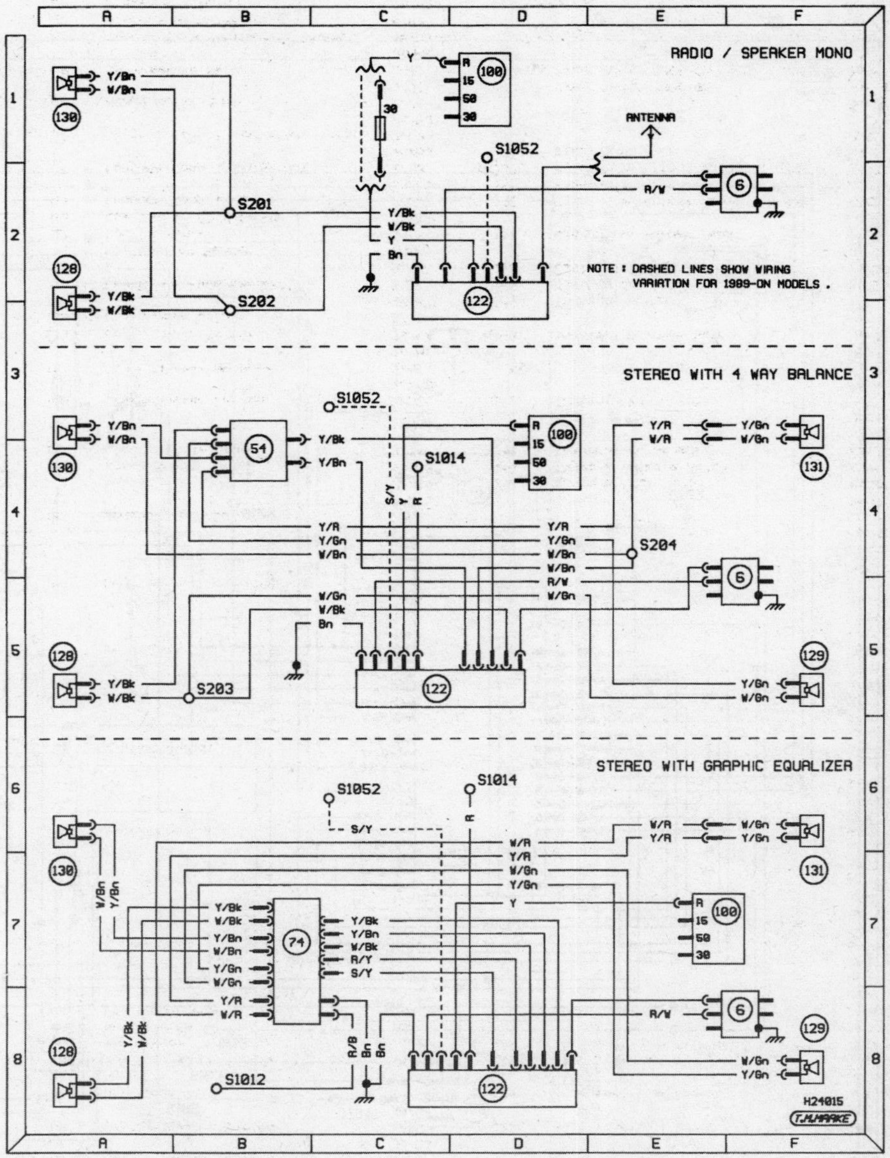

Diagram 5: 1986-on in car entertainment

RADIO / SPEAKER MONO

NOTE : DASHED LINES SHOW WIRING VARIATION FOR 1989-ON MODELS .

STEREO WITH 4 WAY BALANCE

STEREO WITH GRAPHIC EQUALIZER

1980-86 MODEL

COMMON POINT	DIAGRAM/GRID REF.
S103	1/H1
S104	1/H1
S105	2/J2, 2/J2
S106	3/G1, 4/H1, 4/H1, 4b/H1
S107	2/F6, 3/F6, 4/K5, 4a/K5
S108	1/K1, 3/K2, 2/BB, 4/RB
S109	1/H1
S110	2/G1
S113	1/R4, 1a/R4
S120	2/J5, 3/J5
S123	

1986-ON MODEL

COMMON POINT	DIAGRAM/GRID REF.
S116	3a/F6
S1002	4/E6, 1a/G8
S1012	2a/H1, 4b/H1, 1a/F2
S1027	2a/C3, 3a/C3, 5/BB
S1032	1a/J2, 2a/E3, 2a/C5
S1043	5/C4, 5/D6, 1a/RB
S1044	2a/BB, 4/RB, 3a/C4
S1052	5/C3, 5/D1, 1b/E2
S1025	
S1014	
S1021	
S1024	

WIRE COLOURS

B	Blue	Rs	Pink
Bk	Black	S	Grey
Bn	Brown	V	Violet
Gn	Green	W	White
R	Red	Y	Yellow

NOTES:

1. Feed wires are coloured red (black when switched) and originate from diagrams 1 and 1a.
2. Earth wires on all diagrams are coloured brown.
3. The above tables show where common connecting points e.g. S103 common battery +ve, interconnect between diagrams.
4. Earthing points which are identified e.g. G103, denote common earths between diagrams.
5. Not all items are fitted to all models.
6. Brackets show how the circuit may be connected in more than one way.

1983-86 MODEL

FUSE	RATING	CIRCUIT
1	20A	Hazard Warning Lamps, Horn
2	15A	Interior Lighting, Windscreen
3	25R	Washer, Clock
4	25R	Headlamp Washer
5	18R	Spot Lamps
6	18R	RH High Beam
7	18R	LH High Beam
8	18R	RH Low Beam
9	18R	LH Low Beam
10	18R	LH Side, Interior Lamps
11	18R	LH Side, Number Plate Lamps
12	25R	Cooling Fan
13	18R	Flashers, Reversing Lamps
14	28R	Heater Blower
15	15R	Heated Rear Window
16	18R	Stop Lamp, Wipers
17	30R	Door Locking, Tailgate Release
18	30R	Electric Windows
R1	25R	Fuel Injection

1986-ON MODEL

FUSE	RATING	CIRCUIT
1	15A	Hazard Warning Lamps, Horn
2	15A	Cigar Lighter, Interior Lighting
3	30A	Heated Rear Window, Electric Mirrors
4	30A	Headlamp Washers
5	15R	Central Locking
6	10R	Injection Module Voltage Protection
7	20R	Fuel Pump
8	15R	Spot Lamps
9	10R	LH High Beam
10	10R	RH High Beam
11	10R	Heater Blower
12	25R	Cooling Fan
13	10R	Flashers, Reversing Lamps
14	18R	LH Low Beam
15	10R	RH Low Beam
16	18R	Wiper Motor, Washer Pump
17	30R	Stop Lamps, Instrument Illumination
18	30R	Electric Windows
19	18R	LH Side Lamps
20	18R	RH Side Lamps

Table of common points, fuses, wire colours and notes

12

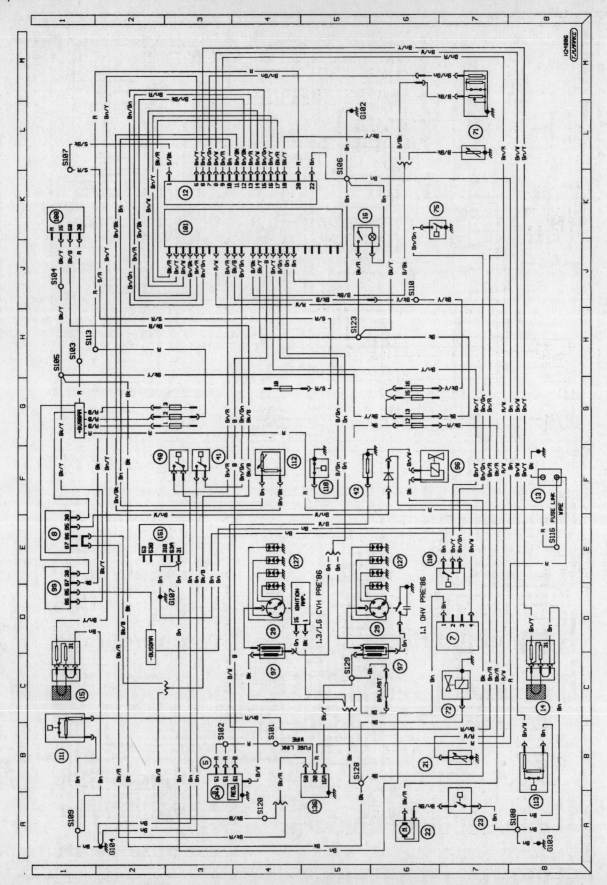

Diagram 1: 1980-86 Starting, charging, and ignition (except fuel injection models)

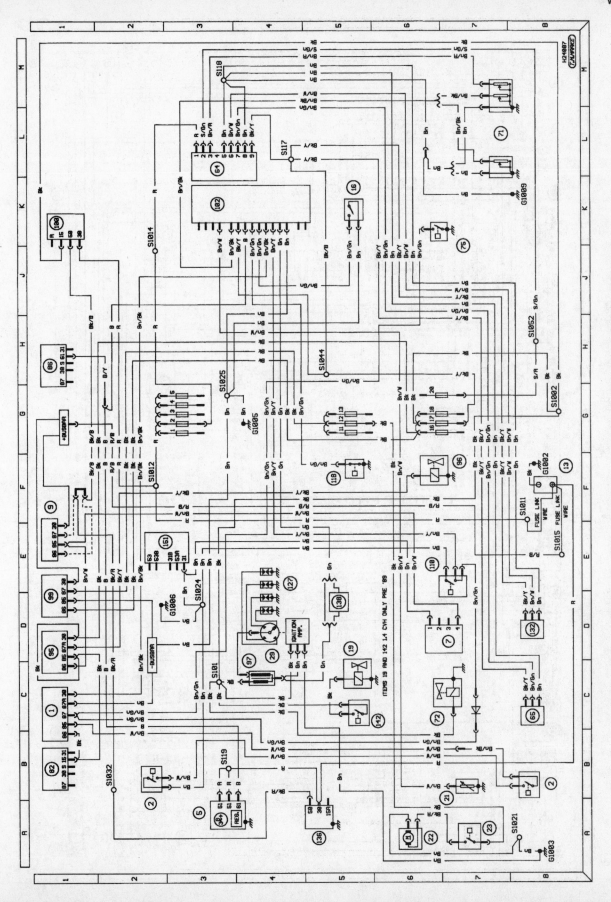

Diagram 1a: 1986-on Starting, charging, and ignition (except fuel injection) all models

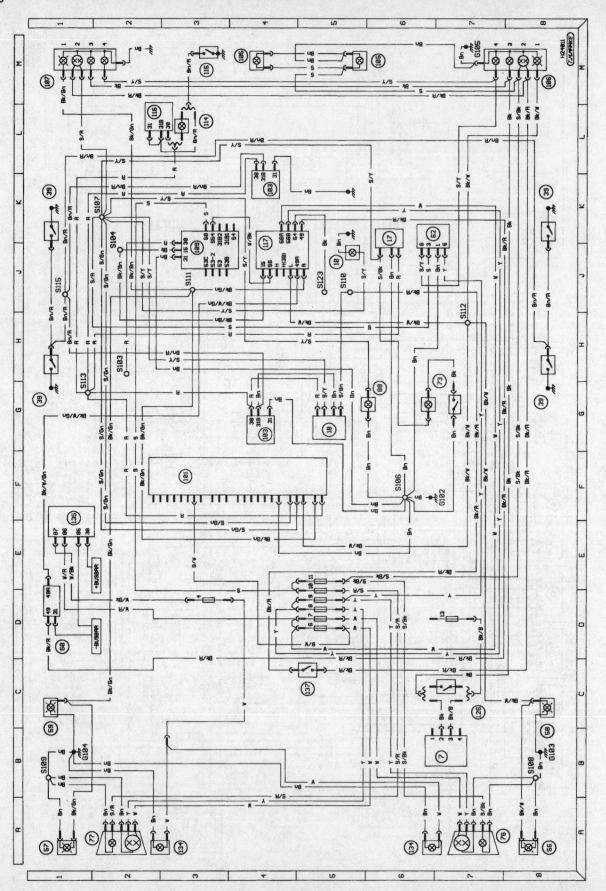

Diagram 2: 1980-86 Lighting all models

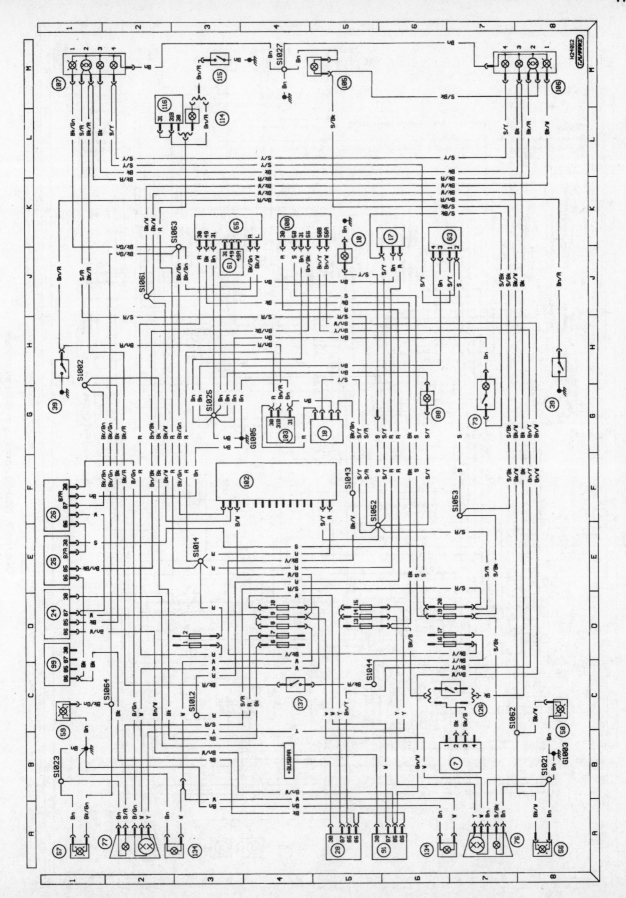

Diagram 2a: 1986-on Lighting all models

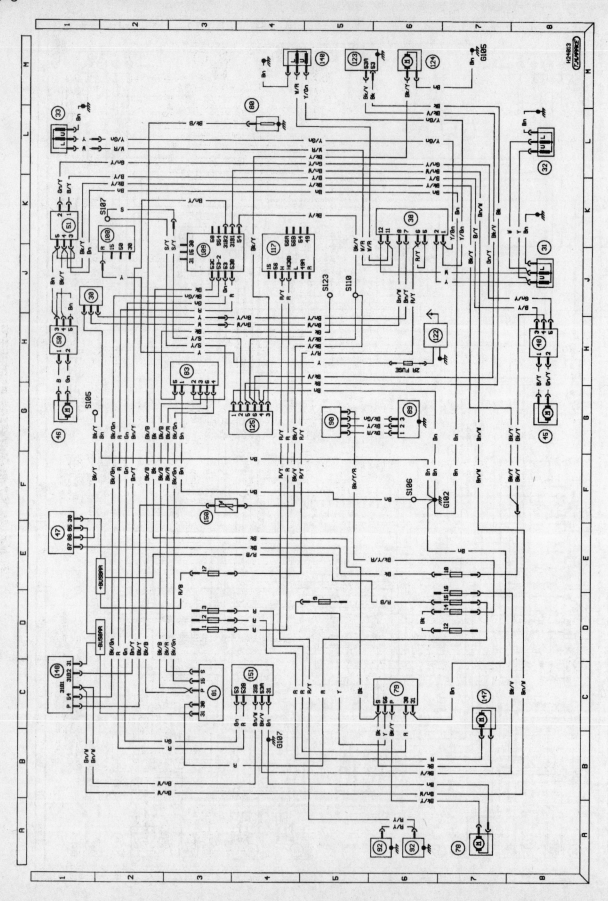

Diagram 3: 1980-86 Ancilliary circuits all models

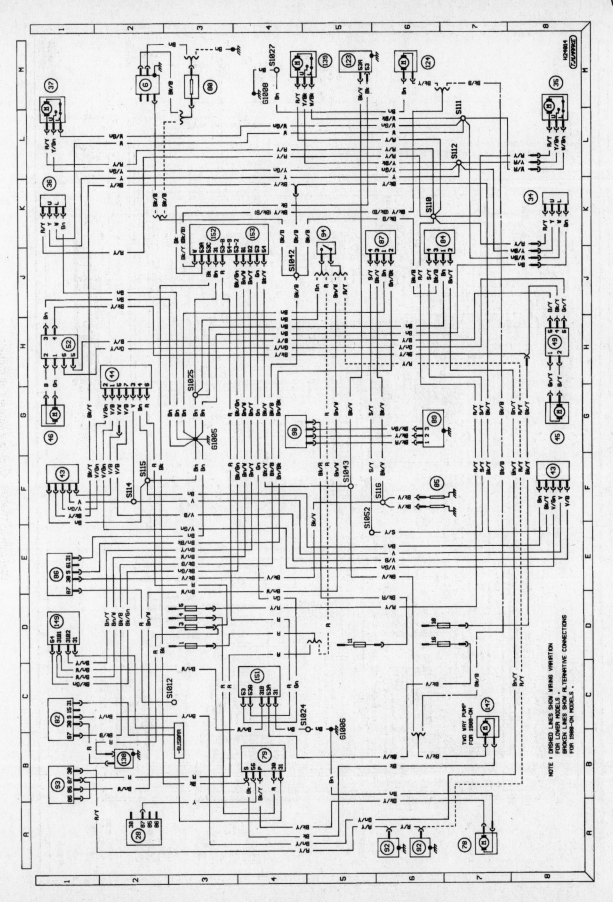

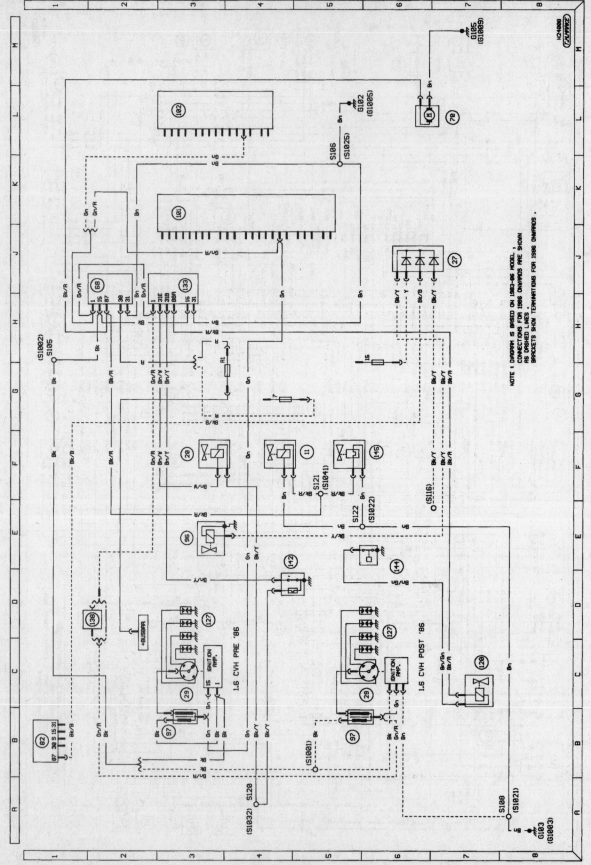

Diagram 4: 1983-on K-Jetronic fuel injection
For starting and charging circuits see Diagram 1

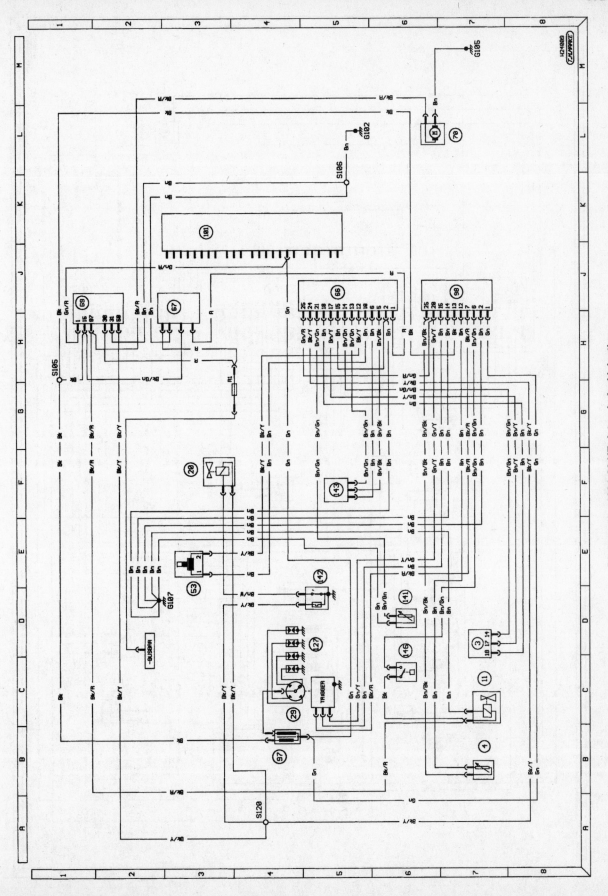

Diagram 4a: 1984-86 KE-Jetronic fuel injection
For starting and charging circuits see Diagram 1

12

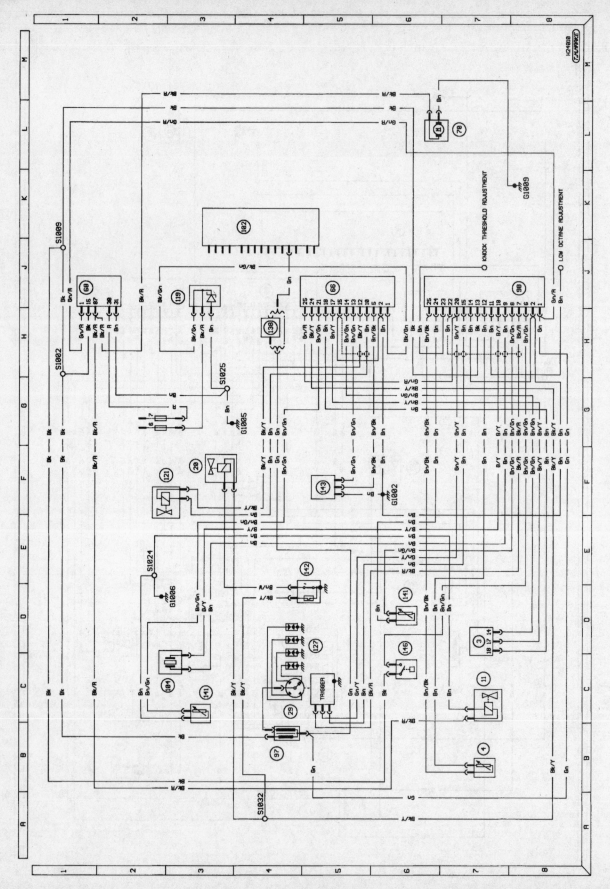

Diagram 4b: 1986-on KE-Jetronic fuel injection
For starting and charging circuits see Diagram 1a

Dimensions and Weights

Note: *All figures are approximate, and may vary according to model. Refer to manufacturer's data for exact figures.*

Dimensions

Overall length:
  Pre-1986 models:
    Saloon and Cabriolet . . . . .4068 mm
    Estate . . . . .4131 mm
    Van . . . . .4129 mm
  1986 models onwards:
    Saloon (except XR3i and RS Turbo) . . . . .4049 mm
    Cabriolet, XR3i and RS Turbo . . . . .4061 mm
    Estate . . . . .4107 mm
    Van . . . . .4181 mm
Overall width:
  Pre-1986 models . . . . .1640 to 1656 mm
  1986 models onwards . . . . .1743 mm
Overall height:
  Pre-1986 models:
    Saloon, Estate and Cabriolet . . . . .1389 to 1400 mm
    Van . . . . .1568 mm
  1986 models onwards:
    Saloon, XR3i, RS Turbo and Cabriolet . . . . .1349 to 1371 mm
    Estate . . . . .1389 mm
    Van . . . . .1594 mm

Wheelbase:
  Saloon, Estate and Cabriolet . . . . .2402 mm
  Van . . . . .2501 mm
Front track:
  Pre-1986 models . . . . .1390 to 1400 mm
  1986 models onwards . . . . .1404 to 1423 mm
Rear track:
  Pre-1986 models . . . . .1384 to 1423 mm
  1986 models onwards . . . . .1384 to 1439 mm

Weights

Nominal kerb weight:
  1.1 litre . . . . .855 to 905 kg
  1.3 litre . . . . .870 to 915 kg
  1.4 litre . . . . .875 to 930 kg
  1.6 litre . . . . .885 to 995 kg
Maximum trailer weight:
  1.1 litre models . . . . .245 kg
  All other models . . . . .408 kg
Van payloads:
  35 Van . . . . .491 kg
  55 Van . . . . .772 kg
Maximum roof rack load . . . . .75 kg

Length (distance)

Inches (in)	x 25.4	= Millimetres (mm)	x 0.0394	=	Inches (in)
Feet (ft)	x 0.305	= Metres (m)	x 3.281	=	Feet (ft)
Miles	x 1.609	= Kilometres (km)	x 0.621	=	Miles

Volume (capacity)

Cubic inches (cu in; in³)	x 16.387	= Cubic centimetres (cc; cm³)	x 0.061	=	Cubic inches (cu in; in³)
Imperial pints (Imp pt)	x 0.568	= Litres (l)	x 1.76	=	Imperial pints (Imp pt)
Imperial quarts (Imp qt)	x 1.137	= Litres (l)	x 0.88	=	Imperial quarts (Imp qt)
Imperial quarts (Imp qt)	x 1.201	= US quarts (US qt)	x 0.833	=	Imperial quarts (Imp qt)
US quarts (US qt)	x 0.946	= Litres (l)	x 1.057	=	US quarts (US qt)
Imperial gallons (Imp gal)	x 4.546	= Litres (l)	x 0.22	=	Imperial gallons (Imp gal)
Imperial gallons (Imp gal)	x 1.201	= US gallons (US gal)	x 0.833	=	Imperial gallons (Imp gal)
US gallons (US gal)	x 3.785	= Litres (l)	x 0.264	=	US gallons (US gal)

Mass (weight)

Ounces (oz)	x 28.35	= Grams (g)	x 0.035	=	Ounces (oz)
Pounds (lb)	x 0.454	= Kilograms (kg)	x 2.205	=	Pounds (lb)

Force

Ounces-force (ozf; oz)	x 0.278	= Newtons (N)	x 3.6	=	Ounces-force (ozf; oz)
Pounds-force (lbf; lb)	x 4.448	= Newtons (N)	x 0.225	=	Pounds-force (lbf; lb)
Newtons (N)	x 0.1	= Kilograms-force (kgf; kg)	x 9.81	=	Newtons (N)

Pressure

Pounds-force per square inch (psi; lbf/in²; lb/in²)	x 0.070	= Kilograms-force per square centimetre (kgf/cm²; kg/cm²)	x 14.223	=	Pounds-force per square inch (psi; lbf/in²; lb/in²)
Pounds-force per square inch (psi; lbf/in²; lb/in²)	x 0.068	= Atmospheres (atm)	x 14.696	=	Pounds-force per square inch (psi; lbf/in²; lb/in²)
Pounds-force per square inch (psi; lbf/in²; lb/in²)	x 0.069	= Bars	x 14.5	=	Pounds-force per square inch (psi; lbf/in²; lb/in²)
Pounds-force per square inch (psi; lbf/in²; lb/in²)	x 6.895	= Kilopascals (kPa)	x 0.145	=	Pounds-force per square inch (psi; lbf/in²; lb/in²)
Kilopascals (kPa)	x 0.01	= Kilograms-force per square centimetre (kgf/cm²; kg/cm²)	x 98.1	=	Kilopascals (kPa)
Millibar (mbar)	x 100	= Pascals (Pa)	x 0.01	=	Millibar (mbar)
Millibar (mbar)	x 0.0145	= Pounds-force per square inch (psi; lbf/in²; lb/in²)	x 68.947	=	Millibar (mbar)
Millibar (mbar)	x 0.75	= Millimetres of mercury (mmHg)	x 1.333	=	Millibar (mbar)
Millibar (mbar)	x 0.401	= Inches of water (inH₂O)	x 2.491	=	Millibar (mbar)
Millimetres of mercury (mmHg)	x 0.535	= Inches of water (inH₂O)	x 1.868	=	Millimetres of mercury (mmHg)
Inches of water (inH₂O)	x 0.036	= Pounds-force per square inch (psi; lbf/in²; lb/in²)	x 27.68	=	Inches of water (inH₂O)

(Pressure subscripts: inH_2O)

Torque (moment of force)

Pounds-force inches (lbf in; lb in)	x 1.152	= Kilograms-force centimetre (kgf cm; kg cm)	x 0.868	=	Pounds-force inches (lbf in; lb in)
Pounds-force inches (lbf in; lb in)	x 0.113	= Newton metres (Nm)	x 8.85	=	Pounds-force inches (lbf in; lb in)
Pounds-force inches (lbf in; lb in)	x 0.083	= Pounds-force feet (lbf ft; lb ft)	x 12	=	Pounds-force inches (lbf in; lb in)
Pounds-force feet (lbf ft; lb ft)	x 0.138	= Kilograms-force metres (kgf m; kg m)	x 7.233	=	Pounds-force feet (lbf ft; lb ft)
Pounds-force feet (lbf ft; lb ft)	x 1.356	= Newton metres (Nm)	x 0.738	=	Pounds-force feet (lbf ft; lb ft)
Newton metres (Nm)	x 0.102	= Kilograms-force metres (kgf m; kg m)	x 9.804	=	Newton metres (Nm)

Power

Horsepower (hp)	x 745.7	= Watts (W)	x 0.0013	=	Horsepower (hp)

Velocity (speed)

Miles per hour (miles/hr; mph)	x 1.609	= Kilometres per hour (km/hr; kph)	x 0.621	=	Miles per hour (miles/hr; mph)

Fuel consumption*

Miles per gallon (mpg)	x 0.354	= Kilometres per litre (km/l)	x 2.825	=	Miles per gallon (mpg)

Temperature

Degrees Fahrenheit = (°C x 1.8) + 32

Degrees Celsius (Degrees Centigrade; °C) = (°F - 32) x 0.56

It is common practice to convert from miles per gallon (mpg) to litres/100 kilometres (l/100km), where mpg x l/100 km = 282

Spare parts are available from many sources, including maker's appointed garages, accessory shops, and motor factors. To be sure of obtaining the correct parts, it will sometimes be necessary to quote the vehicle identification number. If possible, it can also be useful to take the old parts along for positive identification. Items such as starter motors and alternators may be available under a service exchange scheme - any parts returned should always be clean.

Our advice regarding spare part sources is as follows.

Officially-appointed garages

This is the best source of parts which are peculiar to your car, and are not otherwise generally available (eg badges, interior trim, certain body panels, etc). It is also the only place at which you should buy parts if the vehicle is still under warranty.

Accessory shops

These are very good places to buy materials and components needed for the maintenance of your car (oil, air and fuel filters, spark plugs, light bulbs, drivebelts, oils and greases, brake pads, touch-up paint, etc). Components of this nature sold by a reputable shop are of the same standard as those used by the car manufacturer.

Besides components, these shops also sell tools and general accessories, usually have convenient opening hours, charge lower prices, and can often be found not far from home. Some accessory shops have parts counters where the components needed for almost any repair job can be purchased or ordered.

Motor factors

Good factors will stock all the more important components which wear out comparatively quickly and can sometimes supply individual components needed for the overhaul of a larger assembly (eg brake seals and hydraulic parts, bearing shells, pistons, valves, alternator brushes). They may also handle work such as cylinder block reboring, crankshaft regrinding and balancing, etc.

Tyre and exhaust specialists

These outlets may be independent or members of a local or national chain. They frequently offer competitive prices when compared with a main dealer or local garage, but it will pay to obtain several quotes before making a decision. When researching prices, also ask what 'extras' may be added - for instance, fitting a new valve and balancing the wheel are both commonly charged on top of the price of a new tyre.

Other sources

Beware of parts or materials obtained from market stalls, car boot sales or similar outlets. Such items are not invariably sub-standard, but there is little chance of compensation if they do prove unsatisfactory. In the case of safety-critical components such as brake pads there is the risk not only of financial loss but also of an accident causing injury or death.

Second-hand components or assemblies obtained from a car breaker can be a good buy in some circumstances, but this sort of purchase is best made by the experienced DIY mechanic.

Vehicle Identification Numbers

Modifications are a continuing and unpublicised process in vehicle manufacture, quite apart from major model changes. Spare parts manuals and lists are compiled upon a numerical basis, the individual vehicle identification numbers being essential to correct identification of the component concerned.

When ordering spare parts, always give as much information as possible. Quote the vehicle model, year of manufacture, body and engine numbers as appropriate.

The Vehicle Identification Number is located on the plate found under the bonnet above the radiator. The plate also carries information concerning paint colour, final drive ratio etc.

The engine number is located in one of the following places, according to engine type:
Front right-hand side of engine block
Front face of cylinder block
Front left-hand side of engine block
Cylinder block above clutch bellhousing
A tuning decal will also be found under the

bonnet. This illustrates graphically the basic tuning functions, typically plug gap, ignition timing, idle speed and CO level, and (where applicable) valve clearances, points gap and dwell angle.

Additionally, on later models a chassis number is stamped on the floor panel between the driver's seat and door, and is covered by a fold back plastic flap.

Vehicle identification plate location

1 Type Approval Number
2 Vehicle Identification Number
3 Gross vehicle weight
4 Gross train weight
5 Permitted front axle loading
6 Permitted rear axle loading
7 Steering (LHD/RHD)
8 Engine
9 Transmission
10 Axle (final drive ratio)
11 Trim (interior)
12 Body type
13 Special territory version
14 Body colour
15 KD reference (usually blank) or exhaust emission level

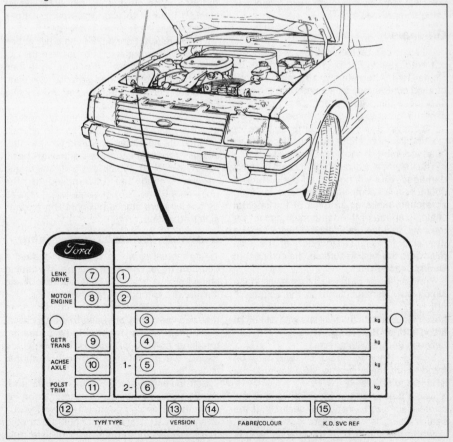

Whenever servicing, repair or overhaul work is carried out on the car or its components, it is necessary to observe the following procedures and instructions. This will assist in carrying out the operation efficiently and to a professional standard of workmanship.

Joint mating faces and gaskets

When separating components at their mating faces, never insert screwdrivers or similar implements into the joint between the faces in order to prise them apart. This can cause severe damage which results in oil leaks, coolant leaks, etc upon reassembly. Separation is usually achieved by tapping along the joint with a soft-faced hammer in order to break the seal. However, note that this method may not be suitable where dowels are used for component location.

Where a gasket is used between the mating faces of two components, ensure that it is renewed on reassembly, and fit it dry unless otherwise stated in the repair procedure. Make sure that the mating faces are clean and dry, with all traces of old gasket removed. When cleaning a joint face, use a tool which is not likely to score or damage the face, and remove any burrs or nicks with an oilstone or fine file.

Make sure that tapped holes are cleaned with a pipe cleaner, and keep them free of jointing compound, if this is being used, unless specifically instructed otherwise.

Ensure that all orifices, channels or pipes are clear, and blow through them, preferably using compressed air.

Oil seals

Oil seals can be removed by levering them out with a wide flat-bladed screwdriver or similar tool. Alternatively, a number of self-tapping screws may be screwed into the seal, and these used as a purchase for pliers or similar in order to pull the seal free.

Whenever an oil seal is removed from its working location, either individually or as part of an assembly, it should be renewed.

The very fine sealing lip of the seal is easily damaged, and will not seal if the surface it contacts is not completely clean and free from scratches, nicks or grooves. If the original sealing surface of the component cannot be restored, and the manufacturer has not made provision for slight relocation of the seal relative to the sealing surface, the component should be renewed.

Protect the lips of the seal from any surface which may damage them in the course of fitting. Use tape or a conical sleeve where possible. Lubricate the seal lips with oil before fitting and, on dual-lipped seals, fill the space between the lips with grease.

Unless otherwise stated, oil seals must be fitted with their sealing lips toward the lubricant to be sealed.

Use a tubular drift or block of wood of the appropriate size to install the seal and, if the seal housing is shouldered, drive the seal down to the shoulder. If the seal housing is unshouldered, the seal should be fitted with its face flush with the housing top face (unless otherwise instructed).

Screw threads and fastenings

Seized nuts, bolts and screws are quite a common occurrence where corrosion has set in, and the use of penetrating oil or releasing fluid will often overcome this problem if the offending item is soaked for a while before attempting to release it. The use of an impact driver may also provide a means of releasing such stubborn fastening devices, when used in conjunction with the appropriate screwdriver bit or socket. If none of these methods works, it may be necessary to resort to the careful application of heat, or the use of a hacksaw or nut splitter device.

Studs are usually removed by locking two nuts together on the threaded part, and then using a spanner on the lower nut to unscrew the stud. Studs or bolts which have broken off below the surface of the component in which they are mounted can sometimes be removed using a stud extractor. Always ensure that a blind tapped hole is completely free from oil, grease, water or other fluid before installing the bolt or stud. Failure to do this could cause the housing to crack due to the hydraulic action of the bolt or stud as it is screwed in.

When tightening a castellated nut to accept a split pin, tighten the nut to the specified torque, where applicable, and then tighten further to the next split pin hole. Never slacken the nut to align the split pin hole, unless stated in the repair procedure.

When checking or retightening a nut or bolt to a specified torque setting, slacken the nut or bolt by a quarter of a turn, and then retighten to the specified setting. However, this should not be attempted where angular tightening has been used.

For some screw fastenings, notably cylinder head bolts or nuts, torque wrench settings are no longer specified for the latter stages of tightening, "angle-tightening" being called up instead. Typically, a fairly low torque wrench setting will be applied to the bolts/nuts in the correct sequence, followed by one or more stages of tightening through specified angles.

Locknuts, locktabs and washers

Any fastening which will rotate against a component or housing during tightening should always have a washer between it and the relevant component or housing.

Spring or split washers should always be renewed when they are used to lock a critical component such as a big-end bearing retaining bolt or nut. Locktabs which are folded over to retain a nut or bolt should always be renewed.

Self-locking nuts can be re-used in non-critical areas, providing resistance can be felt when the locking portion passes over the bolt or stud thread. However, it should be noted that self-locking stiffnuts tend to lose their effectiveness after long periods of use, and should be renewed as a matter of course.

Split pins must always be replaced with new ones of the correct size for the hole.

When thread-locking compound is found on the threads of a fastener which is to be re-used, it should be cleaned off with a wire brush and solvent, and fresh compound applied on reassembly.

Special tools

Some repair procedures in this manual entail the use of special tools such as a press, two or three-legged pullers, spring compressors, etc. Wherever possible, suitable readily-available alternatives to the manufacturer's special tools are described, and are shown in use. In some instances, where no alternative is possible, it has been necessary to resort to the use of a manufacturer's tool, and this has been done for reasons of safety as well as the efficient completion of the repair operation. Unless you are highly-skilled and have a thorough understanding of the procedures described, never attempt to bypass the use of any special tool when the procedure described specifies its use. Not only is there a very great risk of personal injury, but expensive damage could be caused to the components involved.

Environmental considerations

When disposing of used engine oil, brake fluid, antifreeze, etc, give due consideration to any detrimental environmental effects. Do not, for instance, pour any of the above liquids down drains into the general sewage system, or onto the ground to soak away. Many local council refuse tips provide a facility for waste oil disposal, as do some garages. If none of these facilities are available, consult your local Environmental Health Department, or the National Rivers Authority, for further advice.

With the universal tightening-up of legislation regarding the emission of environmentally-harmful substances from motor vehicles, most current vehicles have tamperproof devices fitted to the main adjustment points of the fuel system. These devices are primarily designed to prevent unqualified persons from adjusting the fuel/air mixture, with the chance of a consequent increase in toxic emissions. If such devices are encountered during servicing or overhaul, they should, wherever possible, be renewed or refitted in accordance with the vehicle manufacturer's requirements or current legislation.

OIL CARE
FOLLOW THE CODE

OIL BANK LINE
0800 66 33 66

Note: It is antisocial and illegal to dump oil down the drain. To find the location of your local oil recycling bank, call this number free.

The jack supplied in the vehicle tool kit should only be used for emergency roadside wheel changing unless it is supplemented with axle stands.

When using a trolley or other type of workshop jack, it can be placed under the front lower crossmember (provided a shaped block of wood is used as an insulator) to raise the front of the vehicle.

To raise the rear of a Saloon (except fuel-injected variants) or Estate, place the jack under the right-hand suspension lower arm mounting bracket using a rubber pad as an insulator.

To raise the rear of a Van, place the jack under the centre of the axle tube, taking care not to contact the brake pressure regulating valve or the hydraulic lines.

Axle stands should only be located under the double-skinned sections of the side members at the front of the vehicle, or under the sill jacking points. At the rear of the vehicle (Saloon or Estate), place the stands under the member to which the tie-bar is attached. On Vans, place the stands under the leaf spring front attachment body bracket.

Provided only one wheel at the rear of the vehicle is to be raised, the Saloon and Estate may be jacked up under the rear spring seat, or the Van under the leaf spring-to-axle tube mounting plate.

Never work under, around or near a raised car unless it is adequately supported in at least two places with axle stands or suitable sturdy blocks.

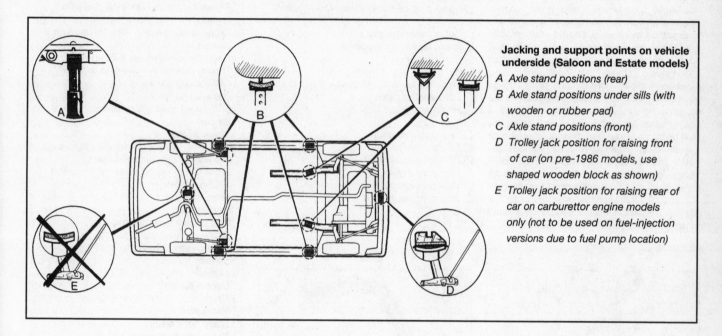

Jacking and support points on vehicle underside (Saloon and Estate models)

A *Axle stand positions (rear)*

B *Axle stand positions under sills (with wooden or rubber pad)*

C *Axle stand positions (front)*

D *Trolley jack position for raising front of car (on pre-1986 models, use shaped wooden block as shown)*

E *Trolley jack position for raising rear of car on carburettor engine models only (not to be used on fuel-injection versions due to fuel pump location)*

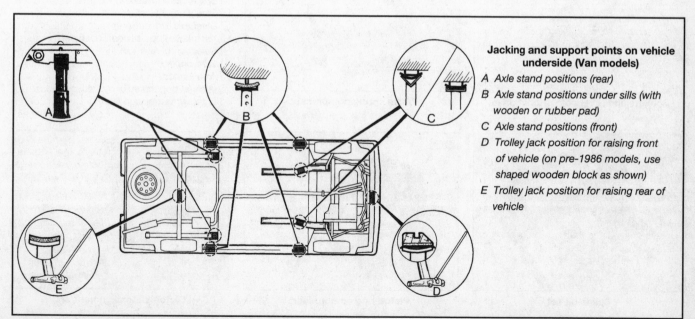

Jacking and support points on vehicle underside (Van models)

A *Axle stand positions (rear)*

B *Axle stand positions under sills (with wooden or rubber pad)*

C *Axle stand positions (front)*

D *Trolley jack position for raising front of vehicle (on pre-1986 models, use shaped wooden block as shown)*

E *Trolley jack position for raising rear of vehicle*

Introduction

A selection of good tools is a fundamental requirement for anyone contemplating the maintenance and repair of a motor vehicle. For the owner who does not possess any, their purchase will prove a considerable expense, offsetting some of the savings made by doing-it-yourself. However, provided that the tools purchased meet the relevant national safety standards and are of good quality, they will last for many years and prove an extremely worthwhile investment.

To help the average owner to decide which tools are needed to carry out the various tasks detailed in this manual, we have compiled three lists of tools under the following headings: *Maintenance and minor repair*, *Repair and overhaul*, and *Special*. Newcomers to practical mechanics should start off with the *Maintenance and minor repair* tool kit, and confine themselves to the simpler jobs around the vehicle. Then, as confidence and experience grow, more difficult tasks can be undertaken, with extra tools being purchased as, and when, they are needed. In this way, a *Maintenance and minor repair* tool kit can be built up into a *Repair and overhaul* tool kit over a considerable period of time, without any major cash outlays. The experienced do-it-yourselfer will have a tool kit good enough for most repair and overhaul procedures, and will add tools from the *Special* category when it is felt that the expense is justified by the amount of use to which these tools will be put.

Maintenance and minor repair tool kit

The tools given in this list should be considered as a minimum requirement if routine maintenance, servicing and minor repair operations are to be undertaken. We recommend the purchase of combination spanners (ring one end, open-ended the other); although more expensive than open-ended ones, they do give the advantages of both types of spanner.

☐ *Combination spanners:*
  Metric - 8 to 19 mm inclusive
☐ *Adjustable spanner - 35 mm jaw (approx.)*
☐ *Spark plug spanner (with rubber insert) - petrol models*
☐ *Spark plug gap adjustment tool - petrol models*
☐ *Set of feeler gauges*
☐ *Brake bleed nipple spanner*
☐ *Screwdrivers:*
  Flat blade - 100 mm long x 6 mm dia
  Cross blade - 100 mm long x 6 mm dia
☐ *Combination pliers*
☐ *Hacksaw (junior)*
☐ *Tyre pump*
☐ *Tyre pressure gauge*
☐ *Oil can*
☐ *Oil filter removal tool*
☐ *Fine emery cloth*
☐ *Wire brush (small)*
☐ *Funnel (medium size)*

Repair and overhaul tool kit

These tools are virtually essential for anyone undertaking any major repairs to a motor vehicle, and are additional to those given in the *Maintenance and minor repair* list. Included in this list is a comprehensive set of sockets. Although these are expensive, they will be found invaluable as they are so versatile - particularly if various drives are included in the set. We recommend the half-inch square-drive type, as this can be used with most proprietary torque wrenches.

The tools in this list will sometimes need to be supplemented by tools from the *Special* list:

☐ *Sockets (or box spanners) to cover range in previous list (including Torx sockets)*
☐ *Reversible ratchet drive (for use with sockets)*
☐ *Extension piece, 250 mm (for use with sockets)*
☐ *Universal joint (for use with sockets)*
☐ *Torque wrench (for use with sockets)*
☐ *Self-locking grips*
☐ *Ball pein hammer*
☐ *Soft-faced mallet (plastic/aluminium or rubber)*
☐ *Screwdrivers:*
  Flat blade - long & sturdy, short (chubby), and narrow (electrician's) types
  Cross blade – Long & sturdy, and short (chubby) types
☐ *Pliers:*
  Long-nosed
  Side cutters (electrician's)
  Circlip (internal and external)
☐ *Cold chisel - 25 mm*
☐ *Scriber*
☐ *Scraper*
☐ *Centre-punch*
☐ *Pin punch*
☐ *Hacksaw*
☐ *Brake hose clamp*
☐ *Brake/clutch bleeding kit*
☐ *Selection of twist drills*
☐ *Steel rule/straight-edge*
☐ *Allen keys (inc. splined/Torx type)*
☐ *Selection of files*
☐ *Wire brush*
☐ *Axle stands*
☐ *Jack (strong trolley or hydraulic type)*
☐ *Light with extension lead*

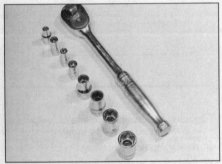

Sockets and reversible ratchet drive

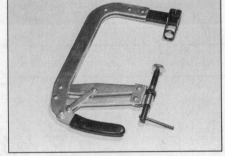

Valve spring compressor

Spline bit set

Piston ring compressor

Clutch plate alignment set

Special tools

The tools in this list are those which are not used regularly, are expensive to buy, or which need to be used in accordance with their manufacturers' instructions. Unless relatively difficult mechanical jobs are undertaken frequently, it will not be economic to buy many of these tools. Where this is the case, you could consider clubbing together with friends (or joining a motorists' club) to make a joint purchase, or borrowing the tools against a deposit from a local garage or tool hire specialist. It is worth noting that many of the larger DIY superstores now carry a large range of special tools for hire at modest rates.

The following list contains only those tools and instruments freely available to the public, and not those special tools produced by the vehicle manufacturer specifically for its dealer network. You will find occasional references to these manufacturers' special tools in the text of this manual. Generally, an alternative method of doing the job without the vehicle manufacturers' special tool is given. However, sometimes there is no alternative to using them. Where this is the case and the relevant tool cannot be bought or borrowed, you will have to entrust the work to a dealer.

☐ Valve spring compressor
☐ Valve grinding tool
☐ Piston ring compressor
☐ Piston ring removal/installation tool
☐ Cylinder bore hone
☐ Balljoint separator
☐ Coil spring compressors (where applicable)
☐ Two/three-legged hub and bearing puller
☐ Impact screwdriver
☐ Micrometer and/or vernier calipers
☐ Dial gauge
☐ Stroboscopic timing light
☐ Dwell angle meter/tachometer
☐ Universal electrical multi-meter
☐ Cylinder compression gauge
☐ Hand-operated vacuum pump and gauge
☐ Clutch plate alignment set
☐ Brake shoe steady spring cup removal tool
☐ Bush and bearing removal/installation set
☐ Stud extractors
☐ Tap and die set
☐ Lifting tackle
☐ Trolley jack

Buying tools

Reputable motor accessory shops and superstores often offer excellent quality tools at discount prices, so it pays to shop around.

Remember, you don't have to buy the most expensive items on the shelf, but it is always advisable to steer clear of the very cheap tools. Beware of 'bargains' offered on market stalls or at car boot sales. There are plenty of good tools around at reasonable prices, but always aim to purchase items which meet the relevant national safety standards. If in doubt, ask the proprietor or manager of the shop for advice before making a purchase.

Care and maintenance of tools

Having purchased a reasonable tool kit, it is necessary to keep the tools in a clean and serviceable condition. After use, always wipe off any dirt, grease and metal particles using a clean, dry cloth, before putting the tools away. Never leave them lying around after they have been used. A simple tool rack on the garage or workshop wall for items such as screwdrivers and pliers is a good idea. Store all normal spanners and sockets in a metal box. Any measuring instruments, gauges, meters, etc, must be carefully stored where they cannot be damaged or become rusty.

Take a little care when tools are used. Hammer heads inevitably become marked, and screwdrivers lose the keen edge on their blades from time to time. A little timely attention with emery cloth or a file will soon restore items like this to a good finish.

Working facilities

Not to be forgotten when discussing tools is the workshop itself. If anything more than routine maintenance is to be carried out, a suitable working area becomes essential.

It is appreciated that many an owner-mechanic is forced by circumstances to remove an engine or similar item without the benefit of a garage or workshop. Having done this, any repairs should always be done under the cover of a roof.

Wherever possible, any dismantling should be done on a clean, flat workbench or table at a suitable working height.

Any workbench needs a vice; one with a jaw opening of 100 mm is suitable for most jobs. As mentioned previously, some clean dry storage space is also required for tools, as well as for any lubricants, cleaning fluids, touch-up paints etc, which become necessary.

Another item which may be required, and which has a much more general usage, is an electric drill with a chuck capacity of at least 8 mm. This, together with a good range of twist drills, is virtually essential for fitting accessories.

Last, but not least, always keep a supply of old newspapers and clean, lint-free rags available, and try to keep any working area as clean as possible.

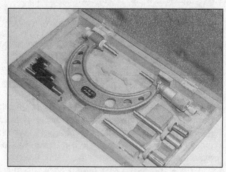
Micrometer set

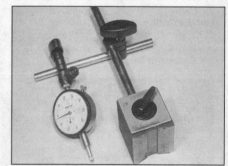
Dial test indicator ("dial gauge")

Stroboscopic timing light

Compression tester

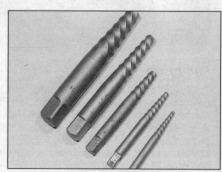
Stud extractor set

This is a guide to getting your vehicle through the MOT test. Obviously it will not be possible to examine the vehicle to the same standard as the professional MOT tester. However, working through the following checks will enable you to identify any problem areas before submitting the vehicle for the test.

Where a testable component is in borderline condition, the tester has discretion in deciding whether to pass or fail it. The basis of such discretion is whether the tester would be happy for a close relative or friend to use the vehicle with the component in that condition. If the vehicle presented is clean and evidently well cared for, the tester may be more inclined to pass a borderline component than if the vehicle is scruffy and apparently neglected.

It has only been possible to summarise the test requirements here, based on the regulations in force at the time of printing. Test standards are becoming increasingly stringent, although there are some exemptions for older vehicles. For full details obtain a copy of the Haynes publication Pass the MOT! (available from stockists of Haynes manuals).

An assistant will be needed to help carry out some of these checks.

The checks have been sub-divided into four categories, as follows:

1 Checks carried out **FROM THE DRIVER'S SEAT**

2 Checks carried out **WITH THE VEHICLE ON THE GROUND**

3 Checks carried out **WITH THE VEHICLE RAISED AND THE WHEELS FREE TO TURN**

4 Checks carried out on **YOUR VEHICLE'S EXHAUST EMISSION SYSTEM**

---

1 Checks carried out **FROM THE DRIVER'S SEAT**

Handbrake

☐ Test the operation of the handbrake. Excessive travel (too many clicks) indicates incorrect brake or cable adjustment.
☐ Check that the handbrake cannot be released by tapping the lever sideways. Check the security of the lever mountings.

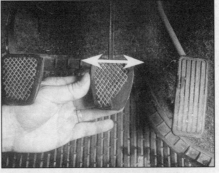

☐ Check that the brake pedal is secure and in good condition. Check also for signs of fluid leaks on the pedal, floor or carpets, which would indicate failed seals in the brake master cylinder.
☐ Check the servo unit (when applicable) by operating the brake pedal several times, then keeping the pedal depressed and starting the engine. As the engine starts, the pedal will move down slightly. If not, the vacuum hose or the servo itself may be faulty.

movement of the steering wheel, indicating wear in the column support bearings or couplings.

Windscreen and mirrors

☐ The windscreen must be free of cracks or other significant damage within the driver's field of view. (Small stone chips are acceptable.) Rear view mirrors must be secure, intact, and capable of being adjusted.

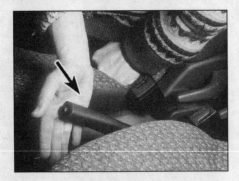

Footbrake

☐ Depress the brake pedal and check that it does not creep down to the floor, indicating a master cylinder fault. Release the pedal, wait a few seconds, then depress it again. If the pedal travels nearly to the floor before firm resistance is felt, brake adjustment or repair is necessary. If the pedal feels spongy, there is air in the hydraulic system which must be removed by bleeding.

Steering wheel and column

☐ Examine the steering wheel for fractures or looseness of the hub, spokes or rim.
☐ Move the steering wheel from side to side and then up and down. Check that the steering wheel is not loose on the column, indicating wear or a loose retaining nut. Continue moving the steering wheel as before, but also turn it slightly from left to right.
☐ Check that the steering wheel is not loose on the column, and that there is no abnormal

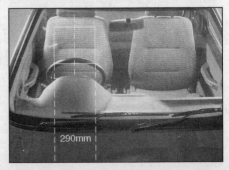

290mm

Seat belts and seats

Note: *The following checks are applicable to all seat belts, front and rear.*

☐ Examine the webbing of all the belts (including rear belts if fitted) for cuts, serious fraying or deterioration. Fasten and unfasten each belt to check the buckles. If applicable, check the retracting mechanism. Check the security of all seat belt mountings accessible from inside the vehicle.

☐ The front seats themselves must be securely attached and the backrests must lock in the upright position.

Doors

☐ Both front doors must be able to be opened and closed from outside and inside, and must latch securely when closed.

2 Checks carried out WITH THE VEHICLE ON THE GROUND

Vehicle identification

☐ Number plates must be in good condition, secure and legible, with letters and numbers correctly spaced – spacing at (A) should be twice that at (B).

☐ The VIN plate and/or homologation plate must be legible.

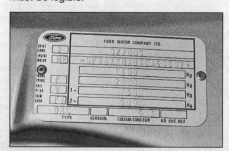

Electrical equipment

☐ Switch on the ignition and check the operation of the horn.

☐ Check the windscreen washers and wipers, examining the wiper blades; renew damaged or perished blades. Also check the operation of the stop-lights.

☐ Check the operation of the sidelights and number plate lights. The lenses and reflectors must be secure, clean and undamaged.

☐ Check the operation and alignment of the headlights. The headlight reflectors must not be tarnished and the lenses must be undamaged.

☐ Switch on the ignition and check the operation of the direction indicators (including the instrument panel tell-tale) and the hazard warning lights. Operation of the sidelights and stop-lights must not affect the indicators - if it does, the cause is usually a bad earth at the rear light cluster.

☐ Check the operation of the rear foglight(s), including the warning light on the instrument panel or in the switch.

Footbrake

☐ Examine the master cylinder, brake pipes and servo unit for leaks, loose mountings, corrosion or other damage.

☐ The fluid reservoir must be secure and the fluid level must be between the upper (**A**) and lower (**B**) markings.

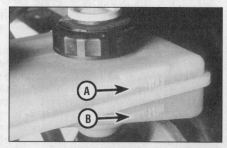

☐ Inspect both front brake flexible hoses for cracks or deterioration of the rubber. Turn the steering from lock to lock, and ensure that the hoses do not contact the wheel, tyre, or any part of the steering or suspension mechanism. With the brake pedal firmly depressed, check the hoses for bulges or leaks under pressure.

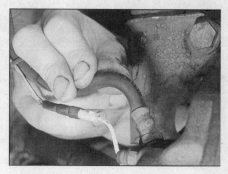

Steering and suspension

☐ Have your assistant turn the steering wheel from side to side slightly, up to the point where the steering gear just begins to transmit this movement to the roadwheels. Check for excessive free play between the steering wheel and the steering gear, indicating wear or insecurity of the steering column joints, the column-to-steering gear coupling, or the steering gear itself.

☐ Have your assistant turn the steering wheel more vigorously in each direction, so that the roadwheels just begin to turn. As this is done, examine all the steering joints, linkages, fittings and attachments. Renew any component that shows signs of wear or damage. On vehicles with power steering, check the security and condition of the steering pump, drivebelt and hoses.

☐ Check that the vehicle is standing level, and at approximately the correct ride height.

Shock absorbers

☐ Depress each corner of the vehicle in turn, then release it. The vehicle should rise and then settle in its normal position. If the vehicle continues to rise and fall, the shock absorber is defective. A shock absorber which has seized will also cause the vehicle to fail.

Exhaust system

☐ Start the engine. With your assistant holding a rag over the tailpipe, check the entire system for leaks. Repair or renew leaking sections.

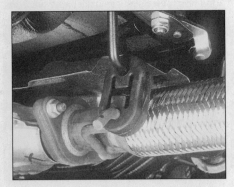

3 Checks carried out **WITH THE VEHICLE RAISED AND THE WHEELS FREE TO TURN**

Jack up the front and rear of the vehicle, and securely support it on axle stands. Position the stands clear of the suspension assemblies. Ensure that the wheels are clear of the ground and that the steering can be turned from lock to lock.

Steering mechanism

☐ Have your assistant turn the steering from lock to lock. Check that the steering turns smoothly, and that no part of the steering mechanism, including a wheel or tyre, fouls any brake hose or pipe or any part of the body structure.

☐ Examine the steering rack rubber gaiters for damage or insecurity of the retaining clips. If power steering is fitted, check for signs of damage or leakage of the fluid hoses, pipes or connections. Also check for excessive stiffness or binding of the steering, a missing split pin or locking device, or severe corrosion of the body structure within 30 cm of any steering component attachment point.

Front and rear suspension and wheel bearings

☐ Starting at the front right-hand side, grasp the roadwheel at the 3 o'clock and 9 o'clock positions and shake it vigorously. Check for free play or insecurity at the wheel bearings, suspension balljoints, or suspension mountings, pivots and attachments.

☐ Now grasp the wheel at the 12 o'clock and 6 o'clock positions and repeat the previous inspection. Spin the wheel, and check for roughness or tightness of the front wheel bearing.

☐ If excess free play is suspected at a component pivot point, this can be confirmed by using a large screwdriver or similar tool and levering between the mounting and the component attachment. This will confirm whether the wear is in the pivot bush, its retaining bolt, or in the mounting itself (the bolt holes can often become elongated).

☐ Carry out all the above checks at the other front wheel, and then at both rear wheels.

Springs and shock absorbers

☐ Examine the suspension struts (when applicable) for serious fluid leakage, corrosion, or damage to the casing. Also check the security of the mounting points.

☐ If coil springs are fitted, check that the spring ends locate in their seats, and that the spring is not corroded, cracked or broken.

☐ If leaf springs are fitted, check that all leaves are intact, that the axle is securely attached to each spring, and that there is no deterioration of the spring eye mountings, bushes, and shackles.

☐ The same general checks apply to vehicles fitted with other suspension types, such as torsion bars, hydraulic displacer units, etc. Ensure that all mountings and attachments are secure, that there are no signs of excessive wear, corrosion or damage, and (on hydraulic types) that there are no fluid leaks or damaged pipes.

☐ Inspect the shock absorbers for signs of serious fluid leakage. Check for wear of the mounting bushes or attachments, or damage to the body of the unit.

Driveshafts (fwd vehicles only)

☐ Rotate each front wheel in turn and inspect the constant velocity joint gaiters for splits or damage. Also check that each driveshaft is straight and undamaged.

Braking system

☐ If possible without dismantling, check brake pad wear and disc condition. Ensure that the friction lining material has not worn excessively, (A) and that the discs are not fractured, pitted, scored or badly worn (B).

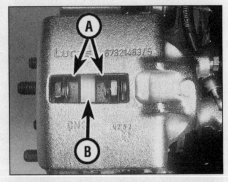

☐ Examine all the rigid brake pipes underneath the vehicle, and the flexible hose(s) at the rear. Look for corrosion, chafing or insecurity of the pipes, and for signs of bulging under pressure, chafing, splits or deterioration of the flexible hoses.

☐ Look for signs of fluid leaks at the brake calipers or on the brake backplates. Repair or renew leaking components.

☐ Slowly spin each wheel, while your assistant depresses and releases the footbrake. Ensure that each brake is operating and does not bind when the pedal is released.

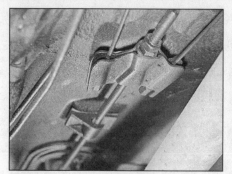

□ Examine the handbrake mechanism, checking for frayed or broken cables, excessive corrosion, or wear or insecurity of the linkage. Check that the mechanism works on each relevant wheel, and releases fully, without binding.

□ It is not possible to test brake efficiency without special equipment, but a road test can be carried out later to check that the vehicle pulls up in a straight line.

Fuel and exhaust systems

□ Inspect the fuel tank (including the filler cap), fuel pipes, hoses and unions. All components must be secure and free from leaks.

□ Examine the exhaust system over its entire length, checking for any damaged, broken or missing mountings, security of the retaining clamps and rust or corrosion.

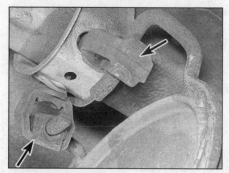

Wheels and tyres

□ Examine the sidewalls and tread area of each tyre in turn. Check for cuts, tears, lumps, bulges, separation of the tread, and exposure of the ply or cord due to wear or damage. Check that the tyre bead is correctly seated on the wheel rim, that the valve is sound and

properly seated, and that the wheel is not distorted or damaged.

□ Check that the tyres are of the correct size for the vehicle, that they are of the same size and type on each axle, and that the pressures are correct.

□ Check the tyre tread depth. The legal minimum at the time of writing is 1.6 mm over at least three-quarters of the tread width. Abnormal tread wear may indicate incorrect front wheel alignment.

Body corrosion

□ Check the condition of the entire vehicle structure for signs of corrosion in load-bearing areas. (These include chassis box sections, side sills, cross-members, pillars, and all suspension, steering, braking system and seat belt mountings and anchorages.) Any corrosion which has seriously reduced the thickness of a load-bearing area is likely to cause the vehicle to fail. In this case professional repairs are likely to be needed.

□ Damage or corrosion which causes sharp or otherwise dangerous edges to be exposed will also cause the vehicle to fail.

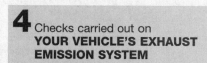

4 Checks carried out on **YOUR VEHICLE'S EXHAUST EMISSION SYSTEM**

Petrol models

□ Have the engine at normal operating temperature, and make sure that it is in good tune (ignition system in good order, air filter element clean, etc).

□ Before any measurements are carried out, raise the engine speed to around 2500 rpm, and hold it at this speed for 20 seconds. Allow

the engine speed to return to idle, and watch for smoke emissions from the exhaust tailpipe. If the idle speed is obviously much too high, or if dense blue or clearly-visible black smoke comes from the tailpipe for more than 5 seconds, the vehicle will fail. As a rule of thumb, blue smoke signifies oil being burnt (engine wear) while black smoke signifies unburnt fuel (dirty air cleaner element, or other carburettor or fuel system fault).

□ An exhaust gas analyser capable of measuring carbon monoxide (CO) and hydrocarbons (HC) is now needed. If such an instrument cannot be hired or borrowed, a local garage may agree to perform the check for a small fee.

CO emissions (mixture)

□ At the time of writing, the maximum CO level at idle is 3.5% for vehicles first used after August 1986 and 4.5% for older vehicles. From January 1996 a much tighter limit (around 0.5%) applies to catalyst-equipped vehicles first used from August 1992. If the CO level cannot be reduced far enough to pass the test (and the fuel and ignition systems are otherwise in good condition) then the carburettor is badly worn, or there is some problem in the fuel injection system or catalytic converter (as applicable).

HC emissions

□ With the CO emissions within limits, HC emissions must be no more than 1200 ppm (parts per million). If the vehicle fails this test at idle, it can be re-tested at around 2000 rpm; if the HC level is then 1200 ppm or less, this counts as a pass.

□ Excessive HC emissions can be caused by oil being burnt, but they are more likely to be due to unburnt fuel.

Diesel models

□ The only emission test applicable to Diesel engines is the measuring of exhaust smoke density. The test involves accelerating the engine several times to its maximum unloaded speed.

Note: *It is of the utmost importance that the engine timing belt is in good condition before the test is carried out.*

□ Excessive smoke can be caused by a dirty air cleaner element. Otherwise, professional advice may be needed to find the cause.

Engine 1

☐ Engine fails to rotate when attempting to start
☐ Engine rotates but will not start
☐ Engine difficult to start when cold
☐ Engine difficult to start when hot
☐ Starter motor noisy or excessively rough in engagement
☐ Engine starts but stops immediately
☐ Engine idles erratically
☐ Engine misfires at idle speed
☐ Engine misfires throughout the driving speed range
☐ Engine hesitates on acceleration
☐ Engine stalls
☐ Engine lacks power
☐ Engine backfires
☐ Oil pressure warning light illuminated with engine running
☐ Engine runs-on after switching off
☐ Engine noises

Cooling system 2

☐ Overheating
☐ Overcooling
☐ External coolant leakage
☐ Internal coolant leakage
☐ Corrosion

Fuel and exhaust system 3

☐ Excessive fuel consumption
☐ Fuel leakage and/or fuel odour
☐ Excessive noise or fumes from exhaust system

Clutch 4

☐ Pedal travels to floor - no pressure or very little resistance
☐ Clutch fails to disengage (unable to select gears)
☐ Clutch slips (engine speed increases with no increase in vehicle speed)
☐ Judder as clutch is engaged
☐ Noise when depressing or releasing clutch pedal

Manual transmission 5

☐ Noisy in neutral with engine running
☐ Noisy in one particular gear
☐ Difficulty engaging gears
☐ Jumps out of gear
☐ Vibration
☐ Lubricant leaks

Automatic transmission 6

☐ Fluid leakage
☐ Transmission fluid brown or has burned smell
☐ General gear selection problems
☐ Transmission will not downshift (kickdown) with accelerator fully depressed
☐ Engine will not start in any gear, or starts in gears other than Park or Neutral
☐ Transmission slips, shifts roughly, is noisy or has no drive in forward or reverse gears

Driveshafts 7

☐ Clicking or knocking noise on turns (at slow speed on full lock)
☐ Vibration when accelerating or decelerating

Braking system 8

☐ Vehicle pulls to one side under braking
☐ Noise (grinding or high-pitched squeal) when brakes applied
☐ Excessive brake pedal travel
☐ Brake pedal feels spongy when depressed
☐ Excessive brake pedal effort required to stop vehicle
☐ Judder felt through brake pedal or steering wheel when braking
☐ Brakes binding
☐ Rear wheels locking under normal braking

Suspension and steering systems 9

☐ Vehicle pulls to one side
☐ Wheel wobble and vibration
☐ Excessive pitching and/or rolling around corners or during braking
☐ Wandering or general instability
☐ Excessively stiff steering
☐ Excessive play in steering
☐ Lack of power assistance
☐ Tyre wear excessive

Electrical system 10

☐ Battery will not hold a charge for more than a few days
☐ Ignition warning light remains illuminated with engine running
☐ Ignition warning light fails to come on
☐ Lights inoperative
☐ Instrument readings inaccurate or erratic
☐ Horn inoperative or unsatisfactory in operation
☐ Windscreen/tailgate wipers inoperative or unsatisfactory in operation
☐ Windscreen/tailgate washers inoperative or unsatisfactory in operation
☐ Central locking system inoperative or unsatisfactory in operation
☐ Electric windows inoperative or unsatisfactory in operation

Introduction

The vehicle owner who does his or her own maintenance according to the recommended service schedules should not have to use this section of the manual very often. Modern component reliability is such that, provided those items subject to wear or deterioration are inspected or renewed at the specified intervals, sudden failure is comparatively rare. Faults do not usually just happen as a result of sudden failure, but develop over a period of time. Major mechanical failures in particular are usually preceded by characteristic symptoms over hundreds or even thousands of miles. Those components which do occasionally fail without warning are often small and easily carried in the vehicle.

With any fault finding, the first step is to decide where to begin investigations. Sometimes this is obvious, but on other occasions a little detective work will be necessary. The owner who makes half a dozen haphazard adjustments or replacements may be successful in curing a fault (or its symptoms), but will be none the wiser if the fault recurs and ultimately may have spent more time and money than was necessary. A calm and logical approach will be found to be more satisfactory in the long run. Always take into account any warning signs or abnormalities that may have been noticed in the period preceding the fault - power loss, high or low gauge readings, unusual smells, etc - and remember that failure of components such as fuses or spark plugs may only be pointers to some underlying fault.

The pages which follow provide an easy reference guide to the more common problems which may occur during the operation of the vehicle. These problems and their possible causes are grouped under headings denoting various components or systems, such as Engine, Cooling system, etc. The Chapter and/or Section which deals with the problem is also shown in brackets. Whatever the fault, certain basic principles apply. These are as follows:

Verify the fault. This is simply a matter of being sure that you know what the symptoms are before starting work. This is particularly important if you are investigating a fault for someone else who may not have described it very accurately.

Don't overlook the obvious. For example, if the vehicle won't start, is there petrol in the tank? (Don't take anyone else's word on this particular point, and don't trust the fuel gauge either!) If an electrical fault is indicated, look for loose or broken wires before digging out the test gear.

Cure the disease, not the symptom. Substituting a flat battery with a fully charged one will get you off the hard shoulder, but if the underlying cause is not attended to, the new battery will go the same way. Similarly, changing oil-fouled spark plugs for a new set will get you moving again, but remember that the reason for the fouling (if it wasn't simply an incorrect grade of plug) will have to be established and corrected.

Don't take anything for granted. Particularly, don't forget that a "new" component may itself be defective (especially if it's been rattling around in the boot for months), and don't leave components out of a fault diagnosis sequence just because they are new or recently fitted. When you do finally diagnose a difficult fault, you'll probably realise that all the evidence was there from the start.

1 Engine

Engine fails to rotate when attempting to start

☐ Battery terminal connections loose or corroded ("*Weekly checks*").
☐ Battery discharged or faulty (Chapter 5, Part A).
☐ Broken, loose or disconnected wiring in the starting circuit (Chapter 5, Part A).
☐ Defective starter solenoid or switch (Chapter 5, Part A).
☐ Defective starter motor (Chapter 5, Part A).
☐ Starter pinion or flywheel ring gear teeth loose or broken (Chapter 5, Part A and Chapter 2).
☐ Engine earth strap broken or disconnected (Chapter 5, Part A).
☐ Automatic transmission not in Park/Neutral position or starter inhibitor switch faulty (Chapter 7, Part B).

Engine rotates but will not start

☐ Fuel tank empty.
☐ Battery discharged (engine rotates slowly) (Chapter 5, Part A).
☐ Battery terminal connections loose or corroded ("*Weekly checks*").
☐ Ignition components damp or damaged (Chapter 1 and Chapter 5, Part B).
☐ Broken, loose or disconnected wiring in the ignition circuit (Chapter 1 and Chapter 5, Part B).
☐ Worn, faulty or incorrectly gapped spark plugs (Chapter 1).
☐ Carburettor or fuel injection system fault (Chapter 4).
☐ Major mechanical failure (eg camshaft drive) (Chapter 2).

Engine difficult to start when cold

☐ Battery discharged (Chapter 5, Part A).
☐ Battery terminal connections loose or corroded ("*Weekly checks*").
☐ Worn, faulty or incorrectly gapped spark plugs (Chapter 1).
☐ Carburettor or fuel injection system fault (Chapter 4).
☐ Other ignition system fault (Chapter 1 and Chapter 5, Part B).
☐ Low cylinder compressions (Chapter 2).
☐ Incorrect valve clearances - where applicable (Chapter 2, Part A).

Engine difficult to start when hot

☐ Air filter element dirty or clogged (Chapter 1).
☐ Carburettor or fuel injection system fault (Chapter 4).
☐ Low cylinder compressions (Chapter 2).
☐ Incorrect valve clearances - where applicable (Chapter 2, Part A).

Starter motor noisy or excessively rough in engagement

☐ Starter pinion or flywheel ring gear teeth loose or broken (Chapter 5, Part A and Chapter 2).
☐ Starter motor mounting bolts loose or missing (Chapter 5, Part A).
☐ Starter motor internal components worn or damaged (Chapter 5, Part A).

Engine starts but stops immediately

☐ Loose or faulty electrical connections in the ignition circuit (Chapter 1 and Chapter 5, Part B).
☐ Vacuum leak at the carburettor/fuel injection unit/throttle body or inlet manifold (Chapter 4).
☐ Carburettor or fuel injection system fault (Chapter 4).

Engine idles erratically

☐ Air filter element clogged (Chapter 1).
☐ Vacuum leak at the carburettor/fuel injection unit/throttle body, inlet manifold or associated hoses (Chapter 4).
☐ Worn, faulty or incorrectly gapped spark plugs (Chapter 1).
☐ Uneven or low cylinder compressions (Chapter 2).
☐ Camshaft lobes worn (Chapter 2).
☐ Timing belt incorrectly tensioned - where applicable (Chapter 2, Part B).
☐ Incorrect valve clearances - where applicable (Chapter 2, Part A).
☐ Carburettor or fuel injection system fault (Chapter 4).

Engine misfires at idle speed

☐ Worn, faulty or incorrectly gapped spark plugs (Chapter 1).
☐ Faulty spark plug HT leads (Chapter 1).
☐ Incorrect ignition timing (Chapter 1).
☐ Vacuum leak at the carburettor/fuel injection unit/throttle body, inlet manifold or associated hoses (Chapter 4).
☐ Distributor cap cracked or tracking internally - where applicable (Chapter 1).
☐ Uneven or low cylinder compressions (Chapter 2).
☐ Disconnected, leaking or perished crankcase ventilation hoses (Chapter 4, Part E).
☐ Carburettor or fuel injection system fault (Chapter 4).
☐ Incorrect valve clearances - where applicable (Chapter 2, Part A).

Engine misfires throughout the driving speed range

☐ Fuel filter choked (Chapter 1).
☐ Fuel pump faulty or delivery pressure low (Chapter 4).
☐ Fuel tank vent blocked or fuel pipes restricted (Chapter 4).
☐ Vacuum leak at the carburettor/fuel injection unit/throttle body, inlet manifold or associated hoses (Chapter 4).
☐ Worn, faulty or incorrectly gapped spark plugs (Chapter 1).
☐ Faulty spark plug HT leads (Chapter 1).
☐ Distributor cap cracked or tracking internally - where applicable (Chapter 1).
☐ Faulty ignition coil or DIS module (Chapter 5, Part B).
☐ Uneven or low cylinder compressions (Chapter 2).
☐ Carburettor or fuel injection system fault (Chapter 4).
☐ Incorrect valve clearances - where applicable (Chapter 2, Part A).

1 Engine (continued)

Engine hesitates on acceleration

☐ Worn, faulty or incorrectly gapped spark plugs (Chapter 1).
☐ Vacuum leak at the carburettor/fuel injection unit/throttle body, inlet manifold or associated hoses (Chapter 4).
☐ Carburettor or fuel injection system fault (Chapter 4).

Engine stalls

☐ Vacuum leak at the carburettor/fuel injection unit/throttle body, inlet manifold or associated hoses (Chapter 4).
☐ Fuel filter choked (Chapter 1).
☐ Fuel pump faulty or delivery pressure low (Chapter 4).
☐ Fuel tank vent blocked or fuel pipes restricted (Chapter 4).
☐ Carburettor or fuel injection system fault (Chapter 4).

Engine lacks power

☐ Incorrect ignition timing (Chapter 1).
☐ Timing belt/chain incorrectly fitted or tensioned (Chapter 2).
☐ Fuel filter choked (Chapter 1).
☐ Fuel pump faulty or delivery pressure low (Chapter 4).
☐ Uneven or low cylinder compressions (Chapter 2).
☐ Worn, faulty or incorrectly gapped spark plugs (Chapter 1).
☐ Vacuum leak at the carburettor/fuel injection unit/throttle body, inlet manifold or associated hoses (Chapter 4).
☐ Brakes binding (Chapters 1 and 9).
☐ Clutch slipping (Chapter 6).
☐ Automatic transmission fluid level incorrect (Chapter 1).
☐ Carburettor or fuel injection system fault (Chapter 4).

Engine backfires

☐ Ignition timing incorrect (Chapter 1).
☐ Timing belt/chain incorrectly fitted or tensioned (Chapter 2).
☐ Vacuum leak at the carburettor/fuel injection unit/throttle body, inlet manifold or associated hoses (Chapter 4).
☐ Carburettor or fuel injection system fault (Chapter 4).

Oil pressure warning light illuminated with engine running

☐ Low oil level or incorrect grade (Chapter 1).
☐ Faulty oil pressure sensor (Chapter 2).
☐ Worn engine bearings and/or oil pump (Chapter 2).
☐ High engine operating temperature (Chapter 3).

☐ Oil pressure relief valve defective (Chapter 2).
☐ Oil pick-up strainer clogged (Chapter 2).

Engine runs-on after switching off

☐ Excessive carbon build-up in engine (Chapter 2).
☐ High engine operating temperature (Chapter 3).
☐ Carburettor or fuel injection system fault (Chapter 4).

Engine noises

Pre-ignition (pinking) or knocking during acceleration or under load

☐ Ignition timing incorrect (Chapter 1).
☐ Incorrect grade of fuel (Chapters 1 and 4).
☐ Vacuum leak at the carburettor/fuel injection unit/throttle body, inlet manifold or associated hoses (Chapter 4).
☐ Excessive carbon build-up in engine (Chapter 2).
☐ Worn or damaged distributor (where applicable) or other ignition system component (Chapter 5, Part B).
☐ Carburettor or fuel injection system fault (Chapter 4).

Whistling or wheezing noises

☐ Leaking inlet manifold or carburettor/fuel injection unit/throttle body gasket (Chapter 4).
☐ Leaking exhaust manifold gasket or pipe to manifold joint (Chapter 4, Part E).
☐ Leaking vacuum hose (Chapters 4, 5 and 9).
☐ Blowing cylinder head gasket (Chapter 2).

Tapping or rattling noises

☐ Worn valve gear or camshaft (Chapter 2).
☐ Ancillary component fault (water pump, alternator etc) (Chapter 3, Chapter 5, Part A and Chapter 10).

Knocking or thumping noises

☐ Worn big-end bearings (regular heavy knocking, perhaps less under load) (Chapter 2).
☐ Worn main bearings (rumbling and knocking, perhaps worsening under load) (Chapter 2).
☐ Piston slap (most noticeable when cold) (Chapter 2).
☐ Ancillary component fault (water pump, alternator etc) (Chapter 3, Chapter 5, Part A and Chapter 10).

2 Cooling system

Overheating

☐ Insufficient coolant in system ("Weekly checks").
☐ Thermostat faulty (Chapter 3).
☐ Radiator core blocked or grille restricted (Chapter 3).
☐ Electric cooling fan or thermoswitch faulty (Chapter 3).
☐ Pressure cap faulty (Chapter 3).
☐ Ignition timing incorrect (Chapter 1).
☐ Inaccurate temperature gauge sender unit (Chapter 3).
☐ Air lock in cooling system (Chapter 1).

Overcooling

☐ Thermostat faulty (Chapter 3).
☐ Inaccurate temperature gauge sender unit (Chapter 3).

External coolant leakage

☐ Deteriorated or damaged hoses or hose clips (Chapter 1).
☐ Radiator core or heater matrix leaking (Chapter 3).
☐ Pressure cap faulty (Chapter 3).
☐ Water pump seal leaking (Chapter 3).
☐ Boiling due to overheating (Chapter 3).
☐ Core plug leaking (Chapter 2).

Internal coolant leakage

☐ Leaking cylinder head gasket (Chapter 2).
☐ Cracked cylinder head or cylinder bore (Chapter 2).

Corrosion

☐ Infrequent draining and flushing (Chapter 1).
☐ Incorrect antifreeze mixture or inappropriate type (Chapter 1).

3 Fuel and exhaust system

Excessive fuel consumption

☐ Air filter element dirty or clogged (Chapter 1).
☐ Carburettor or fuel injection system fault (Chapter 4).
☐ Ignition timing incorrect (Chapter 1).
☐ Tyres underinflated (Chapter 1).

Fuel leakage and/or fuel odour

☐ Damaged or corroded fuel tank, pipes or connections (Chapter 4).
☐ Carburettor or fuel injection system fault (Chapter 4).

Excessive noise or fumes from exhaust system

☐ Leaking exhaust system or manifold joints (Chapter 1 and Chapter 4, Part E).
☐ Leaking, corroded or damaged silencers or pipe (Chapter 1 and Chapter 4, Part E).
☐ Broken mountings causing body or suspension contact (Chapter 1).

4 Clutch

Pedal travels to floor - no pressure or very little resistance

☐ Broken clutch cable (Chapter 6).
☐ Incorrect clutch adjustment (Chapter 6).
☐ Broken clutch release bearing or fork (Chapter 6).
☐ Broken diaphragm spring in clutch pressure plate (Chapter 6).

Clutch fails to disengage (unable to select gears)

☐ Incorrect clutch adjustment (Chapter 6).
☐ Clutch disc sticking on gearbox input shaft splines (Chapter 6).
☐ Clutch disc sticking to flywheel or pressure plate (Chapter 6).
☐ Faulty pressure plate assembly (Chapter 6).
☐ Clutch release mechanism worn or incorrectly assembled (Chapter 6).

Clutch slips (engine speed increases with no increase in vehicle speed)

☐ Incorrect clutch adjustment (Chapter 6).
☐ Clutch disc linings excessively worn (Chapter 6).

☐ Clutch disc linings contaminated with oil or grease (Chapter 6).
☐ Faulty pressure plate or weak diaphragm spring (Chapter 6).

Judder as clutch is engaged

☐ Clutch disc linings contaminated with oil or grease (Chapter 6).
☐ Clutch disc linings excessively worn (Chapter 6).
☐ Clutch cable sticking or frayed (Chapter 6).
☐ Faulty or distorted pressure plate or diaphragm spring (Chapter 6).
☐ Worn or loose engine or gearbox mountings (Chapter 2).
☐ Clutch disc hub or gearbox input shaft splines worn (Chapter 6).

Noise when depressing or releasing clutch pedal

☐ Worn clutch release bearing (Chapter 6).
☐ Worn or dry clutch pedal bushes (Chapter 6).
☐ Faulty pressure plate assembly (Chapter 6).
☐ Pressure plate diaphragm spring broken (Chapter 6).
☐ Broken clutch disc cushioning springs (Chapter 6).

5 Manual gearbox

Noisy in neutral with engine running

☐ Input shaft bearings worn (noise apparent with clutch pedal released but not when depressed) (Chapter 7, Part A).*
☐ Clutch release bearing worn (noise apparent with clutch pedal depressed, possibly less when released) (Chapter 6).

Noisy in one particular gear

☐ Worn, damaged or chipped gear teeth (Chapter 7, Part A).*

Difficulty engaging gears

☐ Clutch fault (Chapter 6).
☐ Worn or damaged gear linkage (Chapter 7, Part A).
☐ Incorrectly adjusted gear linkage (Chapter 7, Part A).
☐ Worn synchroniser units (Chapter 7, Part A).*

Jumps out of gear

☐ Worn or damaged gear linkage (Chapter 7, Part A).
☐ Incorrectly adjusted gear linkage (Chapter 7, Part A).

☐ Worn synchroniser units (Chapter 7, Part A).*
☐ Worn selector forks (Chapter 7, Part A).*

Vibration

☐ Lack of oil (Chapter 1).
☐ Worn bearings (Chapter 7, Part A).*

Lubricant leaks

☐ Leaking differential output oil seal (Chapter 7, Part A).
☐ Leaking housing joint (Chapter 7, Part A).*
☐ Leaking input shaft oil seal (Chapter 7, Part A).*

Although the corrective action necessary to remedy the symptoms described is beyond the scope of the home mechanic, the above information should be helpful in isolating the cause of the condition so that the owner can communicate clearly with a professional mechanic.

6 Automatic transmission

Note: *Due to the complexity of the automatic transmission, it is difficult for the home mechanic to properly diagnose and service this unit. For problems other than the following, the vehicle should be taken to a dealer service department or automatic transmission specialist.*

Fluid leakage

☐ Automatic transmission fluid is usually deep red in colour. Fluid leaks should not be confused with engine oil which can easily be blown onto the transmission by air flow.

☐ To determine the source of a leak, first remove all built-up dirt and grime from the transmission housing and surrounding areas using a degreasing agent or by steam cleaning. Drive the vehicle at low speed so air flow will not blow the leak far from its source. Raise and support the vehicle and determine where the leak is coming from. The following are common areas of leakage.

a) Oil pan.
b) Dipstick tube (Chapter 1).
c) Transmission-to-oil cooler fluid pipes/unions (Chapter 7, Part B).

Transmission fluid brown or has burned smell

☐ Transmission fluid level low or fluid in need of renewal (Chapter 1).

General gear selection problems

☐ Chapter 7, Part B deals with checking and adjusting the selector mechanism on automatic transmissions. The following are common problems which may be caused by a poorly adjusted cable.

a) Engine starting in gears other than Park or Neutral.
b) Indicator on gear selector lever pointing to a gear other than the one actually being used.
c) Vehicle moves when in Park or Neutral.
d) Poor gear shift quality or erratic gear changes.
☐ Refer to Chapter 7, Part B for selector mechanism adjustment.

Transmission will not downshift (kickdown) with accelerator pedal fully depressed

☐ Low transmission fluid level (Chapter 1).
☐ Incorrect selector mechanism adjustment (Chapter 7, Part B).

Engine will not start in any gear, or starts in gears other than Park or Neutral

☐ Incorrect starter inhibitor switch adjustment (Chapter 7, Part B).
☐ Incorrect selector mechanism adjustment (Chapter 7, Part B).

Transmission slips, shifts roughly, is noisy or has no drive in forward or reverse gears

☐ There are many probable causes for the above problems, but the home mechanic should be concerned with only one possibility - fluid level. Before taking the vehicle to a dealer or transmission specialist, check the fluid level and condition of the fluid as described in Chapter 1. Correct the fluid level as necessary or change the fluid and filter if needed. If the problem persists, professional help will be necessary.

7 Driveshafts

Clicking or knocking noise on turns (at slow speed on full lock)

☐ Lack of constant velocity joint lubricant (Chapter 8).
☐ Worn outer constant velocity joint (Chapter 8).

Vibration when accelerating or decelerating

☐ Worn inner constant velocity joint (Chapter 8).
☐ Bent or distorted driveshaft (Chapter 8).

8 Braking system

Note: *Before assuming that a brake problem exists, make sure that the tyres are in good condition and correctly inflated, the front wheel alignment is correct and the vehicle is not loaded with weight in an unequal manner. Apart from checking the condition of all pipe and hose connections, any faults occurring on the anti-lock braking system should be referred to a Ford dealer for diagnosis.*

Vehicle pulls to one side under braking

☐ Worn, defective, damaged or contaminated front brake pads or rear brake shoes on one side (Chapters 1 and 9).
☐ Seized or partially seized front brake caliper or rear wheel cylinder piston (Chapters 1 and 9).
☐ A mixture of brake pad/shoe lining materials fitted between sides (Chapters 1 and 9).
☐ Front brake caliper mounting bolts loose (Chapter 9).
☐ Rear brake backplate mounting bolts loose (Chapter 9).
☐ Worn or damaged steering or suspension components (Chapters 1 and 10).

Noise (grinding or high-pitched squeal) when brakes applied

☐ Brake pad or shoe friction lining material worn down to metal backing (Chapters 1 and 9).
☐ Excessive corrosion of brake disc or drum. (May be apparent after the vehicle has been standing for some time (Chapters 1 and 9).
☐ Foreign object (stone chipping etc) trapped between brake disc and shield (Chapters 1 and 9).

Excessive brake pedal travel

☐ Inoperative rear brake self-adjust mechanism (Chapters 1 and 9).
☐ Faulty master cylinder (Chapter 9).
☐ Air in hydraulic system (Chapters 1 and 9).
☐ Faulty vacuum servo unit (Chapter 9).

Brake pedal feels spongy when depressed

☐ Air in hydraulic system (Chapters 1 and 9).
☐ Deteriorated flexible rubber brake hoses (Chapters 1 and 9).
☐ Master cylinder mounting nuts loose (Chapter 9).
☐ Faulty master cylinder (Chapter 9).

Excessive brake pedal effort required to stop vehicle

☐ Faulty vacuum servo unit (Chapter 9).
☐ Disconnected, damaged or insecure brake servo vacuum hose (Chapter 9).
☐ Primary or secondary hydraulic circuit failure (Chapter 9).
☐ Seized brake caliper or wheel cylinder piston(s) (Chapter 9).
☐ Brake pads or brake shoes incorrectly fitted (Chapters 1 and 9).
☐ Incorrect grade of brake pads or brake shoes fitted (Chapters 1 and 9).
☐ Brake pads or brake shoe linings contaminated (Chapters 1 and 9).

Judder felt through brake pedal or steering wheel when braking

- [ ] Excessive run-out or distortion of front discs or rear drums (Chapters 1 and 9).
- [ ] Brake pad or brake shoe linings worn (Chapters 1 and 9).
- [ ] Brake caliper or rear brake backplate mounting bolts loose (Chapter 9).
- [ ] Wear in suspension or steering components or mountings (Chapters 1 and 10).

Brakes binding

- [ ] Seized brake caliper or wheel cylinder piston(s) (Chapter 9).
- [ ] Incorrectly adjusted handbrake mechanism (Chapter 9).
- [ ] Faulty master cylinder (Chapter 9).

Rear wheels locking under normal braking

- [ ] Rear brake shoe linings contaminated (Chapters 1 and 9).
- [ ] Faulty brake pressure regulator (Chapter 9).

9 Suspension and steering

Note: *Before diagnosing suspension or steering faults, be sure that the trouble is not due to incorrect tyre pressures, mixtures of tyre types or binding brakes.*

Vehicle pulls to one side

- [ ] Defective tyre ("*Weekly checks*").
- [ ] Excessive wear in suspension or steering components (Chapters 1 and 10).
- [ ] Incorrect front wheel alignment (Chapter 10).
- [ ] Accident damage to steering or suspension components (Chapter 1).

Wheel wobble and vibration

- [ ] Front roadwheels out of balance (vibration felt mainly through the steering wheel) (Chapters 1 and 10).
- [ ] Rear roadwheels out of balance (vibration felt throughout the vehicle) (Chapters 1 and 10).
- [ ] Roadwheels damaged or distorted (Chapters 1 and 10).
- [ ] Faulty or damaged tyre (Chapter 1).
- [ ] Worn steering or suspension joints, bushes or components (Chapters 1 and 10).
- [ ] Wheel bolts loose (Chapters 1 and 10).

Excessive pitching and/or rolling around corners or during braking

- [ ] Defective shock absorbers (Chapters 1 and 10).
- [ ] Broken or weak spring and/or suspension component (Chapters 1 and 10).
- [ ] Worn or damaged anti-roll bar or mountings (Chapter 10).

Wandering or general instability

- [ ] Incorrect front wheel alignment (Chapter 10).
- [ ] Worn steering or suspension joints, bushes or components (Chapters 1 and 10).
- [ ] Roadwheels out of balance (Chapters 1 and 10).
- [ ] Faulty or damaged tyre ("*Weekly checks*").
- [ ] Wheel bolts loose ("*Weekly checks*" and Chapter 10).
- [ ] Defective shock absorbers (Chapters 1 and 10).

Excessively stiff steering

- [ ] Lack of steering gear lubricant (Chapter 10).
- [ ] Seized track rod end balljoint or suspension balljoint (Chapters 1 and 10).
- [ ] Broken or incorrectly adjusted auxiliary drivebelt (Chapter 1).
- [ ] Incorrect front wheel alignment (Chapter 10).
- [ ] Steering rack or column bent or damaged (Chapter 10).

Excessive play in steering

- [ ] Worn steering column intermediate shaft universal joint (Chapter 10).
- [ ] Worn steering track rod end balljoints (Chapters 1 and 10).
- [ ] Worn rack and pinion steering gear (Chapter 10).
- [ ] Worn steering or suspension joints, bushes or components (Chapters 1 and 10).

Tyre wear excessive

Tyres worn on inside or outside edges

- [ ] Tyres underinflated (wear on both edges) ("*Weekly checks*").
- [ ] Incorrect camber or castor angles (wear on one edge only) (Chapter 10).
- [ ] Worn steering or suspension joints, bushes or components (Chapters 1 and 10).
- [ ] Excessively hard cornering.
- [ ] Accident damage.

Tyre treads exhibit feathered edges

- [ ] Incorrect toe setting (Chapter 10).

Tyres worn in centre of tread

- [ ] Tyres overinflated ("*Weekly checks*").

Tyres worn on inside and outside edges

- [ ] Tyres underinflated ("*Weekly checks*").

Tyres worn unevenly

- [ ] Tyres/wheels out of balance (Chapter 1).
- [ ] Excessive wheel or tyre run-out (Chapter 1).
- [ ] Worn shock absorbers (Chapters 1 and 10).
- [ ] Faulty tyre ("*Weekly checks*").

10 Electrical system

Note: *For problems associated with the starting system, refer to the faults listed under 'Engine' earlier in this Section.*

Battery will not hold a charge for more than a few days

- [ ] Battery defective internally (Chapter 5, Part A).
- [ ] Battery terminal connections loose or corroded ("*Weekly checks*").
- [ ] Auxiliary drivebelt worn or incorrectly adjusted (Chapter 1).
- [ ] Alternator not charging at correct output (Chapter 5, Part A).
- [ ] Alternator or voltage regulator faulty (Chapter 5, Part A).
- [ ] Short-circuit causing continual battery drain (Chapter 5, Part A and Chapter 12).

Ignition warning light remains illuminated with engine running

- [ ] Auxiliary drivebelt broken, worn, or incorrectly adjusted (Chapter 1).
- [ ] Alternator brushes worn, sticking, or dirty (Chapter 5, Part A).
- [ ] Alternator brush springs weak or broken (Chapter 5, Part A).
- [ ] Internal fault in alternator or voltage regulator (Chapter 5, Part A).
- [ ] Broken, disconnected, or loose wiring in charging circuit (Chapter 5, Part A).

Ignition warning light fails to come on

- [ ] Warning light bulb blown (Chapter 12).
- [ ] Broken, disconnected, or loose wiring in warning light circuit (Chapter 12).
- [ ] Alternator faulty (Chapter 5, Part A).

10 Electrical system (continued)

Lights inoperative

- ☐ Bulb blown (Chapter 12).
- ☐ Corrosion of bulb or bulbholder contacts (Chapter 12).
- ☐ Blown fuse (Chapter 12).
- ☐ Faulty relay (Chapter 12).
- ☐ Broken, loose, or disconnected wiring (Chapter 12).
- ☐ Faulty switch (Chapter 12).

Instrument readings inaccurate or erratic

Instrument readings increase with engine speed

- ☐ Faulty voltage regulator (Chapter 12).

Fuel or temperature gauge give no reading

- ☐ Faulty gauge sender unit (Chapter 3 or Chapter 4).
- ☐ Wiring open-circuit (Chapter 12).
- ☐ Faulty gauge (Chapter 12).

Fuel or temperature gauges give continuous maximum reading

- ☐ Faulty gauge sender unit (Chapter 3 or Chapter 4).
- ☐ Wiring short-circuit (Chapter 12).
- ☐ Faulty gauge (Chapter 12).

Horn inoperative or unsatisfactory in operation

Horn operates all the time

- ☐ Horn push either earthed or stuck down (Chapter 12).
- ☐ Horn cable to horn push earthed (Chapter 12).

Horn fails to operate

- ☐ Blown fuse (Chapter 12).
- ☐ Cable or cable connections loose, broken or disconnected (Chapter 12).
- ☐ Faulty horn (Chapter 12).

Horn emits intermittent or unsatisfactory sound

- ☐ Cable connections loose (Chapter 12).
- ☐ Horn mountings loose (Chapter 12).
- ☐ Faulty horn (Chapter 12).

Windscreen/tailgate wipers inoperative or unsatisfactory in operation

Wipers fail to operate or operate very slowly

- ☐ Wiper blades stuck to screen or linkage seized or binding (Chapter 12).
- ☐ Blown fuse (Chapter 12).
- ☐ Cable or cable connections loose, broken or disconnected (Chapter 12).
- ☐ Faulty relay (Chapter 12).
- ☐ Faulty wiper motor (Chapter 12).

Wiper blades sweep over too large or too small an area of the glass

- ☐ Wiper arms incorrectly positioned on spindles (Chapter 12).
- ☐ Excessive wear of wiper linkage (Chapter 12).
- ☐ Wiper motor or linkage mountings loose or insecure (Chapter 12).

Wiper blades fail to clean the glass effectively

- ☐ Wiper blade rubbers worn or perished (Chapter 12).
- ☐ Wiper arm tension springs broken or arm pivots seized (Chapter 12).
- ☐ Insufficient windscreen washer additive to adequately remove road film (*Weekly checks*).

Windscreen/tailgate washers inoperative or unsatisfactory in operation

One or more washer jets inoperative

- ☐ Blocked washer jet (Chapter 12).
- ☐ Disconnected, kinked or restricted fluid hose (Chapter 12).
- ☐ Insufficient fluid in washer reservoir (Chapter 1).

Washer pump fails to operate

- ☐ Broken or disconnected wiring or connections (Chapter 12).
- ☐ Blown fuse (Chapter 12).
- ☐ Faulty washer switch (Chapter 12).
- ☐ Faulty washer pump (Chapter 12).

Washer pump runs for some time before fluid is emitted from jets

- ☐ Faulty one-way valve in fluid supply hose (Chapter 12).

Electric windows inoperative or unsatisfactory in operation

Window glass will only move in one direction

- ☐ Faulty switch (Chapter 12)

Window glass slow to move

- ☐ Incorrectly adjusted door glass guide channels (Chapter 11).
- ☐ Regulator seized or damaged, or in need of lubrication (Chapter 11).
- ☐ Door internal components or trim fouling regulator (Chapter 11).
- ☐ Faulty motor (Chapter 11).

Window glass fails to move

- ☐ Incorrectly adjusted door glass guide channels (Chapter 11).
- ☐ Blown fuse (Chapter 12).
- ☐ Faulty relay (Chapter 12).
- ☐ Broken or disconnected wiring or connections (Chapter 12).
- ☐ Faulty motor (Chapter 11).

Central locking system inoperative or unsatisfactory in operation

Complete system failure

- ☐ Blown fuse (Chapter 12).
- ☐ Faulty relay (Chapter 12).
- ☐ Broken or disconnected wiring or connections (Chapter 12).
- ☐ Faulty control unit (Chapter 11).

Latch locks but will not unlock, or unlocks but will not lock

- ☐ Faulty master switch (Chapter 12).
- ☐ Broken or disconnected latch operating rods or levers (Chapter 11).
- ☐ Faulty relay (Chapter 12).
- ☐ Faulty control unit (Chapter 11).

One solenoid/motor fails to operate

- ☐ Broken or disconnected wiring or connections (Chapter 12).
- ☐ Faulty solenoid/motor (Chapter 11).
- ☐ Broken, binding or disconnected latch operating rods or levers (Chapter 11).
- ☐ Fault in door latch (Chapter 11).

A

ABS (Anti-lock brake system) A system, usually electronically controlled, that senses incipient wheel lockup during braking and relieves hydraulic pressure at wheels that are about to skid.

Air bag An inflatable bag hidden in the steering wheel (driver's side) or the dash or glovebox (passenger side). In a head-on collision, the bags inflate, preventing the driver and front passenger from being thrown forward into the steering wheel or windscreen.

Air cleaner A metal or plastic housing, containing a filter element, which removes dust and dirt from the air being drawn into the engine.

Air filter element The actual filter in an air cleaner system, usually manufactured from pleated paper and requiring renewal at regular intervals.

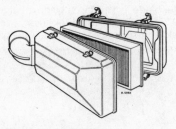

Air filter

Allen key A hexagonal wrench which fits into a recessed hexagonal hole.

Alligator clip A long-nosed spring-loaded metal clip with meshing teeth. Used to make temporary electrical connections.

Alternator A component in the electrical system which converts mechanical energy from a drivebelt into electrical energy to charge the battery and to operate the starting system, ignition system and electrical accessories.

Ampere (amp) A unit of measurement for the flow of electric current. One amp is the amount of current produced by one volt acting through a resistance of one ohm.

Anaerobic sealer A substance used to prevent bolts and screws from loosening. Anaerobic means that it does not require oxygen for activation. The Loctite brand is widely used.

Antifreeze A substance (usually ethylene glycol) mixed with water, and added to a vehicle's cooling system, to prevent freezing of the coolant in winter. Antifreeze also contains chemicals to inhibit corrosion and the formation of rust and other deposits that would tend to clog the radiator and coolant passages and reduce cooling efficiency.

Anti-seize compound A coating that reduces the risk of seizing on fasteners that are subjected to high temperatures, such as exhaust manifold bolts and nuts.

Asbestos A natural fibrous mineral with great heat resistance, commonly used in the composition of brake friction materials. Asbestos is a health hazard and the dust created by brake systems should never be inhaled or ingested.

Axle A shaft on which a wheel revolves, or which revolves with a wheel. Also, a solid beam that connects the two wheels at one end of the vehicle. An axle which also transmits power to the wheels is known as a live axle.

Axleshaft A single rotating shaft, on either side of the differential, which delivers power from the final drive assembly to the drive wheels. Also called a driveshaft or a halfshaft.

B

Ball bearing An anti-friction bearing consisting of a hardened inner and outer race with hardened steel balls between two races.

Bearing The curved surface on a shaft or in a bore, or the part assembled into either, that permits relative motion between them with minimum wear and friction.

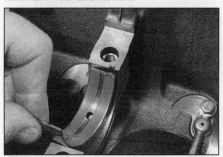

Bearing

Big-end bearing The bearing in the end of the connecting rod that's attached to the crankshaft.

Bleed nipple A valve on a brake wheel cylinder, caliper or other hydraulic component that is opened to purge the hydraulic system of air. Also called a bleed screw.

Brake bleeding Procedure for removing air from lines of a hydraulic brake system.

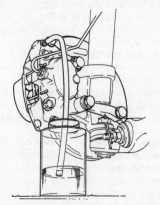

Brake bleeding

Brake disc The component of a disc brake that rotates with the wheels.

Brake drum The component of a drum brake that rotates with the wheels.

Brake linings The friction material which contacts the brake disc or drum to retard the vehicle's speed. The linings are bonded or riveted to the brake pads or shoes.

Brake pads The replaceable friction pads that pinch the brake disc when the brakes are applied. Brake pads consist of a friction material bonded or riveted to a rigid backing plate.

Brake shoe The crescent-shaped carrier to which the brake linings are mounted and which forces the lining against the rotating drum during braking.

Braking systems For more information on braking systems, consult the *Haynes Automotive Brake Manual*.

Breaker bar A long socket wrench handle providing greater leverage.

Bulkhead The insulated partition between the engine and the passenger compartment.

C

Caliper The non-rotating part of a disc-brake assembly that straddles the disc and carries the brake pads. The caliper also contains the hydraulic components that cause the pads to pinch the disc when the brakes are applied. A caliper is also a measuring tool that can be set to measure inside or outside dimensions of an object.

Camshaft A rotating shaft on which a series of cam lobes operate the valve mechanisms. The camshaft may be driven by gears, by sprockets and chain or by sprockets and a belt.

Canister A container in an evaporative emission control system; contains activated charcoal granules to trap vapours from the fuel system.

Canister

Carburettor A device which mixes fuel with air in the proper proportions to provide a desired power output from a spark ignition internal combustion engine.

Castellated Resembling the parapets along the top of a castle wall. For example, a castellated balljoint stud nut.

Castor In wheel alignment, the backward or forward tilt of the steering axis. Castor is positive when the steering axis is inclined rearward at the top.

Catalytic converter A silencer-like device in the exhaust system which converts certain pollutants in the exhaust gases into less harmful substances.

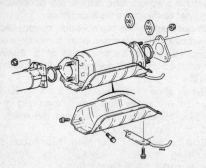

Catalytic converter

Circlip A ring-shaped clip used to prevent endwise movement of cylindrical parts and shafts. An internal circlip is installed in a groove in a housing; an external circlip fits into a groove on the outside of a cylindrical piece such as a shaft.

Clearance The amount of space between two parts. For example, between a piston and a cylinder, between a bearing and a journal, etc.

Coil spring A spiral of elastic steel found in various sizes throughout a vehicle, for example as a springing medium in the suspension and in the valve train.

Compression Reduction in volume, and increase in pressure and temperature, of a gas, caused by squeezing it into a smaller space.

Compression ratio The relationship between cylinder volume when the piston is at top dead centre and cylinder volume when the piston is at bottom dead centre.

Constant velocity (CV) joint A type of universal joint that cancels out vibrations caused by driving power being transmitted through an angle.

Core plug A disc or cup-shaped metal device inserted in a hole in a casting through which core was removed when the casting was formed. Also known as a freeze plug or expansion plug.

Crankcase The lower part of the engine block in which the crankshaft rotates.

Crankshaft The main rotating member, or shaft, running the length of the crankcase, with offset "throws" to which the connecting rods are attached.

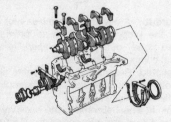

Crankshaft assembly

Crocodile clip See Alligator clip

D

Diagnostic code Code numbers obtained by accessing the diagnostic mode of an engine management computer. This code can be used to determine the area in the system where a malfunction may be located.

Disc brake A brake design incorporating a rotating disc onto which brake pads are squeezed. The resulting friction converts the energy of a moving vehicle into heat.

Double-overhead cam (DOHC) An engine that uses two overhead camshafts, usually one for the intake valves and one for the exhaust valves.

Drivebelt(s) The belt(s) used to drive accessories such as the alternator, water pump, power steering pump, air conditioning compressor, etc. off the crankshaft pulley.

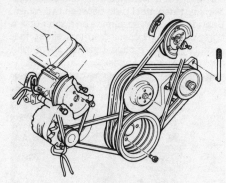

Accessory drivebelts

Driveshaft Any shaft used to transmit motion. Commonly used when referring to the axleshafts on a front wheel drive vehicle.

Drum brake A type of brake using a drum-shaped metal cylinder attached to the inner surface of the wheel. When the brake pedal is pressed, curved brake shoes with friction linings press against the inside of the drum to slow or stop the vehicle.

E

EGR valve A valve used to introduce exhaust gases into the intake air stream.

Electronic control unit (ECU) A computer which controls (for instance) ignition and fuel injection systems, or an anti-lock braking system. For more information refer to the *Haynes Automotive Electrical and Electronic Systems Manual*.

Electronic Fuel Injection (EFI) A computer controlled fuel system that distributes fuel through an injector located in each intake port of the engine.

Emergency brake A braking system, independent of the main hydraulic system, that can be used to slow or stop the vehicle if the primary brakes fail, or to hold the vehicle stationary even though the brake pedal isn't depressed. It usually consists of a hand lever that actuates either front or rear brakes mechanically through a series of cables and linkages. Also known as a handbrake or parking brake.

Endfloat The amount of lengthwise movement between two parts. As applied to a crankshaft, the distance that the crankshaft can move forward and back in the cylinder block.

Engine management system (EMS) A computer controlled system which manages the fuel injection and the ignition systems in an integrated fashion.

Exhaust manifold A part with several passages through which exhaust gases leave the engine combustion chambers and enter the exhaust pipe.

F

Fan clutch A viscous (fluid) drive coupling device which permits variable engine fan speeds in relation to engine speeds.

Feeler blade A thin strip or blade of hardened steel, ground to an exact thickness, used to check or measure clearances between parts.

Feeler blade

Firing order The order in which the engine cylinders fire, or deliver their power strokes, beginning with the number one cylinder.

Flywheel A heavy spinning wheel in which energy is absorbed and stored by means of momentum. On cars, the flywheel is attached to the crankshaft to smooth out firing impulses.

Free play The amount of travel before any action takes place. The "looseness" in a linkage, or an assembly of parts, between the initial application of force and actual movement. For example, the distance the brake pedal moves before the pistons in the master cylinder are actuated.

Fuse An electrical device which protects a circuit against accidental overload. The typical fuse contains a soft piece of metal which is calibrated to melt at a predetermined current flow (expressed as amps) and break the circuit.

Fusible link A circuit protection device consisting of a conductor surrounded by heat-resistant insulation. The conductor is smaller than the wire it protects, so it acts as the weakest link in the circuit. Unlike a blown fuse, a failed fusible link must frequently be cut from the wire for replacement.

G

Gap The distance the spark must travel in jumping from the centre electrode to the side electrode in a spark plug. Also refers to the spacing between the points in a contact breaker assembly in a conventional points-type ignition, or to the distance between the reluctor or rotor and the pickup coil in an electronic ignition.

Adjusting spark plug gap

Gasket Any thin, soft material - usually cork, cardboard, asbestos or soft metal - installed between two metal surfaces to ensure a good seal. For instance, the cylinder head gasket seals the joint between the block and the cylinder head.

Gasket

Gauge An instrument panel display used to monitor engine conditions. A gauge with a movable pointer on a dial or a fixed scale is an analogue gauge. A gauge with a numerical readout is called a digital gauge.

H

Halfshaft A rotating shaft that transmits power from the final drive unit to a drive wheel, usually when referring to a live rear axle.

Harmonic balancer A device designed to reduce torsion or twisting vibration in the crankshaft. May be incorporated in the crankshaft pulley. Also known as a vibration damper.

Hone An abrasive tool for correcting small irregularities or differences in diameter in an engine cylinder, brake cylinder, etc.

Hydraulic tappet A tappet that utilises hydraulic pressure from the engine's lubrication system to maintain zero clearance (constant contact with both camshaft and valve stem). Automatically adjusts to variation in valve stem length. Hydraulic tappets also reduce valve noise.

I

Ignition timing The moment at which the spark plug fires, usually expressed in the number of crankshaft degrees before the piston reaches the top of its stroke.

Inlet manifold A tube or housing with passages through which flows the air-fuel mixture (carburettor vehicles and vehicles with throttle body injection) or air only (port fuel-injected vehicles) to the port openings in the cylinder head.

J

Jump start Starting the engine of a vehicle with a discharged or weak battery by attaching jump leads from the weak battery to a charged or helper battery.

L

Load Sensing Proportioning Valve (LSPV) A brake hydraulic system control valve that works like a proportioning valve, but also takes into consideration the amount of weight carried by the rear axle.

Locknut A nut used to lock an adjustment nut, or other threaded component, in place. For example, a locknut is employed to keep the adjusting nut on the rocker arm in position.

Lockwasher A form of washer designed to prevent an attaching nut from working loose.

M

MacPherson strut A type of front suspension system devised by Earle MacPherson at Ford of England. In its original form, a simple lateral link with the anti-roll bar creates the lower control arm. A long strut - an integral coil spring and shock absorber - is mounted between the body and the steering knuckle. Many modern so-called MacPherson strut systems use a conventional lower A-arm and don't rely on the anti-roll bar for location.

Multimeter An electrical test instrument with the capability to measure voltage, current and resistance.

N

NOx Oxides of Nitrogen. A common toxic pollutant emitted by petrol and diesel engines at higher temperatures.

O

Ohm The unit of electrical resistance. One volt applied to a resistance of one ohm will produce a current of one amp.

Ohmmeter An instrument for measuring electrical resistance.

O-ring A type of sealing ring made of a special rubber-like material; in use, the O-ring is compressed into a groove to provide the sealing action.

Overhead cam (ohc) engine An engine with the camshaft(s) located on top of the cylinder head(s).

Overhead valve (ohv) engine

Overhead valve (ohv) engine An engine with the valves located in the cylinder head, but with the camshaft located in the engine block.

Oxygen sensor A device installed in the engine exhaust manifold, which senses the oxygen content in the exhaust and converts this information into an electric current. Also called a Lambda sensor.

P

Phillips screw A type of screw head having a cross instead of a slot for a corresponding type of screwdriver.

Plastigage A thin strip of plastic thread, available in different sizes, used for measuring clearances. For example, a strip of Plastigage is laid across a bearing journal. The parts are assembled and dismantled; the width of the crushed strip indicates the clearance between journal and bearing.

Plastigage

Propeller shaft The long hollow tube with universal joints at both ends that carries power from the transmission to the differential on front-engined rear wheel drive vehicles.

Proportioning valve A hydraulic control valve which limits the amount of pressure to the rear brakes during panic stops to prevent wheel lock-up.

R

Rack-and-pinion steering A steering system with a pinion gear on the end of the steering shaft that mates with a rack (think of a geared wheel opened up and laid flat). When the steering wheel is turned, the pinion turns, moving the rack to the left or right. This movement is transmitted through the track rods to the steering arms at the wheels.

Radiator A liquid-to-air heat transfer device designed to reduce the temperature of the coolant in an internal combustion engine cooling system.

Refrigerant Any substance used as a heat transfer agent in an air-conditioning system. R-12 has been the principle refrigerant for many years; recently, however, manufacturers have begun using R-134a, a non-CFC substance that is considered less harmful to the ozone in the upper atmosphere.

Rocker arm A lever arm that rocks on a shaft or pivots on a stud. In an overhead valve engine, the rocker arm converts the upward movement of the pushrod into a downward movement to open a valve.

Rotor In a distributor, the rotating device inside the cap that connects the centre electrode and the outer terminals as it turns, distributing the high voltage from the coil secondary winding to the proper spark plug. Also, that part of an alternator which rotates inside the stator. Also, the rotating assembly of a turbocharger, including the compressor wheel, shaft and turbine wheel.

Runout The amount of wobble (in-and-out movement) of a gear or wheel as it's rotated. The amount a shaft rotates "out-of-true." The out-of-round condition of a rotating part.

S

Sealant A liquid or paste used to prevent leakage at a joint. Sometimes used in conjunction with a gasket.

Sealed beam lamp An older headlight design which integrates the reflector, lens and filaments into a hermetically-sealed one-piece unit. When a filament burns out or the lens cracks, the entire unit is simply replaced.

Serpentine drivebelt A single, long, wide accessory drivebelt that's used on some newer vehicles to drive all the accessories, instead of a series of smaller, shorter belts. Serpentine drivebelts are usually tensioned by an automatic tensioner.

Serpentine drivebelt

Shim Thin spacer, commonly used to adjust the clearance or relative positions between two parts. For example, shims inserted into or under bucket tappets control valve clearances. Clearance is adjusted by changing the thickness of the shim.

Slide hammer A special puller that screws into or hooks onto a component such as a shaft or bearing; a heavy sliding handle on the shaft bottoms against the end of the shaft to knock the component free.

Sprocket A tooth or projection on the periphery of a wheel, shaped to engage with a chain or drivebelt. Commonly used to refer to the sprocket wheel itself.

Starter inhibitor switch On vehicles with an automatic transmission, a switch that prevents starting if the vehicle is not in Neutral or Park.

Strut See MacPherson strut.

T

Tappet A cylindrical component which transmits motion from the cam to the valve stem, either directly or via a pushrod and rocker arm. Also called a cam follower.

Thermostat A heat-controlled valve that regulates the flow of coolant between the cylinder block and the radiator, so maintaining optimum engine operating temperature. A thermostat is also used in some air cleaners in which the temperature is regulated.

Thrust bearing The bearing in the clutch assembly that is moved in to the release levers by clutch pedal action to disengage the clutch. Also referred to as a release bearing.

Timing belt A toothed belt which drives the camshaft. Serious engine damage may result if it breaks in service.

Timing chain A chain which drives the camshaft.

Toe-in The amount the front wheels are closer together at the front than at the rear. On rear wheel drive vehicles, a slight amount of toe-in is usually specified to keep the front wheels running parallel on the road by offsetting other forces that tend to spread the wheels apart.

Toe-out The amount the front wheels are closer together at the rear than at the front. On front wheel drive vehicles, a slight amount of toe-out is usually specified.

Tools For full information on choosing and using tools, refer to the *Haynes Automotive Tools Manual*.

Tracer A stripe of a second colour applied to a wire insulator to distinguish that wire from another one with the same colour insulator.

Tune-up A process of accurate and careful adjustments and parts replacement to obtain the best possible engine performance.

Turbocharger A centrifugal device, driven by exhaust gases, that pressurises the intake air. Normally used to increase the power output from a given engine displacement, but can also be used primarily to reduce exhaust emissions (as on VW's "Umwelt" Diesel engine).

U

Universal joint or U-joint A double-pivoted connection for transmitting power from a driving to a driven shaft through an angle. A U-joint consists of two Y-shaped yokes and a cross-shaped member called the spider.

V

Valve A device through which the flow of liquid, gas, vacuum, or loose material in bulk may be started, stopped, or regulated by a movable part that opens, shuts, or partially obstructs one or more ports or passageways. A valve is also the movable part of such a device.

Valve clearance The clearance between the valve tip (the end of the valve stem) and the rocker arm or tappet. The valve clearance is measured when the valve is closed.

Vernier caliper A precision measuring instrument that measures inside and outside dimensions. Not quite as accurate as a micrometer, but more convenient.

Viscosity The thickness of a liquid or its resistance to flow.

Volt A unit for expressing electrical "pressure" in a circuit. One volt that will produce a current of one ampere through a resistance of one ohm.

W

Welding Various processes used to join metal items by heating the areas to be joined to a molten state and fusing them together. For more information refer to the *Haynes Automotive Welding Manual*.

Wiring diagram A drawing portraying the components and wires in a vehicle's electrical system, using standardised symbols. For more information refer to the *Haynes Automotive Electrical and Electronic Systems Manual*.

Note: *References throughout this index are in the form - "Chapter number" • "page number"*

Haynes Manuals – The Complete List

Title	Book No.
ALFA ROMEO	
Alfa Romeo Alfasud/Sprint (74 - 88)	0292
Alfa Romeo Alfetta (73 - 87)	0531
AUDI	
Audi 80 (72 - Feb 79)	0207
Audi 80, 90 (79 - Oct 86) & Coupe (81 - Nov 88)	0605
Audi 80, 90 (Oct 86 - 90) & Coupe (Nov 88 - 90)	1491
Audi 100 (Oct 76 - Oct 82)	0428
Audi 100 (Oct 82 - 90) & 200 (Feb 84 - Oct 89)	0907
AUSTIN	
Austin Ambassador (82 - 84)	0871
Austin/MG Maestro 1.3 & 1.6 (83 - 95)	0922
Austin Maxi (69 - 81)	0052
Austin/MG Metro (80 - May 90)	0718
Austin Montego 1.3 & 1.6 (84 - 94)	1066
Austin/MG Montego 2.0 (84 - 95)	1067
Mini (59 - 69)	0527
Mini (69 - 96)	0646
Austin/Rover 2.0 litre Diesel Engine (86 - 93)	1857
BEDFORD	
Bedford CF (69 - 87)	0163
Bedford Rascal (86 - 93)	3015
BL	
BL Princess & BLMC 18-22 (75 - 82)	0286
BMW	
BMW 316, 320 & 320i (4-cyl) (75 - Feb 83)	0276
BMW 320, 320i, 323i & 325i (6-cyl) (Oct 77 - Sept 87)	0815
BMW 3-Series (Apr 91 - 96)	3210
BMW 3-Series (sohc) (83 - 91)	1948
BMW 520i & 525e (Oct 81 - June 88)	1560
BMW 525, 528 & 528i (73 - Sept 81)	0632
BMW 5-Series (sohc) (81 - 93)	1948
BMW 1500, 1502, 1600, 1602, 2000 & 2002 (59 - 77)	0240
CITROEN	
Citroen 2CV, Ami & Dyane (67 - 90)	0196
Citroen AX Petrol & Diesel (87 - 94)	3014
Citroen BX (83 - 94)	0908
Citroen CX (75 - 88)	0528
Citroen Visa (79 - 88)	0620
Citroen Xantia Petrol & Diesel (93 - Oct 95)	3082
Citroen ZX Diesel (91 - 93)	1922
Citroen ZX Petrol (91 - 94)	1881
Citroen 1.7 & 1.9 litre Diesel Engine (84 - 96)	1379
COLT	
Colt 1200, 1250 & 1400 (79 - May 84)	0600
Colt Galant (74 - 78) & Celeste (76 - 81)	0236
DAIMLER	
Daimler Sovereign (68 - Oct 86)	0242
Daimler Double Six (72 - 88)	0478
DATSUN (see also *Nissan*)	
Datsun 120Y (73 - Aug 78)	0228
Datsun 1300, 1400 & 1600 (69 - Aug 72)	0123
Datsun Cherry (79 - Sept 82)	0679
Datsun Pick-up (75 - 78)	0277
Datsun Sunny (Aug 78 - May 82)	0525
Datsun Violet (78 - 82)	0430

Title	Book No.
FIAT	
Fiat 126 (73 - 87)	0305
Fiat 127 (71 - 83)	0193
Fiat 500 (57 - 73)	0090
Fiat 850 (64 - 81)	0038
Fiat Panda (81 - 95)	0793
Fiat Punto (94 - 96)	3251
Fiat Regata (84 - 88)	1167
Fiat Strada (79 - 88)	0479
Fiat Tipo (88 - 91)	1625
Fiat Uno (83 - 95)	0923
Fiat X1/9 (74 - 89)	0273
FORD	
Ford Capri II (& III) 1.6 & 2.0 (74 - 87)	0283
Ford Capri II (& III) 2.8 & 3.0 (74 - 87)	1309
Ford Cortina Mk III 1600 & 2000 (70 - 76)	0295
Ford Cortina Mk IV (& V) 1.6 & 2.0 (76 - 83)	0343
Ford Cortina Mk IV (& V) 2.3 V6 (77 - 83)	0426
Ford Escort (75 - Aug 80)	0280
Ford Escort (Sept 80 - Sept 90)	0686
Ford Escort (Sept 90 - 96)	1737
Ford Escort Mk II Mexico, RS 1600 & RS 2000 (75 - 80)	0735
Ford Fiesta (inc. XR2) (76 - Aug 83)	0334
Ford Fiesta (inc. XR2) (Aug 83 - Feb 89)	1030
Ford Fiesta (Feb 89 - 93)	1595
Ford Granada (Sept 77 - Feb 85)	0481
Ford Granada (Mar 85 - 94)	1245
Ford Mondeo 4-cyl (93 - 96)	1923
Ford Orion (83 - Sept 90)	1009
Ford Orion (Sept 90 - 93)	1737
Ford Sierra 1.3, 1.6, 1.8 & 2.0 (82 - 93)	0903
Ford Sierra 2.3, 2.8 & 2.9 (82 - 91)	0904
Ford Scorpio (Mar 85 - 94)	1245
Ford Transit Petrol (Mk 1) (65 - Feb 78)	0377
Ford Transit Petrol (Mk 2) (78 - Jan 86)	0719
Ford Transit Petrol (Mk 3) (Feb 86 - 89)	1468
Ford Transit Diesel (Feb 86 - 95)	3019
Ford 1.6 & 1.8 litre Diesel Engine (84 - 96)	1172
Ford 2.1, 2.3 & 2.5 litre Diesel Engine (77 - 90)	1606
Ford Vehicle Carburettors	1783
FREIGHT ROVER	
Freight Rover Sherpa (74 - 87)	0463
HILLMAN	
Hillman Avenger (70 - 82)	0037
Hillman Minx & Husky (56 - 66)	0009
HONDA	
Honda Accord (76 - Feb 84)	0351
Honda Accord (Feb 84 - Oct 85)	1177
Honda Civic 1300 (80 - 81)	0633
Honda Civic (Feb 84 - Oct 87)	1226
Honda Civic (Nov 91 - 96)	3199
JAGUAR	
Jaguar E Type (61 - 72)	0140
Jaguar MkI & II, 240 & 340 (55 - 69)	0098
Jaguar XJ6, XJ & Sovereign (68 - Oct 86)	0242
Jaguar XJ12, XJS & Sovereign (72 - 88)	0478
JEEP	
Jeep Cherokee Petrol (93 - 96)	1943

Title	Book No.
LADA	
Lada 1200, 1300, 1500 & 1600 (74 - 91)	0413
Lada Samara (87 - 91)	1610
LAND ROVER	
Land Rover 90, 110 & Defender Diesel (83 - 95)	3017
Land Rover Discovery Diesel (89 - 95)	3016
Land Rover Series IIA & III Diesel (58 - 85)	0529
Land Rover Series II, IIA & III Petrol (58 - 85)	0314
MAZDA	
Mazda 323 fwd (Mar 81 - Oct 89)	1608
Mazda 323 rwd (77 - Apr 86)	0370
Mazda 626 fwd (May 83 - Sept 87)	0929
Mazda B-1600, B-1800 & B-2000 Pick-up (72 - 88)	0267
Mazda RX-7 (79 - 85)	0460
MERCEDES-BENZ	
Mercedes-Benz 190 & 190E (83 - 87)	0928
Mercedes-Benz 200, 240, 300 Diesel (Oct 76 - 85)	1114
Mercedes-Benz 250 & 280 (68 - 72)	0346
Mercedes-Benz 250 & 280 (123 Series) (Oct 76 - 84)	0677
Mercedes-Benz 124 Series (85 - Aug 93)	3253
MG	
MGB (62 - 80)	0111
MG Maestro 1.3 & 1.6 (83 - 95)	0922
MG Metro (80 - May 90)	0718
MG Midget & AH Sprite (58 - 80)	0265
MG Montego 2.0 (84 - 95)	1067
MITSUBISHI	
Mitsubishi 1200, 1250 & 1400 (79 - May 84)	0600
Mitsubishi Shogun & L200 Pick-Ups (83 - 94)	1944
MORRIS	
Morris Ital 1.3 (80 - 84)	0705
Morris Marina 1700 (78 - 80)	0526
Morris Marina 1.8 (71 - 78)	0074
Morris Minor 1000 (56 - 71)	0024
NISSAN (See also *Datsun*)	
Nissan Bluebird 160B & 180B rwd (May 80 - May 84)	0957
Nissan Bluebird fwd (May 84 - Mar 86)	1223
Nissan Bluebird (T12 & T72) (Mar 86 - 90)	1473
Nissan Cherry (N12) (Sept 82 - 86)	1031
Nissan Micra (K10) (83 - Jan 93)	0931
Nissan Micra (93 - 96)	3254
Nissan Primera (90 - Oct 96)	1851
Nissan Stanza (82 - 86)	0824
Nissan Sunny (B11) (May 82 - Oct 86)	0895
Nissan Sunny (Oct 86 - Mar 91)	1378
Nissan Sunny (Apr 91 - 95)	3219
OPEL	
Opel Ascona & Manta (B Series) (Sept 75 - 88)	0316
Opel Ascona (81 - 88)	3215
Opel Astra (Oct 91 - 96)	3156
Opel Corsa (83 - Mar 93)	3160
Opel Corsa (Mar 93 - 94)	3159
Opel Kadett (Nov 79 - Oct 84)	0634
Opel Kadett (Oct 84 - Oct 91)	3196
Opel Omega & Senator (86 - 94)	3157

Title	Book No.
Opel Rekord (Feb 78 - Oct 86)	0543
Opel Vectra (88 - Oct 95)	3158
PEUGEOT	
Peugeot 106 Petrol & Diesel (91 - June 96)	1882
Peugeot 205 (83 - 95)	0932
Peugeot 305 (78 - 89)	0538
Peugeot 306 Petrol & Diesel (93 - 95)	3073
Peugeot 309 (86 - 93)	1266
Peugeot 405 Petrol (88 96)	1559
Peugeot 405 Diesel (88 - 96)	3198
Peugeot 505 (79 - 89)	0762
Peugeot 1.7 & 1.9 litre Diesel Engines (82 - 96)	0950
Peugeot 2.0, 2.1, 2.3 & 2.5 litre Diesel Engines (74 - 90)	1607
PORSCHE	
Porsche 911 (65 - 85)	0264
Porsche 924 & 924 Turbo (76 - 85)	0397
RANGE ROVER	
Range Rover V8 (70 - Oct 92)	0606
RELIANT	
Reliant Robin & Kitten (73 - 83)	0436
RENAULT	
Renault 5 (72 - Feb 85)	0141
Renault 5 (Feb 85 - 96)	1219
Renault 6 (68 - 79)	0092
Renault 9 & 11 (82 - 89)	0822
Renault 12 (70 - 80)	0097
Renault 15 & 17 (72 - 79)	0763
Renault 16 (65 - 79)	0081
Renault 18 (79 - 86)	0598
Renault 19 Petrol (89 - 94)	1646
Renault 19 Diesel (89 - 95)	1946
Renault 21 (86 - 94)	1397
Renault 25 (84 - 86)	1228
Renault Clio Petrol (91 - 93)	1853
Renault Clio Diesel (91 - June 96)	3031
Renault Espace (85 - 96)	3197
Renault Fuego (80 - 86)	0764
Renault Laguna (94 - 96)	3252
ROVER	
Rover 111 & 114 (95 - 96)	1711
Rover 213 & 216 (84 - 89)	1116
Rover 214 & 414 (Oct 89 - 92)	1689
Rover 216 & 416 (Oct 89 - 92)	1830
Rover 820, 825 & 827 (86 - 95)	1380
Rover 2000, 2300 & 2600 (77 - 87)	0468
Rover 3500 (76 - 87)	0365
Rover Metro (May 90 - 94)	1711
Rover 2.0 litre Diesel Engine (86 - 93)	1857
SAAB	
Saab 95 & 96 (66 - 76)	0198
Saab 99 (69 - 79)	0247
Saab 90, 99 & 900 (79 - Oct 93)	0765
Saab 9000 (4-cyl) (85 - 95)	1686
SEAT	
Seat Ibiza & Malaga (85 - 92)	1609

Title	Book No.
SIMCA	
Simca 1100 & 1204 (67 - 79)	0088
Simca 1301 & 1501 (63 - 76)	0199
SKODA	
Skoda 1000 & 1100 (64 - 78)	0303
Skoda Estelle 105, 120, 130 & 136 (77 - 89)	0604
Skoda Favorit (89 - 92)	1801
SUBARU	
Subaru 1600 (77 - Oct 79)	0237
Subaru 1600 & 1800 (Nov 79 - 90)	0995
SUZUKI	
Suzuki SJ Series, Samurai & Vitara (82 - 94)	1942
Suzuki Supercarry (86 - Oct 94)	3015
TALBOT	
Talbot Alpine, Solara, Minx & Rapier (75 - 86)	0337
Talbot Horizon (78 - 86)	0473
Talbot Samba (82 - 86)	0823
TOYOTA	
Toyota 2000 (75 - 77)	0360
Toyota Celica (78 - Jan 82)	0437
Toyota Celica (Feb 82 - Sept 85)	1135
Toyota Corolla (fwd) (Sept 83 - Sept 87)	1024
Toyota Corolla (rwd) (80 - 85)	0683
Toyota Corolla (Sept 87 - 92)	1683
Toyota Hi-Ace & Hi-Lux (69 - Oct 83)	0304
Toyota Starlet (78 - Jan 85)	0462
TRIUMPH	
Triumph Acclaim (81 - 84)	0792
Triumph GT6 (62 - 74)	0112
Triumph Herald (59 - 71)	0010
Triumph Spitfire (62 - 81)	0113
Triumph Stag (70 - 78)	0441
Triumph TR2, TR3, TR3A, TR4 & TR4A (52 - 67)	0028
Triumph TR7 (75 - 82)	0322
Triumph Vitesse (62 - 74)	0112
VAUXHALL	
Vauxhall Astra (80 - Oct 84)	0635
Vauxhall Astra & Belmont (Oct 84 - Oct 91)	1136
Vauxhall Astra (Oct 91 - 96)	1832
Vauxhall Carlton (Oct 78 - Oct 86)	0480
Vauxhall Carlton (Nov 86 - 94)	1469
Vauxhall Cavalier 1300 (77 - July 81)	0461
Vauxhall Cavalier 1600, 1900 & 2000 (75 - July 81)	0315
Vauxhall Cavalier (81 - Oct 88)	0812
Vauxhall Cavalier (Oct 88 - Oct 95)	1570
Vauxhall Chevette (75 - 84)	0285
Vauxhall Corsa (Mar 93 - 94)	1985
Vauxhall Nova (83 - 93)	0909
Vauxhall Rascal (86 - 93)	3015
Vauxhall Senator (Sept 87 - 94)	1469
Vauxhall Victor & VX4/90 (FD Series) (67 - 72)	0053
Vauxhall Viva HC (70 - 79)	0047
Vauxhall/Opel 1.5, 1.6 & 1.7 litre Diesel Engines (82 - 96)	1222
VOLKSWAGEN	
VW Beetle 1200 (54 - 77)	0036
VW Beetle 1300 & 1500 (65 - 75)	0039

Title	Book No.
VW Beetle 1302 & 1302S (70 - 72)	0110
VW Beetle 1303, 1303S & GT (72 - 75)	0159
VW Golf Mk 1 1.1 & 1.3 (74 - Feb 84)	0716
VW Golf Mk 1 1.5, 1.6 & 1.8 (74 - 85)	0726
VW Golf Mk 1 Diesel (78 - Feb 84)	0451
VW Golf Mk 2 (Mar 84 - Feb 92)	1081
VW Golf Mk 3 Petrol & Diesel (Feb 92 - 96)	3097
VW Jetta Mk 1 1.1 & 1.3 (80 - June 84)	0716
VW Jetta Mk 1 1.5, 1.6 & 1.8 (80 - June 84)	0726
VW Jetta Mk 1 Diesel (81 - June 84)	0451
VW Jetta Mk 2 (July 84 - 92)	1081
VW LT vans & light trucks (76 - 87)	0637
VW Passat (Sept 81 - May 88)	0814
VW Passat (May 88 - 91)	1647
VW Polo & Derby (76 - Jan 82)	0335
VW Polo (82 - Oct 90)	0813
VW Polo (Nov 90 - Aug 94)	3245
VW Santana (Sept 82 - 85)	0814
VW Scirocco Mk 1 1.5, 1.6 & 1.8 (74 - 82)	0726
VW Scirocco (82 - 90)	1224
VW Transporter 1600 (68 - 79)	0082
VW Transporter 1700, 1800 & 2000 (72 - 79)	0226
VW Transporter with air-cooled engine (79 - 82)	0638
VW Type 3 (63 - 73)	0084
VW Vento Petrol & Diesel (Feb 92 - 96)	3097
VOLVO	
Volvo 66 & 343, Daf 55 & 66 (68 - 79)	0293
Volvo 142, 144 & 145 (66 - 74)	0129
Volvo 240 Series (74 - 93)	0270
Volvo 262, 264 & 260/265 (75 - 85)	0400
Volvo 340, 343, 345 & 360 (76 - 91)	0715
Volvo 440, 460 & 480 (87 - 92)	1691
Volvo 740 & 760 (82 - 91)	1258
Volvo 850 (92 - 96)	3260
Volvo 940 (90 - 96)	3249
YUGO/ZASTAVA	
Yugo/Zastava (81 - 90)	1453

TECH BOOKS	
Automotive Brake Manual	3050
Automotive Electrical & Electronic Systems	3049
Automotive Tools Manual	3052
Automotive Welding Manual	3053

CAR BOOKS	
Automotive Fuel Injection Systems	9755
Car Bodywork Repair Manual	9864
Caravan Manual (2nd Edition)	9894
Ford Vehicle Carburettors	1783
Haynes Technical Data Book (87 - 96)	1996
In-Car Entertainment Manual (2nd Edition)	9862
Japanese Vehicle Carburettors	1786
Pass the MOT!	9861
Small Engine Repair Manual	1755
Solex & Pierburg Carburettors	1785
SU Carburettors	0299
Weber Carburettors (to 79)	0393
Weber Carburettors (79 - 91)	1784

01/10/96

Preserving Our Motoring Heritage

< The Model J Duesenberg
Derham Tourster.
Only eight of these
magnificent cars were
ever built – this is the
only example to be found
outside the United
States of America

Almost every car you've ever loved, loathed or desired is gathered under one roof at the Haynes Motor Museum. Over 300 immaculately presented cars and motorbikes represent every aspect of our motoring heritage, from elegant reminders of bygone days, such as the superb Model J Duesenberg to curiosities like the bug-eyed BMW Isetta. There are also many old friends and flames. Perhaps you remember the 1959 Ford Popular that you did your courting in? The magnificent 'Red Collection' is a spectacle of classic sports cars including AC, Alfa Romeo, Austin Healey, Ferrari, Lamborghini, Maserati, MG, Riley, Porsche and Triumph.

A Perfect Day Out

Each and every vehicle at the Haynes Motor Museum has played its part in the history and culture of Motoring. Today, they make a wonderful spectacle and a great day out for all the family. Bring the kids, bring Mum and Dad, but above all bring your camera to capture those golden memories for ever. You will also find an impressive array of motoring memorabilia, a comfortable 70 seat video cinema and one of the most extensive transport book shops in Britain. The Pit Stop Cafe serves everything from a cup of tea to wholesome, home-made meals or, if you prefer, you can enjoy the large picnic area nestled in the beautiful rural surroundings of Somerset.

John Haynes O.B.E.,
Founder and
Chairman of the
museum at the wheel
of a Haynes Light 12.

< Graham Hill's Lola
Cosworth Formula 1
car next to a 1934
Riley Sports.

The Museum is situated on the A359 Yeovil to Frome road at Sparkford, just off the A303 in Somerset. It is about 40 miles south of Bristol, and 25 minutes drive from the M5 intersection at Taunton.
Open 9.30am - 5.30pm (10.00am - 4.00pm Winter) 7 days a week, *except Christmas Day, Boxing Day and New Years Day*
Special rates available for schools, coach parties and outings Charitable Trust No. 292048